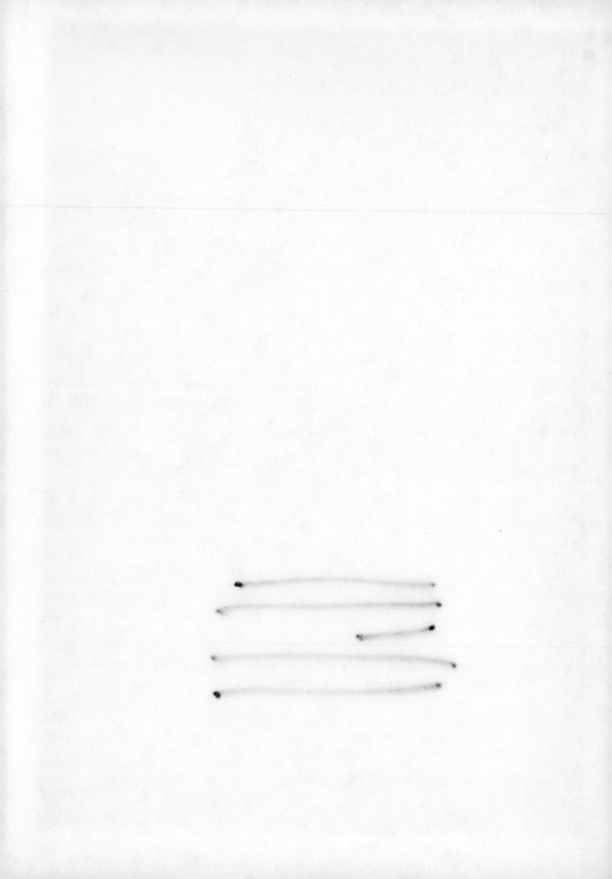

Mental health nursing

A bio-psycho-cultural approach

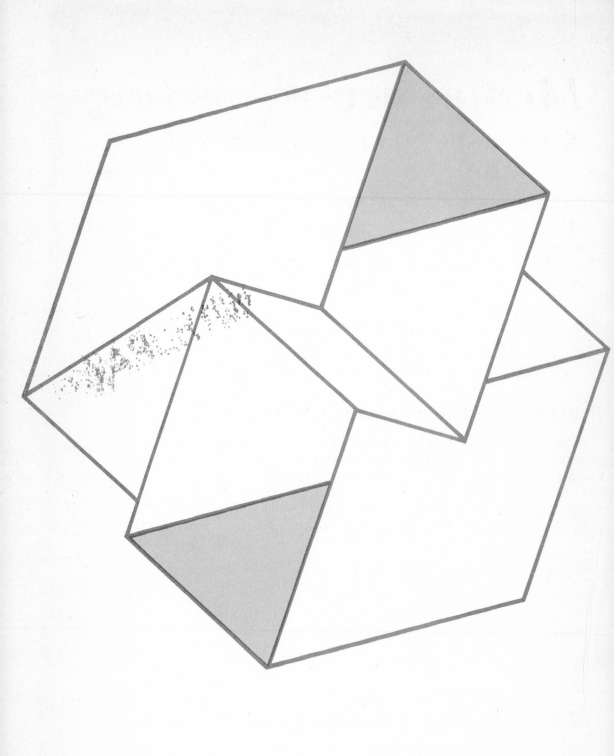

Mental health nursing

A BIO-PSYCHO-CULTURAL APPROACH

ELAINE ANNE PASQUALI, R.N., M.S., M.A.

Doctoral Candidate in Anthropology, Department of Anthropology,
State University of New York at Stony Brook;
Associate Professor of Nursing, School of Nursing,
Adelphi University, Garden City, New York

ELEANORE GORTHEY ALESI, R.N., M.S.

Professor Emeritus of Nursing, School of Nursing,
Adelphi University, Garden City, New York

HELEN MARGARET ARNOLD, R.N., Ph.D.

Candidate for Postdoctoral Certificate in Psychoanalysis,
Institute of Advanced Psychological Studies, and
Associate Professor of Nursing, School of Nursing,
Adelphi University, Garden City, New York;
Clinical Specialist for Group and Marital Therapy,
Mercy Hospital, Rockville Centre, New York

NANCY DeBASIO, R.N., M.A.

Doctoral Student in Human Sexuality Education,
Graduate School of Education, and Associate, School of Nursing,
University of Pennsylvania, Philadelphia, Pennsylvania

The C. V. Mosby Company

ST. LOUIS • TORONTO • LONDON   1981

MOSBY

1906 **75** 1981
YEARS

A TRADITION OF PUBLISHING EXCELLENCE

Printed in the United States of America

The C. V. Mosby Company
11830 Westline Industrial Drive, St. Louis, Missouri 63141

Library of Congress Cataloging in Publication Data

Main entry under title:

Mental health nursing.

    Bibliography: p.
    Includes index.
    1. Psychiatric nursing. I. Pasquali, Elaine Anne,
1940-   [DNLM: 1. Psychiatric nursing. 2. Mental
health—Nursing texts. WY 160 M548]
RC440.M353   610.73'68   80-25234
ISBN 0-8016-3758-9

C/VH/VH 9 8 7 6 5 4 3 2   01/A/077

To
Eleanore
with love, affection, and admiration

Without you this book never
could have been written.

Elaine
Helen
Nancy

PREFACE

What is mental health? What is mental illness? When is a person ill enough to require treatment? These questions have long concerned society in general and mental health practitioners in particular. Of all mental health workers, the nurse is probably the most intimately involved at every level of preventive intervention: primary prevention (health education and health promotion), secondary prevention (case finding and treatment), and tertiary prevention (limitation of disability and rehabilitation).

The concepts and skills of mental health nursing are not limited to a particular setting. General-duty nurses, community health nurses, industrial health nurses, and school nurse–teachers may all be actively involved in the promotion of mental health. The health education and emotional support that these nurses offer to persons facing maturational and situational stress help them to mobilize resources, to resolve crises, and to maintain emotional stability. When mental illness does develop, it is often these same nurses who recognize the early signs of maladaptive behavior and who help people to obtain early treatment. At this point, persons experiencing emotional distress may come into contact with psychiatric nurses, who may be actively involved in all aspects of treatment. Later, community mental health nurses may assist clients to reestablish family and social networks and to reassume social roles. Whether or not nurses function in a psychiatric setting, they may be engaged in a continuum of activities that serves to promote and restore mental health.

This book was written with a particular purpose in mind: to present an integrated and eclectic approach to the practice of mental health nursing. This approach is defined and discussed in Chapter 1. Because care of emotionally ill people is not limited to any particular setting, mental health nursing concepts and skills should be an integral part of all nursing care. We believe that anyone who practices mental health nursing must acknowledge and interrelate biological, psychological, and cultural dimensions of behavior. We do not consider any one factor a prime mover in behavior. Nor do we consider any one theory adequate for explanation of an intervention in human behavior. Instead, we suggest a multifactorial approach to the study of human behavior. We suggest that the reader examine the interrelationships among biological, psychological, and cultural factors, the effects of these factors on each other, and how these effects modify the interrelating process itself.

While many nurses agree with this approach, most textbooks, as well as much of the practice of nursing, tend to emphasize one dimension to the negation or exclusion of the others. We believe, however, that to fail to recognize the biological, psychological, and cultural dimensions of behavior is to fail to meet the primary objectives of mental health nursing: (1) promotion of mental health, (2) intervention in mental illness, and (3) restoration of mental health. This book, written for professional nursing students, therefore integrates the biological, psychological, and cultural dimensions of behavior. This multidimensional approach focuses on *people* and on the myriad interrelated factors that both affect them and are affected by them. Nursing should not be hospital oriented or community oriented but *people oriented*. Nurses need to see people interrelating within a wide social field; they need try to understand the process of this interrelationship.

We believe that people—their behavior and the reasons for their behavior—are the content of mental health nursing. Nurses try to sustain people during stress-producing situations. Nurses endeavor to promote healthy behavior, to intervene in maladaptive behavior, and to restore adaptive behavior.

We believe that people should be actively involved in their own health care. Since the term "client" denotes such a participatory role, this term is predominantly used in this book. However, there are times in the delivery of health care when people are (or have historically been) acted upon, when they assume a submissive, dependent role— the role of patient. Thus, in appropriate instances we have departed from the term "client" and have used "patient" instead.

Behavior needs to be understood within a bio-psycho-cultural context. Such an orientation will enrich the practice of nursing and the education of nursing students.

Many people have contributed in various ways to the development of this book. We are indebted to the hundreds of students who have taken our courses. Their learning needs have motivated us to write the book, and their learning experiences have formed the basis for much that appears in it.

We wish to thank our colleagues for the interest they have expressed at every stage of the development of the manuscript and for their useful comments and advice. We especially appreciate the help of Gail Iglesias, who encouraged us in the early preparation of the manuscript and who participated in long hours of discussion about the ideas presented. We also appreciate Anthony Milazzo's contribution to the section on psychotropic drugs. However, we assume complete responsibility for the content of the book.

Valuable assistance in typing and duplicating was given by Lillian Becker, Elizabeth Becker, Kathleen Becker, Rachel Segal, Helen Stephens, Mary O'Flaherty, and Ruth McKay.

Finally, we want to thank our friends and families, who have patiently lived with the development of the book and who have offered constant encouragement. Without their support this book might never have been written.

Elaine Anne Pasquali
Eleanore Gorthey Alesi
Helen Margaret Arnold
Nancy DeBasio

CONTENTS

Mental health nursing

A bio-psycho-cultural approach

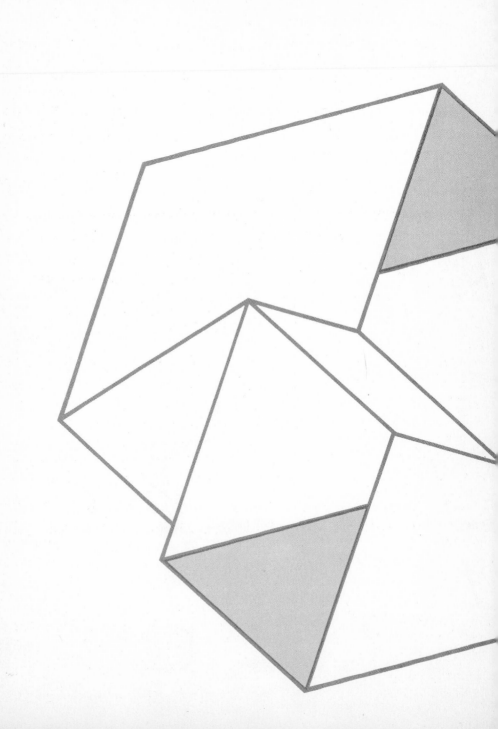

1

INTRODUCTION

Philosophy of professional nursing

Definition of mental health nursing

Relevance of psychiatric nursing to all
areas of professional nursing
practice

Definitions of mental health and mental
illness

Mental health

Mental illness

Theoretical framework

Rationale

Definition

Major theories

Organization of chapters

Concepts basic to understanding
behavior

Concepts basic to therapeutic
nursing intervention

Organization of mental health
services and functions of the
mental health team

Psychiatric disorders

Concepts of power and politics
in mental health care

Organization of nursing intervention

Primary prevention

Secondary prevention

Tertiary prevention

1

PHILOSOPHY OF
PROFESSIONAL NURSING

The activities of the health professions are predicated upon certain beliefs about the nature of human beings, the nature of society, and the role of the professions within that society. These fundamental beliefs provide a philosophical foundation for the attitudes, ideals, and theoretical concepts underlying professional education and practice. Professional philosophy also recognizes the dynamic nature of society and of the health professions and incorporates the ideals toward which the professions strive.

Professional nursing is essentially an interpersonal process, and psychiatric nursing is an integral part of that process (Travelbee, 1970). The primary concern and central focus of nursing is people coping with present and potential health problems. People and the interactions between them are a central component of the nursing process (Peplau, 1952).

Nursing is a humanistic profession. It shares with other health professions the responsibility for meeting the health needs of society. These needs include the maintenance and promotion of health, the prevention and treatment of health problems, and the rehabilitation of clients after treatment. Inherent in the concept of humanism is a belief in the worth, dignity, and human rights of every individual. Among the rights that are of concern to the nursing profession are the right to an optimum level of health and the right to comprehensive health services. Protection of human and civil rights, including the rights to privacy and participation in health care processes, has high priority in professional nursing practice.

Professional nursing acknowledges the complexities of human nature and promotes a holistic view—the person as a biological, psychological, and sociocultural being. Knowledge and understanding of the complex interactions and interrelationships between the biological, psychological, and cultural dimensions of behavior, as each individual continually adapts and adjusts to his internal and external environments, are essential to the practice of nursing. Inherent in the holistic concept is an awareness that many aspects of human nature are universal and that others are unique to the individual. Sullivan's statement (1959) that "we are all more simply human than otherwise" expresses the common humanity that each of us shares with all other people on our planet. The uniqueness can be observed in so basic a biological phenomenon as fingerprints, which are so individual that they are used to distinguish one person from every other. Each personality is even more complex and unique. Each individual is more than a bio-psycho-social being. Each has needs and aspirations as a part of the self, which may be referred to as spiritual being. Recognition of the uniqueness of each personality and of the cultural and ethnic variations in our society is a basic precept of professional nursing practice.

Because nursing is a profession, nurses are responsible for the quality of practice and accountable to the public. A professional level of practice is maintained through a continuing process of formal and informal study. Formal education for professional nursing is a blend of liberal arts and professional education.

Definition of mental health nursing

Mental health, or psychiatric,* nursing is that aspect of professional nursing which is concerned with a person's emotional responses to stress and crisis and with the interplay of bio-psycho-social factors that enhance and/or inhibit the ability to cope with stress. The therapeutic interpersonal process is central to the practice of mental health nursing. Nursing intervention emphasizes interpersonal interactions with individuals and groups coping with present or potential mental health problems. The objectives of nursing intervention are as follows: maintenance and promotion of mental health (primary prevention), early identification and intervention in maladaptive disorders (secondary prevention), and rehabilitation in chronic disorders (tertiary prevention). Psychiatric nursing practice extends across the spectrum of human behavior, from the most adaptive to the least adaptive levels of coping with stress, and involves persons of all stages of the life cycle.

To meet their objectives, psychiatric nursing professionals collaborate with other health professionals and community groups in social, political, and educational activities, among others, that promote the mental health of individuals, families, and communities. Psychiatric nursing is both an integral part of all professional nursing and a specialized area of nursing practice (Travelbee, 1970).

As in all other areas of professional nursing, the level of psychiatric nursing practice varies with the educational preparation and clinical

---

*We use the terms "mental health nursing" and "psychiatric nursing" interchangeably throughout this book since both terms describe the same area of nursing practice.

expertise of the practitioners. The American Nurses' Association's "Statement on Psychiatric and Mental Health Nursing Practice" (1976) identifies two levels of preparation for psychiatric nursing as a specialized area of practice: The *psychiatric nurse practitioner* has educational preparation in the field beyond the baccalaureate degree and has demonstrated clinical ability in psychiatric nursing. The *psychiatric nursing specialist* has educational preparation at the master's or doctoral level and has demonstrated clinical expertise in psychiatric nursing.

Clinical expertise is assessed through a formal review process. Professional nurses who meet the criteria for either of the levels of preparation are prepared to function as members of mental health teams in any clinical setting that provides mental health services. The psychiatric nursing specialist must, in addition, be prepared in research, teaching, clinical supervision, and independent practice. The term "psychiatric nurse" is applied to persons working at either of the two levels of practice.

The professional nurse practitioner with basic preparation in nursing, including bio-psycho-social theory and therapeutic interpersonal skills, incorporates the psychiatric nursing component as an integral part of nursing practice to meet the comprehensive health needs of clients.

Relevance of psychiatric nursing to all areas of professional nursing practice

There is general consensus in the profession that the theories of human behavior and interpersonal skills encompassed in psychiatric nursing are essential aspects of basic nursing education and professional practice. In 1950, the National League for Nursing, the organization responsible for accrediting nursing education programs, required that psychiatric nursing be included in all nursing curricula. Sometime thereafter, the federal government, through the National Institute for Mental Health, provided grant funds for faculty in baccalaureate programs in nursing for the purpose of integrating psychiatric nursing concepts and skills into the curricula.

The practice of mental health nursing is not limited to any particular health care setting or to any one age group of clients. Rather, it is an integral part of nursing in all areas of professional practice and for clients throughout the life span. The nursing profession has long been committed to the concepts of health maintenance and prevention of physical and psychological disorders. Providing emotional support to adults and children who are coping with physical illness and injury has long been part of the nursing process in hospitals, clinics, and the home. Health teaching, supervision, and anticipatory guidance practiced by parent-child nurses are forms of primary prevention in physical and mental health that are accepted aspects of professional practice. Nurses working in community health programs, schools, and industry engage in a continuum of activities that promote mental and physical health.

Recent developments in health care have placed increased emphasis upon the need for the integration of mental health concepts. Among these developments are the public criticism of the health care delivery systems for failure to meet the health needs of many segments of society, particularly the elderly, the poor, and ethnic groups in inner-city ghettos. The demand for comprehensive health care and the focus upon physical and mental health maintenance—in addition to treatment and rehabilitation—place a responsibility upon professional nursing and other health professions for meeting these needs. The report of the 1978 President's Commission on Mental Health emphasized the necessity for primary prevention in mental health and for special mental health services for people with chronic mental health problems (see Chapter 7).

DEFINITIONS OF MENTAL HEALTH AND MENTAL ILLNESS

The terms "mental health" and "mental illness" are used in a very broad, general sense to imply some optimum level of psychosocial functioning or some level of deviation from such a state. Although these terms are widely used in the literature, they have not been clearly defined.

Peplau (1952), one of the outstanding leaders in psychiatric nursing, has written: "Health has not been clearly defined; it is a word symbol that implies forward movement of personality and other ongoing processes in the direction of creative, constructive, productive personal and community living." Leighton (1949) suggests that there are "numerous patterns of psychiatric wellness . . . or many mental healths." Doona (1979) observes: "The problem in defining mental health (and health in general) derives from the fact that health is not a scientific term." Science is concerned with particular, or specific and discrete, aspects that can be clearly defined and measured, while concepts such as "health" and "illness" relate to very general, nonspecific characteristics of an individual or a group or class of a population.

Problems arise when one attempts to apply concepts of health and illness to human behavior—to the complex ways in which people think, feel, and behave in relation to the joys and troubles of life. The ways in which an individual or a group perceives, interprets, and responds to health problems are culturally determined, as are attitudes about which types of treatments are effective. Mental health and mental illness are culturally defined. Each culture sanctions some types of defensive behavior that provides culturally acceptable means of coping with stress, anxiety, and other noxious feelings. Definitions of mental health and illness tend to be based upon particular cultural or ethnic orientations, a situation that may lead to subjective or judgmental attitudes and values being used to assess mental health status.

Kellam and Schiff (1974) observe that "concepts of health and normality tend to reflect the particular orientation or values of the investigator." The term "mental health" also has a static quality: it fails to convey a sense of the dynamic processes through which each personality and environment mutually interact.

Mental health

Such terms as "normal" or "well adjusted," which are sometimes used in preference to "mental health," are vague and subject to cultural bias. "Normal," for example, suggests the existence of a universal standard of mental functioning and a constancy that are inconsistent with the broad range of human experience and the multiplicity of cultural mores and values.

Despite the difficulties involved in finding a satisfactory definition of mental health, there remains a need for some objective standard based on a general concept of mental health or psychological maturity. Cox (1974) has identified "trends or themes of a mature person" that she believes are "most nearly universal and timeless." These include a firm grasp of reality, a value system, a sense of self, and the ability to care for others, to work productively, and to cope with stress. Travelbee (Doona, 1979) views mental health not as something one has but as "something one is." She incorporates themes similar to those listed above into "the ability to love," which includes the love of self, "the ability to face reality," and "the ability to find meaning." Concepts of mental health will be discussed further in Chapter 3.

Mental illness

Mental illness may be defined as psychosocial responses to stress that interfere with or inhibit a person's ability to comfortably or effectively meet human needs and function within a culture. It may be viewed more simply as "problems in living set in motion by stress" (Kolb, 1974). Other terms frequently used include psychiatric or mental disorder, psychopathology, and abnormal or maladaptive behavior.

The use of the term "mental illness" to define or refer to emotional pain and behavioral responses to stress is subject to criticisms beyond those of the ambiguity and imprecision discussed in relation to mental health. Many social scientists and health professionals have raised serious objections to such use. Medical terms such as "illness" or "pathology" suggest the presence of a disease process, which cannot be substantiated in the majority of psychiatric conditions. Of even greater concern is the use of diagnostic categories inherent in the medical model. Diagnostic labeling can have "some very unfortunate effects" (Baron et al., 1978). One such effect is that it tends to "assign the person to the dependent patient status" (Mendel and Greene, 1967). (See Chapter 13.)

In addition, labeling clients by means of psychiatric nomenclature subjects them to public and professional attitudes toward mental illness in general and toward certain diagnostic categories in particular. For example, labeling a person "schizophrenic" in childhood or adolescence may have a profound and lasting impact upon his life, especially if the label becomes known to school systems, employers, law enforcement agencies, and the like.

Questions have also been raised about attempts to fit people of various ethnic backgrounds, and with innumerable behavioral responses to stress, into specific diagnostic categories. Such an effort may lead to a focus upon the diagnostic category rather than upon the person who is suffering. Mendel and Greene (1967) observe that a diagnosis serves the purpose of the physician rather than the client.

Defenders of the medical model point out the need for organizational standards and definitions as a basis for assessment, therapeutic intervention, and prognosis. The American Psychiatric Association, which publishes the *Diagnostic and Statistical Manual of Psychiatric Disorders*, is aware of many of the criticisms and is currently revising the manual to bring it more into line with current needs.

We have attempted to avoid diagnostic labeling in relation to understanding behavior and nursing intervention. Diagnostic categories are, however, utilized in many agencies. It is therefore important for the student of nursing to become familiar with the terminology used in the mental health field and to become aware of both the limitations and the advantages of this form of short-hand communication. Diagnostic terminology is used to facilitate communication and to avoid repetition, and it provides reference points for the study of pertinent literature.

Although mental illness or maladaptive behavior is found in all societies (Murphy and Leighton, 1965; Wittkower and Prince, 1974), the definition, explanation, expression, and treatment of mental illness vary from culture to culture. Culture may in fact contribute to the development of mental illness through child-rearing practices, culture strain, and acculturation pressures. Syndromes or symptoms unique to a particular culture are said to be "culture bound." (Culture and adaptation will be discussed in Chapter 2.)

Regardless of the culture, abnormal or maladaptive behavior can best be understood if we think of it as a way of coping with stress (Baron et al., 1978). As a basis for nursing intervention, we have utilized the concept of *levels of adaptation to psychosocial stress* across the mental health continuum. (This will be discussed further in Chapter 4.)

Psychosocial threat and stress are inherent in the human condition. Threats or stressors may include any perceived threat to the physical or psychosocial self, any loss or threat of loss, and so on. Adaptation to stress is an ongoing process throughout the life cycle. It includes all of the ways in which we cope with anxiety, guilt, fear, frustration, anger, rejection, loss, and so on. Coping processes are strategies for dealing with stress (Lazarus, 1966) and for mastering noxious feelings. They are the processes of adaptation; they include mechanisms of which we are aware and mechanisms of which we are not conscious. Just as physiological adaptation serves the purpose of homeostasis, coping processes serve the purpose of psychological equilibrium. Behavioral responses to psychosocial stress may be expressed through the emotions, through motor behavior, and through thought processes, including language.

Responses to stress become maladaptive (we prefer "least adaptive") when coping processes are unable to control noxious feelings or when the coping mechanisms themselves result in symptoms. For example, in an acute anxiety attack, the defensive or coping mechanisms have failed to contain or master the emotion of anxiety. In obsessive-compulsive behavior, the coping processes result in the behavior. However, all coping processes, regardless of whether they are adaptive to the culture and to external conditions, are adaptive in the sense that they help a person maintain some level of psychological equilibrium. An individual's ability to cope effectively with stress is a combination of biological, psychological, and social factors, the degree of stress perceived, and the current psychosocial situation.

THEORETICAL FRAMEWORK
Rationale

Human behavior can be studied from several perspectives, any one of which can be useful in understanding various aspects of human functioning. The psychologist may study the forces within the individual (the psychodynamic forces), and the anthropologist may study child-rearing practices within a particular culture (sociocultural aspects). Each may extrapolate some general principles that may be used to enhance our understanding of behavior. No single one of these perspectives, however, will provide a complete basis for understanding the complexities of human responses to stress. We believe that the practice of psychiatric mental health nursing requires knowledge of the biological, psychological, and sociocultural dimensions of behavior and of their interrelationships in human responses to stress. We therefore have adopted an eclectic approach as the most effective means of providing a theoretical foundation for nursing assessment and intervention for clients from various ethnic backgrounds who are coping with present or potential health problems.

Definition

The eclectic approach involves selecting from available resources the major theories, concepts and knowledge and inter-relating these concepts to form a comprehensive understanding of the whole. In using the eclectic approach as a basis for mental health nursing, we will introduce major biological, psychological, and sociocultural theories and will interrelate these dimensions of experience to form a comprehensive theoretical basis for understanding human responses to stress. Emphasis will be placed upon behavioral and emotional responses to physiological and psychosocial stress in a culturally plural society rather than upon underlying biological processes.*

---

*We assume that students will have studied the biological and physiological concepts in nursing courses that focus primarily upon that area of nursing intervention.

Major theories

The complex nature of human mental functioning, the large quantity of ongoing research, and the extensive literature available in relation to human behavior make it impossible for a single text to cover the field fully. The mental health practioner is responsible for continued study in order to keep abreast of developments. Selected theories are introduced in this section to provide a historical perspective and some background for the discussions in the various chapters of this book.

Biological theories. A recent report of the National Institute of Mental Health task force on research observed that "more has been learned about the brain and behavior in the last quarter-century than in all previous history" (Segal and Boomer, 1975). Research in neurophysiology has increased our knowledge of the complex processes through which messages or impulses are transmitted in the brain and the central nervous system. This has led to theories about alterations in neurochemical processes that may contribute to such mental disorders as schizophrenia and the depressions. Research in genetics, particularly the discovery by Watson and Crick of the chromosomal structure, and developments in research methodology, such as the electron microscope, have increased the ability to identify genetic abnormalities responsible for some forms of mental retardation and other hereditary disorders. But despite the impressive advances that have been made, knowledge of the complex processes involved in human thought, memory, and emotions, and their interrelationships, is limited.

Genetic theories. At the present time, no single gene aberration has been found that can be cited as a factor in the etiology of schizophrenia (Kety, 1978) or in other functional mental disorders. Genetic defects have, however, been identified in some forms of mental retardation. Phenylketonuria, or PKU, for example, is known to be caused by an "inability to convert the amino acid phenylalanine into tyrosine" (Segal and Boomer, 1975) because of a defect in a single gene that controls the ability to produce the enzyme necessary for the conversion. Phenylketonuria thus is an example of the way in which a genetic defect can alter biochemistry to produce mental retardation.

The observation that such psychiatric disorders as the schizophrenias and the depressions tend to run in families has led naturally to an assumption that these disorders may be hereditary. Research studies of the incidence of schizophrenia in children of schizophrenic parents, and particularly the study of monozygotic and dizygotic twins of schizophrenic parents, has provided statistical evidence to support this theory. Many studies have found that there is a higher incidence of schizophrenia in the children of schizophrenic parents than in children whose parents are not schizophrenic, and an even higher incidence among monozygotic twins of schizophrenic parents. (Studies involving twins will be discussed further in Chapter 13.) In order to avoid the psychological and sociocultural influences that can result from growing up in a family in which the parents are schizophrenic, studies of children and twins raised by adoptive parents who were not schizophrenic have also been conducted. These studies, too, have found the incidence of schizophrenia to be higher in children of schizophrenic parents than in children whose biological parents are not schizophrenic.

Neurophysiological theories. Neurophysiological research has been going on for more than a quarter of a century, during which time many theories about the biological nature of mental disorders have been studied (see Chapters 11 and 13). Fairly recent developments in neurophysiological research have contributed to our knowledge of the complex processes by which messages, or impulses, are transmitted from one nerve cell, or neuron, to another. Several chemicals called neurotransmitters have been identified, among them dopamine, norepinephrine, and serotonin. Because of their chemical structure, neurotransmitters are also referred to as biogenic amines and as monoamines. In the transmission of messages or impulses from the axon, or nerve ending, of one neuron to a receptor site in an adjacent neuron, a chemical neurotransmitter, dopamine for example, is released into the synaptic space between the neurons. Following transmission, the neurotransmitter in the synaptic space is either taken back into the axon of the transmitter neuron through the cell membrane (re-uptake) or metabolized by enzymes or other chemical substances. An enzyme, monoamine oxidase, is believed to be essential to the neutralization of the neurotransmitter and possibly to the re-uptake process (Schildkraut, 1978). Nerve cells are highly specialized in the neurotransmitters that they produce and respond to and in their locations and functions in relation to other neurons (Segal and Boomer, 1975).

Research in neurochemistry has been stimulated and influenced by study of the action and side effects of the psychopharmaceuticals that are effective in the treatment of psychoses and depressions. The dopamine hypothesis, for example, which posits some disturbance in the neurotransmitter dopamine, was stimulated by the observation that parkinsonism was a prominent side effect of treatment with the phenothiazines and other antipsychotic drugs. Since it was known that in Parkinson's Disease there is a deficiency of dopamine or a disturbance in dopamine transmission, the assumption was made that the antipsychotic drugs acted by blocking dopamine receptors (see Chapter 13). Other studies have focused upon the group of antidepressant drugs that are monoamine oxidase inhibitors. Such drugs are effective in treating certain forms of depression (see Chapter 11).

Developmental theories. The relationship between experience and psychological development, particularly in the early years of life and personality development, has been a major concern in psychological theories since the works of Freud, early in this century. Biological research in recent years has focused upon the importance of adequate nutrition and environmental stimulation to brain cell development. Nutritional deficiencies during the prenatal period and during infancy, when the brain is undergoing the most rapid development, have been found to have a direct impact upon brain cell development. Studies in mice have demonstrated that malnutrition during these critical periods "permanently reduces the number of neurons in the brains of mice" (Segal and Boomer, 1975). Lack of environmental stimulation during the early developmental years also has a negative impact upon brain cell development and function (Segal and Boomer, 1975). (See Chapter 3.)

Theories related to brain cell changes. Recent research in relation to Alzheimer's disease has identified changes in the neurons of the cerebral cortex. Alzheimer's disease, a condition occurring in some older people, involves a progressive deterioration in intellectual functioning. Originally described as a condition associated with premature aging, Alzheimer's disease is now believed to be the major cause of severe organic brain dysfunction in older people (National Institute of Health, 1979). The results of neuronal changes that occur in this condition are of two types, often referred to as neurofibrillary tangles and senile plaques. Viewed under the electron microscope, neuronal cell proteins appear as threadlike filaments—hence the term neurofibrillary tangles. The change that produces plaques in the cerebral cortex has been identified as the degeneration of groups of nerve endings (National Institutes of Health, 1979). The cause of the degeneration of nerve cell bodies and terminals is not known. Similar changes have been found in persons with Down's syndrome who survive "beyond 35 to 40 years of age" (Wells, 1978). Further research promises to provide an understanding of the etiology, treatment, and prevention of Alzheimer's disease.

Psychological theories. A variety of psychological theories or schools of psychological thought has developed during the last century. Two major schools of psychological theory began at about the same time with the works of Freud in Austria and Pavlov in Russia. Freud introduced the psychodynamic or intrapsychic theory, which has led to a variety of additional theories of intrapsychic functioning. In his studies of animals, Pavlov introduced behavior theory which has also been expanded upon and applied to human behavior.

Some of the basic concepts of each of these two schools of thought will be presented here. Additional theoretical formulations will be discussed in the chapters in which they are relevant.

Freudian or classical theory. Freud's work spanned more than half a century, during which time he developed several interrelated theoretical formulations of mental functioning. He also developed the psychoanalytic method of psychotherapy. Freud's work aroused controversy in that it challenged accepted beliefs and doctrines. Some of the controversy continues to the present time, although many of the terms and concepts Freud introduced have become part of our language and important to the understanding of human behavior.

Psychodynamic or intrapsychic theory, upon which psychoanalysis is based, is a conceptual framework that aids in the understanding of the complex forces and functions related to human behavior and personality. Several aspects of this theory will be discussed.

LEVELS OF AWARENESS OR CONSCIOUSNESS. The concept of levels of consciousness, often referred to as the topographical theory, is important in psychodynamic theory. According to this concept, there are three levels of awareness, or consciousness, which influence behavior—the conscious level, the preconscious level, and the unconscious level.

The conscious level is that part of experience which is in awareness. This level encompasses the broad range of intellectual, emotional, and interpersonal aspects of behavior, among others, over which we have conscious control. The preconscious level includes those areas of mental functioning that, although not in immediate awareness, can be recalled with some effort. Anyone who has had some difficulty in recalling information necessary to answer a question on an examination, even when the information has been reviewed the night before, has had experience with this level of awareness. The preconscious level serves an important function in screening out extraneous data and incoming stimuli when one is trying to concentrate on a particular matter.

The unconscious level is characterized by mental functioning that is out of awareness and that cannot be recalled. Inherent in Freud's view of the unconscious is the idea that the level of mental functioning in early life, prior to the development of language and logical thought processes, still exists within the psyche and must be maintained on the unconscious level in order to protect one's ability to function as a mature adult. This is accomplished, after the ability for logical thought has developed, through the process of repression. Repression is one of the counterforces or ego defense mechanisms that maintain a hypothetical boundary between conscious and unconscious levels of functioning. Thoughts, wishes, ideas, and so on that are in conflict with one's internalized standards and ideals are also maintained in the unconscious level through repression and other counterforces.

An important aspect of the unconscious level of functioning is that such forces as drives and wishes that are kept out of awareness are dynamic forces that seek expression, even in a disguised form—hence the need for counterforces. Therefore, in topographical theory the unconscious level of functioning is viewed as one of the motivating forces of behavior. Some of the forms through which unconscious forces may be expressed are dreams, slips of the tongue, and impulsive acts. Expression may also be seen in disturbances in thinking and behavior that appear in symptoms of psychoses and neuroses.

The idea of a dynamic unconscious process as one of the motivating forces of human behavior—the idea of unconscious motivation—is one of the freudian views that aroused controversy. The idea that all of our thinking, feeling, and acting is not under fully conscious control is threatening to our view of ourselves as fully rational people. This concept has, however, become a part of our language and can be useful in understanding otherwise inexplicable behavior, such as that often displayed in symptoms of mental disorder.

STRUCTURAL THEORY. Freud's development of a theory of personality—which holds that the personality consists of three parts: id, ego, and superego—occurred after his development of the levels-of-consciousness theory (Fine, 1962). Although often referred to as constituting the structural theory, the id, the ego, and the superego can more accurately be viewed as interacting systems of the personality.

The id is the part of the personality with which one is born and from which the ego and the superego, the more mature parts of the personality, develop as the individual progresses through the stages of psychosexual development from infancy to adulthood (see Chapter 3). The infant is born with the potential for such development and with innate or inborn drives for the survival of the self and the survival of the species. Survival of the self requires that such basic biological needs as those for food, sleep, and shelter be met; since the infant is helpless, these needs must be met by the mother or by others in the environment. The sexual and aggressive drives are also viewed as inborn tendencies or instincts present in the id. The id is therefore often referred to as the seat of the passions.

Freud introduced the term "pleasure principle" to describe one aspect of functioning at the id level of personality. The pleasure principle means that internal needs, experienced by the infant as tension, demand immediate gratification—that is, relief of tension. This principle is in accord with Cannon's theory of homeostasis, which holds that an organism always seeks a return to a steady state. There is no ability to discriminate, at this early level of development, between an object that will satisfy a need and one that will not. Any available vehicle will be utilized to reduce tension. For example, to reduce hunger tension, the young infant will suck upon anything near the mouth. In later life, similar indiscriminate behavior can often be observed as psychiatric sysmptoms. Compulsive hand washing, for example, may be utilized to reduce the tension of anxiety and conflict.

Primary process thinking is another aspect of the id level of functioning that can be helpful in understanding behavior. Primary process thinking is a form of mental functioning that precedes the ability to use logical thought processes. It is the form of thought believed to occur in early life, before the development of language. Dreams are one example of primary process thinking, and it is, perhaps, through dreams that this level of mental functioning can best be understood. One feature of dreams is their incomprehensibility. Dreams are highly symbolic, and much of the symbolism is of the earlier or more primitive level of mental functioning. One symbol may represent more than one unconscious wish, thought, emotion, or object. Put another way, many forces that are seeking expression may be condensed into a single symbolic expression. Another aspect of dreams is the lack of logic. Contradictory or mutually exclusive wishes, thoughts, and so on can occur together.

Dreams serve an important function in mental life in that they provide expression, in a disguised form, of some of the unconscious forces of the personality and thus help to maintain mental health. Primary process thinking can also be seen in some of the behavioral symptoms in mental disorders. For example, the compulsive hand washing mentioned earlier makes no sense from the logical point of view. But in relation to the symbolism of primary process, this symptom becomes more comprehensible when it is viewed as a means of reducing the tension of anxiety, conflict, and guilt.

The ego is the part of the personality that interacts with both the external environment and the somatic and psychic aspects of the individual's internal environment. The ego is, of course, a highly complex system of functions that is sometimes referred to as the executive part of the personality and the site of reason. The ego develops over time as an individual matures physically, psychologically, and socially, and since the ego is involved with learning, reason, and creativity, ego development continues over a lifetime. Ego functions encompass all of the intellectual and social abilities that we think of as being particularly human. Imagination, creativity, and the ability to use spoken and written language, logic, and abstract thought are but a few of these complex human functions. The ego is also the system that experiences emotions, which range from joy to fear, anxiety, and depression. Another major function of the ego that is of special importance to mental health is that of maintaining the integrity of the personality when it is coping with stress. The noxious feelings often aroused by internal and external stress threaten the integrity of the personality by upsetting the balance between unconscious forces seeking expression and counterforces preventing a breakthrough of the unconscious forces into awareness. The ego maintains the delicate balance between the conscious and unconscious aspects of the personality through such mental mechanisms as repression, denial, and projection. Stress and the anxiety that accompanies it can bring about the need for additional, often more primitive, mental mechanisms, or ego-defense mechanisms, to cope with it. When stress is severe, such mechanisms may result in symptoms of mental illness. (Ego-defense mechanisms and concepts of anxiety will be discussed further in Chapter 4.)

The superego represents the internalization of the ethical precepts, standards, prohibitions, and taboos of parents and other authority figures responsible for the acculturation of the child. This complex system develops in childhood through a process of rewards and punishments, approval and disapproval, and through identification with parents, peers, and others in one's culture. The superego provides an individual with a system of internal controls over thoughts, feelings, and actions that is essential to independent, adult functioning in the culture. The ego ideal, a part of the superego system, is an internalized ideal image of the self toward which the ego strives and against which ego functioning is measured. Striving to realize the idealized image provides some of the motivation for achievement of a person's higher aspirations. However, when the idealized image is too far removed from the real self, the struggle to achieve unrealistic ideals can lead to frustration and feelings of hopelessness.

The conscience is another aspect of the complex superego system. The conscience monitors thoughts, feelings, and actions and measures them against internalized values and standards. When one's internalized values are not adhered to in a particular sphere of behavior, feelings of guilt and shame are aroused. A person who has a strict, inflexible superego is highly susceptible to experiencing guilt and other painful emotions. Since portions of ego and superego functioning are unconscious, the person who is unduly susceptible to experiencing guilt is often unaware that the feeling arises from within the self. In such instances, the feeling is perceived as coming from a punitive environment. In contrast, people in whom the superego is weak or non-existent do not experience feelings of guilt or shame, even when behavior grossly violates cultural norms. Such individuals lack the internal controls needed to function responsibly in society.

DEVELOPMENTAL THEORY. One of Freud's major contributions to the understanding of human behavior was the introduction of the theory of personality development, or psychosexual development, as he termed it. Although Freud's ideas about infantile sexuality remain controversial, the concept that there are predictable developmental stages has been generally accepted. The importance of personality development to mental health is implicit in all of the schools of psychoanalytic thought. Since theories of personality development will be the focus of Chapter 4, they will not be discussed here. It is important to note, however, that the degree to which one masters the sequential, developmental tasks of one stage can have an impact upon mastery of the tasks of succeeding stages. For example, difficulty in developing trust in self and others can inhibit the ability to develop autonomy.

The theoretical formulations of Freud have been expanded and given new focus by many theorists during the years following his work. Anna Freud, for example, further developed the concept of the ego and the mental mechanisms utilized in coping with stress. Erik Erikson expanded Freud's theory of personality development to cover the entire life span. Erikson also refocused developmental theory to incorporate social science concepts concerning the interaction of the individual with the environment. Others have advanced different aspects of freudian theory.

Interpersonal theories. The interpersonal theorists, sometimes referred to as neo-Freudians, placed emphasis upon the interaction between the individual and society in relation to mental health and mental illness. Karen Horney, Harry Stack Sullivan, and Erich Fromm utilized modern concepts from such disciplines as sociology and anthropology, to a greater extent than Freud had, in developing their theories.

Horney's theory of neuroses emphasizes the importance of interpersonal interactions in the origin and perpetuation of neurotic behavior. Sullivan also views the individual as primarily a socially interacting organism. Sullivan developed a comprehensive theory to explain human behavior in mental health and mental illness. His theory of personality development and functioning is often considered to be couched more in operational terms than in concepts. Sullivan's terms are often utilized by nurses and other health professionals. Fromm's theory has focused more broadly upon social forces and their impact upon the individual. (The interpersonal theories will be discussed more fully in later chapters.)

Behavior theory. Behavior theory, which was developed in the laboratory through experimental research with animals, had its origins in the work of Ivan Pavlov, in Russia. Interest in this field has steadily expanded, and it is now one of the major branches of psychology in Europe and America. The best known contemporary American in this field is B. F. Skinner, whose *Beyond Freedom and Dignity* (1971) applies some of the behavioral concepts to aspects of society. More recent research in behavior, or learning, theory has also focused upon human, rather than animal, behavior, and advances have been made in the study of human motivation and biological rhythms.

One basic premise of behavior theory is that all behavior is learned—that is, conditioned by events in the development of the organism that arouse the behavior or perpetuate it. From this point of view, psychiatric symptoms are also learned—or, to use the behavioral term, conditioned. Learning occurs in one of two ways—either by respondent conditioning or by operant conditioning.

In respondent conditioning, an event occurs that serves as a stimulus to which the organism responds. A simple type of such stimulus-response conditioning occurs when a child puts a hand on a hot stove. The hot stove causes pain, and the hand is quickly withdrawn. Once an association has been made between the hot stove and the pain in the hand, the response becomes automatic, or the child learns to avoid the hot stove.

Emotional responses may also be the result of this stimulus-response conditioning. For example, a young child who becomes separated from his mother in a department store may become terrified. Subsequent visits to the store may elicit the terror response automatically. Theoretically, many emotional or affectual responses have their origins in such chance occurrences. Once such an emotional response, like the terror response in this example, has been acquired, it may become associated with or extended to other events or situations in the environment, which then arouse the same emotion. For example, the child who experiences terror in a department store may later experience terror in any large space in which many strangers are present. In theory, at least, this could result in a school phobia, one of the more common phobias of childhood.

In operant conditioning, the organism acts upon the environment to produce a response. Or, to put it another way, the organism emits, or exhibits, a type of behavior that produces a response from the environment that may tend to reinforce the behavior. For example, a laboratory animal presses on a bar of its cage, and a food pellet is emitted. Once the animal makes an association between pressing the bar and receiving the food pellet, it quickly learns to press the bar to get the food, even when the bar must be pressed a given number of times to receive the food pellet. The food pellet serves as a reinforcement for the pressing behavior. The learned behavior continues as long as the reinforcement continues. The behavioral pattern may be extinguished, or unlearned, if the pellet, the reinforcement, is withheld when the bar is pressed. Learned behavior also may be extinguished by the substitution of an aversive stimulus (punishment) for the reinforcement—for example, the administration of a small electric shock instead of a food pellet when the bar is pressed. Although stimuli and responses may be somewhat more complex in human behavior, the principles are the same.

Wolpe (1974) and others have applied behavior, or learning, theory to the treatment of some of the symptoms of mental disorders. Many neurotic and psychotic symptoms are regarded by behaviorists as learned but unadaptive behavioral patterns that are maintained by their consequences—that is, by their reinforcements. Behavior therapy, sometimes referred to as behavior modification, focuses upon the overt behavior or symptom that is unadaptive rather than upon the underlying dynamics or subjective experience, which is the focus of the intrapsychic therapists.

The methods employed in behavior therapy for humans include the operant conditioning techniques of positive and negative reinforcement and aversive control or extinction. Positive reinforcement involves the provision of attention, approval, praise, or other forms of reward by people in the environment. Negative reinforcement is accomplished through negative responses to certain behavior, by such means as ignoring the person or the behavior, withholding enjoyable experiences or objects, and administering mild forms of punishment. Positive reinforcement is achieved through consistent, positive rewards for behavior identified as desirable. The "token economy," in which tokens can be exchanged for candy, cigarettes, and so on as a reward for desired behavior, is often used in the treatment of chronically ill clients in mental hospitals (see Chapter 13). Negative reinforcement may be achieved through the consistent ignoring of behavior that is clearly identified as undesirable. Aversive control is achieved through some form of reasonable punishment when clearly identified undesirable behavior occurs. Negative reinforcement and aversive control are often used in adolescent treatment centers, the former by the ignoring of behavior that has been identified as attention seeking and the latter through a system of demerits for undesirable behavior.

Other forms of behavior therapy include desensitization techniques (which are combined with forms of deep muscle relaxation, to enable the individual to cope with anxiety and other noxious feelings), assertiveness training, persuasion, and advice giving. Desensitization techniques have been used extensively in the treatment of phobias. In such a method, the phobic person is repeatedly exposed, in a limited way, to the stimulus that induces anxiety. The therapy is combined with deep muscle relaxation. When the client is completely relaxed, the suggestion is made by the therapist that the person imagine being in the situation that produces the phobic response. An elevator or a bus, for example, may be the object of the abnormal fear. The treatment may be repeated several times until the anxiety response is reduced. Then another step is taken—for example, the client walks toward the elevator with the therapist. This gradual approach is continued until the client is able to overcome the phobia.

Any behavior therapy program should be designed and carried out, or directed, by a skilled behavioral therapist, or by a person who has extensive knowledge of theory and techniques. Prior to any attempt to institute behavior therapy, the particular behavior to be modified must be clearly identified. The contingencies, or events that reinforce the behavior, must also be understood. Then a program can be developed that can be followed consistently by everyone who will participate in the therapy. The client who is the object of the behavior modification techniques should also be informed about the treatment and agree to participate in it.

Sociocultural theories. A sociocultural perspective on mental health focuses on the influence of social definitions, social norms, and social values on human behavior. Sociocultural theory explores social processes in an attempt to better understand mental illnesses and to intervene therapeutically to promote mental health. The sociocultural theories used in this book may be divided into three categories: functionalist model, psychocultural model, and communication model.

Functionalism model. The functionalism model holds that society is an organismic whole. The various parts of society (that is, institutions and groups) articulate smoothly with one another and thereby maintain equilibrium. New ideas and practices that maintain the existing social order are readily accepted by members of society. Ideas and practices that seriously disrupt the existing social order tend to be resisted. Disjunctions in society may produce social strain.

Functionalists like Durkheim, Merton, Srole, and Parsons use social strain theory to explain social deviance and psychopathology. Society stresses certain values, roles, and standards, but the social structure may make it difficult to act in accordance with them. There may be a disjunction between socially sanctioned goals and access to legitimized ways of achieving those goals, or the social system may make the rules contradictory and meaningless. Leighton and Yablonsky suggest that sociocultural disjunctions may result in inadequate socialization of children. Family patterns, kinship obligations, child-rearing practices, and economic activities may be disrupted. Value systems and role relationships may become confused, fragmented, or conflicting. Children may fail to learn socially sanctioned values, standards, and roles. The resultant frustration, alienation, and tension may produce socially deviant or maladaptive behavior.

Psychocultural model. The psychocultural model focuses upon the relationship between the individual psyche and the social field. Society is viewed as having a profound impact upon the development of an individual's personality. Society provides an individual with opportunities for role development, independence, and socially acceptable emotional expression.

Children are born into a family unit. The family unit becomes the first socializing agent. Later in life, children encounter other socializing agents, such as teachers, clergymen, and peers. A socializing agent serves as a cultural ideal. Children identify with socializing agents, emulate their behavior, and thereby inculcate the norms, standards, and values of society. Through the process of socialization, individuals eventually want to act the way society demands and desire what society needs.

Since family units are never identical, what a child learns at home may later come into conflict with what he learns from other socializing agents. The manner of resolving such conflict, as well as the inherent conflict between the desires of the individual and the demands of society, varies from one society to another. While every society defines what is acceptable and unacceptable behavior, each society offers a range of acceptable alternatives from which an individual may choose.

Social scientists like Fromm, Wallace, Whiting, and Child look at the sociocultural context in which individuals develop and at the mechanisms individuals use to adjust to society. While the majority of a society's members are usually able to use socially sanctioned techniques for keeping stress within tolerable limits, some persons may find socially sanctioned stress-reduction behavior ineffective and may try alternative techniques. Some of these alternative types of behavior may be defined by society as social deviance or mental illness.

Communication model. The communication model focuses upon the cultural specificity of communication. Communication is a process of regulating relationships and exchanging ideas, information, values, and feelings with others. Communication occurs on both verbal and nonverbal levels. Verbal communication is the use of spoken language. Nonverbal communication embraces kinesics (the ways people use body parts to communicate) and proxemics (the way people use space to communicate). These different types of communication are systematically interrelated to reinforce, supplement, or contradict one another.

Communication specialists like Birdwhistle, Hall, Scheflen, and Ashcraft maintain that kinesic and proxemic communication are as culturally specific as verbal communication. The form and meaning of linguistic, kinesic, and proxemic behavior are dependent upon the sociocultural context in which they occur. Ethnicity, age, sex, social class, institutional membership, and geographic locale are only a few of the factors that influence the form and meaning of verbal and nonverbal communication.

People from different cultures inhabit different sensory worlds. Selective screening of sensory data results in some information being admitted and other information being filtered out. An experience that is perceived through one set of culturally patterned sensory screens is quite different from the same experience perceived through another set of screens. An encounter or interaction is one type of experience. When persons from different cultural backgrounds interact, using dissimilar linguistic, kinesic, or proxemic cues and having different assumptions and orientations, communication is impaired and role relationships may be disrupted. A sense of nonrelatedness to persons with a different cultural heritage may develop. In addition, culturally determined and culturally acceptable behavior that is foreign to members of a dominant culture may be misinterpreted and labeled as deviant or pathological. (Sociocultural theories will be discussed further in Chapter 2 and in other chapters in which they are relevant.)

General systems theory. A system is a set of interacting and interrelated parts that constitute a whole. General systems theory is an approach to conceptualizing and analyzing relationships between interacting units. It allows us to explore problems beyond the level of the individual person and to see how myriad relationships—biological, physiological, social, economic, and psychological—are involved.

Social scientists such as Moynihan, Janchill, and Hazzard describe systems as being either open or closed. An open system has a permeable boundary, and it is characterized by active interaction with the outside environment. An example of an open system is a family that has many social relationships, that utilizes such social institutions as church, school, and health facilities, and that buys consumer goods from both local and nonlocal merchants. A closed system is self-contained; it has a definite boundary, and interaction with the outside environment is nonexistent. Few families represent such a system, but we may find families whose networks are restricted or limited. For example, an elderly couple living in a depressed urban area may have lost contact with relatives and may be hesitant to make new friends and afraid to venture outside an apartment. The man and the woman in such a couple rely upon each other for support and may have little social interaction with others. However, even such a seemingly closed system has some avenues of interaction with the outside environment. Food must be purchased at the market. Health problems require the services of physicians or nurses. A clergyman may attend to religious needs. Nevertheless, such a family is very vulnerable during crisis periods because of the large expenditure of energy needed to defend its boundaries and the paucity of support resources.

In contrast, a family that is an open system has more access to outside resources and social networks that can provide support and assistance when they are needed. In addition, more energy is available for problem solving and life pursuits, since it is not being expended on maintaining boundaries.

Systems therapy takes into consideration all factors that may contribute to a problem. The illness of one member of a family often indicates that a pervasive, stress-producing problem may exist within the family unit. Treatment may involve all members of the family and may even include other relatives, as well as friends. During a period of hospitalization, other clients may also be included in this social network. Through the inclusion of many vital linkages in a social system, there is increased opportunity for feedback and exploration of alternative avenues of problem solving. Change in any one of the component linkages in a system ultimately affects, and is affected by, the other linkages in the system.

A nurse can become a linkage in the social system of an emotionally ill person. The nurse thus can focus on the person's relationships with other people and with his environment. The actions of either the nurse or the client may affect the entire system. Concentrating on making the system open and adaptable facilitates the evaluation of health care strategems, the development of a holistic approach to health care, and an understanding of the mentally disturbed individual and his place in society. To work on improving an individual's feelings of self-worth, only to discharge him back into a family who scapegoats and derogates him and into a community that is fearful of him and reluctant to employ him, is self-defeating. The hospital, the family, and the community are component linkages in the emotionally disturbed person's social field. Negative feedback from one will undermine the efforts of the other linkages.

ORGANIZATION OF CHAPTERS

The major objectives of mental health nursing are to provide the theoretical background for the understanding of human adaptation to stress and crisis and to serve as a basis for therapeutic nursing intervention to promote, maintain, or restore mental health. In keeping with the holistic, humanistic philosophy of nursing and the belief that psychiatric nursing is both an integral part of all nursing and a specialized area of professional practice, this book focuses upon nursing intervention for persons who are coping both with physical illness and injury and with psychiatric disorders. Some attention is also given to the functions of the nurse as a collaborative member of the mental health team and to the social forces of power and politics as they relate to mental health nursing. The chapters of this book are organized to provide:

1. A theoretical foundation for understanding behavior
2. A theoretical basis for understanding and practicing psychiatric nursing
3. An understanding of the concepts of community mental health and the mental health team
4. An understanding of how people cope with stress at all points of the mental health continuum and of nursing care in primary, secondary, and tertiary prevention
5. An understanding of political and other forms of power inherent in the health field and of the use of such forces to promote positive change in mental health services and the nursing profession

Concepts basic to understanding behavior

Sociocultural concepts. The United States is a multicultural, multiethnic society. The ways in which people perceive and respond to stress and health problems are culturally determined. Chapter 2, "The Sociocultural Context of Behavior," introduces theories that provide a foundation for understanding enculturation and acculturation. Sociocultural determinants that relate to stress and adaptation are explored, as are sociocultural theories that provide an approach to understanding and assessing ethnic or cultural aspects of a particular client or group in relation to health care. The discrepancies that may exist between the cultural values of a client and those of a health care provider are also discussed. A section on attitude clarification focuses attention upon the fact that a professional nurse's own ethnic values may inhibit the nursing process. This section also serves to introduce the function of self-awareness and self-understanding in the therapeutic interpersonal process.

Human development. Experiences early in life help to determine the ways in which each of us experiences and copes with the stress caused by anxiety, fear, frustration, loss, and other threats to well-being (Baron et al., 1978). Chapter 3, "Human Development," discusses the processes of human development from biological, psychological, and sociocultural perspectives. A variety of theories are presented and integrated to provide a comprehensive understanding of the topic. This chapter provides the theoretical basis for nursing intervention for clients at all stages of the life cycle and aids in understanding behavioral responses that may have their origins in early developmental experiences.

Stress and adaptation. Since adaptation to stress is an ongoing process throughout the life cycle, coping with stress is a theme that is integrated throughout this book. Chapter 4, "Adaptation and Stress," discusses physiological, psychological, and cultural concepts and their relationship to adaptation in mental health and mental illness.

In addition, there is some focus upon stressors such as pain, threats to body image, loss, and immobilization, which are commonly encountered in physical health problems. Primary, secondary, and tertiary prevention in cases involving these threats to mental health are discussed in relation to the interpersonal process as a tool of nursing practice.

Concepts basic to therapeutic nursing intervention

The therapeutic interpersonal process is fundamental to the practice of mental health nursing. A knowledge of communication theory and the ability to use therapeutic communication processes with individuals and groups is the heart of psychiatric nursing.

Chapter 5, "Communication," provides a theoretical basis for understanding communication in relation to culture and mental processes. Theories of verbal, kinesic, and proxemic communication are discussed. Communication theory and discussion of the relationships between the levels of communication provide a foundation for understanding the therapeutic interpersonal process with clients from various ethnic backgrounds. The nurse-client relationship is discussed in the latter part of the chapter.

Chapter 6, "The Matrix of Psychosocial Intervention," focuses upon nursing functions in relation to group therapy, milieu therapy, and special therapies utilized in psychiatric settings. Emphasis is placed upon nursing intervention in cases involving maladaptive behavior.

Organization of mental health services and the functions of the mental health team

Chapter 7, "Community Mental Health," focuses upon mental health services as a system of interacting health and welfare systems that are oriented toward a defined community or catchment area. Factors influencing the community mental health movement are discussed from a historical perspective and in relation to future developments. The organization of community mental health systems and the services provided are discussed in terms of primary, secondary, and tertiary prevention.

Chapter 8, "The Mental Health Team," discusses the members of the mental health team and their interrelated, often overlapping, functions. The client is included as a member of the health team. The role of the nurse is emphasized, and levels of psychiatric nursing practice are discussed in relation to mental health team functions.

Psychiatric disorders

Chapters 9 through 14 discuss major psychogenic and psychiatric conditions. Chapter titles focus upon patterns of adaptation to stress rather than upon diagnostic categories, although psychiatric terminology is used when it is appropriate to learning objectives and when it facilitates communication. The various types of maladaptive behavior are viewed as ways of coping with stress so as to maintain psychological equilibrium.

The patterns of adaptation to stress that are discussed in these chapters range across the mental health continuum. The earlier chapters deal with conditions that involve relatively little interference with psychosocial adaptation, such as the psychosomatic and neurotic disorders. The later chapters deal with conditions such as schizophrenia and organic brain disorders, in which there may be great interference with psychosocial adaptation.

Each chapter provides a theoretical foundation for understanding client experiences and for planning and implementing therapeutic nursing intervention for clients from various ethnic groups. Treatment modalities are discussed in relation to particular mental health problems. In addition, each problem is discussed in terms of primary, secondary, and tertiary prevention.

Discussion of the therapeutic nurse-client relationship focuses upon themes or patterns of behavior rather than upon symptom syndromes. Recurrent themes in a disorder are discussed in terms of assessment and the development of goals for nursing intervention.

Since we believe that people should be actively involved in their health care, and that the term "client" denotes such a participatory role, this term is predominantly used in this book. However, we recognize that there are times when, in the delivery of health care, people are (or have historically been) acted upon, when they are placed in a submissive, dependent role—the role of patient. Therefore, in appropriate instances, we depart from the term "client" and use the term "patient."

Concepts of power and politics in mental health care

Since psychiatric nursing is increasingly a collaborative endeavor between mental health professionals, clients, and community members, the last chapter of this book (Chapter 15) provides a theoretical basis for understanding the political forces that are inherent in any situation in which groups of people are working together. This chapter describes strategies for utilizing power and political action to promote mental health and to meet such professional objectives as client advocacy and improvement of mental health facilities and services. The process of change and the roles and functions of agents of change are also discussed.

ORGANIZATION OF NURSING INTERVENTION

Health maintenance and prevention of disease have long been basic goals of professional nursing. Thus psychiatric nursing, as a part of the nursing profession, has a commitment to mental health promotion and maintenance, as well as to treatment of the mentally ill. In addition, the public and many health professionals have been encouraging the health professions to place more emphasis upon maintenance and promotion of health. The chapters on maladaptive disorders therefore include discussion of the nurse's role in primary, secondary, and tertiary prevention in each mental health problem.

"Preventive psychiatry" is a term used by Caplan (1964) to describe a body of theoretical and practical knowledge that can be used to plan and implement programs whose goals are the improvement of the mental health of the community and its residents. Prevention, as defined by Caplan, consists of primary, secondary, and tertiary levels. Primary prevention seeks to reduce the incidence of mental illness in a community, secondary prevention attempts to reduce the duration of mental illness and to prevent sequelae, and tertiary prevention seeks to reduce residual effects of mental disorders through rehabilitation. This concept of prevention has been widely utilized in the community mental health movement in the planning and implementation of treatment and prevention programs to serve the mental health needs of individuals and communities with a variety of sociocultural and ethnic characteristics.

We have found the concept of preventive psychiatry to be an effective approach in professional nursing. It is an approach that can be used in any area of professional practice to meet the comprehensive health needs of clients. Applying the concepts of primary, secondary, and tertiary prevention to the nursing process, on the basis of a holistic philosophy of the nature of human beings, offers a theoretical framework for meeting a client's health needs in the biological, psychological, and cultural spheres. The level of prevention and the priority of needs in each sphere vary from one individual to another and depend on the nature of the health problem and other factors related to it.

Primary prevention

Primary prevention is oriented toward limiting or reducing the incidence of psychiatric disorders in a community. This type of prevention involves an epidemiological, public health approach that has achieved marked success in eliminating communicable diseases. It places emphasis on the community as well as on the individual or family coping with stress. The focus is upon diminishing or removing sources of stress in the community and upon early identification of, and intervention for, persons in crisis situations, with the goal being to prevent the development of psychiatric disorders. Primary prevention of mental health problems is an aspect of many health and social welfare activities that involve cooperation with community groups in the planning and implementation of preventive services. These services include providing consultation and education programs to increase understanding of psychiatric problems, identifying potential threats to mental health, and providing assistance to community groups and residents who may be at risk of developing psychiatric disorders. Preventive measures may also include efforts to strengthen or increase support systems for groups who may be isolated or alienated and participation in social and political action to reduce such sources of stress as poverty, joblessness, and poor or inadequate housing.

Activities aimed at reducing the incidence of alcoholism, a mental health problem found in many communities or catchment areas, are examples of primary prevention. Nurses and other health professionals may:

1. Collaborate with community groups in assessing the level of potential alcohol abuse and the resources available for intervention and in disseminating information about alcoholism to the community through mass media and other means.
2. Provide consultation and education services to special groups, such as teachers, grammar and high school students, and police officers, who may be serving the population at risk or who may be a part of such a population.
3. Provide crisis-intervention and other supportive services to groups and individuals at risk. The population at risk may include anyone who uses alcohol to cope with loss, or the threat of loss, of love, security, esteem, and other basic elements of human existence.

Additional examples of primary prevention will be found in the chapters dealing with the major mental health problems.

Secondary prevention

Secondary prevention is oriented toward reducing the disability rate from psychiatric disturbances in a community through early identification and effective treatment. The underlying theory is that early and effective treatment of many disorders will reduce the duration of illness. Measures to accomplish secondary prevention include screening programs in schools, golden age centers, and other places where groups of residents gather, case finding by public and community health workers, and education programs oriented toward members of the population who may be at risk. Inherent in the concept of secondary prevention is the availability in the community of referral resources for diagnosis and treatment.

Therapeutic modalities utilized in secondary prevention may include any of those used in the treatment of psychiatric disorders. Individual therapy, group and family therapy, brief hospitalization, and chemotherapy may be employed, depending upon the nature of the mental health problem. Brief psychotherapy, crisis intervention, and short-term hospitalization in a psychiatric unit of a general hospital are often employed in secondary intervention.

If we again use alcoholism for purposes of illustration, examples of secondary prevention may be found in programs in industry for early identification and treatment of the alcoholic. Industrial nurses and community health nurses are often involved in such programs. Nurses in any area of practice may also be involved in case finding. For example, clients admitted to general hospitals for treatment of physical disorders may develop withdrawal symptoms, which may be an early indication of physical addiction to alcohol.

Once identified, the client has the right to accept or reject treatment. Early intervention may, therefore, include the development of a supportive therapeutic nurse-client relationship oriented toward helping the client in this decision-making process.

Tertiary prevention

Tertiary prevention is concerned with preventing or reducing the duration of the long-term disability that is often a residual effect of the major psychiatric disorders, such as schizophrenia, organic brain dysfunction, and some of the psychiatric disorders of childhood. The treatment and rehabilitative objectives are to restore the person to his optimum level of functioning.

Treatment in tertiary prevention depends upon the particular psychiatric disorder. Treatment may include any of the somatic therapies, the individual and group psychotherapies, and other measures employed to ameliorate psychological distress and maladaptive coping processes. In addition, rehabilitative measures, which are designed to prevent or to shorten the period of long-term disability, are important aspects of tertiary prevention.

REFERENCES

American Nurses Association Division on Psychiatric and Mental Health Nursing Practice
1976 "Statement on psychiatric and mental health nursing practice." Kansas City: ANA Publications.

American Psychiatric Assoication
1980 Diagnostic and Statistical Manual of Psychiatric Disorders (DMS III). Chicago: American Psychiatric Association.

Baron, Robert, Donn Byrne, and Barry Kantowitz.
1978 Psychology: Understanding Behavior. Philadelphia: W. B. Saunders Co.

Blaney, Paul H.
1975 "Implications of the medical model and its alternatives." American Journal of Psychiatry 132:9.

Caplan, Gerald
1964. Principles of Preventive Psychiatry. New York: Basic Books, Inc. Publishers.

Cox, Rachel Dunaway
1974 "The concept of psychological maturity." In American Handbook of Psychiatry (ed. 2), vol. 1. Sylvano Arieti (ed. and ed.-in-chief). New York: Basic Books, Inc., Publishers, Ch. 9.

Doona, Mary Ellen
1979 Travelbee's Intervention in Psychiatric Nursing (ed. 2). Philadelphia: F. A. Davis Co.

Drellich, Marvin
1974 "Classical psychoanalytic school. A. Theory of neuroses." In American Handbook of Psychiatry (ed. 2), vol. 1. Sylvano Arieti (ed. and ed.-in-chief) New York: Basic Books, Inc. Publishers, Ch. 37.

Erikson, Erik
1963 Childhood and Society (ed. 2). New York: W. W. Norton & Co., Inc.
1968 Identity and Youth in Crisis. New York: W. W. Norton & Co., Inc.

Fine, Reuben
1962 Freud: A Critical Re-Evaluation of His Theories. New York: David McKay Co., Inc.

Fromm, Erich
1962 The Art of Loving. New York: Harper & Row, Publishers, Inc.

Horney, Karen
1945 Our Inner Conflicts. New York: W. W. Norton & Co., Inc.

Jahoda, Marie
1958 Current Concepts of Positive Mental Health. New York: Basic Books, Inc., Publishers.

Kellam, S. G., and S. K. Schiff
1967 "The origins and early evaluations of an urban community mental health center in Woodlawn." In Casebook on Community Psychiatry, New York: Basic Books, Inc., Publishers.

Kety, Seymour S.
1978 "Genetic and biochemical aspects of schizophrenia." In The Harvard Guide to Modern Psychiatry. Armand M. Nicholi, Jr. (ed.). Cambridge, Mass.: The Belknap Press of Harvard University Press.

Lazarus, Richard S.
1966 Psychological Stress and the Coping Process. New York: McGraw-Hill Book Co.

Leighton, Alexander H.
1959 My Name Is Legion. New York: Basic Books, Inc., Publishers.
1974 "Social disintegration and mental disorder." In American Handbook of Psychiatry (ed. 2), vol. 2. Gerald Caplan (ed.). Sylvano Arietic (ed.-in-chief). New York: Basic Books, Inc., Publishers, Ch. 28.

May, Rollo
1974 Love and Will. New York: Dell Publishing Co., Inc.

Mendel, Werner M., and Gerald Allen Green
1967 The Therapeutic Management of Psychological Illness. New York: Basic Books, Inc., Publishers.

Mullahy, Patrick
1955 Oedipus Myth and Complex: A Review of Psychoanalytic Theory. New York: Grove Press, Inc.

Murphy, J. M., and A. H. Leighton (eds.)
1965 Approaches to Cross-Cultural Psychiatry. Ithaca, N. Y.: Cornell University Press

Offer, Daniel, and Melvin Sabshin
1974 The concept of normality." In American Handbook of Psychiatry (ed. 2), vol. 1. Sylvano Arieti (ed. and ed.-in-chief). New York: Basic Books, Inc., Publishers, Ch. 8.

National Institutes of Health
1979 "Alzheimer's disease." Pub. No. 79-6146. Washington, D.C.: U.S. Government Printing Office.

Peplau, Hildegarde
1952 Interpersonal Relations In Nursing. New York: G. P. Putnam's Sons.

Portnoy, Isadore
1974 "The school of Karen Horney." In American Handbook of Psychiatry, (ed. 2), vol. 1. Sylvano Arieti (ed. and ed.-in-chief). New York: Basic Books, Inc., Publishers, Ch. 40B.
1978 Report to the President of the President's Commission on Mental Health. Washington, D.C.: U.S. Government Printing Office.

Rickelman, Bonnie
1979 "Brain bio-amines and schizophrenia: a summary of research findings and implications for nursing." Journal of Psychiatric Nursing and Mental Health Services 17:9.

Riehl, Joan B., and Roy Callistra
1974 Conceptual Models for Nursing Practice. New York: Appleton-Century-Crofts.

Schildkraut, Joseph J.
1974 "Depressions and biogenic amines." In American Handbook of Psychiatry (ed. 2), vol. 6. David Hamburg and Keith H. Brodie (eds.). Sylvano Arieti (ed.-in-chief). New York: Basic Books, Inc., Publishers.
1978 "The biochemistry of affective disorders." In The Harvard Guide to Modern Psychiatry. Armand M. Nicholi, Jr. (ed.). Cambridge, Mass.: The Belknap Press of Harvard University Press.

Segal, Julius, and Donald Boomer (eds.)
1975 Research in the Service of Mental Health: Summary Report of the Research Task Force of the National Institute of Mental Health. Department of Health, Education and Welfare Publication No. (ADM) 75-237. Washington, D.C.: U.S. Government Printing Office.

Seltzer, Benjamin, and Shervert H. Frazier
1978 "Organic Mental Disorders." In The Harvard Modern Guide to Psychiatry. Armand M., Nicholi Jr. (ed.) Cambridge, Mass.: The Belknap Press of Harvard University Press, Ch. 15.

Seltzer, Benjamin, and Ira Sherwin
1978 "Organic brain syndromes: an empirical study and critical review." American Journal of Psychiatry 135:1.

Skinner, B. F.
1971 Beyond Freedom and Dignity. New York: Alfred A. Knopf, Inc.

Spector, Rachel E.
1979 Cultural Diversity In Health and Illness. New York: Appleton-Century-Crofts.

Sullivan, Harry Stack
1953 Conceptions of Modern Psychiatry. New York: W. W. Norton & Co., Inc.

Szasz, Thomas
1961 The Myth of Mental Illness. New York: Harper & Row, Publishers, Inc.
1970 Ideology and Insanity. New York: Doubleday & Co., Inc.

Travelbee, Joyce
1971 Interpersonal Aspects of Nursing (ed. 2). Philadelphia: F. A. Davis Co.

Wells, Charles E.
1978 "Chronic brain disease: an overview." American Journal of Psychiatry 135:1.

Werner, Harold D.
1970 New Understandings of Human Behavior: Non-Freud Readings from Professional Journals 1960-1968. New York: Associated Press.

Wittkower, Eric D., and Raymond Prince
1974 "A review of transcultural psychiatry." In American Handbook of Psychiatry (ed. 2), Vol. 2. Gerald Caplan (ed.). Sylvano Arieti (ed.-in-chief). New York: Basic Books, Inc., Publishers, Ch. 35.

Wolpe, Joseph
1973 The Practice of Behavior Therapy (ed. 2). New York: Pergamon Press, Inc.
1974 The behavior therapy approach." In The American Handbook of Psychiatry (ed. 2), vol. 1. Sylvano Arieti (ed. and ed.-in-chief). New York: Basic Books, Inc., Publishers, Ch. 43.

2
THE SOCIOCULTURAL
CONTEXT OF BEHAVIOR

CHAPTER
FOCUS

The population of the United States is composed of people from many different ethnic groups, each of which has its own culture. Through the process of enculturation, a person learns the conceptual and behavioral systems of his culture. Enculturation is an essential mechanism for cultural continuity. When persons of differing ethnic backgrounds interact, some degree of another process, acculturation, usually occurs. Acculturation refers to the reciprocal retentions, losses, and/or adaptations that occur when members of two or more ethnic groups interact.

Because each culture codifies reality in its own way, members of different ethnic groups act upon different premises in behaving and evaluating behavior. When members of one ethnic group come into contact with the culturally coded orientations of another ethnic group, cognitive dissonance and culture shock may develop. Moving to a foreign country, moving to another neighborhood, or even entering a hospital may precipitate cognitive dissonance and culture shock, which engender stress and make a person more vulnerable to mental illness.

Awareness of ethnic differences and their significance enables nurses to understand the cultural dimension of mental health and mental illness. In addition, a nurse's awareness of his or her own attitudes and the influence of ethnic heritage on them are essential to therapeutic nursing intervention. In order for nurses to engage in the therapeutic use of self, they must have a high degree of self-awareness and self-understanding. Attitude clarification helps them develop insight into many factors that influence their behavior.

2

THE SOCIOCULTURAL CONTEXT OF BEHAVIOR

THE UNITED STATES
AS A MULTI-ETHNIC SOCIETY

The population of the United States is composed of many ethnic groups. An *ethnic group* is a collectivity of people organized around an assumption of common origin. The members of an ethnic group hold basically similar value and ideological systems and share systems of communication, social interaction, and world view. In addition, an ethnic group sees itself and is seen by others as a distinct category.

The characteristics that distinguish one ethnic group from another are not merely the sum of observable differences; they also include the characteristics that members of a group consider signficant. Some characteristics may be emphasized by group members; others may be ignored or underplayed. Cultural traits that produce ethnic differences can be classified into two categories: (1) overt signs and signals, such as language, dress, and house-style, and (2) fundamental values establishing right from wrong and good from bad that serve as standards for judging behavior (Barth, 1960).

Novak (1973) describes several aspects of America's "New Ethnicity" movement: The movement acknowledges the United States as a multi-ethnic society, dispels the melting pot myth, and discourages cultural homogenization. Advantages of ethnic differences are emphasized, and ethnic consciousness raising is encouraged. Awareness of ethnic traditions and practice of ethnic customs are stressed. Involvement in the social and political needs of one's ethnic group is encouraged.

Despite the multi-ethnic nature of the United States, some social scientists believe there is a basic or mainstream American world view. Kluckhohn and Strodtbeck (1961) identify three aspects of any ethnic group's world view: a person's relationship to other people, a person's relationship to time, and a person's relationship to the world about him. The British-American middle class is often referred to as mainstream America or as dominant American society. Central to the world view of this group are the following relationships:

Relationship to other people—individualistic and egalitarian

Relationship to time—extended future perspective and deferment of gratification

Relationship to the world—personal control, autonomy, goal-directed behavior, and self-determination (Schneider and Lysgaard, 1953; Kluckhohn and Strodtbeck, 1961; G. Spindler, 1977)

Dominquez (1975) holds that many minority ethnic group members consider assimilation into mainstream American society either impossible or undesirable. The Glazer-Moynihan study (1970) found that many people prefer to live in ethnic enclaves. An *ethnic enclave* is a geographic area in a city, town, or village that is populated by a minority ethnic group.

ENCULTURATION

Every ethnic group has its unique culture. *Enculturation* is the process of learning the conceptual and behavioral systems of one's culture. The goal of enculturation is to transform a person from a predominantly biogenic being (motivated by physiological states) into a predominantly sociogenic being (motivated by social values, sanctions, and constraints). To achieve this end, a culture must teach youngsters survival skills that provide for the biosocial continuity of society and standards and rules that govern behavior and the distribution of social and material assets (Honigmann, 1967). Through this process, members of an ethnic group learn how their ethnic group is distinguished from all others.

Basic group identity

Basic group identity, which evolves from membership in an ethnic group, results from shared social characteristics, such as world view, language, values, and beliefs. Isaacs (1975) points out that two concepts figure predominantly in the development of basic group identity: body and name.

The body is the most fundamental feature of basic group identity. Because exogamy (marriage outside the ethnic group) threatens the physical similarity of an ethnic group, many ethnic groups have taboos and constraints surrounding exogamy. Many ethnic groups have also created ways of physically distinguishing their members from all others (for example, through tatooing, scarification, or molding the shape of head, nose or lips).

Some people try to "pass" from their own ethnic group to an ethnic group of perceived higher status. Whether passing is achieved through intermarriage or other means, the degree of social mobility possible is closely associated with the degree of physical similarity to the ethnic group of higher status.

The name, or names, associated with an ethnic group carries much meaning. Names that ethnic groups give to themselves and others tell much about interethnic relations. Both names and meaning may change over time (for example, "colored," "negro," black").

Individual surnames may serve as badges of ethnic group identity and current ethnic orientation. For example, "Americanizing" a surname may indicate a desire to be assimilated into mainstream United States society.

Agents of enculturation

Family. The earliest and generally most effective enculturating agent is the family. The family experience is essential to the development of basic group identity. Ethnically specific (unique to an ethnic group) norms, values, role relationships, communication patterns, and world views are taught within the family context.

There are many different family forms, some of which are associated with specific ethnic groups. Two major types of family organization may be distinguished: extended and nuclear.

Extended families encompass three or more generations of kinsmen. The stem family of Japan (composed of eldest son, his wife and their children, and his parents) and the matrilocal family of the West Indies (composed of a woman, her daughters, and her daughter's children) are examples of extended families. The extended family has a potentially larger labor force and more options for the division of labor than does the nuclear family. The extended family also provides many adult members to share in childrearing and with whom children can identify (Davenport, 1961; Scheflen, 1972).

In the Western world, the nuclear family has long been regarded as the "normal" family form. This type of family, which consists of a man, a woman, and their children, emerged as an adaptation to the Industrial Revolution. As farms became mechanized and people began working in factories, large extended families were no longer an economic necessity (Scheflen, 1972).

At each stage of the life cycle, the two basic forms of family organization differ in their potential for meeting the needs of their members. The extended family provides members with security and dignity. Aging members have a place to live and usually hold positions of authority and respect. Children benefit from the presence of older family members, who help rear them and serve as role models. On the other hand, since respect and the exercise of family authority are usually the provinces of age, younger members of the family may live out much of their lives under the supervision of elders. In the extended family, security is often gained at the expense of personal growth and individualism.

The nuclear family usually encourages and facilitates the individual development of young members. However, nonfamily relationships and occupational demands tend to compete with and weaken family ties. Relationships with other relatives are often inadequate. Consequently, during periods of maturational or situational crisis, family members may not receive necessary support or security. For instance, during a divorce, parents may be distraught and unable to offer their children adequate emotional support. At the same time, the children may be physically and affectionally estranged from relatives who could serve as a support system. Aunts and uncles may live many miles away, and grandparents may be isolated from the family or may have little cross-generational contact. In the nuclear family, opportunity for personal development is sometimes gained at the expense of security (Scheflen, 1972).

Whether the ethnic family is extended or nuclear, it often gives its members conflicting messages: Succeed in mainstream America, but do not become part of it. Participate in society, but retain strong bonds with your ethnic group. At the same time, the ethnic family may try to protect children from discrimination by other ethnic groups. This protectiveness may deprive children of opportunities for full participation in mainstream American life and thereby prevent them from successfully competing in society (Gambino, 1974).

Neighborhood. The concept of ethnicity centers around group identity. An ethnic group residing in an enclave feels a strong sense of belonging and community. According to Gans (1962), members of ethnic enclaves have a strong sense of "neighborhood." Neighborhood constitutes a protective social milieu. It encompasses shops with familiar wares, social clubs, a church, often a school, and a supportive social network composed of reliable neighbors.

Neighborhood peer groups often form. Members may be bound together by age and sex, in addition to ethnicity. Because many residents of ethnic enclaves are born, live, and die in the enclave, the same peer group may be influential throughout a person's life. The neighborhood peer group provides support and a sense of belonging. It structures relationships within the neighborhood and with outside communities. It helps its members to cope with the conflict and tension that may be engendered when the values and customs of their ethnic group clash with those of mainstream America.

Within a neighborhood peer group, there is usually consensus about norms and role relationships. There is also pressure to conform. Studies such as those by Bott (1957), Gans (1962), and Young and Willmott (1957) have shown that when marriage is superimposed on peer networks, peer relationships tend to draw spouses into peer network activities and away from their conjugal relationship. Because neighborhood peer groups are often segregated by sex, spouses may receive emotional satisfaction and assistance from peer group members of the same sex. Women usually associate with childhood female friends and help each other with "women's work." Men usually associate with male childhood cronies and help each other with "men's work." The support that such peer relationships provide often reduces the need for emotional support and help from one's spouse and tends to weaken conjugal bonds.

The ethnic association is another type of neighborhood group that contributes to enculturation. In a multi-ethnic society like the United States, ethnic associations help reinforce ethnic identity and ethnic consciousness. Ethnic associations also help members cope with conflict and tension engendered by migration from one's homeland or contact with other ethnic groups. Associations such as the Landman Society (for Eastern European Jews) and the Sons of Italy establish new bonds of fellowship to replace those severed by migration and develop the rudiments of an ethnopolitical consciousness. Children of immigrants often have few, if any, memories of the homeland. Subsequent generations, born in the United States, not only may have few ties with their ethnic heritage but also may experience pressure to "Americanize." By reinforcing ethnic values, standards, and role relationships, ethnic associations serve as reference groups. They also provide mutual aid, promote the interests of the ethnic group, and facilitate the exchange of goods and services (Blau, 1964; Essien-Udom, 1964; Parenti, 1965; Eldersveld, 1966).

Religion. There is a historical association between ethnic groups and religious denominations. In addition to inculcating and reinforcing ethnic values, norms, and behavior, religious groups may act as political reference groups, militating for changes that will advance the ethnic group's aims. For example, black religious sects in the southern United States spearheaded the move for desegregation and justice for Afro-Americans. Religious groups often try to advance ethnic goals by appealing to an abstract and idealistic moral order (Lenski, 1961; Miller, 1961; Manwaring, 1961; Stedman, 1964).

School. When children reach school age, teachers join the ranks of significant others who are instrumental in enculturation. A teacher may be the first significant other with whom a child relates outside the family and the neighborhood. Especially to young children, teachers may represent the end product of the process of enculturation. Neighborhood schools in ethnic enclaves are sometimes staffed with teachers of similar ethnicity or with teachers who are knowledgeable about and supportive of the ethnic group's culture. However, when children of one ethnic group attend school with children of other ethnic minorities or with children from mainstream America, there may be little articulation between values taught at home and those taught at school (Dickeman, 1973).

Ethnic children may quickly realize that there are two value systems: one that reflects the values of their ethnic group and one that reflects the values of mainstream America. For example, Kutsche (1968) points out that American values of equality before the law, of written contractual agreements, and of personal growth and individual responsibility for becoming successful contrast sharply with Spanish values of deference to authority and age, of unwritten personal obligations, and of responsibility to one's extended family even at the expense of personal growth and individuation. Kutsche also notes that while some Spanish-Americans may become anglicized, those who prefer to live in an enclave still hold much of the Spanish value system.

Ethnic children are usually not helped to view the two value systems as complementary. The school may try to socialize ethnic children into the culture of mainstream America by undermining and discouraging any manifestation of ethnicity. Behavior and customs taught and practiced at home may be derogated or forbidden in school.

> Maria was a first-generation Italian-American. When she began kindergarten she was very outgoing and talkative. Her speech was accompanied by gesturing. The teacher was British-American and used little gesturing. The teacher frequently admonished Maria to "calm down" and "not to talk with your hands." Occasionally while Maria was talking the teacher would gently hold Maria's hands.
>
> At the middle of the school year the teacher noticed that Maria had become very quiet. She spoke only when spoken to and then made only brief responses. The teacher consulted the school nurse.
>
> The school nurse spent some time in the classroom observing Maria's behavior. The nurse, who was also Italian, noticed that Maria appeared very tense when speaking and that she used very little gesturing. The nurse shared this observation with the teacher. The teacher then disclosed that

she had tried to help Maria learn to speak without using gestures. The nurse explained that this was an ethnic communication pattern and suggested that interference with it might be related to Maria's noncommunicative behavior. The nurse also referred the teacher to studies on ethnicity and communication.

The teacher decided she had been wrong to try to control Maria's gesturing and explained this to Maria. Maria gradually became more comfortable in the teacher's presence and more communicative.*

Thus criticism of ethnic children by teachers may be aimed at the core of the children's identity. Ethnic customs and values may be derogated or discouraged in the schoolroom, and ethnic literature, art, music, and heroes may be absent. This atmosphere may undermine ethnic identity and make it difficult for ethnic minority students to relate to the aims of formal education. Covello (1972) maintains that such students often find the experience of schooling an experience of cultural criticism.

In school, ethnic children become acquainted with ideas and behavior that are new and different and that may be held up as superior. The culture of mainstream America is attractive because it is the dominant, "superior" culture. The world of ethnic culture is attractive because it is familiar and secure. Thus conflict often occurs. Children may try to resolve this conflict through accommodation, which usually requires the maintenance of a dichotomy between public and private behavior. In public, ethnic children may reject ethnic behavior and try to use the behavior of mainstream America. In the private world of home and enclave, they may use ethnic behavior. The degree of rejection of ethnic behavior depends largely on the ethnic composition of the school population (both students and teachers) and the ethnic homogeneity of the community. When a large percentage of the school population is composed of members of the child's ethnic group and when the child comes from an ethnically homogeneous neighborhood, the probability of culture conflict is smaller than it is when school and neighborhood populations are ethnically heterogeneous (Covello, 1972; Gambino, 1974).

• • •

Ethnicity is inculcated through the process of enculturation. Family, neighborhood, church, and school serve as agents of encultura-

---

*See Chapter 5 for a discussion of ethnicity and communication.

tion. Kin, peers, clergymen, and teachers are profoundly influential in the transmission of norms, values, role relationships, communication patterns, and world view.

ACCULTURATION

During the process of enculturation members of an ethnic group learn the conceptual and behavioral systems of their culture. However, in a culturally plural society like the United States, members of different ethnic groups come into contact and interact with one another. The reciprocal retentions, losses, or adaptations of cultural patterns that result when members of two or more ethnic groups interact constitute the process referred to as *acculturation* (Barnett, 1954; Smith, 1973; L. Spindler, 1977).

The response of members of an ethnic group to inter-ethnic contact may be *assimilation* (becoming integrated with the dominant ethnic group), *separation* (developing, maintaining, or reinforcing ethnic enclaves), or *out-migration* (moving to another locale).

Peterson (1972) studied the reactions of Choctaw Indians to acculturative pressure. Out-migration was high in those Choctaw communities where job opportunities and social services (such as school and health facilities) were limited. Choctaws moved to Choctaw or Anglo communities that offered jobs and social services. Assimilation was high when job opportunities were available in Anglo communities and when Anglos were receptive to Choctaws (that is, when they related to Choctaws as equals and offered them the prerogatives of Anglo status). Separation was high in those Choctaw communities that were large enough to provide necessary social services and where job opportunities were available in nearby communities.

Therefore, the degree of rigidity of ethnic group boundaries and the quality of inter-ethnic relationships influence the response of ethnic group members to acculturative pressures.

Ethnic boundaries

Every ethnic group has its unique culture. Cultures function as systems and have the properties of systems. The properties of interacting cultural systems influence the process of acculturation of ethnic group members.

Cultural systems are bounded. Boundaries maintain the distinctiveness of an ethnic group. *Boundary maintenance mechanisms* are practices and types of behavior that exclude outsiders from the customs and values of a particular ethnic group. Such mechanisms protect the group from foreign influence and create a "we-they" orientation. Some examples of boundary maintenance mechanisms are ritual initiations, secret societies, fear of outsiders, social controls (such as gossip and rumor), racism, and ethnocentrism (Barnet et al., 1954; L. Spindler, 1977).

The degree to which an ethnic group uses boundary maintainance mechanisms largely determines how closed (resistant) or open (susceptible) the group is to acculturation pressures.

A public health nurse had recently been transferred from one district to another. The nurse had observed that the former district had been composed of third- and fourth-generation Americans of many ethnic backgrounds. Neighbors shared recipes for the preparation of ethnic foods. Teachers discussed the ethnic traditions of many countries. It was common for children and adults to have close friends with ethnic backgrounds different from theirs. Ethnicity did not seem to play a role in the selection of a physician.

The public health nurse's new district was different in many respects from the old one. The new district was composed largely of members of a single ethnic group. The residents were primarily immigrant or second-generation Americans. Local grocery stores sold traditional ethnic goods. While teachers in the school came from various ethnic backgrounds, the students were ethnically homogeneous. It was rare for children or adults to have friends from a different ethnic group. Ethnicity played a large role in the selection of a physician. People felt more comfortable with a physician who spoke their language and shared their customs. Residents were reserved in the presence of "outsiders" and seemed to mistrust them. The public health nurse was of an ethnic background different from that of the people in the district and initially had difficulty establishing rapport. Only after many months of attending local activities and events, shopping at local stores, talking with local merchants and residents, and otherwise demonstrating interest in and respect for their culture was the nurse accepted by the people in the district.

The residents of the first district described here exhibit open ethnic boundaries; there is much inter-ethnic exchange. The people in the second district exhibit closed ethnic boundaries. There is a very strong "we-they" orientation. Ethnocentrism and suspicion of outsiders operate to maintain ethnic boundaries, and acculturation is resisted.

Inter-ethnic relationships

In-group–out-group relationships among ethnic groups also influence the process of acculturation.

Coser and Rosenberg (1957) point out that unique socio-politico-economic relationships may exist among the members of an ethnic group and differentiate that group from all other ethnic groups. This results in a "we" (in-group)–"they" (out-group) dichotomy. Relationships within a group are characterized by comaraderie, order, rules, and industry. Relationships between groups are characterized by hostility and conflict. Each ethnic group tends to view its own folkways as superior and right and those of other ethnic groups as inferior and wrong. Each ethnic group uses its culture as a standard for judging all other cultures (ethnocentrism).

> A student nurse had been assigned to a pediatric unit in order to gain clinical experience. One patient that the student cared for was a 4-year-old child who was recovering from meningitis. When the child was discharged from the hospital, the student decided to make a follow-up home visit. During the visit, the student observed the child eating a lunch of beans, rice, hearts of palm, and plantain. The student concluded that this meatless lunch was not very nutritious and that the family's eating habits were poor.

The family had recently emigrated from the Caribbean, where beans, rice, hearts of palm, and plantain are traditional foods. The student nurse was unfamiliar with these foods and therefore viewed them as inferior. The student's judgment was influenced by ethnocentrism, a common in-group theme that contributes to in-group–out-group polarity.

Under certain acculturative conditions, an out-group may become a source of positive rather than negative reference. People may wish to belong to, feel loyalty toward, or emulate the behavior of an out-group and to reject the behavior of their own group. Emulation of out-group behavior tends to be in the direction of the technologically superior culture (Sherif and Sherif, 1953; Merton and Rossi, 1957; Hyman, 1960; L. Spindler, 1977).

Sherif and Sherif (1964) describe some conditions that influence the selection of a reference group:

1. The more unified an in-group is, the more likely that it will serve as a reference group for its members.
2. The more unified an in-group is, the more similar an out-group must be to it before in-group members will select the out-group as a reference group.
3. The more open an out-group is to new membership, the more

likely that in-group members will select the out-group as a reference group.

Horowitz (1975) suggests that the more dominant and prestigious an ethnic group is, the more successful it will be in recruiting and in making itself appealing as a reference group.

Dohrenwend and Smith (1964) believe that the relative dominance of interacting ethnic groups can be determined by analyzing the following three conditions:

1. Which ethnic group(s) can recruit members of other ethnic groups into low-status positions (for example, slave, servant)?
2. Which ethnic group(s) can effectively exclude members of other ethnic groups from positions that confer status equal to or greater than that enjoyed by members of the dominant group (for example, by segregating schools and neighborhoods)?
3. Which ethnic group(s) can assume high-status positions (such as teacher, physician, nurse, and social worker) in the activities of other ethnic groups?

The more completely these conditions are satisfied, the more complete is the establishment of a dominance-submission relationship between ethnic groups. This relationship may not be absolute. For instance, members of a minority ethnic group may be recruited into low-status positions in the economic activities of the larger society, but they may effectively exclude members of the larger society from the kinship and religious activities of the minority group.

When members of different ethnic groups interact, role relationships are established that usually reflect inter-ethnic status, power, values, and needs. These relationships provide culturally patterned ways for people of differing ethnic groups to interact (Barnett et al., 1954).

> The Hsu family followed a very strong Chinese tradition when in their ethnic enclave. The family members spoke Chinese, wore traditional Chinese dress, ate Chinese foods, consulted a herbalist, and followed a Chinese value system. However, whenever they attended a family-practice clinic, they wore Western-style clothes, spoke English, and accepted prescriptions for Western medicines.

Inter-ethnic role relationships thus may produce private and public spheres of interaction, each with its appropriate behavior. By enclosing ethnic differences in a sphere of intra-ethnic articulation (private sphere), members of an ethnic group may maintain ethnic identity and still engage in a sphere of inter-ethnic articulation (public sphere).

The maintenance of dichotomous spheres of behavior is not the only option open to members of minority ethnic groups who wish to participate in mainstream America. Instead, they may try to "pass" and become assimilated into dominant mainstream society, or they may exaggerate their ethnic characteristics and use them to achieve status and desired socioeconomic rewards (Barth, 1960). Social scientists have been unable to determine the variables that influence the selection of an option or to speculate on the degree of success that any one option will provide minority group members who attempt to participate in mainstream society.

Indices of acculturation

The process of acculturation has two stages. In the first stage, cultural acculturation, members of a minority ethnic group accept and use the dominant ethnic group's language, customs, dress, and foods. Members of the minority group may be reluctant to alter their value system. Isolated ideas and values are altered more readily than those that are integral part of their cultural system. In the second stage, structural acculturation, members of the minority ethnic group are incorporated into the dominant ethnic group's social networks (for example, play and peer groups, country clubs, and neighborhoods). This stage of acculturation necessitates acceptance by members of the dominant ethnic group and occurs more slowly than cultural acculturation (Barnett, 1954; Gordon, 1964).

In trying to measure degree of acculturation, anthropologists have considered the type and extent of inter-ethnic contact and the degree to which such contact results in identification with another ethnic group. Kelman (1961) hypothesizes that a change in ethnic identification occurs when people adopt types of behavior that are unique to another ethnic group. The new behavior enables them to establish a relationship with members of the other group and to define their self-image and roles according to the standards of the other group.

Chance (1965) and Shannon (1968) have developed criteria for determining degree of inter-ethnic contact:

1. Knowledge and use of the other culture's language
2. Residential mobility
3. Occupational mobility
4. Access to mass media
5. National Guard or military service

Chance and Shannon have also developed the following indices for measuring identification with the culture of another ethnic group:

1. Preference for activities of another culture over those of one's own culture
2. Preference for foods of another culture when foods from both cultures are equally available
3. Preference for the clothing, hair styles, and cosmetic styles of another culture over one's own culture
4. Use of another culture's language
5. Acceptance of another culture's world view

Cultural assessment tool

Indices of acculturation can be used to develop a tool for assessing cultural orientation. Since a person's cultural orientation and ethnic identity have strong influences on his values and behavior, nurses need to incorporate cultural assessment into overall assessment strategies. Information from the following areas should be included in such an assessment:

1. Place of residence—inter-ethnic neighborhood or ethnic enclave?
2. Family organization—nuclear or extended? Members composing the family unit. Members invested with family authority. Members involved in child rearing. Sense of obligation to family members.
3. Sex-defined roles—stereotyped male and female roles. Amount of independence permitted men and women. Degree of intimacy permitted between married men and women and between unmarried men and women.
4. Communication patterns—languages spoken at home and outside home. Use of touching and/or gesturing. Interpersonal spacing.
5. Type of dress—traditional ethnic dress or Western-style dress?
6. Type of food—ethnic food or "American" food?
7. Relationship to people—individualistic or group-oriented? Egalitarian or authoritative?
8. Relationship to time—past-oriented, present-oriented, or future-oriented?
9. Relationship to the world—personal control? Goal-directed? Fatalistic?
10. Health care patterns—definition of health and illness. Ideas concerning causes of illness. Ideas concerning treatment of ill-

ness. People consulted when ill (for example, family member, native healer, physician, pharmacist).*

CULTURE, COGNITION, AND CULTURE SHOCK
Codification of reality and behavior

Over a span of many years, a person acquires and stores information in his nervous system. *Cognition* is the processing of information by the nervous system. This processing structures reality and gives meaning to human experience. Cognitive activity includes the focusing of attention, comprehension, problem solving, and memory storage and retrieval. When information acquired is consistent with other information being acquired or with information already stored, a person experiences a state of cognitive consistency or equilibrium (Jordon, 1953; Heider, 1958; Rodriquez, 1965; Estes, 1975).

One of the most important aspects of cognition is *coding*, which is the process of categorizing information. Information is sorted and then stored by means of various types of memory codes: iconic codes (visual images), echoic codes (auditory images), motor codes (motor skills), and symbolic codes (representative images) (Hunt and Lansman, 1975). Although culture influences all types of cognitive coding, symbolic codes are especially influenced by culture. For example, communication systems, one type of symbolic coding, vary from culture to culture. Even a sound such as hissing may communicate either approval (in Japan) or disapproval (in the United States).

All cultures provide a cultural code for perceiving, interpreting, and synthesizing reality. This culturally structured codification of reality is referred to as world view. *Culture* is an ordered system of shared and socially transmitted symbols and meanings that structures world view and guides behavior (Geertz, 1957). Members of an ethnic group, by virtue of their shared cultural background, usually have a common world view and similar values, ideologies, and standards of behavior. Although these thought and behavior patterns are similar among members of an ethnic group, they are not identical. Members of a group usually operate within the boundaries of established custom, but there may be a wide range of individual variation (Goodenough, 1961).

---

*Sources consulted in the preparation of this cultural assessment tool include Kluckhohn and Strodtbeck (1961) and Spradley and Phillips (1972).

Because each culture codifies reality in its own way, members of dominant mainstream America may act upon premises for behaving and evaluating behavior that are different from those of members of minority ethnic groups. In the process of inter-ethnic contract and acculturation, change may occur in the culturally structured cognitive order or individual members of an ethnic group. Any such change involves learning new values, beliefs, and attitudes. Three conditions are necessary for such a change to occur:

1. Exposure. Adequate exposure to the cognitive system of another ethnic group must exist so that it may be learned.
2. Identification. Through the mechanism of emulation, another ethnic group must be used as a reference group and must provide motivation for change.
3. Access. Avenues of access to the valued resources of another ethnic group must be provided so that outsiders perceive that a change in their cognitive orientation will gain them desired rewards (Chance, 1965; Graves, 1967).

Individual members of an ethnic group, mindful of alternatives, make choices—usually between a traditional practice, value, or idea and a new one. Ogionwo (1969) analyzed how networks of information and influence are involved in the decision to adopt a new idea. He found that personal communcation is more effective than mass media and that when mass media are utilized, broadcast media (radio and television) are more effective than print media (magazines and newspapers). Ogionwo also found that the flow of information is not simply from the source to the individual. Group interaction is also important. Family, friends, and social norms may all exert pressure on a person either to adopt or to resist a new idea.

> A community mental health nurse identified a need for child care education for new parents. Counseling on a one-to-one basis proved unsuccessful. The nurse evaluated the program and realized that it had not considered the ethnic background of the clients.
> The people in the community were immigrants and first-generation Spanish-Americans. In traditional Spanish culture, child care is the sole responsibility of the women. In addition, the extended family is central to Spanish family life.
> The nurse considered these cultural factors when revising the child care education program. The revised program was designed for the new mother and the female relatives in her extended family. This approach to child care education proved effective.

This vignette illustrates how important it is for nurses to recognize that informational flow is not simply from the nurse to the individual client. Group interaction is also important. The composition of the group and the influence of the group on the individual vary from culture to culture.

Cultural change and cognitive dissonance

When, through inter-ethnic contact and acculturation, change occurs in a person's culturally structured cognitive order, *cognitive dissonance* may develop. Cognitive dissonance is the state of disequilibrium and tension produced when two or more sets of information are at variance with one another (Festinger, 1957; Steiner, 1960; Kogan and Wallach, 1964).

When changes occur in value or ideological systems, people experience cognitive dissonance. They then try to resolve discrepancies in sets of information (such as conflicting value systems) and to reestablish cognitive consistency. People differ in their ability to tolerate cognitive dissonance and in their ways of resolving it and reestablishing cognitive consistency (Festinger, 1957; Heider, 1958; Kretch et al., 1962).

A person tries to cope with the cognitive dissonance engendered by inter-ethnic contact and acculturative pressures by responding in one or more of the following ways:

1. Acknowledging only one set of information and denying the existence of sets of discrepant information
2. Reassessing the value of conflicting information so that one set of information assumes greater value than the others
3. Identifying differences between sets of discrepant information and trying to use one set to explain the others
4. Seeking new information that will be consistent with one set of information and not with the others
5. Tolerating the existence of sets of discrepant information (Festinger, 1957; McGuire, 1966; Wallace, 1970)

Steiner (1968) believes that persons who use a combination of coping responses are usually more successful in resolving cognitive dissonance than those who use only one response.

How or why a person selects a particular response for coping with cognitive dissonance has not been fully determined. Rokeach (1960) maintains that the more rigid and closed-minded a person is, the more he will strive to maintain his existing belief system. The more flexible and open-minded a person is, the more receptive he will be to reconciling his existing belief system with new or different information. The degree of a person's open- or closed-mindedness is an indication of his readiness to change his belief systems. Berlyne (1960) suggests that open-minded people may even view cognitive dissonance as a challenge.

Closed-minded people tend to reject or deny information that does not fit into their existing belief systems. They usually rely on the assessments of authority figures rather than on their own judgments. Closed-minded people also tend to consider fewer factors when making a decision. Open-minded people tend to respond in just the opposite way (Rokeach, 1960; Burke, 1966; Kleck and Wheaton, 1967).

The potential impact of discrepant information on a person's value and belief system also influences his choice of coping responses. Degree of commitment to one's value and belief system, degree of ethnocentrism, and degree of freedom to accept or reject discrepant information all influence a person's selection of coping responses (Zajonic and Burnstein, 1965; Abelson, 1968; Aronson, 1968; Kelman and Baron, 1968).

Cognitive dissonance and culture shock

Culture shock, which results from a drastic change in the cultural environment, is both precipitated by and a response to cognitive dissonance. Culture shock is engendered by unfamiliar cues of social interaction. When ethnic groups use dissimilar cues during interaction with each other, conflicts in communication and role relationships may result. Brink and Saunders (1976) have identified the following factors in social interaction as the ones that most frequently create cognitive dissonance and engender culture shock:

1. Different systems of communication
2. Unfamiliar physical environment
3. Isolation from family and friends
4. Foreign customs
5. Different or new role relationships

Any alternation in a person's verbal or nonverbal system of *communication* creates a barrier in the giving and receiving of behavioral cues. Even if a person is familiar with the language of another ethnic group, he may have difficulty with nuances of meaning, styles of humor, and colloquialisms.

Alterations in the *physical environment* may also prove difficult. If a person has recently immigrated to a country, utilities formerly taken for granted, such as electricity and telephone, may operate differently or be absent. House-styles, clothes, shopping facilities, and food may also seem strange. It takes time and energy to learn to manipulate the mechanical environment. Fatigue and frustration may develop.

In addition, patterns of customary behavior and *role relationships* may be disrupted. A person may have to become accustomed to new and different sex-linked roles, rules of etiquette, and status and kinship systems. Value and belief systems may also be challenged. Since a person's ideological systems are usually implicit rather than explicit, he may not be aware of his own values and beliefs until they are questioned. He may realize only then that his standards and ideology are different from those of his neighbors. These changes in life-style may create cognitive dissonance and result in culture shock.

Cognitive dissonance acts as a stressor and requires adaptive responses. The greater the number of changes required by the new cultural environment, the more difficult the cultural readjustment. Cultural readjustment is part of the process of acculturation. Having to unlearn old cognitive patterns may often prove more stressful than learning new cognitive patterns.

Oberg (1954) was one of the first to observe and describe the phases of adaptation to culture shock: excitement, disenchantment, and resolution. During the excitement phase, a person begins to learn about his new country or neighborhood. He becomes acquainted with new customs, tastes unfamiliar foods, sightsees, and begins to establish new work and social roles. As a person begins to "settle in," he enters the disenchantment phase. Changes in life-style that earlier had seemed exciting now seem frustrating. Ethnocentrism surfaces as a person tends to view the customs, values, and communication system of other ethnic groups as inferior and infuriating. Feelings of inadequacy, loneliness, anger, and nostalgia predominate. If a person remains in a new country or neighborhood and begins to learn the behavioral and communication systems of other ethnic groups, resolution of culture shock is under way. During this phase, new friendships are formed and feelings of inadequacy, isolation, and loneliness dissipate. With the termination of this phase, culture shock is successfully resolved.

However, responses to culture shock are not always adaptive. Spradley and Phillips (1972) have found that when a person's usual coping responses prove ineffective and opportunity to learn new coping responses is unavailable, a person may respond to culture shock with psychosis, depression, suicide, or homicide.

The following operational definition of culture shock describes the dynamic interrelationship between enculturation, cognitive dissonance, and culture shock:

1. A person, through interaction with significant others, learns the skills necessary for participating in a particular ethnic group in a particular society.
2. When this person, through choice or force, interacts with members one or more of other ethnic groups, the skills that were effective in his own cultural system may prove ineffective in varying degrees.
3. The person perceives the situation as stressful. Old role relationships, values, expectations, and types of behavior are either less effective or not effective. Culturally coded meanings for objects and events are not shared by members of the other ethnic groups with whom he has to interact.
4. This drastic change in the cultural environment produces cognitive dissonance, which acts as a stressor and requires accommodation or readjustment of life-style and behavior. This situation is known as *culture shock*.
5. The person develops stress responses to the culture shock. During the process of cultural readjustment involved in resolving culture shock, he either (a) accommodates himself to the other ethnic groups by learning new behavioral, communication, and ideological systems and thus becomes acculturated or (b) is unable to learn the skills required for cultural readjustment and becomes aggressive, depressed, or withdrawn. Mental illness may develop in the latter situation.

Culture shock and mental illness

Social scientists have found a relationship between culture shock and mental illness. Frost (1938) was among the first to study the incidence of mental illness in American immigrants. He found that the first 18 months in a new country is the period when they are most vulnerable. Dayton (1940) found that, for all age groups, the admission rate to psychiatric hospitals in the United States is significantly higher for foreign-born persons than for persons born in this country. More recently, Tyhurst (1955) corroborated the findings of Frost and Dayton by describing some of the maladaptive effects of migration. During the first 2 months in the host country, an immigrant usually experiences a general sense of well-being, with an associated increase in psychomotor activity. This hyperactivity serves to relieve tension. As the immigrant settles into the new country and encounters social difficulties engendered by unfamiliar language, customs, and values, culture conflict and emotional strain develop and gradually heighten. Flights into nostalgia often help an immigrant cope with the realities of culture shock. Approximately 6 months after having arrived in the new country, the immigrant may begin to evidence high anxiety, suspiciousness, depression, psychosomatic disorders, or any combination of these characteristics.

The stress of culture shock is not limited to immigrants. Second- and even third-generation Americans may experience stress engendered by conflict between ethnic ideology and the ideology of mainstream America. Ethnic identity is formed early in life through interaction with family, peers, and significant others. Therefore, social networks are often comprised of members of similar ethnic heritage. However, as Dickeman (1973) points out, in order to succeed in the United States and become assimilated into mainstream American society, members of minority ethnic groups must often deny much of their ethnic heritage. Ethnically oriented customs, behavior, beliefs, and values must often be unlearned and replaced by those of mainstream America. Such denial of ethnicity often requires a person to disavow affiliation with family and other significant members of his ethnic group. Dickeman maintains that disavowal of ethnic identity is demanded of all Americans who wish to participate in mainstream society but have not been born into it.

Spindler (1971), while studying the Menominee Indians of the United States, found a relationship between acculturative pressures and stress. He developed five categories that reflect degrees of social, economic, cultural, and psychological adaptation. Each category represents a different life-style:

1. Native oriented—continued and heavy identification with the traditional past; traditional values, customs, and social controls predominate
2. Peyote cult—synthesis of Christian and traditional behavior and beliefs
3. Transitional—some aspects of the traditional past and many of the values, attitudes, and practices of the Anglo-American lower class; goals of neither culture are meaningful
4. Lower-strata acculturated—cultural patterns and acquisitions of the Anglo-American working class; little social interaction with native-oriented Indians

5. Acculturated elite: cultural patterns and acquisitions of the Anglo-American middle and upper classes; almost no social interaction with native-oriented Indians

Spindler found that members of the transitional group exhibited free-floating anxiety. In an attempt to cope with their transitional stage of acculturation, many Menominee in this group withdrew from social interaction, consumed excessive amounts of alcohol, or both. Although members of the acculturated groups (lower strata and elite) also exhibited high anxiety, they tended to sublimate it into achievement of socially sanctioned mainstream American goals. In contrast, the native-oriented Menominee exhibited little anxiety, while the members of the Peyote cult overtly expressed anxiety through Peyote rituals. Spindler's research thus indicates a relationship between culture shock and emotional stress. It also indicates that the way a person tries to cope with stress engendered by culture shock may be related to upward social mobility and degree of acculturation.

It should not be assumed that acculturation and social mobility must destroy ethnic ties. Gordon (1964) believes that while acculturation does occur during upward social mobility, detachment from one's ethnic group in either values or social relationships is not a necessary end result.

Culture shock and hospitalization

The transition from person to patient* may be marked by culture shock. In a total institution, such as a hospital, a significant number of persons are isolated from society and their lives are organized according to the rules and regulations of a bureaucracy. People in total institutions fall into one of two categories: a large group of supervised inmates and a small group of supervisory staff. Social intercourse and mobility between the two groups are severely limited and usually formally prescribed. Through the bureaucratic management of blocks of people, total institutions try to provide for at least minimal gratification of human needs. A consequence of this enclosed, bureaucratically administered life is the molding of a person's personality and behavior. In order to change a person into an inmate (or a patient), a total institution must use certain techniques, based on the principles of role loss and humiliation, that are built into its structure. These maneu-

---

*The term "patient" is used here instead of "client," to denote a passive, acted-upon role.

vers are part of a "stripping process" that breaks down a person's self-concept and life-style so that he will more readily fit into the institutional mold (Goffman, 1961).

The stripping process may be facilitated in a number of ways. Such procedures as issuing hospital gowns, history taking, and confiscating personal belongings all succeed in undermining a person's self-image. Most people view wearing an open-in-the-back gown, even for a short time, as humiliating. Many people feel dehumanized when aides, technicians, nurses, and doctors do not know their names and have to check name tags to be certain they are talking with the right person. Being known by one's name is very important to one's self-image.

In addition, dependency is fostered by such common practices as being confined in bed, being served meals only at specified times, and having to ask for permission or assistance to get out of bed.

The abrupt transition from a familiar social system to an unfamiliar one is fundamental to the culture shock of hospitalization.* The following factors that are inherent in hospitalization may create cognitive dissonance and engender culture shock.

Communication. A new language, "hospitalese," must be learned. People are asked if they have "voided." It is explained to patients that they will receive IMs, IVs, or ECT. Even previously familiar expressions may suddenly have a different meaning. For example, instead of being an explitive, "S.O.B." stands for "short of breath." A camisole is no longer a type of lingerie but a type of physical restraint.

Mechanical environment. A person must become familiar with new mechanical devices and forms of transportation. In a general hospital, patients often must learn to use bedpans and call buttons and must allow themselves, even when ambulatory, to be transported to various parts of the hospital in wheelchairs or on stretchers. Although a patient in a psychiatric hospital usually encounters fewer mechanical devices, he may encounter physical restraints. He may also have to become accustomed to various types of surveillance systems, such as grating on windows, locked units, and suicide or escape precautions.

Customs. In order to fit into hospital routine, all patients must learn a new life-style. General hospital patients are expected to wear pajamas day and night. Patients in psychiatric hospitals often are not permitted to wear belts or to have access to such sharp objects as razors and mirrors. When to awaken, when to go to sleep, and when

---

*Brink and Saunders (1976) have also discussed this transition.

and what to eat are no longer matters of personal choice. While staff members may intrude into a patient's domain—his room—a patient is usually not permitted to enter the staff's domain—the nurse's station.

Isolation. Another characteristic of hospitals is the isolation of patients from their family and community. Visiting hours are often brief (several hours twice a day) and may be scheduled at times when many people are at work. Children often are not allowed in hospital units. In some hospitals, patients do not have private telephones and may only have access to a telephone in the hall. Such a situation not only makes it difficult to place and receive calls but also violates a person's privacy. One's nearest human contact often is a hospital roommate. Roommates may or may not be compatible and may be from different social classes or ethnic groups. Thus a patient who views the mixing of socioeconomic and ethnic backgrounds as an invasion of privacy may be even further isolated from social interaction. Newspapers, television, or radio may become the major contacts with the outside world.

Role relationships. Patients have to learn a new role, and it is a socially undesirable one. Our society values assertiveness and independence, but the role of patient is often characterized by dependence and subordination. Doctors, nurses, and aides often assume authority roles. Orders are passed from physicians and nurses to aides and finally to the patient. While staff members may both give and receive orders, the patient often can do only the latter. In addition, during the time that a person is assuming the role of patient, other role relationships—those of parent, spouse, employee, or student—may be temporarily interrupted. Occasionally, role reversals occur. For example, a self-supporting, independent father may suddenly have to be cared for by his children.

• • •

An altered communication system, an unfamiliar mechanical environment, different customs, a sense of isolation, and new role relationships are inherent in the experience of hospitalization. These dramatic changes in life-style may create cognitive dissonance and result in culture shock.

During the first days of hospitalization, a patient usually asks many questions and inquires into hospital routines. This period corresponds to Oberg's (1954) first phase of adaptation to culture shock. In phase two, the disenchantment phase, the patient becomes frustrated with hospitalization and responds with depression, anger, or withdrawal. When he learns the communication system and routines of the hospital, becomes friendly with staff and other patients, and demonstrates a sense of humor, he is beginning to resolve the culture shock of hospitalization. However, if a patient stays in the hospital long enough to resolve culture shock completely, problems may develop. Unless he is in a long-term facility or a nursing home, such an adjustment is counter-productive. He feels "at home"; he can function comfortably and easily within the framework of the hospital. He thus has become dependent and institutionalized. He is fearful of discharge and unwilling to face the resumption of life outside the hospital.

Culture, cognition, and the practice of nursing

Nurses and clients as members of ethnic groups. Each person is born into a culture, and his enculturation includes assuming the cognitive system of that culture. It is important to remember that culture is persistent. Through the process of immigration, cultural patterns are transplanted from the country of origin to the new country, and then from the immigrant generation to succeeding generations. These patterns tend to remain viable for many generations. Even when a person from one ethnic group has extensive contact with people from other ethnic backgrounds, many of the thought and behavior patterns he acquired during childhood persist.

Therefore, in the United States, both nurses and clients are usually influenced not only by the American cultural system but also by the cultural systems of their respective ethnic groups, of which British-Americans, Italian-Americans, German-Americans, Afro-Americans, and Sino-Americans are only a few. As a result of inter-ethnic marriage, some people have a mixture of ethnic heritages.

Ethnic heritage can be very influential.

James and Tony were nursing students. Although both young men had been born in the United States, their grandparents had been born in Europe. James was British-American, and Tony was Italian-American.

During a seminar discussion entitled "The Crying Patient," James and Tony evidenced very different reactions. While both young men felt uncomfortable when people cried, James believed it was "unnatural and unmanly" for a man to cry. Tony did not see anything wrong with men crying.

James and Tony were influenced by different ethnic backgrounds. Each young man's ethnically specific values, beliefs, and standards of behavior were reflected in his attitude about crying. James' British heritage sanctioned stoicism as a reaction to stress. Tony's Italian heritage sanctioned crying both for men and women as a response to stress.

An *attitude* is a verbal or nonverbal stance that reflects innermost convictions about what is good or bad, right or wrong, desirable or undesirable. A person's attitudes, which are largely unconscious, are based on value systems that are influenced by his enculturation and on life experiences that are interpreted in terms of that enculturation. Nurses who regard their values, standards, beliefs, and perceptions of reality as absolutes may experience cognitive dissonance when they are confronted with other cultural systems.

> After vacationing in the Carribbean, Jeanette decided to move there. Up to that time, she had lived in the northeastern United States. Initially, she was very happy with the move. She rented a house, did a good deal of sight-seeing, and went to the beach every day. She enjoyed the climate and liked the people.
>
> After a few months of becoming acquainted with her new environment, Jeanette began working as a nurse in a local hospital. The hospital was not air conditioned. She found the heat oppressive, and she could not understand how patients were expected to recuperate under such adverse conditions. She also began to realize that her conception of time was different from that of the native population.
>
> She became increasingly annoyed about "people's inability to be punctual." In addition, she was unable to reconcile folk healing practices with her belief in the efficacy of modern medicine. Eventually Jeanette returned to the United States.

Jeanette's interaction with a foreign culture resulted in culture shock. Her return to the United States and a familiar cultural system was one way of rectifying cognitive dissonance and reestablishing cognitive consistency.

Attitude clarification. The practice of nursing involves three levels of exploration: the factual level, the comprehension level, and the attitudinal level. For example, on the factual level a nurse may learn the definitions of defense mechanisms. On the comprehension level, he or she may consider the function of defense mechanisms and may differentiate between the adaptive and maladaptive use of defense mechanisms. On the attitudinal level, a nurse may explore questions such as the following: What do I consider healthy use of defense mechanisms?

What do I consider unhealthy use of defense mechanisms? What defense mechanisms do I use? When do I use them? How often do I use them?

It is important that nurses look at their own attitudes. They need to understand how ethnic heritage influences attitudes—especially their attitudes about mental health and mental illness. Attitude clarification is one way that nurses may become more aware of their attitudes. Because attitudes are often unconscious, a nurse may need to work with a colleague or supervisor who can provide objective information about behavior that reflects attitudes and who will assist in the clarification process. Attitude clarification can help nurses develop insight into some of the factors influencing their behavior.

The process of attitude clarification involves exploring alternatives and setting personal priorities. Using the work of Smith (1977) and Uustal (1977), we can identify the following six steps in this process:

1. An attitude should be the nurse's own attitude and not one that the nurse thinks is expected. For example, a nurse may believe that a person has a right to self-determination, even when suicide is a possibility. It is this attitude that needs to be acknowledged and explored and not an attitude that the nurse may believe is more acceptable to colleagues.

2. Alternative attitudes should be identified. If we again use the example of the permissibility of suicide, the following attitudes may be considered: Nurses have a moral and/or professional obligation to prevent suicide. A person contemplating suicide is irrational and cannot be allowed to make such an important decision. Suicide is sinful.

3. The consequences and significance of an attitude should be explored. What are the legal ramifications of ignoring a communication that indicates the possibility of suicide? What are the personal ramifications? What are the professional ramifications?

4. Personal priorities should be established. For example, does the nurse believe that being self-sufficient makes life worth living and that it is better to be dead than to be disabled, despondent, or dependent? Does the nurse believe that a person has a right to decide when to die?

5. An attitude should be affirmed. An attitude may be attested to relatives, friends, or colleagues. For example, a nurse might say, "Mr. Jones is terminally ill. He is despondent. If I learned that

he was saving pills to use to commit suicide, I would not try to stop him."

6. An attitude should be incorporated into a person's behavioral system. This is the point at which an attitude is acted upon. When the nurse who believes that a person has a right to decide when to die intentionally ignores clues to suicide, the nurse's attitude has been incorporated into the his or her behavioral system.

Attitude clarification is an essential component of the practice of mental health nursing. In order for nurses to engage in the therapeutic use of self, they must have a high degree of self-awareness and self-understanding. Attitude clarification helps nurses develop insight into many factors that influence their behavior. Raths, Harmin, and Simon (1966) have determined that people who are unclear about their own values and beliefs tend to be apathetic, inconsistent, irresponsible, and either compliant or nonconforming. Such behavior creates barriers to therapeutic communication. Attitude clarification helps nurses become more decisive, consistent, and reliable. These characteristics are fundamental to the formation of therapeutic relationships.

Very often nurses and their clients have different and somewhat conflicting attitudes. When these attitudes are radically different, frustration and misunderstandings may result. How often has a nurse tried to refer a client for psychotherapy, only to have the client hold tenaciously to the belief that "shrink therapy" is useless? How often has a nurse been taken aback at the stigma that is still attached to mental illness? The community health nurse who tries to help the discharged psychiatric client make a place for himself in the community is only too well aware of the prejudice that family, friends, neighbors, and employers still have about mental illness. How often has a nurse shaken his or her head in bewilderment over the number of people who spend a small fortune on over-the-counter drugs while condemning drug abuse?

Attitudes among health professionals frequently differ also. How often has a nurse shivered over incidents involving the too readily prescribed tranquilizer—especially in light of current research suggesting cross-addiction between tranquilizers and alcohol? How often has a nurse been astounded to hear colleagues refer disparagingly to persons with psychosomatic or psychoneurotic symptoms as malingerers and complainers? How often has a nurse encountered sexual bias?

Attitudes are deeply ingrained and are influenced by systems of cultural cognition and codification. Attitudes reflect beliefs, values, and standards of behavior. Attitudes are operative in all aspects of life. Thus it is unrealistic to think that nurses can be attitude free and totally objective. Through attitude clarification, however, they can become increasingly aware of their own behavior and less judgmental about others' behavior. Attitude clarification is essential to therapeutic nursing practice.

CHAPTER SUMMARY

The people of the United States come from various ethnic backgrounds. Each ethnic group has its own cultural system. Through the process of enculturation, people learn the conceptual and behavioral systems of their culture. When people from different ethnic backgrounds interact, some degree of acculturation usually occurs.

Because each culture codifies reality in its own way, members of different ethnic groups act upon different premises in behaving and evaluating behavior. Dissimilar culturally coded orientations often engender cognitive dissonance and culture shock. Moving to a foreign country, moving to another neighborhood, or even entering a hospital may precipitate cognitive dissonance and culture shock. Persons experiencing cognitive dissonance and culture shock are vulnerable to mental illness.

Awareness of ethnic differences and their significance enables nurses to understand the cultural dimension of mental health and mental illness. In addition, a nurse's awareness of his or her own attitudes and the influence of ethnic heritage on those attitudes is essential to therapeutic nursing intervention.

REFERENCES

Abelson, R. P.
  1968 "Comment: uncooperative personality variables." In Theories of Cognitive Consistency: A Sourcebook. R. P. Abelson et al. (eds.). Chicago: Rand McNally & Co., pp. 648-651.
Aronson, E.
  1968 "Discussion: commitments about commitment." In Theories of Cognitive Consistency: A Sourcebook. R. P. Abelson et al., (eds.). Chicago: Rand McNally & Co., pp. 464-466.
Barnett, Homer, et al.
  1954 "Acculturation: an explanatory formulation." American Anthropologist 56:973-1002.
Barth, Fredrik
  1960 "Introduction." In Ethnic Groups and Boundaries. Fredrik Barth (ed.). Boston: Little, Brown & Co.
Berlyne, D. E.
  1960 Conflict, Arousal and Curiosity. New York: McGraw-Hill Book Co.
Blau, Peter M.
  1964 Exchange and Power in Social Life. New York: John Wiley & Sons, Inc.
Bott, Elizabeth
  1957 Family and Social Network. London: Tavistock Publications Ltd.
Brink, Pamela J., and Judith M. Saunders
  1976 "Cultural shock: theoretical and applied." In Transcultural Nursing: A Book of Readings. Englewood Cliffs, N.J.: Prentice-Hall, Inc., pp. 126-138.
Chance, Norman A.
  1965 Acculturation, self-identification and personality adjustment. American Anthropologist 67:372-393.
Coser, L. A. and Rosenberg, B.
  1957 Sociological Theory: A Book of Readings. New York: Macmillan, Inc.

Covello, Leonard
  1972 The Social Background of the Italian-American School Child. Totowa, N. J.: Rowman & Littlefield.
Davenport, William
  1961 "The family system of Jamaica." In Working Papers in Caribbean Social Organization. S. Mintz and W. Davenport (eds.). Social and Economic Studies 10(4):420-454.
Dayton, Neil A.
  1940 New Facts on Mental Disorders. Springfield, Ill.: Charles C Thomas, Publisher.
Dickeman, Mildred
  1973 "Teaching cultural pluralism." In Teaching Ethnic Studies: Concepts and Strategies. James A. Banks (ed.). Washington D.C.: National Council for the Social Studies, pp. 5-25.
Dohrenwend, Bruce, and Robert Smith
  1962 "Toward a theory of acculturation." Southwestern Journal of Anthropology 18:30-39.
Dominquez, Virginia R.
  1975 From Neighbor to Stranger: The Dilemma of Caribbean Peoples in the United States. Antilles Research Program. New Haven, Conn.: Yale University Press.
Eldersveld, Samuel J.
  1966 Political Parties: A Behavioral Analysis. Chicago: Rand McNally & Co.
Essien-Udom, E. U.
  1964 Black Nationalism, A Search for an Identity in America. New York: Dell Publishing Co., Inc.
Estes, W. K.
  1975 "The state of the field: general problems and issues of theory and metatheory." In Handbook of Learning and Cognitive Processes. W. K. Estes (ed.). Hillsdale, N.J.: Lawrence Erlbaum Associates, Inc., pp. 1-24.
Festinger, L.
  1957 A Theory of Cognitive Dissonance. Stanford, Calif.: Stanford University Press.
Frost, Isaac
  1938 "Sickness and immigrant psychoses: Australian and German domestic servants the basis of study." Journal of Mental Science 84:801.
Gambino, Richard
  1974 Blood of My Blood: The Dilemma of Italian Americans. New York: Doubleday & Co., Inc.
Gans, Herbert
  1962 The Urban Villagers. Glencoe: The Free Press.
Geertz, Clifford
  1957 "Ritual and social change: a Javanese example." American Anthropologist, 59:32-54.
Glazer, Nathan, and Daniel Patrick Moynihan
  1970 Beyond the Melting Pot. Cambridge, Mass.: The MIT Press.
Goffman, Erving
  1961 Asylums: Essays on the Social Situation of Mental Patients and Other Inmates. New York: Doubleday & Co., Inc.
Goodenough, Ward H.
  1961 "Comment on cultural evaluation." Daedalus 90:521-528.
Gordon, Milton
  1964 Assimilation in American Life. New York: Oxford University Press, Inc.
Graves, Theordore D.
  1967 "Psychological acculturation in a tri-ethnic community." Southwestern Journal of Anthropology 23:337-350.
Heider, F.
  1958 The Psychology of Interpersonal Relations. New York: John Wiley & Sons, Inc.
Honigmann, John J.
  1967 Personality in Culture. New York: Harper & Row, Publishers, Inc.
Horowitz, Donald L.
  1975 "Ethnic identity." In Ethnicity—Theory and Experience. Nathan Glazer and Danial P. Moynihan (eds.). Cambridge, Mass.: Harvard University Press, pp. 111-140.
Hunt, Earl, and Marcy Lansman
  1975 "Cognitive theory applied to individual differences." In Handbook of Learning and Cognitive Processes. W. K. Estes (ed.). Hillsdale, N.J.: Lawrence Erlbaum Associates, Inc., pp. 81-110.
Hyman, H. H.
  1960 "Reflections on reference groups." Public Opinion Quarterly 24:383-396.
Isaacs, Harold R.
  1975 Idols of the Tribe: Group Identity and Political Change. New York: Harper & Row, Publishers, Inc.
Jordon, N.
  1953 "Behavioral forces that are a function of attitudes and of cognitive organization." Human Relations 6:273-287.

Kelman, Herbert
1961 "Processes of opinion change." In The Planning of Change. W. G. Bennis, K. D. Bennis, and R. Chin (eds.). New York: Holt, Rinehart & Winston.

Kelman, Herbert, and R. M. Baron
1968 "Determinants of modes of resolving inconsistency dilemmas: a functional analysis." In Theories of Cognitive Consistency: A Sourcebook. R. P. Abelson et al. (eds.). Chicago: Rand McNally & Co., pp. 670-683.

Kluckhohn, Florence, and Fred Strodtbeck
1961 Variations in Value Orientations. Evanston, Ill.: Row, Peterson and Co.

Kogan, N., and M. A. Wallach
1964 Risk Taking: A Study in Cognition and Personality. New York: Holt, Rinehart & Winston.

Kretch, D., et al.
1962 Individual in Society. New York: McGraw-Hill Book Co.

Kutsche, Paul
1968 "The Anglo side of acculturation." In Spanish-Speaking People in the United States. June Helm (ed.). Seattle: University of Washington Press, pp. 178-195.

Lenski, Gerhard
1961 The Religious Factor. New York: Doubleday & Co., Inc.

Manwaring, David R.
1961 Render Unto Caesar: The Flag Salute Controversy. Chicago: University of Chicago Press.

McGuire, W. J.
1966 "The current status of cognitive consistency theories." In Congnitive Consistency: Motivational Antecedents and Behavioral Consequents. S. Feldman (ed.). New York: Academic Press, Inc., pp. 2-46.

Merton, R. K., and A. Rossi
1957 "Contributions to the theory of reference group behavior." In Social Theory and Social Structure. Robert Merton (ed.). Glencoe: The Free Press.

Novak, Michael
1973 The Rise of the Unmeltable Ethnics: Politics and Culture in the Seventies. New York: Macmillan Publishing Co., Inc.

Oberg, Kalvero
1954 Culture Shock. Indianapolis: The Bobbs-Merrill Co., Inc.

Ogionwo, W. W.
1969 "The adoption of technological innovations in Nigeria: a study of factors associated with adoption of farm practices." Ph. D. Thesis, University of Leeds. Cited in The Sociology of the Third World: Disparity and Involvement. J. E. Goldthorpe (ed.). New York: Cambridge University Press, pp. 220-224.

Parenti, Michael John
1965 "Black nationalism and the reconstruction of identity." In Personality and Social Life. Robert Endelman (ed.). New York: Random House, Inc.

Peterson, John H.
1972 "Assimilation, separation, and out-migration in an American Indian Group." American Anthropologist 74:1286-1295.

Raths, L. E., M. Harmon, and S. B. Simon
1966 Values and Teaching. Columbus, Ohio: Charles E. Merrill Publishing Co.

Rodriquez, A.
1965 "One of the differential effects of some parameters of balance." Journal of Psychology 6:241-250.

Rokeach, M.
1960 The Open and Closed Mind. New York: Basic Books, Inc., Publishers.

Scheflen, Albert
1972 Body Language and Social Order. Englewood Cliffs, N.J.: Prentice-Hall, Inc.

Schneider, Louis, and Sverre Lysgaard
1953 The deferred gratification pattern: a preliminary study. American Sociological Review 18:142-149.

Shannon, Lyle W.
1968 The study of migrants as members of social systems. In Spanish-Speaking People in the United States. June Helm (ed.). Seattle: University of Washington Press, pp. 34-64.

Sherif, M., and C. W. Sherif
1953 Groups in Harmony and Tension. New York: Harper & Row, Publishers, Inc.
1964 Reference Groups: Exploration into Conformity and Deviation of Adolescents. New York: Harper & Row, Publishers, Inc.

Smith, Maury
1977 A Practical Guide to Value Clarification. La Jolla, Calif.: University Associates, Inc.

Smith, M. G.
1973 Afro-American research: a critique. In Work and Family Life: West Indian Perspectives. Lambros Comitas and David Lowenthal (eds.). New York: Doubleday & Co., Inc., pp. 273-284.

Spindler, George
1971 Dreamers Without Power: The Menomini Indians. New York: Holt, Rinehart & Winston.

Spindler, George
1977 "Changes and continuity in American core cultural values: an anthropological perspective." In Gordon DiRenzo (ed.). Social Change and Social Character. Westport, Conn.: Greenwood Press, Inc.

Spindler, Louise
1977 Culture Change and Modernization: Mini-Models and Case Studies. New York: Holt, Rinehart & Winston.

Spradley, James P., and Mark Phillip
1972 "Culture and stress: a quantitative analysis." American Anthropologist 4:518-529.

Stedman, Murray
1964 Religion and Politics in America. New York: Harcourt, Brace & World, Inc.

Steiner, I. D.
1960 "Sex differences in the resolution of A-B-X conflicts." Journal of Personality 28:118-128.

Tyhurst, Libuse
1955 "Psychosomatic and allied disorders." In Flight and Resettlement. H. B. M. Murphy (ed.). Paris: UNESCO.

Uustal, Diane
1977 "The use of values clarification in nursing practice." The Journal of Continuing Education in Nursing 8:8-13.

Wallace, Anthony F. C.
1970 Culture and Personality. New York: Random House, Inc.

Young, Michael, and Peter Willmott
1957 Family and Kinship in East London. London: Routledge & Keegan Paul Ltd.

Zajonic, R., and E. Burnstein
1965 "The learning of balanced and unbalanced social structures." Journal of Personality 33:153-168.

ANNOTATED SUGGESTED READINGS

Barnett, Homer, et al.
1954 "Acculturation: an explanatory formulation." American Anthropologist 56:973-1002.
A classic exploration of acculturation, this article develops a theoretical framework that stresses the interaction between cultures in contact and factors that may facilitate or impede acculturation.

Brink, Pamela J., and Judith M. Saunders
1976 "Cultural shock: theoretical and applied." In Transcultural Nursing: A Book of Readings. Englewood Cliffs, N.J.: Prentice-Hall, Inc., pp. 126-138.
This essay explores culture shock as a stress syndrome and the implications for nursing care. The authors discuss such categories as stressors, phases of culture shock, coping behavior, and hospitalization as culture shock.

Dunham, H. W.
1976 "Society, culture and mental disorder." Archives of General Psychiatry 33(2):147-156.
Dunham critically examines theories and hypotheses relating societal and cultural factors to the etiology or precipitation of specific emotional disorders. The author identifies many of the unresolved methodological difficulties involved in such research. The article concludes with a summary of definitive results that relate sociocultural factors to specific mental illnesses.

Marcos, L. R., and M. Alpert
1976 "Strategies and risks in psychotherapy with bilingual patients." American Journal of Psychiatry 133(11):1275-1281.
The authors examine the effect of bilingualism on psychotherapy. If only one language is used in therapy, a large segment of a client's experience is excluded. If both languages are used in therapy, a client may change languages in an attempt to avoid emotionally laden material. The article concludes that monolingual psychotherapists need to assess the degree of language independence in bilingual clients.

Oberg, Kalvero
  1954 Culture Shock. Indianapolis: The
      Bobbs-Merrill Co., Inc.
      *In this classic discussion of culture
      shock, the author explores the nature
      and phases of culture shock and briefly
      suggests ways of coping with it.*

FURTHER READINGS

Abernethy, V.
  1976 "Cultural perspective on the impact of
      women's changing roles on psychia-
      try. American Journal of Psychiatry
      133:657-66.
Broverman, I. K., et al.
  1972 "Sex-role stereotypes." Journal of So-
      cial Issues 28:59-78.
Castaneda, Carlos
  1971 A Separate Reality. New York: Simon
      & Schuster, Inc.
Chesler, Phyllis
  1973 "A word about mental health and
      women." Mental Health 57:5-7.
Fabrega, Horatio
  1974 Disease and Social Behavior. Cam-
      bridge, Mass.: The MIT. Press.
Favazza, A., and Oman, M.
  1972 Anthropological and Cross-Cultural
      Themes in Mental Health. Columbia,
      Mo.: University of Missouri Press.
Hill, Robert B.
  1971 The Strengths of Black Families. New
      York: Emerson Hall Publishers, Inc.
Jourard, S.
  1964 The Transparent Self. New York: Van
      Nostrand Reinhold Co.
Paredes, J. A., and Hepburn, M. J.
  1976 "The split brain and the culture-and-
      cognition paradox." Current Anthro-
      pology 17:121-127.
Pasquali, Elaine
  1974 "East meets West: a transcultural as-
      pect of the nurse-patient relationship."
      Journal of Psychiatric Nursing and
      Mental Health Services 12:20-22.

Sapir, Edward
  1963 "Cultural anthropology and psychia-
      try." In Selected Writings of Edward
      Sapir in Language, Culture and Per-
      sonality. D. G. Mandelbaum (ed.).
      Berkeley, Calif.: University of Califor-
      nia Press.
Sizemore, Barbara A.
  1973 "Shattering the melting pot myth." In
      Teaching Ethnic Studies: Concepts
      and Strategies. James A. Banks (ed.).
      Washington, D.C.: National Council
      for the Social Studies, pp. 73-101.
Thomas, A., and S. Sillen
  1968 Racism and Psychiatry. New York:
      Oxford University Press, Inc.
Tyler, S. A.
  1969 Cognitive Anthropology. New York:
      Holt, Rinehart & Winston.
Wallace, A. F. C.
  1970 Culture and Personality. New York:
      Random House, Inc.
Westermeyer, J.
  1976 Anthropology and Mental Health. Chi-
      cago: Aldine Publishing Co.
White, Earnestine H.
  1974 "Health and the black person: an
      annotated bibliography." American
      Journal of Nursing 10:1839-1841.
Wittkower, Eric D., and Raymond Prince
  1974 "A review of transcultural psy-
      chiatry." In American Handbook of
      Psychiatry (ed. 2), vol. 2. Gerald Ca-
      plan (ed.). Sylvano Arieti (ed.-in-
      chief). New York: Basic Books, Inc.,
      Publishers.
Zajonic, R. B.
  1968 "Cognitive theories in social psychol-
      ogy." In The Handbook of Social Psy-
      chology. G. Lindzey and E. Aronson
      (eds.). Reading, Mass.: Addison-Wes-
      ley Publishing Co., Inc.

3
HUMAN
DEVELOPMENT

CHAPTER
FOCUS

That a nurse understand the process of human development is crucial to the accurate assessment of clients. There is a variety of perspectives on how and why a person develops in the manner he does. Cognitive, cultural, economic, physiological, and psychological factors are thought to influence the development of each personality in various ways, making it unique. In this chapter, an eclectic view of the operation of these factors will be presented. The role of culture and its impact on the socialization of a human being will be identified as one of the major theoretical constructs in the process called "development."

Personality can be described as progressing along a chronological schema. The philosophies of human development of four major theorists—Freud, Sullivan, Erikson, and Piaget—will be discussed. Incorporated within this discussion will be the concept of vulnerability and its subsequent impact on healthy adaptation. Mental health and mental illness will be presented as reflect-

ing a continuum on which types of behavior can be placed. Such a continuum reflects the fact that health is a dynamic state, constantly responding to external and internal forces.

Knowledge of the needs and tasks associated with a particular stage of development, and of the tools required to accomplish those tasks, is significant to nurses in making accurate assessments regarding recurrent behavior patterns and their implications. Data from such assessments can then be used to determine areas in which further learning is necessary in order for a client to develop appropriate tools to meet developmental tasks. A brief discussion of Maslow's hierarchy of needs will be presented, along with its implications for personality development. This final portion of the chapter will present each area—infancy, childhood, and so on—being characterized by an interrelationship of the many factors that influence the development of a person's unique personality.

3

HUMAN DEVELOPMENT

Personality is the unique matrix of cognitive and affective modalities of functioning, expressed through behavioral responses, that each human being develops through continuous interaction with others of all cultures and societal norms.

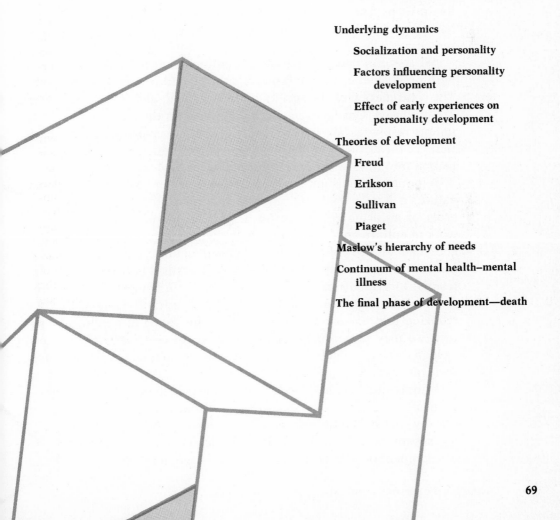

UNDERLYING DYNAMICS
Socialization and personality

The process of personality development is a complex one that is often misunderstood or misinterpreted because everyone who studies personality does so according to his own inclinations. For example, a social-learning theorist may disagree strongly with a cultural anthropologist or a traditional psychoanalyst on the interpretation of a particular incident. Different strategies of intervention result. The question, however, is not which intervention is correct but rather which intervention is most effective in terms of client response and positive directional change. A therapist who refuses to see that an approach is, in fact, ineffective is not helping the client. Nurses therefore must be aware of the varying psychological, sociocultural, and biological factors present. They must have a basic understanding of each factor and its implications. Culture is the first of these variables that will be presented.

We assume that a function of a culture is to inculcate the young with prescribed conceptual, moral, ethical, and behavioral standards. The continuation of the society is thus ensured, and socialized beings are produced. Our focus as nurses, however, is the *individual* and his unique responses. We will be aware of shared personality characteristics, yet the critical emphasis will be on the individual and his socialization into roles within the culture as a whole.

A human being is not a closed system, ruled or governed by a given nature; a human being is an open system. He creates and imposes order of an acquired nature. An individual exists within the framework of culture and society as a being whose needs, attitudes, values, and behavior are defined and made meaningful in the social and cultural milieu. A variety of social types, diversified in time and space, results. Individuals can be viewed as having a common structure of probabilities that can only be realized in a cultural context. By first realizing that personality always comes into being in a cultural context, we may then consider how common cultural materials are utilized by each individual, rendering him a unique being. Although there are similarities in the composition of different personalities, each individual retains differences because of the unique way he responds to and integrates the various cultural patterns and traits. We can say that before his encounter with others, a human being is nothing substantial. He requires the presence of others to stimulate the development of cognition, emotion, and, ultimately, sense of self.

Needs, as an aspect of personality, are noncognitive in origin. They can be divided into two categories: biological needs—such as thirst, hunger, and the need to eliminate—and needs acquired through interaction with society. We need to bear in mind, however, that biological needs are themselves influenced by culture. For example, the need to eliminate is panhuman; however, each society has its own attitudes toward this need. What is considered modesty in one society may be considered inhibition in another. Nurses need to be aware that societal expectations are reflected in behavior clients use to meet needs.

Attitudes, as well as needs, reflect cultural orientation. Like needs, attitudes are major integrative forces in the development of personality; they give a sense of consistency to an individual's behavior. Attitudes are cognitive in origin: they are formed through interactions with the social environment. Attitudes serve to direct an individual's attention to his particular commitments and responsibilities. In a sense, they act as guidelines for his present existence and help shape the future for himself and for his progeny. An individual soon learns to attend to particular aspects of his environment on the basis of his attitudinal system. Ideas, social situations, and other people are grouped according to a person's "frame of reference," his own personal guidelines. Although overall cultural norms are reflected in an individual's tightly knit attitudinal system, they are integrated differently in each personality.

We have been placing various components of the individual into separate categories. Thompson (1975) states that the reconstruction of these parts into some semblance of a being within a cultural context requires an entity that acts as coordinator. That entity is the concept of self—a basic requirement for the sound psychological functioning of the human animal.

Self-concept is a major variable in the development of healthy patterns of behavior. A person's self-concept is his view of his own strengths and weaknesses; it is his perception of himself, based on reflected appraisals from the environment. Self-concept, then, is an accumulation of what others think of a person as well as the person's own exploratory activities that assist him in understanding his world.

One of the most salient features of the self-concept is its ability to grow, to become more sophisticated in acquiring and applying knowledge and experience. In early infancy, the self-concept is virtually nonexistent. However, as the infant begins to see himself as being different from his environment his motor activity increases. As the child develops the tool of language, he becomes more capable of differentiating himself from other objects and persons in the environment. Accomplishments bring positive reinforcement from significant persons, which serves to strengthen his self-concept.

The mores of a culture are internalized and become such an integral part of a person that self-concept cannot be understood without cultural considerations. Internal needs and societal expectations are meshed to permit the individual as a social being to achieve a measure of consistency between his inner and outer selves.

The development of a positive self-concept allows an individual to experience a wide range of activities without feeling threatened. A perception of the world emerges that is unique. As positive experiences accumulate, an individual's self-concept is further enhanced. The individual who repeatedly encounters failure develops a poor self-concept, which is perpetuated through a phenomenon that amounts to a self-fulfilling prophecy. A person with a poor self-concept may continue to perceive his world in the most restricted sense unless he can begin to perceive himself as competent according to societal norms and values. A poor self-concept eventually results in maladaptive coping measures. One of our primary concerns as nurses is assisting such an individual to effect change that will potentiate a positive self-concept. This nursing function will be discussed further in this chapter, in the discussions of self-concept in relation to parent-child interactions and self-esteem.

It is evident that an individual can inherit biological characteristics, such as body size, weight, eye color, and hair color. However, the qualities that identify an individual as a human being are those which may not be genetically transmitted—thought patterns, emotions, and behavioral responses, although some theorists indicate that certain types of behavior are in fact genetically transmitted. Those characteristics identified as congenital are passed on during the gestation period. However, our cultural heritage is acquired through our relationships with others. Even characteristics that seem to be predominantly biological can be related to cultural experience. For example, positive living conditions may be characteristic of a particular civilization because they are valued entities. The same factors may not be in evidence in another civilization, perhaps because they are not valued. A society may limit the availability of affection, physical warmth, and light to the individual. In such a case, an individual's physical growth as well as his emotional development may be retarded. Body size and weight might tend to be less than in a culture that placed a premium on factors that enhance these characteristics.

Locke and Rousseau were the first to oppose the view that the infant entered this world with a built-in set of responses—that he was a mini-adult who had already been programmed for eternity. Locke introduced the concept of the "tabula rasa"—that the newborn infant resembles a blank slate. He learns from the culture, his environment, how, when, and eventually why he should respond. Itard, in his famous work with the Wild Boy of Aveyron, expanded this concept. This young child of about eleven or twelve had the characteristic behavior of a wild animal, posturing himself on all fours, scratching and biting those who came near him. He had no awareness of social restrictions on behavior. He operated on an immediate gratification principle. It was apparent that there was little instinctive basis for rules of socialization. The young boy had adapted to his environment as would any animal in similar circumstances. When the Wild Boy was found by Frenchmen in 1799, he was compared to persons living in a European cultural environment. By European standards he was a freak, a subhuman. Although this case may seem to be an extreme example, it serves to point out the individual differences that result from the socialization process.

It is of little importance to identify one specific factor—biological, psychological, social, cultural—as having more impact on development than another. Behavior and development have a multifactorial base.

However, recognizing the role of culture is particularly relevant nursing. By recognizing the impact of culture on behavioral responses, the nurse makes available a broadened scope of assessment as well as of intervention strategies. Let us consider some examples of what may have previously been identified as having a strictly biological base. The sensory nerve endings respond to heat and cold. However, this response may be culturally as well as biologically induced. A certain element of learned response develops as children are repeatedly warned not to touch something because it is hot. Parents are continually requiring children to put their coats on when the temperature falls to a certain point. Thus a child may not have been biologically triggered, yet he puts on a sweater. In addition, culturally determined dietary preferences affect nutrition, and culturally determined mating preferences affect genetic pools.

Biological factors can be subject to environmental modification. A child who has been locked in a closet for the first 2 years of his life will probably be retarded in motor development. Culture provides a milieu in which an individual can exercise his various options. A person may be biologically ready for a higher level task yet not have learned from his culture what that level means or how to reach it. The tools may be missing. We can look at a variety of situations in which a child may be identified as slow or backward, based on the fact that he is biologically ready for a task but not performing it. For example, the sphincter of the bladder may be developed and functional, yet the child continues to wet his pants. Perhaps he has not been socialized into a realization that this behavior is viewed negatively by his culture. A child's legs and arms may be coordinated sufficiently to propel him over to someone else; however, the question arises of what to do then. Is the answer to that question part of the process of socialization into a particular role by the culture? Socialization into roles continues into adulthood, and each individual may be socialized into a variety of roles. One of the prime examples of the socialization process is learning the role of receiver of health care and health care provider.

In summary, we view the individual as emerging from a cultural context. A human being is born with the biological readiness to perform many functions; however, culture provides the basic materials for personality development, such as value systems, a knowledge base, and fundamental beliefs. Each individual then combines his biological and cultural equipment in a unique way to emerge as a personality different from all others. The culture in turn is molded by the individual in a sort of circular pattern. It is necessary to state at this point that although individuals may share personality traits, a true group personality never exists. As we pointed out in Chapter 2, we use the concept of "basic group identity" to refer to shared traits rather than to a single personality type that is characteristic of an entire culture.

Factors influencing personality development

It seems appropriate to the discussion of personality development that we provide an overview of some of the many "panphasic" factors, or factors that span all the developmental epochs. We suggest that these influences be called to mind as one assesses an individual in relationship to his developmental status. Too often we simply categorize human beings into eras, task groups, or age groups for diagnostic purposes without considering such factors as parent-child relationships, intelligence, self-concept, genetic transmission, age, sex, and child-rearing practices. We have identified three general categories for the purpose of discussion: psychological, biological, and sociocultural.

Psychological factors. The parent-child relationship has been the center of attention during the past decade or so, particularly since the studies of Bowlby and Spitz. The primary concern of theorists has been the impact of the parent, initially the mother, on the early development of the child. Bowlby found that the infant develops a strong sense of attachment to the mothering figure and quite vigorously protests her leaving. The implication is that the persistent attitudes and styles of the parental figures are imprinted on the child at a very early age and that the resulting value system pervades the developmental span until some point in young adulthood, when the individual is able to strike out on his own.

The nature of the family relationships that develop are crucial to each family member. It is within the family system that identification occurs, a major factor in personality development. We note that identification is particularly relevant to the oedipal phase but that it does, in fact, occur throughout the developmental cycle. Shifts in identification result from positive interpersonal relationships with others in the social system.

An infant who is isolated cannot develop into a mature, well-integrated individual. Indeed, physical growth itself must be facilitated by a system that nurtures, educates, and enculturates. The family unit is the chief molder of personality. It is a system that provides an atmosphere for the testing of unfamiliar techniques of adaptation. Within the family, one can become familiar with roles and institutions. There is a sense of stability and integration, a home base to which one may always return. The enculturating capacities of a parent impinge upon the child during whatever phase he may be in; they transcend all phases. Enculturation is a generational process. Each parent brings a value system and characteristics of personality into a mating relationship. Offspring are produced and the values and personality characteristics of the parents influence the development of those offspring.

It is important to note the deleterious influences that parents can have upon the personality development of children. The parent who feels little self-esteem and who has a poor image of himself has difficulty responding to a child in a manner that promotes a positive self-concept in the child. Imagine, for example, that 7-year-old Jamie brings home his first homework assignment. After completing it, he asks his mother to check it for him. She repeatedly makes comments such as "Are you sure this is the way you were supposed to do it?" and "Did the teacher tell you this was alright?" These comments reflect the parent's inability to accept her child's actions as being correct and indicate the parent's dependence on an authority figure. She is uncomfortable with accepting the responsibility for her own actions, and this message is transmitted to her child. The child thus is lead to question his own abilities, a situation that results in a distorted estimation of them.

The effect of parental influence may be quite positive during one phase of development and quite negative during another. A mother may develop a sound relationship with her infant, based on the comfort she experiences in being depended upon. However, if the mother is unable to relinquish this relationship, the child may suffer the consequences in later periods of personality development.

Self-concept evolves out of the parent-child interaction and functions as a mediator of development. Parents and children interact with one another; in this process a self-concept is continually evolving for each family member, as was discussed earlier. Each self-concept reflects the appraisals of significant others in the environment. Thus family life nurtures each child, providing strong affectional and relational bonds. As Satir (1972) points out in *Peoplemaking*, parents have the tremendous responsibility of facilitating the development of a positive self-concept and a sound sense of self-esteem.

It is necessary to identify the meaning of self-esteem as it relates to self-concept. An individual with a healthy self-concept is able to integrate the appraisals reflected from his environment and to accept his own strengths and weaknesses. Self-esteem grows out of this positive self-concept; an individual with high self-esteem feels he is worthwhile in spite of mistakes or defeats. He feels capable of achieving realistically determined goals and accepts responsibility for his actions. He does not have to be right all the time; when he fails, he reassesses his coping skills and develops another plan. He perceives failure not as total defeat but rather as an opportunity to develop an alternative plan of action.

Parents with high senses of self-esteem are able to provide an atmosphere in which each person feels comfortable with his self-concept and his emerging identity. There are no obligations attached to behavior and no conditions for reward. Unmet parental needs do not become a burden to the next generation. Each child is free to "be." Conditions within the family system are such that trust, a secure identity, and a sense of autonomy are valued. In appropriate situations, a child is permitted to explore the decision-making process and to experience independence. He is not forced to play out a symbiotic relationship to meet the needs of his parents.

Parents who are unsure of themselves and their own worth often unconsciously set up circumstances very much like ones they themselves experienced as children. Feelings of "bad me," guilt, and shame, which produce low self-esteem, are evoked in their own children just as they were evoked in themselves many years before. Unreasonable punishment and, ultimately, withdrawal of expression of love cause a child of such parents to feel that his behavior must be unworthy if it has caused these responses from the persons he considers significant—his parents. He believes that he must truly be "bad." A pattern has been established that continues from generation to generation.

One needs to feel positive about one's self—aware of both limitations and strengths—before he can invest actively and positively in another human being. Such is the case in the parent-child relationship. If the parent has experienced a smooth developmental course, and if he is aware of his own needs, he will be more able to share a sound, nurturing relationship with his child.

A positive self-concept, initiated in the toddler period and nurtured throughout the developmental span, enables an individual to meet each challenge as it comes and to deal with it appropriately. Problems are viewed not as insurmountable obstacles but as potential learning situations. It would be unrealistic to say that each possible impediment is viewed with gleeful delight. A person with a strong sense of self recognizes that he has a wide range of capabilities, yet he also acknowledges his limitations. He realizes that it is acceptable to work within the framework of those limitations. At each developmental level, the parameters of those limitations are altered. The individual with a healthy sense of self is able to adapt to those alterations.

Self-concept correlates with many factors, some of which will be discussed at greater length later in this chapter. A person whose self-evaluations are negative tends to experience consistently high levels of anxiety, which in turn lead to less positive interactions with peers. An individual with a poor self-concept feels a sense of powerlessness to change his role, thus perpetuating a cycle of feeling victimized. This sense of inability to bring about change can be connected with the perception of an external locus of control—the feeling that one has no real opportunity to actively effect change, that it is in the hands of fate, so to speak. In contrast, a person with a positive self-concept has a sense of active participation in the environment and feels able to determine realistic life goals. These patterns serve to reinforce the notion that the self is the organizing factor in the personality.

Although each individual is unique, everyone is affected by interactions within his environment, and the process by which interactions affect a person is roughly the same for everyone. All aspects of human development interact, responding continuously to experiential and constitutional factors.

An individual's personality is a reflection of his input into the process of personality development. How he speaks to another person or how he puts thoughts into actions determines the response he receives from the environment. Environmental responses, in turn, determine his behavior. Reciprocity exists in that the behavior of one individual has an impact on that of another and vice versa. There is a continuous exchange of communication (both verbal and nonverbal) between persons (see Chapter 2). Future behavioral patterns are influenced by those interactions.

One individual characteristic that is very relevant to personality development is intelligence. Intelligence is the aptitude or capacity for learning and includes problem-solving ability. Intelligence is biologically determined by virtue of the fact that a person inherits a nervous system. However, experiences provided by the environment may retard or facilitate the development of cognitive skills.

Differences in intelligence appear as early as infancy and gradually become more apparent during the childhood and adolescent years. The ability to reason through complex situations has many implications for personality development. Intelligence has a profound impact on many areas of development and behavior, such as talking, memory, understanding and applying new concepts, and creativity. It seems that children who learn rapidly and who can apply their knowledge develop a more positive self-concept—as a result of praise received from parents and teachers—than children who are poor achievers. They assume positions of leadership more frequently, recognize their limitations more readily, and are able to look at themselves and laugh when appropriate.

Intelligence was once considered completely hereditary. However, published studies have demonstrated that heredity is not the only factor. The effect of environment can no longer be negated. Children who were born to parents with low IQs who were then adopted by parents of average or high IQ have been shown to be able to reach the educational level of their adoptive parents (McCandless and Evans, 1973).

Educational experiences play a definitive role in the development of intelligence, particularly during infancy and the preschool and adolescent periods. Thus parents need to provide an atmosphere that facilitates learning during these critical periods. Personality development will be enhanced, and a positive self-concept will be promoted.

Object loss is discussed at length in the chapter on aggression against oneself (Chapter 11). However, it is relevant here to note the impact that loss has on personality development. Bowlby (1973) compares loss to separation from the mother figure. The manner in which loss is resolved, if in fact it is resolved, is crucial to the development of a positive sense of self and the ability to invest in trusting relationships. Although the interrelationship between positive self-concept and personality development has been emphasized several times in this book, we believe that it bears repetition. The sense of security one has in dealing with loss will be reflected in personality development over and over again. Since life is characterized by a series of losses, it is in this arena that nurses must focus to develop primary preventive strategies.

A person's ability to cope with a variety of situations reflects an awareness of his strengths and limitations and indicates a capacity to tap his resources as necessary. Of great importance to personality development is the type of coping mechanism utilized as well as the degree and frequency to which it is called into play. For example, an individual may learn a coping skill such as the internalization of stress and its expression through a physiological route. This mechanism of reducing tension, learned in early interactions with significant persons in the environment, is then carried on throughout the life cycle. The nature of such early coping experiences and parental response to them have a profound influence on future personality development. Coping skills that include an honest, open sharing of feelings provide the setting for the development of a sound sense of self. Coping skills that are rooted in, or fixated, at early levels of psychosexual development color the emerging personality. The terms "oral personality" and "anal personality" indicate levels of development in which individuals can be rooted. For example, the anal personality is characterized by a coping repertoire that includes retentive kinds of behavior with little sharing of feelings. An individual with this type of personality is stingy on a material level as well as an emotional level.

The nursing profession, by definition, has directed much of its effort toward secondary prevention. However, the potential exists for the awakening of awareness in parents on behalf of their children in order to facilitate the development of healthy coping skills during early childhood periods.

Biological factors. The relationship of neurochemistry to the development of personality is a striking one. Two key hormones, androgen and estrogen, affect not only the biological sexual orientation but also the psychological assumption of sex roles. Aggression and maternalism are two types of behavior that are affected by these hormones. Androgen levels correlate positively with aggressive tendencies, and estrogen levels correlate positively with maternalistic tendencies. The neurochemical effect of hormones also has an impact on growth rates, weight, and bone ossification. Everyone grows at a different rate, a fact that is apparent if we look at a class of first-graders. There may be differences in height of as much as 8 inches. Size definitely affects the kinds of activities a child engages in and how he is perceived by his peers. A boy who is considerably smaller than his classmates is often called a "runt" and may not be asked to participate in physical activities such as football or basketball. He may then assume a passive role among his peers. Because of a biological "hand of fate," his personality development will have taken a particular course; the course might have been different if he had been larger. Thus a simple biological fact of life such as growth rate can have a wide-ranging effect on overall personality development. Again, the interrelatedness of biological and cultural factors is apparent.

The biological factors involved in personality development cannot be discussed without reference to the concept of maturation. Maturation is the process of developmental changes, a process that is controlled by genetic factors.

What is the significance of genetics to personality development? Various personal characteristics, such as physical appearance, motor activity, emotional reactivity, and energy level, are strongly related to genetic composition. Intellectual characteristics—and, to some degree, social characteristics—are shaped by heredity. As an individual matures, he experiences certain expected developmental changes. The timetable that controls these changes is laid down by genes yet may be vastly altered by environmental variables. Even under similar environmental conditions, it is quite possible that two male siblings will reach adolescence at very different times.

The task of nursing involves recognition of two basic facts: (1) each individual occupies his own given space on the developmental continuum and (2) variables such as health care, stress, cultural expectations, and chronic illness affect an individual's rate of maturation irrespective of a genetic timetable. With these facts in mind, nurses can devise primary preventive strategies that promote optimum conditions for the develpment of each individual's unique personality.

Age is probably one of the most common criteria used to categorize human development. Certain observable types of behavior have been identified for each particular age group. Within each age level, these common characteristics are studied in respect to frequency, variety, complexity, and organization. Mental age as well as chronological age need to be considered; individuals in the same chronological age group may have very different mental ages.

There are obviously significant limitations to the discussion of personality development in terms of chronological age. When age is considered alone, the very factors that we have just been discussing—genetic timetables and environmental influences—are negated. To say that a child is older is simply not sufficient to account for increased reading ability, for example. Many experiential factors need to be studied. Since environment plays such a great role in development, we need to identify what may be operating to influence reading ability.

Within an age level of children there is a wide range of variations. It is not appropriate, therefore, to say that a child of 4 will exhibit static characteristics. No child exactly fits the "average" mold. A nursing assessment must consider a range of developmental variations. Parents often believe that their child must exhibit characteristics X, Y, and Z by age 10, for example. They experience a sense of confusion, and panic frequently sets in, when the characteristics are not apparent. Both the child and the parents may then suffer severe consequences of the parents' misapprehensions. Prenatal and well-baby clinics provide excellent opportunities for nurses to discuss behavioral and biological expectations with parents. It is here that nurses can identify wide variations, thus preventing future difficulties in parent-child interaction as well as in the personality development of children.

When considering age as a factor in personality development, most studies have looked at children in "average" environments. This concept constricts one's view of development. More and more, researchers are identifying a variety of environments, both enriching and depriving ones, to broaden their perspectives on personality development. Again, just as biological and maturational factors cannot be put aside in the assessment of personality development, the role the environment plays cannot be ignored.

Sexuality, including sex role behavior, attitudes, and values, is a powerful determinant of personality development. It influences the way a person is perceived, what type of occupations are available to him, and the way he views himself.

Although we are presenting sexuality in this discussion of biological factors, it is important to note that psychological and sociocultural factors are equally as relevant in the development of healthy sexual attitudes and behavior. Such attitudes and behavior in turn promote the growth of a healthy adaptive personality. Concern for the development of a positive sense of sexuality has become an issue for the health professional. It is curious that this change has been such a long time coming, for few subjects touch each human being's life more powerfully. Until recent years the subject was considered taboo. Many educators, health professionals, and others felt that dissemination of information about sexuality would lead to an increase in promiscuity, homosexuality, and so-called sexual deviations, such as oral-genital sex and masturbation. As members of a rational, progressive society, we must realize that a person's interest in his developing sex drives and needs will not disappear magically if he is encouraged to ignore them. Sexuality is a component of a person's self-esteem and sense of identity. He becomes aware of sexual differentiation prior to his knowledge of self as a member of other groups: the child is a boy or a girl before he or she is Irish, Catholic, or American. Although sexuality is becoming a more open topic of discussion, it is still associated with feelings of discomfort for both the client and the nurse. It is thus imperative that nurses understand the biological, psychological, and sociocultural dynamics of human sexuality. From an informed perspective the nurse may then demystify the concept of sexuality, discussing it in a clear, concise format that will enable a client to examine his own sexuality in a less anxious manner. Nurses may reinforce and reaffirm the client's belief that sexuality is an integral part of his self-concept.

What about the nurse's ability to feel comfortable with the issues of human sexuality? Understanding biological, psychological, and sociocultural factors provides the nurse with a sound theoretical framework from which to operate. However, the nurse needs to examine his or her own feelings of sexuality—what values does he or she hold regarding certain sexual orientations and behavior? It is necessary to view sexuality from the client's perspective rather than from one's own frame of reference. Yet it is often difficult to do so, because of the subtle but powerful influence of one's own values. We do not suggest that nurses adopt a free, "valueless" perspective on human sexuality. But it is improtant that nurses be cognizant of their values and that they assess and reassess the impact of those values on clients.

No single determinant can be said to account for sexual behavior. It results from the interaction of biological, psychological, and sociocultural factors.

Biological determinants of sexual behavior have historically been rooted in the concept of instinct. Sex, in one sense, is the innate drive to mate and to reproduce. Yet in lower animals there is no awareness that coitus leads to pregnancy—a fact that leads one to believe that humans as well as lower animals engage in sexual activity for pleasurable reasons. Sex appears to involve a psychological drive that is correlated with feelings of pleasure, which can be traced back to the "pleasure centers"—the thalamus, the hypothalamus, and the mesencephalon. When these centers are electrically stimulated, animals experience pleasurable feelings of varying intensities.

One's sexuality is reflected in the complex interaction of the hypothalamus, the pituitary gland, and the gonads. This system is responsible for the stimulation and regulation of the hormones necessary for sexual development and activity. During intrauterine life the fetus seems to be under the direct influence of hormones that reflect a greater degree of genetic determination of sex roles and behaviors than during the ensuing years of development. It appears that as an individual approaches adulthood, sexual roles and/or behaviors reflect the impact of cultural influences. Indirect data suggests that there is a prenatal influence, by fetal hormones, on the hypothalamus. This influence is exerted in a subtle manner throughout the life cycle. However, there needs to be an awareness of the interaction of these innate, biological, factors and the environmental factors that facilitate the expression of those factors.

Thus it is inaccurate to view sexuality from the singular perspective of biological determination. Psychological factors may be considered expressions of underlying biological sexual instincts. For example, Freud believed that libido (sex drive) was the psychological representation of a biological sexual instinct. Psychological determinants may exist in the form of learned patterns of behavior. Motivation may be mediated through the brain yet have at its base such learned patterns. Sexual behavior, its expression and purpose, may be learned through psychological and sociocultural mechanisms.

Sexuality may be viewed as an interpersonal process in which one individual chooses to share with and relate to a significant other. The process involves the experiencing of interrelated emotional, psychological, and physiological changes that are pleasurable to each partner. Each person enables the other to realize his potential for sexual fulfillment while recognizing his partner's as well as his own strengths and limitations.

A person can experience sexual pleasure without a partner. The most common way of doing so is masturbation, or sexual arousal through either manual or mechanical stimulation of the sex organ—that is, the penis or the clitoris. Masturbation often has been described as "dirty" and considered inappropriate as a means of sexual satisfaction. The myth that masturbation leads to blindness and insanity has long been purported. It is no wonder, then, that masturbation has received little support as an alternative means of sexual stimulation. It is of particular importance that nurses recognize the fallacy of this interpretation of masturbation. They can help parents to see masturbation as a component of the normal growth and development process that occurs during the childhood period, a process that leads to a healthy sexual identity. A determination about the appropriateness of a child's use of masturbation as an adaptive measure may then follow. Masturbation may be a viable alternative for hospitalized clients as well as for persons who have no sexual partner. It is critical, however, that a nurse assess an individual's attitudes and feelings before suggesting masturbation. Achieving sexual satisfaction through this mechanism may be totally unacceptable to a client, and he may cut off communication with the nurse completely.

Sexual identity has traditionally been directly correlated with biological sex (maleness and femaleness), which may also be termed "core gender identity," and to its psychological attributes (masculinity and femininity), which may be referred to as "gender identity." However, recent changes in Western societal norms for men and women have led to a blurring of those characteristics traditionally identified as male and female. The sociocultural context of an individual provides the structure of values, attitudes, and beliefs from which one's sexuality is developed. Again, it is impossible—and inappropriate—to separate the biological dimension from the psychological dimension, or either of those dimensions from the sociocultural dimension.

Sex-role stereotyping has been perpetuated throughout the years by both males and females. Neither group has been willing to risk being identified as "different." Sex roles are defined by characteristics representing masculinity and femininity. These categories emerge from the sociocultural framework inherent in each society. Traditionally, characteristics such as competitiveness, aggressiveness, and intelligence have been considered masculine in Western cultures. Female traits have included gentleness, warmth, and passivity, as well as tendencies toward being understanding and showing emotion.

Recently theorists in the field of human sexuality have suggested the concept of androgyny—the possession of human traits rather than those identified as either masculine or feminine. This concept, which involves a blurring of sex roles, can be viewed as a step toward positive mental health, because it does not require that a person be given a label based on whether a characteristic is appropriate. There is, however, concern that the concept of androgyny may increase the difficulty a child experiences in developing a sound sense of identity. It is important that the child be clearly given the message that he is male or female to prevent ambiguity in core gender identity. He can then be encouraged to select from traits that are identified as "human" rather than "male" or "female." It is indeed important for nurses, counselors, sex educators, and other professionals to recognize that androgyny can be a threatening concept—an unknown. For example, a boy growing up in a tough neighborhood may feel extremely uncomfortable about assuming characteristics not acceptable to his group. He cannot be expected to assume traditionally feminine traits if he is going to be harassed by his peers. Thus the assimilation of human, rather than sex-linked, traits must occur over a period of time, because positive reinforcement from one's cultural group is a necessary ingredient in the process. It can be said, then, that the goal of mental health care is the introjection and expression of human traits.

Sex roles play a part in determining what is considered appropriate or inappropriate behavior. It is not possible to separate sex roles, sexual attitudes, and sexual behavior from one another. Each is interrelated with the others to produce a unique, complex, sexual human being. Likewise, one cannot separate biological, psychological, and sociocultural factors in the determination of gender identity. Each variable reinforces the others; one variable does not operate to the exclusion of the others. It is difficult to separate a biological imperative from one that is imposed by a culture.

Money and Erhardt (1972) proposed a model of psychosexual differentiation that reflects an integration of biological, psychological, and sociocultural dimensions. They believe that gender identity differentiation begins at conception and reaches its conclusion with the emergence of the adult. The sequence is initiated by the chromosomes. The undifferentiated gonads then transmit the message of gender identity through the hormonal secretions of their own cells. As a result of this process, genital dimorphism occurs—the external and internal sex organs develop to correspond to the chromosomal sex. At birth, the impact of social influences begins—sex is assigned by the use of names, the choice of colors (pink or blue), and the choice of toys (doll, football). The process of identifying oneself as male or female becomes part of social learning. As the child grows and develops, he receives reflected appraisals from the environment that serve to facilitate the development of self-concept and its component, body image. The child's understanding of gender identity becomes very concrete. He reaches puberty; his accumulated learning shapes his future behavior—sexual and otherwise. Sexual hormones secreted during this phase result in the development of erotic feelings. The culmination of this process of genital dimorphism, social learning, and secretion of pubertal hormones is what is termed adult gender identity. Money and Erhardt (1972) define gender identity as the "individuality of one as male or female as it is experienced in self-awareness and behavior—it is the private experience of gender role." They define "gender role" as "everything one says or does that indicates one is male or female—it is the public expression of gender identity."

In addition to incorporating the three dimensions mentioned previously, this model of psychosexual differentiation is related to the broader perspective of psychosocial development. An important task connected with identity formation is the development of a healthy, integrated sense of sexuality. Adolescence sees an upsurge in sexual activity; however, intimacy occurs only after an individual has achieved identity formation. As a person moves into adulthood, he shares in relationships—both in a physical sense and an emotional sense. Each person is an individual in his own right yet has the capacity to establish a continuing, sharing relationship—a relationship that can last until death. Thus, it is important to assess psychosexual differentiation *within* the framework of one's psychosocial development.

Finally, the concept of sexual orientation is often confused with core gender identity or with gender identity. The term sexual orientation refers to sexual object choice. The orientation may be toward an inanimate object, as in fetishism (see Chapter 12). The orientation may also be heterosexual, homosexual, lesbian, bisexual, or ambisexual. Although societies often consider sexual orientations other than heterosexual to be deviant, any expression of sexual choice needs to be assessed in terms of its commitment to humanistic values. For example, an individual's sexual behavior must not harm or disadvantage another person. Each member of a relationship must freely consent to that relationship. Thus, heterosexual, homosexual, or lesbian relationships can be satisfying and enriching.

With the advent of increased awareness of sexuality, including sex roles, attitudes, and behavior, it becomes imperative that nurses incorporate a comprehensive sexual history into the health history and assessment format. Nurses need to develop an ability to feel comfortable with the subject of sexuality. As in all other areas of interaction, a nurse must be aware of feelings regarding his or her own sexuality because they affect the assessment of sexual health of clients. Questions nurses should ask themselves might include:

1. What do I consider "male" and "female" traits? Is there a dichotomy between the two?
2. What is "normal" sexual behavior to me? How do I feel about masturbation and oral-genital sex? What are variants of sexual behavior?
3. How do I feel about alternative sexual lifestyles such as homosexuality, lesbianism, and transvestism?
4. How comfortable do I feel discussing sexual issues with a client?

Thus, in order to assess clients' sexual health comfortably and accurately, nurses need to evaluate and reevaluate their own attitudes and values regarding sexuality.

According to Watts (1979) sexuality can be considered a psychophysiological system. Therefore, when conducting a sexual assessment, a nurse should ask questions about sexual functioning at the same time that he or she asks questions relating to the reproductive and urinary systems. Detection of possible sexual dysfunctions (see Chapter 9) can be accomplished through a thorough sexual history.

Other areas that should be included in the sexual history and assessment are: developmental-level tasks; significant family interactions; sexual knowledge, attitudes, and values; current sexual activity; and satisfaction (or lack of it) in sexual relationships. As mentioned previously, the success of a sexual history depends to a large extent on how comfortable the nurse feels in dealing with the subject matter. It is imperative that nurses not neglect sexuality, since it is an integral component of the total individual. A healthy perception of one's own sexuality enhances the development of an adaptive personality.

Sociocultural factors. Child-rearing practices, as a major component of the cultural context, had been relatively ignored by social scientists until the 1950s. Concepts such as Freud's Oedipus complex and the family romance were applied universally with little regard for cultural variations. This is not to say that these psychoanalytic constructs should be negated; instead their usefulness should be expanded. This can be accomplished most readily if they are linked to the cultural environment in which people and their symbols live. For example, Malinowski's (1927) study of the Tobriand Islanders found that a male child developed a hatred of his mother's brother rather than his own father. Thus the Freudian concept has limitations. The primary point to draw from this study is that although the family romance exists, it differs from culture to culture. Thus we could say that Freud's work, although substantially valid, is not necessarily completely valid for every culture.

Whiting and Child (1953) conducted a great deal of research in the area of cultural expectations, child-rearing practices, and individual development. They noted that excessive deprivation of affection during childhood could be correlated with pathological responses in later life and with related cultural beliefs.

As has been stated throughout this book, the impact of cultural context on personality development cannot be minimized. The interaction of biological, psychological, and cultural factors in the lifelong process called personality development cannot be ignored.

Socioeconomic status, social class, and social status are virtually synonymous. The educational level one's parents attained, the occupations they pursue, and the income they receive all contribute to one's social status. It is important to look at these functional correlates of an individual's particular class. What does being a part of an identifiable class mean? How do these correlates affect personality development?

Families of the middle class, whose members are well-educated and have certain advantages, have often been compared to families of the lower class, whose members are poorly educated and have few community resources. There is a marked difference in family stability between the two groups, with a concurrent effect on parent-child relationships. It is within the realm of these relationships that the effects of socioeconomic status on personality development can be noted. The affluent middle class tends to raise children to be high achievers, to control their emotions, and to share thoughts and ideas with their parents. The environment is one in which cultural, physical, and intellectual opportunities are available and encouraged. Value is placed on the appreciation of music and art. Advantaged families may be more liberal than disadvantaged families in child-rearing practices, possibly because, as Zigler (1970) suggests, they have more time and the vocabulary to devote to democracy. Physical punishment is less likely to be used in advantaged families. In contrast, the frustrations of little money, time, and energy may cause the less advantaged family to release pent-up tension through excessive physical punishment or child abuse. Children from less advantaged families tend not to do well on standardized tests (possibly because of cultural variations) or to learn as quickly in school (perhaps because of a self-fulfilling prophecy on the part of teachers). Children from disadvantaged families also tend to feel less secure about their own self-concepts, a situation that has significant effects on personality development.

We do not mean to imply that a person from a lower-class family is always doomed to failure or that a person from a middle-class family always achieves his optimal level of being. The task of nurses is to recognize that the developmental rate can be seriously impeded by conditions of poverty. These conditions need not be restricted to less advantaged families as defined by socioeconomic criteria. As is seen more and more often, children from "good" families can experience difficulty in adjusting to life situations and can have poor self-concepts. A socioemotional poverty can exist in a setting in which material goods are provided but little else. Parents who are caught up in enhancing their own status may show little concern for the emotional needs of their children.

Such data can be useful in the area of primary prevention. By being aware that certain conditions promote positive personality development while others do not, parents can make efforts to provide situations in which learning and growth are facilitated.

Religion is a factor that affects personality development in general and child-rearing practices, family stability, and self-concept in particular. Child-rearing practices may be heavily influenced by religious beliefs. For example, the Protestant ethic ("good, hard work will accomplish all") may be transmitted to a child through a no-nonsense approach on the part of the parent. In such a family, the expression of feelings may be viewed as frivolous and unacceptable. In a family of another religious orientation, discipline may not be considered as important.

Knowledge, attitudes, and problem-solving methods may be influenced by religious affiliation. A child pursuing a parochial school education develops attitudes and values somewhat different from those developed by a child in public school. Differences in motivational levels may be accounted for, in part, by differences in religious background. Even if religion does not play a particularly important role in a family's child-rearing practices, it still can have a profound influence on the development of moral and ethical standards.

Education, although the last factor to be discussed here, is one of the most influential in personality development. Differences in problem-solving capacity, initiative, creativity, and self-concept have been noted among children who have attended different schools. Our goal is not to trace these differences to their respective sources but rather to recognize their implications for the developing personality. Hoy and Applebury (1970) suggest that the most important aspects of the school experience are peer relationships and student-teacher relationships. Students generally see teachers as role models and agents for change. Unfortunately, however, some teachers are instrumental in giving students negative attitudes about themselves. If a teacher considers a student primarily in terms of the student's race, social class, or ethnicity rather than in humanistic terms, a self-defeating cycle can be produced.

It has been shown by various studies that schools are direct reflections of the communities in which they exist. Therefore, it is logical to assume that they meet the needs of their students. However, this is not always the case, particularly in school districts composed of large groups of minorities but administered primarily by members of the middle class. (See Chapter 2 for further discussion.) In order for individual development to be enhanced, the values of the school must be consonant with those of the community. Each group must be working toward the same end. For example, if a school supports the notion of a college education for all its students, but the community views its members as blue-collar workers with little need for a college education, the student is caught in the middle. In such a situation, the effectiveness of the school is impaired and the student is left with unmet needs and a feeling of frustration. Once the values and goals of community, teachers, and students are in consonance, the impact on personality development will be in a more positive, growth-promoting direction (McCandless and Evans, 1973).

• • •

Although a wide range of variables has been considered in terms of their impact on personality development, the most important concept is the interrelatedness of these factors. Biological factors are subject to environmental modification. A child raised in a vacuum, unable to learn from his environment, will be severely retarded in perceptual and motor development. Cognitive processes will also be affected. An individual's self-concept is greatly influenced by constitutional factors such as body height and weight. Genes determine the developmental timetable, but the timetable responds to environmental modifications.

Nurses are not as much concerned with determining the degree each component plays in the development of the individual personality, as they are with recognizing that this interaction occurs and understanding its implications for the emerging personality.

Effect of early experiences on personality development

We have discussed in previous sections the impact of early life experiences on personality development. Adaptive mechanisms in early life may be quite primitive, yet they act as prototypes for future reactions to stress.

Freudian theory has emphasized the fact that a "foundation for pathology" is laid in the early years. This concept may be taken a step further, away from strict psychoanalytic concepts, if we view early sociocultural or environmental experiences as being significant to the development of personality disturbances later in life. It can be said that regardless of whether psychosexual development is maturational, the response of a child's caretaker and the environment in which the child exists at the time of each stage serve to influence personality development.

The energy that is invested in the tasks of each stage, the tension that arises in stressful circumstances, and the coping skills that emerge result in patterns that serve as models for future adjustment to the same circumstances. Freud (1916) states that as a consequence of each stage, a certain amount of libidinal energy is fixated at that stage, building certain defenses and expectations into the personality. Major psychopathology occurs when too much libido or energy is fixated at an early stage, because the coping patterns developed at those early stages are not applicable to problem-solving in adult life. In such an instance, the adult tends to use coping mechanisms that are not effective and that are not appropriate to his level of intelligence.

Probably the very first anxiety experience is that engendered by the birth process. The fetus moves quite rapidly from the warm, dark, quiet, and relatively safe environment of the womb into a bright, almost tumultuous environment. How does the infant respond to this barrage of stimuli? The adaptive mechanisms he develops become models for future adaptations.

The infant devises a number of methods of dealing with incoming stimuli. He may selectively attend to stimuli, filtering out those he cannot or does want to attend to. This cannot be done on a voluntary basis; however, the infant can focus on a specific activity that effectively blocks out other stimuli. He may also become accustomed to a stimulus after it has been occurring for a long period of time. Anxiety then is no longer aroused.

What consequences do these experiences have on personality development? Escalona (1953) suggests that infants differ in responsiveness and in the speed at which they respond. It has been shown that there are infants who react more readily to stimuli—that is, startle more easily. A history of increased sensitivity to stimulation has been identified in children with pathology. Behavior patterns of the schizophrenic child may be maladaptive responses to this sensitivity. Such early mechanisms may serve to reduce anxiety initially, but they are ineffective in the long run.

Sleep is an effective method of reducing anxiety during infancy, and it is frequently utilized and reinforced. Can you recall instances when circumstances around you were overwhelming? It was quite comfortable to retreat to the bedroom, curl up in bed, and pull the covers over your head. Sleep relieves a person of the need to deal with anxiety. The development of this adaptive mechanism need not result purely from an infant experience. In adult life, one is told to "go to bed" or to "get some rest" in order to alleviate the anxiety of a tension-packed day. Sleep allows an individual the luxury of putting off dealing with a situation causing anxiety while realizing that it will be necessary to face the anxiety at some point. Sleep is but one mechanism of adaptation in the early phases of development.

Psychoanalytically oriented theorists believe that certain experiences may be perceived as being comforting because of their similarity to the birth process. A child, when anxious, may seek refuge in a warm, dark place—a place that is similar to the mother's womb. Although this view may stretch one's imagination, it is important to note that early experiences do set the stage for the use of certain adaptive mechanisms in later phases of life.

Factors such as self-concept, interactions with parents and significant others, socioeconomic background, and schooling experiences collectively and individually affect the development of adaptive mechanisms in later life. For example, an individual who feels comfortable with his self-concept is able to relate successfully to others. He is more likely to perceive himself as an integral part of his surroundings, and to provide himself with sources of continuous information about those surroundings. Maladaptive mechanisms tend to occur when a person perceives his environment as threatening. If, in the early phases of life, he encounters continuous negative reinforcement from parents and other significant people, he develops mechanisms to protect his already suffering self-concept. Withdrawal from reality, submission, and psychophysiological responses are utilized to deal with tension. These patterns continue to develop throughout the early periods of life until they become entrenched in the adult personality.

Thus the early periods of life are fertile territory for the development of adaptive (or maladaptive) mechanisms. Nurses need to be cognizant of the many factors that affect personality development. As Freud first pointed out, we need to recognize the implications of early childhood experiences and response patterns in order to understand adult adaptive mechanisms.

THEORIES OF DEVELOPMENT

A wide range of published material is related to the development of personality. We will present the concepts proposed by four major theorists: Freud, Erikson, Sullivan, and Piaget. We believe that these theories present a broad base of knowledge from which students can develop their understanding of the dynamics of personality.

Freud

Freud introduced the principle of epigenetics—the view that development follows a logical, sequential pattern. The critical tasks of each phase in the sequence must be completed in order to successfully move on to the next phase. If there is an interference in development at one of the stages, maladaptive behavior may result. However, since Freud's time it has been found that compensations are possible, to a certain degree. Deficiencies may be converted into strengths if they are recognized at an early stage.

In essence, Freud was arguing that sexual energy or libido is the prime motivator of human behavior. He viewed personality development in terms of libidinal investment, or cathexis, in the oral, anal, and phallic zones. He then correlated the process of physical maturation with the progression of the aforementioned zones.

Before Freud's view of psychosexual development is discussed further, his concept of the partitions of the mind—the id, the ego, and the superego—should be explained. The id represents the instinctual portion of the mind, controlled only by the blind strivings of Eros, the instinct of life, and Thanatos, the instinct of death. Thus the id is the origin of an individual's drives and motives. Normally, the actual forces of the id remain in the unconscious. Their effects are felt, however, as conscious perceptions of thoughts, desires, and feelings. The influence of the id is constantly and subtly felt by the ego, which is the rational, reality-based component. The ego results from interaction with the environment, this interaction forms a boundary for the mind. The ego is the portion of the psyche that others "see" first. It serves a decision-making function in that it determines what kinds and amounts of stimuli are allowed into the mind as well as what is permitted to leave. What we say and do, how we perceive situations—these functions are dictated by the ego. The ego acts as a mediator between the id and the superego, which is the conscience, the dictator of moral and ethical standards. The superego is a differentiation of the ego, as the ego is a differentiation of the id. Both differentiations are a result of the interaction of id and environment and concurrent cognitive development. However, the development of the superego results primarily from interaction with specific parts of the environment, such as parents. The development of the structures of mind can be diagramed as follows:

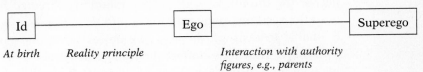

Id	Ego	Superego
At birth	*Reality principle*	*Interaction with authority figures, e.g., parents*

At birth, the infant is predominantly operating under the pleasure principle. He seeks immediate gratification for all his needs and has little concern for the needs of others. He is all-encompassing, a concept that is supported by the orality or literally "eating alive" quality of the infant's responses to the mother. At the interfaces of the pleasure-driven id and reality there arise the beginnings of ego—the reality-oriented component of the mind. It is important to note that the thinking mechanisms associated with the initial, id-driven, behavior can be connected to the dreams and fantasies of adults. This "primary process thinking" is frequently found in adaptive behavior of a regressive nature, such as in various types of psychosis. "Secondary process thinking" is related to reality situations.

Psychosexual development involves the concept of motivation. Freud believed that motivations remain constant throughout life but that the zones through which id gratification is sought vary. Much of motivation remains unconscious; however, in the course of the development of the ego, a person receives a limited insight into his motives. Knowledge that may not be conscious at the moment but that can be recalled at any time is said to exist in the "preconscious." Material that has never been permitted into conscious awareness, as well as repressed material, is said to exist in the "unconscious." The utilization of defense mechanisms to control anxiety points out the fact that individuals often do things for reasons they are unclear about or may even deny (see further discussion of defense mechanisms later in this chapter).

The oral stage of infancy encompasses approximately the first 15 months of life, in which the child is unable to meet his most basic needs on his own. He depends upon others in his environment for that nurturance.

The channel of gratification is the mouth and lips, which are particularly sensitive. The stimulation of the mouth and lips sets off the sucking reflex. Libidinal energy is invested, or cathected, in the relevant channel of gratification, which in this psychosexual stage is the mouth. The gratifying objects are the mother's breast, a bottle, a pacifier, or the thumb. Energies of the infant are directed toward nursing, with the accompanying relationship to the parenting figure. The infant is unable to distinguish satisfying objects as being separate from his own body. They may, in fact, hold more attention than actual parts of his own body. However, by approximately 9 months of age, the infant is able to discern the difference between self and the object of gratification.

Under favorable circumstances, the needs of an infant are met on a consistent basis. A diagram can best illustrate the cycle of need arousal and response from the parenting figure:

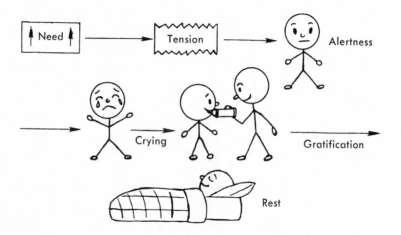

The way in which this cycle operates, particularly the responses of the parenting figure, has a great influence on an adult's ability to relate to another—to develop a sense of trust. If needs are met on a continuous basis by a warm, loving figure, a feeling of trust develops. We will discuss trust further when we consider the theories of Erikson.

It is interesting to note the paradox of infancy. It would seem that the infant is totally helpless, dependent. However, his needs are met repeatedly without his actual recognition and identification of wanted objects. In a sense, then, there is an omnipotence inherent in the infant's personality. Parents of infants, who are often given to discussion of their problems, have frequently expressed the feeling that a mother's or a father's life revolves around the infant. Activities must be planned around the infant's feeding and sleeping schedule. A person cannot simply get in the car and go shopping; such an operation requires very careful consideration of the hours of wakefulness and the "irritable" periods. This feeling of not having one's own life sometimes reaches extreme proportions. In such circumstances a parent may use maladaptive forms of behavior to adjust.

Orality means more than just gratification through the mouth and lips. The infant actually "takes in" various kinds of stimuli in his environment, a process that lays the groundwork for future cognitive and emotional processes. Lest we focus primarily on feeding as the representation of the oral phase, we must be aware that the infant is particularly sensitive to tactile stimulation. This sensation is most highly developed in the oral, or infancy, period. The relationship to the mother's body is very important in this phase; it is an intrinsic component of orality.

Defense mechanisms to reduce tension develop in the phase of infancy or orality. Sublimation, introjection, projection, and denial act as initial tension-alleviating mechanisms in this period.

Sublimation is the directing of unacceptable libidinal energies into socially acceptable channels. These libidinal energies relate more specifically to sexual-aggressive drives or pleasure-seeking drives than to hunger, for example. Thumb-sucking provides physical pleasure; the infant is content with this mechanism, and it is more socially acceptable than sucking on the breast as a comfort measure. Gratification of the need is still achieved but in an indirect manner. The sublimation process also takes place in adults. A young woman on a weight-reduction diet collects thousands of recipes and thus sublimates her desire to eat. A man with intense hostile feelings becomes a lumberjack. The hostile energies are then channeled into vigorous wood chopping.

Introjection develops as a result of the infant's desire to be powerful, an attribute that he has ascribed to the parenting figures. He wants to incorporate this quality into his own personality. By doing so, the infant makes his self-esteem secure enough to last until a time when he is more able to accomplish tasks within his environment on his own. A healthy adult counterpart of this mechanism occurs as a result of the resolution of the grieving process. The bereaved person is able to incorporate qualities of the lost loved one, resulting in decreased separation anxiety and increased ability to invest in other relationships. However, introjection may be an unhealthy mechanism as well. For example, an individual may introject qualities of another person that will result in self-punishment (as when a person incorporates qualities of a punitive mother).

Coupled with introjection is the mechanism of *projection*. Projection involves the attributing of one's own unacceptable thoughts, wishes, fears, and actions to another person or object. In later life this mechanism is the basis for scape-goating. In later phase, mother and infant are perceived as one object by the infant, thereby facilitating the ascribing of feelings and wishes from self to the mothering figure. In later childhood, uncomfortable feelings are attributed to others. For example, a young child who is afraid of the dark might tell his mother that his teddy bear is afraid. In adult life, a person might place the blame for his failures on the circumstances in his environment. The extreme form of projection is paranoia. Although projection is utilized to some degree by healthy individuals, it is a more pathological mode of adaptation than other defense mechanisms.

Denial develops somewhat later in the period of orality. This mechanism involves the rejection or disavowal of elements of reality that may be unpleasant or painful. The infant denies the presence of disturbing stimuli by closing his eyes. This is only a temporary adjustment technique, which eventually disintegrates when an individual is forced to confront reality. However, it is used quite regularly throughout life. The question for nurses thus becomes one of *when* to intervene and present reality without stripping the individual of this defense mechanism. Carter (1971) describes several examples of denial that may be seen in operation in the general population. Some people postpone diagnostic testing or, when confronted with results of tests, refuse to acknowledge that illness exists. Persons with chronic illnesses such as diabetes or cardiac problems sometimes ignore the disability and fail to take the prescribed medications or to follow the planned regimen. Each of these situations reflects a denial of painful information and an attempt to continue life on a "business as usual" level.

Since denial ranges along a continuum, it is important for nurses to determine whether denial is harmful or therapeutic in a given situation. Involved in this assessment is the nurse's understanding of his or her own feelings regarding the client and the illness. What are the nurse's own expectations of client behavior? Is the nurse fostering denial or preventing denial from following a natural course? Denial has many faces. Because of its complex nature, nurses must view its operation as multidimensional and must be aware that it has far-ranging implications. It is no longer sufficient to say that denial is healthy or unhealthy. A client's utilization of denial must be assessed carefully before its importance in the maintainance of a healthy, integrated ego can be understood.

It must be pointed out that defense mechanisms do not operate on a conscious level. Even in adulthood they operate below the awareness levels. The results of these mechanisms, however, are apparent.

The degree of libidinal energy invested during the oral phase is reflected in later activities such as gum chewing, nail biting, excessive eating and drinking, and smoking. All of these activities are said to satisfy oral needs. Problems that develop during the oral phase may prohibit the release of energy for utilization during later stages, thereby causing a fixation in that stage. In such a situation, the individual's physical development progresses according to schedule while psychosexual objectives remain the same as they were during that early period.

The toddler period is the stage in which the child begins to move throughout his environment, to exercise control, to be free to some degree. There is a shift of libidinal energy from the mouth as a channel of gratification to the anus. This area becomes highly sensitive and responds to stimulation. Baldwin (1967) suggests that the shift is not maturational but rather follows the attention that is directed toward the anus by the toilet-training process. The focus of the anal period is toilet training. Here the child finds himself in a bind. He wants to please parents by having a bowel movement in the right place at the right time, yet this intention impinges upon his developing sense of autonomy. He also desires the immediate gratification of the pleasurable feeling of the act of defecating. The question becomes one of either delaying gratification in order to receive parental approval or risking disapproval for immediate pleasure. There is a sense of ambivalence, a combination of positive and negative feelings directed toward the same object or situation.

According to Freud, various features of the anal period are crucial to later development. The retention of feces and "giving" them to the parents increases the significance attached to possessions. The person fixated at the anal stage of development is often characterized as parsimonious and unable to tolerate ambiguity or confusion. The anal personality considers love objects as possessions and acts to control them rather than to permit them to act independently. This tendency may be reflected in the marital situation, with each partner "belonging" to the other.

The mechanism of sublimation is carried over into the anal phase, as are other mechanisms. The small child finds pleasure in playing with feces, yet this is unacceptable to parents. Such activities as playing with mud, finger paints, sand, and modeling clay satisfy this instinctual drive in a socially acceptable fashion.

Reaction formation is the shift in feelings or attitudes from one point on a continuum to the extreme opposite point. The first utilization of this defense mechanism is the shift in attitude toward bowel and bladder function in order to avoid unacceptable impulses. For example, the desire to play with feces may be transformed into scrupulous cleanliness. Although the visible behavior is more socially acceptable, the original attitude is not erased. It is merely relegated to a lower level of consciousness. Another example, seen frequently in adult males, is concern about feelings of warmth and tenderness. Masculine characteristics of physical prowess are overdeveloped to replace unacceptable "feminine" traits.

Repression, one of the major defense mechanisms, arises during the anal phase in order to push unpleasant thoughts, feelings, and emotions out of conscious awareness. It is an attempt to prevent feelings of unpleasantness caused by the recollection of the desire to play with feces or of the sexual fantasies aroused by the parent during the phallic phase. Repression is the cornerstone of defense mechanisms, its major goal being to preserve ego boundaries.

Regression, the last of the primary defense mechanisms, is a return to an earlier stage of development, where modes of gratification were more satisfying and needs were met. The most important aspect of regression is that it happens *to* the ego; the ego is *acted upon* rather than doing the action. The child in the anal phase, feeling the pressure to conform to bowel and bladder training, may go back to the previous phase, in which he sought gratification primarily through the oral mode. Another example of regression in the toddler-age child is his seeking of attention from parents after the arrival of a new sister or brother, by soiling his diaper.

The phallic stage, or self-centered sexual stage, revolves around the concept of the Oedipus complex (or in the female, the Electra complex). There is a shift of libidinal energies from the anal region to the genitals. The male child directs his energies toward the mother, in direct competition with his father. He alternately loves and hates the father (ambivalence). The preschooler's ideas of sexual relations are often vague. The child sometimes places his hands all over the mother's body, particularly on the breasts. He imitates the way his father transmits affection to the mother. The mother tends to feel uncomfortable, particularly if she is unaware of her son's internal struggles at this time. The child, in any case, is not permitted to live out his fantasy. His feelings are condemned by both parents, yet those same feelings are accepted *between* the parents. The young boy fears the retaliation of his father in the form of castration. The subsequent aspect of this phase is the relinquishing of the sexual wishes because of fear of castration. Rather than be a rival of his father, the boy identifies with him. Hostility is repressed, as are sexual desires for the mother. In this way, the young boy begins to acquire masculine desires and values.

The Electra complex has not been as well defined as its male counterpart. Similar components exist: sexual desires are repressed, rivalry with the mother cannot be tolerated, so identification occurs, and acceptance of femininity results. The concept of castration anxiety is quite different for the female, since there is no penis. The resolution of this part of the complex lies in the fact that women can reproduce and men cannot.

The beginning of the resolution of the Oedipus complex occurs in the phallic stage, as does the beginning of the development of the superego. As we will see, this resolution is carried over into the latency period. To present a clear picture of the development of the superego, we will discuss the mechanisms of introjection and identification. The child takes on aspects of the personality of the parent of the same sex. This process, termed introjection was discussed previously. As a result of this internal process, identification comes about. The child introjects the values, attitudes, and goals of his parents—a ready-made conscience—into his ego structure. Identification is the process whereby the child imitates the desired qualities of the significant other. This process concurs with the child's concrete cognitive level of development. Introjection serves as the basis of the superego, yet it can be carried to an extreme. In such a situation, an individual may replace his entire ego structure with the characteristics of the significant other, losing his own identity in the process. As a person matures, the superego becomes more reality based and less harsh and demanding. The development of the superego relieves the child's castration anxiety or penis envy.

Faulty resolution of the Oedipus complex has far-reaching effects on later personality development. It can be said that at the base of almost all neurotic difficulties lies an inadequate resolution of the Oedipus complex. The adult who is fixated at this phase of development is characterized by poor sexual identity and difficulty with authority figures.

The period corresponding to the school-age years is referred to as the latency period. As we noted, there is a tremendous flow of energy in the phallic stage. Then there is a quieting of that energy in the latency period, perhaps a "calm before the storm" type of effect. It is the valley between the two peak periods—the phallic and the genital phases. A great deal of energy is devoted to intellectual pursuits. Sexual achievement and curiosity are replaced by a quest for knowledge and the motivation to achieve in school. Through sublimation, sexual drives are channeled into the socially accepted activity of the pursuit of education. The latency period is a time when culturally determined skills and values are acquired. The child moves out of the family system and is subjected to the values and attitudes of others. Throughout this period, the superego matures and becomes more organized, integrating the viewpoints of a variety of significant people in the environment.

The latency period, ranging from ages 6 to 12, is characterized by increasing sex-role development, which is facilitated by identification with the parent of the same sex. Testing of new sex roles can be seen in the development of sex-segregated gangs and cliques, which are quite common during this phase. Aggressive behavior, valued in males, takes the form of rebellion against authority. Reaction formation is in operation when the male child rejects not only sexuality but the whole opposite sex. This phenomenon can be noted in the attitude of boys toward girls in this age bracket. A 9-year-old boy would not be caught dead having a conversation with a girl! Adults fixated at this stage of development are often characterized by a lack of motivation and by an inability to appraise situations and solve problems creatively.

Freud did not actually include adolescence as a stage of personality development. It was his feeling that the personality is established by the beginning of adolescence. The genital stage differs from the phallic stage in that the genital stage is characterized by an overwhelming supply of sexual drives. But there is now a concern for others' feelings. The primary goal of this stage is the development of satisfactory relationships with persons of the opposite sex. The manner in which the Oedipus complex is resolved may have a definitive effect on an individual's choice of a partner. A girl often seeks out a boyfriend whose expectations in regard to her behavior are similar to her father's expectations about her mother. A man will often marry a girl who is quite similar to his own mother.

As a result of the Oedipus complex, the male identifies with the father. In the genital phase, repressed sexual feelings are allowed into conscious awareness, and acceptance of these feelings begins. It is at this point that libidinal energies are directed toward a relationship with the opposite sex.

TABLE 3-1. Miscellaneous defense mechanisms

Defense mechanism	Definition	Example
Isolation	Ego allows actual facts of experience, either past or present, to remain in consciousness, but breaks the linkage between facts and the emotions that belong with them	Nursing student giving postmortem care walls off emotions usually elicited by dead human bodies
Displacement	Certain strivings or feelings are unconsciously transferred from one object, activity, or situation to another	Husband is mad at his boss, so he comes home and yells at his wife
Rationalization and intellectualization	Plausible reasons for one's behavior, feelings, and attitudes are constructed (rationalization) Anxiety is controlled through the transporting of conflict to the realm of secondary process thinking and talking (intellectualization)	Man cheats on his income tax but explains it away by telling himself, "Everyone does it"
Undoing	A specific action is performed that is considered to be the opposite of a previously unacceptable wish or action; mechanism is related to the magical thinking of childhood	Ritual undoing of wrongs through penance

Another major component of the adolescent phase is the development of a sense of self-worth. Inherent in this development is the defining of one's role in society. Up until this point, the adolescent had occupied a fairly secure role—he knew where he belonged, who his friends were. But during this phase of life he must move out of his comfortable niche and find his own place in society. This process may encompass a wide range of possibilites, such as further education, a vocation, and marriage. Finding one's place in society is, at best, a difficult task!

An adult who is fixated at the genital phase of development is characterized by an inability to enter into an intimate relationship with another individual and by a tendency to "float" from one occupation or educational setting to another.

In addition to the defense mechanisms already presented, several others are commonly utilized. They are summarized in Table 3-1.

In summary, according to Freud two series of changes take place concurrently in the development of the personality. The first is the maturation of the ego, with the attending recognition of reality and development of defense mechanisms. The final product of this series is an interpersonally oriented being. Second, cognitive processes develop that permit an individual to assess and interpret his environment, to give meaning and rationality to what he perceives. This framework leads to the discussion of the view of development of another psychoanalyst—Erik Erikson.

Erikson

Erikson added a new dimension to Freud's psychosexual stages: psychosocial development. He viewed society as having a profound impact on the emerging personality. Erikson identified critical tasks for each phase of development. These graduated tasks must be met in order for a person to move successfully on to the next phase. Society assures the proper socialization of the child by providing him with opportunities for (1) role development, (2) attainment of independence, and (3) healthy expression of emotions. The accomplishment of these tasks occurs differently in each culture.

Development, according to Erikson, is a gradual process. The ultimate goal is an individual who not only feels comfortable with his own identity but also is sensitive to the needs of others in his environment: a *social* animal. Like Freud, Erikson believed that the success or lack of success of adaptation in one phase influences an individual's ability to master the critical tasks of the next period. It is not a question of a child selecting the tasks that he would like to master. Tasks occur on a continuum, each leading to the next, with an ever-increasing repertoire of coping abilities being made available on a regular basis.

A sensory phase lasts from birth to approximately 18 months. The most crucial task to be dealt with is the development of a sense of being able to rely on others, to establish a sense of trust. During this period the infant is totally dependent upon others in his environment. As his needs are consistently met, he begins to attain a basic sense of trust. The significant relationships that occur during this phase set the tone for all future relationships. An infant who is able to trust others, to be confident that his needs will be met, is more likely to achieve a feeling of confidence in himself. This feeling of trust in others and the increasing sense of self-confidence permit the individual to feel secure in the knowledge that his needs will be met should he find himself in a helpless, dependent position in later life. The adult who has not experienced trusting relationships in early life will be more pessimistic in his expectations of others. His relationships with others are frequently doomed to failure. His lack of self-esteem is often projected onto others in the form of attitude "he doesn't like me." This attitude elicits responses that reinforce it. The cycle then comes full circle. The individual does not have a basic sense of self, which prevents him from investing in open, two-way interactions with others.

The muscular, or toddler, phase approximates the period of ages 1 to 3. The critical task of this phase is the achievement of a sense of autonomy, as opposed to arousal of feelings of self-doubt. Lidz (1968) suggests that this cannot truly occur until the child achieves a sense of initiative, the critical task of the next developmental phase.

Perhaps the crucial concept here is the interrelationship of phases. The young child becomes independent of the parent as the parent provides opportunities to do. He feels comfortable in seeking out new experiences in his environment because there has been the initial development of basic trust. He soon realizes that he can take the initiative to explore his world, knowing full well that mother or father will be there if the need should arise. In this way the child begins to feel independent, autonomous. He begins to be aware of the effects his body has on the environment around him.

Parents greatly influence the degree to which a child attempts to master his environment. When constant barriers, both physical and verbal, are placed in the path of the development of autonomy, there is little room for growth of initiative. The child feels he is "bad" for not conforming to rules and regulations. Parents who lack confidence in their own abilities often project their inadequacies onto their children. In such a case, the child does not feel capable of extending his horizons further into the environment. Again, a basic lack of trust in oneself prevents the development of a satisfying relationship.

The critical task of the next stage, the locomotor stage, is the achievement of a sense of initiative. During the period from ages 3 to 6, the developing child seeks to balance initiative and guilt. Erikson (1950) suggests the child achieves this balance by identifying with the parent of the same sex, thereby reducing the guilt produced by the rivalry between the child and that parent. As a result of this phase, the child develops a conscience that serves to regulate primary id impulses.

The locomotor phase is characterized by a greater organization of personality. The child gains an appreciation of his own sense of identity, his own place as a system in relation to many other systems. He becomes increasingly aware of his influence on others as well as of his limitations. In a later section, we will discuss the impact of the broadening range of cognitive processes on the child's personality organization and development.

The latency period, ages 6 to 12, is concerned with task of industry versus inferiority. The child utilizes his energies in creative activities or in the pursuit of learning. He seeks to become part of a group; a sense of belonging is crucial to this phase. He begins to internalize the values and attitudes of those around him. There are new environments with which he now becomes familiar. He finds a place for himself among his peers. The child gains feelings of self-worth as a result of appraisals from other persons in his environment—adults, playmates, and schoolmates. Recognition that some people like him and value his word while others do not is critical to the development of a capability for a healthy self-evaluation. The quality of leadership is one that becomes apparent in this period. The child learns he can lead; or he sees himself primarily as a follower. Or he may see himself as never being a part of the group and thus becomes habitually rebellious or alienated. In such a situation, the child often feels a sense of inferiority, which causes him to act out in defiance against others—a protective shell made necessary by his lack of self-worth.

The adolescent phase, encompassing ages 12 to 20, is the transition phase between childhood and adulthood. It is characterized by turmoil and change. There are individual variations in the rate of sexual maturation, as well as in the pace of emotional, intellectual, and social development. During this phase the child is expected to integrate all his life experiences up to that point into a coherent sense of self and to emerge as an adult.

The achievement of an integrated self requires the successful accomplishment of the tasks of previous phases. The child comes equipped with a basic sense of trust, an ability to make some decisions regarding his life, and an ability to relate to others individually and in groups. These factors enable the personality to gel into a workable, integrated whole.

During the transition period the individual can prepare for independence, yet he is still under the protective umbrella of his parents. This situation may have a negative influence on successive development if parents do not permit children to exercise some of their options. If an adolescent remains in a children's world within the family but is confronted with adult expectations in the total society, a sense of role confusion results.

Erikson (1950) stresses the significance of the next phase—young adulthood or late adolescence, which lasts from ages 18 to 25. The crucial task of this phase is the achievement of intimacy as opposed to isolation. The young person must gain an ego identity that reflects an individual who is a human being in his own right. He is no longer considered someone's daughter or son. Once a firm sense of self has been established, the young adult is able to extend himself into an intimate relationship with another individual. Interdependence—the sharing with another of all that one values without fear of loss of self—is the crux of this period. (It seems that an inability to achieve a true sense of intimacy in our current society is being reflected in a rising divorce rate, although the divorce rate is influenced by many other factors as well.)

The phase of adulthood, ages 21 to 45, is concerned with the task of generativity as opposed to stagnation. As the young adult moves through the life cycle, he begins to identify life goals, including occupational and marital choices. The period of adulthood thus is a logical extension of the period of young adulthood, during which the capacity for a sharing relationship develops. The adult's choices reflect the successful achievement of a sense of self-worth and belonging, and the transition from operating under parental values and attitudes to operating under his own.

During this period, a dyad is often transformed into a triad with the addition of a child. The partners who feel comfortable with themselves and who have had their needs met are able to direct their love and energy into the development of a new human being. We have come full circle; the phases of development begin again—with another life.

The final phase of development, according to Erikson, is maturity, in which the task is to accomplish ego integrity as opposed to despair. The individual reviews his life experiences, considering those objectives he has successfully completed and those he has not. A person who can accept his life for what he has achieved undergoes a renewed sense of ego integrity. Life has meaning for him, in both its positive and negative events. He does not despair for what might have been. The end of life is perceived as a culmination of his many experiences rather than as something to be feared. The older person has thought a good deal about death and has usually had many experiences with it. Death is a phase of development that one must pass through, with the ultimate goal being achievement of a positive sense of self in this final stage.

Sullivan

Harry Stack Sullivan believed that individuals need to be socialized into their environments. His theory was based on the premise that each individual seeks to avoid anxiety. Inherent in this theory is the view that coping mechanisms are developed in order to reduce anxiety. Sullivan differed from Freud and Erikson in that he viewed biological changes as the stimuli for emerging needs and growth trends.

As an individual grows, there are changes in his inherent ability to relate to objects and persons in his environment. Abilities and body parts are considered an individual's *tools*. The goal of each developmental phase is considered the *task*. For example, the task of the infancy stage is to receive fulfillment of needs from others in the environment. In order to accomplish this goal, the infant utilizes his mouth, his ability to cry. The mouth and his ability to cry are considered the tools. As the child moves through the stages of development, the tasks become more sophisticated, as do the tools. During late adolescence, the individual utilizes his genital organs and the process of experimentation (tools) to develop an intimate, loving relationship with another (task). Like Freud, Sullivan described the individual who successfully completed the tasks of each developmental phase as being interdependent, capable of forming a lasting relationship, and comfortable with his concept of self.

In order to facilitate the understanding of sullivanian theory, we will discuss some of its dynamic concepts. Reality orientation is referred to in terms of "mode." The prototaxic mode, occurring in infancy, is characterized by a lack of differentiation between self and the environment. Thus Sullivan's and Freud's concepts of self and its relationship to the environment are similar.

The parataxic mode is characterized by the breaking up of the undifferentiated whole. The resulting parts are illogical and disjointed and occur inconsistently. This mode is in operation primarily during childhood, but it also extends into the juvenile period. It is necessary for the child to separate the parts of the whole into discrete units so as to better understand their individuation and subsequent relatedness to the physical and social environment.

The ability to perceive whole, logical, coherent pictures as they occur in reality characterizes the syntaxic mode. The syntaxic mode is used as a means of understanding the environment and relating to others. In order to gain assurance that perceptions are real, the adult seeks consensual validation. He is then able to identify areas that need development as well as those that do not.

Sullivan refers to the organization of experiences that defend against anxiety as the "self-system." In order to to make an accurate assessment of an individual's feelings of worth, it is important to understand the concepts of "good-me," "bad-me," and "not-me." The child, based on his interpesonal experiences, assumes one of the above postures. Behavior that is regarded as valued by the parents is then learned and incorporated by the child as good-me. Behavior that does not receive parental approval is identified as bad-me. The child perceives from verbal and nonverbal cues that such behavior is not acceptable. For example, he may hear a parent talk about the unacceptability of tardiness. Behavior that generates large amounts of anxiety is denied and identified as not-me. A parallel can be drawn between the freudian mechanism of reaction formation and the concept of not-me. Each involves an unacceptable feeling being denied, the opposing feeling being verbalized, and anxiety being reduced for the moment. For example, a person who is experiencing feelings of hostility may say, "I love everyone as a brother." He is saying, in effect, that the hostility is "not me."

The focus of sullivanian strategies is to develop appropriate, healthy responses as components of the syntaxic mode. Reduction of anxiety caused by developmental deficits is also a primary goal. One of the purposes of the nurse-client interaction is to permit the client to identify these deficits and to correct them. (See Chapter 5 for discussion of nurse-client interaction.

Sullivan identified six basic phases of development, which are similar to those of Freud and Erikson. In *infancy*, the period from birth to approximately 1½ years, the primary task is the development of basic sense of trust in others. The gratification of needs ensues as a result of the foundation of trust. The mouth, the ability to cry, the satisfaction response, empathic observation, autistic invention, exploration, and emergency responses such as rage and anxiety are the developmental tools—the means by which the child accomplishes the task.

As an individual moves through the developmental phase, he increases his repertoire of coping mechanisms as each task becomes more complex. The focus of the *childhood* period, 1½ years to about 6 years, is learning to delay gratification in order to receive long-term reward—for example, parental approval. Through the use of mouth, anus, autistic invention, experimentation, manipulation, identification, and emergency responses such as anxiety, guilt, shame, doubt, and anger, the child begins to develop a more realistic sense of his own influence on the environment, which leads to a greater sense of independence and self-worth.

The *juvenile* period, ages 6 to approximately 9, is characterized by the development of a sense of belonging within one's peer group. It is especially important for a child in this period to form a satisfying relationship with a child of his own age group. Sullivan refers to this as the "chum" relationship. Often the child will place his family second in order to meet the needs of his peers. The tools available to the child in this period include competititon, compromise, cooperation, experimentation, manipulation, and exploration.

Following the juvenile period is *preadolescence*, which includes ages 9 to 12. During this time there is a marked switch of loyalty from family to peers. A friend of the same sex is the primary relationship. Exploration, manipulation, and experimentation, coupled with the capacity to love, consensual validation, and collaboration, are the primary tools of the period.

Early adolescence, ages 12 to 14, reflects the child's beginning attempts to be independent of his parents and their set of values, attitudes, and beliefs. There is a sense of rebelliousness. It seems as though the child longs to be both independent and dependent at the same time, and anger arises from this seemingly impossible situation. The task at hand is learning to develop satisfactory relationships with members of the opposite sex. Another primary goal is the achievement of a sense of identity concurrently with a delineation of life goals. Lust, experimentation, exploration, manipulation, and anxiety are the tools most commonly utilized during this phase of development.

The last phase, *late adolescence*, encompasses ages 14 to approximately 21. The major task of this phase is similar to that of Erikson's late adolescent or young adulthood phase—achievement of an intimate, love relationship without the fear of loss of self. This is a culmination of the previous phases in that a sound sense of identity has developed, along with the ability to form trusting relationships with others. The appropriate tools of this period include genital organs, exploration, manipulation, and experimentation.

Sullivan believed that once an individual had completed the tasks of late adolescence, he would be capable of functioning interdependently in society. He thought it unnecessary to continue the discussion of personality development farther than this point, since the most crucial tasks would already have been accomplished.

Piaget

Piaget describes personality development as a progression of cognitive processes. Initially the child is quite egocentric: he believes that all others in his environment share his feelings, thoughts, and beliefs. As he matures, he becomes aware of others' viewpoints and develops an ability to integrate those concepts into his own framework.

Like the other theorists discussed, Piaget views development as a series of stages. When a stage has been completed successfully, the child moves on to a more complex one. For Piaget, mature, intelligent behavior is the ability to critically assess and problem-solve in virtually any situation. Thought processes progress from a concrete level to "formal operations," or abstract, logical thinking.

Four factors concurrently influence the development of cognition: biological maturation, experience with the physical world, social experience, and equilibration. Equilibration is the balancing and integrating of new experiences with those of the past as an individual progresses along the developmental course.

Two behavioral factors inherent in equilibration are *assimilation* and *accommodation*. Through the interaction of these two components, the child (and eventually, the adult) is able to reconcile and integrate any new behavior.

Assimilation is the ability to comprehend experiences. An individual is constantly being bombarded with new situations that require his response. What he learns as a result of new interactions with the environment needs to be incorporated into his already existing body of experiences. Thus new interactions are given meaning in terms of the experiences an individual has had up to that time. In other words, assimilation occurs.

When new concepts are introduced, a certain degree of upset or disequilibrium ensues, depending on the nature of the concept and its perceived effect. An individual directs his energies toward identifying and eliminating the cause of the disequilibrium. As the disequilibrium decreases, the perception of the event becomes more accurate. The process is termed accommodation. For example, the infant views the mothering figure as an extension of self. Through the process of development, he begins to differentiate self from environment. New experiences impinge upon the infant. The meanings of these experiences need to be integrated with the meanings of past experiences. The infant must change the manner in which he perceives the mothering figure in order to develop a differentiated self. Thus the process of differentiation occurs as a result of assimilation and accommodation, in that order.

In summary, assimilation is the mechanism whereby the comprehension of a new experience occurs, up to the point where previous experience left off. Therefore, assimilation frequently results in incorrect plugging in (because of lack of experience). Accommodation occurs to rectify the inaccurate plugging in. This leads to restoration of equilibrium at a higher level of functioning. A parallel can be drawn between disequilibrium and anxiety; the ultimate goals of an individual are the reduction of anxiety and the incorporation of experiences—and thus higher-level functioning—cognitive, emotional, psychological, and biological.

Piaget divides his cognitively based developmental schema into four periods. The first is the *sensorimotor* period, which lasts from birth to 2 years of age. This period is characterized by the infant's moving around in his environment. Meaning is attached to objects by way of manipulation. The young child begins to differentiate himself from his environment through goal-directed behavior. One of the primary concepts a child learns in this period is the permanence of objects, a concept that is basic to logical thought. Objects continue to exist, whether they are seen or not. Another concept that is basic to logical thought is that objects retain their identity even though the context in which they appear may change. The child in this period learns that Grandma is the same person with her glasses off as she is with them on.

The second major period is that of *preoperational thought.* In order to describe the progression of cognition more clearly, Piaget divided this period into two phases—preoperational and intuitive.

The preoperational period, ages 2 to 4, reflects the child's growing ability to use language as a tool to meet his needs. The seedlings of thought begin to appear as the child becomes more aware of the representation of objects by words. For example, a table is an object; we do not eat at the word "table" but at the actual object. The ability to make this distinction prepares the child for symbolic mental activity.

Children in this phase cannot categorize objects in more than one dimension—for example, an object cannot be both yellow and rectangular. He is capable of attending to only one primary characteristic at a time. The child is also unable to classify a group of similar objects in terms of their multifactorial similarity.

Another general feature of thinking of the preoperational period is egocentrism. The child believes that his viewpoint is the only one—it is difficult for him to understand thoughts, perceptions, and ideas as being different from his own. The child cannot understand why an event does not occur as he had thought it would. He cannot allow for factors other than his own. When a parent admonishes him, saying, "Don't do that—you wouldn't like it if someone did that to you," the child does not understand, because he is unable to place himself in the position of another.

As the child becomes older, he is able to conceive of groups or classes as having relationships. In the intuitive phase, ages 4 to 7, he comprehends basic rules and is able to integrate concepts based on more than one dimension. The number of objects in a group no longer changes as the context of presentation changes—another cornerstone of logical thought. For example, the child is able to discern that one set of dots is equal in number to another set of dots even though the presentation is different.

By the end of the preoperational phase, the child sees that each block contains six dots.

In the period of *concrete operations*, ages 7 to 11, the child begins to use logic and objectivity. Reasoning is related to concrete or real events—for example, all apples are fruit; then this apple is fruit. As a result of this phase, the child can organize objects into hierarchies as well as reduce a whole into its component parts and combine it differently without causing a change in the whole.

The final step—abstract thinking—is reached during the period of *formal operations*, ages 11 to 15. By age 11, the child is able to conceptualize a plan based on hypothetical events, consider more than one variable, and identify appropriate strategies of action. Potential relationships among objects can be visualized. As in the adolescent phases of Freud, Erickson, and Sullivan, there is emergence of self, recognition and validation of one's own identity, and then the development of relationships with others in the environment. The individual is able to reflect on himself, review his experiences to that point, and evaluate their influence on his self-appraisals.

Thus man's interaction with his environment is a fundamental premise of the piagetian philosophy of personality development. The child moves from simple cognitive processes, such as understanding object permanence, to formal, abstract thought processes.

MASLOW'S HIERARCHY OF NEEDS

The previous section dealt primarily with the phases of development a child must complete in order to reach maturity. Parallels among four theorists discussed were drawn when appropriate; the tasks or crises of corresponding phases often seemed to be similar. It is important to understand the implications of this statement. Nurses must not assess client on the basis of only one developmental theory; they must correlate the relevant aspects of many theories.

Maslow (1954) views individuals from a perspective that is somewhat different from those of the four theorists discussed—but one that is equally important for heath care providers to understand and apply. Maslow suggests that there is a priority or "hierarchy" of needs, that seeks to satisfy basic needs before moving on to complex ones.

The individual must be motivated to meet challenges, to satisfy needs. Motivation, a concept crucial to the understanding of human behavior, has been discussed in a variety of formats. It can be defined as the rationale or logical thought behind an individual's actions, plans, or ideas. A rationale operates on three levels—conscious, preconscious, and unconscious. Most of what motivates individuals operates on an unconscious level. This fact is of critical importance not only in a nurse's assessment of a client's behavioral responses but also in the nurse's understanding of his or her own reciprocal responses. Maslow proposed a list of five basic needs, each of which reflects a higher level priority than the preceding one. The needs are as follows: (1) physiological, (2) safety, (3) love and belonging, (4) self-esteem, and (5) self-actualization. What meaning do these needs hold for the development of nursing care strategies? Nurse and client could be operating on two different levels. Imagine, for example, that a community health nurse enters a woman's home to discuss her feelings about becoming a mother for the first time but that the mother does not seem interested. Observations of the surrounding environment reveal leaky ceilings, no food in the refrigerator, little furniture, tattered clothing. What are this woman's priorities of needs? Obviously, the nurse is concerned about a higher-level need (love and belonging) than the client. The client is concerned about physiological necessities and safety. Initially, lower-level needs must be satisfied. The client may then be more able to share her feelings about being a new mother. Nursing strategies must take into account the fact that lower-level needs must be satisfied to a greater extent than higher-level needs.

When the first three needs are, for the most part, satisfied, a person seeks out appraisals and assurance from significant others in the environment. He needs to feel a sense of self-respect and self-confidence. Individuals value the appreciation and recognition received from their peers; however, the last two of the five needs are rarely satisfied. Self-fulfillment needs and the recognition of one's potential for continued self-development tend to remain below the level of consciousness. These two needs thus tend to be unconscious motivators of behavior (Maslow, 1954). This fact should alert nurses to be critically aware of verbal and nonverbal behavior that may be motivated by a client's desire for self-respect, autonomy, and self-development.

Maslow's levels of need overlap, just as the phases of development of the various theorists overlap. Higher-level needs emerge before lower-level needs are totally satisfied. Most people tend to be partially satisfied in each area and partially unsatisfied.

CONTINUUM OF
MENTAL HEALTH–MENTAL ILLNESS

We have noted that developmental "lags," fixations at early levels of development, or unsuccessful accomplishment of developmental tasks set the stage for mental illness. However, we must point out the fact that mental health, or mental illness, exists on a continuum. Behavior varies from minute to minute, day to day, month to month. Mental health can be likened to a series of peaks and valleys with plateaus interspersed periodically. Many factors interact, resulting in behavior. In addition, as we will note in succeeding chapters, culture influences the identification of mental illness. Sapir (1963) points out the role of culture as an etiological factor in mental illness—through child-rearing practices and stressful roles, for example—and as a symptom-molder, as in the case of syndromes peculiar to one culture. For example, in the United States, value is placed on rational, logical thought processes. Persons unable to behave in a rational manner are labeled "ill." The same behavior in another culture may be perceived as normal. Thus the criteria used to define and identify mental illness are linked to cultural heritage. It is necessary for nurses to appreciate the arbitrary, culture-bound bases of what is viewed as "normal." Oddities of behavior in another culture are easily identifiable as culture bound. However, the identification of psychiatric disorders within one's own society as being culture bound is not readily accepted.

Jahoda (1953) describes six characteristics developed in infancy and childhood that reflect positive mental health. The first of these indicators is a positive attitude toward oneself. A person who understands his strengths and accepts his limitations possesses a strong sense of identity and is relatively secure in his environment.

Appropriate growth and development as well as achievement of self-actualizing ability, constitute the second positive indicator. Erikson's eight stages of man can be used to measure this particular criterion. The individual who is unable to successfully complete developmental tasks may become maladapted. Positive reinforcement of self-concept is of great importance in enabling an individual to achieve his maximum level of functioning.

The third indicator of positive mental health is the ability to integrate and synthesize life events in such a way as to maintain equilibrium and to reduce anxiety or make it tolerable. Each person develops a philosophy of life that reflects an assessment of the environment and his relatedness to, or isolation from, that environment.

Autonomy is the ability to make appropriate decisions and to be self-directed, with specific goals and objectives in mind. A parallel can be drawn between this fourth indicator of positive mental health and Erikson's second phase of development—autonomy versus shame and doubt. Can a person separate himself from the environment and its social influences? Is he able to make decisions on his own and willing to accept the consequences of his actions, whatever they may be? Throughout the life span, vast amounts of energy are directed toward achievement of independence, which is an important indicator of mental health.

The fifth indicator of positive mental health is the ability to perceive reality without distortion. A person's perceptions of the "real" world as opposed to what is fantasized are influenced by cultural values and mores. Through consensual validation, a sullivanian concept, a person receives support from others in perceiving the environment validly. Similarly, we consider an individual to be mentally healthy if he is sensitive to another human being's wants and needs—that is, if he is empathic. One of the most significant indicators of mental disorder is the inability to grasp reality. However, this factor must be assessed in relationship to the predominant culture, as well as to family constellation and significant others.

The sixth indicator of positive mental health is the ability to love others and to be loved. The ability to love others and be loved includes all aspects of interpersonal relationships, such as work and play. Environmental mastery is the crux of this criterion. The ability to adapt—to meet situations head-on, assess them appropriately, draw relevant conclusions, identify goals, and plan strategies—is a complex component of environmental mastery. The individual is no longer a slave of the environment; he is aware of his *impact* on those around him, that he does have input. Environmental mastery begins shortly after birth and continues through senescence. At each level, different tasks serve to increase an individual's ability to problem-solve in new and varied settings. Energy is directed toward mastering the tasks at hand. A paralyzed young adult devotes his energies toward mastering an environment that functions on the concept of mobility. A perceptually or visually impaired person seeks to master his environment. Each individual assesses his environment to discover what meaning it holds for him at the time. He then devotes energy toward the accomplishment of tasks that will reinforce environmental mastery.

Thus far in this chapter, some of the major aspects of personality development have been presented. Assessment of clients must be based on an overview of psychosexual, biological, cognitive, interpersonal, and social characteristics, as well as of other factors that combine to form an integrated, whole being. Table 3-2 illustrates such an integration of the concepts we consider to be significant to the understanding of the unique personality of each client.

Text continued on p. 134.

TABLE 3-2. Overview of developmental stages

Stage of development	Play/social activities	Health promotion	Language/cognitive development
Infancy	Playing with self Understanding environment through movement Infant needs colorful, mobile, cuddly toys	Immunizations essential during this period Safety precautions relate to falls, burns, oral ingestion of foreign objects and poisons, drowning	Sensorimotor period—ability to recognize change and to adjust accordingly Vocalization begins about 4 months of age—relates to recognition of people and definition of needs; language in this phase is autistic; communication is goal-oriented by the end of the period

*According to Duvall (1971).

Body image	Emotional development	Developmental tasks*
Diffuse feelings of hunger, pain, comfort, but no real body image; self not differentiated from environment; basis for positive perception of body image laid in early mother-child relationships By end of first year, internalization of sensory experiences into body image occurs Ego development and body image development occur simultaneously	Parent-child bonding crucial foundation for basic sense of trust and patterns of future relationships; essential that primary needs are gratified promptly	Achieve physiological equilibrium following birth Establish self as dependent person but separate from others Become aware of alive versus inanimate and familiar versus unfamiliar and develop rudimentary social interaction Develop feeling of and desire for affection and response from others Adjust somewhat to the expectations of others Manage the changing body; learn new motor skills; begin eye-hand coordination Learn to understand and control the world through exploration Develop beginning symbol system, preverbal communication Direct emotional expression to indicate needs and wishes

Continued.

TABLE 3-2. Overview of developmental stages—cont'd

Stage of development	Play/social activities	Health promotion	Language/cognitive development
Toddler	Play is primary mode through which child organizes world, releases tension, improves muscular coordination, and develops spaciotemporal perception Stage characterized by solitary or parallel activities	Primary concerns are respiratory infections and accidents; parents "childproof" the home by removing scatter rugs and sharp or breakable objects and putting poisons out of reach	Preoperational/parataxic period—learning through imitation; lack of understanding of cause and effect relationships Child communicates in an understandable manner yet may not use words with meaning Syncretic speech—one word represents a certain object; emotions, objects, actions are fused to have one meaning Speech is autistic, Vocabulary enlarges

Body image	Emotional development	Developmental tasks
Body image gradually evolves as a component of self-concept	Developmental task: autonomy versus shame and doubt—"Me do it!";	Settle into healthy routines
Child becomes more aware of his body as having physical and emotional components	Child relies greatly on parental responses and support; need for attention and approval acts as primary motivator for socialization process	Master good eating habits
Child not fully aware of the interaction of his body with the environment—i.e., the impact each has on the other	Toilet-training is major developmental accomplishment	Master the basics of toilet-training
Body products—e.g., feces—are not perceived as separate from self		Develop physical skills appropriate to stage of motor development
Self-concept develops from reflected appraisals of significant others; concept of "good-me" develops as a result of positive responses from others; critical period for development of positive self-concept		Become a family member
		Learn to communicate effectively with others

Continued.

TABLE 3-2. Overview of developmental stages—cont'd

Stage of development	Play/social activities	Health promotion	Language/cognitive development
Preschool	Pre-gang stage; peers assume a new importance; child progresses from solitary play to cooperating with others in group; learns to follow rules, to compare self to others, and to be concerned about others; appraisals begin to come from persons other than parents—provides for reality testing and allows expression of emotion and creativity	Accident prevention—e.g., motor vehicles, burns, falling, drowning, child needs clear-cut safety rules explained consistently, simply; adult supervision is also warranted Immunization boosters Dental and medical check-ups important on a regular basis	Concept formation begins—child moves from lack of differentiation to awareness of objects as concrete and separate from the environment Inability to differentiate own feelings from external events—everything is important on an equal basis Language is used to get attention, to maintain interpersonal relationships, and to gather information Reading becomes significant factor in language development

Body image	Emotional development	Developmental tasks
Ego boundaries become more differentiated, as do physical body boundaries; in part because of an increase in sexual awareness, an increase in motor coordination, more mature play experiences, and positive parental relationships Fear of mutilation is quite common in this period	Child learns social roles and responsibilities and behaves more like adult counterparts, Continuation of mastery of self and environment Developmental task—initiative versus guilt Child uses imagination and creativeness to greater degree Increasing awareness of feelings of love, hate, anger, tension—child learns modes of coping to reduce anxiety	Settle into healthful daily routine of adequate eating, resting, and playing Master skills of gross- and fine-motor coordination Become a participating family member Conform to others' expectations Express emotions healthfully and for a wide variety of experiences Learn to communicate effectively with others Learn to use initiative tempered by a conscience Develop ability to handle potentially dangerous situations Lay foundations for understanding the meaning of life, self, the world, and ethical, religious, and philosophical ideas

Continued.

TABLE 3-2. Overview of developmental stages—cont'd

Stage of development	Play/social activities	Health promotion	Language/cognitive development
School age	Peer groups provide a broader circle of friends outside home environment Six- or seven-year old enjoys assuming roles—e.g., fireman, mailman, teacher, doctor, nurse Older school-age children enjoy table games of a simple nature, riding bikes, swimming Later in this period, creativity appears in the areas of music, art, dance, drama Predominant partner is "chum"—of same sex and age, actually is an extension of child's self; sharing of very special thoughts and feelings occurs	Illness occurs for first time as child enters school; upper respiratory infections are common Immunization boosters are important Safety precautions in relation to motor vehicle accidents and drownings	Stage of concrete operations—reasoning through real or imagined situations Child progresses to greater understanding of meanings and feelings Child uses language to establish relationships and to increase his knowledge base Syntaxic communication is utilized—cause and effect relationships are beginning to be recognized Child learns to express his feelings and thoughts in a way that is meaningful to others

Body image	Emotional development	Developmental tasks
School experience reinforces or weakens child's perceptions of body and self Fluidity of body image/self-concept, due to rapid physical, emotional, and social changes	Developmental task—industry versus inferiority Child progresses from self-centered to more other-directed behavior Child evidences concern for others—particularly "chum" in latter part of period More self-direction—continued imitation of adults Child still unaware of effects of self on others, yet becoming more tolerant of others' behavior	Decrease dependence on family and gain satisfaction from peers and adults Increase neuromuscular skills in order to participate in games and work with others Learn adult concepts, as well as concepts related to problem-solving Learn to communicate with others realistically Become active family member Give affection to; and receive affection from, family and friends without expecting immediate return Learn socially acceptable ways of handling and saving money Learn to deal with strong feelings Adjust to changing body image and come to terms with sex roles Discover healthy ways to become an acceptable person Develop positive attitude toward own and other social, racial, and economic groups

Continued.

TABLE 3-2. Overview of developmental stages—cont'd

Stage of development	Play/social activities	Health promotion	Language/cognitive development
Adolescence	Peer groups most important; Status and recognition derived from the group; behavior defined by group members Sense of identity results from appraisals by others in the social setting	Mood swings quite common in this period Accidents involving motor vehicles of some sort are leading cause of death Obesity, excessive loss of weight (anorexia nervosa), acne, venereal disease, and pregnancy are current health issues Drug and alcohol abuse are, historically, very characteristic of period	Period of greatest ability to acquire and use knowledge; adolescent is able to perform active problem-solving to reach realistic solutions; considers alternatives to problems; is highly imaginative—this can be a very creative time

Body image	Emotional development	Developmental tasks
Body image and self-concept closely tied to identity formation; experiences of a positive nature enable development of positive body image; adolescent is sensitive to rapid change in physical characteristics; may be overly aware of a defect, resulting in undervaluation of self Body is the channel through which rejection or acceptance occurs	Developmental task—identity versus role diffusion completion of task rests on successful completion of previous tasks—leads to secure sense of self Values, attitudes, beliefs of parents are internalized Adolescent feels a sense of wholeness—recognizes uniqueness of self	Accepts changing body size, shape, and function Learn a variety of physical skills Achieves a satisfying and socially acceptable sex role Find the self as a member of one or more peer groups; develop interpersonal skills Achieve independence from parents and other adults yet maintain interdependence Select a satisfying occupation in line with interests and abilities Prepare to settle into a close relationship with another individual based on love rather than infatuation Develop intellectual and work skills and sensitivity to others Develop workable philosophy of life, mature values, and worthy ideals

Continued.

TABLE 3-2. Overview of developmental stages—cont'd

Stage of development	Play/social activities	Health promotion	Language/cognitive development
Young adulthood	Review of life options to decide what focus of life will be—e.g., marriage, work, family Person continues to have close circle of friends, usually based on similar interests, values occupations Chooses social and recreational activities as pleasure-promoting as well as outlets for energy	Accidents—especially motor vehicle, industrial, drowning—are the leading cause of death	Full mental capacity has been attained, although knowledge may be increased in college or trade schools Person assumes more responsibility for own learning rather than expecting it to be handed to him Is able to make contributions to society of a social or intellectual nature

Body image	Emotional development	Developmental tasks
Body continues to be channel of connection to the world; disturbances of the body influence self-concept If body undergoes changes, person must explore those changes and incorporate them into existing picture Body type and size influence personality development Illness causes changes in body image/self-concept that need to be integrated	Developmental task— intimacy versus isolation Inadequate resolution of identity crisis may lead to disturbances in sex role identity Stress reactions, including physiological changes, may occur as a result of intolerable levels of anxiety Suicide is third leading cause of death Alcoholism and drug abuse are two other chronic problems	Accept self and stabilize self-concept and body image Establish independence from parental home and financial aid Become established in a vocation or profession that provides satisfaction and financial recompense Learn to appraise and express love responsibly through more than sexual contacts Establish an intimate bond with another Manage a residence Decide whether to have a family Find congenial social group Formulate a meaningful philosophy of life Become involved as a citizen in the community

Continued.

TABLE 3-2. Overview of developmental stages—cont'd

Stage of development	Play/social activities	Health promotion	Language/cognitive development
Middle age	Leisure time becomes a concern; as individual progresses toward retirement, assessment of leisure time is important; person needs to feel that it is acceptable to put aside time for leisure Recognition of the era in which one was raised and subsequent values developed Relationship with spouse is especially important—provides security and stability in a period of much change	Menopause—both male and female—occurs, with concurrent physiological changes Consideration of safety factors to prevent falls, burns Coronary artery disease is leading cause of death in men Other health problems include cancer, pulmonary disease, diabetes, depression, alcoholism	Learning enhanced by individual's resource of life experiences Motivation to learn is greater—increasing numbers of individuals in this age bracket are continuing their education Ability to integrate cognitive function with experiential factors, resulting in more meaningful interpretation of life experiences

Body image	Emotional development	Developmental tasks
Additional physical changes occur—graying hair, wrinkled skin, decreasing sensory functions	Developmental task— generativity versus stagnation	Rediscover and develop new satisfactions as a mate
Need to accept body changes as part and parcel of maturation process	Reassessment and evaluation of one's life are critical	Assist growing children to become more responsible
Need to recognize positive aspects of self, body, and other persons in age group	Acceptance of goals that were accomplished as well as those that were not	Create pleasant, comfortable home, appropriate to own values
	Enjoyment of watching children and their children carry on traditional values and beliefs	Find pleasure in generativity and recognition in work
	Orientation toward needs and goals of others— willingness to extend self	Adjust to role reversal with aging parents
		Assume mature social and civic responsibilities
		Develop and maintain active organization membership
		Accept and adjust to physical changes
		Make an art of friendship
		Use leisure time with satisfaction
		Continue to form a philosophy of life

Continued.

TABLE 3-2. Overview of developmental stages—cont'd

Stage of development	Play/social activities	Health promotion	Language/cognitive development
Older adulthood	Older individual often surrounds himself with his few special friends; period characterized by great sense of loss—loss of close friends, loss of function/independence, and eventual loss of self Person is comfortable with daily routines and same people Needs to maintain contact with outside world in order to preserve reality orientation and to prevent loneliness Retirement affects number and type of relationships—person may feel cut off from meaningful people	Safety factors are of prime consideration; impaired sensory input hampers the accurate perception of environment; falls, burns, forgetfulness in regard to the taking of medications are examples of potentiallly dangerous situations Alterations in all major systems begin; regular physicials and early detection of illness help to reduce ensuing problems	Many factors affect learning: reduced motivation, sensory impairment, educational level, deliberate caution; capacity to learn continues—logical associations between words and events are easily recalled Apprehension in new learning situations Slowness in reaction time

Body image	Emotional development	Developmental tasks
Physical changes cause alterations in function and appearance and thus in body image; sensory deficits cause individual to believe that he is weak and less worthy; feels the loss of independence; perceives prostheses, hearing aides, glasses, etc. as being threats to wholeness	Developmental task—ego integrity versus despair; person defends his beliefs and life-style—because they hold meaning for him; views life as worthwhile, productive rather than futile, and too short; individual who has had an intact ego throughout the life cycle is better equipped to deal with aging—feels completeness and satisfaction with his life; death then is not feared but accepted as part of life	Decide where and how to live out remaining years; find satisfactory home and living arrangements Continue a warm, supportive relationship with significant other Adjust living standards to a retirement income Maintain maximum level of health Maintain contact with children, grandchildren Maintain interest in people outside family Pursue new interests and maintain former activities Find meaning in life after retirement Work out significant philosopy of life Adjust to loss of loved one

THE FINAL PHASE OF DEVELOPMENT—DEATH

Death—an unavoidable aspect of life yet probably one of the most difficult to accept. Modern society tends to place the dying in hospitals or other places outside the home. They are isolated from family and friends. Grieving often takes on a superficial character, stilted by unfamiliar surroundings and faces. Although each person who faces death experiences the situation uniquely, six phases are commonly associated with the process of dying. These phases, identified by Elizabeth Kubler-Ross as a result of her extensive work with the dying, were incorporated into her book *On Death and Dying* (1969).

The first stage is characterized by shock and denial. Many dying persons react with the statement, "No, not me; it can't be true!" Kubler-Ross says this reaction occurs whether a person is told at the outset of an illness or comes to his own conclusions at a later time. Denial is a healthy mechanism; at this point, it acts as a buffer. It also permits a person to collect himself and to mobilize adaptive responses that are more effective on a long-term basis and that are most comfortable for him. The types of responses that he develops depend upon his previous experiences with loss situations, the time he has to gradually prepare for his death, and the manner in which he received the information that he was going to die.

Anger and rage are the responses associated with the second stage. "Why me?" That is the question the dying person most frequently asks of those around him. These feelings are often projected onto family and hospital staff at random, causing the arousal of many feelings in them that ultimately affect the responses of the client. At this point, the client feels that nothing is going well; the doctor is not helping him and the nurses do not care. He directs anger at his family but at the same time desperately needs their support. He has difficulty sifting out and sharing his emotions. Very often his anger takes the form of a desire to control his situation. Family and staff should allow him to make some of the decisions regarding his own care.

After the period of anger, the dying person becomes less agressive; in this third stage he directs his energies toward bargaining for more time. This is an attempt at postponement, a delay for the accomplishment of some important task. Assume, for example, that a woman of 54 is dying of lung cancer. Her one wish is to see her daughter married. Once this wish has been realized, she sets another goal. Such a mechanism permits a client to cope with dying, but a piece at a time. These bargains are usually made with God and are kept secret. However, the message can be read between the lines.

The fourth stage is depression. As the illness of the terminally ill client progresses, he is no longer able to keep up a stoical appearance, and his rage is replaced by a great sense of loss. He is going to lose everything around him—his friends, his family, all that holds meaning for him. Financial burdens may become heavier as a result of the loss of employment. Feelings of guilt and shame often accompany the depression.

Kubler-Ross calls the fifth stage "preparatory depression." This type of depression helps to prepare the client for his future losses and thus eventually to give him a sense of acceptance. It is important that a nurse recognize the client's need to express sorrow, to be sad. This is a quiet period with little need for words. A stroking touch is sufficient to let the client know he is understood during this most difficult of times.

The final stage is acceptance. In this stage the client is neither depressed nor angry. He is able to admit being envious of the living, angry at those who do not have to die now. The struggle is over and the battle won. The dying person may prefer to have one significant individual with him rather than to surround himself with visitors. However, he needs to know he is not alone. This is the period of disengagement; it is especially important that family and friends understand the nature of this period.

Death is the final stage of growth (Kubler-Ross, 1975). It is essential that nurses accept the finiteness of their own and their clients' existences.

Although it is important to recognize the phases that the dying client passes through, they are simply a framework for understanding. Each person lives uniquely—and dies uniquely.

Caring for the dying client and his family should be based on the development of an approximated relationship, which Barton (1977) describes as a "need-discerning relationship that is more than just talking." A level of relatedness is promoted that facilitates both verbal and nonverbal communication. Needless prattle is unnecessary. The sincere listening of one individual to another or a simple touch may be all that is needed. There should be an appreciation by the nurse not only of the facts of the client's situation but also of his wide range of experience.

A relationship that is based on avoidance does not recognize or accept the concerns, needs, or perceptions of the client and his family. The nurse who focuses exclusively on seemingly relevant details, such as financial concerns, may avoid discussion of the client's personal experiences. Published studies indicate that nurses are quicker to respond to the physical needs of clients than to their emotional needs. In order to facilitate the expresssion of the client's feelings about the experience of dying, a nurse needs to understand the "metacommunication" that is being transmitted. "Metacommunication is a message about a message" (Satir, 1972). Metacommunication can also be described as the implicit content or the nonverbal interchange of an interaction. Understanding a client's metacommunication leads a nurse to a more accurate assessment and to more appropriate nursing responses. For example, a woman states during a physical examination, "I have a lump in my breast." This statement carries many implicit messages: "I have cancer." "Am I going to lose my breast?" "Will I die?" On the basis of unconscious personal priorities, the nurse responds to the client. However, communication may be cut off if the nurse does not explore the implicit meaning of the client's message. The nurse's message also carries an implicit meaning. In order to clarify the metacommunication, the nurse might respond in this situation by saying, "It sounds as though you have some concerns—can you share them with me?" The client perceives her feelings as being legitimate and worthwhile. An open, direct relationship can then be developed.

Nurses often are overwhelmed by their own feelings while caring for a dying client. Barton (1977) describes a process of controlled distancing, "a therapeutic maneuver which permits the care-giver to maintain emotional integrity in the face of a continuous care process." It is sometimes critical that the nurse move back from the situation in order to more objectively understand what is occurring. This action allows the nurse to maintain a sense of control while at the same time maintaining sensitivity. A successful manner of accomplishing controlled distancing is to become more aware of one's own identity and one's own feelings that dying arouses. Nurses need to share these feelings with their colleagues. A support system can readily be developed that fosters sharing, permits each nurse to feel comfortable with his or her feelings, and ultimately maximizes the relationship between nurse and client. Both nurse and client should be permitted to legitimately be persons.

Of course, working with a dying client and his family also involves the assessment of physical needs, toward which, as mentioned previously, nurses generally direct most of their energies. Comfort measures, such as providing adequate pain medication, positioning the client appropriately, and maintaining sufficient hydration, can be instituted by the nursing staff on the basis of assessment of the client and collaboration with the physician.

To maintain a position within his social context is a concern for the dying client. Often he is shut off from significant others in the environment—by the physical setting such as a hospital or by fear of others becoming emotionally involved. He needs to continue to feel a sense of being alive by participating in all facets of life, including his dying. Nurses can allow clients to experience their illness by recognizing these feelings as being valid and worthwhile. Grieving with the client and his family is acceptable. Clients have described nurses who share in the grieving process as being genuinely concerned and interested in them as human beings rather than only as clients.

Nurses can minimize interpersonal conflict between the client and his family. Anticipatory planning can be utilized to identify possible changes in existing relationships and to develop a problem-solving approach to avert a crisis. When a member of a family is terminally ill, responsibilities shift. For example, a wife may have to balance the checkbook, take out the garbage, and do other jobs that had previously been taken care of by the husband. After this pattern continues for a period of time, the wife may become excessively demanding of her children, the nursing staff, and other significant people in the environment. She may feel that her needs are being neglected even though she is carrying a greater portion of the household responsibility. The emotional drain of dealing with the eventual loss of her husband of course can also contribute to the pattern of demanding behavior. Nurses can facilitate the discussion of shifts in responsibility and the resultant emotional conflicts so that each member of a family is aware of the others' feelings. By maintaining open lines of communication and recognizing each individual's needs as valid, family members can continue to maintain a supportive interaction pattern. The maximizing of each individual's feelings of worth as a person during the dying process decreases feelings of guilt and hostility among the survivors. There is less need to say, "I should have said more" or "I should have done this."

Other supportive measures include the provision of spiritual comfort and continuous care by all staff members. Nurses need to recognize emotional problems. Is a client severely depressed? Has he considered taking his own life? Is there a history of suicide in his family or a history of suicide attempts by this particular individual? It is not sufficient to say that depression is normal because a person is dying. Further data needs to be collected.

The client who is dying must be met on his level. The nurse who sits and truly listens, who goes beyond the disease to the individual, develops a relationship that permits everyone involved—client, family members, nurses, physicians, social workers—to experience an active, open, approximated interaction.

CHAPTER SUMMARY

The process of personality development can be viewed from many perspectives. We have presented for discussion the many factors that influence this process.

There are numerous theories regarding the sequence of development. Our intention has been to present four major developmental theories, as well as to discuss Maslow's theory of the hierarchy of needs. It is essential that nurses assume an eclectic approach. The ultimate goal is to recognize each client as a unique human being. When a nurse keeps this fact in mind, a nursing assessment will reflect an accurate appraisal of all the elements that combine to form an integrated human being.

REFERENCES

Baldwin, A. L.
1967 Theories of Child Development. New York: Wiley & Sons, Inc.
Barton, D.
1977 Dying and Death. Baltimore: The Williams & Wilkins Co.
Bowlby, J.
1973 Attachment and Loss: Separation, Anxiety, and Anger, vol. I. New York: Basic Books, Inc. Publishers, pp. 101-120.
Carter, F. M.
1971 Psychosocial Nursing (ed. 2). New York: Macmillan, Inc.
Duvall, E.
1971 Family Development (ed. 4). Philadelphia: J. B. Lippincott Co.

Erikson, E.
1950 Childhood and Society (ed. 2). New York: W. W. Norton & Co., Inc.
1968 Identity: Youth and Crisis. New York: W. W. Norton & Co., Inc.
Escalona, S., and M. Leitch
1953 "Early phases of personality development: a non-normative study of infant behavior." Monographs of the Society for Research in Child Development 17(1):33-49.
Flavell, J.
1963 Developmental Psychology of Jean Piaget. Princeton, N. J.: D. Van Nostrand Co.
Freud, S.
1916 A General Introduction to Psychoanalysis. New York: Liveright Publishing Corp.
Hauck, B.
1970 "Differences between the sexes at puberty." In Adolescence: Readings in Behavior and Development. E. D. Evans (ed.). Hinsdale, Ill.: Dryden Press.
Hoy, W. K., and T. Applebury.
1970 "Teacher-principal relationships in "humanistic" and "custodial" elementary schools. Journal of Experimental Education. 2:161-170.
Jahoda, M.
1958 Current Concepts of Positive Mental Health. New York: Basic Books, Inc., Publishers.
Kubler-Ross, E.
1969 On Death and Dying. New York: Macmillan, Inc.
Kubler-Ross, E.
1975 Death: The Final Stage of Growth. Englewood Cliffs, N. J.: Prentice Hall, Inc.
Lidz, T.
1968 The Person. New York: Basic Books, Inc., Publishers.

Malinowski, B.
1927 Sex and Repression in a Savage Society. New York: Harcourt Brace.

Maslow, A. H.
1954 Motivation and Personality. New York: Harper & Row, Publishers, Inc.

McCandless, B., and E. Evans.
1973 Children and Youth: Psychosocial Development. New York: Dryden Press.

Sapir, E.
1963 "Cultural anthropology and psychiatry." In Selected Writings of Edward Sapir in Language, Culture, and Personality. Berkeley: University of California Press.

Satir, V.
1967 Conjoint Family Therapy. Palo Alto, Calif.: Science & Behavior Books.
1975 Peoplemaking. Palo Alto, Calif.: Science & Behavior Books.

Sheldon, W., S. Stevens, and W. Tucker
1940 The Varieties of Human Physique. New York: Harper and Brothers.

Stone, L. J., and J. Church
1968 Childhood and Adolescence: A Psychology of the Growing Person (ed. 2). New York: Random House, Inc.

Sullivan, H. S.
1953 The Collected Works of Harry Stack Sullivan. New York: W. W. Norton & Co., Inc.

Thompson, R.
1975 "Culture and personality." In Psychology and Culture. Dubuque, Iowa: Wm. C. Brown Co., Publishers.

Whiting and Child
1953 Child Training and Personality: A Cross-Cultural Study. New Haven, Conn.: Yale University Press.

Zigler, E.
1970 Social Class and the Socialization Process. Review of Education Research.

ANNOTATED SUGGESTED READINGS

Barton, D.
1977 Dying and Death. Baltimore: The Williams and Wilkins Co.
Barton presents a multidimensional approach to the understanding of the process of dying. Spiritual, medical, and psychological issues are explored in depth. An outline that can be utilized by nurses as well as by other health professionals delineates the areas that need to be considered by persons who work with dying clients. Difficulties encountered by nurses, such as lack of adequate preparation to deal with dying clients, are identified and discussed.

Lidz, T.
1968 The Person. New York: Basic Books, Inc., Publishers.
This classical work presents an overview of the developmental cycle from birth to death. The discussion of each phase incorporates an assessment of biological, psychological, and cultural factors affecting growth and development. This excellent text provides a framework for a holistic understanding of the client as a person.

Watts, Rosalyn
1979 Dimensions of Sexual Health. American Journal of Nursing, September, pp. 1568-1572.
Watts presents sexuality as an integrated component of self that, like any other component, needs to be assessed. Brief synopses of sexual physiological responses and psychosexual development and gender identity, as well as a classification of disorders, are presented. The book explores sexuality concurrently with a review of the reproductive system of the female and the genitourinary system of the male.

FURTHER READINGS

Jourard, S.
1971 The Transparent Self. New York: Litton Educational Publishing, Inc.

Masters, W. H., and V. E. Johnson
1966 Human Sexual Response. Boston: Little, Brown & Co.

Michel, B., and E. Michel
1971 "The nature and development of psychological sex differences." In Psychology and Educational Practice. G. Lesser (ed.). Glenview, Ill.: Scott, Foresman, & Co.

Money, J., and A. Erhardt
1972 Man and Woman, Boy and Girl. Baltimore: The Johns Hopkins University Press.

Rogers, C.
1961 On Becoming a Person. Boston: Houghton Mifflin Co.

Woods, N. F.
1979 Human Sexuality in Health and Illness (ed. 2). St. Louis: The C. V. Mosby Co.

4
ADAPTATION AND STRESS

CHAPTER FOCUS

Adaptation, stress, anxiety—these are terms of significance for the health care team as well as for clients. The concepts these words represent will very often be the basis for clinical assessment and intervention.

A person's position along the mental health–mental illness continuum flucuates according to his ability to adapt to stress. Through the process of adaptation an individual meets needs that are dictated by internal and external factors. Adaptation may be equated with survival. The degree of ability to adapt inevitably influences the ability to survive. Adaptation may also be viewed as the changes an individual experiences as a result of a reaction to stress. These changes act as a defense system by which a person attempts to deal with stress—whether by limiting its impact or by neutralizing its effects. Thus adaptation permits the body to continue to function in an effective manner. It promotes forward movement by reducing or alleviating the negative aspects of change. Adaptation can be viewed as a lifelong process that is neither permanent nor static; it involves constant change.

The nurse's role is unique. The nurse can be instrumental in assisting clients to develop successful adaptative mechanisms in both the psychosocial realm and the physiological realm. Nurses are in a position to facilitate the efforts of their clients to deal with obstacles that may interfere with the ability to respond appropriately and realistically to the demands of their environment, situation, or condition.

4

ADAPTATION AND STRESS

Adaptation encompasses the
internal and external changes that
interrelate to ensure the survival of
the individual in his environment.

Underlying dynamics

    Stress

    Anxiety

    Adaptation

Commonly encountered stressors

    Threats to body image

    Pain

    Immobilization

    Loss and change

Nursing intervention

    Primary prevention

    Secondary prevention

    Tertiary prevention

UNDERLYING DYNAMICS
Stress

What then is stress? How does it differ from anxiety? What are the causative factors of stress? Are there different types of stressors? How does one adapt to stress? These are but a few of the areas that need to be discussed.

Selye (1956) describes stress as being nonspecific in nature and requiring a person to make some type of change. Engel (1962) defines stress as any process, either in the external environment or within an individual, that demands a response from the individual. He views stress as an inducer of action rather than as an effect of that action. It is important to note that stress is not always a negative entity: pleasurable experiences such as marriage, delivery of a baby, or beginning a new job also produce stress. In fact, a person is constantly under stress—even when he is asleep. Stress is inherent in the process of life—respiratory and cardiac activity and gastric secretion are but a few examples of physiological processes that may be considered stressors. It is not until stress becomes intensified and appears repeatedly that a person becomes aware of it.

Factors in one's external environment may act as stressors, while factors in one's internal environment may determine how one adapts to those stressors. Stressful external factors may include physical aspects of the environment—for example, climate or amount of daylight. Living in a city that is frequently smog bound can be stressful to a person who is predisposed to lung disease. Social factors such as crowding can be stress producing. Freedman (1971) states that high population density is a potential stressor—it can increase the occurrence of psychological maladaptation and physiological dysfunction. The critical factor is not the limited space itself; the most important factors are the shortage of needed resources and the substantial amount of forced interaction with large groups of people. When these factors remain within acceptable parameters, there does not seem to be an adverse effect on emotional or physical health.

Internal factors mediate the effect that stressors have on an individual. One's personality, degree of ego strength, and temperament affect the perception one has of a stressful situation. One person's crisis is another person's everyday situation. Past experiences with and reactions to stressful situations affect a person's perception of similar events in the present. Genetic endowment predisposes each individual to emotional and/or physical vulnerabilities. In conjunction with certain external factors such as life experiences, these vulnerabilities or weaknesses can appear in the form of a dysfunctional organ. This organ becomes the "organ of choice," or the organ that expresses or channels tension. This concept will be discussed more fully in Chapter 9. The chronological age and the developmental level of the individual also influence the perception of an event as being stressful. As a person progresses through the life cycle, stressful events become growth promoting if the person is able to manage his environment comfortably. Stressful situations take on crisis proportions when an individual reaches the point where developmental capabilities are no longer able to meet the increasing demands imposed by the environment.

Thus both internal and external variables affect the stress state, which is a reflection of a delicate interrelation of the two. Stress is growth promoting until it exceeds certain parameters, which depend upon individual temperament.

Anxiety

Anxiety is a result of stress. Engel (1962) describes anxiety as the psychological response to great amounts of energy running unchanneled as a result of a stressful situation. As was previously stated, stress is the inducer, not the effect, of an action. Anxiety is often described as a feeling of apprehension, of impending doom. The behavior of a person who is experiencing anxiety may run the gamut from maintainance of a state of alertness to panic of such severity that the individual either becomes immobilized or attends to every minute cue in his environment. Anxiety is a subjective experience that results from a fear of an undetermined nature. Anxiety may have its roots in past experiences, or it may be produced by a threatened or perceived loss of inner control or by a threat to self-esteem. Feelings of isolation, helplessness, and insecurity are associated with anxiety.

Freudian theory considers anxiety to be the major motivating factor in behavioral change. Freud used the term "anxiety" to refer to that anxiety which results from the trauma of the birth process itself. Then, throughout the developmental span, anxiety is generated by conflict between the id and the superego. The ego acts as referee between the two conflicting forces. Freud (1936) proposed that anxiety acts as a signal system, warning that a conflict may become overwhelming. He also believed that the object of anxiety is unconscious and related to earlier object loss. Freud differentiated fear from anxiety by arguing that fear has its origins in a threatening external event.

It is an acute response whose precipitating factors are real and immediate, while anxiety has its origins in intrapsychic conflict. According to freudian theory, ego defense mechanisms defend the ego against anxiety. These mechanisms operate outside the level of conscious awareness, acting to repress all material that is anxiety producing (see Chapter 3 for a discussion of defense mechanisms).

Sullivanian, or interpersonal, theory proposes that anxiety is a tension state that is transmitted through an empathic process from mother to infant, with the infant responding as though mother and self were one. In order for this process to occur, the ego must have some awareness of the environment. Sullivan (1953) believes that the infant fears disapproval from the mothering figure and that later experiences with significant others thus may generate feelings of anxiety if the individual perceives that his behavior will not receive approval. The lack of parental approval during childhood therefore affects adult interpersonal situations.

Peplau (1963) bases much of her theoretical framework on Sullivan's theory. She defines four levels of anxiety, which are summarized in Table 4-1.

As anxiety increases, a person attempts to meet the demands of the stress-producing situation. Patterns of coping are established as an individual utilizes certain mechanisms repeatedly to control or allay anxiety. Pathological behavior results when intrapsychic defense mechanisms are used to excess and become ineffective. For example, a young child who is constantly subjected to fighting between his parents retreats into his own world to protect himself from intense anxiety. If he retreats too often, this mechanism acts to distort reality and to interfere with the development of interpersonal relationships.

Some persons suffering from anxiety use behavior that serves to justify actions by placing blame elsewhere or by directing anger outward onto society. Other anxious persons turn their anger inward—as in depression—as a mechanism of tension relief. Finally, some persons control or allay anxiety by directing the energy created by anxiety through psychological and/or physiological channels. The resulting neurotic patterns of behavior—for example, phobias, obsessive-compulsive behavior, dissociative tendencies—are commonly referred to as "psychological conversions" (for further discussion of neuroses, see Chapter 10). Physiological responses to relieve anxiety are termed "psychosomatic dysfunctions" or "physiological dysfunctions." These dysfunctions can affect any part of the body. Permanent structural

TABLE 4-1. Levels of anxiety*

Mild (+1)	Moderate (+2)	Severe (+3)	Panic (+4)
Person is alert; sees, hears, grasps more than he previously would ordinarily; learning is enhanced	Perceptual field is narrowed, but person can attend to more if directed to do so (person makes use of selective inattention—i.e., directing attention to a primary focus with little attention to the periphery)	Perceptual field greatly reduced	Attention is narrowed severely, or speed of scatter is sharply increased
May protect self by limiting close interpersonal relationships		Person may become preoccupied with one detail or focus on many details simultaneously ("scattering")	Feelings of awe, dread, terror, personality disintegration are common
Uses coping mechanisms to relieve tension; such as nail biting, walking, crying, sleeping, eating, laughing, smoking, drinking	Increased powers of concentration	Selective inattention continues to be operative	Exhaustion and death occur if panic continues for prolonged period
Anxiety is controlled with little conscious effort	Problem-solving capacity still available		
		Dissociation occurs to permit escape; tension relief behavior predominates	

*Data adapted from Peplau, H. 1963. "A working definition of anxiety, "In Some Clinical Approaches to Psychiatric Nursing. S. Burd and M. Marshall (eds.). New York: Macmillan, Inc.; and Menninger, K. 1963. The Vital Balance. New York: Viking Press.

change and eventually irreversible organic damage may result from prolonged use of a particular organ for anxiety relief (for further discussion of psychophysiological disorders, see Chapter 9).

Clients who are experiencing anxiety are unable to identify their feelings specifically. They may refer to "tenseness," "apprehension," "impending doom," "nervousness," or an "all-encompassing feeling that something terrible is going to happen." Various emotions are often associated with anxiety. The energy created by anxiety may be expressed in anger, depression, guilt, jealousy, low self-worth, helplessness, or hopelessness.

Anxiety cannot be easily discerned, yet both the recognition of anxiety and the understanding of its expression are crucial to the nurse-client relationship. The nurse needs to be cognizant of a client's level of anxiety—as well as his or her own level—throughout the relationship. The following adaptation of Peplau's (1962) interpersonal techniques can serve as a model for nursing intervention for the anxious client.

1. Assess the client. Note physiological and psychological indicators of anxiety. Identify the level of anxiety.
2. Explore the feelings that the client is experiencing at the moment by asking, "Are you feeling uncomfortable or tense?" Determine whether any behavior observed—for example, smoking, getting up in the middle of a conversation, changing the subject—is connected with the feelings of anxiety.
3. Begin to explore the reasons for the anxiety by identifying what had been happening in the client's situation prior to the increase in anxiety. Identify precipitating stressors.
4. Connect stressors with a perceived or real threat that the client is experiencing. The threat may then be related to past emotionally charged experiences or situations.
5. Assist the client to relate the present experience to experiences in the past that may have involved arousal of similar feelings of anxiety.
6. Once the threat has been identified, determine the effectiveness of current coping mechanisms. State the nursing diagnosis.
7. Encourage the client to reevaluate the threat. Is his assessment of it realistic? Many times a client fears that others will reject him or that he is inadequate. Bring overly critical assessments into realistic proportions by allowing the client to share his feelings with supportive staff members, family members, and peers.
8. Facilitate the development of effective coping mechanisms through the use of role modeling, which can be accomplished in the following manner. Provide an atmosphere that is conducive to the testing of new behavior. Realistic appraisal of behavior enables the client to integrate more adaptive measures into his repertoire. Open, honest communication between nurse and client can be carried over into other interpersonal relationships. Self-esteem will thus increase, with a concurrent decrease in anxiety.
9. Include significant others in the nursing care plan so as to facilitate the further exploration of anxiety-producing situations.
10. Continue to evaluate levels of anxiety throughout the relationship.

Anxiety leaves no person untouched. In mild forms it contributes to growth, while in severe forms it can cause total personality disintegration. An understanding of the behavior and emotions associated with anxiety enables nurses to make inferences relating to the presence of anxiety in a client. The goals of the nurse-client relationship are (1) to assist the client to recognize anxiety as the cause of certain behavior that may be harmful and (2) to develop alternative methods of coping. In later chapters, anxiety will be discussed in relation to the development of pathological forms of behavior.

Adaptation

Adaptation to stress occurs physiologically, culturally, and psychologically.

Physiological adaptation. What occurs on the physiological level during a stress reaction? Stress stimulates the release of adrenocorticotropic hormone (ACTH) from the anterior lobe of the hypothalamus. Continued stimulation causes the production of cortical hormones. These hormones have various effects on the body, one of which is to act on the pituitary, when necessary, to reduce the production of ACTH. Stress acts first on the brain and then on the sympathetic nervous system to stimulate the production of norepinephrine and epinephrine. How is this hormone activity perceived by the individual? The body prepares itself for the stressor by increasing the heart rate and respiratory activity; the pupils dilate to provide a wider range of vision; the skin may become cold and clammy, and the person may become pale; "butterflies," muscle stiffness, weakness, increased perspiration, and chest pain often occur as well. Norepinephrine stimulates arteriolar vasoconstriction to increase blood pressure; the adrenal glands produce epinephrine, which stimulates the release of glucose by the liver; and peristaltic activity is slowed. Blood is diverted from the gastrointestinal tract to the cardiovascular system for the purpose of "fight or flight." The parasympathetic system may act simultaneously to produce diarrhea and excessive urination.

Let us briefly look at Selye's (1956) General Adaptation Syndrome as a correlate of the sympatho-adreno-medullary response to stress. Selye divides adaptation into three states or stages: Stage I is the initial "call to arms," which serves to alert the sympathetic nervous system. Stage II is the stage of resistance and prolonged abnormal physiological functioning in an attempt to deal with the stressors. Stage III is the final stage—exhaustion. Selye's emphasis on the pituitary-adrenal mechanism as a response to stress serves as a foundation for his concept of "diseases of adaptation." He sees stress—rather than inherent physiological defects—as responsible for the various disease states.

Cultural adaptation. In order to live productively, individuals develop patterns of living and relationships with others that allow them to interact with the physical environment rather than be controlled by it. Cultural systems provide parameters for behavior and physiological functioning yet permit individual diversity. They allow individuals to adapt to various situations and problems and to be informed about the environment.

Adaptive changes often have been achieved through genetic, physiological, and constitutional means and have then been transmitted for generations through natural selection or conditioning by a culture.

Cultural adaptation in regard to the mental health–mental illness continuum may take place in a variety of ways. For example, modification of the environment may enable a client to adapt to a condition that interferes with optimum health.

Culture plays an important role in determining a client's definition of stress and how he responds to that stress. Alland (1970) views evolution of human behavior, or rather how one adapts, in light of Darwin's theory of biological evolution. Alland argues that there is an interrelationship between organic and social life that is significant to the understanding of adaptation.

Two types of cultural adaptation are significant. Inward-directed adaptation, including internal homeostasis or integration, results in continuous change and/or motion. Outward-directed adaptation is the result of encounters between a person and his environment. The total of these interactions results in the development of an effective self-regulatory system, one that is capable of functioning within a variety of environments.

The interaction between evolutionary concepts (the development of effective feedback or self-regulatory systems) and cultural concepts results in a change in the human system in the direction of a better environmental "fit." For example, organisms with higher developmental levels of homeostatic mechanisms will produce more offspring, leading to increased populations of these more highly adapted organisms. Eventually, less adaptable organisms will be overshadowed by organisms that more readily "fit" the environment.

It is important to point out that both inward-directed adaptation and outward-directed adaptation have physiological, environmental, and cultural modes. Thus, cultural adaptation is as much a biological process as the inherent genetic process is.

How does this fact relate to the development of a "disease process"? Individuals are in a constant state of interaction with and reaction to the environment. In the study of human stress, then, it is impossible to negate cultural and environmental factors, because they are interrelated with specific biological stressors. When the human organism adapts to reduce stress of biological origin, the organism also moves towards consonance with environment and culture.

Psychological adaptation. In order to effectively enable clients to cope with stressful situations, the nurse must understand the process of psychological adaptation. The three stages of adaptation that make up Selye's General Adaptation Syndrome can be correlated with a psychological model of adaptation. The alarm stage, which corresponds to Peplau's mild or +1 level of anxiety, alerts the system to stress. The client is able to perceive data. He can visualize connections. He can engage in problem-solving. However, he may not be able to relieve the anxiety by his normal adaptive mechanisms. In such a case, anxiety increases and less adaptive types of behavior occur (for example, irritability, anger, withdrawal, denial, and silence). During the second phase, the resistance stage, characteristics of the moderate level of anxiety are apparent (see Table 4-1). Ego adaptive mechanisms may be called into action if anxiety continues to heighten. The mechanisms utilized are sublimation, rationalization, displacement, and compensation. Should these mechanisms fail, the client moves into the exhaustion stage, in which mechanisms of a more disintegrative nature are utilized for adaptive purposes. Unless he changes his behavior, the client may become chronically ill and may even die. The exhaustion stage is correlated with a severe state of anxiety (+3 to +4); the client's attention is either focused on one particular detail or directed toward many scattered details. Adaptive mechanisms in this phase may include hallucinations, compulsive behavior, or severe psychophysiological illness.

• • •

If a nurse is to help a client adapt to stress, many variables need to be thoroughly investigated. All factors are of equal import—sociocultural, physiological, constitutional, psychological, familial, and economic. A client often needs direct assistance in accomplishing behavioral change that will be most satisfying in terms of goal achievement.

A nurse is able to increase a client's sensitivity to the environment, which at the same time increases his ability to adapt. To accomplish this task, the nurse must consider three factors: mental state of the client (over which there is no direct control), cognitive state (that which the client knows about his life situation), and interpersonal activities (both the client's ability to relate to others and the nurse's utilization of this ability).

Stress may be seen as a precipitator of a very individualistic response on the part of the client. There continue to be unanswered questions: Why do some people respond in a psychophysiological manner while others respond in a neurotic manner? Why are some people able repeatedly to meet life's challenges with seemingly little difficulty while other people have great difficulty? In the next section, commonly encountered stressors and nursing intervention will be presented.

COMMONLY ENCOUNTERED STRESSORS
Threats to body image

As was discussed in Chapter 3, body image is an integral part of self-concept. A person's body image is reflective of the attitudes he holds about his body. Related to body image is sense of identity—a person's perception of his strengths and weaknesses and his relationship to others.

Body image may be altered by the addition of artifacts or by a threat to body integrity. The disruption of body image may be caused by many situations, including weight loss or gain, surgical intervention, and pathophysiological and psychopathological conditions. Because certain areas of the body may hold more meaning for an individual than others, threats to these areas may be considered more significant and require more action by the individual. Throughout the life cycle, varying dimensions of body image are developed and redeveloped. Feelings of self-worth may correlate with positive body image. A person who has difficulty developing an integrated self-concept has a corresponding difficulty relating to others. It is only after the development of positive feelings about self that a person seeks to invest in others.

Many factors contribute to the development of body image. The most pertinent factors include responses from others in the environment (such as parents and peers), one's own attitudes and emotions regarding the body, one's degree of independence and motivation, physical appearance, how well the body functions, and perception of body territoriality. Body image thus is multidimensional rather than unidimensional. Nursing assessment and intervention must include a survey of the various factors in an effort to develop a realistic appraisal and plan of action. A client's feelings about particular aspects of body image depend on whether he perceives them as functional tools or as central personal attributes. For example, dentures may be accepted as a tool rather than as a central attribute, while hair may be viewed as essential to one's identity.

A sense of body space and self-concept emerges during the first year of life. As the child moves through the developmental stages, changes occur in the physical aspects of the body. During adolescence, the body is viewed as a social creation; however, as middle age and old age approach, the body becomes wrinkled, skin sags, and sensory functions decrease. As the actual physical appearance of the body changes, the feelings one has about one's self may also change. Therefore, it is important that nurses assess the impact that disturbances in body image may have on an individual and his relationships with others.

Kolb (1959) groups body image disturbances into five categories: (1) neurological dysfunctions that affect sensorimotor status, such as paraplegia or hemiplegia; (2) metabolic dysfunction, such as thyroid disease or obesity; (3) dismemberment (such as loss of a limb); (4) personality dysfunctions, such as neuroses, psychoses, and psychophysiological diseases; and (5) dysfunctions related to progressive deformities, such as arthritis. Body image is a vulnerable entity. It may be distorted, as in a person experiencing pain, or diminished, as in a person with decreased sensory function. Although a client in pain often focuses his attention on the area of pain, his whole self is consumed by the pain. The body image is grossly distorted, as this cartoon of an individual experiencing a headache shows:

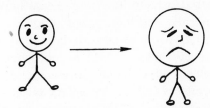

Threats to body image are sources of stress because body image is related to various areas of function. The choice of a life's work, sexual behavior, the ability to respond appropriately to stress, and relationships with others are related to the concept of self and body image.

Surgical removal of a body part (for example, amputation of a limb or removal of the gall bladder) or alteration of a body function (for example, colostomy or ileostomy) often constitutes a threat to body image. Gross changes in body size and shape may also serve as threats to one's self-concept. Changes result, for example, from the increases in weight caused by pregnancy or overeating and from excessive weight loss. Finally, pathological processes, such as coronary artery disease, cause changes in the functioning of critical body parts, such as the heart. Even though there may be no outward manifestation that the body is not functioning properly, one's self-concept is definitely altered.

Surgical removal of a body part such as a breast or a limb often implies that an individual is no longer a whole human being. Breast cancer is on the rise in the United States, and its impact is being felt in all social classes. The changes in self-concept that result from a mastectomy depend upon the significance a woman places on the breasts and her perception of the seriousness of the threat posed by the loss of a breast. Various values are placed on the breast—it is a symbol of femininity for many, and it is often closely linked with sexual functioning. Loss of a breast may mean loss of a job, if performance in the job relies on use of the whole body, as in modeling. With the loss of a breast, a woman comes face to face with her feelings of self. She will depend on the reactions of significant others to help her assimilate the change in body image into the self-concept. The loss of a limb causes a similar disturbance in body image. The degree of the threat to self-concept that results from such a loss depends upon the value placed on the limb and the ability of the individual to successfully adapt to the loss.

A colostomy or an ileostomy often poses a threat to body image and self-concept. Defecation and urination traditionally have been considered private functions. Feces have often been considered dirty, both literally and figuratively, and odors and sounds related to bowel function have been considered taboo. Thus, to release feces into a small plastic bag that may leak or smell is often regarded as repulsive, and a client may display a tendency toward social isolation in order to protect his self-concept. Very often he resists accepting the reality of body image change. However, the changes—the stoma, the odor, the plastic bag—need to be incorporated into a restructured body image.

Coronary artery disease is frequently described as a psychophysiological response to stress. Coronary artery disease therefore may be viewed both as a threat to body image and self-concept—a stressor—and as a *result* of maladaptation to stress. The heart is the "organ of choice" (refer to Chapter 9). It is important to recognize this dual position that coronary artery disease holds. The disease process is commonly interpreted in nursing assessments as being stress-induced; however, it is equally important to assess the impact that coronary artery disease has on body image and self-concept. (Coronary artery disease as a psychophysiological response to stress is discussed further in Chapter 9.)

An increase in body weight is one of the prominent changes that occurs during pregnancy. Women often speak of feeling "like a balloon." A woman's body space enlarges, possibly restricting her movement through territory that had originally been familiar and accessible. Everyday functions such as bending down to tie shoes, driving a car, and turning around in a small space are no longer as easy to accomplish. The increased size may result in a disturbance in body image and a threat to self-concept, depending upon a woman's feelings toward the pregnancy.

Obesity and anorexia nervosa are considered psychophysiological responses to stress (see Chapter 9 for further discussion). However, as in the case of coronary artery disease, obesity and anorexia nervosa, which produces excessive weight loss, can be considered to be both stressors and stress responses. For example, obese persons may have body image disturbances that both result from over eating and contribute to overeating. This dual concept may be diagramed as follows:

Stressor (increase or decrease in body size) → possible disturbance in body image and altered self-concept

Stress response (overeating [obesity] or excessive weight loss [anorexia nervosa]) → perpetuation of disturbance in body image and probably lowered self-concept.

Thus it is critical that a nurse determine the impact of a client's body size on body image and self-concept. The physical changes that an individual experiences may result in increased anxiety levels and the utilization of pathological defense mechanisms.

Several commonly encountered stressors that may cause disturbance in body image and alteration of self-concept have been presented. In a nursing assessment, it is important to determine the client's perception of the meaning of a threat and its implications for his life-style. The client calls varying levels of defense mechanisms into action, depending on the seriousness of the threat. The goal of nurse and client is to recognize the implications of the alterations and to maximize the client's adaptive capacities.

Pain

Pain, which is associated with many disease processes, may be considered a stressor. Pain may also be considered a response to psychological stress, in either an adaptive or a maladaptive sense. Pain will be discussed in this section as a stressor—a personal, subjective experience that elicits various types of responses, depending on physiological, biological, and sociocultural factors. Pain may be defined as a stressor in that it causes anxiety levels to rise; the greater the pain, the higher the level of anxiety. Adaptation to pain may be retarded if the pain receptors are no longer functioning properly or if one's culture places restrictions on the expression of pain. In the latter instance, excessive denial of pain may be used to the detriment of a client's nursing care.

In order to understand the significance of pain as a stressor, we must consider briefly the various theories of pain. The "gate" theory holds that accelerator, nerve fibers carry impulses to the brain and that the impulses return via the spinal cord. Here they close the "spinal gate" and prevent slower-transmitting nerve fibers from carrying impulses upward, unless the intensity of the impulses is such that they can push open the "gate." This theory takes into consideration the influence of memory and cognitive processes as well as past and present pain experiences. The specificity theory is the most widely accepted notion of pain perception. According to this theory, pain can be produced only by certain stimuli, and these stimuli are always interpreted as pain. A third theory, the pattern theory, supposes that a pattern of impulses is generated by pain receptors. This pattern forms the basis of an internal code that supplies the message that there is pain.

What influences the behavior of a person experiencing pain? Does each person respond according to a predetermined "set"? Because cultural, physical, and physiological factors influence the pain response, it is important to recognize that a client may not fit into any specific category of responses. The following factors are presented as guidelines for nursing assessment and intervention.

The duration and intensity of pain will be reflected in client behavior. For example, the chronic pain involved in terminal cancer is best described as all-consuming. The focal point of behavior is relief of pain. Superficial pain, on the other hand, prepares the body for "fight or flight." Two additional factors that affect the perception of pain are sensory restriction and prolonged loss of sleep. Clients often experience more pain during the night than they do during the day, because the number of incoming stimuli decreases during the night, and their type and pattern change. The body responds to stimuli of lesser intensity during periods of quiet, such as nighttime; during the day the number and variety of stimuli bombarding the client are greater. The other factor, sleep deprivation, lowers the adaptive capacity of the client, thus intensifying the perception of pain. The client who has been undergoing a rigorous series of diagnostic tests, the preparations for which preclude normal sleep, may cry pitifully following the pinprick for a blood sample. This is not irrational behavior. It should be expected in light of our understanding of pain perception.

Culture may dictate very detailed and specific responses to pain. Reactions to pain vary according to a person's age, sex, and occupation. Culture also determines whether curative or palliative treatment is sought and whether the intensity and duration of pain are sufficient to merit reporting. Recognition of cultural influences allows a nurse to understand the significance of pain for each individual client as well as the overt response to that pain. Nurses thus can develop a wide range of approaches when intervening in the process of pain perception.

Since there are many ethnic groups within American society, nurses need to identify the influences that the culture has upon pain expectancy and pain acceptance. Zborowski (1969) has done an extensive amount of work in the field of pain perception and its cultural components. McCaffery (1972) supports Zborowski's belief that cultural background exerts more influence on behavioral response than the pain situation itself.

Each culture defines its own parameters of pain response, determines the necessity for pain relief, and dictates the type and duration of use of defense mechanisms employed to control increased levels of anxiety. For example, the "old American," typically a third-generation American of white, Anglo-Saxon background, does not often verbalize his pain. His reflex response to pain is to withdraw rather than to cry out. This type of client is frequently future oriented and optimistic about treatment plans. He is often labeled a "good" patient because he rarely asks for assistance. This type of behavior can be misleading to the nurse and can discourage the sharing of feelings regarding the pain experience.

Members of another group, Jewish Americans, may describe pain as being "terrific" or "unbearable." Tolerance or acceptance of pain is usually low. Outward expressions of the stress of a pain experience are considered acceptable. Crying and moaning elicit sympathetic responses from others and serve to draw others close to the client. The Jewish American is future oriented yet pessimistic about his treatment plans. He may seek several medical opinions

Latin Americans and Americans of a Mediterranean background respond in a manner similar to that of Jewish Americans. A low tolerance for pain exists, along with the need to verbalize one's inner response to a painful experience. There is, however, a an orientation to the present; palliative relief is sought immediately.

Irish-Americans present another distinct response to the pain experience. The client is stoic, almost to the point of being unable to admit to experiencing pain. Withdrawal behavior is the means most frequently utilized to control overt responses. Pain is viewed as something one must face with the attitude of "grin and bear it." This group is future oriented, and its members accept the validity of information provided by the health care team.

Black Americans also have parameters of pain response. There is a denial of the existence of pain until it reaches an emergency state. Clients describe pain in general terms, and there is a reluctance to seek pain relief.

Each cultural group has its own parameters of pain tolerance and response behavior. The goal of a nursing assessment is not to rigidly categorize each client's subjective pain experience based on ethnic group. However, as Larkin (1977) points out, "the experience of pain defies explanation in purely physiologic or biological terms; the sociocultural aspect of pain must be taken into account. The patient's cultural background influences not only attitudes towards pain but his response to it as well."

An important consideration in the assessment of the expression of pain is the reward or gain that a client derives from that expression. For example, a client who verbally expresses pain may elicit a sympathetic response from family, staff, and friends. He is placed in a dependent, "sick" role that releases him from the responsibilities of the adult-parent-spouse role. The client who needs to receive such a reward for the expression of pain may be attempting to adapt to a situation that has become excessively stressful, such as the increased responsibility associated with a new job, marriage, or parenting. Psychogenic pain (for further discussion, refer to Chapter 9) is considered a psychological response used to control the anxiety caused by the arousal or previously unconscious conflicts. Pain, therefore, may be viewed from two perspectives—as a commonly occurring stressor and as a psychophysiological response to a stressful life situation.

Pain is a subjective personal experience. Pain responses are altered by physical and physiological factors as well as by cultural and psychological determinants. In order to decide upon and implement a plan of action, a nurse should consider the overt as well as covert expressions of pain and their implications. The "bad" client is not necessarily the one who is most vocal about his pain, nor is the "good" client necessarily the one who stoically keeps his complaints to himself. Observation of responses to the pain experience will promote the accurate assessment of the implications of that experience for each client.

Immobilization

Immobilization commonly causes stress that may affect all areas of function—physical, emotional, sociocultural, and cognitive. Prolonged immobilization has a profound impact on the psyche. Feelings of powerlessness occur. A reorganization of territory results. There may also be a redefining of self in terms of the immobilization.

In order to discuss the concept of immobilization as a stressor, we must consider the effect of immobilization on sensory status. When an individual is immobilized, there are multiple changes in the patterning and variation of incoming stimuli. One of the primary nursing actions is to identify each client's sensory status in order to maintain perceptual and responsive function. There is no clear-cut mechanism to determine at what point sensory overload or deprivation begins. But it is certain that there are gross changes in behavior when overload or deprivation does occur.

What occurs as a result of sensory overload and/or deprivation? The client experiences a decrease in the ability to solve problems. His ability to perform tasks requiring eye-hand coordination is decreased, as is his perceptual alertness. Often there is disorientation to time, and he feels as though his body parts were floating. Hallucinations and illusions are described vividly by clients who have spent extended periods of time in intensive- or coronary-care units, where restrictions regarding visitors, flowers, clocks, and reading materials are imposed. In these units, sensory overload may be experienced because of the constant humming of monitors or other types of machinery and the constant lighting, whether it be day or night. Clients rapidly lose orientation to time and place, since the familiar objects that act as cues are absent. Clients who are isolated in such units, as well as those who are restricted to their own homes or rooms, often experience a sense of overwhelming anxiety and depression.

Who fares well in these situations? Does everyone respond similarly, or are there persons who do not develop behavioral changes? The person who needs to be amused continuously—to be on the go or always engaged in some kind of activity—is the type of client who adapts poorly to sensory deprivation or overload. It has been found that, as in many other situations, the client who has developed successful adaptation mechanisms before his illness and whose ego is sound is better able to cope with the multiple effects of sensory deprivation or overload. This is not to say, however, that such a client relies solely upon his own resources for the development of adaptation mechanisms. Nursing intervention to prevent or reduce the effects of sensory deprivation or overload will be presented later in this chapter.

Immobilization and sensory deprivation or overload are stressors that are interwoven with one another. Each system of the body responds differently to prolonged periods of immobility. Often the immobilized client must deal with many crisis situations at once. For example, associated with immobilization there are often changes in body image as well as in such normal bodily functions as breathing, urinating, and defecating. Concurrently, the client experiences profound changes in emotional, social, and cognitive status. Nursing measures, therefore, must be directed toward identifying these changes as stressors and mobilizing the client's resources in order to help him adapt to the new situation.

Loss and change

In recent research, loss and change have been identified as predominant stressors; they have been shown to precipitate varying degress of anxiety. Life changes correlate with major health disruptions. Individuals who experience many changes over a short period of time seem to be more susceptible to illness. Toffler (1970) believes that too much change in too short a period of time can cause adverse physical as well as emotional reactions. Although this statement is not necessarily true for all individuals, it is imperative that nurses recognize the correlation between change and illness.

Holmes and Rahe (1967) developed a "social readjustment rating scale" on which are ranked stressful life events of both a positive nature (such as marriage, pregnancy, and promotion) and a negative nature (such as death of a spouse, divorce, or illness). Each event is rated in "life change units" (LCUs); the number of LCUs ranges from 100 to 19. Holmes and Rahe's hypothesis was that the greater the number of LCUs, the greater the probability of a client experiencing a health crisis. Table 4-2 lists the various stressful events and their corresponding numbers of LCU's.

The scale ranks life events or changes according to their "stress value"—that is, the amount of coping that is required to adapt to them. The stressors listed include those that are threats to physiological integrity as well as those that are threats to self-esteem. Clients perceive stressful events differently, depending on their past experiences, and their current emotional and physical health. By observing clients' responses to stressors, nurses can formulate comprehensive nursing care plans.

Why do some people become ill as a result of stress while others are much more capable of adapting to stress with a minimal amount of health change? Are some people more vulnerable as a result of certain variables? Do some individuals have better outside support systems, more optimistic outlooks on life, or better health habits? Pesznecker and McNeil (1977) sought to discover whether good health habits, strong support systems, and a positive outlook could act as forces in assisting people to adapt to increased change. They noted that although the above variables made slight differences in the likelihood that major illness would occur, change was still the most significant factor. There are many ways in which a nurse, particularly in a community setting, can intervene on the primary level to help persons experiencing stress. The goal is to help a person become the manager of his own life changes rather than simply to help him cope with the crises that occur as a result of those changes.

Loss, like change, cannot be avoided during a lifetime. As an individual moves through the life cycle, he is continuously experiencing some degree of loss—the loss of instant gratification of all demands, the loss of total dependence through learning to crawl and to walk, the loss of control over the environment through illness, the loss of hearing and sight, the loss of close friends through separation or death, the lost of independence through the aging process, and, finally, the loss of his own life. How well a person adapts to new losses depends, to a great extent, on past experiences with loss. If they have been positive in nature, an individual can successfully assimilate new losses and changes. However, the more negative past experiences with

TABLE 4-2. Social readjustment rating scale*

Rank	Life event	Mean value
1	Death of spouse	100
2	Divorce	73
3	Marital separation	65
4	Jail term	63
5	Death of close family member	63
6	Personal injury or illness	53
7	Marriage	50
8	Fired at work	47
9	Marital reconciliation	45
10	Retirement	45
11	Change in health of family member	44
12	Pregnancy	40
13	Sex difficulties	39
14	Gain of new family member	39
15	Business readjustment	39
16	Change in financial state	38
17	Death of close friend	37
18	Change to different line of work	36
19	Change in number of arguments with spouse	35
20	Mortgage over $10,000	31
21	Foreclosure of mortgage or loan	30
22	Change in responsibilities at work	29
23	Son or daughter leaving home	29
24	Trouble with in-laws	29
25	Outstanding personal achievement	28
26	Wife begin or stop work	26
27	Begin or end school	26
28	Change in living conditions	25
29	Revision of personal habits	24
30	Trouble with boss	23
31	Change in work hours or conditions	20
32	Change in residence	20
33	Change in schools	20
34	Change in recreation	19
35	Change in church activities	19

*Reprinted with permission from Holmes, T., and Rahe, R.: The social readjustment rating scale, J. Psychosom. Res. 11:213-218, 1967. Copyright 1967, Pergamon Press, Ltd.

loss have been, the greater the potential that a person will have difficulty in adapting to current losses.

This concept can be stated in another way: early modes of adaptation to loss are the foundation of future patterns. To cite an example, the infant who is being weaned from the breast may receive nonverbal messages that this is a traumatic experience, and the experience may therefore be a negative one. For a more positive picture, consider the situation of a school-age child who moves away from his best friend. He and his parents discuss his feelings as well as theirs. There are open lines of communication and a sense of honesty. There is an understanding of the meaning of the loss to all involved. The child develops healthy patterns of adaptation, which are supported by his parents. The course has been set for the continuation of these healthy mechanisms in the future.

NURSING INTERVENTION

PRIMARY PREVENTION

Primary prevention is a critical concern for nursing. A person's ability to adapt to stress depends on his ability to identify potential stressors in his life situation. These stressors may stimulate a positive growth response. Continued stress, however, causes exhaustion and the eventual development of psychopathology and/or pathophysiology. The goal of primary prevention is to help people develop healthy patterns of coping with stress during the early years of life in order to prevent later maladaptive responses. The family becomes the unit of focus. Intervention with the family directs the family's attention toward (1) the development of a positive self-concept, including healthy feelings towards one's own body; (2) the facilitation of interaction with others in the environment; (3) the sharing of feelings in an open, honest, caring manner; (4) the utilization of the problem-solving process to resolve disagreements; and (5) the acceptance of each individual as a separate being with unique behavior. A healthy family environment provides an atmosphere in which members can communicate their needs and identify potential stressors without feeling ashamed or afraid of repercussions. Each member feels unique and important. To minimize the effects of stressors, family members support one another in their attempts to plan their lives. Children grow up feeling confident in their ability to cope and able to reach out for support from others when it is necessary.

The adult client can be educated to recognize potential life stressors. Nurses and other members of the health care team may assist the client to manage his own environment through anticipatory planning—that is, by helping him to determine the number and type of stressors he can cope with comfortably. Education, role modeling, and supportive counseling with families and individuals are primary nursing measures for promoting effective coping patterns and healthy adaptation.

SECONDARY PREVENTION

Secondary prevention includes nursing measures to reduce the impact of stressors and to help clients understand the implications of those stressors. Specific nursing measures for persons facing common life stressors are as follows:

Alteration in body image

1. Identify areas of concern to the client by listening and observing for nonverbal messages. Explore feelings and validate his statements in relation to his changed body image. Rather than probe directly into this emotionally charged area ask open-ended questions.
2. Emphasize the client's areas of strength—accentuate the positive! By mobilizing his own strengths, the client begins to regain a sense of worth and a more positive self-concept.
3. Encourage physical movement, since it enhances the client's ability to integrate body changes into a new body image. He develops competence through mastering his own body again.
4. Facilitate the interaction of the client with others in his environment. Provide an atmosphere in which he may gradually resume his previous social roles as well as develop new ones. It is imperative that nurses allow the client to progress at his own pace. It is often helpful for the client to discuss his feelings with others who have experienced similar alterations. Nurses can act as resource persons by contacting such groups as Reach for Recovery (for mastectomy clients) and ostomy, heart, and stroke clubs.
5. Include the client in self-care activities that will increase his opportunities to become reacquainted with his body. Such activities as looking at a wound, participating in dressing changes, feeling the bandages or cast, and handling equipment (for example, colostomy bags, prostheses) are crucial in the restructuring of body image and self-concept.
6. Recognize that the client will take his cues from the nurse's reactions to his changed body image. He is acutely aware of responses from his environment, and he assimilates those responses into his newly developing body image.
7. Facilitate the expression of unresolved feelings such as anger, fear, hopelessness, and dependence by providing open lines of communication at all times.
8. Include family and significant others in all aspects of the client's course of recovery. Encourage the sharing of feelings and concerns that they may have regarding the care of the client and his eventual resumption of previous roles (or assumption of new ones). As was previously noted, responses from significant others are crucial.

Pain

1. Recognize that the pain experience is real to the person who is describing it.
2. Explore the meaning of the pain experience with the client. Perhaps a desire for gain or reward is an important aspect of his behavior.
3. Remain with the client during the painful experience. Perceptions of pain increase during the night or at other times when he is left alone to focus on the pain.
4. Reduce environmental stimuli of a noxious nature, such as excessive lighting and noise. Often a quiet, slightly darkened room serves to alleviate pain.
5. Provide periods of rest and relaxation. It has been noted that fatigue potentiates the pain experience.
6. Educate the client as to the various pain relief measures that are available to him. This enables him to maintain a sense of control over his pain.
7. Touch the client. Touching and other means of sensory input often reduce pain perception.
8. Observe verbal and nonverbal expressions of pain. Are they congruent with one another? For example, does the client describe excruciating pain while lying casually on the bed watching television? Does he deny pain even though he maintains a rigid posture while in the supine position?
9. After careful observation of pain behavior, administer analgesics in a prudent manner. Document pain relief and attendant behavior.
10. Behavior modification and hypnosis are used successfully in the management of pain. Surgery such as chordotomy may be indicated in the case of intractable pain.

Immobilization

1. Provide such physical activities as turning and moving of unaffected parts of the body within the confines dictated by the client's situation. Movement helps the client to determine his own body space, which may have been altered by the immobilization. Activity also serves to reduce the severity of the negative physiological effects of prolonged immobilization.
2. Identify individual effects of sensory overload or deprivation. For example, while one client may quietly accept all the medical procedures being done for him, another client may evidence hypersensitivity to the environment by being acutely aware of and involved in all the activities around him. This type of client needs to feel a sense of control over his environment. We must facilitate this control as much as possible.
3. Maintain sensory-perceptual stimulation by means of newspapers, television, radio, visitors, and so on.
4. Reduce environmental stimuli of a monotonous nature, including noise, lighting, and personnel impinging on the client's space.
5. Identify adaptation mechanisms, along with their efficiency levels in the current situation and in past situations of a similar nature. What are similarities and differences? Accentuate ego strengths. How can

they be developed in the client's best interests?

6. Describe the client's immediate environment, and explain the various sights, sounds, and smells. This enables the client to understand the patterns of what is going on around him.

7. Allow the client to resume activities at his own pace. Introduce changes in routine slowly and with brief explanations of rationale.

8. Structure the environment and activities so that the client is not expected to accomplish tasks that require in-depth problem-solving processes. Sensory overload or deprivation decreases his capacity to learn and to solve problems.

9. When you consider a roommate for an immobilized client, it is often wise to place the immobilized client with a person who is oriented toward and involved with his environment.

10. Provide an atmosphere of open communication whereby the client may verbalize concerns or fears relating to his immobilization.

11. Point out inappropriate responses, such as prolonged hallucination, hostility, withdrawal, or belligerence, to the nursing team. Consultation with a psychiatric nurse-clinician and/or a physician may be necessary.

12. Include family members and significant others in the nursing care plan of the immobilized client. Assist them to recognize and understand the effects of prolonged immobilization (for example, sensory overload or deprivation). They may also be instrumental in enabling the client to resume his former social roles.

13. The primary goal of nursing care is to recognize situations that may cause sensory overload or deprivation and the clients who are potentially at risk. Nurses should consider not only those clients who are physically immobilized but also those who have social, emotional, or cognitive impairments. Individuals in mental institutions or orphanages, the elderly, the blind, the deaf, and the mute—these are just a few of the target populations that deserve attention in regard to the effects of sensory overload or deprivation.

Change and loss

1. Encourage the verbal expression of feelings of anger, helplessness, fear, or hopelessness by maintaining open lines of communication.

2. Support the client, yet allow him his own space to grieve. Be there when he feels the need to relate to another human being. (See Chapter 11 for further discussion of grief.)

3. Facilitate participation in activities of daily living. Support attempts to engage in such new behavior as managing the checkbook or putting on the storm doors.

4. Gradually encourage the client's reinvestment in new object relationships. Since this process often reemphasizes the sense of loss it should be paced cautiously.

5. Identify ego strengths. Help the client to perceive himself as a

worthwhile human being who is capable of experiencing life to its fullest in spite of his loss.

6. Direct the client in anticipatory planning by preparing him for what changes and/or losses lie ahead. Persons who are most in need of such planning include expectant parents, couples contemplating marriage, adolescents who are experiencing maturational crises, clients in low-income housing projects, individuals whose spouses have chronic or terminal illnesses, couples that are separating or divorcing, clients who move frequently, clients who are about to experience menopause, and individuals who are about to retire. To focus on these groups before the onset of illness is a major nursing priority!

7. Assess the client's previous life changes in light of adaptive mechanisms used—their effectiveness or ineffectiveness in coping with the stress incurred as a result of the change or loss. What symptoms does the client have?

8. Educate the client—on either an individual or a group basis. The client learns through his relationships with group members and nursing staff how to become a manager of his life. He need not wait for a major health crisis to occur. Instead, his preparation for and understanding of change and loss enable him to develop successful adaptation mechanisms. Pressures of life will no longer seem insurmountable. Some changes may be delayed while he is adapting to those of higher priority. The goal of intervention is the recognition of changes and their impact on life-style.

TERTIARY PREVENTION

A stressor can generate so much anxiety that an individual is overwhelmed. Maladaptive responses then occur in the form of psychophysiological patterns, withdrawal patterns, and acting-out patterns. In some cases these behavior patterns are inevitable. Tertiary measures are directed toward assessment of the effects of the maladaptive responses. Nursing intervention in this phase serves to preserve the client's positive feelings of self, even though a crisis may have arisen, and to explore alternative styles of coping rather than accept the maladaptive response as a permanent pattern.

CHAPTER SUMMARY

Every person is in a continual state of flux, always responding to internal and external cues. Adaptation is the series of changes that occur in response to a stressor. The way a person adapts to stress is influenced by cultural, physiological, and psychological factors. If a stressor is not perceived as very threatening, anxiety levels are mild. Mild anxiety can be utilized in the service of learning. As anxiety levels increase, however, problem-solving capacities become impaired and previously successful coping behavior becomes inadequate. If severe anxiety continues for a prolonged period, physical exhaustion and maladaptive patterns of behavior result. Recognition of anxiety levels and their implications for nursing intervention are critical to the process of healthy adaptation.

Several commonly encountered stressors that pose varying degrees of threat to self-concept have been presented. Key concepts in the understanding of these stressors include the perception of the event and the degree and type of coping mechanisms utilized. In some instances a change, such as an increase in body size, is both a stressor and the *result* of a stress response. Nurses need to keep in mind the difference between *stressor* and *stress response*.

Primary, secondary, and tertiary preventive measures in relation to stress, anxiety, and adaptation have been presented. Primary prevention directs its efforts toward identification and management of potential stressors. Secondary prevention involves the early detection of actual stressors and the implementation of nursing strategies to cope with them. Tertiary prevention deals with the assessment of maladaptive responses arising from prolonged periods of uncontrolled anxiety and intervention to keep these maladaptive responses from becoming permanent.

Nurses need to be aware of the implications of the stress response and the attendant anxiety levels—both for themselves and for their clients. One goal of the nurse-client relationship is the identification of motivators of behavior. An understanding of anxiety and its effect on behavior enables nurse and client to explore present and future coping mechanisms. The nursing diagnosis and the subsequent nursing intervention should reflect this understanding. Nursing care of the person experiencing stress includes all areas of prevention—primary, secondary, and tertiary.

REFERENCES

Alland, Alexander
  1970 Adaptation in Cultural Evolution: An Approach to Medical Anthropology. New York: Columbia University Press.
Engel, George
  1962 Psychological Development in Health and Disease. Philadelphia: W. B. Saunders Co.
Freud, S.
  1969 A General Introduction to Psychoanalysis. New York: Pocket Books.
Holmes, T. H., and R. U. Rahe
  1967 "The social readjustment scale." Journal of Psychosomatic Research II: 213-218.
Kolb, Lawrence
  1959 "Disturbances of the body image." American Handbook of Psychiatry, vol. 1. Silvano Arieti (ed.). New York:Basic Books, Inc., Publishers.
Larkins, F.
  1977 "The influence of one patient's culture on pain response." Nursing Clinics of North America 12 (4):156-162.
McCaffery, M.
  1972 Nursing Management of the Patient with Pain. Philadelphia: J. B. Lippincott Co.
McNeil, Jo, and Betty Pesznecker
  1977 "Keeping people well despite life change crises." Public Health Reports 92(4):343-348.
Menninger, Karl
  1963 The Vital Balance. New York: The Viking Press.
Peplau, H.
  1962 "Interpersonal techniques: the crux of psychiatric nursing." American Journal of Nursing 62:53-54.
Peplau, H.
  1963 "A working definition of anxiety." In Some Clinical Approaches to Psychiatric Nursing. S. Burd and M.

Marshall (eds.). New York: Macmillan, Inc.

Schilder, Paul
1950 The Image and Appearance of the Human Body. New York: International Universities Press, Inc.

Selye, Hans
1956 The Stress of Life. New York: McGraw-Hill Book Co.

Sullivan, H. S.
1953 Interpersonal Theory of Psychiatry. New York: W. W. Norton & Co., Inc.

Toffler, Alvin
1970 Future Shock. New York: Random House, Inc.

Zborowski, Mark
1969 People in Pain. San Francisco: Jossey-Bass, Inc., Publishers.

ANNOTATED SUGGESTED READINGS

Pasquali, E.
1975 "Personification: patient and nurse problems." Perspectives in Psychiatric Care 13:58-61.
The author discusses the problem of personification. She identifies the difficulties that occur when a client is unable to integrate an alteration in body image into his view of self. Appropriate nursing strategies are presented.

Peplau, H.
1963 "A working definition of anxiety." Some Clinical Approaches to Psychiatric Nursing. S. Burd and M. Marshall (eds.). New York: Macmillan, Inc.
Peplau's classic discussion of anxiety presents the various levels of anxiety and their behavioral and physiological manifestations. This clear-cut and concise presentation serves as a framework for the understanding of anxiety and for the development of relevant nursing strategies.

Smith, Marcy, and Hans Selye
1979 "Reducing the negative effects of stress." American Journal of Nursing 79 (10):1953-1957.
This article points out that nurses need (1) to have a sound understanding of the concept of stress, (2) to recognize the manifestations of stress, and (3) to apply strategies to reduce stress. Each individual responds differently to stressors, depending on past experiences, coping mechanisms, and perception of

a stressful event. Consideration therefore must be given to all factors affecting the response to stress. The authors conclude that a holistic approach is necessary for the rehabilitation of clients. Education provides clients with the information to manage both potential and actual stresses.

FURTHER READINGS

Bell, J.
1977 "Stressful life events and coping methods in mental illness and wellness behaviors." Nursing Research 26:136-141.

Breeden, S., and C. Kondo
1978 "Using biofeedback to reduce tension." American Journal of Nursing 75:2010-2012.

Garfield, Charles A. (ed.)
1979 Stress and Survival: The Emotional Realities of Life-Threatening Illness. St. Louis: The C. V. Mosby Co.

Gruendeman, B.
1975 "The impact of surgery on body image." Nursing Clinics of North America 10:635.

Hurst, M., C. D. Jenkins, and R. Rose
1976 "The relation of psychological stress to onset of medical illness." Annual Review of Medicine 27:86-95.

Kerr, N.
1978 "Anxiety: theoretical considerations." Perspectives in Psychiatric Care 16:36-46.

Lambert, Vicki, and Clinton Lambert
1979 The Impact of Physical Illness and Related Mental Health Concepts. Englewood Cliffs, N. J.: Prentice-Hall, Inc.

Maguire, P.
1975 "Emotional responses after mastectomy." Contemporary Obstetrics and Gynecology, pp. 34-48.

Murphy, L., and A. Moriarity
1976 Vulnerability, Coping, and Growth. New Haven, Conn.: Yale University Press.

Selye, H.
1977 Stress without Distress. Toronto: McClelland & Stewart, Ltd.

Williams, C., and T. Holmes
1978 "Life change, human adaptation and onset of illness in clinical practice." In Psychosocial Nursing: Assessment and Intervention. D. Longo and R. Williams (eds.). New York: Appleton-Century-Crofts.

5
COMMUNICATION

CHAPTER
FOCUS

Communication is a process involving three levels of interaction: verbal, kinesic, and proxemic. Just as language varies from culture to culture, kinesic and proxemic behavior are also culturally variable. When members of different cultures interact, dissimilar verbal, kinesic, and proxemic cues may contribute to misunderstandings and disruption of role relationships. Therapeutic communication involves more than learning a body of interviewing skills. It involves understanding the process of communication and the influence of culture on communication.

Ruesch and Bateson (1968) view communication as the social matrix of psychiatry. Until recently, health workers have focused primarily on verbal communication. Now they are beginning to recognize the importance of nonlinguistic communication—kinesics, the use of body parts in communication, and proxemics, the use of space in communication.

Silverstein (1977) states that meaning is communicated each time one member of a society interacts with another member. This is known as a *cultural event*. For instance, think of all the verbal and nonverbal ways that people communicate the message of dominance-submission.

The United States is a nation of immigrants. Its population is an ethnic mix. Even though most of its people speak English, they may use ethnically patterned kinesic and proxemic behavior. Scheflen (1972) cautions that, even when people speak the same language, it cannot be assumed that there is shared meaning. Communication may be misunderstood; communication problems may arise. Knowledge of the process of communication and the influence of culture on communication may prevent the development of communication barriers and may help to establish therapeutic communication.

Communication is the act of imparting and exchanging ideas, information, and feelings with others. People communicate through both verbal and nonverbal expression. Verbal communication is spoken language: the words we use and the way we use them. Nonverbal communication embraces kinesics and proxemics: the way we move body parts and the way we use the space around us. The two modes of communication—verbal and nonverbal—are neither separate nor unrelated. Instead, they are different *levels* of communication that systematically interrelate to reinforce, supplement, or contradict one another. Dr. Albert Mehrabian (1969, 1972) has calculated that 7% of the total impact of a message comes from verbal expression, 38% from vocal expres-

5

COMMUNICATION

sion, and 55% from facial expression. We may agree or disagree with Dr. Mehrabian's figures or argue that "facial expression" is too narrow a category and that all body movements need to be considered, but most of us will agree that verbal and nonverbal expressions interrelate in the act of communication.

Verbal communication

Nonverbal communication

Kinesics

Proxemics

Relationships among levels of communication

Therapeutic communication

Process of exploration, assessment, and intervention

Guidelines for promoting therapeutic interaction

Barriers to the therapeutic process

VERBAL COMMUNICATION

"In the beginning was the word. . . ." Whorf (1956) maintains that language structures thought. While most anthropologists do not accept this concept of linguistic determinism, they do hold that language and thought are interrelated. Language influences the way people perceive, interpret, and respond to the world around them. For instance, the grammatical forms of American Indian languages influence Indians' perception of relatedness. Many of these languages do not contain coersive or possessive words. The Wintu Indians of California cannot say "I have a child" or "I took my child to the doctor." Wintu language does not permit such expression. Instead, the Wintu say, "I live with the child" or "I went with the child to the doctor." Similarly, the Navaho Indians of Arizona and New Mexico guide rather than command their children to observe numerous Navaho taboos. Navaho parents do not speak of teaching children to obey or of punishing children. Instead, they explain that when a taboo is broken a specific unpleasant consequence follows. When a child violates a taboo, parents view it as a mistake that the child must rectify and not as a consequence of something that parents either did or did not do. As a result, neither parents nor children experience a sense of overwhelming guilt (Lee, 1959). Thus language plays an important role in reinforcing the concepts of permissiveness and personal integrity that are central to the interpersonal relationships of many American Indians.

Any group of people may create arbitrary meanings for words and phrases. An ethnic group, an age group, a social class, or an occupational group may have its own vocabulary (Ervin-Tripp, 1977). For example, when an adolescent refers to a "square" he is not referring to the concept that a mathematician refers to when he talks about a square. The abbreviation "S.O.B." has a different meaning to nurses than to the general public. The shared meaning and understanding of language help to create and maintain a sense of identity, belonging, and exclusivity.

Peplau (1953, 1954) and Ujhely (1968) have pioneered in helping nurses focus on the *meaning* of verbal communication. One needs to listen to the messages being conveyed—the *themes* of communication. Listening is an essential ingredient in talk therapy.

A *communication theme* is a recurrent idea or concept that underlies communication and ties it together. There are three types of communication themes: content theme, mood theme, and interaction theme.

The *content theme* is the idea that underlies or links together seem-ingly varied topics of discussion. It is the "what" of communication.

Elvira Johnson, 31 years old, was hospitalized after an attempted sui-cide. She had been married for 3 years to Stuart Johnson, a successful insurance agent. Barbara, a student nurse, began meeting biweekly with Mrs. Johnson to talk about her concerns. After 3 weeks, the student nurse became very disheartened and frustrated. She believed that Mrs. Johnson was using the time to socialize and that she was only talking about super-ficial topics. Barbara's verbatim notes showed that Mrs. Johnson fre-quently spoke as follows: "When I was younger, I had several girl friends. None of us were any beauties. We would go bowling or out for pizza. We had a lot of laughs. We didn't need boyfriends to have a good time."

"My husband is an insurance agent, and many of his clients are pretty young student nurses like you. They take out professional liability insur-ance." Then she would laugh and ask, "Do you think I can trust him with those students?"

"I had a beautiful wedding. Many friends were invited. My sister was my maid of honor, and my husband's best friend, Jeff, was his best man. They really are good friends—best buddies they call each other. I think if my husband had to choose between the two of us he would choose Jeff."

In discussing this interaction with her instructor, Barbara began to see that low self-esteem was a recurrent theme. Mrs. Johnson saw her-self as an unattractive woman. She felt threatened by her husband's young clients and believed that her husband preferred his male friend to her. Mrs. Johnson had not been engaging in superficial conversa-tion. The underlying message or theme in her interactions was that of low self-esteem. Once this theme was identified, nursing intervention could be planned.

The *mood theme* is the affect or emotion a person communicates. In order to identify the mood theme, one needs to listen for speech patterns and tone of voice. In addition, gestures, facial expressions, posture, and personal appearance should be observed. The mood theme reflects an individual's affect. Is he angry? Hopeless? Apathetic? Any adjective describing a mood may be a possible mood theme. The mood theme is the "how" of communication.

Mrs. Barnes had recently been diagnosed as diabetic. A public health nurse was counseling her in diabetic care and helping her work through her feelings about being diabetic. The nurse noticed on each of her visits that Mrs. Barnes' 14-year-old son, Matthew, appeared listless. His face was expressionless. Regardless of what was happening or what he was speaking about, Matthew's face was expressionless and his voice was monotone.

The public health nurse identified Matthew's mood as apathetic. She recognized that this flatness of affect or apathy might be an indicator of deep emotional conflict. The nurse referred Matthew to a neighborhood counseling center.

By identifying the mood theme of apathy and recognizing its import, the public health nurse was able to make an appropriate referral.

The *interaction theme* is the idea or concept that best describes the dynamics between communicating participants. Are the partners in communication relating to one another in a pattern of dominance-submission? Collaboration? Power struggle? Parallel play? If the interaction theme is reinforcing well-established patterns of pathology or if it is destructive of therapeutic communication, it may need to be identified so that the problem can be resolved.

> After a 1-year stay in a psychiatric hospital, John Toomey had been discharged to his home. Carlos Rodriquez, a psychiatric nurse, was visiting John on a weekly basis. Carlos' purpose was to help John readjust to living in the community. The focus of these visits was to assist John in finding employment, to teach him to shop for and prepare meals, and to help him to budget his money. Whenever John had to make a decision or initiate a plan of action he would ask Carlos "What do you think I should do?" Carlos would usually respond with his assessment of the best course of action. After several visits, Carlos realized that the interaction theme had become one of dominance-submission. He had taken the dominant role, and John had assumed the submissive role. Once Carlos had identified these dynamics, he pointed out to John the pattern their interactions had taken. Carlos explained that in the future he would help John explore alternatives and arrive at a decision but would not make the decision.

Had Carlos failed to identify the interaction theme, he might have continued to reinforce unhealthy patterns of communication and behavior.

These vignettes illustrate what is meant by content, mood, and interaction themes. Although these hypothetical cases have been drawn from nursing situations, any one or combination of themes can be identified in any sequence of communication, be it social or therapeutic.

NONVERBAL COMMUNICATION

Nonverbal communication is any type of communication other than verbal. We will focus on two areas of nonverbal communication: kinesics and proxemics. *Kinesics* refers to the way we use body parts when we communicate while *proxemics* refers to the way we use space when we communicate. Observation will show that body movements and spatial arrangements *do* communicate significant information. We may think of kinesics as body language and of proxemics as space language.

Kinesics

Birdwhistle (1963, 1970), a pioneer in the field of kinesics, recognized certain similarities between spoken and written language and body language. His research was guided by two basic assumptions: that individuals are constantly maneuvering to accommodate the presence and activities of other individuals and that the system of kinesic movement is learned and ultimately analyzable. In order to understand the way people communicate kinesically, we must have some knowledge of the properties of kinesic behavior.

Properties of kinesic behavior. Kinesic behavior is most often unconsciously performed. It is found both among primates and among other mammals. Socialization plays an important role in transmitting kinesic systems from generation to generation. Body movements are responsive to an individual's bio-psycho-cultural state and usually vary in form and meaning according to ethnic background, sex, age, and social class (Efron, 1942; Birdwhistle, 1970; Scheflen, 1972).

The point of origin, speed, and destination of a gesture, empathic assessment, a person's psychophysiological state and cultural background, and the context in which a gesture is made are all involved in the way a person reads and responds to the body movements of another. For example, when a person with whom we are conversing raises his arm, we rapidly and unconsciously ask ourselves: "What is he doing? Is he friend or foe? What do I mean when I do that? What has happened in similar situations when someone has raised his arm like that? Who is he aiming at?" The interpretation we arrive at and the way we respond will vary greatly—they depend on our answers to these questions. Certainly the raising of an arm by a stranger on the street has a different meaning from the same gesture performed by a friend at a cocktail party, an opponent in a sports arena, or a person receiving physiotherapy.

Body movements, then, are very important to our understanding of others and to being understood by others. Just as an individual has the physical capacity for producing thousands of sounds, but is limited by his language to the use of only a very few, each individual, on the basis of his culture, uses only a relatively small number of the many motions available for communication. Kinesic behavior can be classified according to function. Scheflen (1972) has distinguished and described three types of body movement that aid in communication: markers, reciprocals, and territorials.

Markers act as punctuation points and indicators:

> During a group therapy session, it was observed that participants lowered their heads, eyebrows, and hands at the end of statements, but raised one or all of these body parts when they asked questions. Moreover, when one participant accused another of monopolizing the session, he pointed his head and right hand in the direction of the accused and said, "Harry doesn't give any of us a chance to get a word in edgewise."

Can there be any question that these group members were using their bodies to clarify or dramatize situations?

When a person makes one gesture as he says one word and another gesture as he speaks the next word and so on, we say that he is using a marker of speech. Gestures are also used to mark the beginnings and endings of sentences. For example, at the end of a sentence, a person not only lowers the pitch of his voice but also lowers his hands and head. On the other hand, when a person asks a question, he raises his voice, head, and eyebrows. When a person has completed an idea, he usually signals this fact by shifting his eyes and head and changing his posture. When he begins to express another idea, he again shifts kinesically.

While markers of speech involve only the speaker, markers of discourse involve both speaker and listener. A person may try to obtain speaking rights in one of several ways, depending on the situation. He may stand, as when making a form presentation. He may remain seated, but lean forward and extend one or both hands into the space in front of him. He may lean back in his seat and either steeple his fingers or place the palms of his hands behind his head. These latter types of posturing often indicate that the person about to speak has some status, and they are usually differentiated by sex. Women tend to steeple, while men tend to place the palms of their hands behind their heads. Meanwhile, listeners are looking in the direction of the speaker, occasionally making eye contact with the speaker and intermittently making such listening movements as nodding. In addition, if speaker and listeners are in rapport, they indicate this by posturing and moving in synchrony. Finally, when discourse is completed, a terminal marker signals the end of the encounter. Participants lower their eyes and engage in some parting ritual such as shaking hands, kissing, or palm brushing.

Reciprocals indicate affiliation between people. Reciprocals include bond-servicing behavior (for example, behavior such as exchanging food and drink or giving affection and attention that reinforces interpersonal bonds) and empathic behavior (such as looking sympathetic or exchanging winks and smiles).

Courtship behavior and quasi-courtship behavior are also reciprocals. Courtship behavior is characterized by increased muscle tonus and preening. A message of intimacy is conveyed. Women protrude their breasts and display their wrists or palms. Men display their chests by straightening up, contracting abdominal muscles, and squaring their shoulders. Voices are kept low so that conversations will not be overheard. Quasi-courtship behavior, on the other hand, contains qualifiers or metacommunication signaling that courting should not be taken seriously. Voices may be loud enough for conversations to be overheard. References may be made as to the inappropriateness of the situation for courting, or an incomplete postural-kinesic configuration may be given. For instance, participants may be facing each other, but their torsos may be turned toward other people or their eyes may dart around the room.

Quasi-courtship behavior has a systems-maintenance function. In situations in which one participant either withdraws or is excluded, quasi-courtship behavior calls back the errant participant and thereby maintains the interaction. Quasi-courtship behavior thus facilitates rapport and sociability, necessary elements in group cohesion.

To avoid the misunderstanding of communication, nurses must be able to distinguish between courtship and quasi-courtship behavior.

> A student nurse observed a psychiatrist interacting with a 23-year-old female client in the sitting room of a large hospital. They were facing each other, with their bodies turned toward the staff in the nurses' station. The client frequently brushed hair away from her face, presenting the palm of her hand to the psychiatrist. The psychiatrist adjusted his tie several times. They were speaking loudly enough so that the student nurse could hear that they were discussing plans for the young woman's imminent discharge.
>
> The student misinterpreted this quasi-courtship behavior for courtship behavior and felt that the psychiatrist was encouraging his client's "seductive behavior." After talking the situation over with her instructor, the student was able to identify the behavioral qualifiers that signaled the message that courting should not be taken seriously (participants' torsos were turned away from each other and toward the rest of the staff, they were talking in a large sitting room and in the midst of other people, and they were speaking loudly enough so that their conversation could be easily overheard).

Occasionally, individuals may inadequately learn either the courtship behavior or the behavioral qualifiers. Since both sets of behavior are essential for quasi-courtship, deviance or pathological behavior ensues when *either* set is performed in the absence of the other. Schizophrenic persons often use courtship behavior without including behavioral qualifiers. Instead of quasi-courting they court. We usually say that they are exhibiting inappropriately seductive behavior. Or an individual may be unable to deal with quasi-courtship behavior and may respond by "decourting"—withdrawing or criticizing. This type of behavior is often associated with such sexual dysfunctions as impotence and frigidity (Scheflen, 1965, 1972).

Scheflen (1965) states that misinterpretation of quasi-courtship behavior results, at the individual level, in a loss of courtship readiness and rapport and, at the social level, in a loss of group cohesion.

Other types of reciprocals, those of dominance and submission, indicate status. A dominant male may place his hands on his hips, scowl, or place the palms of his hands behind his neck. A dominant female may steeple her fingers. The person in the submissive position will usually "reciprocate" by lowering his head. It is important for a nurse who is working with a submissive client to avoid assuming a dominant role either verbally or kinesically. By being aware of reciprocals of dominance and submission, the nurse can be more attuned to patterns of dominance and submission in the nurse-client relationship.

Unlike reciprocals, *territorials* frame an interaction and define a territory. When someone wants to pass through or intrude on another person's territory, certain behavior patterns are displayed. The intruder will bow his head, curl his shoulders inward so that his chest does not protrude, keep his arms at his side, and look downward. In addition, he may mumble a "pardon me."

> A nurse noticed that whenever Mrs. Bowens walked past the library section of the sitting room, she looked downward and curled her shoulders inward. The nurse mistakenly assumed that Mrs. Bowen was intimidated by Mr. Jackson, who usually spent his free time in the library. After discussing the situation with another nurse, who was more knowledgeable about kinesics, the first nurse recognized that, since Mr. Jackson had staked out the library section as his territory, Mrs. Bowen was displaying normal behavior for passing through or intruding on another's territory.

We have seen how kinesic signals help interacting participants recognize what is happening. We will now explore the regulatory nature of kinesics.

Regulatory nature of kinesics. Nonverbal behavior, especially kinesic behavior, serves to regulate the pace of a relationship and to monitor deviant behavior. Regulatory behavior occurs many times during an interaction. When deviance appears, a new pattern of behavior may emerge to monitor the deviant behavior; it will continue until the deviant behavior ceases.

> A nurse-therapist had received a family's permission to videotape its family therapy session. After the session, the nurse studied the videotape and tried to identify group dynamics. She noticed that every time the husband-father leaned in to speak to her, he would lower his voice. This excluded the rest of the family from the interaction. The wife-mother and two daughters would then cross their legs and rub their noses. At the appearance of this behavior, the husband-father would lean back in his chair and raise his voice, so that the rest of the family could hear what he was saying. By interrupting any alliance with the nurse that excluded other family members, the wife-mother and the two daughters were monitoring the husband-father's behavior.

Thus we see how monitoring gestures and signals can occur synchronously among members of a group and can serve to check deviant behavior.

Whenever we try to interpret the meaning of kinesic behavior, we have to look beyond the individual or the group to the interrelationship between behavior and context. This is what is meant by a systems approach to understanding behavior.

Kinesic behavior is learned and passed on from generation to generation. Scheflen (1972) points out that the nuclear family or household is the first group to which a person belongs. It is here that most kinesic behavior is learned. Family or household members function interdependently to obtain food, affection, status, and self-esteem. Should a member deviate from culturally defined behavior, some of these ministrations may be withheld as a sanction. Therefore, at one and the same time, family interactions physically sustain a young child while servicing social bonds and teaching culturally approved values and behavior.

As an individual grows to maturity, he belongs to other groups and expands his social network. In each of these groups, he plays specific roles. Should he deviate from the expected role behavior, metacommunications occur that serve to discipline and reindoctrinate him or to keep him out of the mainstream of society. Bateson (1955) defines *metacommunication* as communication that tells how verbal communication should be interpreted.

A public health nurse was visiting with a woman who was the mother of a toddler and an infant. The nurse was discussing sibling rivalry with the mother. The toddler was sitting at the kitchen table eating cookies and drinking milk. As the toddler reached for a cookie, he knocked over the glass of milk. The mother jumped up and said sweetly, "Don't worry, Johnny—accidents will happen." However, from the frown on her face and her brusque behavior in cleaning off Johnny's wet clothes, both the public health nurse and Johnny were very aware that the mother was annoyed with Johnny's behavior.

The behavior that communicated the message of annoyance contradicted the verbal message; it indicated how the verbal message should be taken. This is the function of metacommunication. It may support or contradict verbal communication and thereby reinforce the values, behavior, and standards of society. Interactions continue in their customary manner, and unusual experience and information are kept to a minimum.

Taken together, metacommunication, marking, and territorial and reciprocal behavior serve to clarify ambiguous communication, signal deviance in an interaction, and bring about a return to conventional behavior. It is primarily through this regulatory function of kinesics that social order is maintained.

Cultural influences on kinesic behavior. Communication specialists like Birdwhistle (1952, 1970) and Scheflen (1972) believe that kinesic behavior is culturally variable. Ruesch and Kees (1969) agree with this view and have postulated that body movements are a function of their cultural context. Ruesch and Kees argue that climate, population density, mode of subsistence (for example, agricultural versus industrial economy), availability of raw materials, and historical heritage all influence the cultural specificity of body movements.

Some researchers have identified culturally specific body movements. For example, considerable time has been spent exploring the culturally specific form and meaning of eye movements. Ashcraft and Scheflen (1976) have found that while most British-Americans seek eye contact as a means of establishing affiliation and rapport, West Indians and Afro-Americans usually avoid direct eye contact, for such behavior invites the escalation of hostility. British-Americans often misinterpret the black American's avoidance of eye contact as being indicative of submissiveness or of having something to hide. Black Americans often misinterpret British-American eye contact as either a put-down or a confrontation. Hispanic women tend to hold eye contact slightly longer than women from other ethnic groups, and this behavior is often interpreted by non-Hispanic people as seductive.

Hall (1966) has found that even in the "British-American world" eye contact differs. The British tend to blink their eyes to show they are listening and understanding conversation, while Americans, who have conventions against staring, do not look directly into people's eyes. Instead, Americans indicate attentiveness by nodding and making listening noises. While an American's gaze wanders over the face and sometimes off the face, an Englishman fixes his gaze on the eyes.

Needless to say, the cultural variability of the form and meaning of eye movements can result in many misunderstandings.

> A young Hispanic nurse was assigned as primary nurse to an Irish-American male client. The client had been hospitalized for treatment of a myocardial infarct. The nurse spent much time listening to the man's fears, explaining his diet to him, and helping him to establish a prescribed exercise program. Because the young man was unaccustomed to women maintaining prolonged eye contact except when inviting or involved in intimate encounters, he interpreted the nurse's slightly prolonged eye holding as seductive behavior. He responded by inviting her out for a date. To the nurse, whose behavior was customary for someone from her Hispanic culture, the client's behavior was unwarranted. She could not see why this young man had acted as he had. In talking the situation over with a nurse-anthropologist, she was able to identify the kinesic behavior that had resulted in the misunderstanding. Once she understood the cultural dynamics of the situation, she was able to explain to the client that she was not trying to establish a social relationship and to point out why he might have thought that she was. The confusion was resolved, tension between them was lessened, and a more therapeutic relationship was established.

Misinterpretation of the culturally specific form and meaning of another's kinesic behavior can cause misunderstandings and produce barriers to communication. And without effective communication, a therapeutic relationship cannot be established.

The cultural specificity of kinesic behavior is also revealed in the form and meaning of gestures. Scheflen (1972) has noted that British-Americans tend to gesticulate less frequently than persons from Mediterranean countries and Eastern European Jews. When British-Americans do gesticulate, they usually keep their forearms in fixed positions and move either or both hands from the wrist in a circle approximately 6 inches in diameter.

Effron (1942) found that in day-to-day communications, Italians tend to use their hands, faces, arms, and shoulders to emphasize and illustrate their words. Gestures may become so flamboyant that Italians need approximately an arm's length of lateral space in order to avoid striking things with their sweeping arms. Eastern European Jews tend to use motions to "support" words. Instead of the sweeping arm movement of Italians, which starts at the shoulder and involves the entire arm, they tend to hold their upper arms close to their bodies and use only their lower arm to gesture. Eastern European Jews usually stand within touching range as they converse. They are able to poke, pull, and push as they embellish, punctuate, and accent their conversations.

Scheflen (1972) observed that black Americans tend to gesticulate much like British-Americans but that working-class blacks often use more gestures than middle-class blacks. Black Americans generally gesticulate with the index finger and also display their palms more frequently than British-Americans.

One might wonder of what import this knowledge of the cultural specificity of gestures is to nursing. We will look at two examples.

> Ms. Galiano, a nursing instructor, was a second-generation Italian-American. After several years of teaching, she found herself becoming increasingly tense during clinical seminars. One day, she sat down and tried to identify the dynamics of the situation. Everything was similar to previous semesters with one exception: this semester her clinical group was sitting in a tight circle with barely 6 inches of space between the chairs. Ms. Galiano suddenly realized what was happening. Her clinical group was composed of British-American students and Eastern European Jewish students, none of whom needed lateral space for body movements. Ms. Galiano, however, used the gesticulatory behavior common to her ethnic group. In order to kinesically communicate, she needed lateral space. Without such space, her body language was being stifled. As a result, she was becoming tense. She explained the dynamics of the situation to the group. They spread open their circle and allowed Ms. Galiano the space she needed to gesticulate. The problem was solved. Both students and teacher had received a first-hand lesson in the role of kinesic behavior in the process of communication.

> Ms. Thompson, a 60-year-old British-American, had been admitted to a psychiatric hospital. A student nurse established a one-to-one relationship with her. The student became concerned about Ms. Thompson's lack of body movement during their interactions. He told his instructor: "Either Ms. Thompson is scared to death of me or she's catatonic. She never moves." His instructor helped the student to look at the dynamics of the interaction. The student was of Eastern European Jewish extraction and used much gesturing and touching during conversation. Ms. Thompson

was British-American and accustomed to little gesturing. Her behavior was neither rooted in fear nor pathological. It was completely normal for someone of her ethnic background.

Postures and gestures thus can have various causes and various meanings. Form and meaning are dependent on cultural context. Probably because culturally specific behavior is unconscious and not formally learned, it is one of the last types of behavior to be acculturated. As a result, when people of different ethnic backgrounds interact, misinterpretation of behavior may cause misunderstandings.

Body language, then, like speech, is very much a part of any communication system. Kinesic behavior communicates needs, feelings, and intentions that are universal, but the form and meaning of body movements are culturally specific. In looking at the communicational value of kinesic behavior, we have seen the importance of understanding the interrelationship between kinesic behavior and the context in which it occurs. We will now explore another level of human communication: proxemics.

Proxemics

The proxemic level of communication—the use of space—has only recently become an area for study. Hall (1966) was a pioneer in proxemic research. Scheflen and Ashcraft (1976) see space as neither thing defined nor people defined. They refer to bounded space as territory that is framed and used by people but that does not consist of people. Instead, it surrounds people or exists between them. It is defined by a relationship or pattern of behavior and movement. Therefore, a "territory" is a space claimed by a person through his behavior. People claim space either through the direction in which they orient their bodies or by the way they project their gazes or voices. Even though claims may be of a temporary nature, once a space has been claimed and the claim has been acknowledged, a territory has been established.

Mr. Jefferson was recovering from abdominal surgery. He spent a great deal of time in bed watching television. The television set was located on a shelf on the wall opposite his bed. Any time that a nurse came in to care for the person in the next bed, he or she had to walk through the space between Mr. Jefferson's bed and the television set. Each time that the nurse did this, if Mr. Jefferson was watching television, the nurse said, "Excuse me." By orienting his body and his gaze toward the television set, Mr. Jefferson had claimed this territory.

Proxemics, as a legitimate area of research, grew out of studies of animal territoriality. Once it was recognized that animals organize space, it was a short step to the realization that human beings also organize space.

Animal behavioralists (Wynne-Edwards, 1962; Lorenz, 1966; McBride, 1964; Goodall, 1967) have observed that each animal species occupies a life-supporting ecological niche. Within each niche, groups mark off territorial boundaries that keep their members inside the territory and intruders out. Within their territorial boundaries, the members of the animal group are able to maintain visual, auditory, or olfactory communication. This communication may be maintained on a prolonged basis or only during the mating season, depending on the species.

Many animal behavioralists have studied distance regulation among animals. Hediger (1950, 1955, 1961) identified three types of distance: flight distance, personal distance, and social distance. Flight distance is the distance that a wild animal will tolerate between itself and an enemy before fleeing. Usually, the larger the animal the greater the distance it keeps between itself and a predator. For example, while an antelope has a flight distance of 500 yards, a lizard's flight distance is only 6 feet. Personal distance is the normal spacing maintained between animals of the same species. Dominant animals tend to have larger personal spaces than subordinate animals. Moreover, subordinate animals tend to yield personal space to dominant animals. Therefore, spacing often reflects social organization. Social distance, the third type of distance, is found only among social animals. It is the maximal distance that an animal will travel from the group before the animal begins to feel either psychologically threatened or physically and socially isolated (unable to maintain visual, auditory, or olfactory contact with the group). Social distance serves to contain a group of animals; it varies from species to species.

Christian (1960), Calhoun (1962), and Southwick (1964) have found that during prolonged overcrowding of animals, dominance hierarchies break down, territorial boundaries are violated, and a stress syndrome develops. The stress syndrome includes elevated eosinophil counts, adrenocortical hyperactivity, and enlarged adrenal glands. If left unchecked, the syndrome may result in the death of the animals.

Properties of human spacing. Now that we have looked at some studies of spacing in animal behavior, we will note some properties of human spacing. Scheflen and Ashcraft (1976) have been pioneers in the examination of the properties of space. By studying territories of orientation, these researchers have shown how we can better understand the ways in which human beings organize space.

Scheflen and Ashcraft use the term *point behaviors* to refer to the way in which body parts move within a space and orient themselves in some direction. For example, the gaze of an instructor's eyes may be directed toward a student in order to warn him, reprimand him, or focus attention upon him. A nurse's head may be cocked so that is can be oriented toward a client. The small space that becomes the object and extension of point behavior is called a "spot."

Positional behaviors involve four body regions: head-neck, upper torso, pelvis-thighs, and lower legs–feet. These regions may be oriented in the same direction or in different directions. When saying a fast "hello" to fellow classmates, a student may orient his head, chest, and arms toward his friends while orienting the lower part of his body in the direction in which he is walking. When a single body region or a cluster of body regions is pointed in a specific direction, it claims a space beyond that occupied by the body region. People usually avoid looking into or walking through this space. It is through such acknowledgment that a space is claimed and a territory established.

Besides being organized by identifying spatial orientations, space can also be organized by degree of affiliation. In Scheflen and Ashcraft's terminology, people who are affiliated ("with" one another) share *"with" space*. In "with" spaces, participants use body parts and regions to show that they are affiliated and that they share a similar spatial orientation. For example, a nurse and a client may, during the course of their interaction, assume congruent body positions or mirror-image stances ("book-ending") and thereby define a common focus of attention. In addition, people show they are affiliated by leaning toward each other, forming links through touching, and using arms and legs to demarcate spatial boundaries.

In *"non-with" spaces*, participants use body parts and regions to show that they have different spatial orientations and that they are unaffiliated with one another. For example, during a nurse-client interaction, the nurse and the client may assume stances that show that they are affiliated but may position their extremities to form a barrier between themselves and others. They are indicating that they are temporarily unaffiliated with the others.

So far we have looked at how body parts and regions define spatial orientation and organization. However, body parts and regions belong to and are part of the total body. When looking at the orientation of the total body in space, we are describing relationships. People may commit all or only part of their bodies to an interaction. We will now look at patterns of low commitment and patterns of high commitment.

While *low-commitment configurations* may result in the dissolution of a relationship, *high-commitment configurations* reinforce a relationship. Low-commitment configurations are characterized by the involvement of only one body part, the positioning of a body region so that a person is only partially oriented toward the focus, the maintenance of maximal interpersonal distance, the crossing of extremities, or the covering and/or immobilization of body regions so that body movements are minimal. High-commitment configurations are characterized by the involvement of several body regions, the positioning of body regions toward the focus of orientation, the maintenance of minimal interpersonal distance, the uncrossing of extremities, and the display of mutual point and positional behavior. In the following hypothetical situation, patterns of both high and low commitment affect an interaction.

Ms. Zender, a student nurse, was sitting outdoors with her client, Mr. Morrow. They were seated on chairs and facing each other. Each was leaning forward as they talked. After about 20 minutes, Ms. Zender gazed over at a softball game that was being played nearby. Within minutes, not only was she looking at the game but her head and upper torso were turned away from Mr. Morrow and toward the softball field. A silence fell between nurse and client. Five minutes later, Mr. Morrow said he had nothing more to say. He got up and left. Ms. Zender was frustrated and confused. She told her nursing instructor that the interaction had been going "so well and then suddenly Mr. Morrow got up and left." The instructor had been sitting outside and had observed the changing behavioral configurations. In the beginning of the interaction, both Ms. Zender and Mr. Morrow were engaged in high-commitment configurations. When Ms. Zender turned her gaze and her body toward the softball game, she changed her spatial orientation and assumed a low-commitment configuration. From that point on, the interaction deteriorated. Once the student became aware of her behavior, she stopped blaming Mr. Morrow for interrupting the interaction and recognized how her own spatial orientation had affected the interaction.

Spatial orientations and relations do not exist in isolation. They are formed by people who cluster together at a given time. Scheflen and Ashcraft (1976) use the term *formations* to refer to these clusters of people and the term *sites* to refer to the spaces these formations define and occupy.

One type of site, a solo site, is the space occupied when a person is alone or with very few other people. The size of a solo site is determined by such factors as ethnicity, age, affiliation, role, activity, social class, and sex. Scheflen and Ashcraft (1976) have found that a British-American or Afro-American man, when standing and conversing with acquaintances, usually occupies a site of approximately 1 square yard. Since persons from the Mediterranean area and from Eastern Europe are inclined to stand closer together, each person's site tends to be smaller than the site occupied by a British-American or a black American. Latin Americans stand even closer together than Mediterraneans. Since Cubans stand only about 18 inches apart when conversing, their sites tend to be even smaller than those of Mediterraneans or Eastern Europeans.

Another type of spacing, unaffiliated rows, is found when strangers sit side by side in a public area (for example, when strangers sit on a park bench). They may try to separate themselves from others by maintaining space around themselves, orienting themselves in different directions, or erecting barriers.

On the other hand, persons who know each other may show affiliation by huddling together and maintaining a distance from others, erecting barriers to separate themselves from others, and orienting themselves toward each other and away from the strangers present.

Obviously, it is important for nurses who work with clients of various ages, social classes, and ethnic backgrounds to recognize how these variables may influence the way people occupy and use space and show affiliation.

A nurse was explaining hospital visiting regulations to a Cuban visitor. Both nurse and client were standing in a face-to-face formation. The nurse, who was British-American, suddenly began feeling very uncomfortable. She started moving around, side-stepping, and taking occasional steps backward. Everytime she moved, the visitor would take a step toward her. Each person was doing a "distance dance." The British-American nurse was trying to maintain slightly more than an arm's length of space between herself and her client. The Cuban client was trying to maintain a much smaller (approximately half an arm's length) interpersonal space. Each was trying to establish and maintain the interpersonal distance that was common to his or her ethnic background, and each was confused by the distancing maneuvers of the other. Had the nurse been aware of what was occurring, she might have felt less uncomfortable and might have been able to use her energy to interact more effectively with her client. Unfortunately, she did not have this awareness. Because she felt uneasy, she terminated the interaction prematurely.

Up to now, we have been focusing on relationships. Scheflen and Ashcraft (1976) have shown that another way to examine the properties of space is to look at the characteristics of fixed spaces and built spaces. Because it sets a focus of orientation, provides a place in which to interact, and defines what is going to happen, furniture establishes *fixed spaces*. For instance, wheeling a medicine cart into a hospital room, building a nurses' station in the center of a hospital unit, or placing a television set in the sitting room of a day hospital sets a focus and defines the type of activity that is going to occur.

Built spaces are bounded by such physical structures as curbs, walls, and fences. Areas may be marked off by lines or low barriers across which people can see and interact, or they may be marked off by walls through which participants cannot see one another. The latter type of built space obviously provides a greater degree of privacy.

The use of fixed and built spaces has many implications for nurses. Sommer (1969) observed that in a certain state psychiatric hospital all chairs were arranged in straight lines against the walls. Although people sat side by side, rarely in the course of a day did they engage in more than two brief conversations. Sommer hypothesized that conversation was inhibited by the fact that clients had to turn their heads at a 90-degree angle in order to talk to persons sitting alongside. As a result, clients usually sat quietly, staring at the floor or ceiling. Sommer wondered why the chairs were arranged side by side and arrived at the following answers:

1. The arrangement made it easier to clean the room.
2. It was easier for nurses to supervise the unit.
3. The arrangement was a function of "institutional sanctity." Since the furniture had always been arranged that way, it had become a fixed routine.

Rather than the environment being arranged to meet the needs of the people inhabiting it, the people had been arranged to fit the environment. Sommer received permission to rearrange the furniture. He began by placing chairs around square tables. He chose square tables because the boundaries of a square table can be determined and demarcated more easily than those of a round table. Shortly after the furniture was rearranged, client interactions increased in both number and duration.

We have seen how built and fixed spaces, point behavior, and positional behavior occur within some larger pattern of behavior. Types of behavior are hierarchically arranged and occur within a broad context that is both temporally and spatially defined. Now we will look at the way culture influences the meaning, ordering, and use of space.

Culture and proxemics. The organizational, social, and symbolic meaning and use of space have been explored by archeologists, social anthropologists, psychologists, geographers, and ethnographers.

Hall (1966) has looked at man's perception of space. He sees people as surrounded by expanding and contracting perceptual fields that at all times provide them with information. He believes that people interact in four spatial zones: intimate, personal, social, and public.

The intimate zone is the zone of physical contact. It is the area within 18 inches of the body. This is the zone of lovemaking and comforting. Sight is often blurred or distorted. The perception of odors, heat, and breath from another's body is heightened. The voice, if used, is kept to a whisper. Americans feel uncomfortable if forced into the intimate zones of strangers. For instance, when crowded onto an elevator, Americans respond by becoming immobile, holding their arms at their sides, fixing their eyes on some spot, and tensing their bodies. Many nurses have experienced this same response when comforting clients with whom they have not established rapport, trust, and confidence.

The personal zone comprises the area 18 inches to 4 feet from the body. This area is sometimes visualized as a "bubble" that a person keeps between himself and others. The bubble expands and contracts according to circumstances. At a small personal distance, one can hold and touch another person. At a great personal distance, one is just within reach when both parties extend their arms. Vision is not distorted, as it is in the intimate zone. In fact, a person is able to see the texture of the hair, the pores in the skin, and the three-dimensional qualities of objects. The breath and body heat of another person are imperceptible, and the voice level is moderate. During a nurse-client interaction, participants usually maintain personal distance.

Social distance is approximately 4 to 12 feet. At this distance people cannot touch one another. This is the distance at which most business is conducted; it is also the distance maintained by student and teacher during a classroom lecture.

Public distance, 12 to 25 feet or more, separates public figures from the public. It is used in formal situations. Fine details of the other person are lost, as is the three-dimensional quality of the body. This is the distance maintained between student and lecturer in a large lecture hall.

These zones of interaction are neither static nor absolute. They are related to the way people organize their senses, a process that is culturally determined. What is considered intimate distance in one society may be considered personal or public distance in another society.

Although there are areas of cultural similarity among societies of the Western world, there are also many areas of cultural difference. People who are unaware of these differences risk misunderstanding others and being misunderstood. Behavior that differs from that of the dominant culture is usually interpreted as rudeness, ineptness, or apathy. We will now explore some proxemic differences among cultures.

Scheflen (1972) has observed that when people place themselves in a vis-à-vis position for the purpose of communication, the amount of space between them depends on their ethnic background, their degree of intimacy, their previous relationship, the reason they assembled, and the amount of available physical space. Should the people interacting come from different ethnic backgrounds or have different ideas about the purpose and circumstances surrounding the interaction, they will have difficulty agreeing on the distance between them. They might do a "spatial dance" until they arrive at a spatial compromise. For example, Englishmen and British-Americans usually arrange themselves just beyond touching distance, and they touch very little while interacting. Latins and Eastern European Jews tend to position themselves within easy tactile range and to use varying degrees of touching during conversation. A nurse who has been culturally conditioned to use little touching while conversing may be made very uncomfortable by the small interpersonal distance and the use of touching by a client or colleague, and vice versa.

What is regarded as intrusive behavior in one culture is not necessarily regarded as such in another culture. Ashcraft and Scheflen (1976) point out that while urban Americans and Englishmen try to avoid touching when in crowds and apologize if they do touch, this is not the case in all cultures. Frenchmen often collide with one another without apologizing, and Russians, who often slip on the ice, knocking one another down, usually get up without paying any attention to those they have knocked over.

The definition of intrusive behavior is also influenced by social class. Ashcraft and Scheflen (1976) have noted significant differences in the way members of the middle and lower classes define intrusiveness. Middle-class American family members usually lay claim to specific household chairs. There is mother's chair, and there is father's chair. Children are usually not permitted to sit in these chairs without parental permission or must vacate them when the parent appears. On the other hand, in a lower-class home, where furniture may be at a premium, there are usually more family members than there are chairs. This shortage of chairs does not afford the luxury of "owning" a chair.

As we have seen, we all have a sense of territoriality that is operative in our daily lives. As we interact with others, we both acknowledge other people's claims to space and expect them to acknowledge our claims. Problems arise when the use of different spacing signals results in ambiguous or disputed claims. When this occurs, we do not realize that a claim has been made and therefore do not respect it.

Deviant proxemic behavior. We have discussed how the use of space may be misinterpreted by persons of differing backgrounds. However, some people exhibit behavior that is deviant even by the standards of their own ethnic, economic, or regional group. A person might touch persons with whom he does not have tactile rights, or might fail to touch persons with whom he has such rights. He may orient his body away from persons with whom he is interacting, or may stand at a distance that is too close even for his own ethnic background. Such deviant territorial behavior is called "distance maneuvering."

Ashcraft and Scheflen (1976) have advanced several possible explanations of deviant territorial behavior. One is decreased living space. Traditionally, less living space has been available to the poor and to city dwellers than to the wealthy and to suburbanites. Since 1900, the amount of living space has decreased for those living in the American Northeast, without an accompanying decrease in the number of persons in a household. Large apartments have been subdivided into small apartments. New, high-rise apartments have been built smaller than older apartments. Open spaces surrounding dwellings have given way to homes and industrial parks. The change that has taken place is obvious if one simply looks around and counts the number of vacant lots that exist now as compared to 10 to 20 years ago. How many people have the luxury of living on an acre or more of land? Space is indeed at a premium. This all results in increased population density.

As population density has increased, we have developed behavior to try to ensure some modicum of privacy. Such territorial behavior includes not only actions that stake out private areas but also actions that show respect for privacy. Rooms in a house or an apartment are arranged so that a person goes from communal areas to increasingly private areas. The central hallway and the living room are open to guests, but access to the kitchen is usually only by permission. In fact, sometimes the kitchen is even off limits to certain family members. How often is a family member shooed away by a mother so that she may work in "her" kitchen? Bedrooms are very private areas. In fact, adolescents often mark this privacy with "no trespassing" and "keep out" signs. Rooms thereby become a means of ensuring some degree of privacy.

However, crowding can be defined only by looking at the context in which it occurs. For instance, Ashcraft and Scheflen (1976) have observed that children are better able to tolerate sleeping in a crowded bedroom if they can study and play in another room. Ashcraft and Scheflen have also found that crowding is culturally defined. While black Americans and British-Americans tend to disperse throughout the available space in a house, Puerto Ricans tend to cluster in one room. While Italian-Americans, British-Americans, black Americans and Jewish Americans usually define being "alone" as being physically removed from *family members* (they go outside or into another room), Puerto Ricans usually define being alone as being physically separated from *strangers* but being among their families.

In light of such information, nurses need to recognize that the crowded and cramped living conditions of ghetto apartments have conceptually different meanings to people of different ethnic groups. If a nurse suggested to a harried Puerto Rican mother that she try to get some rest and privacy by relaxing in her bedroom away from the noise and activity of family members, the nurse would be imposing his or her concept of privacy on someone whose definition of privacy was very different. The Puerto Rican mother would probably view the idea as strange and unworkable. The nurse, unless aware of the ethnic variation in the definition of privacy, would not even realize that he or she was being ethnocentric. A misunderstanding might result as both nurse and client become frustrated in working toward their goal of decreasing the mother's sense of fatigue and harassment.

Patterns of proxemic communication may vary. By looking at these patterns, nurses can discover cultural frames that influence the structure of a person's perception of the world. Since a person's perceptual structuring of the world influences his definitions and interpretations of the use and meaning of space, people of differing ethnic backgrounds often misinterpret the meaning of each other's proxemic behavior. Territorial intrusion occurs, and conflicts of varying intensity develop. When we study proxemic communication, we are studying how people of different cultures use their senses to screen perceptual data, admitting some information and filtering out other information. Culture therefore serves as a medium for proxemic communication.

RELATIONSHIPS AMONG LEVELS
OF COMMUNICATION

We have heuristically examined all three levels of communication: verbal, kinesic, and proxemic. We will not consider how these levels are interrelated. For years, communication specialists have realized that the process of communication involves more than speech. Until recently, however, they have lacked the tools to study the nonverbal aspects of communication. They therefore have focused their attention on the aspect of communication that they have had the tools to study—the verbal aspect.

Scheflen (1972) explains that as language evolved and attempts were made to clarify and punctuate speech, specific body motions such as gestures, posturing, and spacing behavior began to be used. Interaction thus came to involve the interpretation of kinesic and proxemic behavior, both as autonomous means of communication and as mechanisms integrated with speech.

The investigation of the relationships between various levels of communication probably owes its inception to Trager's (1964) collaborative efforts with Smith, Hall, and Birdwhistle. Fromm-Reichman later joined them. Research commenced on kinesics, proxemics, and metalinguistics. The process of communication was defined as including three coexisting levels: verbal, kinesic, and proxemic.

Out of this early research, interest was stimulated in communication as a system of interrelated levels. Birdwhistle (1972) recalls that "circum-speech" behavior was identified. Circum-speech includes such behavior characteristics of conversation as instrumentals, interactional behavior, markers, demonstratives, and stress kinesics. Instrumentals are such task-oriented movements as walking, smoking, eating, and knitting. People often carry on these activities while they are speaking. Interactional behavior is found in both verbal and nonverbal interactions. It includes shifts or movements of all or part of the body that increase, decrease, or maintain space between interacting individuals. Remember the "spatial dance" that people do when trying to adjust the distance between them? Markers are body movements that illustrate ambiguous words. For example, hand sweeps that indicate direction and accompany such phrases as "here" or "there" and head nods that clarify pronominal references are all markers. Demonstratives, like gestural mapping, are actions that accompany and illustrate speech. When someone indicates with his hands that a toddler has grown "this tall" or that a melon is "this big," he is using a demonstrative. The term stress kinesics refers to movements of the head, hand, or eyebrow that serve to mark the flow of speech; these movements generally coincide with linguistic stress patterns. When a student raises his eyebrows as well as the pitch of his voice to state in amazement, "I received an 'A' on my nursing process paper," he is using a stress kineme.

Until recent years, we paid little attention to the interrelationship of linguistics, kinesics, and proxemics. Anthropologists, psychologists, and nurses focused almost all of their attention on verbal communication. What people said and how they said it were analyzed extensively. It was not until the 1950s that kinesic behavior became the object of study. Proxemic behavior was not studied until the late 1960s.

THERAPEUTIC COMMUNICATION

In order to cope with and profit from an experience, one must be able to learn from that experience. Learning is an active process that utilizes intellectual and perceptual capacities as well as acquired knowledge to explain events, to engage in problem solving, and to plan and implement change.

Both client and nurse bring intellect, perception, knowledge, and experience to the therapeutic interview. Together they explore the client's perception of events—events that the client regards as important or as a matter of concern. Although occasionally comparisons may be made with past experience or reminiscing may occur, the focus is on the here and now—what the individual is presently experiencing that is of import or concern to him.

The nurse tries to sustain the individual in this experience by helping him cope with and profit from it. Such therapeutic intervention is possible only after the predominant themes in the client's communication have been identified. It is only then that long- and short-range goals can be set. The example of Mrs. Johnson, cited earlier (see p. 171), will illustrate this point.

Once the student nurse had identified the content theme of low self-esteem in Mrs. Johnson's communication, she was able to establish goals and develop plans for implementing them. The student set goals that would aid Mrs. Johnson in coping with and profiting from her experience. The plan of action included:

A. Long-range goals—assist Mrs. Johnson to:
　1. accept both her strengths and her weaknesses
　2. develop insight into sources of low self-esteem
　3. develop feelings of adequacy and security
B. Short-range goals—assist Mrs. Johnson to:
　1. assess her level of self-esteem
　2. recognize that low self-esteem is a predominant communication theme
　3. recognize that feelings of low self-esteem are causing her discomfort and that new ways of coping should be explored
　4. identify some positive qualities in herself
　5. set realistic goals for herself
　6. develop skills and talents that will build self-confidence
　7. engage in activities that present a challenge but that can be readily completed and thus provide a sense of accomplishment
C. Nursing principles—the student nurse needs to remember that:
　1. Negative appraisals have contributed to Mrs. Johnson's feeling of low self-esteem. It is important to provide an environment that is nonjudgmental. The nurse should accept Mrs. Johnson's negative as well as positive attributes.
　2. When an individual sets unrealistically high goals, the result will be failure. When failure consistently occurs, feelings of inadequacy are reinforced. The setting of challenging but realistic goals will help Mrs. Johnson to overcome some of her feelings of inadequacy.
　3. Feelings of neglect tend to reinforce feelings of low self-esteem. It is important to approach Mrs. Johnson in a consistent, accepting manner and to make her realize that the nurse considers her a worthwhile person.

Thus it is very important to correctly identify predominant communication themes. It is only after these themes have been identified that goals based on nursing principles can be established.

Process of exploration, assessment, and intervention

Identifying predominant communication themes and helping an individual learn appropriate and effective coping behavior require that nurse and client actively explore the client's experiences.

The first step of the process of exploration involves establishing the focus of the interaction. It is the client who decides what he wishes to discuss. The client thus can talk about events of concern or importance to him and also feel assured that only subject matter that he is psychologically able to tackle will be explored. Should the nurse introduce a topic, he or she might inadvertently select one that is traumatic to the client (Ujhely, 1968; Sayre, 1978). The nurse encourages the client to take the initiative in setting the focus by offering such broad opening questions as "What have you been thinking about?" or "What's been going on with you?" The client will usually initially speak about many different areas but will not delve deeply into any one area. This is to be expected. During this stage, which is called the orientation phase, the nurse and the client are getting to know one another and the client is mapping out areas that are of concern to him. At some point, the client will begin to repeat areas and will assume a high commitment configuration and/or postures of affiliation. This should indicate to the nurse that the individual is ready to discuss these areas in greater detail. This repetition also signals the beginning of the next step in the process of exploration: description and clarification. This step is also referred to as the working phase in a therapeutic relationship.

As the client observes and describes what he perceives of his experience, the nurse assists him in this description. The nurse encourages the client by saying, "Start at the beginning and tell me what happened" or "Tell me more about that." Occasionally the nurse might assist the person to clarify his thoughts by seeking to clarify his speech. We have all had the experience of being unable to put something into words until we have thought it out clearly in our heads. Therefore, when a client uses vague pronouns, speaking of "them," "they," "he," "she," or "it," the nurse needs to seek clarification. The nurse may ask, "Who is 'she'?" or "Who are you referring to when you speak about 'all of them'?"

> Mr. Graph, a 62-year-old man, had been admitted to the hospital after slipping in the bathtub and fracturing his leg. Following surgery to reduce the fracture, Mr. Graph was resting in his hospital bed. When his meal was served, he became very upset. He could not eat because he did not have his dentures. Repeatedly he ranted, "How do you expect me to eat when they took my teeth?" Nurses and aides hastily looked through his bedside stand and in his closet but found no dentures. Yet the hospital record indicated that he had been wearing dentures when he was admitted. The staff activity seemed only to further aggravate Mr. Graph. He continued to rant, "They took my teeth." Finally a nurse asked, "Mr. Graph, *who* took your teeth?" Mr. Graph answered, "My daughter and son-in-law took my teeth home with them. They were afraid they'd get lost or broken if left here. Now how am I going to eat?" Once the situation was clarified, a phone call was made to the daughter, and she brought Mr. Graph's dentures to him. The problem had been resolved.

Occasionally during the process of exploration, a nurse may have to provide information to compensate for some lack in a client's ability to perceive or to correct a client's tendency to subjectively and selectively perceive and interpret an experience. For example, a nurse might give concise instructions to a person experiencing moderate to severe anxiety or might try to help a client perceive an experience more objectively by expressing doubt as to the reality of his perceptions and asking, "Isn't that a bit unusual?" However, a nurse must be careful to word such an expression so that it does not threaten the client, increase his anxiety, and further distort his perception of reality.

Once a client has described and clarified an experience, he is ready to progress to the next step of exploration. It is at this point that the nurse and client *together* look at the data. They try to place events in sequence, to determine in what way the experience is similar to or different from other events, and to evaluate the impact of the experience on the individual. In helping a client explore the experience, a nurse might inquire, "What happened first?" or "In what way was this the same as (or different from) . . .?"

> A 70-year-old woman, Mrs. Rich, had just completed the first week in a home for the aged. She appeared lonely and explained, "I feel so alone and afraid. I don't know anyone here. I have no one to talk to. I've never been in a place like this before. I've never even been in a hospital. I had all my children at home." A nurse inquired, "Was there ever a time in your life that you had some of these same feelings?"
>
> Mrs. Rich thought a while and said, "Yes, when I was first married. My husband brought me to this small town where he had found work. I didn't know a soul, and all my family lived miles away. I felt so alone—I thought I'd never feel like I belonged. I'd go for long walks, and before long I'd begin to see some of the same faces. I'd sort of smile, and they'd smile, and before you'd know it we would be talking."

The nurse had assisted Mrs. Rich to find similarities between the present experience of loneliness and a past experience.

Once nurse and client have sifted through the data, putting events in sequence and establishing similarities to and differences from other experiences, the client is ready to draw conclusions and to formulate the meaning of the experience. The nurse assists the client in this process by facilitating summarization or by suggesting a tentative conclusion. The nurse might say, "Then what you are saying is . . ." or "What do you conclude from all this?" or "It sounds like what you're saying is . . . . Does that sound right to you?" In the case of Mrs. Rich, once she had made the comparison between her experience as a bride and her present experience in the nursing home, the nurse would be able to ask, "Might you be able to handle this new experience in a similar way?" Ideally, Mrs. Rich would state that it might be possible and would agree to give it some thought.

Now the client is ready to decide whether events should be allowed to progress as they have been or whether new behavior is needed to better cope with the experience. The nurse might inquire, "The next time this happens, what might you do?" By asking a client to consider what behavior might be more appropriate in the future, the nurse encourages the client to formulate a plan of action. In the example of Mrs. Rich, once she had recognized similarities between her past and present experiences, the nurse would be able to help Mrs. Rich deal with the situation. Mrs. Rich might decide that since, in the past, taking long walks had helped to familiarize her with her new neighbors, she might start strolling around the nursing home and into scheduled activites.

"Perhaps," Mrs. Rich stated, "taking walks will help me get to know people." The nurse agreed that this plan was worth a try and suggested that they evaluate the results after a week. At the end of the week, Mrs. Rich proudly reported that she had made one "pretty nice friend" and that several other people were stopping and chatting with her.

Thus a nurse helps a client plan a course of action, supports the client while he is trying out the plan, and assists him in evaluating how effectively the plan has helped him cope with the situation. Should the evaluation show the new behavior to be ineffective, nurse and client need to identify the reasons why it does not work and to develop a new course of action.

Guidelines for promoting therapeutic interaction

Establishing and maintaining a therapeutic relationship requires thoughtful assessment and intervention. It is not uncommon for a student or beginning practitioner to be fearful of "prying" or "saying the wrong thing." All too often, principles and techniques of interacting abound with "don'ts." *Don't* pry! *Don't* ask questions merely to satisfy your own curiosity! *Don't* give out personal information! *Don't* push for too much too soon! Certainly, such "don't's" are important to keep in mind, but a therapeutic relationship should not be based solely on them. There are also a great many "do's." During an interaction it is just as important, if not more important, to be mindful of these positive guidelines. In fact, if nurses can focus on such positive parameters, they may find that they are less hesitant, better able to establish therapeutic relationships, and more confident in establishing them.

The following are some important "do's" of therapeutic communication.

1. *Do* select a quiet, private area in which to hold interactions. Imagine how it may feel to discuss personal feelings and problems within hearing range of others or in a place subject to frequent intrusion.

2. *Do* provide for comfortable seating arrangements. Standing is not conducive to in-depth interaction. People cannot stand for too long in one place without becoming tired and restless. Also, sitting on a bed in a client's room is neither comfortable nor conducive to therapeutic interaction. The nurse should be seated in a chair. This enables the nurse to see the client without staring at him and without blocking his avenue of egress. It is often a good idea to sit down first and let the client arrange his chair so that he feels comfortable with the seating arrangement. Remember that staring may heighten anxiety. A client is already carrying around enough anxiety. The interview situation should not add to it.

3. *Do* provide an avenue of egress. An already anxious person frequently leaves the interview situation to get a cigarette or a drink of water. Whatever the reason given for a client's physical departure from the interview situation, leaving provides him with an opportunity to gain both physical and emotional distance from what he might perceive as a stressful situation. Keep in mind that by providing an area of "escape" the nurse is also providing an area of reentry. If he does not have to climb over people and furniture, a client is much more likely to return to an interview.

4. *Do* be aware that behavior usually satisfies several needs at the same time. For example, bragging serves to build the braggart's self-esteem, but, by making others feel insecure, it may also serve to manipulate and control people. Eating is another example of multipurposeful behavior. When a person eats during a time of stress—for example, exam week—he may be meeting not only a physiological need but also a psychosocial need. Food symbolizes love and security. From infancy on, many people associate being fed with being cared for. Everyone has his own special "security" food. For some, it is chocolate; for others, warm milk or some other goody. While eating such food, a person gains a sense of security and well-being.

5. *Do* keep in mind that when a person is trying to satisfy a need that is of primary importance to him, he may either ignore or fail to recognize that other needs exist. Many public health nurses have encountered parents who must devote almost all of their time and energy to earning enough money to keep food on the table and a roof over their heads. As a result, these parents may give a lower priority than does the nurse to such preventive health measures as immunizations and annual physical examinations. This is an example of focusing on a felt primary need and ignoring other needs.

6. *Do* recognize that a person should be accepted as he is. To accept a person as he is means to recognize that he has strengths and weaknesses and positive and negative emotions. For instance, if a person is angry, allow him—even help him—to express his anger. Saying to him, "Calm down," "Be more rational," or "Put it all in the past and forget it" is not only fruitless but also ignores the reality and importance of his feelings.

7. *Do* allow a person to proceed at his own pace. The less threatened a person feels, the more quickly rapport can be established. The person will also be better able to look at his experience and to learn from it.

A student nurse had established a pattern of asking a client questions about her family. The student was "pushing" the client to talk about an area that was not of her own choosing. The client would tersely answer these questions and then fall silent. The student soon became frustrated because the client would not "open up." One day the student developed laryngitis. Student and client agreed they would spend the allotted time sitting together. The student would listen to whatever the client wanted to talk about. Much to the student's amazement, the client began to talk about the difficulties she had experienced on her last weekend pass home!

Once the pressure to talk about traumatic material was lifted, the client was able to discuss areas that were meaningful to her.

8. *Do* observe a client's behavior. Is he depressed? Elated? Apathetic? Does he appear alert? Confused? Hyperactive? Pay attention to a client's physical appearance. Is he appropriately dressed? Bizarrely dressed? Slovenly dressed? Does he hold himself in a sagging posture? Does he move rigidly? What is

his facial expression? Physical appearance reflects how people feel about themselves. Nurses may learn much about their clients' emotional states by observing behavior and physical appearance.

9. *Do* be consistent when interacting. Consistency facilitates the establishment of security, rapport, and trust in a relationship.

> A nurse and a client decided that between 4 PM and 5 PM each day they would talk over the events of the day and assess how the client had dealt with them. One day, the client was particularly talkative and continued talking beyond the agreed-upon limit. The nurse reminded the client of their agreement and helped the client summarize and terminate their conversation.

Thus the nurse was consistent in maintaining the boundaries of their relationship. To talk an hour one day, half an hour the next day, and perhaps 2 hours another day would create an ambience of uncertainty. The client might begin wondering: "What is expected of me? How long will the nurse stay with me today? How much time do I have to discuss my problems?" As such feelings of uncertainty grow, it is very likely that the client will question the nurse's reliability. Certainly, if a particular need arose, a nurse and a client might agree to extend their time together. By doing so, they would be acknowledging that the situation warranted an exception to their usual arrangement. By maintaining the boundaries of the relationship, consistency and trust are reinforced rather than undermined.

10. *Do* try to keep a client's anxiety to a minimum. High anxiety decreases one's ability to perceive, and learning is less likely to occur. The nurse needs to help the client decrease his anxiety. Altering the environment may have a therapeutic effect. By controlling the noise level and avoiding overcrowding, the nurse can make the environment less stressful. For instance, in a crowded unit, it is important to provide a quiet area. It is not uncommon in a psychiatric unit for a very anxious individual to request some time in a seclusion room. The individual recognizes that by limiting external stimuli he may decrease his stress level. A nurse's being available so that an anxious client can verbalize his concerns may also help reduce anxiety. Finally, a nurse should remember that physical activity, such as gardening and participating in sports, serves to dissipate

anxious energy and to help an anxious individual feel more comfortable.

11. *Do* explain routines and procedures in terms that a person can understand. A nurse needs to assess a person's level of anxiety and level of understanding, evaluate the influence of the person's past experiences and explain technical terminology. For example, when a nurse is establishing a therapeutic relationship, a client's past experiences with psychotherapy may have a great influence on his present experience. If a client has participated in a relationship in which a nurse pushed him to discuss material with which he was not yet ready to deal, he may be reluctant to enter into a new therapeutic relationship. In addition, if a nurse orients a client to the purpose of a therapeutic relationship by saying, "We are entering into a one-to-one relationship, and you can discuss your problems during these interviews," the client may hesitate to talk with the nurse for several reasons. He may not understand what is meant by a "one-to-one relationship." He may associate the word "interview" with probing questions. He may be frightened by the focus on "problems." He may feel that he does not have enough "problems" to fill up the "interview" time. When a nurse explains that during an interaction a client may discuss anything that is of interest or concern in his daily life, the nurse is using vocabulary that is more understandable and less threatening.

12. *Do* offer your client realistic reassurance. To give false reassurance or to reassure a client before a situation has been explored blocks communication. For example, to reassure a crying person that everything will be "all right" before you know why he is crying cuts off communication. To tell someone who has had mutilating surgery "Things will look brighter once you get out of the hospital" denies that there will be difficult times ahead. By acknowledging that there will be some difficult times but that rehabilitation and psychotherapy will help with readjustment, a nurse offers realistic reassurance. The nurse is providing the person with an opportunity to explore his concerns and is also pointing out treatment modalities that will assist him in dealing with the stress caused by his situation.

13. *Do* remember that there is always potential for growth. There are no "hopeless," "hard-core" individuals. People who do not show progress or seem resistant to therapy may not yet be

ready to change. Readiness to profit from therapy is not much different from readiness to learn how to walk or talk. A person must see a need for change before change can take place. Also, it is possible that the staff may need additional knowledge of therapeutic tools in order to help a client work through his difficulties. If client and nurse are ready and able to utilize an opportunity for therapy, there is potential for growth.

The process of therapeutic communication focuses on the client's experience. By helping a client to learn more appropriate and effective coping behavior, a nurse encourages him to move beyond mere tolerance of a stressful situation to understanding and profiting from it.

Barriers to the therapeutic process

Up to now we have concentrated on the unimpeded process of therapeutic communication. Therapeutic principles have functioned as a guide to effective interaction. However, the process does not necessarily progress from stage to stage without some difficulties being encountered. Difficulties may arise out of characteristics of the client, the nurse, or both. We will describe some of the most frequently encountered barriers to the therapeutic process. It is important to note that these barriers are not restricted to the therapeutic process; they may be found in any situation in which two or more people interact.

Egocentrism. Egocentrism is the attitude that one's own mode of living, values, and patterns of adaptation are superior to all others. This attitude is often accompanied by contempt for life styles that differ from one's own. Egocentrism tends to manifest itself in superior, proselytizing, moralizing, rejecting, hostile, or aggressive behavior.

When a nurse and a client have different values, especially if one or both are unaware of how strongly they are influenced by these values, conflict may result.

A public health nurse had been visiting the Smith household to assist Mrs. Smith in the care of her 72-year-old mother-in-law. The mother-in-law had suffered a stroke that had left her aphasic and that had paralyzed her right side. After several weeks, Mrs. Smith confided to the nurse that she found it very time consuming and fatiguing to take care of her mother-in-law. Mrs. Smith said, "My primary responsibility is to my husband and children, and now I feel like I have no time or energy left for them." She feared that the strain was also being reflected in her children. She pointed out that her 5-year-old son had begun bedwetting and that her 8-year-old daughter, complaining of stomach aches, had seen the school nurse three times in the past 2 weeks. Mrs. Smith said that she and her husband were considering placing her mother-in-law in a nursing home.

The public health nurse had strong feelings about the duty of children to care for their aged parents. In fact, he came from a family background that regarded it as disgraceful to place parents in a nursing home. He responded to Mrs. Smith, "Oh, that would be such a shame. I'm sure you'll be able to manage once you get a routine. After all, you have to remember that you're setting an example for your children. The way you treat your mother-in-law is probably the way your children will treat you when you're older."

The public health nurse inadvertently was imposing his values on the client.

Sometimes it is the client's values and attitudes that function as a barrier to therapeutic interaction.

Marcia Henderson, 22 years old, went to a neighborhood mental health center for counseling. Ms. Henderson complained of feeling "tired and sad." She added that she cried easily and had no appetite. During a subsequent session, Ms. Henderson asked the nurse, "What is your religion?" The nurse responded, "Catholic. Why do you ask?" Ms. Henderson replied, "Oh, no reason, I'm just nosey I guess." At the following session, Ms. Henderson requested another nurse, explaining, "I'm living with a man whom I have no intentions of marrying. I can't talk about this to someone who's Catholic. I don't want any moralizing at my expense."

The client's values and attitudes led her to assume that the nurse would pass judgment on her. The client erected a barrier to the therapeutic process and terminated the relationship.

Thus problems may arise when a nurse and a client have different value systems. Conflict is especially apt to result when participants are unaware of the influence their values exert on them. Even the most self-aware people have values that operate outside their full awareness. Only as nurse and client become more aware of the values that influence their thoughts and feelings can they being to free themselves from subjectivity and to accept that another person's value system can be adaptive. (See Chapters 2 and 3 for discussion of attitudes.) Egocentrism then ceases to exist as a barrier to effective communication, and nurse and client can begin to set mutually agreed-upon goals.

Denial. Denial is the unconscious evasion or negation of objective reality. Denial functions to reduce anxiety, to stabilize and define relationships, and to retain or regain a sense of autonomy.

When either a nurse or a client uses denial, a barrier to the therapeutic process is erected. Eventually, the nondenying participant becomes bored, frustrated, or angry with the other's systematic avoidance of certain topics and may respond either by ignoring the pattern of denial or by confronting the use of denial. Ignoring the pattern of denial serves to reinforce its use. Confronting denial too early or too severely almost certainly will threaten the denying individual, provoke anger in him, and cause him to try to cope with reality by further reliance on denial. The therapeutic process then becomes characterized by anxiety.

> A student nurse, Marty Hendricks, was working with Julie, a verbally and physically abusive adolescent girl. Without any observable warning, Julie would suddenly lash out at people. Only recently, she had severely scratched her psychiatrist's face.
> During supervisory conferences, Marty consistently assured his instructor that he felt comfortable in Julie's presence, that he trusted Julie, and that he did not think Julie would strike out at him. The more his instructor questioned him about his feelings, the more adamantly he asserted that he was unafraid. The instructor believed that Marty was denying reality and decided to stop challenging his description of his feelings and instead to be increasingly supportive of him during this experience. As Marty began to feel more comfortable with his instructor and less threatened by possible recriminations from her, he began to talk about how he felt "uneasy" with Julie.

Thus, challenging a person's use of denial can cause him to feel threatened and to rely increasingly on denial in order to cope with reality. When attempts are made to alleviate the anxiety underlying denial, the need to use denial usually decreases.

Resistance. Resistance is conscious or unconscious reluctance to bring repressed ideas, thoughts, desires, or memories into awareness. By preventing the entry of such threatening material into consciousness, resistance functions to maintain an individual's security or self-esteem.

Therapeutic intervention involves helping a client explore experiences that are of concern to him. If a client is trying to avoid material that threatens his self system, attempts to help him verbalize his feelings, evaluate his patterns of behavior, or examine his interpersonal relationships may be met by resistance. Should a nurse fail to recognize a client's use of resistance and try to force him to talk about a painful area from which he feels a need to retreat, the nurse may only succeed in increasing the client's anxiety.

Peter Mulally had been experiencing auditory hallucinations. The nurse assigned to work with Peter noticed that whenever she questioned him about the content of these hallucinations, he would change the subject. The nurse became very impatient with his behavior and began pressuring him to talk about the hallucinations, explaining, "I can't help you unless I know what's troubling you." Peter began rocking back and forth in his chair. Instead of changing the subject, he got up and walked away.

Resistive behavior, then, can escalate when a nurse does not recognize that resistance is being used to avoid extremely anxiety-producing material. Had the nurse allowed the client to retreat from the areas that were painful to him, the client's anxiety might have decreased rather than increased. At the same time, the nurse would have contributed to an atmosphere of trust. The client might eventually have felt free to explore threatening material without fearing loss of security or self-esteem.

The use of resistance is not restricted to clients. Sometimes nurses use resistance.

Joan Bellows, a student nurse, was consistently absent the last day of each clinical experience. During her community mental health experience, her instructor pointed this pattern out to her. Joan responded, "I'm coming down with a cold and don't want to talk about it right now." The instructor said, "Maybe you'll feel like discussing it some other time."

As the day for terminating with her client approached, Joan's instructor again pointed out her habit of being absent on the last day of each clinical experience. Joan explained, "One time I was sick. Another time I had car trouble—and the last time the alarm clock didn't ring and I overslept." The instructor replied, "Sometimes good-byes are difficult to say."

The next time Joan and her instructor discussed Joan's plans for termination with her client, Joan began to cry. She explained that she never could say good-bye to anyone and would do anything to avoid good-byes. She was ready to talk about an area that up to then had been too painful to explore.

Given an accepting relationship, an individual can be helped to deal with previously resisted material. By gradually calling an individual's attention to his resistive behavior and slowly and nonjudgmentally exploring or pointing out possible reasons for the behavior, a nurse can resolve resistance. The individual can then begin to deal with the threatening material. It is important to remember that since resistance is a mechanism used to maintain security and self-esteem, attempts should not be made to pointedly confront the person using resistance or to argue the person out of resistance.

• • •

Characteristics of the client, of the nurse, or of both may set up barriers to the therapeutic process. Egocentrism, denial, and resistance are three frequently encountered barriers. However, they need not be insurmountable. If they are recognized and understood, steps can be taken toward resolution of the difficulties and reestablishment of the therapeutic process.

Listening is essential for effective communication. Listening requires moving beyond the words used in order to hear the meaning or messages (themes) being conveyed. In the process of therapeutic communication the focus is on the client's experience as he perceives it. Client and nurse become actively involved in moving beyond mere tolerance of the experience and toward an increased understanding of the situation and a plan for developing appropriate and effective coping behavior. During this exploration, some barriers to the therapeutic process may arise. Once these barriers have been understood, they can be surmounted and the therapeutic process can be reestablished.

CHAPTER SUMMARY

People from different cultures not only speak different languages but also inhabit different sensory worlds. Selective screening of sensory data admits some information and filters out other information. An experience that is perceived through one set of culturally patterned sensory screens is quite different from the same experience perceived through another set. An encounter or interaction is one type of experience. When two interacting cultural groups use dissimilar verbal, kinesic, or proxemic cues, assumptions, and orientations, misunderstandings may occur and role relationships may be disrupted. A sense of nonrelatedness to the members of the other cultural group may develop. Culturally determined and acceptable behavior that is different from that of a dominant culture may be mistaken for pathological or deviant behavior.

Therapeutic communication involves more than learning a body of interviewing skills. It involves understanding the process of communication and the influence of culturally determined communication cues and meanings. With this knowledge, barriers to effective communication may be avoided and therapeutic communication may be promoted.

REFERENCES

Ashcraft, Norman, and Albert Scheflen
1976 People Space: The Making and Breaking of Human Boundaries. New York: Anchor Press.

Bateson, Gregory
1955 "The message, "This is play." In Group Processes. B. Schaffner (ed.). Madison, N.J.: Madison Printing Co.

Birdwhistle, Ray
1952 Introduction to Kinesics. Louisville, Ky.: University of Louisville Press.
1963 Some Relationships Between American Kinesics and Spoken American English. Section H-AAAS.
1970 Kinesics and Context. Philadelphia: University of Pennsylvania Press.
1972 "A kinesic-linguistic exercise: the cigarette scene." In Directions in Sociolinguistics: The Ethnography of Communication. John J. Gumperz and Dell Hymes (eds.). New York: Holt, Rinehart & Winston, pp. 381-404.

Calhoun, John B.
1962 "Population density and social pathology." Scientific American 206:139-146.

Christian, John J.
1960 "Factors in mass mortality of a herd of sika deer (Cervus Nippon)." Chesapeake Science 1:79-95.

Efron, D.
1942 Gesture and Environment. New York: King's Crown Press.

Ervin-Tripp, Susan M.
1977 "Language and thought." In Horizons of Anthropology. Sol Tax and Leslie G. Freeman (eds.). Chicago: Aldine Publishing Co.

Gesell, Arnold, and Catherine Amatura
1946 The Embryology of Behavior. New York: Harper & Row, Publishers, Inc.

Goodall, Jane
1967 The Wild Chimpanzee. Washington, D.C.: National Geographic Society.

Hall, Edward T.
1966 The Hidden Dimension. Garden City, N.Y.: Doubleday & Co., Inc.

Hediger, Heini
1950 Wild Animals in Captivity. London: Butterworth and Co.
1955 Studies of the Psychology and Behavior of Captive Animals in Zoos and Circuses. London: Butterworth and Co.

1961 "The evolution of territorial behavior." In Social Life of Early Man. S. L. Washington (ed.). New York: Viking Fund Publications in Anthropology, no. 31.

Lee, Dorothy
1959 Freedom and Culture. Englewood Cliffs, N.J.: Prentice-Hall, Inc.

Lorenz, Konrad
1966 On Aggression. M. Wilson (Trans.). New York: Harcourt, Brace & World, Inc.

McBride, Glen
1964 A General Theory of Social Organization and Behavior. St. Lucia, Australia: University of Queensland Press.

Mehrabian, Albert
1969 "Significance of posture and position in the communication of attitudes and status relationships." Psychological Bulletin 71(5):359-372.
1972 Nonverbal Communication. Chicago: Aldine-Atherton.

Peplau, Hildegard
1953 "Themes in nursing situations." American Journal of Nursing 53:1221, 1343.
1954 "Utilizing themes in nursing situations." American Journal of Nursing 54:325.

Ruesch, Jurgen, and Gregory Bateson
1968 Communication, The Matrix of Psychiatry. New York: W. W. Norton & Co., Inc.

Reusch, Jurgen, and Weldon Kees
1969 Nonverbal Communication. Berkeley: University of California Press.

Sayre, Joan
1978 "Common errors in communication made by students in psychiatric nursing." Perspectives in Psychiatric Care 4:175-183.

Scheflen, Albert E.
1965 "Quasi-courtship behavior in psychotherapy." Psychiatry: Journal For Study of Interpersonal Processes 28:245-257.
1972 Body Language and Social Order: Communication as Behavioral Control. Englewood Cliffs, N.J.: Prentice-Hall, Inc.

Scheflen, Albert E., and Norman Ashcraft
1976 Human Territories: How We Behave in Space-Time. Englewood Cliffs, N.J.: Prentice-Hall, Inc.

Ujhely, Gertrud
1968 Determinants of the Nurse-Patient Relationship. New York: Springer Publishing Co., Inc.

Whorf, Benjamin Lee
  1956 "Language, thought and reality." In Selected Readings of Benjamin Lee Whorf. J. B. Carroll (ed.). New York: John Wiley and Sons, Inc.

ANNOTATED SUGGESTED READINGS

Ruesch, Jurgen, and Gregory Bateson
  1968 Communication, The Social Matrix Of Psychiatry. New York: W. W. Norton & Co., Inc.
  Ruesch and Bateson develop a theory of human communication that includes social context, networks (intrapersonal, interpersonal, group, and cultural), technical characteristics (coding and informational state), interaction, and self-correction. Communication is viewed as a system, and the interrelationship between communication, mental illness, and psychiatric intervention is discussed.

Sayre, Joan
  1978 "Common errors in communication made by students in psychiatric nursing." Perspectives in Psychiatric Care 4:175-183.
  Sayre discusses errors in communication that are frequently made by students and that impede therapeutic intervention. The author takes a chronological approach, identifying communication errors that may occur in the orientation, working, and termination stages of a relationship. Verbatim transcripts of student-client interaction exemplify the communication errors being discussed.

Scheflen, Albert E.
  1972 Body Language and Social Order. Englewood Cliffs, N.J.: Prentice-Hall, Inc.
  Scheflen examines kinesic behavior within the contexts of verbal communication, group processes, ethnicity, and social order. The book is divided into four sections: the fundamentals of kinesics, the regulatory nature of kinesics, communication in institutional and political control, and communication in the creation of deviance. Photographs and used to illustrate examples of kinesic behavior.

Scheflen, Albert E., and Norman Ashcraft
  1976 Human Territories: How We Behave in Space-Time. Englewood Cliffs, N.J.: Prentice-Hall, Inc.
  The authors explore human territoriality within a context of space-time and show how territorial behavior is integrated into ever enlarging contextual units. The book is divided into five parts: territories of orientation, formations and sites, built territories, use of territorial forms, and territorial disturbance. A photogrpahic format is used to illustrate the dimensions of human territoriality.

FURTHER READINGS

Boucher, Michael L.
  1971 "Personal space and chronicity in the mental hospital." Perspectives in Psychiatric Care 9:206-210.
Condon, W. W., and W. D. Osgood
  1966 "Sound-film analyses of normal and pathological behavior patterns." Journal of Nervous and Mental Disorders 143:338-347.
Ekman, Paul, and Wallace Friesen
  1972 "Constants across cultures in the face and emotion." Journal of Personality and Social Psychology 17:124-129.
Ekman, Paul, et al.
  1969 "Pancultural elements in facial displays of emotion." Science 164:86-88.
Gerber, Claudia B., and Deanne F. Snyder
  1970 "Language and thought." Perspectives in Psychiatric Care 8:230-237.
Newman, O.
  1972 Defensible Space. New York: Macmillan, Inc.
Roberts, Sharon L.
  1969 "Territoriality: space and the schizophrenic patient." Perspectives in Psychiatric Care 7:28-33.
Sarles, Harvey B.
  1970 "Communication and ethology." In Anthropology and the Behavioral and Health Sciences. Otto von Mering and Leonard Kasdan (eds.). Pittsburgh: University of Pittsburgh Press.
Scheflen, Albert E.
  1963 "Communication and regulation in psychotherapy." Psychiatry 26:126.
  1964 "The significance of posture in communication systems." Psychiatry 27:316-331.

6
THE MATRIX
OF PSYCHOSOCIAL
INTERVENTION

CHAPTER
FOCUS

In addition to individual-relationship therapy, the nurse who works in a psychiatric setting is usually involved in other forms of psychosocial intervention. Important elements of treatment include milieu therapy, group therapy, family therapy, and special activity therapies such as art therapy and psychodrama. In working as a cooperative member of an interdisciplinary team, a nurse will find that his or her functions and responsibilities overlap or even duplicate those of other team members. Because of the nature of nursing education and clinical nursing experience, nurses bring some unique attributes and abilities to team participation. Health teaching from a holistic point of view is a prime example. In psychiatric settings the natural tendency is to focus on psychosocial problems. But a human being is also a biological organism. The nurse, with knowledge of physiology, psychology, sociology, nutrition, pharmacology, and health in general, can be the catalyst that helps the team members to approach the client as a whole person. A nurse is also the one professional member of the team who is in a unique position as far as milieu therapy is concerned. Nurses are the only professionals who are always present in the milieu—24 hours a day, 7 days a week. Indeed, maintenance of the therapeutic milieu is the responsibility of the nurse. Thus, the nurse is able to be instrumental in managing the milieu in a way that facilitates a consistent progression in the psychosocial growth of the client.

6

THE MATRIX OF PSYCHOSOCIAL INTERVENTION

THERAPEUTIC COMMUNITY OR MILIEU THERAPY
History and description

"Milieu" is the French word for "middle" or "middle place"; in English we use it to mean "environment."

Milieu therapy implies utilization of the *whole environment* as a therapeutic agent—hence Maxwell Jones' term "the therapeutic community."

A useful definition of milieu therapy is "scientific manipulation of the environment aimed at providing changes in the personality of the patient" (Cumming and Cumming, 1962, p. 5).

The concept of therapeutic community, or milieu, therapy is a spin-off of Maxwell Jones' (1953) work in Britain. Jones, a Scottish psychiatrist who has also done a great deal of work in America, developed a treatment modality that uses the environment—its physical facilities, various therapies, and interpersonal relationships—to foster a healthy personality. A therapeutic community is a protective setting. It provides relationships that will help its residents learn more effective and more socially acceptable means of coping. The therapeutic community becomes a microcosm of society. The individual is made to look at how he interacts and functions in this small and specially structured segment of society. Individuals who are acting out their inner conflicts are confronted by the entire community with their hostility, alienation, manipulation, insensitivity, lack of responsibility, and poor judgment.

A therapeutic community is characterized by a team approach. Residents are part of the team and share in the responsibility and the process of decision-making. They are included in the planning and implementation of treatment approaches and in the evaluation and reevaluation of their effectiveness. All aspects of the therapeutic community are seen as presenting opportunities for residents to examine their behavior and, when indicated, to grow in the direction of more socially acceptable behavior. There are three phases to treatment in a therapeutic community:

1. Adjustment to the setting
2. Observation, examination, and discussion (often confrontation) of adaptive and maladaptive responses (socially acceptable and unacceptable behavior)
3. Development of new, socially acceptable patterns of coping and communicating

Residents are included in all phases of treatment (both planning and implementation). Many different types of therapy may be used to facilitate change in behavior: encounter therapy, sociodrama, recreational and work activities, educational therapy, and community government.

Community government is an outstanding characteristic of a therapeutic community. Jones (1953) and Cumming and Cumming (1962) view community government as a primary means of implementing the goals of milieu therapy. Meetings are used to inculcate the social standards, values, and behavior that have never been internalized by acting-out individuals. Community government provides opportunities to explore behavior, try out new roles, make decisions, and engage in problem solving. In the process, group identification is fostered.

Late one afternoon, Jean was admitted to a therapeutic community that worked with drug abusers. After a brief orientation to the house in which the community members lived, Jean was introduced to the residents and staff. Then she was shown to the room that she would share with two other girls. Jean settled in, had dinner, and then attended a group "sing." Residents played guitars, sang, and generally had fun. After the sing, Jean was *told* to help others clean up. She was directed, rather than asked, to take some responsibility for the evening's recreation. After helping with the clean-up she went to bed.

At 6 o'clock the following morning, a bell rang. The residents got up and busied themselves with washing, dressing, and straightening their rooms. During orientation Jean had been told that unless her section of the room passed morning inspection, she would not be able to join others at breakfast. Jean was hungry, so she quickly tidied up her dresser and made her bed. Then she went down to breakfast.

After breakfast, everyone attended a community government meeting. The "president" presided. He led a discussion of jobs that needed to be done in the house, activities that had to be planned, and problems that had arisen. Then he read a list of names of people who had been repeatedly ignoring rules. Each person was permitted to speak in his own defense. However, if he attempted to rationalize or manipulate he was "blown away." This means that in front of the entire group one of the several staff members who had formerly been addicts would verbally attack the offender's behavior. Then the community would decide how to handle the situation. It is important to emphasize that the person's *behavior*, not the person himself, was attacked. Next, the president read the names of those residents whose behavior had improved and who were eligible for privileges. The entire group, including the person under consideration, decided whether privileges had been earned. Then work assignments were made. The community's house was run entirely by the staff *and* the residents. Community members were assigned to groups for cooking, doing laundry, shopping, and housekeeping. Jean was assigned to the housekeeping group.

Thus the residents are fully involved in every aspect of life in a therapeutic community. From the very first, Jean was included in the routine and incorporated into the process of community socialization.

According to one writer (Abroms, 1969), the goals of milieu therapy are the same as those of any other form of psychiatric care: to *set limits* on symptomatic behavior and to foster the learning of some basic *psychosocial skills*.

Psychosocial skills

Abroms has organized the teaching of psychosocial skills into four broad categories: orientation, self-assertion, occupational activities, and recreational activities.

Orientation can be as basic as the adjustment to time, place, and person that is necessary for a confused person. It can be as general or as extensive as the fostering of an understanding of the workings of an institution's social system, which would be appropriate to a tertiary-care, transitional-service setting.

Self-assertion implies the learning or relearning of direct, self-regulated ways of expressing feelings or attitudes—for example, learning to "talk it out" in the encounter groups of a therapeutic milieu for drug abusers. The adoption of such socially accepted behavior is evidence of growth from a stage in which chemical substances were used to avoid the pain of interpersonal relationships.

Occupational activities can include the learning of basic skills for managing one's life, such as the ability to adhere to a schedule. These activities may also include formal occupational or vocational counseling, training, and placement.

Recreational activities are important to help clients develop the ability to engage in various leisure pursuits, to enjoy them, and to cooperate with others in enjoying them. The development of such ability helps to increase a client's self-confidence and self-esteem.

Setting limits

In discussing the types of behavior that necessitate the setting of limits, Abroms describes "five Ds" of pathology and lists them in order of decreasing severity:

Destructiveness—suicide, homicide, and other forms of behavior that harm persons or property

Disorganization—for example, the autistic and bizarre behavior and thinking of an acutely psychotic person

Deviancy—for example, acting-out behavior, illegal activities, and rule breaking

Dysphoria—for example, depression, hypochondriasis, schizoid detachment, elation, obsessions, and phobias

Dependency—avoiding responsibility for one's own feelings, thoughts, and actions

Physical structure of a therapeutic milieu

Structure and physical surroundings are important in enhancing therapy—ideal hospitals and units are set up in such a way as to provide a homelike, attractively decorated setting for the clients. Nursing stations are open and accessible and are not "cages" where staff members can retreat and withdraw from clients. The change from uniforms to street clothes for staff members has been part of an attempt to minimize interpersonal barriers between staff and clients, and the present-day architecture of psychiatric settings has the same purpose. Furniture is arranged to promote increased socialization among clients. Fortunately, the large, barren day room with chairs rigidly placed against the wall has, for the most part, disappeared. Safety is considered without the obvious accoutrements of an old-style "asylum." For example, instead of barred windows, the newer facilities use a special break-proof glass in a tamper-proof window. Rooms are designed with the goal of maximum utility. Pleasant day rooms convert from sitting rooms to dining rooms to recreation rooms to group therapy rooms. Often the clients' bedrooms are designed to look more like comfortable and attractive motel rooms than hospital "sick rooms." Children's psychiatric facilities are designed in family-type arrangements—units are set up to resemble a home living situation as closely as possible, with a central living room, a kitchen, several bedrooms, and an outside yard.

Program of a therapeutic milieu

Several important elements may be, and usually are, integral parts of the program of a therapeutic milieu:

1. Some form of *self-government*. Self-government can be accomplished in the form of structured meetings such as client-staff meetings, large community meetings, and clients' business meetings. An expectation in many facilities is that patients or residents will have some input into all of the unit activities. Some enlightened units expect clients to participate in team decisions about their fellow resi-

dents, around such issues as weekend passes, discharges, and changes in status while in the hospital. Meetings may provide a healthy, open forum for the discussion of everyday living problems in the unit. For example, at a meeting in one facility, the staff members' habit of not knocking before entering clients' rooms during the daytime hours was brought up by some of the annoyed clients. Feelings were expressed, ideas were exchanged, and clients and staff were able to work through a potentially milieu-destructive situation in a growth-enhancing manner.

2. *Graded responsibility.* Treatment plans often reflect the principle of allowing the client to proceed at his own pace. Graded responsibility is a system that can demonstrate to the client his own progress in a very real way as he passes through "levels," "groups," or other structures for conveying status. This system also allows a reduction in responsibility for the client who needs a situation in which he can temporarily regress. For example, he may need a "quiet room" in which he can be isolated whenever he feels the need for fewer stimuli. A quiet room, if it is to be a therapeutic experience, must be used by staff and clients in a way that is protective of self-esteem and that does not imply any sort of punishment by the staff. Nor should it provide clients with a means of avoiding responsibility. Some units have "open charting" systems wherein clients may read their own charts at any time—the belief is that this practice fosters trust in the staff and the expectation of responsibility for oneself.

3. Programs that provide *sufficient stimulation and activity.* To prevent unnecessary, nontherapeutic regression, most units or hospitals have recreational and occupational therapy situations and some means of maintaining the clients' link between hospital and community.

4. *Individualization of treatment.* Overall rules and regulations are necessary to run any sort of community. However, since the treatment needs of clients vary, the focus is on maximum individualization of treatment.

5. An *optimistic philosophy.* The philosophy of one therapeutic milieu may differ somewhat from that of another milieu, depending on the client population each serves. The needs of acutely psychotic or confused clients differ from the needs of acting-out, sociopathic individuals. Certainly, the needs of adolescents differ from those of a geriatric population. Maxwell Jones did his original work with sociopathic individuals, but the basic principles can apply to several

settings. One part of any milieu's philosophy, however, remains crucial: there needs to be *an air of optimism about the prognosis for mental disorders*. This is necessary for clients *and* staff.

6. An *adequate communication system for staff*. It is to be hoped that optimum communication will help resolve conflicts among personnel and prevent any harmful projection onto the clients. Staff members need to feel secure in their positions, and they need to obtain job satisfaction. A staff member who feels good about himself and about his job is a much more effective therapeutic agent than one who does not have these feelings. Adequate communication among staff members regarding the problems, progress, and daily activities of clients is likewise important. The *confidentiality* principle that operates within a therapeutic milieu is *not* one of confidentiality between client and single therapist. This type of confidentiality is not compatible with the fact that each staff member must be an actively involved member of the therapeutic team. Complete and full communication among staff members is crucial to a program's success. The client must be assured that no personal information will leave the unit. However, since observation of clients' behavior is an important and valuable part of milieu therapy, the results of observation need to be shared with all staff members for maximum benefit to the client. Such information can be used effectively to modify treatment plans, and it can also help dilute possible distortions resulting from negative countertransference situations (see p. 243). Some important ways of communicating among staff members include report meetings, weekly case conferences, and charting of observations.

Milieu therapy and the primary nursing model

Using primary nursing as the model for nursing care delivery is gaining in popularity throughout the United States. The model's popularity is, for the most part, well earned. This trend is bringing back the personal, involved, and professional aspects of nursing care in a variety of settings. It has been particularly effective in medical-surgical units of general hospitals. Psychiatric units probably are among the last of the holdouts against assimilation of the model into nursing practice.

The most obvious reason for the difficulties encountered in applying primary nursing in psychiatric units is a basic antagonism between the principles of milieu therapy and those of primary nursing. For example, milieu therapy necessitates a close, cooperative team effort in which *all* staff members work together to facilitate the growth and autonomy of the client. This effort makes possible flexible, fluctuating roles among workers. Primary nursing, however, is defined as "individualized, total patient care by the same care giver from the time of admission to discharge" (Smith, 1977). In the primary nursing model, assignment of staff members to clients may be done in an *arbitrary* manner. The staff of a therapeutic milieu, though, ideally includes persons of a variety of ages, ethnic groups, and professional disciplines and of both sexes. Such a staffing pattern is specified so that a client's relationship with the staff can vary according to his changing needs and abilities. The goal is to help the client increase his ability to relate to others by having him interact with several different people. Arbitrary assignment of staff members to clients can defeat this purpose. In addition, arbitrary assignment may fail to adequately address the problems of countertransference (see p. 243) in workers who should not be expected to work equally well in an intensive relationship with all clients.

Primary nursing also implies an *exclusive* staff-client assignment. This exclusivity can be a problem within the therapeutic milieu because it may lead to excessive dependency on one staff member. Abroms (1969) has described excessive dependency as one of the "five Ds" that milieu therapy aims to decrease. Exclusive assignment of a client to one worker may erode staff responsibility for *all* clients. Such assignment may be interpreted by the client as meaning that he *must* wait for his staff member to be on duty before he seeks counseling.

Another problem with an unmodified primary nursing model superimposed on a therapeutic milieu is the word "primary" itself. In one unit where such a model was introduced, the term "primary therapist" was objected to by the admitting psychiatrist, who had been the clients' therapist for many years and who continued to view himself in that role. The term was changed to "primary nursing therapist," which created another problem, since other members of the interdisciplinary team (such as social workers and occupational and recreational therapists) legitimately objected to the designation. Perhaps a better choice would be "primary milieu therapist."

Primary nursing, as it is utilized in traditional medical-surgical settings, does not take into account the special needs and problems involved in the treatment of certain types of clients, such as one who is in the middle of an escalating and exhausting *manic* episode (see Chapter 11). The behavior of such a client is too demanding, too taxing of the coping abilities of any *one* staff member for a prolonged period of time. For the sake of both client and worker, the care of such a client needs to be shared. Caring for a chronically schizophrenic client is another example of a situation that can require the involvement of more than one staff member. Such involvement would help prevent devastating reactions to the inevitable interruptions in a therapeutic relationship, such as sickness, vacation, and termination of employment.

Primary nursing, as practiced in medical-surgical units, has had as one of its legitimate and laudable goals the assignment of personnel to clients on the basis of nursing care problems and the educational background of staff members. However, in many psychiatric units, the interdisciplinary team includes both staff members whose educational preparation is equivalent to that of baccalaureate nurses and staff members who have more complex educational and experiential backgrounds than the baccalaureate nurse.

Finally, some of the traditional nursing functions that require a *professional* nurse as a primary giver of care (such as the administration of medication and the administration and supervision of treatments) are, because of the nature of the disabilities of clients in psychiatric units, of secondary importance. Medication routines are fairly simple—intravenous infusions and complex monitoring procedures and machines are not usually used.

These are some of the problems inherent in attempts to simply transfer the primary nursing model to the psychiatric unit. There *are* benefits that primary care could provide for the psychiatric client who is hospitalized. For instance, the continuity of care from emergency room admission to discharge from the facility would certainly be enhanced. There might also be a built-in mechanism for avoiding the "woodwork client" phenomenon—the not-so-interesting client becoming lost in the shuffle. The phenomenon of the "problem client," whose taxing behavior elicits avoidance from staff, is another situation that might be prevented through primary nursing. Certainly, it has been reported that primary nursing can lead to increased job satisfaction. Psychiatric nursing, with its long tradition of therapy involving one-to-one relationships, seems expecially compatible with a primary nursing philosophy. The benefits may be as numerous as the problems in adapting the primary nursing model to milieu therapy. What is needed is a creative blending of the goals of primary nursing with the requirements for an effective and therapeutic milieu. *Primary care* that is flexible in its administration and not arbitrary in its assignment could be one aspect of the total milieu that enhances the effectiveness of treatment.

GROUP THERAPY

An aspect of milieu therapy that is already well established on psychiatric units is group therapy. Group therapy came into existence at the turn of the century when a Boston physician, Dr. Joseph H. Pratt, used it to enhance the medical treatment of tuberculosis patients by attempting to deal with their emotional problems. During and immediately after World War II, when there was a shortage of psychiatric personnel, group therapy was seen as an economical form of psychotherapy. Eventually, a body of theory developed surrounding group treatment, and it became quite evident that in addition to its economy advantages group therapy had other important advantages over individual therapy. These advantages include provision of a protective environment for trying out new patterns of behavior, opportunities for learning new patterns of behavior, the availability of a role model for interpersonal relating (the leader or leaders), and the opportunity for multiple transference situations within the group, which can lead to the development of greater insight.

One authority (Yalom, 1975) has delineated the *curative factors* that group treatment can offer:

1. *The instillation of hope.* A group member sees the progress of others in the group, and he feels that something is being done for him.
2. *Universality.* When a group member sees that others in the world share similar feelings or have similar problems, his anxiety is decreased.
3. *Imparting of information.* Information about interpersonal relating, developmental tasks and stages, medications and other somatic treatments, and the structure of the setting are only a few examples of information that may be given.
4. *Altruism.* The opportunity to support another group member or to help him increase his self-awareness gives the helping individual increased self-esteem. It also encourages a preoccupied individual to "come out of himself."
5. *Corrective recapitulation of the primary family group.* Multiple transference opportunities may help an individual in group treatment to develop insight into his background and its effects on his present relationships. (See page 228. The individual dis-

places and projects feelings and attitudes onto the therapist *and* onto other group members.)

6. *Imitative behavior.* The group leader, a recovering group member, or a group member who has already mastered a particular psychosocial skill or developmental task can be a valuable role model.

7. *Interpersonal learning.* The group offers many and varied opportunities for relating to other people on a here-and-now basis.

Approaches to group therapy

Group treatment may be based on any of the many schools of psychotherapy (Freudian, Sullivanian, transactional analysis, gestalt, Jungian, and so on), or it may be based on an eclectic viewpoint. Leadership style varies: it may be directive or nondirective, authoritarian or democratic, or laissez-faire.

As a general rule and for most group therapy situations, it is best for a leader to start out in a somewhat authoritarian role (authoritarian only in the sense that the leader gives the group its basic ground rules and perhaps states some goals for the group sessions). As the members begin to express trust and confidence in the leader, the leader gradually relinquishes this moderately authoritarian role by fostering interaction among the group members. The goal of the leader is to become a "facilitator," a "referee," a "consultant," or a "clarifier," or to assume any combination of these roles.

Carl Rogers (1971) has described several characteristics of an effective group leader.

1. The leader is a *facilitator* rather than a *director* of the therapeutic process; he works toward becoming a participant and toward being able to move comfortably back and forth between the stances of leader and participant.

2. The leader is responsive to *meaning* and *feelings*, which are more important than the details of *what* happened to the group member. However, it may be necessary to explore these details before he can get to the meaning.

3. The effective leader accepts the group where it is *now*. This implies an acceptance of the individual group member and his degree of participation. The group may not accept a particular member's degree of participation, but the leader must. Silence is acceptable if it is not unexpressed pain.

4. Sympathetic understanding of the individual member's intellectualizations and generalizations and the ability to select the self-referent meanings of these and respond to them are crucial.

5. The facilitating leader operates in terms of his own feelings but with a degree of caution. A leader who is *too* expressive *too* early in the group's evolution may be unaware of his own feelings, and he may be doing a kind of "acting-out" by expressing his feelings without adequate thought.

6. The leader should confront appropriately and provide constructive feedback without attacking a group member's defenses. The group leader should use his or her *own* feelings responsibly and therapeutically in confronting group members and providing them with feedback.

7. An effective leader is able to use self-disclosure in a manner that is tempered by professional conscience and that serves a therapeutic purpose.

8. An effective leader avoids excessive planning and group "gimmicks." He usually uses gimmicks only as a last resort, because they rarely work.

9. A leader who is successful at being therapeutic tends to avoid interpretive comments, which only serve to make group members self-conscious. Commenting on group process* *can* be helpful sometimes but should not be overdone.

The following are some techniques that are effective in group therapy.

1. Provide a safe, comfortable atmosphere. Generally, when people feel secure, they are able to participate more easily in self-disclosure. Putting group members "on the spot" and attempting to force self-disclosure are the actions of an inexperienced and misinformed group leader.

2. As a general rule, focus on the "here and now." While some discussion of past events can be helpful, an obsession with them may be a way of avoiding current problems in living. Berne (1967) has described this game played in group therapy situations as "archeology."

3. Use any transference situations, as they become evident, as

---

*Group *process* refers to everything that happens within a group—who talks to whom, who "pairs" with whom, who sits where, the tone of the group, who acts as "assistant therapist," the "norms" of the group, the degree of group cohesiveness, and so on. Group *content* simply refers to *what* is discussed.

learning and insight-development opportunities. Point out the *differences* between the transference object and the group member's significant other. The increasing ability to be aware of one's own distortions is a sign of improving mental health.

4. Whenever necessary, protect individual members from verbal abuse or from scapegoating. This is an *important* role of the leader, and it also enables the leader to act as a model for constructive communication and interpersonal relating.

5. Whenever appropriate, point out any change a group member has made. One group member in an inpatient unit, for example, was not able to tolerate sitting with her group for an entire session. But with encouragement she gradually became able to stay for the entire session and then even began to participate. Another group member, who was prone to using a good deal of circumstantiality, was able, after participation in the group, to control this behavior effectively. In both of these situations, positive reinforcement provided ego support and encouraged future growth.

6. Handle *monopolization*, *circumstantiality*, *hallucination*, or *disclosure of delusional material* in a manner that protects the self-esteem of the individual but that also sets limits on the behavior in order to protect the other group members. Other group members may feel threatened by psychotic behavior because they do not know how to respond to it, because they are afraid that they, too, may come to such a point, or both. Disclosure of delusional material is particularly threatening to other group members. Quite often, the delusional beliefs have *not* been totally accepted by the individual and thus are somewhat open to therapeutic intervention. Since there is usually this doubt on the part of the delusional client, it usually helps to connect the beliefs to real feelings—of fear, anxiety, anger, and so on. For example, a leader might say, "Sometimes when we get frightened or feel insecure, we become suspicious of other people." The next step is to avoid dwelling on or exploring the delusional material in the group session. These steps on the part of the leader can help decrease the anxiety within the group, which is partially the result of members not knowing how to respond to their fellow group member.

7. Develop the ability to intuitively recognize when a group member (particularly a new member) is "fragile." Chances are that

the member is indeed in a precarious mental and emotional state and should be approached in a gentle, supportive, and nonthreatening manner.

8. Use silence effectively, to encourage self-responsibility within the group. Silence should not be allowed to continue when it is nonproductive or when it becomes too threatening to the group members. A good rule of thumb is that usually the most anxious person in the group will break the silence—sometimes it is the leader.

9. Laughter and a moderate amount of joking can act as a safety valve and at times can contribute to group cohesiveness.

10. The "assistant therapist" in the group can be a useful phenomenon. A group member may assume this role; he is often extremely insightful and can provide valuable feedback and suggestions. The group leader should be able to use this help without allowing the assistant to completely avoid focusing attention on himself and his problems.

11. Role playing and role reversals can sometimes be useful in short, modified versions. They may help a member develop insight into the ways he relates to others.

12. The promotion of interaction among group members is one of the main goals. Some techniques include:
    a. Reflecting or rewording comments of individual group members
    b. Asking for group reaction to one member's statement
    c. Asking for individual reactions to a member's statement
    d. Pointing out any shared feelings within the group
    e. Amplifying an individual situation to include either some or all of the group members
    f. Summarizing at various points within the session and at the end (A. J. Smith, 1970)

13. Encourage the cohesiveness of the group. Group cohesiveness includes all of the factors, both evident and subtle, that interplay to encourage the group to "stick together." The following factors may enhance group cohesiveness:
    a. The ability of the members to be *interdependent*
    b. A uniformity of standards among group members concerning behavior, communication, goals, and so on
    c. A mutually supportive attitude
    d. An attitude of responsibility toward one another

e. An atmosphere that is protective and that enhances security and self-esteem

The following factors may contribute to group dissolution:

a. Frequent absenteeism of members or leader
b. Loss of a leader
c. Addition of new members without adequate preparation
d. Cancelled meetings
e. Structural changes—time, day, size of group
f. Subgrouping, pairing, or polarization

Phases of a group

As in individual treatment, there are phases to the life and natural history of a group. Most ongoing groups will proceed from the *orientation phase* through the *working phase* toward *termination*. Testing of the therapist and the group norms tends to occur in the early, orientation stage, which is generally characterized by only superficial discussion of the group's area of concern. The emerging group responsibility, cooperative therapist-client efforts, and identification with the leader occur in the working phase. Group cohesiveness than becomes evident. As in individual treatment, the termination phase requires that the leader prepare the group well ahead of the group's ending. A summary of the group's history and progress and the formulation of any future plans for individuals are appropriate during this phase.

Types of groups

There are several ways of using group therapy and many ways of describing groups.

Play therapy groups are specifically used for therapy with children, because of their limited verbal ability. Conflicts and problems are acted out in the play of the children, and interpersonal learning takes place.

Psychoanalytically oriented group therapy is an "uncovering" type of therapy aimed at helping group members delineate and understand their intrapsychic and interpersonal conflicts and problems. The group and the leader may follow any one of the various theoretical schools of psychoanalysis, such as Freudian, Sullivanian, or Jungian. This type of group therapy is most often done in an outpatient setting, with clients who are neurotic rather than psychotic and who are functioning on an adequate level of adjustment.

Repressive-inspirational group therapy provides the framework for such self-help groups as Alcoholics Anonymous and Overeaters Anonymous. Repressive-inspirational groups try to alter socially unacceptable behavior while developing and emphasizing socially acceptable qualities. These groups, which consist exclusively of acting-out or formerly acting-out individuals, usually meet in a community setting.

> Michelle had been overweight for as long as she could remember. Even in kindergarten she had been taunted by other children, who gave her the nickname "fatty." She had been on and off diets all of her life. She would lose 50 or 60 pounds and then regain them. Now that Michelle was the mother of two children, she was afraid that her children would follow her poor eating habits and develop weight problems. She joined Overeaters Anonymous. With the support of the group members, all of whom either had been or were presently overweight, she was able to acknowledge her problems—that she ate when she was unhappy and that eating was a means not only of satisfying hunger but also of feeling secure. Michelle and another member of Overeaters Anonymous were teamed as "buddies." When one of them experienced an uncontrollable craving for food, she called her buddy and "talked it out." If necessary, the other person came to the house and stayed with her buddy until the craving for food passed. In this way, food binges were avoided.

It is obvious that a fundamental idea underlying repressive-inspirational therapy is that with the help of persons who have experienced the same problem, acting-out individuals can face up to their socially unacceptable behavior, vow not to repeat it, and help others who are struggling with the problem.

Although nurses may not be directly involved in repressive-inspirational groups, they do play important roles as facilitators and resource persons. In hospitals, self-help groups such as Alcoholics Anonymous and Narcotics Anonymous frequently hold meetings for patients who are potential members. Nurses who have established some degree of rapport with acting-out individuals can be influential in encouraging them to attend the meeting of the appropriate group. When nurses provide them with adequate time, privacy, and space for their meetings, they give them the message "This is important therapy." In the community, public health nurses, occupational health nurses, and school nurse–teachers serve as important sources of information. In their role as case finders, these nurses come in contact with many people who may be in need of but unaware of existing self-help groups. It is often through the encouragement and support of these nurses that acting-out individuals make their initial contacts with these groups.

Encounter groups, or T-groups (the "T" stands for "training in human relations"), originated with Kurt Lewin in 1946. Lewin had been asked by the Connecticut Interracial Commission to help resolve some of the state's interracial problems. He and his colleagues assembled some of Connecticut's black and white leaders in an attempt to help them resolve their differences. Lewin appointed four observers to record the group process. After each session, these recorders discussed the group's dynamics with the group's leaders. Group members insisted on being present at these "postmortems." Lewin found that the conferees learned more from these feedback sessions than from the group meetings themselves. This was the inception of encounter group therapy.

Encounter groups focus on the here and now—on what group members experience as they meet. Members are urged to be completely candid and to shed their facades of adequacy, competence, and self-sufficiency. These groups are peer-oriented rather than leader (authority)-oriented. Members are encouraged to tell one another how they come across to others (that is, to provide feedback). Brutal verbal attacks often develop. Encounter group therapy seems to crack the shell of maladaptive communication patterns used by acting-out individuals. They then can begin to develop insight and to change their behavior. An encounter group thus functions as a microcosm of society.

Yablonsky (1965) describes an encounter group session at Synanon, the original therapeutic community for drug addicts in this country. The meeting becomes an emotional battlefield. Complete candor is the order of the day. Maladaptive defenses and socially unacceptable behavior of members are repeatedly attacked. The encounters are designed to help acting-out individuals see themselves as society sees them. They are forced to look at both their strengths and their weaknesses.

Although nurses do not usually participate in encounter sessions, it is important for them to understand the therapeutic function of what might appear to be destructive group techniques.

A student nurse was trying to establish a therapeutic relationship with Jamie, who had been using alcohol since elementary school and drugs since he began high school. Jamie, aged 16, was now part of a therapeutic drug community. One of the treatment modalities used by this community was encounter group therapy. After a session in which the group had "attacked" Jamie's behavior and attitudes, Jamie complained to the student nurse. The student, who was not acquainted with encounter therapy, sympathized with Jamie and told him that it sounded as though he was being scapegoated. She explained, "They are probably ganging up on you so that no one will focus on them."

When the student recounted this episode to her instructor, the instructor explained the therapeutic rationale underlying the group's approach. After that, the student was able to support Jamie through the experience by helping him listen to what the group was saying. She also helped him realize that although his socially unacceptable behavior was under attack, he as a person was not being rejected.

As members of health teams, nurses need to be involved in developing and implementing therapeutic goals. It is also the function of nurses to sustain acting-out individuals during their experience with encounter therapy. Moreover, because nurses work closely with families, it is important for nurses to understand the therapeutic rationale underlying encounter group therapy so that they can explain it to family members. Otherwise, the families of acting-out individuals could become alarmed at what might appear to be a brutally destructive or punitive group process.

The approaches of all health team members must be coordinated in order to ensure that the therapeutic goals of encounter group therapy are implemented and that socially acceptable behavior is promoted.

Activity group therapy is task oriented. A variety of recreational and occupational forms of therapy is utilized for the purpose of assessing and developing social skills. Activity groups are found in both hospital and community settings. The goals of activity group therapy are as follows:

1. To encourage communication
2. To facilitate the expression of feelings
3. To provide opportunity for decision making
4. To increase a person's concentration span
5. To teach a person how to cooperate, share and compete

Activity group therapy is especially well suited for acting-out individuals. Such persons are action oriented—they try to cope with inner conflicts by doing and not by talking. Activities necessitating gross physical movements therefore provide socially acceptable outlets for the hostility and aggressiveness that underlie most acting-out behavior. Woodworking, sports, and arts and crafts are only a few of the activities that are suitable for acting-out individuals.

A group of student nurses brought construction paper and paints to a unit for newly admitted acting-out individuals. One young man had been admitted after he had taken LSD and experienced a "bad trip." He would not talk about the experience. Midway through a session in which the patients were using the art supplies, the young man sat down at the table. He picked up a piece of green construction paper and, using the colors yellow, purple, orange, red, and black, drew a demonic face. One student asked, "Who is that?" The young man answered, "That's how I felt—just like a devil." He was beginning to admit his experience and to assimilate it into his self system.

Activity therapy thus can facilitate communication and the expression of emotion. In addition, when people set up the equipment for an activity, share materials and tools, and put everything away afterward, they are engaged in interaction, interplay, and interdependency.

Few formal demands are made on activity group members. In this relatively nonthreatening atmosphere, they can "do" to things rather than to people. This is an important phase in treatment of acting-out behavior. It serves the dual purpose of redirecting and sublimating aggression and hostility. New, socially acceptable behavior can supplant the older, socially unacceptable behavior.

Multifamily therapy groups and *couples groups* are composed of more than one family unit. These groups help members to work with the problems of intrafamily communication and relationships. Individuals and families help one another in a supportive, learning atmosphere.

In *groups for persons with special problems*—for example, colostomy groups, laryngectomy groups, and mastectomy groups—feelings are expressed and support and suggestions are offered in a way that helps members adjust to and accept their changed body images and decreased ability to function. Members are encouraged to function at their maximum potential levels.

Other groups found in community and hospital settings include *sensory awareness groups, transactional analysis groups* (based on the theory of Eric Berne [1967]), and *problem-solving* or *brainstorming groups,* which are found in business and used by the staff members of health care facilities.

Therapy groups may be short-term, open-ended groups—the type most often formed in the psychiatric units of general hospitals—or they may be of the close-ended, long-term type found in community outpatient settings. "Open-ended" simply means that as one group member is discharged and leaves the group, another member may be added. The composition of the group is flexible and always changing. A close-ended group begins with a certain composition, and if someone leaves the group, no additional member is added. And while a close-ended group is long term, there is often a specific time at which it is to disband.

Composition of a group and frequency and duration of meetings

The size of a group and the frequency and duration of meetings can, of course, vary greatly. As a general rule, however, an ongoing therapy group meets once a week, its optimal size is eight to ten members, and a session lasts an hour to an hour and a half.

A group may be *homogeneous*—that is, composed of people who share characteristics such as age, sex, diagnosis, or particular problem—or it may be *heterogeneous*. There are advantages to each situation, and which is used generally depends upon the goals of the group.

Phenomena occurring in groups

Communication problems such as *monopolization, intellectualization, circumstantiality*, and *tangentiality* may occur. It is necessary for the leader to confront—in a gentle, nonthreatening way—the client who has any of these problems. If the client is confronted in the proper manner, he may be able to use the group experience as a way to grow, and the other group members will be protected from the effects of his behavior.

Scapegoating may be carried out against a group member who is present at a meeting, or it may be directed toward an individual who is not present. The leader must protect the scapegoated individual, point out what the group is doing, and use the phenomenon as a means of increasing the self-awareness of individual group members.

Transference can be directed toward the leader or toward other members of the group. Within any one group there may be transference reactions based on past or present relationships with mother, father, siblings, husband, wife, children, or boss. If one person's transference reaction is based on two or more relationships, the phenomenon is called *multiple transference*.

Relationships among group members can take several forms. For example, there may be pairing, subgrouping, or polarization. Such developments can be destructive if they interfere with honest and constructive confrontation or if they result in scapegoating or infighting.

Pseudomutuality within a group can also interfere with honesty relating and communicating. Sometimes *sadomasochistic* relationships will erupt between group members. Such relationships are often reflections of the way members relate outside of the group, and they can be used as learning opportunities. Some group members may display their tendencies to *withdraw* and *isolate* themselves or to *conform* as a pattern of relating.

The group member who assumes the role of "assistant therapist" or *group catalyst* can be helpful to the leader. Often this individual is insightful and supportive and able to confront constructively and appropriately. However, he may be attempting to avoid looking at his own problems or exposing himself to the group process.

Catharsis, is an outpouring of emotional tension through verbalization or display of feelings, can occur in any group session. It can be a tension-reducing and growth-enhancing phenomenon. A cathartic release of pent-up emotions has sometimes been a crucial turning point in a group member's life. In addition, an individual's strong expression of emotions has effects on the other group members; it is a vital part of the group process. It may be instrumental in producing group cohesiveness (Yalom, 1975).

A group leader should be aware of *seating arrangements*. Where an individual sits in relation to the leader may be an important clue to his personality. Members who always sit next to the leader may be indicating a need to associate with the leader for some reason—perhaps for protection. Habitually sitting directly opposite the leader may indicate a desire to engage in direct communication or confrontation with the leader. That "pairing" has occurred between two group members may be demonstrated by their choice of seats. The need to withdraw or isolate oneself or the feeling of being threatened by the group may result in placing one's seat at a point *outside* the group circle. While all group members are expected to sit within the circle, an exception to the rule may need to be made for a threatened and timid schizophrenic client (Berne, 1966, p. 56).

It is sometimes helpful for co-therapists to sit opposite one another to maximize nonverbal communication between them and to enlarge their view of the nonverbal communication of other group members.

SPECIAL THERAPY

In addition to milieu therapy and the more conventional forms of group treatment, other types of group therapy are either led by or participated in by nurses who work in psychiatric settings. Among these special types of therapy are poetry therapy; psychodrama; art therapy; graffiti therapy; dance, exercise, and yoga groups; music therapy; and videotape therapy. A brief description of each of these modalities follows.

Poetry therapy

Poetry is a useful tool for reaching many psychiatric clients. Poetry therapy can be handled in more than one way. A single poem may be chosen ahead of time by the leader for the group members to react to in a personal way. The leader may choose a poem that he or she thinks is particularly meaningful to many of the patients in the group, that addresses the problems, feelings, and life-style of the group members. It is hoped that the feelings the poetry evokes will be communicated and discussed by the group members. Many of Robert Frost's and Walt Whitman's poems seem ideally suited to such a purpose, but the choice is as wide as the therapist's experience with poetry. Another way of proceeding is for the leader to present several poems, concerned with various themes, to the group and have each member choose the one that is most meaningful to him and discuss it in a personal way. Still another method is to have the members write their own poetry—an activity that can have the added benefit of increasing an individual's self-esteem through creativity.

Whichever method is used, the poetry serves to stimulate self-understanding (perhaps even catharsis), self-expression, and interpersonal interaction and to increase self-esteem. According to Arthur Lerner (1973) the important qualities of an effective poetry therapist are an acquaintance with a wide variety of poems, a genuine concern for people, an authentic love of poetry, and sensitivity and openness to the possible meanings of poems.

Psychodrama

Psychodrama, a form of group therapy that was originally developed by the late Dr. Jacob Moreno, is becoming widely used in short-term psychiatric units and in such places as alcoholism rehabilitation centers. Various institutes and continuing education courses train professionals in psychodramatic techniques, which focus on dramatizing an individual's conflicts, problems, and past and present relationships. A therapist directs the scene, and other clients or staff members play key roles or act as "alter egos" (roughly, persons who provide uninhibited versions of what the client is saying). There are opportunities for insight development through such methods as role reversals and for catharsis through such activities as conversations with a dead parent. The therapist keeps the action rolling as a stage director does, steps in to protect when necessary, interprets at times, and intentionally reduces group anxiety at the end through the use of a low-key "sharing session." Warm-up techniques and gimmicks are used at the beginning of the session to promote group and individual interaction. Psychodrama is a powerful tool and should not be used in psychiatric settings except under the supervision of a trained person.

Art therapy

Art therapy is useful in three ways:
1. It can be used as a tool for stimulating self-expression in a client (particularly clients who have difficulty expressing their feelings—for example, regressed schizophrenics or children before they can express feelings or conflicts verbally.
2. It can be used as a diagnostic tool from which modifications in a treatment plan can be made.
3. It can provide opportunities for increasing self-esteem and for promoting sublimation and personal growth.

Deep, analytical interpretation of a person's conflicts can be made on the basis of the art he produces. Interpretation, of course, should only be done by persons who have extensive knowledge of psychoanalysis and art therapy and diagnosis. However, using art therapy to stimulate expression, provide recreation and sublimation, increase interpersonal interaction, and enhance self-esteem is an appropriate method for nurses who work with psychiatric clients. Various materials may be used—water colors, oil paints, crayons, modeling clay, felt-tipped pens. Felt-tipped pens are particularly useful—they are easy to store and use, inexpensive, and colorful. Sometimes a group leader will offer a theme to the group and ask the members to draw their responses to it (for example, "What do you look forward to?" "What was your happiest time?" "What makes you sad?"). Group members usually need a good deal of encouragement and support—an invariable complaint is "I simply cannot draw at all!" They need to be reassured that artistic ability is not a requirement; it often helps if the leader is willing to participate in the project as a member of the group. Each drawing is viewed by the group, and discussion follows. Any interpretation of a drawing is best given by the person who produced it. Another way of using art therapy is to have the group participate in the production one large mural or collage. Such an activity promotes cooperation and interaction among members.

A specialized form of cooperative art therapy is *graffitti therapy*, which is a way of stimulating clients' expressions of self and communication with others. Participants are provided with a large piece of brown paper or a blackboard, and they are given pencils, crayons, chalk, or other writing instruments with which to scribble messages and comments. Clients are free to write whatever they choose and to remain anonymous. Themes or topics may be suggested, and staff *and* clients are encouraged to participate.

Movement therapy

Several forms of movement therapy are used in psychiatric settings; dance, exercise, and yoga are examples. Movement therapy provides several benefits. It can increase physical well-being and reduce the tension of anxiety and it can increase self-esteem. Exercise and dance can be particularly helpful to depressed clients, who tend to immobilize themselves in despair. Such group activities can also encourage interpersonal interaction—and to put it simply, they can be fun. Rhythmic dance movements to music have been found to be especially beneficial for psychotic children—such movements help them to improve body coordination (Gunning and Holmes, 1973). Many nurses working in psychiatric settings who have had training in dance, yoga, or calisthenics—or who simply have an interest in these arts— are participating in movement therapy groups.

Music therapy

Music therapy has a long history in psychiatric care. The ancient Greeks believed that music could be a healing agent for persons in disturbed emotional states. In the seventeenth century, music was a specific part of the treatment of madness.

The goals of music therapy include increased self-esteem through pride in achievement, increased interpersonal relating, improved abilities to communicate and problem-solve, and an increased attention span. Music therapists are trained in psychology, sociology, anthropology, and education. Of course, they have a background in music, and they are required to complete a 6-month clinical internship. Some elements inherent in music are thought to have specific curative effects (Parriot, 1969). For example, a consistent rhythm is seen as having a calming effect, a regular but interrupted rhythm is thought to hold a person's attention and to create suspense, and an uneven or irregular rhythm is said to produce surprise and humor. In addition, music can encourage reminiscence, which is considered therapeutically valuable for geriatric clients. A "sing-along" featuring favorite tunes from the past is one possibility. While nurses may not be trained music therapists, many of them can certainly use their musical talents—or encourage clients to use theirs—to make use of the therapeutic value of music.

Videotape therapy

Some clinicians, units, and hospitals are using videotape equipment as a therapeutic modality. For instance, the technique of videotaping family therapy and group therapy sessions and having the participants view the tapes immediately afterward has been used to increase awareness of self and of communications patterns. The technique has also been used to help staff members to increase their own self-awareness. *Informed consent* is a very necessary requirement in the use of videotaping equipment.

•   •   •

While nurses are not art therapists, occupational therapists, or recreational therapists, their interest in—and recognition of the therapeutic value of—various activities can encourage clients to participate in them. Because nurses are often able to spend longer periods of time with clients than activitiy therapists can, nurses may be more knowledgeable about individual interests and talents and thus may be able to suggest activities to the therapists. In addition, nurses can plan and participate in activities that promote interpersonal communication, sharing, decision-making ability, and cooperation. Unlike activity therapists, nurses do not use activity groups for diagnosis and interpretation of clients' behavior. Instead, they use these groups to promote socialization—the learning of communication skills and social values.

Group therapy and activity therapy are important parts of the treatment of emotionally ill persons. Such therapy results in personal insight, the learning of socially acceptable behavior, and the development of positive group identification, all of which facilitate an individual's integration into social groups and the learning of social values and constraints.

FAMILY THERAPY

Family systems theory and family therapy began in the mid-1950s (Bowen, 1976). In the United States, individuals and groups at first worked independently in the area of family treatment. They eventually began to communicate with each other, and a body of theoretical knowledge began to evolve. Today, family therapy is an effective tool for alleviating emotional problems. Graduate psychiatric nursing programs include family systems theory and clinical courses in family therapy as parts of their curricula. Psychiatric nursing clinical specialists are often actively involved as family therapists; many have increased their understanding and knowledge through attendance at workshops and enrollment in family therapy institutes throughout the country.

In conducting family therapy, the goals of the therapist are to clarify and improve *family communication patterns* and *family relationship patterns.* The family itself is viewed as the client. Individual family members are supported and encouraged to be separate from one another instead of being fused to one another in unhealthy, neurotic states. It is thought that through reinforcement of healthy, clear boundaries between individuals, family members will be able to relate to one another in a meaningful way—and in a way that protects healthy individual autonomy. There will not be the threat of loss of self through engulfment *or* the need to defend against this threatened loss through destructive distancing maneuvers. When necessary, the family therapist protects family members who are potential scapegoats and acts as a role model for more mature functioning in the family environment. The therapist *clarifies* and *educates* and thus *facilitates* healthier functioning within the family system. In working with a family, a therapist usually wants to know something of the family history of both the husband and the wife. This information is helpful in assisting the family members to connect their past experiences to the present situation and to gain insight into their tendencies to use certain patterns of communicating and relating.

Family theorists identify certain patterns of communicating and patterns of relating among family members as pathological. The member who is using the pathological pattern is referred to as the "identified patient." If one family member uses such a pattern, they consider the whole family system to be dysfunctional, and the family as a unit thus becomes the focus of therapy.

Murray Bowen, a prominent family theorist, views anxiety within a family system and the lack of *differentiation* of one family member from another as important parts of a pathological system that leads to a family *projection process* and, in turn, emotional illness. Family projection may be manifested in one of three ways:

1. Overt conflict between spouses
2. Impairment of the functioning of one of the spouses (for example, alcoholism, physical illness, obesity, schizophrenia)
3. Impairment of the functioning of one or more children (for example, acting-out behavior, juvenile delinquency, physical illness, schizophrenia) (Bowen, 1976)

Pathological patterns of relating

Many factors may determine why one child develops severe impairment of functioning while his siblings do not. Parental preference for one sex; parents' reaction to fretful, colicky behavior in infancy; nonresponsiveness in an infant; and a high level of anxiety between spouses at the time of birth are all possible explanations.

Scapegoating. The process of consciously or unconsciously singling out one child to be the carrier of the family problems has been termed scapegoating by family theorists. Possible explanations for a child's acceptance of this role include the fear of annihilation of the family system if he does not accept the role and the desire to defend against unconscious incestuous feelings.

Emotional divorce. Emotional divorce occurs when emotional investment between the spouses has been withdrawn. They may be "staying together for the children" or for any number of other reasons, but there is little real involvement with one another.

Pseudomutuality. Pseudomutuality includes the actions, conscious and unconscious, that represent an attempt by the family members to make the family system appear smooth running and conflict free to the outside world. This pattern of relating involves the creation of a facade; in reality there is much overt and covert conflict and confusing communication.

Coalition across generational boundaries. Sometimes a parent tends to enter into or even initiate conspiracies and alliances with a child. Such a conspiracy, which is usually against the other parent, undermines the marital relationship and instills guilt and fear in the child, who sees himself as betraying one parent and being too close to the other.

Assume that a child has asked his father for money to buy an ice cream cone from a street vendor. The father replies, "No, it's 15 minutes before your supper!" The child then asks his mother, who has overheard the exchange. She might respond in one of the following ways:

1. "No, your father is right; it's too close to supper!"
2. "OK, here's the money, but let's not tell your father!"
3. "I don't agree with your father, and I will tell him so—here's the money."

Response 1 is probably the healthiest; response 3 indicates a certain amount of marital discord—disagreement over child-rearing. However, it is a healthier response than response 2, since it is out in the open and the child is not engaged by the parent in a conspiracy against the other.

Pathological patterns of communicating

The following are pathological ways of communicating within a family. An understanding of these concepts is particularly relevant in the treatment of the schizophrenogenic family.

Vagueness. Vague ways of communicating, with a tendency to use universal pronouns ("they") and loose associations, lead to ambiguity and to confusion on the part of the listener.

Tangentiality. Tangentiality means never really answering a question or responding to a statement in a direct way. This "going off on tangents" confuses a listener, who is not sure whether a question has been answered or, if it has been answered, what the response was.

Double-bind communications. A double-bind communication involves the giving of two conflicting messages at the same time. One message may be verbal and the other nonverbal—for example, saying something affectionate to a child when body language says the opposite. Or both messages may be verbal: "Son, your mother and I want you to be an independent person who makes his own decisions, so we have decided that you must go to a school out of town." The individual who receives such a message is not aware that it contains two conflicting messages, but the conflict serves to immobilize and confuse him. "Damned if you do and damned if you don't" messages are also double-bind messages—for example, a mother asking her adolescent schizophrenic son, "If your father and I were drowning and you could only save one of us, which one would it be?"

Family myths. Some families engage in a perpetual denial of reality. For example, a father who is an alcoholic tyrant has a wife who denies this fact to the world and to herself and insists that her children participate in the myth that the father is a sober and loving person. Any attempts by a child to state the real facts or to discuss his feelings about them are met with strong denial and guilt-producing accusations.

Mystification. Mystification is a habitual communication process that might include any or all of the patterns described above. The following are some key characteristics of this schizophrenogenic process:

1. A child being mystified does not realize that his family uses faulty communication patterns and thus blames himself for his confusion.
2. The child unconsciously senses that to question these patterns would threaten the equilibrium of the family system and his security.
3. His family continually uses these way of communicating.

For further discussion of family theory and its importance in the etiology and treatment of emotional disorder, see Chapter 13.

NURSING THERAPY
The nursing process in psychiatric settings

The steps followed in the nursing process in any setting have been delineated in various ways. But basically, each way has been a form of the scientific method. Briefly outlined, the steps include:

1. Making an assessment—in other words, collecting data
2. Making inferences based on data collected
3. Developing a nursing care plan
4. Intervening
5. Evaluating the intervention

In a psychiatric nursing setting, *assessment* of a client may include *listening for themes* (see Chapter 5) and observing the client's participation in one-to-one relationships, group therapy sessions, and recreational and unit activities. *Making inferences* based on collected data involves an understanding of psychosocial theories and of one's own life experiences and applying this understanding to the client's behavior. This stage of the nursing process is often facilitated through *clinical supervision*—either with the help of a teacher or supervisor or in the form of "peer supervision," which implies a mutual exchange of ideas and suggestions among co-workers. The nursing care plan is developed on the basis of *psychiatric nursing principles*, the psychiatric literature, and the nurse's own experience with helpful approaches to specific nursing problems. After the nurse has *intervened*, it is necessary to *evaluate* the effect of the intervention on the client's behavior. Since each client is a unique person with a unique background, the nursing proces must be flexible and dynamic. It is often necessary to "go back to the drawing board" when a set of interventions does not seem to be having the desired effect. It is important to remember that although "principles" and "approaches" can be extremely helpful, they should not be rigidly adhered to when the complexity of an individual case calls out for reevaluation of a care plan. Like step 2 (making inferences), evaluation is an integral part of the supervisory process in its various forms, and it is a continuous process. Part of the evaluation process involves the charting of observations of client behavior in order to increase communication among team members. In most psychiatric facilities, the nurse is not the only team member who charts observations. Each team member is expected to record observations of any client with whom he works.

Principles of psychiatric nursing. Some of the important concepts underlying psychiatric nursing intervention include:

1. Freud's dictum that *all behavior is meaningful* and that most behavior, in the complex human organism is designed to satisfy several needs. For example, an individual who strives to do his job well may be attempting to satisfy the following needs:
   a. The need for approval
   b. The need for security
   c. The need for affection and companionship
   d. The need for self-respect
   e. The need for increased knowledge
   f. The need to create and to express creativity

   Several other needs could be added to the list. Pathological behavior also may represent attempts to satisfy several needs. For example, a person who maintains a delusion of being persecuted by the FBI or the CIA may be satisfying the following needs:
   a. The need to disown one's negative and aggressive thoughts and to project them onto the outside world
   b. The need to feel important (as a result of being singled out)
   c. The need to provide some reasons for the existence of a chaotic inner world and thus restore some measure of order to that world

2. Maslow's hierarchy of needs (Maslow, 1967). A person tries to meet his most pressing needs first and, in doing so, may not rec-

ognize other important (perhaps even life-supporting) needs. For example, a person who is in a manic state seeks immediate release of tension through physical exertion. Sometimes the need for rest and adequate food are completely ignored in deference to the need for physical release of energy. Individuals whose needs have been satisfactorily met in the past are generally able to tolerate delays in the satisfaction of present needs.

3. The humanistic-existential stance that *all human beings have potential for growth.* Many psychiatric clients have led chaotic lives in the past and are experiencing a multitude of severe problems in the present. A feeling of hopelessness about a situation can become contagious, affecting even the nurse, or it can take the form of a self-fulfilling prophecy. In order to be truly helpful, the nurse must appeal to, cultivate, and reinforce the client's "healthy part." This belief in an individual's potential for change and for growth is also the antidote for any other dissatisfaction that can arise out of the nurse's own hopelessness.

4. The use of "themes" in psychiatric nursing (see Chapter 2) as a way of collecting and organizing data about the needs, problems, and goals of a client.

Matheney and Topalis (1965) have compiled a very useful and concise list of psychiatric nursing principles. The following discussion incorporates several of them, as well as some additional principles and some illustrations of important points.

In interaction with psychiatric clients, *consistency* is important. When there is intrapsychic turmoil, a consistent, fairly well-ordered outer world can be a calming influence that provides the client some security. When a person has the painfully low self-esteem that is so common with psychiatric clients, he may automatically blame himself for inconsistency on the part of others. A "You're OK—I'm *not* OK" stance (Harris, 1969) is taken by such a client, who tells himself, "I'm the sick one, so it must be *me* who made the mistake."

Acceptance as a worthwhile human being is what we are all looking for. Because of traumatic past experiences, the need of the psychiatric client for acceptance is exquisite. However, acceptance of a client does not include automatic acceptance of all of his behavior. Self-destructive acts or aggressive acts that constitute a danger to other people are some obvious examples of behavior that cannot be accepted. *Limit setting* may be necessary in order to control some types of behavior, but the setting of limits can be done in a respectful, accepting manner that is therapeutic and not destructive of the client's self-esteem.

For example, when a nurse is involved in a "one-to-one," confidential interaction with a client, and another resident of the unit keeps interrupting their conversation by asking to be included, some action is mandated. It would probably be most helpful if the nurse were firm in setting limits on such behavior, explaining to the interrupting person that the conversation is confidential, as any similar conversation with him would be. An appointment for a one-to-one conversation with the interrupter, or for a three-way casual conversation, could be made for the very near future. Such a response by the nurse recognizes the needs of both clients. It fosters self-respect and respect for others, and it helps promote the client's trust of the nurse.

When they first begin to work with psychiatric clients, nurses are often reluctant to employ any form of limit setting. This reluctance probably arises out of the fear that setting limits may hurt the client, whom they view as having suffered sufficiently already, and also out of the nurse's need to be accepted. *Therapeutic* limit setting, however, is not harmful, and it can be very beneficial for the client who is unable to exercise control over his own behavior. The validity of this statement has been demonstrated by the case of a young woman who, after having recovered from a period of confusion and florid psychosis, thanked her nurse for having set limits on some of her bizarre behavior.

In dealing with *unacceptable behavior*, nurses need to remember some important points. First, is the behavior truly unacceptable? The ability to express negative feelings verbally is a necessary part of living. On a continuum of communication, verbal expression of anger is a more mature and socially acceptable form than physical expression of anger. Therefore, the expression of negative feelings, although it can be threatening to the nurse, should be encouraged and supported. Nurses do, however, sometimes need to protect other clients—especially *vulnerable* clients—from verbal abuse.

When behavior is truly *unacceptable* or when *safety* requires that some amount of physical force be used, the least amount possible should be employed. An example of a situation that might prove very distressing to a nurse working with psychiatric clients would be the need for several staff members to restrain a client who simply must be given medication.

A small, frail-looking elderly woman who had a severe heart condition and who was also psychotic was expressing her psychosis with hyperactivity that was threatening her life. Sedation was absolutely necessary; the woman had only recently been admitted, and the behavior was a continuation and escalation of what had been happening at home. Since she refused all medication and exhibited a degree of strength that was extraordinary for her age and size, it was necessary for several staff members to restrain her while an injection was administered.

While it was not possible in this case, many such situations could be avoided through judicious use of medication *before* anxiety has escalated. A cooperative nurse-client relationship that facilitates good communication and close observation can alert staff and client to a build-up of anxiety or aggression that might be alleviated by appropriate use of sedative medication.

The legitimate goals of psychiatric nursing intervention allow for acceptance of the individual as he is and for the fostering of personal growth. Control of behavior, while sometimes necessary, is never completely benign, and it is certainly not one of the main goals.

In interacting and communicating with clients, *nurses use themselves as therapeutic tools.* But they should keep some important points in mind. Responding to a client's emotional or mental problems with an appeal to logic is usually not much help to the client. If the client were able to be logical about his inner turmoil, he probably would not be in the hospital or clinic and under psychiatric care. Murray Bowen, a noted family therapy theorist, points out that persons who are most vulnerable to emotional illness live in a feeling-dominated world in which it is often impossible to distinguish feeling from fact (Bowen, 1976).

Sometimes clients deny their real feelings or feel guilty about them. "They aren't logical" is a common remark. Allowing for the expression of feelings is probably the best course at such a time. For some clients, the ability to take a more logical stance toward their problems may be a longer-term goal. This particularly true of the acutely ill psychiatric client.

Giving advice, like appealing to logic, usually is not helpful. If we could simply visit every psychiatric unit and hospital and advise clients of the best courses of action for their future, we could probably empty most of these facilities. Not only is giving advice a naive approach but it does not allow for differing value systems. It would be better to remember that when a person is troubled and looking for answers to his problems, he often has most of those answers inside his own head. The way to help is to facilitate the process of getting to those answers. This is why *listening* can be such a valuable tool.

The nurse should avoid raising the client's *level of anxiety* unnecessarily. An increase in anxiety level will only exacerbate symptoms, because the symptoms of psychopathology are exaggerations of the normal defense mechanisms used to control anxiety. There are times, however, when some provocation of anxiety may be justified in order to facilitate growth. Encouraging a client to begin to participate in group therapy may be an example of such justified provocation. For the client who has had difficulty learning to relate to others at all and for the client who has never had a "group experience," the thought of participating in a group can be frightening. The nurse can help by *supporting* the client through the necessary stages. The client can develop increased self-respect and optimism as a result of having accomplished a difficult task.

Support and reassurance, in the situation just described and indeed in any situation, must be given in a realistic manner and with authenticity if they are to be effective. Telling the truth is the best approach; sometimes the amount of information or detail may need to be modified, but to lie to a client to protect his self-esteem is not a good idea. For example, a nurse who praises a client falsely or intentionally loses games in order to bolster a client's self-esteem, is participating in self-defeating behavior. The client is likely to spot this dishonesty, and it may destroy any trust he had in the nurse and to result in a *decrease* in his self-esteem.

In using the nursing process in the psychiatric setting, the nurse often needs to analyze the client's behavior. The goal of this analysis is to try to understand what the client is attempting to communicate or what some of his needs may be. The analysis is done in the nurse's head, and the client's behavior should *not* be interpreted to him. There are several reasons for this:

1. The nurse may indeed be right on target with an interpretation that is told to a client, but the client may not be emotionally ready to accept the information or knowledge about his underlying motivations. Information of this kind can exacerbate psychotic or neurotic symptoms.
2. The nurse may be wrong in the interpretation; nurses are not mind readers.
3. Communications that even hint at mind reading are not helpful. Many psychiatric clients have habitually used unclear commu-

nication patterns, and verbalized interpretations of their behavior serve to reinforce these faulty communication patterns. In addition, some clients have delusions that others can read their minds, and it is thus not therapeutic to reinforce these delusions through communication that might suggest mind reading.

Countertransference is a universal phenomenon in helping relationships. It can be a helpful tool in understanding a client, or it can be a significant nursing problem. Countertransference is experienced by the therapist; *transference* is experienced by the client. Both are intrapsychic concepts. Transference, as it occurs in the helping relationship, has been defined as "those feelings and attitudes that were originally experienced with regard to significant others in the past but are now displaced or projected upon the therapist" (Saretsky, 1978). Countertransference has been defined as

> . . . The emotional process present in the therapist [that] . . . (1) is in relationship to the patient, (2) has a bearing on the therapeutic process, (3) involves unconscious feelings of the therapist, (4) has a component of conscious or unconscious anxiety, and (5) represents a blending of appropriate, defensive and fixated responses (Eisenbud, 1978).

A nurse must ensure that countertransference becomes an effective agent for understanding and relating to a client rather than an obstacle to relating. A nurse's acceptance and awareness of countertransference are the first steps in avoiding some its pitfalls. In order to use the self as a therapeutic tool, one should know as much as possible about the tool. *Reasonable objectivity* is the ideal, but this does not mean cold underinvolvement (what was referred to years ago in nursing as "being professional"). Goldsborough (1969) points out that the therapeutic use of self is not effective unless a nurse is open to involvement and committed to going beyond the imparting of learned skills. Holmes and Werner (1968) see underinvolvement as being as damaging and as useless as overinvolvement. They cite three factors from which underinvolvement may arise: the need of the nurse for a facade, lack of knowledge of how to be effectively therapeutic, and apathy toward and dissatisfaction with one's work.

There is, therefore, an optimum level of involvement between nurses and clients in psychiatric settings. Maintaining that level is rather like walking a tightrope, with overinvolvement on one side and underinvolvement on the other. Perhaps a better way to describe the situation would be to refer to the "art" of psychiatric nursing—this branch of nursing is characterized by a dynamic state of relative equilibrium, as far as involvement with clients is concerned. How does the nurse reach this state of relative equilibrium? One thing that can help is the availability of an objective person with whom the nurse can discuss clinical work and problems—in other words a person with whom the nurse can establish a supervisory relationship.

The supervisory process. Ideally, anyone involved in therapeutic relationships with psychiatric clients should also be involved in a supervisory relationship. Problems of countertransference, overinvolvement, manipulation, or mutual withdrawal between staff members and clients may all be dealt with in a supervisory relationship. In addition, increased self-awareness—a necessary and important goal for the nurse working in a psychiatric setting—can be promoted through the supervisory process. It is also helpful to have another source of ideas for modifying a care plan.

The supervisory process can be part of scheduled staff meetings or team conferences, or it can be the focus of separate meetings. Regardless of which format is used, meetings held on a regular basis, with sharing of clinical material and with peer supervision, can help to meet the goals of supervision. Where a fairly open and trusting atmosphere exists, interpersonal conflicts among staff members are appropriate topics for discussion. Otherwise, the effects of staff conflicts may be projected onto clients, and certain clients may even act some of the conflicts out.

Constructive supervision that involves the sharing of information can facilitate a dynamic, creative approach to carrying out the nursing process in a psychiatric setting.

Charting of observations of behavior. The purposes of charting are as follows:
1. To facilitate the sharing of information among the entire staff
2. To provide information for planning and revising a treatment plan
3. To keep a record of changes in a client's behavior that may lead to a better understanding of his problems

Nurses should observe the following basic principles of charting:
1. Record accurately, using concise, simple language.
2. Be objective and nonjudgmental.
3. Give concrete examples (for example, what *was* the behavior that suggested hostility?)
4. Quote *exactly* what a client says. This is especially important in reporting delusions and hallucinations. Use quotation marks.
5. Sign, date, and record the time of each entry.
6. If a mistake is made, cross through it and initial.

There are five broad areas of reporting and charting: general behavior, patterns of communication, content of communication, affect, and physical signs and symptoms. Some examples of what to report and some possible ways of recording specific observations follow.

General behavior

Changes in behavior
Ways of relating to
staff, patients, visitors
Involved in unit activities or tending to be
seclusive and avoiding staff?
Personal hygiene
Giggling and laughing
inappropriately
Refusing to take medication

Seeking attention from
the staff
May be experiencing
memory defects
Seemed to be hallucinating
Tends to withdraw
(give example to
illustrate)
Tends to be suspicious
(give example to
illustrate)

Patterns of communication

Circumstantial
Tangential
Incoherent
Mute
Demonstrates blocking
Slurred speech
Flight of ideas
Loose association

Content of communication

Any problems, plans,
ideas, hopes, or complaints the client
discusses that may be
important as far as his
progress or treatment
plan is concerned

Affect

Flat affect
Inappropriate affect
Seems depressed
Seems apathetic
Seems anxious
Seems preoccupied
Seems hostile

Physical signs and symptoms

Any physical signs and
symptoms, if significant
Sore throat (important phenothiazine
side effect?)
Appetite changes
Constipation
Skin rash
Edema
Unusual gait, fine hand
tremor, or any extrapyramidal symptom

A particular form of charting is done at the time of admission—the admission assessment. Each agency has its own way of eliciting such an assessment or "mental health history," but the following information is usually obtained, generally through interviewing the client and, if possible, a family member.

1. The event that precipitated hospitalization
2. Prior psychiatric problems
3. Past school and childhood relationships; relationships with parents and siblings
4. Sexual and marital history
5. Relationships with children

6. Job, vocational, and avocational history
7. Any special physical conditions
8. History of allergies
9. List of medications taken recently or within past 2 or 3 weeks (does the client have any medications with him *now?*)
10. Blood pressure, temperature, pulse and respiration rates, weight and height
11. List of clothing and valuables
12. Phone number of family member or friend

Liaison nursing

Liaison nursing has become an important part of the health care system. Clinical specialists in psychiatric nursing provide consultation services for their nursing colleagues in medical-surgical, maternal-child, and geriatric settings. They also provide these services to other professionals, such as physicians and social workers. Another aspect of liaison nursing is the giving of care directly to clients in settings outside of the psychiatric unit. For example, the anxious client awaiting life-threatening surgery, the severely depressed victim of a stroke, or the family of a dying person may all be included in the case load of a psychiatric nurse involved in liaison nursing.

The liaison nurse may be called in to conduct group sessions for staff members who are working in high-stress environments such as terminal care units, intensive care units, or pediatric inpatient units. The goal of these sessions is to help staff members to discuss and express their feelings about the difficult and painful aspects of their work and to provide group support for individuals who are experiencing stress.

Thus, the functions of the psychiatric nursing clinical specialist who performs liaison work may include consultation; client assessment; teaching of staff, clients, and their families; and direct intervention with clients. In a hospital, a good deal of this intervention with clients may be in the form of crisis intervention.

Crisis intervention

Crisis intervention is short-term therapy whose goals are limited to assisting an individual or a family to cope with a crisis situation. A crisis state arises when habitual methods of coping become ineffective in resolving or dealing with a stressful situation.

A crisis is experienced as an increase in tension and anxiety, accompanied by feelings of helplessness and some decrease in the ability to function. A crisis may be precipitated by any event that poses a threat or a potential threat to a person's ability to meet biological, social, or psychological needs. Caplan (1961) notes that crisis states are self-limiting in that a person must resolve a problem at some level in order to return to a state of equilibrium.

A crisis poses a threat to an individual's adaptive abilities, but it also may offer opportunities for personality growth. The resolution of a crisis may, therefore, result in a return to the level of adaptation or coping that preceded the crisis, the development of a less adaptive coping status, or the achievement of a higher level of coping ability.

Crises may be classified as either maturational or situational. Maturational crises occur during the periods of vulnerability that exist when a person progresses from one developmental stage to another (see Chapter 3). For example, in modern society the transitional state from adolescence to adulthood often precipitates a crisis. Many factors that are culture bound, such as the prolonged period of dependence upon parents and the competitive pressures for scholastic and other forms of achievement, are artifacts of modern society that can contribute to stress in the adolescent period and that may lead to crises in some circumstances.

Crisis situations may arise from any stressful event. Physical illness and disability are causes of crisis that are seen frequently in professional nursing practice. Other events that may precipitate crises include loss of a loved one through, for example, death, divorce, or marriage; loss of a job or of economic security; failure in school or at work; and isolation from family and other social network systems.

Such stressful situations occur periodically in the life of everyone. A crisis develops when the event, or the individual's perception of the event, becomes so threatening that attempts to cope with it and with the emotions that the event arouses are effective neither in resolving the crisis situation nor in relieving the anxiety, helplessness, and disequilibrium that the person in crisis experiences. The ability to cope with stressful situations varies in relation to mental health status—including the ability to maintain equilibrium—and the availability of support systems.

The ability to cope effectively with stressful events therefore varies from one individual to another, and it may even vary within the same individual from time to time. Some people cope effectively with emergencies and catastrophic events such as the sudden death of a loved one, while others may experience a crisis as a result of the temporary disruption of a close relationship.

The individual who loses several family members at the same time through an accidental occurrence (such as a fire) or as a result of a natural disaster (for example, a flood or an earthquake) experiences the grief associated with the loss of loved ones and, in addition, loses the family network that could provide support and comfort. In such a situation, the magnitude of the stressful event and the loss of the family support network combine to promote an especially severe crisis.

A person's ability to cope effectively with a stressful situation is also related to his mental health status at the time. Caplan (1961) views the following as important aspects of mental health status: (1) the state of the ego—that is, the capacity of an individual to cope with stress and anxiety and maintain ego functioning; (2) the level of ego maturity—in other words, the degree of reality present in the perception of stress and in problem-solving responses to it; and (3) the quality of the ego structure, which can be determined through assessment of the effectiveness of the coping mechanisms.

Crisis theorists have suggested specific procedures that have proved to be useful guides in crisis intervention for both individuals and families. The following is a summary of a procedure developed by Aguilera and Messick (1978).

1. Assessing the client and his problem (the precipitating event and the resulting crisis)
2. Planning the therapeutic intervention (to restore the person to at least his pre-crisis level of equilibrium)
3. Intervening
    a. Helping the client to gain an intellectual understanding of his crisis
    b. Helping the client bring into the open his present feelings, of which he may not be aware
    c. Exploring coping mechanisms (to find alternate ways of coping)
    d. Reopening the social world (important for the crisis precipitated by loss—of significant other, position in life, or particular view of oneself)
4. Resolving the crisis and engaging in anticipatory planning (reinforcing adaptive coping mechanisms the client used successfully in the past, assisting him to develop realistic plans for the future, and discussing how the present experience can be applied to future coping situations)

In the assessment stage, Aguilera and Messick recommend a focus upon the details of the precipitating event and the client's view of it. Of importance is determining whether the client's view is realistic and to what extent the crisis has disrupted the client's life and the lives of others in the environment. Aguilera and Messick also suggest that assessment should include a review of a client's strengths and weaknesses and the availability of support systems.

Letting the client know that his stressful situation is understood and assuring him that he will receive support are important aspects of intervention. In planning intervention, the therapist evaluates the client on the basis of the data collected in the assessment, as well as his or her own theory and experience. The immediate goal of intervention is a reduction of tension and anxiety. Supporting adaptive mechanisms and gratifying dependence needs during the period of stress are two anxiety-reducing measures that may be employed.

CHAPTER SUMMARY

Psychosocial intervention for clients who are experiencing emotional problems includes individual and family psychotherapy, group therapy, milieu therapy, and special-activity therapies such as art and music therapy and psychodrama. Nurses who work in psychiatric settings are involved, in varying degrees, in these treatment modalities, in addition to individual-relationship therapy. Because of the nature of nursing education and nurses' clinical experience, milieu therapy is probably the area in which the responsibility of the nurse is most evident. However, nurses are becoming increasingly involved in group therapy, and their special interests and talents are also being used effectively in special-activity therapies.

The nurse brings a background in science and the humanities, as well as an understanding of psychiatric nursing principles, to the mental health team. A crucial element of the nurse-client relationship is the degree of self-awareness in the nurse. Self-awareness is enhanced through the supervisory process, which is also a stimulus for a creative and dynamic nursing process.

Communication among team members is essential to an effective treatment plan. One way of promoting communication is the charting of observations of clients' behavior. In many psychiatric facilities, charting is not solely the responsibility of the nurse; it is done by every member of the interdisciplinary team. Ideally, the mental health team works together to engage the client in cooperative, goal-oriented involvement in his own treatment. This effort can foster responsibility for self and facilitate growth.

REFERENCES

Abroms, G. M.
1969 "Defining milieu therapy." Archives of General Psychiatry 21:553-60.

Aguilera, D., and J. Messick
1978 Crisis Intervention: Theory and methodology (ed. 2). St. Louis: The C. V. Mosby Co.

Berne, E.
1966 Principles of Group Treatment. New York: Oxford University Press, Inc.
1967 Games People Play: The Psychology of Human Relationships. New York: Grove Press, Inc.

Bowen, M.
1976 "Theory in the practice of psychotherapy." In Family Therapy. P. J. Guerin (ed.). New York: Gardner Press, Inc.

Caplan, G.
1961 An Approach to Community Mental Health. New York: Grune & Stratton, Inc.

Cumming, J., and E. Cumming
1962 Ego and Milieu. New York: Atherton Press.

Eisenbud, R.
1978 "Countertransference." In Psychoanalytic Psychotherapy. G. Goldman and D. Milman (eds.) Reading, Mass.: Addison-Wesley Publishing Co., Inc.

Goldsborough, J.
1969 "Involvement." American Journal of Nursing 69(1):65-68.

Gunning, S., and T. Holmes
1973 "Dance therapy with psychotic children." Archives of General Psychiatry 28:707-714.

Harris, T.
1969 I'm OK—You're OK. New York: Grossman Publishers.

Holmes, M., and J. Werner
1966 Psychiatric Nursing in a Therapeutic Community. New York: MacMillian, Inc.

Jones, M.
1953 The Therapeutic Community, A Treatment Method in Psychiatry. New York: Basic Books, Inc., Publishers.

Lerner, A.
1973 "Poetry therapy." American Journal of Nursing 73(8):1336-1338.

Maslow, A. H.
1967 "A theory of metamotivation: the biological roots of the value of life." Journal of Humanistic Psychology 7:93-127.

Matheney, R., and M. Topolis
1965 Psychiatric Nursing (ed. 4). St. Louis: The C. V. Mosby Co.

Parriot, S.
1969 "Music as therapy." American Journal of Nursing 69(8):1723-1726.

Rogers, C.
1971 "Carl Rogers describes his way of facilitating encounter groups." American Journal of Nursing 71(2):275-279.

Saretsky, L.
1978 "Transference." In Psychoanalytic Psychotherapy. G. Goldman and D. Milman (eds.). Reading, Mass.: Addison-Wesley Publishing Co., Inc.

Smith, A. J.
1970 "A manual for the training of psychiatric nursing personnel in group psychotherapy." Perspectives in Psychiatric Care 8(3):106.

Smith, C.
1977 "Primary nursing care—a substantive nursing care delivery system." Nursing Administration Quarterly 1(2):1.

Yablonsky, L.
1965 Tunnel Back Synanon. New York: MacMillan, Inc.

Yalom, I.
1975 The Theory and Practice of Group Psychotherapy (ed. 2). New York: Basic Books, Inc., Publishers.

ANNOTATED SUGGESTED READINGS

Lipkin, G., and R. Cohen
1973 Effective Approaches to Patients. New York: Springer Publishing Co., Inc.
This manual describes problem behavior, discusses the underlying dynamics of the behavior, and suggests helpful approaches. The work is a practical, concise, and informative guide to working with clients with emotional problems.

Parad, H. (ed.)
1965 Crisis Intervention: Selected Readings. New York: Family Service Association of America.
This collection of readings on the work of various theorists in the field of crisis intervention gives the reader an overview of theory and the application of theory to clinical practice. Maturational and situational crises, problems in the delivery of services, and various aspects of crisis theory are among topics discussed.

Rogers, C.

1971 "Carl Rogers describes his way of facilitating encounter groups." American Journal of Nursing 71(2):275-279.

This excellent article describes Carl Rogers' philosophy of working therapeutically with groups. It is particularly helpful for nurses leading or participating in group therapy sessions in the psychiatric units of general hospitals. Appropriate, therapeutic use of self and self-disclosure is discussed.

Satir, V.

1967 Conjoint Family Therapy: A Guide to Theory and Technique (rev. ed.). Palo Alto, Calif.: Science & Behavior Books.

Written in the format of a training manual, this easy-to-read book focuses on clarification of communication among family members and ways of negotiating various relationships within families. Numerous clinical examples are included.

Smoyak, S. (ed.)

1975 The Psychiatric Nurse as a Family Therapist. New York: John Wiley and Sons, Inc.

This book is a compilation of the works of 25 authors writing on various aspects of family therapy. Included are such topics as scapegoating, the use of analogies in family therapy, family myths, relationship models, and communication patterns.

Termini, M., and M. Hauser

1973 "The process of the supervisory relationship." Perspectives in Psychiatric Care 11(3):121-125.

This article clearly describes the dynamics of the supervisory process in psychiatric nursing. Included are aspects of transference and countertransference in the nurse-client relationship and in the supervisory relationship.

Williams, F.

1971 "Intervention in maturational crises." Perspectives in Psychiatric Care 9(6):240-246.

Crises such as marriage, parenthood, and the beginning of school are discussed as periods requiring role changes. Assessment and intervention are described, and clinical examples are provided.

FURTHER READINGS

Byrne, A., et al.

1972 "Graffiti therapy." Perspectives in Psychiatric Care 9(1):34-36.

Challela, M.

1979 "The interdisciplinary team: a role definition in nursing." Image (Sigma Theta Tau) 11(1):9-15.

Ciske, K.

1979 "Accountability—the essence of primary nursing." American Journal of Nursing 79(5):890-894.

Fagin, C.

1967 "Psychotherapeutic nursing." American Journal of Nursing 67(2):298-304.

Fink, P. J., et al.

1973 "Art therapy: a diagnostic and therapeutic tool." International Journal of Psychiatry. 11(1):104-125.

Fitzgerald, R., and I. Long

1973 "Seclusion in the management of severely disturbed manic and depressed patients." Perspectives in Psychiatric Care 11(2):59-64.

Hyde, N. D.

1970 "Play therapy: the troubled child's self-encounter." American Journal of Nursing 71(7):1366-1370.

Jourard, S.

1964 Transparent Self. Princeton, N.J.: D. Van Nostrand and Co.

Leone, D., and R. Zahourek

1974 " 'Aloneness' " in a therapeutic community." Perspectives in Psychiatric Care 12(2):60-63.

Lyon, G.

1970 "Limit setting as a therapeutic tool." Journal of Psychiatric Nursing and Mental Health Services 8(6):17-21.

North, M.

1972 Personality Assessment through Movement. Boston: Plays, Inc.

Pesso, A.

1969 Movement in Psychotherapy. New York: New York University Press.

Rogers, C.

1970 On Encounter Groups. New York: Harper & Row, Publishers, Inc.

Ujhely, G. B.

1960 "Basic considerations for nurse-patient interaction in the prevention and treatment of emotional disorder." Nursing Clinics of North America 1:2.

Yalom, I.

The Theory and Practice of Group Psychotherapy (ed. 2). New York: Basic Books, Inc., Publishers.

The matrix of psychosocial intervention **251**

7
COMMUNITY
MENTAL HEALTH

CHAPTER
FOCUS

Mental health care has been undergoing an evolutionary, some even say a revolutionary, process for more than a quarter of a century. The community mental health movement has been an important part of this process since its implementation on a nationwide basis in the 1960s.

The Comprehensive Mental Health Centers Act, passed by the United States Congress in 1963, along with subsequent legislation, has changed the mental health care delivery system. The 1963 legislation was unique in that it increased the involvement of the federal government in mental health care. Prior to the passage of the community mental health legislation, major responsibility for mental health care was a function of state and local governments and the private sector. The federal government had been involved only in funding research, education, and other aspects of mental health care and in providing health services to special groups such as the armed forces and veterans. The legislation established national guidelines for mental health services and provided some funding in the form of grants for construction and staffing of mental health centers. The guidelines were broad enough to allow programs to meet local and regional mental health needs to be developed (Brown and Isbister, 1974).

Community mental health care involves a complex, multifaceted approach to meeting one of the nation's major health problems. Concepts of community mental health place emphasis upon reducing the incidence of mental disorders through locally available and comprehensive services for prevention, early treatment, and rehabilitation. As a means of achieving these objectives and of bringing mental health care into the mainstream of modern health practices, an integrated system of health, social welfare, and other human services was conceived.

Implementation of the goals of the community mental health movement is an evolving process in which communities, governmental, health, and social agencies, professional practitioners, and consumers develop collaborative, cooperative programs to promote mental health. Because of variations in population density and the multiplicity of ethnic and sociocultural groups in the United States, the mental health needs and the organization of mental health services to meet those needs vary considerably from one community to another. Certain concepts, however, are characteristic of all community mental health programs. Among these concepts are the following:

1. Emphasis upon preventive psychiatry and the availability of comprehensive services for the prevention, treatment, and rehabilitation of mental disorders

COMMUNITY MENTAL HEALTH

2. Provision of mental health services in a setting in which there is the least possible disruption of social and kinship support systems and the least possible interference with personal and civil liberties
3. Responsiveness to consumer needs through community involvement in the planning and evaluation of programs to meet mental health needs
4. Provision of mental health services by interdisciplinary mental health teams

The community mental health movement has had a major impact upon the treatment of persons with psychiatric disorders. There has also been an influence upon the roles and functions of health professionals involved in providing health services. As a basis for understanding current mental health practices, this chapter will focus upon major aspects of community mental health. Attention will be given to the historical antecedents of the movement, including developments in therapeutic modalities for treating emotional disorders and the legislative and judicial actions that have influenced mental health care. The present status of community mental health care and some of the factors that have influenced the realization of the goals of the movement will be discussed.

Concepts underlying community mental health care

Historical aspects of mental health care

Factors influencing the community mental health movement

Scope of the mental health problem

Developments in therapeutic modalities

Impact of expanding institutional populations

Legislative action

Judicial action

Report of the President's Commission on Mental Health

Characteristics of community mental health services

The mental health team

Concepts of preventive psychiatry

Essential services

Organization of services

Legal aspects of mental health care

Involuntary commitment

The right to treatment

Basic civil rights

Current status of community mental health

CONCEPTS UNDERLYING
COMMUNITY MENTAL HEALTH CARE

The community mental health movement embraces a broad-spectrum approach to meeting mental health needs. Theoretical concepts place emphasis upon the interrelationship of biological, psychological, and sociocultural forces inherent in a *holistic view* of the individual interacting with the environment (see Chapter 1). Developments in psychopharmacology and biochemical research and advancements in the knowledge of the effects on mental health of such sociocultural stressors as poverty, racism, and unemployment have emphasized the importance of a bio-psycho-social approach to mental health promotion (Greenblat, 1973). The community mental health concept utilizes *systems theory* in the organization of services to meet the mental health needs of a community and to provide therapeutic intervention for individuals, families, and communities. In addition, any one of several conceptual models may be used.

The *medical model*, as its name implies, involves the organization of mental health services in much the same way that services in an acute care hospital are organized. The major focus is upon the individual and his symptoms and pathology. Treatment is oriented toward the amelioration of symptoms through brief psychotherapy and somatic and activity therapies. The medical model is often found in inpatient psychiatric units of general hospitals. These units provide short-term hospitalization for community residents who are in crisis, as a part of the community mental health system. Such units usually have outpatient clinics, which provide additional and longer-range services.

The *public health model* embraces many of the aspects of the public health movement that were so effective in eliminating communicable diseases. An approach based on this model is concerned with decreasing or eliminating mental disorders from the population or community, in addition to providing treatment and rehabilitation services. A community is a geographically defined area with a population of 75,000 to 200,000 people. A community, for purposes of community mental health, is also known as a catchment area. Preventive efforts in a catchment area include case finding, consultation, and education of community groups. In addition, community members participate in planning, implementing, and evaluating programs to meet mental health needs. Mental health workers functioning in the public health framework may have an eclectic view of the nature of mental disorders. Such a view makes use of several theoretical constructs as a basis for understanding and intervening in psychopathology. For example, the concepts of personality development of Freud, Erickson, and Sullivan may be utilized in consultation and education programs with parents and school systems, as a means of primary prevention. Or vulnerability to stress may be understood in terms of psychodynamic theory. This may be combined with a view of the interaction between an individual and sources of stress in his environment, such as poverty—a view that is inherent in systems theory. Mental health workers then might join with community groups in social and political action to reduce the level of stress in the environment.

Within a catchment area there may be many ethnic and sociocultural groups, each of which may consider itself a community (Hume, 1974) and within which mental health needs and beliefs and practices related to health and illness may vary considerably. The involvement of the members of such communities in mental health programs thus is important.

The social model, which traces its origins to Adolph Meyer but which has more recently been expanded by many social scientists, focuses upon the way in which the individual functions in society. Schulberg (1969) points out that, when this model is used, mental disorders are no longer perceived as primarily intrapsychic processes but are viewed as reflections of disequilibrium between the individual and the environment. He terms this model the "problems in living" model. Factors such as poverty and segregation often inhibit or prevent a person from assuming socially expected roles and functions. The behavioral responses to such deprivations and frustrations are often viewed as being normal within the social context, rather than as symptoms of pathology. Mental health workers in community agencies that function according to the social model attempt to become cognizant of the problems, attitudes, and broad aspects of the environment as they apply to a particular population and not simply to the individual. Ideally, the resources and strengths of the community are mobilized in helping individuals and families to cope with crises and problems of daily living. Mental health workers may also join with community groups to improve the social milieu through social and political action.

HISTORICAL ASPECTS OF MENTAL HEALTH CARE

Mental disorders are believed to have been a part of human experience throughout recorded history. Insanity was mentioned by Homer in the *Iliad*. Plato distinguished between "divine madness," the madness given by the gods, and "natural madness." Hippocrates, a Greek physician who lived from 460 to 370 BC, described depressed states. Claudius Galen, a Roman physician who lived from 138 to 250 AD, wrote a treatise on melancholia that remained an important work on the subject for many centuries (Manfreda and Kampritz, 1977). Justinian, an emperor of the Eastern or Byzantine Empire, in the sixth century AD, established many charitable institutions, including some for the care of the mentally ill (Ellenberger, 1977).

As early as the thirteenth century, the people of Gheel, Belgium, had pioneered in community psychiatry to meet the needs of the mentally ill, many of whom made pilgrimages to the Shrine of St. Dymphna, the patron saint of the mentally ill. Some of the pilgrims to St. Dymphna's shrine stayed on in Gheel, and a practice of foster family care evolved that has continued to the present time.

Attitudes toward mental illness and the treatment of people regarded as being mentally ill have not always been so enlightened. During the Middle Ages, a theory of demonology, or possession by the devil or evil spirits, was prevalent in some areas of Western Europe. Such views persisted at least into seventeenth century—for example, in the town of Salem, Massachusetts. In some cases, people who may have been mentally ill were regarded as witches and, at times, burned at the stake. In other instances, rites of exorcism were practiced as a means of driving out evil spirits.

Developments in mental health care have always been influenced by cultural attitudes, the level of knowledge available, and the religious beliefs and sociopolitical events of particular eras. For example, Phillipe Pinel, who has been credited with liberating mental patients from their chains in Salpetrière in France in 1795, was undoubtedly influenced and his work given public support by the spirit of "liberté, egalité, and fraternité" that prevailed in France around the period of the French Revolution. The spirit of humanism and concern for humane treatment of the mentally ill was greatly influenced by Pinel's philosophy that mental illness was caused by an individual's experiences in life rather than by some lesion in the brain or by demons or devils. The humanistic philosophy and the enlightened treatment of the mentally ill embraced by Pinel could also be found in the work of Vincenzo Chiarugi in Italy and William and Samuel Tuke in England.

Benjamin Rush (1745-1813), an American physician who is sometimes described as the "father of American psychiatry," provided humane treatment for the mentally ill in the late eighteenth and early nineteenth centuries (Greenblatt, 1971; Manfreda and Kompritz, 1978). During this time the people of the United States were fairly homogeneous in cultural background, and they often were highly dependent upon one another for survival because they lived predominantly in small, largely agricultural, communities. The shared sense of responsibility was reinforced by the Christian ethic. These factors influenced Rush and others to provide humanistic treatment and care for the mentally ill. The humanistic movement lasted until about the middle of the nineteenth century (Greenblatt, 1971).

In the latter half of the nineteenth century there was a decline in public interest in mentally ill persons and a concurrent decline in the number and quality of facilities available for their care. This change in public attitude was related to the wave of poor immigrants from Europe. Many of the immigrants suffered from poverty and culture shock, which increased the incidence of mental disorders and the need for mental health services.

Dorothea Lynde Dix (1802-1887), a retired Boston schoolteacher, became alarmed by the condition of the mentally ill and the prevailing practice of incarcerating mentally ill persons in filthy almhouses and jails. She traveled thousands of miles in the United States and abroad, urging state legislatures and other governmental agencies to assume responsibility and to establish hospitals for the care of mental patients. Miss Dix's reform effort was successful in that the individual states assumed responsbility for mental health care and built state hospitals to care for persons with emotional disorders. The state hospitals, often large, understaffed, and built in locations remote from population centers, served primarily to provide custodial care. These hospitals were a major mental health resource until the community mental health movement of the 1960s.

In 1903, a book by Clifford Beers entitled *The Mind That Found Itself*, in which he described his experiences in such a custodial institution, attracted the attention of several prominent people. Among them were William James, the great American psychologist, Adolph Meyer, a leading American psychiatrist, and William Welch, the father of American pathology. They joined with Beers and others to form the National Committee for Mental Hygiene. Under the leadership of Adolph Meyer, the movement took a preventive approach to mental illness similar to that of the community mental health movement of the 1960s. The movement failed, however, to attract public and governmental support.

The work of Freud, in the late nineteenth and early twentieth centuries and that of his contemporaries and of the neo-Freudians who followed, dominated psychiatric thought in the first half of the twentieth century. Although Freud's work markedly increased our knowledge of human behavior, it had a limited effect upon the treatment of patients in the large state hospitals, where canvas restraints and locked doors often replaced the chains of Salpetrière.

FACTORS INFLUENCING THE COMMUNITY MENTAL HEALTH MOVEMENT
Scope of the mental health problem

Word War II, which brought universal conscription of young men for military service in the United States, focused national attention upon the extent of the nation's mental health problems. Levenson (1974) notes that "approximately 40% of the 5,000,000 men rejected for military service for medical reasons, during this time, were rejected because of some neuro-psychiatric defect." Levenson also notes that such disturbances were responsible for the greatest number of medical discharges from the armed services during the war. In addition, the success of military psychiatry in returning soldiers to active duty following brief crisis intervention treatment near the front lines (Glass, 1955) served to alert the nation to the possibility of more effective treatment of mental disorders.

Developments in therapeutic modalities

World War II focused attention upon the scope of the nation's mental health problem, but it was not until the 1950s that several important developments in the therapeutic measures available for treating the mentally ill occurred. These developments improved the quality of health care and changed the attitudes of both the public and health professionals about psychiatric disorders. Among the developments were group therapy, which was adaptable to meeting a variety of treatment goals; crisis intervention; the therapeutic community concept developed by Maxwell Jones in England; and chemotherapy, which was in wide use by the mid-1950s. (See Chapter 5.) In addition to improving the treatment of people with psychiatric disorders, the advances spurred research into etiology and treatment modalities for such disorders.

Impact of expanding institutional populations

Levenson (1974) notes that in 1945 there were approximately 450,000 people in state psychiatric institutions in the United States and that the number had increased to 550,000 10 years later. The impact upon the state budgets, which had to be increased to provide essential services and the capital spending needed to expand the institutions to meet the mental health needs of the steadily increasing institutional populations, was profound. In many states, the cost of mental health services became a major budgetary expense—and therefore a sociopolitical concern that served to focus attention upon the mental health problem.

The ever-rising costs of services gave impetus to the utilization of newer therapeutic modalities, particularly chemotherapy, and also served to focus the attention of the federal government upon the nation's mental health needs.

Legislative action

In 1955 the United States Congress passed the Mental Health Studies Act, which directed that a Joint Commission on Mental Health and Mental Illness be appointed to study "the needs and resources of the mentally ill in the United States and to make recommendations for a National Mental Health program" (Joint Commission Report, 1961). The Joint Commission, appointed by the National Institute for Mental Health, was an interdisciplinary group drawn from 28 national organizations concerned with mental health. The American Nurses' Association and the National League for Nursing were among the professional organizations supporting the study.

In 1961 the Joint Commission issued its final report in the form of a book entitled *Action for Mental Health: A Program for Meeting the National Emergency*. The report included the following recommendations:

1. The Commission strongly recommended that action be taken to promote publicly supported research and the development of research centers. The report noted that education and scientific knowledge should be regarded as national resources.
2. To achieve better use of present knowledge and experience, the report recommended that "psychiatry and the mental health professions should adopt and practice a liberal philosophy of what constitutes and who can do treatment. . . . " The report noted that certain examinations and treatments should be done by physicians and that psychoanalysis and related forms of insight therapy must be conducted by persons with special training. It recommended, however, that nonmedical mental health workers "with aptitude, sound training, practical experience and

demonstrated competence should be permitted to do short term psychotherapy."

3. To increase the number of mental health professionals, the report recommended federal support of education in the mental health professions. The report also recommended that the mental health professions conduct national recruitment drives and training programs for all categories of mental health workers and that professional leaders become actively engaged in supporting constructive legislation for general and professional education.

4. The report made a number of recommendations concerning services provided to people with emotional disturbances. Among the recommendations were increases in the number of community mental health clinics and in the number of psychiatric units in general hospitals; provision of counseling services in the community as secondary prevention measures; improvement in facilities for the chronically ill as tertiary prevention measures; and dissemination of information aimed at increasing public understanding and attitudes about mental illness.

5. The Commission recommended vastly increased federal funding for mental health care and improvement in mental health services.

President Kennedy's interest in mental health served to give further impetus to the community mental health movement. In 1963 he spoke to the crisis in mental health. Congress responded by passing the Community Mental Health Centers Act, which allocated monies for mental health care and developed guidelines for mental health services.

The Community Mental Health Centers Act incorporated many of the recommendations of the Joint Commission. The basic principles of the act included the following:

1. Providing services for mental health care that are readily available to community residents

2. Providing comprehensive services to meet the varying needs of community residents

3. Providing services appropriate to the individual's problems

The original intent of the act was to establish 2,000 community mental health centers, in locations throughout the nation, to serve populations of from 75,000 to 200,000 people (Levenson, 1974). Although many mental health centers were built or organized as a result of the act, the original goal of 2,000 was not achieved.

A major effect of the Mental Health Studies Act and subsequent legislation on nursing and other, nonmedical health professions was a resolution of the problem of who was qualified to do short-term psychotherapy. The practice of short-term psychotherapy by qualified nurses, social workers, and other professionals became accepted.

Judicial action

During much of the history of the United States, the civil rights of persons involuntarily hospitalized because of mental illness or mental retardation were given little more than cursory attention by either the health and legal professions or the public at large. Laws governing involuntary commitment to mental hospitals were established under state judicial systems and therefore varied somewhat from state to state. In general, laws and legal procedures related to the process of involuntary commitment to a mental hospital; judicial involvement often ended when the hospital doors closed upon a client. There were, of course, mental hygiene laws or codes established by each state to administer and supervise mental health care. But such codes were the responsibility of the mental health profession, not the legal profession. The length of time a person was detained in a hospital and the treatment or lack of treatment given were regarded as medical problems and hence came under medical jurisdiction.

It should be kept in mind, however, that neither the states nor the hospital administrations, who were increasingly faced with burgeoning populations and limited finances, were eager to admit more people to state hospitals than seemed absolutely necessary. There was no motivation for keeping clients in the hospitals any longer than necessary. But, for many people there were no alternatives. Families were often unable or unwilling to assume responsibility for the care of mentally ill members, and the few community resources that were available were unable to meet the needs. Furthermore, the nature of the hospitalization itself and the forms of treatment available tended to encourage chronicity and long-term hospitalization rather than improvement in mental health. Perhaps of even greater detriment to mental hospital patients was the rejection of the mentally ill by society at large. Not only were the civil rights of the mentally incapacitated ignored, but the people themselves were in large part ignored except by those providing direct care and by the branches of state government responsible for providing funding and services.

No major public movement arose to prevent the abrogation of the civil rights of mental hospital populations. Even the small movements that did arise, often led by families and friends of patients, failed to attract much public support or financing.

In 1963, however, shortly after the Community Mental Health Centers Act was passed, a series of legal actions was brought in state courts that was ultimately to have a profound impact upon the civil rights of person deprived of freedom as a result of being declared mentally ill or incompetent. These suits focused primarily upon two major issues: deprivation of liberty and the right to treatment. Following are pertinent aspects of two of the major suits.

> *Rouse v. Cameron* (1966). In the District of Columbia Circuit Court, Judge Bazelon found that commitment to a mental hospital, without provision of treatment, in a criminal case, violated District of Columbia statutes and may have violated the Eighth amendment to the Constitution, which prohibits cruel and unusual punishment, and the Fourteenth Amendment, which guarantees the right to due process of law. Judge Bazelon recommended that a bona fide effort be made to provide treatment and that there be periodic review of the client's mental health status. He further noted that lack of treatment cannot be justified on the basis of insufficient funds (Stone, 1975).

> *Mason v. Superintendent of Bridgewater State Hospital* (1968). The Supreme Judicial Court of Massachusetts, the state's highest court, ruled that a constitutional right to treatment exists for persons who are found incompetent to stand trial and who must return to competence before they can be tried. The judge based his decision upon the Fourteenth Amendment (equal protection and due process of law) and threatened to free the defendant if treatment was not provided (Stone, 1975).

Each of these suits resulted from involuntary commitment to mental hospitals as a result of criminal proceedings in which the defendants were found not guilty of their crimes or were deemed unfit to stand trial for their crimes because of mental disorders. A precedent had been set earlier, in 1952, in court rulings related to involuntary hospitalization of sexual deviants (Stone, 1975). However, since these cases involved criminal behavior they had little effect upon the commitment of clients who were not charged with crimes.

In 1971 and 1972, however, a class-action suit involving civil commitment to state hospitals in Alabama resulted in court rulings that were to have a major impact upon the legal rights and treatment of persons involuntarily hospitalized simply because they were found to be mentally ill.

> *Wyatt v. Stickney* (1971). Judge Johnson ruled that deprivation of liberty and failure to provide treatment violated the fundamental principles of due process of law.

Wyatt v. Stickney (1972). Judge Johnson issued a decree setting forth standards for mental hospitals in Alabama, to guarantee minimum constitutional and medical requirements. Among the basic rights of patients set forth were the right to privacy, presumption of competence to handle personal affairs, and the right to communicate with persons outside the hospital. The decree also required a consent procedure for such treatments as electroconvulsive therapy. In addition, Judge Johnson established minimum standards for staff-to-patient ratios, floor space, sanitation, and nutrition. The decree further ordered that individual treatment plans be developed, that medical orders be filed and periodically reviewed, and that a Citizen's Commission be appointed to monitor the enforcement of patients' rights. Although Judge Johnson's decision was appealed, it was upheld by the Court of Appeals for the Fifth Circuit in 1974 (Stone, 1975).

In June, 1975, the United States Supreme Court handed down a unanimous decision on the constitutional rights of a person who was committed simply because he was found to be mentally ill. In *O'Connor v. Donaldson*, the Court found that "a State cannot constitutionally confine without more a nondangerous individual who is capable of surviving safely in freedom by himself or with the help of willing and responsible family members or friends." (The phrase "without more" is legal language—in other words, without evidence beyond that of mental illness. Dangerousness to self or others is the usual criterion.) The Court avoided rendering a decision on the right-to-treatment issue and left to a lower court the decision of whether to award damages to Donaldson for having been involuntarily kept in a Florida mental hospital for 15 years. The lower court later assessed monetary damages against O'Connor, who had been the hospital superintendent, thus establishing personal liability of hospital officials for violations of patients' constitutional rights to liberty.

Many additional lawsuits have since been adjudicated in state courts across the nation, and the legal procedures for the protection of clients' civil rights appear to be firmly established. Although the changes that have resulted are not usually referred to as one of the revolutions in psychiatry, they have indeed revolutionized many aspects of mental health care. The Department of Health, Education, and Welfare established guidelines for Medicaid reimbursement for institutions providing mental health care that were similar to ones set down by Judge Johnson (Stone, 1975). The various states revised their mental health laws to protect clients' civil rights. For example, the New York State Mental Hygiene Law, revised in 1973, set stringent controls on involuntary admission to state hospitals and established the client's rights to appeal and to review by the courts. This law also established a Mental Health Information Service, under the jurisdiction of a state court, through which lawyers are provided to represent patients and protect their rights. Other states have similar laws.

Although the right-to-treatment issue has not been resolved by action in the courts, that a client has a right to treatment has become fairly well-established policy and has been reaffirmed in the goals set forth by the President's Commission on Mental Health.

Report of the President's Commission on Mental Health

Shortly after taking office, President Carter established a Commission on Mental Health. The Commission, a 20-member interdisciplinary group whose honorary chairperson was the President's wife Rosalynn, submitted its report to the President in April, 1978. The Committee members were selected from among the leaders of national organizations concerned with mental health care, among them the American Nurses' Association and the National League for Nursing. Serving on the Commission was Martha L. Mitchell, Chairperson of the American Nurses' Association Division of Psychiatric Nursing Practice. Three additional registered nurses served on task panels.

The Commission identified several mental health needs. Among them were prevention of mental illness, removal of financial barriers to mental health care, better distribution of mental health care providers, and improvement of services to persons most in need, including children, adolescents, the elderly, minorities, and people with chronic mental health problems.

The following were among the major recommendations of the Commission:

1. A mental health service system through which services could be provided in the least restrictive settings so that the maximum possible independence of clients could be maintained. The report noted that community-based services should be the keystone of the mental health system.
2. Improved services for the underserved groups already mentioned, through a new federal grant program
3. Continued phasing out of large state hospitals and upgrading of services in those that remain. Also recommended was community planning of services for formerly hospitalized patients.
4. Protection of the civil rights of persons needing mental health care

5. Stipulation that clinical services be rendered only by, or under the direct supervision of, a psychiatrist or a psychologist, social worker, or nurse with an earned master's or doctor's degree
6. Coordination of mental health services and integration of a mental health system into other human service systems; inclusion of a mental health component in health systems agencies' plans
7. Recognition and strengthening of natural social support networks in mental health services and development of linkages between social support systems and mental health service systems as a means of improving mental health care
8. Giving more attention to prevention, with a strong emphasis on primary prevention of mental disorders
9. Expansion of the knowledge base through research and rebuilding of the nation's mental health research capacity
10. Improving public knowledge and understanding of mental health problems
11. Changing present laws governing third-party payment for mental health care to include additional health care providers and to give clients a broader choice of providers (Report to the President of the President's Commission on Mental Health, 1978)

Legislation that allowed the implementation of these recommendations to begin was passed by the Congress and signed by the President in 1980.

CHARACTERISTICS OF COMMUNITY MENTAL HEALTH SERVICES
The mental health team

Staffing patterns in community mental health facilities vary from one agency to another. Ideally, however, a health team includes one or more of each of the following: psychiatrist, psychologist, social worker, clinical nurse specialist, professional nurse, recreational therapist, and occupational therapist. Paraprofessional therapy aides and community volunteers are also frequently team members. The structure and functioning of a mental health team depend upon the conceptual model utilized by the particular facility. The mental health team approach differs from the traditional hierarchical or authoritarian structure that characterizes many health facilities, in which decision-making is done at the top and decisions are passed down through lines of authority. Ideally, authority and responsibility are shared by mental health team members, although it should be emphasized that the professional responsibilities that define professional practice are retained. The physician, for instance, retains the responsibility for prescribing medications. The nurse and the physician share the responsibility for drug administration. Team members share in the evaluation of clients and in the planning, implementation, and evaluation of treatment. Team leadership may rotate among team members, depending upon which member has the greatest expertise in a given situation or the most information about a particular client. The team approach offers staff members the opportunity to share experiences and responses and to receive validation and support from each other. It also permits any tensions between team members to be worked through before they encroach upon the therapeutic milieu. The team concept is particularly valuable in mental health care because a cooperative, collaborative effort in planning therapeutic intervention promotes consistency in the treatment of a client. (The team approach will be discussed in greater detail in Chapter 8.)

Concepts of preventive psychiatry

The purposes of primary prevention services are to identify potential health problems and to plan and implement preventive programs. Primary prevention services involve a cooperative effort between mental health professionals and institutions and organizations in the community. Although the individual health professional may practice mental health prevention as a part of the provision of professional services in any area in which he or she may function, preventive programs on a community-wide basis are a cooperative endeavor among health care and social welfare systems, educational institutions, courts and penal institutions, police precincts, industrial organizations, and health and safety organizations. Additional community resources may include the news media, social and religious groups and individual residents. For example, an emergency room nurse who becomes aware of a drug abuse problem in a local high school population might institute a collaborative relationship with community agencies to provide preventive measures such as health education and to refer individuals and families to mental health facilities. Developing a program for prevention of drug abuse in the particular population would involve a variety of additional steps. Working with other professional persons, such as the school nurse, teachers, and school officials, could be an initial step in the assessment of the extent of the potential danger.

Health and welfare institutions could be sources of information about the availability of facilities for early treatment. Planning educational and other programs for prevention of drug abuse would involve collaboration among law enforcement agencies, community groups such as the Parent-Teacher Association, religious organizations, local news media, and mental health consultants.

Secondary prevention, the objectives of which are early identification and effective treatment of mental disorders, also necessitates a cooperative effort between community agencies and residents and mental health practitioners. Clients with mental health problems may come to the attention of, or seek assistance from, a community mental health center, a general hospital, private practitioners, or various health services. Or they may seek assistance from family, friends, religious leaders, or other members of the community who are not health professionals. In some situations, people in need may not seek assistance from anyone. A community health nurse visiting a home may be the first health professional to identify depression in an elderly client living alone and to recognize that he is in need of treatment. Or a maternal child nurse providing services in a well-baby clinic may identify an emotional disturbance in a new mother. School nurse—teachers, nurses in medical-surgical units or other units of general hospitals, operators of "hot line" telephone services for drug and alcohol abusers and persons contemplating suicide, and persons working in abortion clinics and emergency rooms all may be involved in secondary prevention of mental disorders.

Tertiary prevention is oriented toward providing treatment and rehabilitative services, in the least restrictive setting possible, to persons with chronic psychiatric disorders and to persons who are developmentally disabled. Many clients who have been hospitalized for long periods of time suffer from the effects of institutionalization, or the "social breakdown syndrome." Rehabilitation of such clients often requires therapeutic measures designed to remotivate and resocialize them. In addition, the provision of basic subsistence needs and sheltered living facilities is often essential to any therapeutic endeavor.

Gerald Caplan (1964) noted several principles that are important in the rehabilitation of the psychiatric client. Among them is that rehabilitative treatment should be instituted as soon as a psychiatric problem has been recognized and a diagnosis has been made. According to Caplan, the major goals of rehabilitation are to maintain or reestablish social network systems and to counteract or reverse the social breakdown syndrome.

The term "social breakdown syndrome" was introduced in 1962 by the American Public Health Association's Committee on Mental Health (Gruenberg, 1974). This syndrome begins when an individual who is experiencing psychiatric symptoms becomes unable to meet the behavioral expectations of his culture and develops feelings of isolation and estrangement. Such feelings are intensified by his being labeled mentally ill and being admitted to a mental hospital. Long-term hospitalization then tends to foster helplessness, isolation, dependence, compliance, and identification with fellow patients. The social isolation and the loss of minimum social skills are major components of chronic mental disability. Beard et al. (1978) note that the debilitating effects of long-term hospitalization are reflected in apathy, inactivity, excessive dependence, and profound deficiencies in the skills of daily living.

The community mental health movement and current treatments for the major psychiatric disorders are oriented toward preventing or reversing the social breakdown syndrome. Brief hospitalization for treatment of acute psychotic states, in a therapeutic milieu, with follow-up care in outpatient departments of mental health centers in the community, is utilized to achieve this goal.

The support systems that compose the social network include family, neighborhood, and religious and other groups through which an individual receives the physical, emotional, and psychological support that is essential to being able to meet basic human needs. Such needs include social contact, a sense of belonging and participation, and opportunities for achievement and mastery in interaction with group members (Caplan, 1974).

Although the family is often the most important part of a social network, a major psychiatric disorder may cause a breakdown in a person's relationship with his family. A family member who is regarded as mentally ill may be stereotyped and thus become alienated from the family. Nurses may ameliorate or prevent such stereotyping and alienation of psychiatric clients by working with family members as part of the treatment and rehabilitation process and by facilitating communication between clients and their families and other social network systems. Treatment in community settings, with minimal restrictions on client's freedom and maximum opportunity for the maintenance of social contacts, is another important measure.

For some clients with chronic disabilities, or for clients who have experienced long-term isolation from their social support systems, efforts to develop new social networks may be necessary. Ethnic and religious groups and community mental health services may provide such networks. For example, Alcoholics Anonymous often serves as a major social support system for persons with disorders related to alcoholism.

Essential services

The Community Mental Health Centers Act of 1963 established guidelines for mental health care and defined five essential services that a health center must provide in order to be eligible to receive federal funds. The five essential services were (1) around-the-clock inpatient care, (2) outpatient clinic services, (3) facilities for partial hospitalization (for example, day or night hospitals), (4) walk-in facilities for emergency services, and (5) community consultation and education services for prevention of mental illness and promotion of mental health.

The 1963 legislation listed additional services that could be provided but that were not mandatory: diagnostic services, rehabilitation services, research, and evaluation and training of mental health workers.

A subsequent law, the Mental Health Centers Act of 1975, required that all of these services be provided. In addition, this legislation required services for special groups—particularly children, the aged, ethnic minorities, and persons with special problems such as drug or alcohol addiction—and recommended coordination of health and human services systems to meet mental health needs.

The 1975 legislation had less of an impact upon mental health care than the earlier legislation, in part because federal funding to implement the legislation was not provided and in part because of the evolving nature of community mental health. Some of the recommendations of the 1978 report of the President's Commission on Mental Health were similar to the stipulations of the 1975 Mental Health Centers Act.

Organization of services

The manner in which community mental health services are organized and the programs that are developed to provide comprehensive services may vary from one community to another. Many factors can influence the way in which community mental health programs are implemented. Variations in geographic distribution of population, population density, and mental health needs necessitate variations in the organization of mental health services. Socioeconomic factors and the availability of already-existing mental health and human services systems may also affect the ways in which programs are planned to meet mental health needs. Many patterns of organization have developed (Macht, 1978). In some communities, services are organized under the auspices of a single agency, often with a single center serving as the hub of a mental health program. In other communities, several agencies develop a collaborative arrangement or system to promote community mental health. Such a system is referred to as a multiple-agency system.

The ideal toward which the community mental health movement strives is a system characterized by a collaborative endeavor of all agencies and personnel providing human services. Macht (1978) points out that to promote such collaboration, 26 states have established human services or human resources departments.

In a single-agency system, primary, secondary, and tertiary services are organized under one center, although some services are frequently provided in satellite clinics or other facilities in the community. In a multiple-agency system, services are divided among several agencies. For example, a voluntary hospital might provide in-hospital emergency and diagnostic services. Follow-up clinics and transitional services might be provided by nonprofit organizations, branches of state, local, or federal government, or the private sector. Outreach programs and services to meet the needs of special groups such as children or the elderly might be offered through a variety of resources in the community. Each type of agency would collaborate in the training of mental health professionals and the planning of primary prevention programs.

Many large state hospitals have decentralized their operations by making their various units relatively autonomous and assigning each one to a particular community or catchment area. In addition to providing in-hospital treatment for persons with acute and chronic disorders, such units may function as community mental health centers that can provide further treatment, follow-up services, and health supervision in a community. Follow-up and satellite clinics are often staffed by members of an in-hospital mental health team. Such clinics offer clients some level of continuity of care and often provide special services such as the following:

1. Day and night treatment centers and follow-up clinics
2. Occupational and recreational training and rehabilitation programs
3. Transitional services such as halfway houses, foster homes, and supervised hostel arrangements
4. Vocational counseling centers and sheltered workshops
5. Emergency services, such as crisis intervention and other brief forms of therapy to provide support to clients in their homes in crisis situations

Rehabilitation programs for clients whose chronic disabilities lead to institutionalization and the social breakdown syndrome may need to include special or long-range therapeutic measures and mental health services to prepare them for discharge from the hospital and to enable them to function in the community. Such measures may include a variety of therapies and activities designed to promote social, cognitive, and daily living skills.

Special living arrangements may be necessary for some clients. Halfway houses, for example, serve as transitional living facilities between the hospital and independent living in the community. For clients who have chronic disabilities or health problems that necessitate a continuing form of supervision, foster homes, adult homes, health-related facilities, or nursing homes may be utilized.

LEGAL ASPECTS OF MENTAL HEALTH CARE

Practitioners of professional nursing, particularly those who are directly involved in the care and treatment of clients with mental disorders, have a professional responsibility to protect clients' civil rights and to serve as client advocates when such rights appear to be abrogated.

Protecting the civil rights of individuals and groups is a responsibility of the courts and the legal profession. Mental health professionals often become involved in legal proceedings when expert testimony is essential to the administration of justice. Traditionally, psychiatrists have been the professionals regarded as expert witnesses before the courts in matters related to mental health. The interface between psychiatry and the courts has been named forensic psychiatry, and psychiatrists who are experts in the legal aspects of mental health have been termed forensic psychiatrists.

A mental disorder in which there are disturbances in cognitive, emotional, and behavioral functioning frequently results in a person becoming more dependent on others and therefore more vulnerable to infringements upon his civil rights. Thus, although the civil rights of clients is a topic of importance to all nurses, it is of particular importance to nurses who work in psychiatric settings.

Involuntary commitment

Most persons who enter mental hospitals for inpatient treatment do so voluntarily. In some instances, however, involuntary hospitalization is deemed necessary. Since involuntary commitment deprives an individual of liberty, the decision to commit a person involuntarily rests with the courts. Involuntary commitment results from either civil or criminal court proceedings. The procedures relating to involuntary commitment are specified by state laws and may, therefore, vary from one state to another.

Civil commitment. When it is determined through psychiatric evaluation that an individual has a mental disorder and that he is dangerous to himself or others, and the person refuses hospitalization, a petition for involuntary commitment may be made to a civil court. In any such proceeding, the person is entitled to legal counsel and has the right to appear in court in his own defense. The court (often a judge, rather than a judge and a jury) hears evidence from psychiatrists representing the petitioning agency and the person involved, as well as any other information that is relevant or admissable. On the basis of the evidence presented and the laws of the particular state, the judge grants or denies the petition.

There is usually some provision in state laws or codes for very *brief* involuntary commitment in an emergency situation (see Chapter 15).

A major concern of the legal and mental health professions is the requirement for assessing—and in effect predicting—whether an individual will be dangerous to himself or others because of mental disease or disorder. If a person who is expressing suicidal ideation, predicting that he will be dangerous to himself may be easy. But in many, if not most, instances, a prediction of dangerousness is more difficult.

In *Addington v. Texas* (1979), the United States Supreme Court considered the question of "what standard of proof is required by the Fourteenth Amendment to the Constitution in a civil" commitment proceeding. The Court ruled that involuntary commitment to mental hospitals of citizens who are unable to care for themselves or who are dangerous to the community because of mental disorder requires proof "more substantial than mere preponderance of the evidence." The Court also ruled, however, that "due process does not require states to use the 'beyond a reasonable doubt' standard of proof applicable in criminal prosecutions . . . . "

Commitment as a result of criminal proceedings. Involuntary commitment to a mental institution as a result of criminal proceedings may come about in one of two ways. A person accused of a crime may be found incompetent to stand trial because of a mental condition, or he may plead not guilty on the basis of insanity and be so found by a jury.

A determination that a person is incompetent to stand trial is based upon the person's lack of ability to understand the charges against him and to participate with his lawyer in his own defense because of mental disorder (Stone, 1974).

Many of our laws and legal procedures have developed from English common law. This is true of one of the more frequently invoked rules in cases involving the insanity plea—the *McNaughton Rule*. This rule, which was handed down in England in 1843, holds that a person is not guilty of a crime if he did not understand the nature and quality of an act or did not know that the act was wrong (Stone, 1974; Jones, 1965). Although the McNaughton Rule has been criticized by legal scholars and members of the psychiatric profession, it has remained an important aspect of the insanity defense in many jurisdictions in the United States.

Another defense that is valid in some states is the *Irresistible Impulse Test*, which was introduced in Alabama in 1887 and has since been adopted by many states. The Irresistible Impulse Test expanded upon the McNaughton Rule by adding criteria for determining a person's ability to control his behavior (Stone, 1974).

Both the McNaughton Rule and the Irresistible Impulse Test have been criticized by legal scholars and members of the psychiatric profession because of their moralistic quality and because they do not reflect current knowledge of human psychology. The most recent attempt to develop a test or rule governing responsibility for criminal acts in relation to mental disorders is the *American Law Institute Test* (1962). According to this test, a person is not responsible for criminal behavior if at the time of committing a crime he lacked substantial capacity either to appreciate the criminality of the act or to make his behavior conform to the law (Stone, 1974; Jones, 1968). (See Chapter 15).

The right to treatment

The right to treatment has become a generally accepted precept in mental health care during the past decade. That persons in mental hospitals have a constitutional right to treatment has been established by the courts in many states. Many of these court decisions have been discussed earlier in this chapter (for example, *Rouse v. Cameron*, and *Wyatt v. Stickney*). Although the courts have established the right to treatment, the responsibility for prescribing, implementing, and evaluating treatment remains with psychiatrists and other mental health professionals. Stone (1975) points out that the increase in the amount of litigation relating to mental health care treatment makes it important that institutions providing mental health services have access to expert legal counsel.

Two corollaries of the client's right to treatment are the client's right to refuse a specific treatment and the need for health professionals to obtain "informed consent" for any treatment given. The right to refuse treatment and the need to obtain informed consent pose definite problems for mental health professionals and institutions. The individual who is experiencing an emotional crisis and who is aggressively "acting out," or the person who is extremely depressed or who is experiencing an acute psychotic episode, may be unable to comprehend a proposed treatment or may oppose any form of treatment. A minor who is hospitalized by his parents against his will, or an adult who is involuntarily committed to a hospital, may reject the need for any treatment.

Many state laws and mental health codes contain provisions governing treatment in emergency situations. The responsibility of protecting clients' civil rights requires both a knowledge of state laws and institutional policies on the part of the mental health team and skill in coping therapeutically with clients who reject treatment. (The right to treatment and to "informed consent" will be discussed further in Chapter 15.)

Basic civil rights

In addition to the constitutional rights relating to conditions of confinement and treatment, the basic civil rights of hospitalized people must be maintained. In *Wyatt v. Stickney*, Judge Johnson pointed out such rights as "a presumption of competency" to handle personal affairs, the right to communicate with people outside the institution, and the right to privacy (Stone, 1975). Also important is the right to treatment in the "least restrictive" setting, a right that was upheld by the United States Supreme Court in *Donaldson v. O'Connor*, which was discussed earlier in this chapter.

CURRENT STATUS
OF COMMUNITY MENTAL HEALTH

During the past two decades there has been remarkable progress in the implementation of the community mental health concept. This progress is reflected in major changes in services for the treatment of persons with psychiatric disorders and developmental disabilities.

Stickney (1974) has aptly described the characteristics of public mental institutions, which were the major resource for mental health care for about a century prior to the mental health movement. He notes that such institutions "became progressively more overcrowded, underfunded, understaffed and stagnant." Others have described such institutions as warehouses for people.

Long-term hospitalization in institutions has largely given way to brief hospitalization in times of crisis and the development of treatment and prevention services in local communities throughout the country. State hospital populations have declined, despite a relatively stable number of admissions or, in some institutions, even a slight increase in admissions. For many persons with chronic disabilities, forms of supervised housing in the community have replaced the institution as a home. This pattern has become increasingly prevalent as the constitutional rights of persons with mental health problems have been affirmed by the courts.

There has been an increase in the number of mental health professionals, a phenomenon that has been made possible by government funding of professional education. Government funding has been important in improving the quality of care. For example, many nurses have earned graduate degrees in psychiatric nursing through government-funded educational programs. These nurses' contributions to nursing literature and research and to the quality of care provided in the agencies in which they are employed attest to the value of government funding of higher education. Unfortunately, the level of such funding has declined in recent years.

Progress has also been made in primary prevention, including public education about mental disorders, and in the promotion of collaborative efforts between health and social service systems for the improvement of mental health care.

Despite the progress that has been made, many problems and difficulties lie ahead. Borus (1978) refers to the community mental health movement as being "in a state of developmental crisis." As in any developmental crisis, he points out, there exist both the opportunity for growth and development and the danger of regression to a less healthy state.

Much criticism has been leveled against the community mental health movement in recent years by health professionals and the public at large. Community mental health has been cited by many authors as moving too far too fast, of failing to live up to early expectations and promises, and of moving people out of the back wards into the back alleys. That problems would be encountered and criticisms would arise as a result of a change in health care of the magnitude of that brought about by the community mental health movement was to be expected. Challenges to long-standing beliefs, attitudes, and practices and to areas of vested interest were threatening to many people.

In many communities, for example, there has been public resistance to the presence of mental health treatment and rehabilitation facilities. This problem has been exacerbated in some areas because of the large numbers of people with chronic disorders who have been housed or "dumped" in some communities. The problem, to some extent, reflects a lack of funding by state, local, and federal governments, which could have made possible the wider distribution of the mental health facilities necessary to provide care and treatment of persons with chronic disorders.

The maldistribution of health professionals is another major concern, particularly since the persons most in need of mental health services often reside in poor neighborhoods or in rural areas, where few health professionals practice and where the services that are available are often provided by local residents or self-help groups with inadequate preparation. Borus (1978) points to the "lack of adequate and stable rewards" as one of the causes of the maldistribution of health professionals.

Although there is general acceptance among health professionals of the concept of community mental health, there are differences of opinion concerning the scope and function of community programs. Schulberg (1969) points out that one school of thought holds that the focus of treatment and rehabilitation efforts should be on persons who seek help. This group is critical of the broader concepts of primary prevention, maintaining that too little is known about primary prevention at the present time. To other mental health professionals, a holistic orientation toward the treatment of mental health problems and a public health approach in developing programs for the total population of a community involve primary prevention and outreach programs in addition to treatment and rehabilitation services. The latter view has prevailed in many areas. But implementation of programs based on this view has been a slow and evolving process. Christmas (1979) points out that there are problems in developing the cooperative, collaborative effort essential to the concept of a system of human services to meet mental health needs. But, as she also observes, change, although slow in coming, eventually does occur. There is a need at all levels of government for legislation and funding to provide improved prevention, treatment, and rehabilitation facilities, professional education, and support of research.

There is also a need for continuing education of the public about modern concepts of mental health, in order to overcome long-held myths and negative attitudes about psychiatric disorders and to gain public support for mental health maintenance programs as well as treatment and rehabilitation services. Although the community mental health movement has made progress in educating the public, much remains to be done, particularly in the area of seeking assistance from members of the communications media and from local, state, and federal legislators, all of whom are in a position to benefit the movement.

Whether the community mental health movement can survive during a period of economic uncertainty is a question that is frequently raised and one that is important both for the public at large and for mental health professionals. Budget reductions in times of inflation and recession are often made in areas of public services such as community mental health. The mentally ill have traditionally failed to attract the support of advocacy groups that could provide the social and political action essential to optimum mental health care.

Several factors, however, favor the continuation and possibly the expansion of the community mental health movement, even during a period of economic uncertainty. One factor is economic. Providing services through which to treat people with psychiatric disorders and disabilities in the community is less costly—in human as well as economic terms—than maintaining large inpatient populations in public hospitals. Although it is necessary in times of fiscal restraint to establish priorities in relation to mental health programs, economic considerations favor the community mental health approach. Prevention of disorders is also far less costly in human and economic terms than secondary and tertiary programs.

Another factor that augers well for community mental health programs is the court actions that have upheld the constitutional rights of persons with psychiatric problems. Our legal system is based upon precedents established by decisions of the courts. The many lawsuits adjudicated in state courts across the nation and in the United States Supreme Court during the past two decades have established precedents and upheld clients' constitutional rights concerning mental health care, including the right to such care in the least restrictive setting.

The strong commitment to the community mental health movement that has been demonstrated by many mental health professionals and many consumers of health care holds promise for the development of the movement in the future. Participation in social, political, and community action to promote mental health programs and facilities is an important function of nurses and members of the other health professions.

CHAPTER SUMMARY

The community mental health concept embraces an interacting system of health, welfare, and social services oriented toward meeting the mental health needs of a community. Programs are organized to provide mental health services for populations in geographically defined communities termed catchment areas. Each catchment area may have a population of from 75,000 to 200,000 people. Programs to meet community needs are, ideally, developed through a cooperative effort between health and social agencies, community organizations, and residents of the community served.

Although many factors influenced the development of the community mental health movement, the Community Mental Health Centers Act, passed by Congress in 1963, was a major factor in the implementation of mental health programs on a national basis. The act provided some federal funding for mental health care and established principles and guidelines to meet comprehensive mental health needs of residents in their local communities. Subsequent legislative and judicial actions further defined mental health care and upheld the constitutional rights of persons who have psychiatric disorders.

Although it continues to be an evolving process, the community mental health movement has significantly changed the treatment of mentally retarded persons and persons with psychiatric disorders. Before the community mental health movement, mental health care had usually been available only in public hospitals, where long-term hospitalization was often a major form of treatment.

The community mental health concept utilizes a public health approach to meeting mental health needs. This approach involves primary, secondary, and tertiary prevention. Primary prevention seeks to reduce the incidence of psychiatric disorders, secondary prevention seeks to reduce the disability rate through early and effective intervention, and tertiary prevention seeks to prevent or reduce the severity or duration of long-term disability.

Mental health services are provided by an interdisciplinary mental health team, and consumer interests are protected through the participation of community members in the planning and evaluation of mental health services.

The characteristics of agencies providing mental health services and the ways in which mental health teams function vary from one agency to another and according to the philosophies and professional orientations of health team members. The mental health services offered also vary according to the priorities established by a particular community.

REFERENCES

"Addington v. Texas."
 1979 U.S. Reports 441:418.
Baldwin, Ann C.
 1978 "Mental health consultation in the intensive care unit: toward greater balance and precision of attribution." Journal of Psychiatric Nursing and Mental Health Services 16(2):17-21.
Beard, Margaret T., Cathy T. Enelon, and Jeanette G. Owens
 1978 "Activity therapy as a reconstructive plan on the social competence of chronic hospitalized patients." Journal of Psychiatric Nursing and Mental Health Services 16(2):33-41.
Beers, Clifford
 1953 A Mind That Found Itself. New York: Doubleday & Co., Inc.
Bellak, L., and H. Barton (eds.)
 1975 Progress In Community Mental Health, vol. 3. New York: Brunner/Mazell, Inc.
Blaney, Paul H.
 1975 "Implications of the medical model and its alternatives." American Journal of Psychiatry 132(9):911-914.
Bohm, Evelyn
 1978 "Interdisciplinary teamwork in a community SRO." Journal of Psychiatric Nursing and Mental Health Services 16(7):23-28.
Borus, Jonathan F.
 1978 "Issues critical to the survival of community mental health." American Journal of Psychiatry 135(9):1029-1035.
Brown, Bertram S., and James D. Isbister
 1974 "U.S. governmental organization for human services—implications for mental health planning." In American Handbook of Psychiatry (ed. 2), vol. 2. Gerald Caplan (ed.). New York: Basic Books, Inc., Publishers, Ch. 37.
Butler, Robert N.
 1975 "Psychiatry and the elderly." American Journal of Psychiatry 132(9):893-900.
Caplan, Gerald
 1974 Principles of Preventive Psychiatry. New York: Basic Books, Inc., Publishers.
 1974 Support Systems and Community Mental Health: Lectures on Concept Development. New York: Behavioral Publications.
Chodoff, Paul
 1976 "The case for involuntary hospitalization of the mentally ill." American Journal of Psychiatry 133(5):496-501.
Christmas, June J.
 1979 "The many faces of psychiatry—innovation, initiative or inertia." Journal of Psychiatric Treatment and Evaluation 1(1):11-15.
David, Henry P.
 1976 "Mental health services in the developing countries." Journal of Psychiatric Nursing and Mental Health Services 14(1):24-28.
Ellenberger, Henry F.
 1974 "Psychiatry from ancient to modern times." In American Handbook of Psychiatry (ed. 2), vol. 1. Sylvano Arieti (ed.). New York: Basic Books, Inc., Publishers.

Fieve, Ronald E.
  1977 "The revolution defined: It is pharmacologic." Psychiatric Annals 7(10):10-18.
Frank, Deborah
  1974 "The process of implementing the nurse's role in a neighborhood center." Journal of Psychiatric Nursing and Mental Health Services 12(2):33-38.
Greenberg, Ernest M.
  1974 "The social breakdown syndrome and its prevention." In American Handbook of Psychiatry (ed. 2), vol. 2. Gerald Caplan (ed.). Sylvano Arieti (ed.-in-chief). New York: Basic Books, Inc., Publishers.
Greenblatt, Milton
  1977 "Introduction to psychiatry and the third revolution." Psychiatric Annals 7(10):7-9.
  1977 "To complete the revolution." Psychiatric Annals 7(10):105-109.
  1977 "The revolution defined: it is sociopolitical." Psychiatric Annals 7(10):24-29.
Greenblatt, Milton, R. H. York, and E. L. Brown
  1955 From Custodial to Therapeutic Care in Mental Hospitals. New York: Russell Sage Foundation.
Hume, Portia Bell
  1974 "Principles of community mental health practice." In American Handbook of Psychiatry (ed. 2), vol. 2. Gerald Caplan (ed.). Sylvano Arieti (ed.-in-chief). New York: Basic Books, Inc., Publishers.
Joint Commission on Mental Health and Mental Illness
  1961 Action for Mental Health: A Program for Meeting the National Emergency. New York: Basic Books, Inc., Publishers.
Katz, J.
  1969 "The right to treatment—an enchanting legal fiction." University of Chicago Law Review 362(H55):755-783.
Laing, R.
  1967 The Politics of Experience. New York: Ballantine Books, Inc.
Levenson, Alan I.
  1974 "A review of the federal Community Mental Health Centers programs." In American Handbook of Psychiatry (ed. 2), vol. 2. Gerald Caplan (ed.). Sylvano Arieti (ed.-in-chief). New York: Basic Books, Inc., Publishers.
Lewis, Nolan D. C.
  1974 "American psychiatry from its beginnings to world war II." In American Handbook of Psychiatry (ed. 2), vol. 1. Sylvano Arieti (ed.). New York: Basic Books, Inc., Publishers.
Liss, Robert, and Frances Allen
  1975 "Court mandated treatment: dilemmas for hospital psychiatry." American Journal of Psychiatry 132(9):924-927.
Macht, Lee B.
  1978 "Community Psychiatry." In Harvard Guide to Modern Psychiatry. Armand M. Nicholi, Jr. (ed.). Cambridge, Mass.: Belknap Press of Harvard University Press.
Manfreda, Marguerite, and S. D. Krompitz
  1977 Psychiatric Nursing. Philadelphia, F. A. Davis Co.
Mora, George
  1974 "Recent psychiatric developments (since 1939)." In American Handbook of Psychiatry (ed. 2), vol. 1. Sylvano Arieti (ed.). New York: Basic Books, Inc., Publishers, Ch. 3.
Mueller, John F., and Terrie Schwerdtfeger
  1974 "The role of the nurse in counseling the alcoholic." Journal of Psychiatric Nursing and Mental Health Services 12(2):26-33.
Musto, David
  1977 "Whatever happened to community mental health?" Psychiatric Annals 7(10):30-55.
"O'Connor v. Donaldson."
  1975 U.S. Law Week 43:4929.
Olin, Grace B., and Harry S. Olin
  1975 "Informed consent in voluntary mental hospital admissions." American Journal of Psychiatry 132(9):938-941.
Report to the President of the President's Commission on Mental Health.
  1978 Washington, D.C.: U.S. Government Printing Office.
Robinson, Karen Meier
  1978 "Working with a community action group." Journal of Psychiatric Nursing and Mental Health Services 16(8): 38-42.
Sabshin, Melvin
  1977 "Politics and the stalled revolution." Psychiatric Annals 7(10):98-102.

Schulberg, Herbert C.
1969 "Community mental health: fact or fiction?" Canada's Mental Health Supplement, no. 63. Ottawa: Department of National Health and Welfare.
Sedgwick, Rae
1974 "The family as a system: a network of relationships." Journal of Psychiatric Nursing and Mental Health Services 12(2):17-20.
Singh, R. K., William Tarnawer, and Ronald Chen (eds.)
1971 Community Mental Health and Crisis Intervention. Palo Alto, Calif.: National Press Books.
Stickney, Stonewall
1974 "Wyatt vs. Stickney: the right to treatment." Psychiatric Annals 4(8):32-45.
Stone, Alan
1975 "The right to treatment." American Journal of Psychiatry 132(11):1125-1134.
Sullivan, Mary Ellen
1977 "Processes of change in an expanded role in nursing in a mental health setting." Journal of Psychiatric Nursing and Mental Health Services 15(2):18-24.
Szasz, Thomas
1963 Law, Liberty and Psychiatry. New York: MacMillan, Inc.
Timmreck, Thomas C., and Loreem H. Stratton
1978 "The schedule of recent events; a measure of stress due to life change events translated for the spanish speaking." Journal of Psychiatric Nursing and Mental Health Services 16(8):20-25.
Topalis, Mary, and Donna Aguilera
1978 Psychiatric Nursing (ed. 7). St. Louis: The C. V. Mosby Co.
Walters, William E.
1977 "Community psychiatry in Tutuila, American Samoa." American Journal of Psychiatry 134(8):917-919.
Wilson, Holly Skodal
1978 "Fairing: control of staff work in a healing community for schizophrenics." Journal of Psychiatric Nursing and Mental Health Services 16(3):24-38.
Zusman, Jack, and Richard Lamb
1977 "In defense of community mental health." American Journal of Psychiatry 134(8):887-890.

ANNOTATED SUGGESTED READINGS

Lancaster, Jeanette
1980 Community Mental Health Nursing: An Ecological Perspective. St. Louis: The C. V. Mosby Co.
This recent work provides a good theoretical background in community mental health. A holistic view of the individual interacting dynamically with his environment is the approach utilized by the author. The book also provides a preventive approach to meeting mental health needs. There is some discussion of particular mental health problems, as well as the problems of various age groups, persons who abuse drugs or other substances, and other persons at risk.
Robinson, Karen Meier.
1978 "Working with a community action group." Journal of Psychiatric Nursing and Mental Health Services 16(8): 38.
This article provides a theoretical framework and a process for assessing the functioning of a community action group. Utilizing systems theory and group dynamics, the author provides a step-by-step description of the formation and development of a community action group and the role of professional nurses serving in a consultant capacity to the group. The steps and principles outlined can be used for assessing and promoting positive change in any group.
Stone, Alan.
1975 "The right to treatment." American Journal of Psychiatry 132(11):1125-1134.
Dr. Stone, an expert on psychiatry and the law, reviews recent legislative and judicial actions that have had a profound impact upon the civil rights of people with mental problems and therefore upon mental health care. The involuntarily hospitalized client's right to treatment and his right to refuse treatment, as well as other aspects of the question of clients' rights, are discussed in terms of their import for institutions and psychiatrists. Many of the points made, however, are equally applicable to nursing and other health professions.

8
THE MENTAL
HEALTH TEAM

CHAPTER
FOCUS

Staffing patterns in mental health facilities vary from one agency to another. Ideally, the mental health team includes one or more of the following: psychiatrist, psychologist, social worker, clinical nurse specialist, professional nurse, recreational therapist, and occupational therapist. In addition, paraprofessional therapy aides and community volunteers are frequently team members. The mental health team concept differs from the traditional hierarchical or authoritarian structure found in many health facilities, in which decisions are made at the top and passed down through lines of authority. In the mental health team concept, authority and responsibility are shared by team members, although the responsibilities that define professional practice are retained.

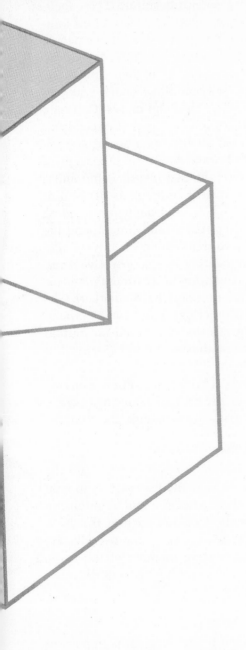

8

THE MENTAL HEALTH TEAM

People are treated for mental illness in a variety of settings—for example, community mental health clinics, day-care centers, psychiatric hospitals, and psychiatric units of general hospitals. These facilities become part of the social network or support system of an individual, and they are social systems in and of themselves. Some people (for example, workers and "outpatients") spend part of the day within such a system, while others ("inpatients") spend all of their time there. Each of these systems is rather like a self-contained society; subcultures may evolve with their own customs, rules, and mores (Goffman, 1961). Goffman and the Cummings (1970) are among many social scientists who have studied the psychiatric facility as a social system. Maxwell Jones (1953), a psychiatrist, helped develop the concept of that social system as a treatment factor—the therapeutic community. The therapeutic community—or therapeutic milieu, as it is also called—is based on the belief that the whole environment, including the architecture, the furniture, the rules of the establishment, and the *entire* group of workers, can be utilized to treat clients effectively. Ideally, the various workers will function together as a cooperative *team.*

In most psychiatric facilities the formulation of treatment plans for clients is the responsbility of several different health care workers. The way this group of individuals works together as a team can be crucial to the success of a treatment plan. A relationship based on mutual respect and equality not only facilitates the team's functioning but also promotes the well-being of the client.

In a therapeutic milieu or community a certain amount of blurring of the distinctions between the roles of the various team members is considered appropriate. This role blurring may include the designation of an interdisciplinary team leader. While some agencies follow the medical model, in which a psychiatrist serves as team leader, other agencies allow any member of the helping professions to fill the role. Role blurring is based on the belief that the best person to help an individual is one who has developed a meaningful relationship with him. This belief does not negate the fact that each of the disciplines brings something unique to the team and to the overall care plan for a client. The nurse, as a cooperating member of the team, needs to have an understanding of the roles and functions of the other persons who make up the team.

THE CLIENT

The most crucial member of the team is the client. It is important for nurses or any health professional to remember that no amount of treatment can be successful if the client is not engaged as a responsible partner in a therapeutic alliance. In the last analysis, it is the client who will, in one way or another, decide the outcome of therapy. Today, in many enlightened treatment centers, this fact is acknowledged through efforts to include the client in the process of making decisions about treatment or about goals for the future. Unfortunately, however, this philosophy is not always carried through; too often the client's views are considered *after* the ideas of other team members.

Self-government

Most units and facilities allow clients some form of self-government within the overall treatment plan. The amount of self-government varies considerably. In some units clients participate only in once-a-week "client-staff" or "community" meetings that deal with here-and-now situations affecting staff and clients. In other units clients are expected to be responsible for many day-to-day decisions. Such decisions may involve the planning of recreational events and outings, the granting of weekend passes, and changes in the status of individual clients. In such units, clients also may be involved in decisions about discharge. In some alcoholic rehabilitation units, before a client is readmitted to the community, he must meet with the entire treatment staff to discuss what he sees as his problems and his goals, as well as the degree of commitment he has to his treatment plan. Some facilities have "open charting"—clients are allowed to read their own charts at any time. All of these policies are based on the belief that encouraging an individual to be responsible for himself and to assume some responsibility for his fellows will facilitate recovery and growth.

Advocacy

Inspired in part by the "radical therapists" (see Chapter 13), consumer advocacy is beginning within the ranks of the mentally ill—or, more accurately, among recovered, or formerly mentally ill, persons. Advocacy takes energy, and someone in the midst of trying to cope with severe mental illness has little strength to spare. A significant portion of this advocacy is also carried out by relatives of clients, and they have been successful in making some major changes in large state-run facilities. Because of their efforts federal and state funds for certain mental health institutions have been withheld until services and facilities were improved.

Clients have won some important court cases concerning their rights to freedom and to adequate and appropriate treatment while under psychiatric care. In addition to the right to treatment, other rights are being promoted by advocacy groups, including the following:

1. The right to the least restrictive form of housing
2. The right to education (particularly in the cases of mentally handicapped and emotionally ill children)
3. Employment rights, including restrictions on the use of institutionalized persons to perform labor without receiving *at least* the minimum wage and protection against discrimination in employment in the community
4. The right to live in the community without being subject to discriminatory zoning codes
5. The right to refuse treatment (*Science News,* July 12, 1975)

THE SOCIAL WORKER

Social workers function in many settings—for example, medical services, public welfare programs, family and adoption agencies, prisons, clinics, and psychiatric facilities. While the largest portion of social workers work in psychiatric settings, the term "psychiatric social worker" is considered obsolete. Most professional social workers are prepared at the master's level (M.S.W.); a smaller number are graduates of baccalaureate programs with a major in social welfare. Some social workers have doctorates in social work (D.S.W. or Ph.D.) or in related fields. Some states have licensing or certification laws for social workers (C.S.W.). The national professional organization is the National Association of Social Workers (N.A.S.W.). A social worker who has a master's degree, who has completed 2 years of supervised practice, and who has passed a qualifying examination may be admitted to the Academy of Certified Social Workers. The worker is then entitled to use the designation A.C.S.W.

Social workers are particularly concerned with the family, community, and social networks of clients, and they have a good deal of expertise in carrying out appropriate referrals. At the master's level, social workers are trained in individual, group, and family treatment. At this level there seems to be a good deal of overlapping with the functions of the master's-trained clinical specialist in psychiatric nursing. Social workers and clinical specialists work cooperatively in many settings. Some social workers and clinical specialists are enrolled in postdoctoral programs that provide training in psychoanalysis.

THE CLINICAL PSYCHOLOGIST

The clinical psychologist is educated at the Ph.D. level. Four to five years of graduate school and one year of clinical internship are usually required. Psychologists are trained in individual, group, and family psychotherapy. In several states they are licensed through qualifying examinations and other criteria. Some psychologists also receive several years of postdoctoral training in psychoanalysis. A unique facet of the psychologist's education is preparation in the area of psychological testing. Tests are used for diagnostic purposes, modification of treatment plans, and research projects. The professional organization is the American Psychological Association, which maintains standards and sponsors various professional activities.

THE PSYCHIATRIST

The psychiatrist is a medical doctor who has specialized in psychiatry. Some psychiatrists are "board certified," a designation that involves meeting clinical requirements and passing written examinations. Like psychologists, some psychiatrists seek additional training as psychoanalysts. The professional organization for psychiatrists is the American Psychiatric Association. Psychiatrists make diagnoses; they are usually the professionals who admit or discharge clients from hospitals, and they prescribe and supervise the administration of medication and other somatic treatments, such as electroconvulsive therapy.

THE PHYSICIAN

The client is a bio-psycho-social organism, a *whole person*. Too often in psychiatric settings, however, there is a tendency to focus only on the psychological aspects of a client's case and to neglect the physical aspects. Most general hospital psychiatric units therefore include a medical internist or general practitioner as an active team member. Another important role that such a physician plays is in the area of referral. Indeed, many referrals of clients to psychiatric care originate with family doctors.

THE OCCUPATIONAL THERAPIST

Occupational therapists have been educated and trained to promote the recovery and rehabilitation of clients through manual creative and self-help activities. After assessing clients and participating in team conferences, occupational therapists may prescribe activities that involve learning new job skills or relearning old ones, learning crafts and hobbies, and mastering the activities of daily living.

THE RECREATIONAL THERAPIST

Recreational therapists assess the needs of clients in the area of recreation, sports, and cultural enrichment, and they plan programs that will enhance the treatment plans for individuals and groups. Being involved in leisure-time pursuits can increase an individual's self-esteem, encourage him to interact with others, and help him gain ego strength as a result of increased competence in dealing with the environment. Most recreational and occupational therapists have majored in their areas in colleges, and some have advanced degrees (M.A. or Ph.D.). In addition to their specialties they are educated in counseling and other social sciences. Recreational therapists often utilize volunteer services in order to maintain the necessary link between client and community. They also plan and supervise trips from the agencies to such places as shopping centers, theaters, and beaches.

THE PSYCHIATRIC AIDE OR CLINICAL ASSISTANT

The preparation of psychiatric aides varies greatly. Many are high school graduates, but an increasing number of people with additional education—including persons who have master's degrees in psychology and are either working toward a doctoral degree or awaiting admission to a doctoral program—are functioning as psychiatric aides in order to increase their clinical experience and competence.

In traditional state hospital settings, an aide works under the direction of a nurse and is often the person who spends most time in direct client care. Thus, adequate and extensive in-service training programs for aides are essential in order to maximize effective and therapeutic interaction with clients.

THE NURSE

The nurse is an important member of the interdisciplinary team in psychiatric settings; nursing actions are many and varied. According to the American Nurses' Association's "Statement on Psychiatric and Mental Health Nursing Practice," the functions of a psychiatric nurse include the following:

1. Responsibility for maintaining a therapeutic milieu
2. Working with clients to help resolve some of their problems in living

3. Acceptance of the surrogate parent role
4. Supervision of the physical aspects of the client's health needs, including responses to medications and treatments
5. Health education, particularly in the area of emotional health
6. Helping to improve the client's recreational, occupational, and social competence
7. Providing supervision and clinical assistance to other health workers, including other nurses
8. Psychotherapy
9. Involvement in social action related to the mental health of the community

The A.N.A. statement also defines various levels of practice in psychiatric nursing. Nurses who are prepared at the diploma, associate degree, or baccalaureate level may be found working in psychiatric facilities. According to the statement, they are referred to as "nurses working in a psychiatric setting." The term "psychiatric nurse" is reserved for nurses who have demonstrated, through a formal review process and examinations, a depth of knowledge of psychiatric nursing and an ability to provide quality care to psychiatric clients. The "clinical specialist" in psychiatric nursing is a nurse who has completed graduate education, who has been involved in supervised clinical work, and who has attained a substantial base of theoretical knowledge and clinical competence. The minimal level of education for a clinical specialist is a master's degree in psychiatric nursing. Activities of the clinical specialist include individual therapy; group psychotherapy; family therapy; intake screening and evaluation; home visits; provision of a therapeutic milieu, counseling, health education, and support; medication surveillance; and community action. Many clinical specialists are engaged in private practice, either on an independent basis or in a group-practice situation. Others work in education, research, or administration, sometimes in addition to being engaged in private practice.

• • •

Since mental health services are provided through a system of cooperating health, welfare, and social systems in a geographically defined community, the mental health team may function in any one of a variety of settings. The therapeutic services offered in any setting depend upon whether the major focus is primary, secondary, or tertiary prevention, although some treatment modalities may be utilized in all three levels of prevention. The therapeutic milieu, for example, is an important aspect of therapy in both secondary and tertiary treatment centers, although styles of implementing the concept may vary.

The roles and functions of each member of the health team will also vary according to the needs of the population being served and the organization of the particular agency.

Certain professional responsibilities, however, may not be divided among the members of the mental health team. The physician, for example, always retains professional responsibility for such functions as prescribing medications. The nurse shares with the physician the responsibility for the administration of drugs and the evaluation of their effectiveness and side effects.

But many aspects of psychiatric treatment can be provided by all professionals and by some paraprofessionals. Individual and group therapy and maintaining a therapeutic milieu are some examples. It is in these areas, in which there is an overlapping of professional roles and responsibilities, that the professional expertise and experience of particular team members determine who is responsible for intervention. For example, a nurse with training and experience in crisis intervention or psychodrama would be the team leader when these therapeutic modalities are employed. Or a member of the team who is of the same ethnic group as a client may be more effective than other team members when ethnicity is an important consideration in therapy. Evaluation of client behavior and of the effectiveness of treatment plans are additional areas in which team leadership may shift from one team member to another.

CHAPTER SUMMARY

Team members share in the evaluation of clients and in planning, implementing, and evaluating treatment programs. Team leadership may shift or rotate among team members, depending upon which member has the greatest expertise in a given situation or the most information about a given client.

Clients are considered to be members of the team. In many aspects of milieu therapy clients may be active participants in planning and implementing team goals. Clients may be allowed a degree of self-government, for example, or they may serve as group leaders in staff-client meetings. They may also assume some responsibility for providing support and supervision for clients who are unable to assume responsibility for themselves.

The team approach offers opportunities for staff members to share their experiences and responses and to receive validation and support from other staff members. It also permits the working through of tensions between team members, a process that tends to prevent staff anxieties from encroaching upon the therapeutic milieu. The team concept is of particular significance in mental health care in that the cooperative, collaborative effort involved in planning therapeutic intervention promotes consistency— the treatment plan for each client can be followed through by all members of the mental health team.

Community relations are an important aspect of community mental health. Maintaining liaison with other agencies providing services in a community is essential to meeting local health needs and coordinating services within the health care system.

REFERENCES

Cumming, J., and E. Cumming
    1970 Ego and Milieu. New York: Atherton Press.
Goffman, E.
    1961 Asylums: Essays on the Social Situation of Mental Patients and Other Inmates. Garden City, N. Y.: Anchor Books.
Jones, M.
    1953 The Therapeutic Community, A Treatment Method in Psychiatry. New York: Basic Books, Inc, Publishers.

FURTHER READINGS

Abroms, G. M.
    1969 "Defining milieu therapy." Archives of General Psychiatry 21:553-560
Davis, E. D., and E. M. Pattison
    1979 "The psychiatric nurse's role identity." American Journal of Nursing 79(2): 298-299.
Lego, S.
    1973 "Nurse psychotherapists: how are we different?" Perspectives in Psychiatric Care 11(4):144-147.
O'Toole, A.
    1973 "Doctoral study for psychiatric nurses." Perspectives in Psychiatric Care 11(4):161-164.
Rouslin, S.
    1972 "On certification of the clinical specialist in psychiatric nursing." Perspectives in Psychiatric Care 10 (5):201.
    1976 "Commentary on certification." Perspectives in Psychiatric Care 14 (3):107-111.
Sayre, J.
    1974 "Radical therapy—a challenge to psychiatry." Perspectives in Psychiatric Care 12(1):26-31.
Strachyra, M.
    1973 "Self-regulation through certification." Perspectives in Psychiatric Care 11(4):148-154.
Ujhely, G. B.
    1973 "The nurse as psychotherapist: what are the issues?" Perspectives in Psychiatric Care 11(4):155-160.
    1979 "Credentialing in nursing: a new approach." Report of the Committee for the Study of Credentialing in Nursing. American Journal of Nursing 79(4):674-683.

9
COPING THROUGH PSYCHOPHYSIOLOGICAL RESPONSES

CHAPTER FOCUS

This chapter focuses on psychophysiological responses to stress. It emphasizes the fact that such responses have many causes—including environment, genetic considerations, and interpersonal and intrapersonal factors—and that they all require equal weighting in the assessment process. Nurses as health care providers must begin to view the psychophysiological response as a two-way rather than a one-way process of interaction. Psychological factors, such as anxiety, guilt, and shame, affect the development of physiological responses. The reverse also occurs: a physiological response may then reinforce or intensify the feelings of anxiety, guilt, or shame. The two components act together to maintain a psychophysiological dysfunction.

The chapter includes a classification of dysfunctions. For each dysfunction, the underlying dynamics and the methods of expression of anxiety and communication of needs are described briefly. Specific etiological theories are presented in detail in a section devoted to that topic. Emphasis is placed on an *integrative* approach to the understanding of the client who expresses his needs through a psychophysiological response. The modalities of treatment described in this chapter reflect the fact that persons who exhibit psychophysiological responses to stress are seen more frequently in general hospitals than in psychiatrists' offices. This fact has implications for primary, secondary, and tertiary levels of prevention. Primary prevention deals with the identification of high-risk individuals or groups—for example, persons with type A personality (individuals who continually subject themselves to high levels of stress, such as high-powered business executives and persons whose families utilized psychophysiological responses as appropriate methods of communicating needs). The chapter emphasizes the importance of parental counseling in relation to early interactional patterns within the family group as well as the significance of unmet needs and the eventual expression of those needs or feelings in later years. Secondary prevention directs attention to behavioral problems and appropriate nursing responses. Tertiary prevention involves the use of value clarification to help clients understand the origins of the stress they are experiencing. In addition, the utilization of adaptive methods to express needs should be encouraged by the nurse. The family and other significant social support systems are necessary components of tertiary care. The client who communicates his needs through a psychophysiological response should be assessed from a multifactorial frame of reference. A nurse must consider all relevant information in order to determine a nursing care plan that reflects the interaction of predisposing factors and precipitating events.

292

COPING THROUGH PSYCHOPHYSIOLOGICAL RESPONSES

The psychophysiological response is a result of the delicate interrelationship among genetic, environmental, biochemical, and psychodynamic factors—rather than a unidirectional correlation of stress to disease.

Historical perspectives

Underlying dynamics

   Dependence

   Hostility

   Self-esteem

Classification of psychophysiological dysfunctions

   Peptic ulcer

   Ulcerative colitis

   Asthma

   Obesity

   Anorexia nervosa

   Migraine headaches

   Cardiovascular dysfunctions

   Essential hypertension

   Arthritis

   Cancer

   Sexual dysfunction

Etiology

   Psychological theory

   Biological theory

   Family theory

   Interrelationship of theories

Treatment modalities

   Medication

   Individual and group therapy

   Family therapy

Nursing intervention

   Primary prevention

   Secondary prevention

   Tertiary prevention

HISTORICAL PERSPECTIVES

Traditionally, the intricate interrelationship of physiology and psychology has been a question of interest and consternation. Cannon (1929) demonstrated that changes in secretions of organs and tension of muscles occur as a result of arousal of emotions. Selye (1956) suggested that stress causes the arousal of psychological as well as physiological responses and that the two kinds of response combine to cause organ changes. Freud, in his study of conversion reactions, also noted the significance of the interrelationship of emotions and physiological responses.

We can no longer consider the dichotomy between mind and body appropriate when we assess an individual's health status. Nor can we predict that a stressor will lead to a certain set of responses. Each human being represents a complex interrelationship of internal and external factors. As we propose in the section on etiology that appears later in this chapter, cognitive, genetic, communication, learning, and psychoanalytic theories all must be used to explain psychophysiological responses, because experience, environment, personality type, and defense and coping strategies all combine to produce the responses. It is from such a perspective that a nurse must work in order to be able to determine an appropriate and comprehensive nursing care plan.

UNDERLYING DYNAMICS

Illness frequently is related to personality type and predetermined patterns of response to stress. Various physical symptoms may be related to the experience of stress in the environment. As we pointed out before, however, such a process does not operate in isolation from other significant factors. It is thus important to identify issues such as dependence, hostility, and self-esteem that arise as nursing problems when we care for clients experiencing psychophysiological dysfunctions.

Dependence

Some clients are unable to express feelings of dependence and to feel comfortable being taken care of. Early patterns of interaction may have prohibited the expression of dependence needs. These needs then may have been translated into "words" that were expressed through the autonomic nervous system. Implicit messages from significant others as well as from society as a whole may prevent a person from acting out his dependence needs. For example, an active middle-aged man who experiences a heart attack may be unable to accept staying in bed. Denial of dependence needs is often a key issue in such a situation.

Hostility

Inability to express anger or resentment is another critical behavioral problem. Unacceptable hostile impulses and frustrations may be chronically repressed. This repression may be a response learned from early interactions with significant persons. Environmental factors may further accentuate the repression of these emotions. Expression of anger or resentment through psychophysiological responses may have been implicitly encouraged through the very same interactional patterns that prohibited the verbal expression of such emotions. Nurses need to remember that the development of a psychophysiologic response is the result of a complex interaction among many factors.

Self-esteem

Self-esteem is always a significant factor in a person's health status. When an individual is unable to communicate needs directly, there is a resulting loss of self-esteem. The degree of loss depends upon the length of time such a pattern has existed, the repertoire of coping and defense mechanisms and their efficiency, the availability of active support systems, and the number and type of stressors operating at any given time. Loss of self-esteem may result from a client's inability to accept a less independent state. Increasing the client's ability to directly express needs will increase the likelihood that he will feel better about himself.

• • •

Through the process of exploring issues of dependence and anger, the client can identify his role in the interaction with significant others. With their support, he can be assisted to deal with the anger and hostility associated with dependence. He can be helped to see that anger or resentment can be discussed during interactions with others.

It is important to reemphasize the complex interrelationship of factors that results in a psychophysiological response. Intrapsychic issues, life stresses, personality organization, environmental supports, and biochemical factors act in conjunction to *increase the probability* that a psychophysiological response will occur.

CLASSIFICATION OF PSYCHOPHYSIOLOGICAL DYSFUNCTIONS
Peptic ulcer

The client experiencing a peptic ulcer is not necessarily of any one personality type. Characteristically, there is a longing to be cared for and loved, which is repressed and replaced by aggressive behavior. In some cases, however, the client may be overly dependent or demanding a situation that causes him to feel that he is being repudiated because of his dependent state. Thus, unconscious conflicts and negative responses from the environment for dependent behavior may be two factors forcing a client to maintain an independent stance. When needs for love cannot be met through a relationship, they are converted into a wish to be fed. The stomach then remains in a constant state of preparation for food. It is interesting to note that ulcer pains are relieved by food and exacerbated by hunger. In essence, food is equated with being loved.

No single factor is responsible for ulcer formation. Genetic predisposition to hypersecretion, relatively strong oral-dependent traits, increasingly high levels of stress in life experiences—these characteristics coupled with thwarted dependence needs encountered in later life and a limited repertoire of coping and defense strategies increase the probability of the occurrence of ulcers.

Ulcerative colitis

Ulcerative colitis may develop as a result of unmet dependence needs as well as feelings of guilt. The capacity for ego integration in a person with this condition is poor, and he frequently uses projection—diarrhea literally becomes a way of projecting unacceptable impulses onto the environment.

The onset of ulcerative colitis is frequently associated with periods of emotional stress. Experiences relating to loss—of a body part, a relationship, or status, for example, with concurrent loss of self-esteem—are significant factors in the development of colitis. The response to loss is often characterized by hostility and depression. Relationships with other persons are often shallow and lack the capacity for an appropriate affective response. The inability to form a relationship of significance may result from the early mother-child relationship. In many cases the mothering figure was domineering while at the same time hostile and rejecting. The individual was left feeling helpless and unable to express his rage. A nurse must be aware of genetic predisposition, personality pattern, strategies of coping, the degree to which stress is perceived as threatening, and the degree of unmet dependence needs in order to determine a nursing care plan that reflects the interrelationship of all factors.

Asthma

Asthma has historically been identified as the "typical" psychophysiological response. Asthma's notoriety results in part from its relationship to a vital function—breathing. The influence of emotions on the functioning of the respiratory system is evidenced in such statements as "The scenery was breathtaking" or "The experience took my breath away." The etiology of asthma involves many factors—organic as well as psychological. Many personality types are seen among asthmatic clients. Some are aggressive-compulsive; others are hypersensitive to other people. Some asthmatic clients have an exaggerated dependence on the mothering figure that arouses conflict when the relationship is threatened. This situation does not result in a wish to be fed, as in the case of an ulcer client, but in the need to be protected. A recurrent theme of maternal rejection or attempts on the part of parents to make a child independent too quickly is often noted. The child is assumed to be mature; however, he is not mature, and, as he is forced to be mature, his insecure feelings about himself rapidly heighten. Dependent longings are viewed negatively. The child is not allowed to express feelings—particularly to cry. Thus an asthmatic attack can be viewed as being symbolic of the wish to reestablish a relationship with the mothering figure.

No single factor or theory can accurately account for the asthmatic response. Some suggest a strong correlation between stressful events—for example, seeing a picture of a dead parent or going to a place that the individual had frequented with the parent—and the onset of an asthmatic attack. According to this theory, hyperventilation occurs as a conditioned response to a conditional stimulation (the stressful event). Bronchial spasms and increased mucous secretions then occur, which may increase the individual's anxiety. The increase in anxiety then results in the asthmatic attack.

According to another theory, psychosocial stressors that threaten a person's current relationships activate familiar unpleasant feelings from past relationships with significant others. Fear of rejection and feelings of helplessness, lack of control, and dependence are generated, which have the *potential* to initiate an asthmatic response.

Obesity

In order to understand obesity, it is necessary to clearly identify two physiological processes—satiation and the act of feeding. The hypothalamus controls these processes. However, such physiological functions are also affected by parental influences, genetic predisposition, sociocultural determinants, amount of activity, psychological or physical stressors, and level of development. Within the family environment, the infant begins to develop an awareness of eating and hunger as well as satiety of hunger. It is believed that satiety is not discriminated; thus it is not learned. In other words, the young child does not learn, through parental interaction and feedback, to eat to satisfy his hunger but rather eats in an indiscriminate fashion.

Assessment of early family relationships is significant since a pattern leading toward obesity often develops in early childhood. Parents are often frustrated with their own lives and tend to live vicariously through the lives of their children. Parents frequently believe that they had difficult lives as children, and they are therefore determined that their own children will not experience the same frustrations they did.

However, feelings of resentment may be nonverbally transmitted to the child. The child may be viewed as an extension of the parent. As this view is perpetuated through infancy and early childhood, the child may be unable to develop an adequate sense of self. In adolescence, such an individual experiences difficulty in the accomplishment of a sense of identity. He becomes a passive, submissive person who has internalized feelings of resentment and hostility.

Instead of verbalizing feelings of affection, parents, particularly the mother, sometimes force food on a young child as a means of demonstrating love. The critical factor seems to be that often these children are not wanted. This message is transmitted to the child. Food then is equated with love and satisfaction. This dynamic can be demonstrated repeatedly in later, adult relationships. Forceful feeding rather than allowing a child to eat according to his hunger and satiety leads to his developing a distorted perception of his body. Bruch (1973) believes that the child who does not learn to respond to his own cues regarding hunger and satiety is unable to determine how much he should eat. Bodily distortion becomes an integral component of such an individual. By the time he reaches adulthood, the obese body image will have become a means to receive attention and praise. It may be the single factor that draws others close to him.

Characteristically, an obese person has poor ego strength, he lacks a sound self-concept, and he harbors repressed feelings of hostility toward the parental pair—particularly the mother. Because of the underlying low self-worth, the obese individual may experience difficulty in love relationships. Frustration results, and the excessive eating behavior is reactivated, as in past situations. Parents pushed food as a means of controlling anxiety and giving love; the obese client has internalized this mechanism, which is reactivated in an anxiety-provoking situation. Eating is equated with satisfaction and thus becomes a predominant defense.

An assessment of the strength of the need to eat as a means of maintaining personality integration is a necessary nursing measure. A weight-reduction program may be very anxiety provoking; it can cause a severe shift in the psychological equilibrium of a client.

Many factors can be involved in the development of obesity. For example, social factors such as class are relevant. It has been noted that members of lower-class families are more likely to become obese than are members of middle- and upper-class families. This situation may be caused by the frustration and hostility generated as a result of being unable to meet the most basic needs for survival.

Anorexia nervosa

The cluster of symptoms that characterize an anorectic client includes severe weight loss, absent or irregular menstrual periods, loss of sexual desire, and decrease in endocrine function with a resultant decline in growth rate. There is a mortality rate of 10% to 15%. Anorexia nervosa occurs primarily in adolescent girls. The adolescent experiences a fear of being rejected by the mothering figure and often desires special attention in order to feel loved. Unconscious aggressive impulses take the form of envy and jealousy toward persons—often siblings—who receive such attention. Ambivalence is characteristic of the mother-daughter relationship. Hostility toward the mother exists, yet the daughter feels threatened by the thought of having to assume independence. The adolescent's cessation of eating may be a rebellion against parents. A feeling of loss of control and a sense of ineffectiveness and helplessness are also characteristic of the anorectic adolescent.

Several factors, then, interact to lead to anorexia: intrapsychic conflicts, overall personality traits, early parent-child interactions, past experiences, and present situations that reactivate feelings of dependence and helplessness. Current situations in an adolescent's life, such as the establishment of the first sexual relationship, may act as precipitants. Loss of the sense of one's childhood and of one's dependent status may also initiate the anorectic syndrome. The illness causes the family to shift its attention toward the anorectic child—an unconscious secondary gain for the child.

Minuchin and associates (1978) place a great deal of emphasis on the view that the syndrome involves the entire family even though the symptoms are expressed only through the adolescent member. They argue that anorexia encompasses the behavior of all family members. Overprotection in the form of excessive concern for psychobiological needs is apparent in such a family. The child develops the same excessive awareness of bodily needs. The child is also quite aware of her effect on the interactions in the family. There is a dependence on parental assessment, leading to inhibition of the development of independence and control over one's life. In addition, there is usually an excessive concern with eating and dieting. Members of the anorectic family are overinvolved in each other's lives, with a resultant loss of individuation. Conflict is negated by the use of the children—particularly through the use of the anorectic child's symptoms. In essence, the anorectic child is charged with maintaining the status quo of the family. When the status quo has been maintained, the symptoms are reinforced. This pattern continues even though family members may feel exploited. In a sense, everyone wins but also loses in such a situation. The anorectic child receives attention and feels in control, while other family members are able to avoid conflict once again. The dysfunction continues even though all members of the family are experiencing some level of discomfort. The ultimate goal of avoiding conflict is maintained.

Bruch (1973) delineates two types of anorexia nervosa. Primary syndrome anorexia is characterized by hyperactivity, continual seeking of perfection, preoccupation with food, and the pursuit of a thin state of being. The last aspect is often perceived as crucial in the anorectic person's search for identity. Food is frequently taken in only to be regurgitated—possible because of overwhelming guilt for having eaten. The atypical syndrome is characterized by an overconcern for the actual function of eating. There is little evidence of the other characteristics.

The nursing assessment should reflect a consideration of all factors and their implications for client and family behavior. A comprehensive nursing care plan may be determined. There does not seem to be one specific therapy that has achieved success. The most important considerations are the predominant themes and the degree of starvation.

Migraine headaches

The client who releases anxiety through migraine headaches is best described as a perfectionist who sets exceptionally high standards for himself and others in his environment. He is compulsive in his attention to detail and is not likely to delegate responsibilities. There is a characteristic repression of hostile impulses. Although he is of superior intelligence, this type of client may not be as emotionally mature as his peers. He has a genetic predisposition to vasodilation. The onset of a migraine can often be related to a stressful event. The occurrence of a migraine frequently leads to episodes of vomiting, diarrhea, and vertigo. The client is virtually immobilized until the persistent headache subsides. A lesser form of migraine is the "tension" headache, which is commonly experience as a response to stress. When completing an assessment, a nurse should rule out the possibility of organic causes before attributing the headache to stress factors.

Cardiovascular dysfunctions

Cardiovascular dysfunctions are frequently identified as being stress related. When stress becomes chronic, the cardiovascular system experiences changes in heart rate, blood pressure, and strength of contractions. As was stated in Chapter 4, these changes can then act as stressors in and of themselves, with resulting increases in anxiety levels.

Much emphasis has recently been placed on the type A personality as described by Friedman (1969). Such an individual is characterized as hardworking, competitive, and aggressive; he invests a great deal of energy in many commitments. These individuals usually occupy upper-level management positions. They frequently feel that their jobs or businesses cannot go on without them; they pay little attention to vacations or to time that could be spent pursuing personal or family interests.

It is imperative, of course, that nurses also consider other factors that are relevant to the increased incidence of cardiovascular disease (which includes coronary artery disease, angina, myocardial infarction, and congestive heart failure). Genetic and constitutional factors such as cholesterol levels are interrelated with personality factors, socioeconomic factors, and cultural factors.

The individual who experiences a cardiovascular dysfunction is characterized as being controlled; he does not readily display emotions. Dependence needs and hostile impulses are repressed. Denial of dependence needs can take the form of not adhering to the cardiac regimen after myocardial infarction. In such a situation, the denial can be life-threatening. Being controlled by hospital routine can be perceived as threatening, which may result in increased anxiety and further cardiac dysfunction.

Stressors in the environment—social, economic, cultural—may threaten an individual's sense of control, leading to increased incidence of cardiac dysfunction. An example of a stressor might be a change in job status that has social, economic, and cultural implications for the individual.

Nurses might care for a cardiac client who has excessive needs for dependence but is unable to express those needs verbally. Hospitalization and illness might permit an individual to give up some of his responsibilities—for example, to self, family, and job. It is often difficult for a client to make strides toward improvement if the secondary gains of illness are attractive.

Cardiac neurosis or "effort syndrome" is not characterized by structural changes in the cardiovascular system or by electrocardiogram changes. An individual with this condition does, however, experience shortness of breath, chest pain, rapid heart rate, dizziness, and several other symptoms of cardiac dysfunction. The condition seems to be related to an underlying conflict that involves unmet dependence, needs and repression of hostile impulses. Personality factors, particularly immaturity, interact with stress occurring within the individual's interpersonal, social, and/or cultural spheres. It is important for the nursing assessment to include a physical examination to determine whether any physiological changes have occurred. If the results are negative, concern should be directed toward the identification of bio-psycho-social factors that may be precipitating the cardiac neurosis.

Essential hypertension

Bottled-up rage, a phenomenon that resembles the action of a pressure cooker—this is the concept underlying the expression of tension through the cardiovascular system. The client's conscience will not permit the expression of angry impulses, even though dependent relationships are being threatened. His sense of guilt acts as a stopgap measure. This mechanism continues until a pattern of repression of hostility is developed. The repeated vasoconstriction that results leads to irreversible changes in the cardiovascular system—particularly in persons who seem to be predisposed to hypertension. Characteristically, during early life experiences the individual was charged with an increased sense of responsibility. He was not permitted the luxury of being angry, because of the implied message that a responsible individual does not show his anger. This behavior may have been learned from significant others in the environment and positively reinforced as a method of coping. The personality of the individual who has hypertension masks the intrapsychic conflict by displaying a calm, serene, facade. This facade permits the individual to maintain relationships and thus to meet dependence needs. Socioeconomic, genetic-consitutional, cultural-ethnic, interpersonal, and intrapsychic factors interact to increase the probability that hypertension will develop. For example, a black American who is experiencing high levels of stress—perhaps as a result of divorce proceedings or loss of a job—may be prone to developing hypertension. No one factor is responsible alone for the development of hypertension, although the emotional component does seem to be significant.

Arthritis

The client who expresses his tension through the musculoskeletal system in the form of arthritis is often described as an extrovert—jovial, happy, and interested in athletic activities. Arthritic clients may experience a chronic state of inhibited rebellious hostility, which is frequently related to strong dependence needs. One dynamics pattern involves an overprotective parental influence, particularly on the part of the mother, which eventually causes a repression of hostile tendencies. Hostility is sublimated into physical exercise—particularly competitive sports. The arthritic individual maintains control over his environment to prevent the expression of hostile impulses. Increased muscle tonus results from this prolonged inhibition of hostile impulses. The degree of inhibition is directly proportional to the degree of contraction of the muscle; the more repressed the hostile tendencies, the greater the contraction.

Although personality factors and intrapsychic conflicts seem to play a significant role in the development of arthritis, genetic and constitutional factors, biochemical changes, and precipitating stressful events must be considered. For example, stressful events cause changes in the levels of hormones and adrenocorticoids. These substances play a role in the development of collagen, a form of connective tissue. As hormone and adrenocorticoid levels change, there is a resulting change in the nature of the connective tissue formed, leading to arthritis. Stressors that precipitate the onset or reappearance of symptoms may be bio-psycho-social or cultural in nature. Oftentimes the stressor occurs in the form of a loss that is perceived as threatening to the dependence needs of an individual. Unresolved feelings of anger are then transferred to the musculoskeletal system. The interrelationship of genetic factors, intrapsychic conflicts, biochemical changes, and precipitating stressors—particularly those revolving around loss—must be an integral part of the nursing assessment.

Cancer

The correlation between psychological stress and the onset of neoplastic disease has been suggested by several research studies. There seems to be a complex set of interactions rather than a direct cause-and-effect relationship.

LeShan (1966) and Bahnson and Bahnson (1966) noted that the loss of a significant, intensely dependent relationship often occurs just before (within 12 months) the appearance of symptomatology. The loss may reactivate unmet dependence needs that were generated in the early mother-child relationship. Hostility, which the client cannot express openly, is aroused as a result of the loss. The loss may center around a personal relationship, a job, status in the community, or control over one's environment. As a result of responses that were learned in early parental interactions, the individual must repress his hostility in order to be "the good person." The early mother-child relationship is characterized by an impoverishment of affection, by strong unresolved tensions, and by poor communication lines. The child learns not to express feelings, not to expect much from anyone, and not to become angry.

As in the other psychophysiological responses, there is no single cause leading to the outcome. Biological factors, including changes in endocrine and metabolic function, occur as a result of stress. Genetic and constitutional predisposition may cause an individual to be more vulnerable to these endocrine and metabolic changes. A decreased immunological response resulting in a reduced antibody reaction may have occurred as a result of early infantile relationships. Stress in current life situations may act as a precipitant leading to a reduced antibody response in adult life. Greene (1966) suggested that anxiety and depression related to precipitating loss events such as death of a spouse or separation from spouse, children, or significant others were often factors in the etiology of cancer. This statement implies that, in such cases, early resolution of loss situations was not handled appropriately. Coping mechanisms were utilized to deny or repress the hostility and feelings of dependence, generated by the unresolved loss situations.

Studies are not conclusive, however, concerning the impact of unresolved loss situations on the development of cancer. More definitive data needs to be collected on what constitutes psychological stress as opposed to physiological (biochemical, genetic) risk factors and on the role of previous life events. Some evidence has suggested a relationship between stress and the development of leukemia and lymphoma (Greene, 1966). However, there is no consistent data indicating that the life stress theory is applicable to other types of neoplasms.

Consideration must be given to all factors—genetic and constitutional traits, intrapsychic conflicts, personality traits, past interpersonal experiences, and biochemical and autoimmune responses—and the interaction of these factors with precipitating events (life stress).

Sexual dysfunction

Sexual dysfunctions have historically been related to intrapsychic conflicts—particularly the repression of hostility. This factor retains considerable significance; however, biological, interpersonal, and sociocultural factors must be considered as well. Impotence, premature ejaculation, and retarded ejaculation are included among male sexual dysfunctions; female dysfunctions include preorgasmia, vaginismus, and dyspareunia. In order to determine a comprehensive plan of care, a nurse must consider all factors that may be relevant to a dysfunction.

Biological or organic factors play a part in the evolution of sexual dysfunctions. Organic causes may be natural in the developmental sense, such as aging, or they may be pathological, as in the disease processes. Sexual functioning may be impaired as a result of chronic illness or degenerative disease. Diseases of the genitalia can alter sexual functioning—even to the point of total abstinence from coitus, depending upon the degree of discomfort incurred as a result of sexual relations. Other disorders, such as diabetes, hypothyroidism, hepatitis, and cirrhosis, may also alter sexual functioning. Neurological impairment, including spinal cord trauma and diseases of the frontal and temporal lobes, may cause impotence or inorgasmia. Finally, drugs can have an effect on sexual performance—either a permanent one or a temporary one, depending upon the drug. Antihypertensive medications, estrogen, steroids, and anticholinergics may cause impotence. When administration of such a drug is stopped, sexual dysfunction usually disappears. However, in some cases, permanent dysfunction may result.

Intrapsychic conflict that generates anxiety may be detrimental to sexual functioning. Unconscious conflicts, particularly those surrounding the oedipal period, have been identified as being responsible for dysfunction. Castration anxiety is a common cause of impotence, according to the psychoanalytic school of thought. Incestuous wishes that are repressed in the oedipal phase may be reexperienced in later life, leading to guilt and the inability to perform sexually. Hostile impulses resulting from early conflicts may be precipitated by a current sexual relationship. The hostility is repressed; tension may be released through the penis in the form of impotence or through the vagina in the form or preorgasmia or frigidity.

Children often learn at an early age that sex and their bodies are "dirty." This belief as well as other values and attitudes regarding sex are learned via an intricate network of experiences. Behavior in later life may reflect those early experiences. The original stimulus—for example, a parent telling a child that masturbation will lead to mental illness—is no longer necessary; the imprint from that original message will last a lifetime.

Fear may also play a significant role in the development of sexual dysfunctions. There is the fear of pregnancy for the female, as well as the fear of being found out and the fear of venereal disease. Situations may develop in which partners fear engaging in sex—for example, because visitors are staying in the house, the children are still awake and may come in or call out for the parents, or the partners are visiting in a friend's home. The environment must be as free of tension as possible so that each partner feels comfortable expressing himself sexually.

Interpersonal conflicts may indicate poor lines of communication between the partners. When one partner is distressed or angry at the other, the anger may be expressed through the sexual act or may inhibit the sexual act. Each partner needs to feel that his wishes are being considered. Feeling as though one is a sexual object rather than an active participant in a relationship has deleterious effects upon sexual functioning. Innuendos regarding sexual competence—for example, comparison of the current partner with previous partners—lead to feelings of inadequacy and impaired sexual functioning. Sensitivity to one another's needs and respect for each other's bodies is a crucial interpersonal factor. Consideration of individual needs reduces the incidence of sexual dysfunction.

Sociocultural factors have a significant impact upon the development of sexual attitudes and the sexual interaction that a couple experiences. Changes in attitude toward the role of the woman have had a significant effect on sexual functioning. The woman may no longer be considered the "passive recipient" of the sexual act. The male who has operated under the assumption that he is the dominant figure in the sexual relationship may perceive this change in mores as threatening. Much more emphasis has been placed on performance and competence. Anxiety has been generated, followed by a fear of failure. Sensitivity to one another's needs in a relationship has been replaced by the philosophy "Do it more and do it better!" This emphasis on function will surely lead to increased dysfunction.

Each of the factors mentioned must be considered in order to understand the evolution of sexual dysfunction. Again, no one theory is sufficient to explain a dysfunction, and it cannot be said that each type of conflict leads to one specific dysfunction. Precipitating events need to be considered in light of their interaction with bio-psycho-social factors. A brief description of each dysfunction follows.

Impotence is the inability to achieve or maintain an erection. It results from an inhibition of the vasocongestive phase of sexual response. Men who have never had an erection are said to have primary impotence. Impotence that occurs in individuals who have experienced successful erections in the past is called secondary impotence. Impotence may be general—that is, it occurs in any and all sexual experiences. Or it may be situational—occurring only in certain situations. For example, a man may be potent with his wife yet unable to achieve erection while having a relationship with another woman, or vice versa. Impotence prior to old age is a devastating experience that may lead to a loss of self-worth and ultimately to failures in other areas of life.

Premature ejaculation is the ejaculation of semen before the partners reach a state in which mutual enjoyment is experienced. The man has not learned voluntary control over ejaculation; orgasm is reached quickly once he is sexually aroused. Although there is no real time limit for ejaculation, many men state that they are not able to delay ejaculation. Both partners can learn to be responsive to ejaculation; the man can begin to learn voluntary control, while the woman may also learn techniques to control ejaculation.

Retarded ejaculation is the opposite of premature ejaculation. This occurrence is normally associated with the aging process. In this dysfunction, the male is able to achieve erection but is unable to ejaculate.

Orgasmic dysfunction is the inability of the female to achieve orgasm. Orgasmic dysfunction may be situational or general. Women who have never achieved orgasm are said to have primary inorgasmia. These women may also be termed "preorgasmic." Women who have achieved orgasm through masturbation or intercourse but are presently unable to achieve orgasm are said to have secondary inorgasmia.

Dyspareunia refers to pain during intercourse. This situation may result from inadequate lubrication of the vagina.

Vaginismus refers to the development of spasticity in the pelvic muscles surrounding the opening of the vagina. The spasticity results in contractions, which lead to decreased probability of penetration.

Each dysfunction must be assessed in terms of the intricate relationship of many factors. Helen Singer Kaplan (1974) believes that the development of an erotic environment provides the atmosphere for the development of healthy sexual relationships. Feelings, needs, and concerns need to be openly expressed. Pressure to perform should not be the overriding principle. Couples should concentrate on making sexual experiences exciting, stimulating, and enjoyable for both partners.

• • •

Kolb (1977) states that there is strong support for the view that there is a close association between physical and psychological dysfunctions. Psychophysiological responses are commonly treated by a physician rather than a psychiatrist. In fact, psychiatrists often view clients with such responses as not being "sick" enough or at least not "mentally sick" enough to be treated. Often these persons are referred from physician to physician with little attention being given to their psychological needs. Such clients are typically found in medical and surgical units of general hospitals. It becomes the nurse's responsibility to accurately and comprehensively assess the needs of these clients in order to prevent further neglect of psychological dysfunction.

Diagnostic and Statistical Manual III no longer classifies psychophysiological dysfunctions as such but includes these disorders under the heading "Psychological Factors Affecting Physical Illness." This change in classification attests to the strong link between physical illness and psychological, social, and cultural factors.

ETIOLOGY
Psychological theory

Psychoanalytic-intrapsychic theory. Franz Alexander (1950) claims that each physiological response specifically corresponds to an uncon-

scious emotional conflict. For example, a client who has the need to be taken care of cannot accede to that need but must instead maintain the appearance of being independent. The tension or anxiety arising from the arousal of this unconscious conflict in a dependent individual is discharged through a peptic ulcer. Another client is unable to directly discharge his anger or hostility. The symptom that may appear is rising blood pressure. This "specificity theory" implies that there is a specific physiological response to each emotional conflict or emotional stimulus. The physiological response is under the control of the autonomic nervous system.

This theory assumes a one-to-one cause-and-effect relationship between particular conflictual issues and physiological responses. Little or no consideration is given to genetic predisposition, personal coping strategies, or past experience, to cite a few factors.

Psychodynamic-interpersonal theory. Dunbar (1954) argues that clients have particular personality "profiles". Such a theory implies that there is a definitive correlation between a particular personality type and a particular disease entity. To cite an example, this theory holds that the client who is most likely to develop peptic ulcers is the high-powered, goal-oriented, aggressive, long-term planner. The accident-prone client is an impulsive, unsystematic, and hostile individual.

Personality, however, cannot account in full as an explanation for the development of psychophysiological disorders. Friedman (1969) incorporates this fact into his description of the correlation between the type A personality and an increased incidence of coronary artery disease.

Conditioned or learned response theory. Nurses need to consider how and if learning affects a response. Does the behavior result in dependence needs being met? Does it provide positive reinforcement from significant others in the environment? For example, does the onset of ulcer symptoms engender caring responses that the client cannot normally accept? Behavior may be learned from significant others such as family members. A child finds that one parent "uses" his ulcer pains to gain attention from others in the family. Others take care of him and perform the tasks that are part of that parent's responsibility. The child "learns" that such a technique is an effective way to be dependent while maintaining a facade of independence. This may be particularly true for men, since men generally are permitted neither to express emotions nor to be dependent—although this attitude does seem to be changing as society continues to emphasize the importance of sharing feelings openly. It is imperative that we recognize that the expression of tension through the autonomic nervous system may be a learned response that is well entrenched by the time a person reaches a point where he seeks treatment.

Biological theory

The discussion of psychophysiological disorders is not complete without the inclusion of Selye's theory that pituitary-adrenal responses to stress lead to "diseases of adaptation." Selye suggests that when sufficient stress occurs, anxiety arises, which in turn leads to the arousal of psychological and physiological responses. If coping strategies are unable to deal with the increased stress, a change in somatic functioning results. Selye further suggests that which organ is affected depends to a greater extent on physiology and genetic predispostion than on psychology. (For further discussion of this disorder, known as Selye's General Adaptation Syndrome, see Chapter 4.)

Family theory

The concept of family has become increasingly important over the last 20 years. The family transmits the mores and values of society to its members. The child is influenced by the manner in which parents communicate to one another and by the adaptation mechanisms they use to reduce stress and anxiety. The family structure provides an arena in which the offspring develop a sense of identity or a lack of identity. They learn to communicate with others, and they learn to relate in a healthy manner to others in their environment and in society as a whole. Satir (1972) points out not only that the family is charged with helping a child to accomplish these tasks, but that the child emerges as a mentally healthy adult as a result of their successful achievement. Satir therefore views the family as a complex, continuous interaction of individuals who assume various roles at various times, accomplish developmental tasks, cope with conflicts, and become active members in society. When discussing this concept of family, we often do not realize the full impact the family has upon its individual members. As you will note in later sections, adaptive behavior that clients utilize in response to stressors such as changes in body image, pain, immobilization, sensory overload or deprivation, and loss or change are greatly influenced by previous experiences with these stressors in the family setting. Parents act as role models for the handling of conflict situations. Communication patterns utilized by parents are adopted by children to be transmitted to their children.

As we know, this role modeling may be either positive or negative.

How is the concept of family related to the utilization of psychophysiological processes as modes of adaptation? How can it not be related? Minuchin (1974) believes that there is a "psychosomatogenic family." Reviewing what has previously been discussed, we see that the child's adaptation mechanisms, as well as his roles, are learned through the family process. Within the psychosomatogenic family, the child learns that his psychophysiological dysfunction serves as a source of concern for family members. This allows the family to focus on something other than family conflict. Minuchin feels that there is a particular type of family organization that submerges or denies outright conflict; conflicts are never resolved in such a family. As the psychophysiological dysfunction continues to mask the conflicts within the family, the child receives positive reinforcement for his symptoms, which in turn serves to maintain the ritual of conflict avoidance. Minuchin also discusses the question of physiological vulnerability. The child may have a particular physiological weakness that determines the organ of choice, but the operation of the family and its impact on its members is a crucial aspect of the dysfunction.

Ackerman (1966) supports the concept that a psychophysiological dysfunction in a child serves to control conflict within the family. The dysfunction maintains patterns of communication and prevents the occurrence of psychosis.

Interrelationship of theories

A delicate interrelationship of genetic, intrapsychic, psychodynamic, cognitive, biochemical, and familial factors must be considered before a psychophysiological response can be understood. This interrelationship operates in a multifactorial sense; that is, when several factors are present, there is an increased probability of a particular psychophysiological response. Precipitating stressful events, such as the perceived or actual loss of a relationship, act as catalysts. Individual coping strategies and personality traits also affect the development of psychophysiological responses. A nurse must consider many theories in order to determine a plan of care that is suited to a particular client and to his psychophysiological response at the time.

TREATMENT MODALITIES
Medication

A primary goal of the nurse is to assess the meaning that a dysfunction holds for the client. Why does he choose to adapt to stress in this manner? However, it is often necessary to deal with the high levels of anxiety and the symptoms of depression that precipitate and exacerbate psychophysiological dysfunctions. Tranquilizers, antidepressants, and sedatives are the drugs most frequently indicated. They should be administered judiciously and according to the needs of each individual client. Medications are not replacements for therapy but should be utilized in conjunction with appropriate modes of intervention. Other types of medication, directed toward specific disease processes, are often indicated as well.

Individual and group therapy

There are various psychological modalities for the treatment of psychophysiological dysfunctions. Treatment plans are based on the theory that is most relevant to the client's situation. Psychotherapy is directed toward the long-term goal of initiating new adaptive measures. Intensive psychotherapy is successful in the treatment of most psychophysiological dysfunctions. However, the decision to engage in this interpretive form of therapy depends upon the fragility of the client's ego. This type of therapy is not recommended for clients with ulcerative colitis or peptic ulcers, since the exacerbation of symptoms may be potentially life threatening.

Supportive one-to-one therapy is essential until the client is able to accept himself and his role in his environment. He then will no longer "need" the psychophysiological dysfunction and will seek more realistic and self-satisfying modes of adaptation.

Anaclitic therapy may be utilized, but only in a well-controlled situation. This form of therapy involves the regression of the client to an earlier stage of development—a stage where he feels comfortable. He then is gradually moved back through the developmental eras and helped to deal with feelings of dependence and/or guilt when appropriate.

Rest, diet, and other supportive measures, as well as medical intervention, are also utilized, as needed, in individual therapy.

Group therapy may be used as an adjunct to the supportive or psychotherapeutic one-to-one relationship. Initially, a client needs to feel comfortable with one helping person. He may then move into a group situation with greater self-confidence.

It is important to note that clients rarely seek psychiatric help for any of the dysfunctions discussed in this chapter. Frequently it is in the general hospital setting that nurses deal with clients who are experiencing stress-related dysfunctions. Society may, in fact, subtly condone the occurrence of such dysfunctions as ulcers or coronary artery disease as part of becoming successful—they are often seen as marks of an aggressive, ambitious individual. Although therapy is important, it is more relevant for nurses to assist clients to gain an understanding of the interaction among dysfunction, stress, and lifestyle. In many instances, nurses can provide short-term supportive therapy that can enable a client to gain more control over his environment and to express needs in a more open, direct fashion. Follow-up treatment in the form of family therapy can then serve to support the use of alternative methods of coping.

Family therapy

Proponents of systems theory view the individual as a subsystem that is in continuous interaction with many other subsystems in the environment. The underlying premise is that one cannot successfully treat an individual client without considering him as an integral part of the total system. Family therapy involves all family members or significant others in the client's environment. As was previously discussed, the goal of family therapy is to enable the *family*, not just the individual client, to resolve conflict and express needs directly, rather than force the client to use maladaptive behavior to maintain family patterns.

NURSING INTERVENTION

PRIMARY PREVENTION

Primary prevention is a key concept in the area of psychophysiological dysfunctions. As Chapter 4 pointed out, it involves the identification of potential stressors and the education of individuals and families to enable them to develop healthy patterns of adaptation. It is important to identify high-risk groups, such as members of families in which one or both parents express needs primarily through psychophysiological behavior. This task may seem monumental, particularly since such clients do not usually seek psychiatric treatment. Nurses often see these clients in general hospital settings and physicians' offices. Assessment data should reflect the fact that the client is an integral part of his family and community system. Nursing intervention can be directed toward identifying the significance of early patterns of interaction within a family in which physical illness is directly affected by psychological factors. Since these issues are often quite emotionally charged, a client may deny that he has any difficulty expressing needs or feelings.

Parental education on an informal level may stimulate parents to become more aware of the role they play in influencing their children's methods of adapting to stress—particularly the use of psychophysiological behavior. As was discussed in Chapter 4, the family is the target client system for nursing intervention. Nurses can enable clients to provide an atmosphere in which their children can feel safe and comfortable in sharing their needs to feel taken care of and to feel that they are whole, interdependent, unique beings. In such an atmosphere, expressions of anger, fear, and rage are dealt with in an open, honest manner. Providing open lines of communication may be difficult for a parent who has never experienced such a situation himself. In spite of the significance of early parental interaction and direct lines of communication, it is important not to neglect the impact of genetic predisposition, personality factors, and precipitating factors that may interact to increase the use of psychophysiological responses as adaptive mechanisms.

Primary prevention is concerned with the identification of potential stressors and the education of the individual to deal with them. If a client has already developed a psychophysiological response as an adaptive measure, the focus of primary prevention shifts to the children of the client, with an increased emphasis on the influence of parental adaptive measures.

SECONDARY PREVENTION

Whether the primary theme is unmet dependence needs or unexpressed hostility, certain basic elements are important in the assessment of a client's status and in the determination of the overall nursing care plan.

Nurses need to consider what meaning the behavior holds for the client. Does he feel more important or more in control of his environment when releasing tension through psychophysiological processes? Has he always utilized such an adaptive process? Have significant others in his past made use of similar behavior? Does the behavior allow him to be dependent in an acceptable manner? Does it provide a relief from bearing what seems to be an inordinate amount of responsibility? Is it the only means by which he receives attention from the environment? A dysfunction may be perceived as a less painful manner in which to deal with such unacceptable feelings as dependence or hostility.

Nurses need to identify what precipitated a particular crisis. Gradually the assessment is directed toward perceptions of self. What are the client's values, strengths, weaknesses, and developmental status? What are his attitudes toward the physical side of his illness as well as his knowledge about the illness? How has the dysfunction changed his life-style or that of his family? Have roles been changed?

Since these areas are often emotionally charged, they need to be approached with care and sensitivity. An understanding of such factors provides a basis for an understanding of a psychophysiological dysfunction as an adaptive response.

What overall nursing measures are relevant? Utilization of self as a support system of the client as he interacts with his environment is a primary function. Nurses are in a unique position in that they are able to reach clients during their most vulnerable periods. Direct intervention can be provided to meet a crisis, and supportive measures then can be continued for as long as necessary. The development of a relationship that facilitates open exchanges of feelings is the key to effective nursing intervention. Such an atmosphere permits a client to test new adaptive behavior in a safe setting.

A nurse must identify the positive points of a client, maximize his potential, and capitalize on his problem-solving capabilities—the effective communication patterns he utilizes. Nurses often see or hear only the negative aspects of a client's behavior. They need to focus on how he utilizes self positively as a tool and to reinforce such positive behavior. Initially it may be difficult for the client who is very independent or hostile to accept outward signs of support. Support needs to be indicated repeatedly and in a genuine manner in order for a client to integrate it into his behavior.

A nurse needs to define predominant content, mood, and interaction themes so as to be aware of parallel areas of relevance to a client. The interaction theme is particularly pertinent because patterns of behavior that have been utilized in past interactions may be reactivated in the present relationship with the nurse. The client, however, is not usually aware of this interactional pattern.

Reduction of the number or intensity of environmental stimuli that may increase stress and anxiety is an important nursing measure. For example, the presence of certain visitors may exacerbate symptoms.

Teaching a client and his family about presenting clinical symptoms is also a part of secondary prevention. Diet, activity, and clinical changes that may occur should be the focus of a teaching plan.

Inclusion of family members or significant others in the therapy process is essential. Since the client interacts on a continuous basis with all these individuals, their involvement is crucial to the nurse's understanding of the dynamics of the client's adaptation process.

Nurses need to objectively evaluate the progress of their relationships with clients in order to identify what goals have been accomplished and what short- and long-term goals remain. Have the approaches utilized been acceptable and comfortable for both nurse and client? Is the relationship ready to be terminated? If so, what support systems are available for the client? Evaluation and reevaluation are critical to the ongoing success of the nurse-client interaction.

The following are useful nursing responses to the behavioral problem of dependence:

1. Develop a sensitivity to the dependence needs of the client. Recognize that the problem re-

sults from an inability to express feelings openly and that the client needs to maintain a facade of independence.

2. Initially, meet the dependence needs of the client. Permit him to assume a dependent role. For example, give him a bath or assist him in making decisions. Provide him with nourishment, praise, and gestures of concern, all of which are associated with mothering.

3. Recognize that dependence arouses feelings of anger and fear. Facilitate the expression of these feelings by maintaining open lines of communication.

4. Anticipate the client's needs prior to his asking. The need to remain independent prevents the client from asking to have even his most basic needs taken care of.

5. Gradually direct the client to a greater degree of independence. Encourage him in his decision-making process. At the same time be available to assist him when necessary. A sincere, interested nurse can point out that accepting assistance in the accomplishment of a task does not necessarily have a negative connotation. Often the secondary gains received as a result of a dysfunction are very difficult to relinquish. Nurses can assist the client to develop more adaptive methods of obtaining much-needed love and attention.

6. Denial is a common adaptation mechanism in a dependence-independence situation, just as it is in many other stress-produc-

ing situations. Permit the client to deny his dependence needs until his ability to accept them can be enhanced and his rejection of the need to deny can be facilitated. Forcing a client to relinquish the denial mechanism before he is ready may cause another mechanism to arise in its place.

7. Define the client's strengths, particularly in relation to dependent behavior. Is there a part of him that enjoys being cared for? On occasion, does he feel more comfortable as a follower than as a leader? Assist him in viewing these as positive attributes. Respond positively to the client as he experiments with this change in attitudes. It is in such a manner that he develops more mature, as well as more successful, patterns of adaptation to stress-producing situations.

The following are useful nursing responses to the behavioral problem of hostility:

1. Repression is a primary adaptation mechanism. Recognition of its use as well as an understanding of the client's rationale for hostile behavior are necessary prerequisites for intervention. We need to be aware that society frowns upon the open expression of anger and hostility. Therefore, intervention must be directed toward the development of satisfactory ways to handle these feelings.

2. Facilitate the open expression of anger and hostility. This must be accomplished on a gradual basis, since a long pe-

riod of time and many societal pressures are involved in the development of psychophysiological modes of dealing with anger. Discuss alternative ways in which a client might feel comfortable handling his hostility (for example, taking walks, using a punching bag, or participating in sports of a competitive nature).

3. Be sensitive to the fact that a client may feel that others will reject him if he directs his hostility outward. This does not mean that a nurse must take the brunt of unchained aggression! Acceptable modes of expressing hostility and anger must be developed within the learning environment of the nurse-client interaction. The client will soon discover that openly handling feelings of rage and bitterness is much more effective and comfortable than suppressing them.

4. Set limits on such behavior as self-mutilation or verbal self-degradation. Inherent in such behavior are a fear of not being loved as well as an aspiration for high levels of achievement that cannot realistically be attained.

5. Self-assertiveness techniques are often helpful in facilitating a client's ability to outwardly direct his anger.

6. Recognize the effects of guilt upon the client. He may magnify his purported wrongdoing out of proportion. This is usually indicative of an immature conscience. Assist the client to realistically assess his guilt. Identify other mechanisms that may be utilized to handle guilt.

7. Reduce environmental stress and anxiety. The alleviation of adverse stimuli is instrumental in promoting a therapeutic milieu.

TERTIARY PREVENTION

Tertiary prevention is directed toward the avoidance of further impairment of a client's physical, psychosocial, and emotional status. The nurse-client interaction continues, with the focus of intervention being placed on efforts to understand the client's need for the particular mode of adaptation.

Nurses are also concerned with how a client's perception of himself and his roles is related to the mode of adaptation. As mentioned previously, certain psychophysiological responses are perceived as status symbols or marks of success, as in the case of ulcers. The issue that arises is the extent to which such an adaptation mechanism impairs the individual in his current life situation. The primary focus of tertiary prevention then becomes one of clarification of values and life goals. The nurse does not step in and immediately imply that the client must change his value systems and reorder his priorities. Instead, nurses can facilitate the understanding of the relationship between stress, personal life-style, and a psychophysiological dysfunction. The client must then choose whether he wants to commit himself to the long-term process of change. Active support of the use of alternative methods of expressing needs and adapting to stress becomes the focus of the nurse during this phase of prevention.

CHAPTER SUMMARY

Physical symptoms cannot be viewed simply as reflections of physiological dysfunctions. A delicate interweaving of physiological, psychological, and sociocultural factors can result in psychophysiological illness. This chapter has presented a discussion of the dysfunctions that have been traditionally identified as psychophysiological. Predominant behavioral problems have been identified, and nursing intervention has been presented in terms of the three levels of prevention—primary, secondary, and tertiary. Every day nurses in general hospital settings meet clients who exhibit physical illnesses that are related to psychological factors. These clients' cases are frustrating yet also most challenging! Such clients are not candidates for traditional therapeutic approaches. In fact, a client may be unwilling to acknowledge that he is experiencing any difficulty. Society compounds an already frustrating situation by subtly condoning a number of psychophysiological dysfunctions as being "job related" or "success related" hazards. The challenge for nurses, therefore, is to assess the physiological, psychological, and sociocultural components of dysfunctions. A nursing care plan must reflect a complete portrait of a client in the context of his own world. Nurses have the knowledge and skills to enhance a client's potential for change, through the use of short-term, flexible treatment measures. In the future, nurses will continue to be instrumental in assisting clients to assess their values, to identify and manage actual and potential stressors, and to develop alternative methods of adaptation.

REFERENCES

Ackerman, Nathan
  1966 Treating the Troubled Family. New York: Basic Books, Inc., Publishers.
Alexander, Franz
  1950 Psychosomatic Medicine. New York: W. W. Norton & Co., Inc.
Bruch, Hilde
  1973 Eating Disorders: Obesity, Anorexia Nervosa and the Person Within. New York: Basic Books, Inc., Publishers.
Dunbar, H. F.
  1954 Emotions and Bodily Changes. New York: Columbia University Press.
Friedman, M.
  1969 Pathogenesis of Coronary Artery Disease. New York: McGraw-Hill Book Co.
Greene, W. A.
  1966 "The psychosocial setting of the development of leukemia and lymphoma." Annals of the New York Academy of Sciences 125:794-801.
Kaplan, Helen Singer
  1974 The New Sex Therapy. New York, Brunner/Mazel, Inc.
Minuchin, S., B. Rosman, and L. Baker
  1978 Psychosomatic Families. Cambridge, Mass.: Harvard University Press.
Satir, Virginia
  1972 Peoplemaking. Palo Alto, Calif.: Science and Behavior Books.
Selye, H.
  1956 The Stress of Life. New York: McGraw-Hill Book Co., pp. 20-36.

ANNOTATED SUGGESTED READINGS

Dubovsky, S., et al.
  1977 "Impact on nursing care and mortality: psychiatrists on the coronary care unit." Psychosomatics 18 (August):20-27.
    This study explores the effects of psychiatric consultation on a group of critical care unit nurses. The study was

prompted by research that suggested that the CCU milieu in general and nurses in particular affect patient outcome. This research showed that nurses can affect patient outcome directly by recognizing dangerous situations and indirectly by decreasing adverse physiological changes associated with the emotional climate of the ward.

The authors report that the psychiatric consultation resulted in an increase in the time the nurses spent in direct patient care and an increase in the importance assigned to and the enjoyment of that activity. There was also a significant increase in charting efficiency. Nurses seemed to become more acutely aware of situations that might trigger an arrhythmia, and they felt more comfortable with their own emotions.

The implications are striking: Nurses need to become more aware of their own responses to stressful situations in the CCU—for example, the impending death of a client resulting in depression and anxiety; increased workload; and excessive responsibility. Nurses must openly communicate their responses to these stressors in order to reduce the transmission of anxiety to the CCU client and thus to avoid or decrease the severity of any adverse physiological changes in the client that might result.

Herbert, D. J.
  1976 "Psychophysiological reactions as a function of life stress and behavioral rigidity." Journal of Psychiatric Nursing, May, pp. 23-27.
  This study hypothesizes that disease occurs when a significant level of life stress is reached and that an individual's behavioral rigidity plays a role in the disease process. The hypothesis is supported by data collected from subjects. The important factor presented in this study that has not been discussed in other studies on life stress is the individual's ability to assume a flexible rather than a rigid approach to a problem. Nursing intervention can be directed not only toward the identifica-

tion of life stressors but also toward assisting an individual to utilize a variety of methods of adaptation rather than be inflexible.

Minuchin, S., B. Rosman, and L. Baker
  1978 Psychosomatic Families. Cambridge, Mass.: Harvard University Press.
  This book applies family therapy techniques to the treatment of anorexia nervosa. The authors draw upon their clinical experience to suggest that the focus of therapy should be not on the individual but rather on the entire family. The therapist is viewed as an active agent for change who acts as a catalyst—with the catalytic activity resulting in new and healthier patterns of interaction. The book presents an eclectic model for treatment that can be utilized in any type of case involving psychophysiological dysfunction.

FURTHER READINGS

Caplan, Gerald
  1964 Principles of Preventive Psychiatry. New York: Basic Books, Inc., Publishers.

Kimball, C.
  1970 "Conceptual developments in psychosomatic medicine: 1939-1969. Annals of Internal Medicine **73**:101–126.

LeShan, L.
  1966 "An emotional life-history pattern associated with neoplastic disease." Annals of the New York Academy of Sciences **125**:780-793.

Menninger, Karl
  1963 The Vital Balance. New York: The Viking Press.

Nemiah, J. C.
  1975 "Denial revisited: reflections on psychosomatic theory." Psychotherapy and Psychosomatics **26**:140-147.

Shontz, Franklin
  1975 The Psychological Aspects of Physical Illness and Disability. New York: Mac Millan, Inc.

Titchener, J.
  1971 "Families of psychosomatic patients." In the Theory and Practice of Family Psychiatry. New York: Brunner/Mazel, Inc., Ch. 37.

10
COPING THROUGH
DEPENDENCE, DOMINATION,
AND DETACHMENT

CHAPTER
FOCUS

An understanding of human responses to stress is essential to the professional practice of nursing. This chapter will focus on the neuroses, which are psychiatric disturbances in which stress, anxiety, and conflict are ever-present phenomena. Neurotic persons consistently cope with anxiety by making use of interpersonal patterns of dependence, domination, or detachment. Horney (1945) regarded such patterns as compromise solutions to conflicts present in neuroses.

Many books that deal with the neuroses discuss only such disorder as the phobias, dissociative reactions, and anxiety reactions. There are, however, many persons whose modes of adapting to life and to their culture are not characterized by observable symptoms but who are more vulnerable to anxiety and have fewer options for coping with it than the average person. Many such people can be found among the clients requiring nursing services in any health care setting. Making psychiatric diagnoses is not, of course, part of a nurse's function, and such an effort would not serve a particularly useful nursing purpose. It is, however, important that the professional nurse be able to identify clients whose anxiety levels and coping responses are so significantly different from those of the average client that efforts to promote health are inhibited.

In keeping with the philosophy of professional nursing presented in this book, this chapter will focus on mental health maintainance (primary prevention) in persons coping with physical illness and injury, who may be more vulnerable to stress than the average person. Attention will also be given to aspects of primary prevention for families in which children may be at risk of developing neurotic coping patterns.

The concept of character neuroses (Horney, 1945; Drellick, 1974) will be utilized as a theoretical framework. A character neurosis may be defined as a personality organization that is characterized by excessive anxiety and by unconscious conflicts. Although there is no gross impairment of intellectual functioning, the defense mechanisms and compromise solutions needed to maintain adjustment and to control anxiety result in some degree of rigidity of personality and in interpersonal patterns that inhibit relations with others.

This chapter will, of course, also focus upon nursing intervention in cases involving the phobias, dissociative reactions, anxiety reactions, or other disorders. Some emphasis will be placed upon early identification and treatment (secondary prevention), in various health care settings, of clients who have symp-

COPING THROUGH DEPENDENCE, DOMINATION, AND DETACHMENT

tom neuroses. "Symptom neuroses" is the term used to denote dysfunctional coping mechanisms that appear as clinical symptoms. The symptoms represent either direct manifestations of anxiety or the automatic, unconscious defense mechanisms utilized to contain it. The predominant observable symptoms give the various forms of neurosis their names.

As a foundation for nursing intervention, major etiological theories, underlying dynamics, and treatment modalities pertinent to neuroses will be discussed. Emphasis will be placed upon the theories of Karen Horney.

To be neurotic is to be in conflict, to be more vulnerable to anxiety than the average person, and to settle for a compromise solution which includes pathological symptoms.
Cameron, 1963

Epidemiological and sociocultural aspects of neuroses

Theories of neurosis

Intrapsychic theories

Sociocultural theories

Characteristics and underlying dynamics of neuroses

Personality patterns

Symptom neuroses

Treatment modalities

Individual psychotherapy

Group psychotherapy

Brief hospitalization

Use of psychopharmaceuticals

Nursing intervention

Primary prevention

Secondary prevention

Tertiary prevention

Problems in nursing intervention

"Neurosis," or "psychoneurosis" has become a commonly used term in our culture. Neuroses frequently figure prominently in works of literature and the cinema. Likewise, as diagnostic categories, the neuroses are subject to current societal attitudes toward mental illness. Because of the detrimental aspects of the labeling of complex human behavior (see Chapter 1), the current revision of the American Psychiatric Association's *Diagnostic and Statistical Manual of Mental Disorders* has, in fact, eliminated neuroses as diagnostic categories.

We have attempted to avoid a disease orientation and to focus the mental health nursing process toward identifying and intervening in patterns or themes of behavior that are distressing to a client and his family. In this chapter, the terms "character neuroses" and "symptom neuroses" have been utilized to provide an understanding of responses to stress.

EPIDEMIOLOGICAL AND SOCIOCULTURAL ASPECTS OF NEUROSES

Although there are no definitive demographic studies available, it is believed that the neuroses are among the more prevalent functional disorders in our society. Reliable data on incidence are difficult to obtain for a variety of reasons. Nemiah (1978) points to the lack of "universally accepted diagnostic criteria." Another factor may be that many people function effectively and successfully despite neurotic problems until or unless they are confronted with unbearable situational stress. Kubie (1974), for example, mentions that "a neurotic process . . . need never manifest itself in formal symptomatology." Another factor is that many people are treated by private physicians for a variety of complaints or seek assistance from private resources that may not be involved in any diagnostic data collecting system.

There are, however, many indications that substantial numbers of people are seeking help in coping with psychological stress. Among these indications is the extensive use of minor tranquilizers. Diazepam (Valium), for example, is currently one of the most frequently prescribed pharmaceuticals in the United States. The rapid growth in the popularity of such short-term group modalities as encounter sessions, assertiveness training classes, and EST (Erhard Seminar Training) also indicates a widespread need for help in coping with life's problems. The growing number of self-help books dealing with a wide range of psychological problems and the many works of fiction dealing frankly with neuroses also suggest that many people are interested in finding ways to function more comfortably.

The relationship between culture and mental disorders has long been recognized. The interpersonal psychiatrists (Horney and Sullivan) incorporated sociocultural concepts into their theories of neuroses and other psychiatric disorders. Some of the research that has been done during the past quarter-century has been concerned with the relationship between social status and the incidence of mental disorders. Hollingshead and Redlich (1958), in an extensive study of social stratification and mental disorders, found a much higher incidence of neuroses in the upper and middle classes than in the lower classes and a higher incidence of psychoses in the lower classes than in the upper and middle classes.

Other researchers have studied psychiatric disorders in relation to urban and rural populations. Dohrenwend and Dohrenwend (1974) found the incidence of neuroses and personality disorders to be higher in urban areas than in rural areas. These authors also noted that neuroses occur as frequently in social classes other than the lowest socio-economic class as they did in the lowest class. This finding suggests that socioeconomic status is less important in the etiology of neuroses than it is in the etiology of psychoses. (Transcultural epidemiological studies, however, have often focused upon the utilization of psychiatric facilities and the incidence of psychoses more than upon the incidence of neuroses.)

According to David (1976), a summary report of the World Health Organization's Expert Committee on Mental Health found that the incidence of neuroses and personality disorders in the developing countries was "difficult to ascertain." The report indicated that there is evidence that more than 40 million people in the developing countries suffer from "serious untreated mental disorders" and that the major functional psychoses are the most prevalent. David noted that statistics on the incidence of neuroses in developing countries are difficult to obtain.

Some anthropological studies have attempted to identify national character traits and to relate them to child-rearing practices. Among the better known of such studies is Ruth Benedict's work on Japan, *The Chrysanthemum and the Sword*. Benedict attempts, for example, to correlate compulsive behavioral patterns with toilet training practices.

Cultures may differ considerably in the traits they seek to encourage in their people. In Japan, for example, strong group identification and social conformity are emphasized. In contrast, in the United States individuality, competitiveness, and personal freedom are considered important. The group orientation of the Japanese involves rather strict rules and formalities for social behavior, even within the immediate family. Child-rearing practices in Japan promote group identification through direct teaching, role modeling, and the use of the group as the punisher of persons who engage in undesirable behavior. The admonition "People will laugh at you," given by the Japanese mother to her child, tends to induce feelings of shame in the child, which help to reinforce group identification. A culturally specific neurosis, termed Taijin Kyofu, appears in Japan. It is manifested as a phobic fear that one's gaze can hurt other people and a corresponding reluctance to meet with others (Massafumi, n.d.).

The advances in science and technology of the last quarter-century have had a profound impact upon the people of many cultures. Technological advances have taken much of the drudgery out of the struggle for survival that prior generations experienced. These advances have often been accompanied by changes in long-established social mores and values. In the United States, changes in the status of women and in religious practices are but two examples. When a culture is in a state of transition, or when an individual who is sensitive to stress moves from one cultural environment to another, a form of culture shock may occur (see Chapter 2). In the United States, values and life-styles have been undergoing rapid change during the past two decades. The stress that such change has induced has caused increasing feelings of helplessness and alienation in many people (May, 1975).

THEORIES OF NEUROSIS

The neuroses are generally considered to be functional disorders because, as far as is known, there is no biological or physiological basis for their occurrence. The etiology of neurotic functioning lies in the psychological and sociocultural experiences that tend to shape personality.

Major emphasis will be placed upon some of the theories of Karen Horney. Horney's holistic approach to understanding neuroses, which incorporates sociocultural and psychodynamic concepts, is congruent with our philosophy of health care. Horney's theoretical formulations are adaptable to nursing applications, since many of them are explained in terms of themes and patterns of behavior that may aid the professional nurse to understand otherwise puzzling actions and to adapt nursing intervention to meet mental health needs. Some attention will also be given Freudian and behavior theory.

Intrapsychic theories

Intrapsychic, or psychodynamic, theories focus upon the forces within the mind, or psyche, that influence human development and functioning. Freud's concept of a dynamic unconscious is fundamental to intrapsychic theories (see Chapter 1). There is general agreement among intrapsychic theorists that unconscious or intrapsychic conflicts are major factors in neurotic functioning. The anxiety associated with intrapsychic conflict is one of the most prominent symptoms in neuroses (Drellich, 1974). The origins of neurotic conflict lie in a person's experiences—and his responses to them—during the period of psychosocial development. The defense mechanisms and/or compromise solutions utilized to cope with conflict and anxiety shape the personality.

Concepts of Karen Horney

Psychosocial development. The origins of neurotic conflict are in the early developmental years. The young child who consistently or frequently experiences feelings of fear, distrust, and conditional love in experiences with parents and other significant people may well acquire enduring attitudes of fear and distrust of significant people in the environment. He may also experience helplessness, confusion, and rage in a world he perceives as frightening. Since the young child is dependent upon the care-giving people in the environment, the ways in which he can cope with such traumatic experiences are limited. During childhood, submitting, rebelling, or withdrawing may be the only alternatives available for coping with noxious situations and with the rage, helplessness, and other emotions such situations arouse. Whether the child surrenders, fights back, or withdraws into himself depends upon the particular situation and the innate characteristics of the child. Surrendering, fighting back, or withdrawing may begin in early life as a conscious effort to adapt to a confusing or frightening situation. When such experiences repeatedly occur, the child's response may become automatic or unconscious. Over a period of time, the child develops attitudes about the self and other people that become internalized and part of the neurotic conflict (Portnoy, 1974).

Many factors in a child's environment can contribute to such a development. Parents who are themselves remote or unable to provide the quality of love and guidance that the growing child requires can be important factors. Parents who favor one child over another can cause a child to feel insecure and to distrust both himself and others. Making demands for achievement that a child is unready or unable to meet, or an overcautiousness on the part of a parent that prevents a child from testing out skills and abilities that he is ready for, may inhibit the development of autonomy and the ability to achieve. Parents who teach a child a moral code but regularly violate it themselves, or who demand certain behavior in school or in relations with peers but subtly approve the opposite behavior when it occurs, can cause confusion and anger in a developing child. The absence of parents because of illness during one of the developmental crises can have an impact. Schools can also influence development through such practices as preferential treatment of some children and subtle degradation of others (Horney, 1945).

It should be kept in mind that it is never a single event in the life of a developing child that is important in shaping personality, but the whole complex of interpersonal and other experiences, and the child's responses to them, during the developmental years.

Psychosocial development is, of course, strongly influenced by the ethnic group within which a child grows up. A neurosis can be understood only in relation to the culture in which it occurs or within which a person is acculturated.

The human child's long period of helplessness and dependence provides the opportunities not only for learning and developing the language, mores, values, and other elements essential to maturation and the assumption of the adult role but also for developing attitudes and feelings about himself and other people. The demands of a child's culture and the attitudes and behavior of the persons responsible for the care and nurturing of the child play important roles in personality development and the adaptation of the child to the culture. The child who is valued, accepted, and respected by members of the culture with whom he has intimate contact tends to develop self-respect, confidence, and inner security. Such a child also develops trust in and respect for others—a quality that enables him to function effectively and comfortably.

Intrapsychic conflict. To be in conflict is not in and of itself neurotic. Everyone must frequently make decisions between opposing goals. The driver on a superhighway who has a desperate need for sleep is in conflict, since he has an equally impelling need to stay awake until he can safely leave the highway. He is in a conflict that places him in a life-threatening situation. One would assume that he is fully aware or conscious of both aspects of the conflict and that he will resolve it according to a priority of needs, through a rational decision.

Neurotic conflicts are different from the one just described. Neurotic conflict differs in intensity and in the variety and flexibility of compromise solutions available (Drellich, 1974).

According to Horney's theory, the conflicts in neurosis center around meeting the basic interpersonal needs that we all share. The needs for affection, attention, approval, and recognition from others and the opportunity for expressing aggression and sexuality are some of the familiar human needs. In meeting such needs, everyone at times experiences distress, anxiety, guilt, and conflict within himself and between himself and others.

The experience of conflict during the satisfaction of needs is, of course, not limited to persons with neurotic personalities. Each of us, from time to time, feels pulled in two directions in our relations with family members, friends, peers, and co-workers. Each of us makes choices to resolve such conflicts. The way in which a conflict is resolved depends upon the circumstances or the quality of a need in a given situation. Sometimes we submit to the wishes or demands of another. At other times we assert ourselves and insist that our ideas or choices prevail. Occasionally, the need for privacy and to be alone may take precedence over all demands on our time. Such choices are made frequently and with relative comfort by the average person. This give and take, competition and compromise, in life is essential to the satisfaction of needs and the achievement and fulfillment of personal goals. But for the person trapped in a neurotic conflict, this flexibility in relations with others is less possible. Horney (1945) viewed the basic conflict in neuroses as a disturbance in human relationships. An individual is pulled or driven by a compelling need or striving to move toward others, to become dependent upon others. This striving is blocked, however, by an equally compelling need or striving to move against others (to dominate them) or away from others (toward detachment).

Trapped between such powerful and opposing forces in meeting fundamental needs, the individual is immobilized and unable to function unless some adaptive compromise can be achieved. Such a compromise can be achieved, and the conflict somewhat defused in its ability to generate unmanageable anxiety, if the person accedes to one aspect of the conflict in all interpersonal situations and forces opposing aspects out of awareness.

For example, one compromise solution is to move toward others by being compliant, submissive, and dependent—in a sense, to seek protection of others as a means of containing fears and anxiety and maintaining self-esteem. Another compromise is to move against others by gaining power or domination over them. A third compromise solution is to move away from others—to become detached and, when possible, to limit interpersonal interactions (Horney, 1945).

Such compromise solutions represent defensive maneuvers that serve to control anxiety and to enable an individual to function despite underlying conflict. It must be emphasized, however, that both the compromise and the conflict are unconsious. Once a particular compromise solution has been adopted, and the other aspects of the conflict repressed, the compromise becomes a part of the personality structure of the individual; it is used compulsively and indiscriminately in every interpersonal situation, whether it is appropriate or not (Horney, 1945).

The compromise solutions discussed thus far have been in relation to conflicting attitudes toward other people. However, neurotic conflicts also involve attitudes about the self. The use of a number of compromise solutions to cope with underlying conflicts brings about an alienation from the self and a lack of genuine self-awareness or self-understanding. Such a situation also results in some inflexibility or rigidity in behavior.

One form of inflexibility or rigidity, which may be observed in some people, is compulsive behavior. This kind of behavior can be interpreted as an unconscious extension into the external world of an effort to maintain internal order. While a little compulsive neatness and organization may lend order to our lives, carried to extremes it can be a burden to others, who may have to comply with rigid demands and prescribed methods of carrying out various endeavors.

For example, a noncompulsive student who shares a dormitory room with a highly compulsive student runs into difficulties in trying to maintain harmony. Frustration of the compulsive person's need to maintain strict order in the surroundings, or in ways of accomplishing certain tasks, arouses anxiety that may be expressed as overt anger. The presence of anxiety when compulsive needs are frustrated is a clue that the compulsivity is an ego defense mechanism.

Idealized image. The need to maintain unity within the self despite feelings of anxiety, helplessness, insecurity, and inferiority can also lead to a compromise solution that is designed to counteract and force out of a awareness, or deny, the existence of internal conflict—the idealized image (Horney, 1945; Portnoy, 1974).

The particular qualities that are incorporated into an idealized image depend upon the ideals, beliefs, and needs of the individual. For example, one may regard himself as intellectually or morally superior to others. Although the attitude may initially arise as a fantasy, the idealized image may be internalized as an unconscious defense and thus come to be regarded as the real self. Like other compromise solutions, the idealized image is compulsively adhered to and defended against any efforts on the part of others to point out discrepancies between the way the person sees himself and the way others see him. Although the idealized image serves the defensive purpose of reinforcing feelings of self-worth and denying conflicts, it also tends to alienate the person from himself. In addition, such a compromise solution prevents the experiencing of pride in genuine achievements, a situation that can lead to new conflicts. Additional defense mechanisms may then be necessary to cope with them.

Anxiety. We have noted before that anxiety plays a leading role in neuroses but that anxiety is also a universal experience. It is therefore important to distinguish between normal and neurotic anxiety. Anxiety is normal when the degree or intensity experienced is appropriate to the situation that arouses it and when its effects are not disorganizing and maladaptive but rather serve to focus the attention and to increase the ability to take action against the impending threat. Anxiety is neurotic when the degree or intensity is not appropriate to the situation that arouses it, or when it occurs without apparent stimulus. Anxiety that is of exaggerated intensity, that lasts too long, and that gives rise to excessive tension that requires immediate discharge through hyperactivity or aggression can be said to be neurotic.

Neurotic anxiety can have a disorganizing effect upon the personality. When this occurs, additional defense mechanisms or compromise solutions become essential. Such additional defenses may result in pathological behavior. Horney viewed such feelings as helplessness, hostility, and isolation as elements of the basic anxiety in neuroses (Portnoy, 1974).

It should be kept in mind that everyone has a need for relief from anxiety from time to time and that everyone makes use of defense mechanisms and other measures for this purpose. Thus neurotic behavior differs from normal behavior only in the degree of anxiety experienced and the extent and flexibility of defenses available to cope with it.

Freudian or classical theories. According to freudian theory, neuroses originate during the period of psychosexual development (see Chapter 3). They are related to innate drives or instincts, particularly the libidinal (sexual) and aggressive drives and to the struggle to master them in order to conform to cultural standards. The eventual outcome of psychosexual development depends upon the experiences of the early years. The child who experiences repeated trauma, or in whom excessive fears are generated during the developmental sequences, may develop a neurotic character structure (Drellich, 1974).

In freudian theory intrapsychic conflict is viewed as a universal experience. The basic conflict is between the unconscious fantasies, wishes, and so on that are seeking overt expression and the forces (ego defense mechanisms) that are striving to prevent overt expression and keep such fantasies out of awareness. The drives or instincts most frequently involved are libidinal and aggressive drives. Such thoughts or fantasies, termed "drive derivatives" in freudian terminology, are considered primitive, since they have their roots in early developmental eras. The overt expression of such primitive fantasies and wishes represents a danger to the person. The danger may come from external reality, or it may result from a conflict with the individual's moral standards and values. For example, acting out aggressive or sexual wishes impulsively against another person may result in punishment or pain. Such action may also result in feelings of shame and guilt.

One of the functions of the ego is to keep unacceptable thoughts or fantasies out of awareness and to prevent their overt expression. Covert or disguised expression takes place through dreams, humor, and sublimation and in other forms.

Drellich (1974) points out that when the two forces are in balance, there is little interference with a person's daily functioning or personality. In a neurosis, however, there is an imbalance between the two forces. The degree or intensity of inner turmoil is greater. The person with a neurotic character has less variety of defenses and fewer options for gratification of unconscious strivings than does the "normal" personality. Available defenses or compromise solutions are used more frequently and more rigidly than in the normal personality. Anxiety is aroused when unconscious wishes threaten to become conscious. Additional defenses are then needed to control anxiety.

Sociocultural theories

The intrapsychic theories focus upon the etiology of neuroses in terms of psychosocial development and coping strategies. Many aspects of psychosocial development, of course, are directly related to the culture in which an individual is born and reared.

Leighton and Murphy (1965) point out that cultures determine the symptoms and patterns of behavior in neuroses and other disorders. These authors note that the ways a culture may produce a vulnerable personality include placing emphasis on teachings that promote feelings of shame and guilt, putting people in stressful roles and promoting fears and unrealistic expectations. Horney (1939) viewed the person with a neurosis as a "stepchild of [his] culture."

Culture fosters the development of neuroses through factors that promote or create feelings of helplessness, insecurity, tension, hostility, or emotional isolation. Among these factors are competitiveness and emphasis upon success, which often leads to economic exploitation and inequality of rights and opportunity (Portnoy, 1974). Horney (1939) pointed to the contradictions in Western culture that promote confusion, conflict, and feelings of helplessness. The emphasis upon humility and brotherly love, for example, conflicts with the emphasis upon achievement, success, and competition; the stimulation and exploitation of needs, wishes, and desires by the mass media are in conflict with the frustration of needs in many instances. There are also conflicts between such ideals as brotherly love and charity and the often exploitative characteristics that society rewards.

Arieti (1974) points out that many of the teachings and beliefs of Western culture are in conflict. He, too, mentions the concept of brotherly love that is taught to children and the competitiveness and exploitation that are rewarded in society. The precept that men are created equal conflicts with the inequalities that are so prevalent. Arieti also notes that we are taught to cherish freedom, when, in reality, personal freedom is increasingly infringed upon. He suggests that such societal conflicts become "internalized by the individual and transformed into personal conflicts."

Kubie (1974) observes that the freedom to change is an essential aspect of mental health. He notes, however, that many factors in Western culture inhibit the freedom to change. These factors reinforce the compulsive aspects of the personality. Since compulsivity, or in Kubie's terminology, "obligatory repetition," is so prominent a feature in neuroses, the reinforcement of this quality can be neurotigenic. Kubie suggests that educational practices that emphasize "drill and grill" contribute to the loss of freedom by encouraging the automatic repetition inherent in the neurotic process.

CHARACTERISTICS AND UNDERLYING DYNAMICS OF NEUROSES

Anyone who has worked in one of the health professions for any length of time soon becomes aware that it is more difficult and challenging to provide needed health services to some individuals than it is to others, regardless of the health problems involved or the complexity of the services required. Every professional nurse has, from time to time, encountered the helpless, dependent client whose demands upon staff time and attention seem excessive and disproportionate to the client's needs. Also familiar is the client who rejects the dependent role necessitated by a particular health problem and who defies medical orders and staff efforts designed to promote recovery. Such a client is often frustrating to nurses providing health services. Less frustrating, perhaps, but still of concern, is the detached individual, who resists involvement with staff in the meeting of health care needs.

Nurses generally recognize the hypochondriac, the compulsive hand washer, or the severely phobic client as a person who is suffering from severe psychological distress. There is an awareness that the behavior or symptoms represent coping mechanisms essential to the individual's ability to adapt. There is often less recognition that consistent interpersonal patterns of dependence, domination, or detachment are indicative of a similar type of psychological distress, or that such interpersonal patterns also represent unconscious coping mechanisms needed to control anxiety in a stressful situation.

It is important for the professional nurse serving clients who display such patterns to be aware that they represent unconscious efforts to cope with stress. Such interpersonal patterns may become exaggerated when a client is confronted with a health problem and placed in a dependent role in the health service structure.

In general, people who adapt through neurotic coping patterns are functioning members of society. Many such individuals pursue careers in business, the professions, or the arts and often are highly successful in our competitive industrial society. Since there is little or no impairment in intellectual functioning, the achievement of educational and other goals is not impaired. Indeed, some neurotic trends may provide the impetus needed to achieve positions of dominance in society. A mild degree of compulsivity, for example, can be a definite asset in certain fields of endeavor requiring precision and attention to detail. A neurotic coping pattern thus may be adaptive for an individual.

Neurotic individuals remain in contact with reality, in contrast to psychotic persons, who experience delusions and hallucinations (see Chapter 13). Even when such symptoms as phobias or compulsions are being experienced, there is an awareness that the behavior is in response to some internal force that cannot be resisted.

Some characteristics of persons with neuroses may, under certain circumstances, be interesting and charming. For example, the dramatic flair and histrionic features often associated with the hysterical personality are frequently regarded as attributes in such professions as the performing and creative arts. In addition, such characteristics may lend a certain richness to the lives of friends and relatives.

It should be kept in mind that each of us responds to experiences in an infinite variety of ways. Each person has innate and learned interests, attitudes, strivings, and ideals, as well as a multitude of other motivating forces. These may be expressed in innumerable ways at different times and under differing circumstances. Everyone needs relief from anxiety from time to time and makes use of defense mechanisms and other coping measures for this purpose. Neurotic behavior differs from normal behavior only in the degree of anxiety experienced and in the extent to which defense mechanisms are needed or available to help a person cope with it. The degree to which anyone is neurotic may vary with circumstances, with the individual's biological and psychological status, and with the culture in which he lives.

There may be no overt symptoms or specific complaints on the part of clients with character neuroses. Vague expressions of dissatisfaction with life, concerns about developing lasting and meaningful relationships with others, or complaints about job satisfaction or working relationships may be the only problems mentioned even by those who seek psychiatric help. Family members or co-workers who have long associations with such people may be aware of certain inflexibilities or peculiarities in their personalities. They may even regard such a person as being, in modern parlance, "uptight" and as having "hang-ups" in certain.areas.

Some of the inflexibilities revolve around the ways in which such a person relates to others. Always assuming the submissive, dependent role or the dominant role can be frustrating to family, friends, and co-workers, who may themselves be more flexible. But such fixed attitudes and patterns in relations with others represent unconscious solutions to underlying conflict. The person compulsively utilizing such inflexible behavior is aware of neither the underlying conflict nor his own inflexibility. He can readily justify or rationalize, to the self and others, actions in any situation.

Personality patterns

Dependence on others. The individual who functions on a submissive, dependent level in relations with others has excessive needs for attention, affection, and approval. To such a person, acceptance by other people is essential to maintaining security. In order to achieve these ends, this type of person may view other people as superior and adopt their attitudes and opinions. Since he considers the approval of others to be essential to the maintainance of self-esteem, the dependent person may function in a manner that is in accord with other people's beliefs and judgments rather than his own. Such traits may initially cause a hospitalized client to assume the "good patient" role, since submissiveness and dependence are often encouraged in health agencies. However, excessive demands for attention and approval and an inability to tolerate criticism or anything perceived as rejection will soon become apparent.

Each of us has a friend, relative, neighbor, or classmate who always needs to be coaxed and pleaded with to join some group activity and who becomes hurt and upset when such urging is not sufficiently forthcoming. Each of us knows someone who is often anxious and who becomes more tense and emotional when he is involved in a "fender-bender" automobile accident or other type of minor crisis. We are all familiar with people who need frequent emotional support, confirmation of any proposed activity, and approval of even minor achievements. Most of us are also flattered when our advice is sought in relation to the solution of problems or when we are effusively praised for our superior knowledge or experience. We may not often recognize the underlying needs being expressed, although we may tend, at times, to become skeptical when our advice is ignored, or to become annoyed or angry when demands exceed our ability or willingness to comply with them.

Such submissive, dependent behavior does not, of course, resolve the individual's underlying conflict. The dependent role itself may lead to resentment, anger, or despondency.

Domination of others. The person who copes with interpersonal relationships by dominating other people has underlying feelings that everyone is hostile to him. The strong need to maintain control over other people may be expressed in a variety of ways. Taking command in any situation may serve to threaten other people and thus maintain control. Overt expressions of anger when orders are challenged or not carried through may be effective in maintaining control and, in addition, may serve as outlets for the person's own anxiety. At other times, particularly in circumstances in which such direct methods would be ineffective, forms of subtle manipulation may be employed. Such manipulation may take the form of flattery, excessive concern about the plight of others, or efforts to make others feel obligated (Horney, 1945).

As in the case of the dependent person, such behavior is motivated by anxiety and conflict. Although the dependent aspects of the conflict are forced out of awareness, and partially maintained there by the dominating behavioral patterns, the dependence needs are still present. Situations, such as hospitalization, that place the person who distrusts others in a dependent role may be particularly threatening for such an individual.

In such a situation, there is often an inability to admit to oneself or others any feelings or fears, since to do so could be overwhelming. There is a strong need to prove to oneself and others that one is strong and right, in order to maintain equilibrium and contain anxiety. Efforts to establish any other than a superficial relationship usually fail, since relationships tend to be regarded as dangerous.

Although such methods of relating with other people tend to distort human relations, the feelings and attitudes about the self are even more distorted. The vignette that follows may serve to demonstrate this point.

Mr. H. was admitted to a hospital in the small community where he lived; the diagnosis was peptic ulcer. Married and a father of two children, Mr. H. was in his late thirties and held an important position in a bank. While in the hospital, he continued to carry on business on the phone and through visits from employees of the bank.

During the visits Mr. H. on several occasions shouted at a co-worker and made disparaging remarks about his intelligence in front of hospital staff and the other client in the room. At other times, Mr. H. was heard to flatter the co-worker and then send him off on a personal errand. When the charge nurse attempted to set limits on such business activities, Mr. H. became very angry and threatened to report her. Efforts to explain to Mr. H. that his own recovery was not being helped by the business activity and that the other patient in the room was very ill and needed a quieter atmosphere only served to increase Mr. H.'s anger.

When the supervisor appeared to discuss the matter with Mr. H., he became very conciliatory and expressed concern about the other patient. He flattered the supervisor about the way in which she ran the unit and expressed interest in her personal likes and dislikes. The next day he sent her tickets to a play they had discussed. The unit staff received a large box of candy.

Mr. H. continued to conduct business from the hospital room. When the subject was raised with him again, Mr. H. explained to the staff that his position was very important and that he was unable to rely upon the people under him. He attempted to convince the staff that he rested easier knowing that things were under control at the bank.

Since all of the nursing staff members were becoming frustrated in working with Mr. H., a group meeting was held to work out a plan of care. Underlying anxiety was identified as one of the major problems, and a plan of care that emphasized emotional support and health teaching through a one-to-one relationship was developed and implemented. However, Mr. H. initially thwarted any efforts to establish any other than a superficial discussion. He said that he regarded talking about his experience as "sentimental hogwash." He resisted just as adamantly any interest in health teaching, and responded to the nurse's efforts to open any avenue of communication with sexually seductive remarks.

In a supervisory session with a mental health nurse, the staff nurse mentioned the frustration and humiliation she was experiencing in working with Mr. H. After a review of the content of the interactions, the nurses were able to identify Mr. H.'s responses as "distancing maneuvers," or unconscious attempts to keep the nurse from getting too close psychologically. Once this theme of the relationship had been identified, the staff nurse was able to utilize an approach that encouraged the client to take the lead in discussing areas of concern to him. This approach was less threatening to the client and more effective in meeting some of the nursing care objectives.

Detachment from others. The characteristics of the individual who resolves a neurotic conflict by becoming detached from others are in sharp contrast to those of the dependent, submissive person. The detached person has strong needs to maintain independence and self-sufficiency. He has a strong drive to keep a distance between himself and others and to avoid becoming emotionally involved. Intellectualization and a superior manner are some of the means used to accomplish this end. Although such a person does not like being taken for granted, he often prefers being alone. Superficial relations with others may be amicable, but any effort to place such a person in a dependent position or a position in which there must be submission to others' expectations arouses uneasiness, rebellion, and further emotional withdrawal.

As might be predicted, illness is bitterly resented by a person with such strong needs for detachment from others (Horney, 1945). Any question about such an individual's personal life is likely to be regarded as a shocking intrusion, and attempts to give advice of any kind are apt to be perceived as attempts to dominate and to be met with resistance. Any health problem that results in dependence upon a health agency is likely to be resented and highly emotionally unsettling (Horney, 1945).

Symptom neuroses

Neurotic conflicts are believed to originate during childhood. The onset of symptoms usually occurs in late adolescence or early adulthood, although it may occur at any point along the life span, during periods of developmental or situational crisis. Developmental crises are the periods of vulnerability encountered as a person moves from one developmental stage to the next (see Chapter 4). Situational or incidental crises occur when people are confronted with stressful events of such unusual intensity or duration that customary methods of coping are no longer effective. In the crisis state, additional defensive mechanisms are brought into play. For the individual who is particularly sensitive to stress, such defensive measures may include neurotic symptoms. People may be especially vulnerable to emotional crises when stressful events coincide with crisis points in development, such as adolescence or old age. Health problems that involve admission to a hospital or dependence upon a community health agency for treatment and rehabilitation are examples of stressful situations that may lead to development of conditions that are even less adaptive than the three personality patterns just discussed—symptom neuroses.

As we noted earlier, the ways in which neuroses are expressed are determined by culture. It is interesting to note that even within the same culture, the ways in which neuroses are expressed vary from one period to another, much as fashions in clothing and other aspects of life change. This is not to imply that neurotic symptoms are as whimsical as dress styles. Rather, such symptoms reflect many aspects of our constantly changing environment, and our relationships to it. As lifestyles change, the ever-creative human being utilizes whatever resources are available to achieve both healthy and neurotic ends.

Neuroses are classified according to observable symptoms. The primary symptom in a neurosis gives the neurosis its name. Symptoms represent, to a great extent, either direct manifestations of anxiety or defense mechanisms utilized to control anxiety.

Anxiety reactions. Anxiety reactions are overt manifestations of anxiety; they are classified according to the physiological and psychological effects the anxiety has upon an individual. Although anxiety is a prominent feature and one of the motivating forces in all neuroses, the anxiety neuroses differ from the other symptom neuroses in the degree of anxiety and in the lack of any stable defense mechanisms or symptom formation to counteract the anxiety. This form of neurosis may be chronic, or it may occur in acute attacks.

Chronic anxiety. Experiences of chronic anxiety closely resemble the physiological and psychological responses to fear. The emotional responses are often described as feelings of apprehension, awe, and dread and fear of impending disaster. In the chronic form, anxiety neurosis is exhibited through such character traits as timidity, indecisiveness, self-doubt, inability to concentrate or organize activities, and aggressive outbursts. Vague fears and feelings of inferiority may be verbalized. Insomnia and nightmares may occur.

The physiological symptoms of muscle tension, chronic fatigue, restlessness, palpitation, and somatic complaints are common. Since a sustained high level of anxiety has an effect upon the autonomic nervous system—and, indeed, upon the functioning of all body systems—psychosomatic and other physiological disorders may coincide with chronic anxiety or be precipitated by it.

Acute anxiety attack. The most dramatic form of anxiety neurosis is the acute anxiety attack, which, as its name implies, comes on suddenly and overwhelms a person with a terrifying anxiety that is akin to panic. The sudden onset, without apparent cause, often occurs when the person is alone and away from home. Although he is acutely aware of the anxiety and its physiological aspects, the reason for the occurrence is not known to him. The source is, of course, within the self, internal and unconscious, although it may be associated with or triggered by environmental stress.

An attack may last from several minutes to several hours. The emotional response is accompanied by rapid breathing and heart rates, muscle tension, and restlessness. Palpitation, trembling, profuse perspiration, faintness, and dizziness as well as nausea, vomiting, and diarrhea may convince the sufferer that he is having a heart attack or even that he is going to die.

To an observer, the face is flushed, and the pupils are dilated; pulse rate and respiratory rate are very rapid. The person is extremely restless; he perspires heavily. The ability to answer questions or follow directions may be very limited. Since many of these symptoms may also occur in some physical illnesses, the possibility of such an illness should be ruled out before a diagnosis of acute anxiety attack is made.

Anyone who has experienced the anxiety that occurs when one awakens from a nightmare may have some understanding of the distress of an acute anxiety attack. The following vignette may help to clarify some aspects of such an attack and of anxiety neurosis in general.

> Mary J., a young college student enrolled in a social work program, was very shy and retiring in class. She rarely participated in classroom discussion, and when called upon to express an idea or opinion, she became very tense, restless, and obviously uncomfortable. She readily acceded to the opinions and decisions of other students in the class, even on controversial issues about which she privately expressed different opinions. When course assignments required that she speak before the group or participate in panel discussions, her obvious level of anxiety made other students uncomfortable. Mary's achievement on written assignments and examinations indicated that she was intellectually mastering the material, and she was receiving fairly high grades.
>
> During the course of the semester Mary became very dependent upon the teacher, constantly seeking approval and guidance outside of the classroom. When the teacher was unable to spend as much time with her outside of class as Mary demanded, or when the suggestion was made that she discuss in class some of the points she brought to the teacher, Mary reacted with an outburst of anger at the teacher. The outburst was followed shortly by submissive and conciliatory actions, including excessive praise and compliments.
>
> Mary, who had an older brother and a younger sister, described her family as being religious and very strict. High moral standards and demands for achievement had been stressed throughout her life. Failure in either area had been severely punished. Mary believed that her parents favored her brother because he was a boy and her sister because she was

prettier and more like the mother. The mother and the younger sister often went on vacations together and shared many other activities—a practice that at times left Mary with the feeling of being alone and abandoned. Mary often expressed envy of her college classmates, whom she described as being more independent and having more fun than she did.

When Mary was placed in a social agency for field work practice, she continued to seek out the former teacher and even attempted to have the teacher intervene on her behalf with her agency supervisor, whom she described as being very difficult and impossible to please. Mary described her efforts to memorize all of the procedures and techniques the agency used, and she expressed the wish that she could exchange places with the clients she was serving. The agency supervisor described Mary as being disorganized and unable to plan or conduct even the simplest interview.

Mary experienced an acute anxiety attack in her car while driving to the agency one day. Following the attack, she became so fearful of leaving her immediate neighborhood that she had to temporarily withdraw from the program and seek professional help in coping with her anxiety.

Hysterical reactions. Hysterical reactions may be viewed as psychological flight from overwhelming anxiety. Such flight is somewhat comparable to physical flight from a feared object or incident. Psychological flight may take the form of a *conversion reaction.* In such a reaction, unconscious conflict and the attendant anxiety are transformed, through several defense mechanisms, into a physical symptom in a body part. As in a phobia, the conflict is changed, through condensation, displacement, and projection, from an internal phenomenon into a physical symptom. The symptom is usually expressed as impairment of one of the senses or as paralysis of a limb or other body part. A symptom such as hysterical blindness or paralysis of a hand or a forearm may symbolically express some aspect of the underlying conflict and may, temporarily, eliminate the anxiety.

Conversion reactions produce self-limiting symptoms that serve as emergency responses to situations that generate overwhelming anxiety. Such reactions occur most often in persons who have chronic anxiety levels, and they occur more often in persons who tend to believe in magic and mysticism than in persons who are science-oriented.

A young woman was brought into an emergency room of a general hospital from a family court session, with the complaint that she had suddenly become blind. Physical examination revealed no pathology that could account for the symptom. The examining physician was struck by the complete absence of any anxiety or other emotional response to what could be presumed to be a terrifying experience. Following a psychiatric consultation, a diagnosis of conversion reaction was made and the woman was admitted to the psychiatric unit, where, after a few days of supportive treatment, she recovered her sight and was discharged to an outpatient clinic.

The woman had become blind during the family court session moments after her husband had refused to consider a reconciliation and had demanded a divorce and custody of their children. The couple had been having marital difficulties for several years following their immigration to the United States from Puerto Rico.

The blindness symbolically expressed, in part, the woman's unwillingness or inability to "see" or accept the abandonment by her husband.

The total lack of observable anxiety is a common feature of conversion reaction. Termed "la belle indifférence," this feature often serves as a clue that the problem is a psychological one rather than a physical one. Hysterical paralysis of an arm or a hand, which may be found in battle neuroses and other situations that involve an underlying conflict centering around aggression, is another clue that a problem is psychological rather than physical. Such symptoms rarely conform to the neurological pathways that they would normally follow if there were a physiological basis for their occurrence.

Phobic reactions. A phobia is a persistent pathological fear. The object of a phobia can be almost anything in the environment to which fear can be attached. Some of the more common phobias currently found in Western culture involve closed spaces, open spaces, heights, and various means of travel. A number of phobias have been given Greek names—for example, claustrophobia and agoraphobia.

Phobias are believed to occur far more commonly than statistics indicate (Kolb, 1973); they are often associated with anxiety reactions and other forms of neurosis.

A phobia represents a transfer of internal anxiety to some object in the environment. Two major mechanisms, projection and displacement, are combined in a complex and unconscious process to accomplish this end. The mechanism of projection transforms an internal psychic threat into a fear of some object in the environment; displacement serves to transfer the emotional investment—the anxiety—to the selected object. These maneuvers have the effect of changing anxiety into a more manageable form—fear. The feared object can then be avoided, thereby further controlling the anxiety. Although the avoidance may inhibit one's life-style, it does serve to maintain functions in other spheres. Thus, as in other neuroses, the containment of anxiety and the preservation of functioning are the primary gains.

Fear of an elevator—to cite one fairly common type of fear—is not necessarily a pathological experience. Many of us have qualms when we step onto an elevator. But this mild fear differs from that of a phobia. Instead of having a pathological origin, it often stems from having been stuck in an elevator between floors; it is relatively easily overcome, and we get on the elevator. The person with a phobia is unable to do so; he avoids riding an elevator even if he resides on an upper story of a tall apartment building and becomes, in effect, a prisoner of his apartment.

For the person who is trapped in such a phobic pattern, many needs, such as shopping for food and other necessities, must be met by other people, and many of the onerous chores of living can thus be avoided. These kinds of effects and the additional attention often given the phobic individual by family and friends provide the secondary gain that is typical of many of neuroses. Such secondary gains may serve to reinforce the phobia.

It is interesting to note that the object of a phobia may change to meet changing conditions in the environment. For example, the pathological fear of being bitten by a horse, described by Freud in 1903 in "The Analysis of a Phobia In a Five Year Old Boy," would not serve as a substitute for anxiety in current society, where horses are relatively rare. But it may well have been a very prevalent phobia in an era when the horse was the major means of land travel and transport. A bus phobia would serve the same psychodynamic purpose today.

Phobic responses that begin in the adult years in persons who live in a highly industrialized, mobile society such as that of the United States often involve less specific phobic objects than those discussed thus far. Agoraphobia, the fear of open spaces, in current terminology refers to the fear of entering public places alone. Manifestations of this phobia can vary in degree from an inability to leave one's own home to a somewhat less restrictive inability to travel any distance from one's own neighborhood without experiencing overwhelming anxiety. Agoraphobia is currently one of the most prevalent forms of phobia (Mark, 1970).

The fear of being promoted in one's work, which may be manifested as acute anxiety attacks or depression, and an abnormal fear of contracting a disease such as cancer are also common in modern society.

It should be noted that not everyone who experiences phobic fears succumbs to the inhibiting restrictions. Some individuals attempt, by sheer force of will and repeated exposure, to overcome their phobias. For example, a person who has a fear of heights may attempt to master his phobia by becoming a mountain climber. (This is not to imply that all mountain climbers are phobic.) But it is probable that a phobic person does not derive the same quality of joy and pleasure from mountain climbing as the nonphobic person. This effort at mastering a phobia is termed "reactive courage."

Obsessive-compulsive reactions. The most observable symptom that characterizes an obsessive-compulsive reaction is the repetitious performance of ritualistic acts. When one observes a person with this disorder, one is struck by the persistent performance of behavior that, in itself, is useless or that is made useless by the repetition. For example, washing one's hands or flushing a toilet are perfectly reasonable acts unless they must be repeated some magical number of times, as occurs in a compulsion. The observer of such a compulsive person is also struck by the intensity and concentration with which such acts are performed and by the obvious tension and discomfort of the performer.

Not available to the eyes of the observer are the obsessive thoughts or impulses that keep recurring despite the individual's efforts to banish them. The life of the obsessive-compulsive neurotic is beset by such thoughts.

As in all neuroses, the compulsive behavior represents an effort to control or contain anxiety arising from unconscious conflict. The intrusion of the obsessive thoughts into consciousness signals the danger that repression may not be completely effective in keeping the conflict out of awareness. The obsessive thoughts, which represent the expression of a part of the conflict as an unacceptable idea or impulse, increase the anxiety and further threaten the ability to function.

The compulsive behavior also serves as a mechanism for banishing obsessions and controlling guilt and anxiety. The conflicts in this disorder frequently concern one's views of good and evil—particularly aggressive and sexual thoughts and impulses that come into conflict with internalized standards and beliefs. The ritualistic behavior expresses, at least symbolically, aspects of the underlying conflicts and the self-punishing efforts at controlling guilt. The hand-washing compulsion is clearly an effort to wash away something, although the ritualistic aspects and magical quality indicate that it is a far more complex process. The ritualistic behavior may appear meaningless or useless to the observer and sometimes is also so regarded by the performer. However, it cannot be interrupted or prevented without extreme anxiety or even panic being aroused.

Compulsive behavior may consist of a single act, carried out some magical number of times, or it may involve complex rituals, but the repetitive nature of the behavior remains in both instances. In addition to hand washing, which is frequently seen, compulsions may take many forms having to do with aspects of living and working. Complex rituals in bathing and dressing are very common.

In the milder forms of obsessive-compulsive behavior, a single compulsive act may serve to contain anxiety and enable a person to reestablish character defenses and to return to the premorbid state. In the more severe forms, anxiety is not contained, and increasingly more elaborate rituals develop, and steadily greater portions of the individual's life are devoted to carrying them out. The more severe forms are quite resistant to treatment and may become chronic.

An obsessive-compulsive neurosis can begin at any period of life, although it most often appears in adolescence. The onset is usually associated with developmental or family crisis or situational stress.

The following vignette illustrates a severe form of obsessive-compulsive neurosis.

> Jane M., a young woman of 24 was brought to a mental health clinic by her husband, who said that she had developed such elaborate rituals for getting dressed each morning that she was unable to get to work on time. The rituals included repeated hand washing and a pattern of dressing and undressing that took several hours to accomplish. These activities were interfering not only with Jane's life but also with her husband's, since he was unable or unwilling to leave home until she was ready to leave also.
>
> Jane's compulsive behavior began shortly after their marriage. It started with an inability to throw away dirt after she swept the kitchen floor. The hand washing started shortly after that incident, and the other rituals soon after that. At the time of the visit to the clinic, Jane was unable to do any of the housework because of her preoccupation with dirt. As a consequence, her husband had assumed these chores. The history revealed that Jane had refused to have sexual relations with her husband after the first month of marriage.
>
> Jane had always done well in school and had graduated from college with honors. She was currently employed as an accountant. Her employer thought highly of her work and, despite the current difficulties, continued to employ her.

Jane was the only child in a middle-class family that she described as being very strict and upright. Her mother took great pride in maintaining her home in an immaculate condition, and was completely unable to understand Jane's current inability to do the same. Although the parents had always placed demands upon Jane to excel in school and to conform to their precepts, they were also very proud of her and rewarded her for her achievements.

During the course of treatment at the clinic, Jane was very consistent in arriving on time. However, the hand-washing ritual increased to the point that, even though she arrived at the clinic on time, she would be late for appointments. She also developed an additional ritual, which symbolically expressed her anxiety and ambivalence. This ritual consisted of repeatedly walking up to the front door of the clinic and then retreating back to the sidewalk.

Psychotherapy and the administration of anti-anxiety drugs were combined in the treatment. Although Jane made some progress, the therapy was not completely effective in eliminating the symptoms.

This vignette hints at some additional features of obsessive-compulsive neurosis. For example, the hand-washing ritual results in painfully chapped hands. The obvious embarassment and discomfort that accompany the activity—particularly when it is done in a public rest room—are evidence of the self-punitive, masochistic nature of the symptom. The treatment of the husband—and, to a lesser degree, the therapist, in keeping him waiting for each appointment—demonstrates the sadistic nature of the behavior. Such sadistic and masochistic traits, although unconscious rather than deliberate, are common features of the disorder. They may represent a reenactment of earlier experiences in the life of the neurotic person. The secondary gains that the symptoms provide Jane are fairly obvious. The concern and attention of her husband and the avoidance of the boring chores of housework, which were taken over by the husband, may well have served to reinforce the symptom picture.

Dissociative reactions. Dissociative reactions represent a form of psychological flight from the self in which a part of all of the personality is denied, or dissociated. The most frequently occurring form of dissociative reaction is *amnesia*, in which a part or all of a person's past life is forgotten or, more accurately, forced out of awareness through repression. In partial amnesia the person may be unable to recall or remember a significant portion of his experience. Total amnesia is characterized by failure to recall any aspects of past life, including such vital information as name, place of residence, names of family and friends, and occupation.

Amnesia comes about in response to extremely anxiety-provoking situations experienced by persons who exist in chronic states of anxiety. The precipitating events often are traumatic situations that involve loss of or rejection by a loved one. Amnesia may be preceded by dream-like or trance states, during which a person may travel distances from home, act out impulsively, or engage in childish behavior. The defense mechanisms that are involved in amnesia are repression and denial.

To the casual observer, the person with amnesia appears normal and often seems quite calm. Intellectual functioning in spheres other than those involved in the amnesia remains normal, and there is little overt evidence of anxiety.

Typically, a person with amnesia comes to psychiatric attention when he is brought to an emergency room or psychiatric hospital by the police, who have found him wandering aimlessly during the trance-like state or to whom he has appealed for help because of his memory loss.

Although in popular fiction persons with amnesia sometimes take up new lives and live them for years, amnesia is usually an emergency response from which a person recovers in a relatively short time. A psychiatrist may use hypnosis to treat the disorder. During a hypnotic trance, the person may be able to provide information about himself that has been repressed, although it will not usually be available to the client's consciousness when he comes out of the hypnotic state. In some instances the therapist may suggest to the client that he will be able to recall certain facts when he comes out of the trance.

Somatiform reactions

Hypochondriasis. Hypochondriasis is a morbid preoccupation with the state of one's health. Such concern can range from a series of minor complaints to the conviction that one has some serious disease.

Hypochondriacs are frequently seen in acute health care settings. Their repeated visits with the same, or similar, complaints often arouse anger or indifference on the part of health professionals. A person's persistent belief that he has a physical illness should, of course, always be taken seriously and evaluated medically.

Hypochondriasis represents an unconscious transformation of internal conflicts into physical symptoms, which are more acceptable to the individual and to others than is a psychological disorder. As in other forms of neurosis, the symptoms represent attempts to contain anxiety and maintain integration of the personality. It should be kept in mind that the symptoms seem very real to the person experiencing them and that they may result in as much physical discomfort as they would if they were real. Attempts to reason such symptoms away, or to explain them on a logical basis, will at best be rejected and at worst may result in increased anxiety and the need for additional defense mechanisms to cope with it. The less adaptive defense mechanisms that might then develop could take a psychotic form, since the false belief that one has a physical disorder is a delusional idea. The individual who entertains such a belief is on the borderline between neurosis and psychosis. Fenichel (1945) observed that hypochondriasis may be a transitional state between neurosis and psychosis.

Anorexia nervosa. Anorexia nervosa is a condition that is not usually included among the neurotic disorders. We have included it in this chapter because it has many features in common with neuroses and also because it is a condition that is seen fairly often in Western society. Anorexia nervosa resembles a neurosis in that, apart from the symptom formation, there is little interference with intellectual functioning and reality testing and in its compulsive nature. Kolb (1977) cites a compulsive drive to be thin as a prominent feature of this disorder.

Anorexia nervosa is characterized by excessive dieting, which is often carried to the point of severe malnutrition and emaciation. In some instances the disorder results in death. The condition appears to involve a disturbance in body image, since, even in an emaciated state, the individual tends to perceive himself as overweight. Anorexia nervosa often has its onset in adolescence; it may have been preceded by an overweight condition. Although it can occur in men, the majority of people with this disorder are young women. Such women are often highly intelligent, well-educated people, some of whom are found in the health professions. The equation of thinness with beauty in modern culture and the focus upon diet foods and activities may influence, somewhat, the incidence of this condition, but these factors cannot account for the severity and persistence of the disorder.

The origins of anorexia nervosa are believed to lie in the early developmental stages, in which disturbances in the mother-child relationship result in ambivalent feelings toward the mother. A wish to remain a child is sometimes fostered by the mother. Resistance to food and to attempts at treatment, even in extreme states of health, is a prominent feature of the condition.

TREATMENT MODALITIES

The therapeutic modalities used in the treatment of neuroses include many of the measures employed in the treatment of the other emotional disorders. The most frequently employed modalities in the treatment of neuroses are individual psychotherapy, group psychotherapy, behavior therapy, administration of psychopharmaceuticals, and brief hospitalization. The therapeutic milieu and recreational, occupational, and other activity therapies are included in the brief-hospitalization modality.

Individual psychotherapy

Several forms of individual psychotherapy are employed in the treatment of neuroses. These include psychoanalysis, psychoanalitically oriented psychotherapy, and short-term psychotherapy. These types of therapy differ from each other in objectives, duration and intensity, and degree to which a client must be able or willing to participate and cooperate.

Psychoanalysis. Psychoanalysis is the method developed by Freud for the treatment of neurosis. It has been adopted as a therapeutic modality by analysts in all of the schools of psychoanalytic thought, including those of Horney, Sullivan, and Fromm. Psychoanalysis is a long-term and intensive form of therapy that is oriented toward the restructuring of the personality. Emphasis is placed upon growth of the ego and resolution of unconscious conflicts. In the process, there is a focus upon the transference and resistance that arise in the interpersonal relationship between the client and the analyst during therapeutic sessions. Psychoanalysis may last over a period of two or more years, with sessions being held as often as three times a week.

Becoming a psychoanalyst requires extensive education in the psychoanalytic method and a supervised clinical practicum. In addition, the trainee must undergo a personal analysis. Psychoanalytic training generally entails a period of study and supervised practice of three years beyond the doctoral degree. The majority of analysts are psychologists or psychiatrists. However, an increasing number of nurses and social workers have become certified analysts.

Psychoanalysis is often considered the treatment of choice for neurosis. However, many people are unable to enter into the intensely personal relationship and the rigorous self-exploration that are required in this form of therapy. In addition, some people—for economic, sociocultural, or psychological reasons—are not suited to analysis.

Psychoanalytically oriented psychotherapy. Psychoanalytically oriented psychotherapy is a modified form of psychoanalysis in which the goals are more limited. The method of treatment is much the same as that in psychoanalysis, but the objective is symptom reduction or change in areas of the personality that are troubling to the client. Psychoanalytically oriented psychotherapy may extend over a period of a year or more. It is often the method of choice for clients who are unsuitable for analysis or unwilling or unable to undergo analysis but who could benefit from a limited form of therapy.

Short-term psychotherapy. Short-term, or brief, psychotherapy is, as the name implies, a brief form of psychotherapy designed for people in emotional crisis. Such a crisis can arise in a neurotic person as a result of any form of situational stress perceived as a threat or danger. As had been noted earlier, almost anything can precipitate a crisis response in a vulnerable individual. Sifneos (1972) describes two forms of brief psychotherapy: in *anxiety-provoking, or dynamic, psychotherapy,* the goal is to achieve some change in the client's problem-solving ability and interpersonal relationships, rather than simply symptomatic relief. Clients are carefully selected. In *anxiety-suppressive, or supportive, psychotherapy,* the aim is the reduction of anxiety through the interpersonal techniques discussed in connnection with the nurse-patient relationship (see Chapters 5 and 6). Supportive psychotherapy is often used as a crisis intervention measure, in combination with brief hospitalization and other forms of therapy, in the treatment of clients who have the more disabling forms of symptom neuroses.

Group psychotherapy

Many forms of group therapy are used in the treatment of neuroses. In addition to being more economical for the individual client, group therapy also makes it possible to serve a larger number of people than can be treated through individual therapy. Group therapy thus allows more effective utilization of the available professional practitioners. Of greater significance, however, is the fact that, for some people, the group method may be a more effective means of treatment. For example, the client who is unable to participate in an intensive one-to-one relationship may be able to participate effectively in a small group of peers.

Psychoanalytically oriented group therapy is perhaps the most effective and the most common type of group therapy used in the treatment of the less maladaptive forms of neurosis. The psychoanalytic method is utilized, and the therapist is either an analyst or a person who is skilled in both the analytic method and group process. The group is usually limited to about eight members, who are carefully screened by the therapist. The therapist is concerned with putting together a group whose members will be able to work together in the therapeutic process. The overall goal is to resolve basic conflicts that are anxiety provoking and that interfere with the ability to function.

A relatively brief or short-term form of group therapy can be used for the treatment of people in emotional crises. This form of group therapy may be either anxiety provoking or anxiety suppressive, as in individual short-term therapy. The focus is upon problems in the client's current situation, with the objective being to improve the ability to cope effectively and comfortably with crises and other life situations.

Family therapy is a relatively new form of group therapy that is being utilized in a variety of situations for treatment of emotional disorders. Family therapists do not use the psychoanalytic method; instead, they focus upon the interactional patterns within the family system. The objective in family therapy is the promotion of the individuation of family members through intervention in maladaptive alliances and communication patterns.

The family differs significantly from other therapy groups. The family is the living system in which interpersonal patterns and coping processes, both adaptive and maladaptive, have their origins and in which they are maintained. Thus the transference phenomena or parataxic distortions that occur in other forms of group therapy may not occur in family therapy. While family therapy offers unique opportunity for the therapist to observe and assess the psychodynamics of individual members and the family system, it also requires special skill and knowledge on the part of the therapist if the therapeutic intervention is to be effective.

Although family therapy is too new to have been adequately evaluated as an effective therapy in neuroses, it could conceivably provide an important addition to treatment modalities in both primary and secondary prevention in cases in which families are available and able to participate in such an endeavor. Nurses with post-baccalaureate degrees and special training in the method are among the practitioners of family therapy.

Psychodrama is a group method, developed by J. L. Moreno, in which group members act out an interpersonal problem volunteered by one of the members. Under the direction of the group leader, who serves as director of the drama, selected group members enact the roles described by the client who volunteered the problem. That client, called the protagonist in the enactment, plays himself. Additional members of the group serve as doubles for each of the participants in the drama. The doubles serve as auxilliary or alter egos. As the problem is acted out, the doubles attempt to portray the inner and often hidden feelings and thoughts of the participants in the drama. Role reversal—the switching of roles between the protagonist and another significant person in the drama—is another technique utilized to increase self-awareness. The director shares with other group members the responsibility for providing needed support and empathy for the participants in the psychodrama. The therapist or director is also responsible for protecting members from psychological trauma as the drama is enacted.

Psychodrama is often employed as a treatment modality in neuroses, especially when short-term hospitalization is part of the therapeutic regimen. Persons in crisis situations are often considered good candidates for psychodrama. The therapist who uses psychodrama should be skilled and should have special training in psychodramatic method. Nurses with special training in psychodrama often participate in this form of therapy.

Brief hospitalization

The broadening of insurance coverage so that it includes brief in-hospital treatment for psychiatric disorders has led to the expansion of psychiatric units in general hospitals and has made facilities for in-hospital treatment of persons in crisis situations more generally available. Many of the clients in general hospital psychiatric units are suffering from neurotic reactions.

In order to provide optimum service in the brief span of time available for client hospitalization, such units make use of all of the treatment modalities available. The concept of the therapeutic community is stressed. All aspects of the environment are oriented toward promotion of health. In addition to the therapies already discussed, many of which may be employed, recreational therapy, occupational therapy, and various forms of creative therapy are also utilized.

Nurses in in-patient psychiatric units function as members of the interdisciplinary mental health team (see Chapter 8) and participate in all of the ongoing therapeutic measures. In many settings the nursing staff also works directly with families of clients and provides follow-up care when clients are discharged.

Use of psychopharmaceuticals

Minor tranquilizers, or anti-anxiety agents, are widely used in the treatment of neuroses and other anxiety states, either alone or in combination with other therapeutic modalities. Baldessarini (1977) points out that two of these drugs—Valium and Librium—are among the most commonly prescribed drugs in the United States. Although the current era has been described as the "age of anxiety," human beings have, throughout recorded history, used a variety of substances to help them cope with the noxious feelings labeled anxiety. Such substances have included alcohol, opium derivatives, and barbiturates. Research is continuously being conducted in an effort to find chemical substances that are more effective and less toxic in controlling anxiety. The following substances are among the drugs most commonly used in the treatment of neuroses at the present time.

Benzodiazepines (the most effective and least toxic of the minor tranquilizers)

Generic name	Trade name	Daily dosage
Chlordiazepoxide	Librium	15-100 mg
Diazepam	Valium	5-60 mg
Oxazepam	Serax	30-120 mg
Clorazepate	Tranxene	15-60 mg

Glycerol derivatives (related to muscle relaxants)

Generic name	Trade name	Daily dosage
Meprobamate	Miltown, Equanil	200-1200 mg
Tybamate*	Solacen	750-3000 mg

*Not widely used—effective only in some severe neuroses.

Diphenylmethane (antihistamine)

Generic name	Trade name	Daily dosage
Hydroxyzine	Atarax, Vistaril	100-400 mg

Barbiturates

Generic name	Trade name	Daily dosage
Phenobarbital	Luminal	60-150 mg
Butabarbital	Butisol	60-150 mg

Pharmacologic action. All of the minor tranquilizers are central nervous system depressants. The degree to which central nervous system depression occurs depends upon dosage and varies according to the particular drug group. The barbiturates and the antihistamines have a greater sedative effect than the benzodiazepines and the glycerol derivatives. The benzodiazepines are among the safest and most effective in the treatment of anxiety. They also have anticonvulsant and muscle relaxant properties and produce little effect on autonomic functions such as blood pressure. All of these drugs can produce physiological addiction, but the benzodiazepines are less addictive than the others and have fewer side effects. The side effects of the minor tranquilizers, which are often dosage related, are daytime drowsiness and sedation, decreased mental acuity, and decreased coordination. Overdoses produce muscle weakness, lack of coordination, sleep, and coma (Baldessarini, 1977).

Contraindications. Since the minor tranquilizers are central nervous system depressants, they should not be used in combination with other central nervous system depresssants such as the phenothiazines and alcohol. They are also contraindicated in pregnancy, particularly in the first trimester, and, because of the potentially addicting effect, in people known to be addicted to alcohol or other drugs.

Clients should be alerted to the possible side effects of anti-anxiety medications, and they should be cautioned against the use of other sedatives such as sleeping pills and alcohol. They should also be alerted to the possible dangers involved in driving a car or operating tools or machinery that require alertness and attention—especially in the early weeks of administration, when side effects are most apt to appear. Withdrawal symptoms, which can occur if the administration of a drug is suddenly ended, can be avoided through a gradual decrease in dosage over a week or so. Nurses in health care settings are responsible for the administration of medication and the assessment

Coping through dependence, domination, and detachment **353**

of client responses, including side effects. Nurses are also responsible for health teaching in relation to dosage and side effects.

NURSING INTERVENTION

PRIMARY PREVENTION

A major aspect of primary prevention in mental health nursing is the identification of persons at risk and intervention to prevent psychopathology. Although primary prevention is an evolving process in all areas of mental health, there is increasing emphasis upon maintaining the mental health of clients who are coping with health problems and the health care system.

The practice of nursing brings members of the profession into contact with persons of all ages and various states of physical and mental health. This professional contact in the community offers nurses the opportunity to participate in the primary prevention of neuroses and other mental health problems. A nurse who provides services to clients in a community agency, a general hospital, or any setting other than a psychiatric one often has little information about the emotional status of clients. Indeed, in many instances, clues to emotional status are masked or distorted by the phsyical disorder being treated and by the role of patient into which an individual is cast in many health care settings. Under such circumstances, a nurse must rely upon his or her knowledge and skill in assessing anxiety responses and behavioral patterns that indicate the need for nursing intervention to support clients who are attempting to maintain positive mechanisms of adaptation. The identification of themes or patterns of behavior and the development of goals and methods of intervention based upon the identified themes are particularly important aspects of primary prevention.

The major themes that emerge in character neuroses are (1) mood themes—themes of anxiety, anger, guilt, or fear; (2) interaction themes—themes of dependence, domination, or detachment; and (3) content themes. Content themes will vary; they depend upon the particular matters being discussed. They may or may not be in agreement with the mood and interaction themes (see Chapter 5).

The content theme, which is conveyed through verbal communication, is also known as the subjective data. It is the means through which a client communicates information about himself and his experience that he is able to share or wants to share. A practitioner who is skilled in listening and observing notes the manner in which the content is communicated and also such details as gaps or omissions in the content and any areas that are emphasized or discussed with reluctance.

The mood theme is the emotional tone; it may be expressed verbally or nonverbally. For example, some people who experience high levels of anxiety may be able to verbally communicate their feelings of uneasiness or their fears, and they may be able to identify what they perceive to be the sources of the discomfort. Other people may be quite unaware of such emotions as fear and anxiety but may convey them to the observer through restlessness, sighing, and other forms of nonverbal communication.

The interaction theme is the characteristic way in which an individual relates to other people. Inherent in the interaction theme is a covert communication, or metacommunication, that conveys a person's expectation of the way in which other people will respond. For example, a person who approaches others in a dependent manner conveys the expectation that others will care for and protect him.

Identification of themes of behavior
Anxiety. Nearly everyone experiences some anxiety when he is confronted with a health related problem that requires the services of health professionals. Many factors contribute to the arousal of anxiety. The decision to seek professional assistance for any health problem signifies a recognition that something is significantly different in a person's life—something that requires outside help. The degree to which a particular health problem is perceived as threatening is, to some extent, related to the purpose for which health care is sought and the extent of services required. Since

anything perceived as a threat to physical safety or psychological security is a source of anxiety, some evidence of anxiety is manifested by anyone who needs health care services.

The acceptance of health care means giving up some autonomy and becoming dependent upon others to some extent. Practices routinely used by nursing and medical personnel may be experienced as invasions of privacy. Nursing and medical histories may inquire into areas of life that are regarded as personal and private matters. Questions about dietary habits or alcohol and drug use, for example, may be perceived as containing implied value judgments. Physical examinations and treatment measures may cause physical pain and invade the privacy of the body, arousing shame and psychological discomfort.

Like pain, anxiety serves to alert a person to danger and enables him to institute measures to protect or defend himself. The pain resulting from a fractured bone helps to immobilize the part, preventing further damage and thus protecting physiological integrity. The defensive mechanisms and maneuvers brought into play by anxiety serve much the same purpose in protecting psychological integrity. When anxiety is mild and proportional to the threat to health, it may enhance the ability to participate effectively in a health care plan.

Some people, however, suffer from chronic anxiety, which is kept under control until stressful situations develop. Such persons are particularly vulnerable to stress; they may respond to any health problem with excessive anxiety.

The ways in which anxiety is communicated vary to some extent, according to a person's age, his cultural background, the health problem being coped with, and the milieu involved. A child may express anxiety through crying or nightmares, for example. An adult may respond through silent brooding or symptoms of depression. Anyone may feel far more threatened in a general hospital than in his own home, where support systems are available and the surroundings are familiar. However, people from a southern European cultural background, for example, may express such a feeling openly and overtly, while people from northern European heritages may be restrained and stoic. A person coping with a major threat to life may well experience greater anxiety than a person coping with a minor, temporary ailment. The nurse who becomes knowledgeable about the clients he or she serves and the usual coping mechanisms utilized in response to stress will become more effective in assessing anxiety responses and in intervening to support and sustain clients.

Physical evidence of anxiety includes rapid pulse and heart rates, increases in the rate and depth of respirations, muscle tension, restlessness, and dizziness. Gastrointestinal disturbances, which can range from "butterflies in the stomach" to nausea, vomiting, and diarrhea are not uncommon. Headache, chronic fatigue, and insomnia may be indicative of chronic anxiety. These symptoms represent physiological responses through which the autonomic nervous system prepares the body to take action against a perceived threat. Prolonged anxiety—a state that is characterized by constant readiness for flight or fight—may induce chronic fatigue and may even contribute to disorders in the cardiovascular, gastrointestinal, and other systems.

Psychological evidence of anxiety may include disturbances in perception of and response to stimuli, ability to concentrate, memory, and ability to focus attention, as well as difficulty in relating to other people. Ego defense mechanisms such as denial and regression, which may include dysfunctional symptoms, can occur.

Disturbances in perception, memory, and ability to concentrate may be indicated by an inability to comprehend accurately, a situation a person perceives as traumatic. Focusing upon a detail of a situation or communication may indicate a narrowing of the perceptual field, which can occur when a person's anxiety level is elevated. The inability to retain or fully comprehend information, instructions, or health teaching or to remember appointments may be a clue to a anxiety.

Perception is a complex process that includes the ability to interpret, organize, and integrate into one's experience stimuli arising from sources internal and external to the self. Inherent in the process is the ability to exclude excessive stimuli present in the environment. This ego-maintaining function, which protects personality integration by selectively limiting incoming stimuli, involves the use of what is termed a "stimulus barrier" (Carter, 1976). The ability to study and concentrate in a large room, with many activities going on, and within hearing distance of rock-and-roll music, illustrates how such a barrier works.

When a person is in a state of heightened tension and anxiety caused by physiological and psychological stress, he may be overwhelmed by the situation. In such a case, he may overreact to any stimuli, either external or internal. The noise level in many hospitals, as well as the number of people and the degree of activity, may increase tension and irritability. Strange equipment, which is taken for granted by the staff, may be misperceived and therefore terrifying. The experience of pain may be markedly heightened as a result of such an environment.

The perception of time may also be distorted. Anyone who has been in a frightening situation will recall that an event that lasted a few moments seemed to take hours when it was occurring. The inability to wait one's turn for an appointment or services or impatience with any delay is indicative of a low frustration threshold, which serves as another clue to anxiety.

A person may utilize any resource available in coping with anxiety. Sometimes, especially in mild anxiety, thinking through a situation in a problem-solving manner may be effective. At other times, a person might escape from a situation by means of food, alcohol, or drugs. But in many other instances, particularly when anxiety is high, ego defense mechanisms will come into play. The most frequently encountered defense mechanism in relation to health problems is denial. This mechanism, which is an unconscious phenomenon, serves to protect the ability to cope with experience by keeping out of awareness intolerable thoughts, feelings, and aspects of reality. Denial may take many forms. The ways in which it is manifested depend in part upon the degree to which a person's life, autonomy, life-style, mobility, body image, and so forth are perceived to be threatened. Anxiety responses also depend upon the charactersitic ways in which an individual has previously coped with stressful situations. Whatever the source of anxiety, nurses and other health workers who are confronted with a client who denies the reality of a serious health problem, or who exhibits behavior that is contraindicated by the particular situation, may well respond with anger, frustration, and helplessness. An understanding of the need for the denial and the purpose it serves in the overall coping strategy of the client will enable health professionals to provide the emotional support he requires.

Dependence. Nearly everyone is placed in a somewhat dependent role when he is confronted with a health problem requiring professional assistance. The decision to seek such assistance indicates that a person recognizes that he has a problem with which he is unable to cope without assistance. The health agency and the type of services required may foster feelings of dependence. Health professionals, to whom a particular health problem may be an everyday occurrence, and who are familiar with its course and treatment, may automatically assume an authoritative manner toward a client without fully comprehending the emotional response of the client toward his situation. In addition, many people experience a degree of regression when they are ill and feeling helpless. These and many other factors increase a client's feeling of dependence when he is coping with a health problem.

The behavior of the client who characteristically relates to others in a dependent manner differs from the behavior of the average client only in the degree or extent to which dependence needs are expressed and in the persistent, often indirect way in which such a client communicates these needs. The complexity and variability of human behavior, the diversity of cultural response to health problems, and the differences in the quality of stress inherent in physical conditions complicate the problem of assessment.

Persistent and repeated demands for attention or services, which do not diminish when they are met, provide a clue to anxiety and to the fact that the attention and approval of the staff are necessary to the individual's psychological security. Hypersensitivity to anything viewed as rejection, criticism, or neglect, which may be expressed through increased anxiety, overt expressions of anger, or depression, indicates that the person is striving to maintain the ability to function in a crisis situation. Excessive compliance with the demands of others and excessive praise—or unrealistic expectations about—the abilities of staff members may be subtle forms of manipulation, which communicate feelings of helplessness and a need for emotional support.

Domination. The individual who copes with experiences by attempting to dominate other people seems, on the surface, to be the exact opposite of the overly dependent person. But this facade is misleading. During stressful situations such a person is just as vulnerable to anxiety and its disruptive forces as a dependent person. Instead of depending upon others to bolster self-esteem, the person who copes by domination must take command of the environment and project an image of competence. An underlying view of the world as a threatening, hostile place makes it difficult, if not impossible, for him to place the degree of trust in others that is often necessary during a health crisis. In addition, the dependent role necessitated by admission to a hospital may arouse anxiety, unconscious dependence needs, and the underlying conflict of which such needs are a part. An inability to admit to himself or othes such feelings as apprehension, fear, and anxiety makes it difficult for this type of person to deal with these feelings when they emerge. The need to be dominant may also result in conflict with physicians, nurses, and other health care providers in their professional roles of authority figures.

Although overt evidence of anxiety may not be discernable in such clients, many other clues may be detected that suggest an underlying struggle to maintain equilibrium. Consistent disregard for or defiance of medical orders or a prescribed treatment plan may indicate that the need to preserve psychological equilibrium is of higher priority than the threat to physical well-being. For example, the refusal of a person with diabetes to adhere to a prescribed diet, or of a person with a coronary occlusion to accept restrictions on his activity, frequently results in annoyance and frustration for nurses and other health professionals.

Aggression, whether expressed overtly through angry outbursts or covertly through sarcasm or being late for appointments, may indicate underlying anxiety. Resentment of questions about personal life and habits and resistance to accepting advice, suggestions, or health teaching may be indications of the need to remain in control in order to contain anxiety and preserve psychological integrity.

Professional nurses, who are confronted daily with the more extreme manifestations of disorders, may respond with frustration and even anger to a client who resfuses to allow a treatment plan or to accept advice or instruction. Such a response to a client's behavior on the part of a nurse may itself be a clue that a client is experiencing psychological distress or anxiety. Anxiety is often contagious; it can be communicated nonverbally in a way that arouses anxiety in others.

Detachment. The person who copes with stress by becoming detached from other people is especially vulnerable when he experiences physical illness or injury, which of necessity may bring him into closer contact with other people than can be tolerated. The need to feel self-sufficient or even superior may result in conflict with professional authority. Medical orders, a treatment plan, or the requirement that the routine of a health agency be adhered to, may be perceived by the detached person as coercion and responded to with uneasiness and rebellion.

The need for privacy, which is of great importance to the detached individual, may be violated in several ways in the health care setting. A medical or nursing history often probes into aspects of life regarded as private and personal. Resistance and evasion in responding to such questions, and accompanying signals of anxiety or withdrawal, can alert the questioner to the client's distress. Sharing a room in a hospital with one or more other clients may be particularly distressing; it may increase the use of defense mechanisms to control the discomfort and maintain some degree of privacy. Intellectualization and an air of superiority may be employed to keep other people at a distance. Indifference and disinterest in others and even in one's own condition may be clues to detachment. Conversely, the person who furnishes many clues that he prefers to be alone may become angry if he feels that he is being ignored or taken for granted. Such inconsistent messages demonstrate the very human need such clients have for contact and acceptance by other people. They also indicate the incompatability of the needs and strivings of individuals who cope through detachment. (This incompatibility also characterizes the situation of persons who cope through domination.)

Nursing goals. Nurses should keep the following principles in mind when they develop goals for primary prevention of neuroses:

1. Interpersonal patterns of dependence, domination, and detachment are means of coping with unconscious conflicts in order to maintain the ability to function.
2. Neurotic conflict cannot be resolved by rational decision.
3. Anxiety is present whether or not there are overt symptoms.
4. A behavioral response in any situation is aimed primarily at maintaining psychological security and keeping anxiety under control.
5. During periods of crisis, anxiety increases and regression may occur.
6. Awareness of feelings and interpersonal behavior is low during such periods.
7. Such periods are characterized by excessive vulnerability to criticism, rejection, or desertion.
8. Nurses and other health care workers will have emotional responses to client behavior.

Ujhely (1968) best expresses the major objective of nursing intervention for clients struggling to maintain adaptation while coping with a physical health problem. Ujhely regards "sustaining the person in his experience" as a major concern of professional nursing. She includes in the sustaining process all of the professional activities that assist the person in coping with any experience in which he requires health services. Inherent in the concept of sustaining the client is designing nursing intervention to provide the emotional support required by the client and avoiding, as much as possible, actions that increase anxiety, isolation, or other emotions that may inhibit the achievement of health care goals.

Ujhely (1968) points out that permitting the client to be the way he can or must be at any given time, and protecting him from the necessity to defend his behavior against outside assault, help to conserve his energy for coping with the health problem at hand. This is a form of emotional support. For the client who is struggling to contain anxiety and to maintain psychological security, accepting behavior may also prevent regression and the development of maladaptive coping measures.

Providing emotional support has long been accepted as a major tenent of professional nursing practice. The therapeutic nurse-patient relationship is regarded as the means through which this goal is accomplished in any health care setting. Since the interpersonal process has been discussed earlier in this book, it will not be discussed further here. At this point it will be sufficient to emphasize again the importance of this process in the achievement of nursing goals.

The increasing demands of technology in health care settings today tend to force both nurses and patients into roles or models in which technology takes· precedence over humanism. For the client, this can be a terrifying experience. For the nurse, it often means combining the nurse-client relationship with the more technical aspects of health care and with close supervision of and planning with nonprofessional staff members, who may have extensive contact with clients.

In developing a relationship with a person who is coping with a crisis situation, a nurse must orient the goals and expectations of the relationship toward the provision of the level of support the client needs or can accept. For example, some clients may have difficulty tolerating or participating in a supportive relationship. An expectation that a substantial level of trust can be achieved in a relationship with such a client may thus be unrealistic, since this is often an area in which the client is in conflict. The establishment of a basic rapport may be more realistic.

The focus of discussion should be on the client's current experience with the health problem and its treatment. The major objective is alleviating some of the underlying anxiety. The nurse's presence and demonstration of interest and empathy may have a more therapeutic effect than the content of the discussion. The ability to empathize with a client whose interpersonal patterns may appear to be unreasonable and self-defeating can only come about when a nurse understands and accepts the client's need for the behavior. The recognition that such a client is as immobilized psychologically as a patient with a fractured femur is immobilized physically, and that the psychological pain—anxiety—may be as acute as the physical pain, may contribute to the ability to empathize. Respecting a client's need for privacy and avoiding questioning except when the information sought is essential to the treatment plan are also important.

Some alteration in usual nursing procedures may be helpful in alleviating anxiety. For example, the individual who copes by means of dependence and submissiveness is often highly susceptible to increased anxiety from anything perceived as a threat. Many medical and nursing procedures may be particularly anxiety provoking; they may arouse hysterical outbursts or even panic reactions. For such a person, information about a procedure may provoke the least amount of anxiety if it is given as near the time the procedure is to be performed as possible. In addition, such information should be limited to the amount the individual wants or is able to accept. Very often, interest is limited to "Will it hurt?" and "How long will it take?" Procedures such as enemas and catheterizations may be especially threatening, since they not only invade privacy, but their intrusive nature may arouse repressed fantasies and fears from earlier developmental eras.

In contrast, persons who cope through domination may wish to know all the technical details and to be consulted early when procedures are planned. For the client who needs to be in a dominant position, engaging his participation in planning and implementing health care may be the most therapeutic approach. However, a nurse should also be alert to any dependence needs that may emerge. Such needs should be accepted without comment and met to the extent possible or appropriate.

Primary prevention during the developmental years. Up to this point the focus has been upon preventive measures for adults, whose personality patterns are fairly well established. We shall now turn our attention to a brief discussion of primary prevention in childhood and to the points of vulnerability in the early developmental years, a period during which preventive efforts may be most effective. A child born into a family in which one or both parents use neurotic coping patterns is in a vulnerable state. Poverty or other environmental stresses that contribute to a chronic crisis situation may cause a child to experience difficulty in accomplishing the tasks of normal development. Identification of and preventive intervention for such families are particularly pertinent in the prenatal and perinatal periods, during developmental crisis in the child, in family developmental crises, and in situational crises.

Practitioners of family nursing have long been active in promoting physical and mental health in prospective parents. Natural childbirth, health education, anticipatory guidance, and genetic counseling, as well as the support of persons who are adapting to the role of parent, are but a few areas of concern that have been extensively studied. Much of this effort, however, has focused on the normal family or on prospective parents who are relatively mentally healthy. Less attention has been given to persons whose character structures suggest the need for intermittent intervention in periods of family crisis. For example, a prospective parent who has excessive dependence needs may be unable, without ongoing support, to meet the dependence needs of an infant and, later, the developing child. A person who copes by means of patterns of domination may be unable to allow a toddler the degree of freedom necessary to develop autonomy, or an adolescent the degree of independence essential to the development of identity. Identification of such prospective parents before their children are born and supportive follow-up care during their children's early developmental years are aspects of primary prevention. Referral to mental health resources in the community is an additional step toward primary prevention that nurses can initiate for clients who need such referrals and who are willing to accept them. It should be kept in mind, however, that the decision to seek treatment rests with the individual client. A client's willingness to seek professional help when it is needed may be increased by a supportive nurse-client relationship and a knowledge of resources in the community that are available for help.

Situational crises such as the loss of a parent through illness, death, or divorce or the death of a sibling can be psychologically traumatic to a developing child. Schwartz and Schwartz (1972) have written extensively about the effects of hospitalization on children, particularly about the traumatic effects on children in the preschool years. Anxiety engendered by separation from parents, regression to an earlier stage of development, and fears and fantasies aroused by intrusive nursing and medical procedures are some of the factors these authors mention as contributing to the trauma of the experience. Modern hospitals have taken many steps to minimize or prevent psychological trauma in hospitalized children. Encouraging parents to participate in the care of children and providing play and other activities in which children can act out fears and fantasies related to their hospital experiences are important preventive measures.

Adolescence is another period in which illness, injury, and hospitalization are potentially traumatic. The young person who is coping with rapid changes in body image and who is attempting to establish psychosocial identity and independence is particularly vulnerable to additional threats to body image caused by illness or injury and to the dependent role in which such health problems place him. The invasion of privacy and intrusive nursing and medical procedures often increase feelings of shame and guilt associated with rapidly developing sexuality. The degree to which the resulting anxiety and regression have any lasting effect upon the personality depends, to a great extent, upon how successfully earlier developmental tasks have been mastered and the degree of threat and trauma in the current situation.

Parker and Gibson (1977), noting the prevalence of anxiety among hospitalized adolescents and the difficulties involved in relying upon behavioral assessment in the measurement of anxiety in this age group, developed a tool for the purpose. The authors believe that their "Hospitalized Adolescent Anxiety Tool" (HAAT) would be effective in identification of and early intervention in adjustment problems experienced by hospitalized adolescents.

Early therapeutic intervention is important as a preventive mental health measure. Group discussions in which adolescent patients can share experiences with peers, under the guidance of a psychiatric nurse or another mental health professional, constitute an important preventive measure. In addition, follow-up mental health services for adolescents and children in whom chronic anxiety persists and regression and other defenses appear are important in preventing neurosis.

SECONDARY PREVENTION

Like "primary prevention," "secondary prevention" is a public health term that came to be used during the community mental health movement. The philosophy in the secondary prevention of neuroses, as in all areas of mental health nursing, is that early identification and effective treatment will prevent long-range sequelae and limit the incidence of neurotic disorders in a community. Inherent in the concept is the availability of necessary resources in the community to meet these objectives.

Although professional nurses have traditionally been involved in the treatment of the more severe psychiatric disorders, such as the psychoses, changing patterns of health care and the expanding role of the nurse in community health and mental health are placing increasing demands upon the profession to participate in secondary prevention in the neuroses. Such prevention involves meeting the following objectives:

1. Early identification of cases of neurosis in the community
2. Obtaining prompt and effective treatment to restore the individual to optimum mental health
3. Assessment of available community resources for referral
4. Participation with community groups in expanding needed resources

Early identification. Early identification, or case finding, is important in neuroses since many individuals suffering from them do not seek professional help until or unless the symptoms severely inhibit the ability to function. The professional involvement of nurses in many aspects of community life brings them into contact with families and individuals. Nurses thus have opportunities for early identification that may not be available to other health professionals. A nurse may be the first health professional to come into contact with a person with a neurotic disorder. In such an instance, the nurse may be concentrating primarily on family health or social problems that may or may not be related to the neurosis. A public health nurse, for example, providing services to a family in a home, may be the first health professional to learn of a phobia in a mother that is undermining the mental health of the entire family. A school nurse may be the first to recognize an anxiety reaction in a parent that is interfering with child's learning. An industrial nurse may be the first to recognize symptoms of an underlying neurosis that is contributing to alcohol abuse in an employee.

Such early assessments are tentative and should be validated through consultation and, when possible, through referral of clients to other health professionals, before further intervention is planned. The amount of consultation and the manner in which it is carried out depend upon the circumstances and on the way in which a client and a nurse come together. A public health nurse will have an opportunity to discuss a plan of action with a supervisor and a mental health nurse in an agency, as well as opportunities for repeated visits to a client's home. A school nurse may be able to encourage the mother of a child to meet with a school psychologist. An industrial nurse may have the services of a physician or a psychiatrist available.

The objective of early identification in secondary prevention is the referral of the client to a mental health resource for treatment. Many clients, however, are highly resistant to any form of psychiatric intervention. In such a case, the person's right to refuse treatment must be respected. For persons who are reluctant to accept treatment or who are ambivalent about becoming involved, a supportive nurse-client relationship, with the limited goal of providing emotional support while the client is in a crisis, may be effective in motivating the individual to accept further treatment.

Intervention in symptom neuroses. The role of the nurse in the treatment of neuroses depends upon several factors, including the treatment setting and the level of professional practice at which the nurse is prepared to function.

Clients with neuroses may be found in all of the settings in which professional nurses function, including the home, community clinics and health centers, and psychiatric and other units of general hospitals. The mental health staff available and the treatment modalities utilized may vary considerably from one agency to another, and the functions of the nurse may vary with them. For example, a nurse working with an interdisciplinary team in a psychiat-

ric unit would function in a collaborative relationship with other members of the team in meeting treatment objectives for a group of clients, while a nurse in a community health center might work with a client in his home, be the only professional in contact with him, and thus serve as the primary therapist.

The educational preparation of nurses also varies. The number of nurses who have post-doctoral preparation in psychoanalysis is steadily growing, these nurses are prepared to practice psychoanalysis and intensive psychotherapy. Many nurses have master's degrees in psychiatric nursing, with training and experience in individual and group therapies; they often practice as individual or group therapists, both independently and in psychiatric clinics and hospitals. Many more nurses have baccalaureate degrees in nursing and interest and experience in psychiatric nursing that prepares them to provide supportive therapy to individuals and groups. (See Chapter 1.)

In planning a supportive relationship with a neurotic client, a nurse should keep the following principles in mind regardless of the symptom picture:

1. The focus should be upon the client as a person who is suffering, and not upon the symptom.
2. Whether or not it is observable, underlying anxiety is present.
3. The symptom is a defense mechanisms designed to contain anxiety and to preserve ego integrity.

4. Nurses and other staff members will have emotional responses to client behavior. A nurse should protect the client's right to the symptom and, when necessary, should serve as an advocate for the client during interaction with other staff members.
5. Nursing interventions and activities should permit the patient to carry out demands of the disorder, such as an obsessive-compulsive ritual.
6. The client needs acceptance and approval; he is vulnerable to any form of rejection.
7. If the disorder is characterized by indecisiveness, any pressure to have the client make decisions should be avoided.
8. Although the client is in contact with reality and able to think logically, he may be out of touch with his own feelings.
9. Repressed hostility may be overtly expressed when the client feels pressured or frustrated.
10. Since the client fears his own hostility and anger, and his anxiety increases when they become overt, actions that may arouse anger should be avoided.
11. Any attempt to rationally explain symptoms or underlying dynamics should be avoided. Such attempts would be met with resistance and increased anxiety.

Specific goals for the supportive nurse-patient relationship should be established to meet the needs of the individual client as expressed in the relationship. The general objectives for any client include reducing anxiety and sustaining or supporting him. In many instances, communication may be established with relatively little difficulty and with less threat to the nurse than might be encountered in working with a client with a psychosis. Maintaining the relationship on a therapeutic rather than a social level may be more difficult. The focus of the relationship should be on the current experience of the client and on the areas of concern that he is willing or able to discuss. Ongoing supervision is important for the nurse who is working in an interpersonal process with a neurotic client.

Acute anxiety attacks. An acute anxiety attack comes on suddenly and lasts from several minutes to a few hours. During such an attack, a person is in or near a panic state. He may be immobilized by the anxiety, or he may place himself in danger by attempting to run away from it, perhaps into a busy street. The ability to perceive what is happening around him is severely restricted, but he may also overreact to external stimuli. The physiological symptoms may convince him that he is having a heart attack or experiencing some other physical disorder.

A major aspect of nursing intervention is the protection of the client. Lipkin and Cohen (1973) note the importance of staying with the client until the anxiety level subsides. As they point out, a nurse can prevent the client from taking any action that might be dangerous. More importantly, the calm, accepting manner of the nurse can provide some sense of security. Communications with the person in panic should be brief, clear, and concrete and should be made in a calm, slow manner. If he is able to do so, the client may be encouraged to talk about the feelings he is experiencing. Any probing or pressure should be avoided. Since the source of anxiety is unconscious, any suggestions about the possible cause may only increase the anxiety (Lipkin and Cohen, 1973). Comfort measures such as loosening tight clothing, giving hot or cold fluids, and providing calm, quiet surroundings are also important in supporting the client in a panic state.

Anxiety reactions are often associated with phobias. For example, a person with agoraphobia—an abnormal fear of leaving one's home—who travels even a short distance from home alone may experience an acute anxiety attack.

Phobic reactions. Many aspects of nursing intervention for the phobic person have been discussed already. Focusing upon the client as a person and not on the phobia is an important aspect of the nurse-patient relationship. Protecting the client's right to the symptom and supporting his efforts to avoid contact with the feared object help him to contain the underlying anxiety. A phobic person is aware of the irrationality of the symptom and very often is able to discuss it and to examine the impact it is having upon his life. The degree to which a phobia is disruptive of a person's life depends upon the nature of the fear. The fear of flying in an airplane may be far less inhibiting than the fear of rid-

ing in an elevator, when one lives on an upper floor of a high-rise building. The degree of disruption in a person's life may also be related to the degree to which he is motivated to give up the symptom or to seek professional help. A nurse must be alert to the secondary gains that may result from a phobia. A client who has a bus phobia may be able to avoid some boring chores and to obtain additional attention from others, who must provide the needed services. At times a nurse may be able to modify a phobic person's environment slightly, and with the cooperation of family and friends, limit some of the services provided that tend to reinforce the symptom. In a hospital setting, it may be possible, through careful study of the situation, to limit secondary gains that reinforce the symptom, while at the same time permitting the client to avoid the feared object. Although such a plan may be more easily carried out in the controlled environment of a hospital, the benefits may be greater when it is carried out in the home, where the problem originated.

Plans for such environmental manipulation should be made with the client and appropriate family members and friends when the client appears to be ready for such a step and agrees to participate in the planning.

A community health nurse had met several times with Mrs. M, the mother of three children, in her home. Because of a phobia, Mrs. M was unable to leave her home even when accompanied by her husband and children. She eventually had reached the point where she was motivated to contact a nearby mental health clinic. During each of the past two visits by the community health nurse, a plan to leave the home in the company of the husband and the nurse had been agreed upon by the client. But it had to be canceled each time because the client had an anxiety attack and could not follow through. During a supervisory meeting with a mental health nurse, the community health nurse expressed her frustration with Mrs. M and mentioned that she believed the client was enjoying her disability. After examining this idea for evidences of secondary gain in the situation, both agreed that the perception was valid. Together they developed a plan for intervention. In a subsequent meeting between the community health nurse and the client, the client agreed to the plan and with the nurse began to examine aspects of her lifestyle that might be subtly reinforcing the symptom. Several factors were identified. The husband regularly brought Mrs. M a variety of magazines and books, in addition to doing all of the shopping for the family, which the client admitted had always bored her. The husband also was very good about buying the foods and delicacies she preferred and about keeping her informed about affairs of the community. Many small comforts were provided by a friend who visited regularly and shared Mrs. M's interest in fashion and design. In the next session, in which both the husband and the friend participated, everyone agreed upon a plan that would eliminate all but necessities from Mr. M's shopping list. The friend's visits would be suspended for a time. The nurse would continue to hold regular sessions and would be available by phone for crises that might ensue from the plan. Several small crises did arise, but the husband and the friend, with the support of the nurse, held firmly to the agreed upon plan. The client was eventually able to keep an appointment at the mental health clinic.

Hysterical and dissociative reactions. Such symptoms as conversion reactions and amnesias are among the most dramatic events found in psychiatry. For the patient they represent emergency defenses against situational crises which are intolerable and from which temporary relief is achieved by the symptom. To the viewer, the client who is suddenly struck blind in the face of hardship or who wipes out his past by means of amnesia appeals to the sense of drama and symbolism that we all share. Who among us has not had fantasies about wiping the slate clean and starting over again or, through some magical act of omnipotence, rejecting unpleasant reality? Vicarious pleasure may, indeed, be one of the responses of staff members to a client who has a conversion symptom or a form of amnesia; staff members may pay much superficial attention to such a patient when he is first admitted to a psychiatric unit. This situation can be detrimental to the client, because it derives from the needs and curiosity of the staff and because staff members may later experience vague feelings of guilt and wish to avoid the client. It is thus particularly important that nurses who work with persons experiencing hysterical reactions understand their own responses to the patients.

Protecting the person's right to the symptom may also be difficult. The absence of anxiety, which is often the case in conversion reactions, may tempt staff members to prematurely convince the client with a conversion symptom that medical evidence does not support the existence of the symptom, or to provide the amnesia victim with information about himself that he is denying or repressing. When successful, such efforts may result in psychosis.

Hysterical symptoms usually indicate an immature personality. Feelings and responses are often acted out in a hystrionic fashion, which masks low self-esteem. Establishment of therapeutic milieu, in which the client can be encouraged to achieve gratification in activity therapies and in which appropriate and reasonable limits can be maintained, is an important nursing measure. In a nurse-patient relationship, the objectives should be to provide needed emotional support and to encourage verbalization of feelings and responses. The focus should be upon the person and not upon the symptom or the events that led up to it. A conversion symptom should be dealt with in much the same way that a delusion is dealt with—that is, by accepting the client's need for the symptom and by neither denying nor confirming its existence.

Obsessive-compulsive reactions. In working with an obsessive-compulsive client, a nurse must set realistic goals. This form of neurosis tends to be chronic and quite resistant to almost any form of therapy. Unless the onset is recent and the symptom limited, any expectation of results other than some reduction in the level of anxiety and the severity of symptoms is unrealistic in most cases. Obsessive-compulsive behavior can be a source of frustration to the nurse who works with such a client. Setting unrealistic goals only increases the frustration the nurse experiences.

Many aspects of nursing intervention discussed in relation to the person who is detached are relevant to intervention for the obsessive-compulsive client. There is difficulty in establishing an interpersonal relationship, since the obsessive-compulsive client has difficulty feeling close to other people. Frequently, such a client finds it difficult to express thoughts and feelings, and he often needs to maintain some physical distance. Underlying hostility and a need to control the environment pose problems for both the client and the nurse.

In establishing a nurse-client relationship, a calm, quiet approach is important. After a statement of interest and availability, it is important to wait for clues from the client before proceeding with further verbal communication. It is necessary that communication move at a pace that is comfortable for the client. The focus of interaction should be the person, not the symptom, and any form of pressure or prying should be avoided. Once a relationship has been established, goals and intervention can be determined by the themes that emerge and the client's ability or willingness to work with them.

Any level of nursing intervention for obsessive-compulsive clients should take into account the fact that they are tense and anxious. They have little tolerance for frustration, and the strong need to control the environment may conflict with the established routines of a health agency. Efforts to make a client comply with fixed routines may result in increased anxiety and possibly in overt expressions of anger. Since the client is struggling to contain underlying hostility, situations that increase frustration or provoke anger may be detrimental to the progress of his treatment. Demands made and limits imposed on the client should be reasonable, and their purpose should be made clear to him. It should be kept in mind that obsessive-compulsive people are ambivalent; they have difficulty making even minor decisions or choices. Pressuring such a person to make decisions should be avoided.

To protect the client's right to the symptom, it is necessary to allow time for the ritual to be performed and to schedule therapeutic activities so that they do not interfere. Protecting the client from the criticism or ridicule of other clients, as well as staff members, is frequently necessary. In the event that limits must be set on ritualistic behavior, they must be stated clearly, concisely, and reasonably, and they should be consistently maintained. Such limits should, of course, only be established to achieve a therapeutic goal.

At times, ritualistic symptoms may interfere with or threaten the health of the client. Such situations may range from dermatitis of the hands as a result of compulsive hand washing to malnutrition as a result of ritual concerning food. Appropriate measures must be taken in such instances to maintain physical health.

Hypochondriasis. Hypochondriasis is one of the more severe neuroses;

it can result in regression to a psychotic state. Hypochondriasis appears in an immature person who has an underlying dependence-independence conflict. Strong dependence needs are thwarted by fear and distrust of others. The individual is often self-centered or narcissistic; he is often preoccupied with the body and its functions. His chronic anxiety is expressed in the form of physical symptoms. Hypochondriacal symptoms differ from psychosomatic symptoms in that the hypochondriacal symptom, although very real to the person affected, has no physical basis. The psychosomatic symptom is caused by a disease process.

A young woman who has one or more children is one typical victim of hypochondriasis. If such a woman has strong dependence needs, having young children dependent upon her may be intolerable. Chronic physical complaints offer some acceptable escape, and the resulting medical and nursing attention serve to meet some of the dependence needs.

Persons with hypochondriasis often come to the attention of nurses in acute health care settings such as clinics, emergency rooms, or general hospitals. Although the symptoms are very real to the client and the suffering is as great as, or greater than it would be in a physical illness, nursing and other staff members often respond with impatience, anger, or frustration when such a client rejects medical findings that indicate that no underlying disease is present. Family and friends often respond with similar contempt and rejection. Such responses only increase the client's anxiety and his need for the symptoms.

A common feature of hypochondriasis is strong resistance to any challenge to the validity of the physical complaint or to any form of referral for psychiatric therapy. The symptom (or symptoms) represents a strong effort to maintain ego integrity and the ability to function. Nursing intervention that is designed to provide support during crisis situations can prevent regression to a less adaptive level of functioning. Some principles of nursing intervention for the hypochondriacal patient follows.

1. Recognize the underlying dependence needs of the client.
2. Accept the client as he is, and adapt nursing intervention to meet his dependence needs.
3. Recognize negative staff responses to the client, and protect him from subtle forms of rejection, isolation, or derogation.
4. Provide staff members an opportunity for ventilating and sharing feelings and responses.
5. Identify social networks within the family and community that may be able to provide support when necessary.
6. Attempt to enlist the cooperation of family members and other persons in the client's social network who can provide support.
7. Make use of discussion groups in health care settings, such as prenatal or child care clinics, for sharing problems in coping with children or with daily living. Health teaching and antic-

ipatory guidance can offer support for the hypochondriacal client who is often isolated in the home.
8. Make the client aware of the resources available for crisis intervention when it is needed.
9. Refer the client to family therapy resources when the client and his family can accept this form of intervention, and when such resources are available.

Anorexia nervosa. The person with anorexia nervosa most often comes into contact with professional nurses only after the behavioral pattern of self-starvation has been well established and he has become so emaciated and malnourished that survival is threatened. If this is the case, the person must be admitted to a medical or psychiatric unit of a general hospital as an emergency measure. The following are aspects of nursing intervention for such clients:

1. Maintaining nutritional needs is usually the major concern in the treatment of anorexia. The clients, who are usually young women, are resistant to treatment and adept at thwarting efforts to improve nutrition. Close supervision is necessary in order to identify and circumvent evasive measures designed to avoid food intake.
2. An anorectic client has a strong need to maintain control. Although superficially compliant, such individuals use manipulation and evasiveness to achieve this end. Schlemmer and Barnett (1977) point out that this manipulation, which is constantly en-

countered in the treatment of anorexia appears to be an effort on the part of the anorectic person to control himself as well as the environment. They recommend that in controlling behavior, nurses should set limits, when necessary, and consistently and firmly maintain them. Clients should be informed of the limits and their purpose, and infractions should not be overlooked. Inconsistency on the part of the staff members in maintaining limits are noticed by patients and may be used as a weapon against them later. Schlemmer and Barnett note that anorectic patients fear loss of control over their own behavior and seem to welcome staff intervention.

3. The anorectic client has a distorted view of himself and a distorted body image. Such a person has an underlying lack of self-worth, which may be masked by an air of superiority, and a sense of helplessness and hopelessness. Displaying an accepting attitude, being available when needed, consistently pointing out misperceptions, and verbally recognizing and reinforcing authentic communication of feelings and perceptions are important ways in staff members can enhance an anorectic client's self-worth and increase his trust in others.

4. Opportunities should be provided, when possible, for patients to have control over their lives and environment. They need to be helped to understand that they do have control over, and responsibility for, weight gain.

5. Frequent opportunities for nursing and other staff members to ventilate and share their feelings and frustrations in response to manipulative behavior and self-destructive actions are essential. Staff meetings also offer opportunities for planning consistent and therapeutic intervention.

Bruch (1978) points out the importance of early identification and treatment of potentially anorectic persons before the starvation pattern is well established. She suggests that professionals involved with the education of young people are in a position to identify the over-compliant, over-conscientious, over-studious young person as potentially anorectic. School nurses and other health professionals who work with children, adolescents, and young adults also have opportunities to identify potential victims of this disorder, as well as roles to play in the education of teachers in early identification. The potentially life-threatening nature of anorexia nervosa and the resistance to treatment that occurs once the starvation syndrome has developed make prevention essential.

TERTIARY PREVENTION

Relatively little attention has been given to the long-range effects of neuroses upon the personality and the ability to function. The level of maladaptive functioning that occurs in neuroses does not produce the severe psychological crippling that is seen in schizophrenia, for example, and the other psychoses. Except for individuals with hypochondriasis, which is sometimes a stage preliminary to schizophrenia, persons who have neuroses often function satisfactorily in society, although they may require some psychiatric intervention in times of crisis.

However, everyone arrives at the so-called golden years with the personality characteristics and coping patterns that have developed over a lifetime. The sociocultural and physiological problems that beset people in the older age group may be made more severe by any neurotic coping patterns that, under less stressful circumstances, have been used to maintain the ability to function. When confronted with the loss of family and friends, who earlier provided needed support, and with decreasing economic status, a neurotic individual is often less able to cope with the problems of aging than the average person is. Many such individuals can be found, somewhat isolated, in single-room dwellings and health-related facilities, where they are often viewed as problem clients by staff members and other residents.

Tertiary prevention should include the provision of mental health centers where crisis intervention and individual and group psychotherapy are available for such persons and for others who may be similarly isolated in the community. In addition, tertiary prevention should include the identification of individuals in the community who have chronically displayed neurotic symptoms, such as obsessive-compulsive behavior or phobias, and the provision of psychiatric services for them.

Problems in nursing intervention. A problem frequently encountered in working with clients who cope with stress by means of an interpersonal pattern of dependence, domination, or detachment is the emotional responses that such clients' interpersonal behavior arouses in nursing and other staff members. Anger, anxiety, frustration, helplessness, and guilt may be aroused in staff members in response to client behavior. An angry, defensive outburst on the part of a client may well evoke a similar response in a staff member. Since anxiety is often communicated from one person to another on an emotional, nonverbal level, anxiety in a client may be met by anxiety in a nurse. Helplessness and frustration in staff members may stem from excessive demands on their attention and from the fact that they may have to regard one client's needs as less urgent than those of another. Transference and countertransference phenomena may increase anxiety levels in both clients and staff.

Transference is a complex, unconscious process in which a client transfers feelings and attitudes toward a significant person from the past to someone in his present situation—often a health care professional. Countertransference is a similar unconscious response on the part of a therapist toward a patient. Both terms were originally used in psychotherapy, but such phenomena may occur in many other situations, including the nurse-client context. Schwartz (1972) points out the similarities between the nurse-client and parent-child roles; he notes that both relationships are conducive to transference distortions in many situations.

Coping through dependence, domination, and detachment   **373**

Sullivan (1953) refers to transference phenomena as "parataxic distortion."

Nurses and other staff members need to find opportunities to discuss such emotional responses in a nonjudgmental atmosphere. Small group discussions in which staff members can receive support and guidance from respected peers serve to defuse emotional responses. Peer group discussions can be utilized to increase staff members' understanding of behavioral responses and to build team spirit. In addition, consultation with clinical nurse specialists or mental health staff members can be valuable in the planning of nursing intervention.

Distinguishing behavioral patterns that are culturally determined from those that arise as a result of chronic anxiety and unconscious conflict may at times be difficult. For example, A client from Japan, who typically has a strong group identification, may be confronted with culture shock when he is admitted to a Western hospital, where he is isolated from his family group. He might respond with submissiveness and dependence or with detachment. But the overall goals of supporting him in his experience would still be applicable.

CHAPTER SUMMARY

A neurosis can be defined as a personality organization characterized by excessive anxiety and unconscious conflict. Although such a disorder involves little or no distortion of reality or impairment of intellectual functioning, the use of various defense mechanisms and compromise solutions to maintain functioning and to control anxiety results in rigidity of the personality and the development of interpersonal patterns of dependence, domination, or detachment. When a neurotic person experiences stress, symptoms that are more pathological may appear.

Neurotic conflicts have their origins in the early developmental years—during the long period in which a child depends upon significant others for nurturing and acculturation. Neurotic behavior differs from normal behavior only in degree, and a neurosis can be understood only in relation to the culture in which a child is reared.

Neuroses are believed to be among the most prevalent psychiatric disorders in Western culture, although no reliable demographic studies are available. Whether neuroses exist in all cultures is not clear at this time.

Treatments for neuroses include individual and group psychotherapy, administration of psychopharmaceuticals, and behavior therapy, as well as brief hospitalization in certain crisis situations. Primary prevention includes early identification of and intervention for persons who experience chronic anxiety states and who display interpersonal relationship patterns that indicate that maladaptive coping patterns could develop during a crisis. Adapting nursing intervention to meet the needs of such clients during health-related crises is another important aspect of primary prevention.

The role of the nurse in secondary prevention depends, to some extent, upon the type neurosis and the setting in which the nurse intervenes. A fundamental aspect of nursing intervention, however, is a supportive nurse-patient relationship. Collaboration with other health professionals and utilization of available therapies are other important measures. Tertiary prevention includes case finding and collaboration with community groups in securing and utilizing resources for treatment.

REFERENCES

Aguilera, Donna C., and Janice M. Messick
   1978 Crisis Intervention: Theory and Methodology (ed. 3). St. Louis: The C. V. Mosby Co.
Allport, Gordon W.
   1955 Becoming. New Haven, Conn.: Yale University Press.
Arieti, Sylvano
   1974 "The cognitive volitional school." In American Handbook of Psychiatry (ed. 2), vol. 1. Sylvano Arieti (ed. and ed.-in-chief). New York: Basic Books, Inc., Publishers, Ch. 40, Section C, pp. 877-903.
Baldessarini, Rose J.
   1977 Chemotherapy in Psychiatry. Cambridge, Mass.: Harvard University Press.
Bellak, Leopold, Marvin Hurvich, Helen K. Gediman
   1973 Ego Function in Schizophrenics, Neurotics, and Normals. New York: John Wiley & Sons, Inc.

Benedict, Ruth
   1934 Patterns of Culture. Boston: Houghton Mifflin Co.
   1946 The Chrysanthemum and the Sword: Patterns of Japanese Culture. Boston: Houghton Mifflin Co.
Bruch, Hilde
   1978 The Golden Cage, The Enigma of Anorexia Nervosa. Cambridge, Mass.: Harvard University Press.
Cameron, Norman
   1963 Personality Development and Psychopathology: A Dynamic Approach. Boston: Houghton Mifflin Co.
Carter, Frances Monet
   1976 Psychosocial Nursing. New York: MacMillan, Inc.
Coelho, G. V. (ed.)
   1974 Coping and Adaptation. New York: Basic Books, Inc., Publishers.
Cohen, Roberta
   1971 "Anxiety in a Jewish patient." Journal of Psychiatric Nursing and Mental Health Services 9(6):5-8.
David, Henry P.
   1976 "Mental health services in the developing countries." Journal of Psychiatric Nursing and Mental Health Services 14(1):24-29.
Dikowitz, Sally
   1976 "Anorexia nervosa." Journal of Psychiatric Nursing and Mental Health Services 14(10):28-37.
Dunham, H. W.
   1976 "Society, culture and mental Disorder." Archives of General Psychiatry 33(2):147-156.
Dohrenwend, Bruce P., and Barbara Snell Dohrenwend
   1974 "Psychiatric disorders in urban settings." in American Handbook of Psychiatry (ed. 2), vol. 2. Gerald Caplan (ed.). Sylvano Arieti (ed.-in-chief). New York: Basic Books, Inc., Publishers, Ch. 29.
Drellich, Marvin
   1974 "Classical psychoanalytic school. A. Theory of neuroses." In American Handbook of Psychiatry (ed. 2), vol. 1. Sylvano Arieti (ed. and ed.-in-chief). New York: Basic Books, Inc., Publishers, Ch. 37.
Duval, Evelyn Mills
   1977 Marriage and Family Development (ed. 5). Philadelphia: J. B. Lippincott Co.

Epstein, Charlotte
1974 Effective Interaction in Contemporary Nursing. Englewood Cliffs, N.J.: Prentice-Hall, Inc.
Erikson, Erik
1968 Identity and Youth in Crisis. New York: W. W. Norton & Co., Inc.
1963 Childhood and Society (ed. 2). New York: W. W. Norton & Co., Inc.
Fenichel, Otto
1945 The Psychoanalytic Theory of Neuroses. New York: W. W. Norton Co., Inc.
Fine, Reuben
1962 Freud: A Critical Re-Evaluation of His Theories. New York: David McKay Co., Inc.
Freud, Sigmund
1936 The Problem of Anxiety. New York: W. W. Norton & Co., Inc.
1960 Group Psychology and the Analysis of the Ego. New York: Bantam Books, Inc.
1969 A General Introduction to Psychoanalysis. New York: Pocket Books.
Fromm, Erich
1962 The Art of Loving. New York: Harper & Row, Publishers, Inc.
Haber, Judith, et al.
1978 Comprehensive Psychiatric Nursing. New York: McGraw-Hill Book Co.
Hoff, Lee Ann
1978 People in Crisis: Understanding and Helping. Menlo Park, Calif.: Addison-Wesley Publishing Co., Inc.
Horney, Karen
1937 The Neurotic Personality of Our Time. New York: W. W. Norton & Co., Inc.
1939 New Ways in Psychoanalysis. New York: W. W. Norton & Co., Inc.
1945 Our Inner Conflicts. New York: W. W. Norton & Co., Inc.
Jarvik, Murray E.
1977 Psychoparmacology in the Practice of Medicine. New York: Appleton-Century Crofts.
Kolb, Lawrence C.
1977 Modern Clinical Psychiatry (ed. 9). Philadelphia: W. B. Saunders Co.
Klingbeil, G. Antoinette, and Ona M. Alvandi
1975 "Concepts of transactional analysis and anxiety with persons in crisis." Journal of Psychiatric Nursing and Mental Health Services 13(3):5-10.
Kubie, Laurence
1974 "The nature of the neurotic process." In American Handbook of Psychiatry (ed. 2), vol. 3. Sylvano Arieti and Eugene Brody (eds.). Sylvano Arieti (ed.-in-chief). New York: Basic Books, Inc., Publishers, pp. 3-16.
Laing, R. D.
1965 The Divided Self. Baltimore: Penguin Books, Inc.
Lidz, Theodore
1968 The Person. New York: Basic Books, Inc., Publishers.
Lipkin, Gladys B., and Roberta G. Cohen
1973 Effective Approaches to Patients' Behavior. New York: Springer Publishing Co., Inc.
Massafumi, Nakakuki
n.d. "Japan's homegrown neurosis." In Psychiatric Perspectives, Roche Reports, Frontiers of Psychiatry.
May, Rollo
1967 Man's Search for Himself. New York: The New American Library, Inc.
1974 Love and Will. New York: Dell Publishing Co., Inc.
1975 The Courage to Create. New York: W. W. Norton & Co, Inc.
Niemeier, Diane, and Tom S. Allison
1976 "Nurses can be effective behavior modifiers. Journal of Psychiatric Nursing and Mental Health Services 14:1.
Portnoy, Isadore
1974 "The school of Karen Horney." In American Handbook of Psychiatry (ed. 2), vol. 1. Sylvano Arieti (ed. and ed.-in-chief). Basic Books, Inc., Publishers.
Robinson, Lisa
1977 Psychiatric Nursing as a Human Experience. Philadelphia: W. B. Saunders Co.
Rogers, Carl R.
1970 Carl Rogers on Encounter Groups. New York: Harper & Row, Publishers, Inc.
Schwartz, Lawrence H., and Jane Linker Schwartz
1972 The Psychodynamics of Patient Care. Englewood Cliffs, N. J.: Prentice-Hall, Inc.
Schlemmer, Janet K., and Patricia Ann Barnett
1977 "Management of manipulative behavior of anorexic patients." Journal of Psychiatric Nursing and Mental Health Services 15:11.
Schreiber, Flora Rheta
1973 Sybil. Chicago: Regency Press.

Shapiro, David
   1965 Neurotic Styles. New York: Basic
        Books, Inc., Publishers.
Sifneos, Peter E.
   1972 Short Term Psychotherapy and Emo-
        tional Crisis. Cambridge, Mass.: Har-
        vard University Press.
Skinner, B. F.
   1971 Beyond Freedom and Dignity. New
        York: Alfred A. Knopf, Inc.
Specter, Rachel E.
   1979 Cultural Diversity in Health and Ill-
        ness. New York: Appleton-Century-
        Crofts.
Stevenson, R. L.
   1961 The Strange Case of Dr. Jekyll and Mr.
        Hyde and Other Famous Tales. New
        York: Dodd, Mead & Co.
Sullivan, Harry Stack
   1953 Conceptions of Modern Psychiatry.
        New York: W. W. Norton & Company,
        Inc.
Thigpens, C. H., and H. M. Cleckley
   1957 The Three Faces of Eve. New York:
        McGraw-Hill Book Co.
Ujhely, Gertrud Bertrand
   1963 The Nurse and Her "Problem" Pa-
        tients. New York: Springer Publishing
        Co., Inc.
   1968 Determinents of the Nurse-Patient Re-
        lationship, New York, Springer Pub-
        lishing Company, Inc.
Wolpe, Joseph
   1974 "The behavior therapy approach." In
        American Handbook of Psychiatry (ed.
        2), vol. 1. Sylvano Arieti (ed.). New
        York: Basic Books, Inc., Publishers,
        Ch. 43.

ANNOTATED SUGGESTED READINGS

Gelfman, Morris, and Emilee J. Wilson
   1979 "Emotional reactions in a renal unit."
        In Stress and Survival: The Emo-
        tional Realities of Life-Threatening
        Illness. Charles A. Garfield (ed.). St.
        Louis: The C. V. Mosby Co.
        The authors discuss emotional re-
        sponses to the stress caused by severe
        renal disease, in which dialysis and or-
        gan transplant are treatment modalities.
        Emphasis is placed upon the personal-
        ity of the client coping with such
        stress, rather than upon the fear of
        death, as the important factor in the
        emotional responses to this life-threat-
        ening disorder. One of the cases cited is
        that of a woman with a neurotically de-
        pendent personality who became psy-
        chotic after attempts by family members
        and health agency staff to make her
        more independent.
Horney, Karen
   1945 Our Inner Conflicts. New York: W. W.
        Norton & Co., Inc.
        Horney presents her theories of neu-
        roses. The nature of neurotic conflict
        and the impact upon personality of at-
        tempts at resolution are discussed. Hor-
        ney writes with great clarity and in lan-
        guage that is readily understood.
        Instead of using the terms "depen-
        dence," "domination," and "detach-
        ment" to describe interpersonal themes
        of behavior, Horney uses the terms
        "moving toward," "moving against,"
        and "moving away" from others to de-
        scribe the compromise solutions in neu-
        roses.
Mullahy, Patrick
   1955 Oedipus Myth and Complex. New
        York: Grove Press, Inc.
        Mullahy reviews psychoanalytic theo-
        ries of Freud and his contemporaries
        Adler, Jung, and Rank and interper-
        sonal theories of Sullivan, Horney,
        and Fromm. This work serves as an ex-
        cellent introduction to the major psy-
        choanalytic or psychodynamic theories.

11
COPING THROUGH
INWARDLY DIRECTED
AGGRESSION

CHAPTER
FOCUS

Depression is currently one of the most prevalent mental health problems in the United States. Discussion of depression as a disorder dates back to 1500 BC. The term is well-known to many yet has several different connotations: mood disorder, change in affect, clinical syndrome, or cluster of behavioral symptoms.

Depression accompanies a significant proportion of physical illnesses, particularly those that are severe. Suicide is positively correlated with depression. Few individuals have not been touched by depression, at least in its mildest form, as a reaction to loss or change.

An understanding of depression begins with an understanding of the concepts of grief and loss. Depression occurs as a response to any form of loss—loss of function, body part, status or responsibility or significant other. Depression, of course,

is also experienced by a person who learns that he is going to lose his own life. Phases of mourning will be discussed, and implications of healthy and maladaptive responses to loss will be identified.

Maladaptive responses to loss are discussed in terms of whether they are *exogenous* or *endogenous*, *neurotic* or *psychotic*, *unipolar* or *bipolar*. The discussion of depression also includes the concept of a continuum and the relationship of this continuum to these currently used terms.

The presentation of major theoretical constructs provides a framework for a thorough understanding of the complex underlying dynamics of depression. Predominant themes, coping mechanisms, and nursing interventions are discussed in relation to the manic-depressive response, involutional melancholia, and suicide.

COPING THROUGH INWARDLY DIRECTED AGGRESSION

Depression can be described
as sadness or disappointment;
in its most profound form
it is a syndrome characterized
by the wish to withdraw, the need
to deprecate self, and intense
feelings of guilt.

GRIEF AND LOSS

Grief is the process of separation. It is a universal process that is generally taken for granted. According to Engel (1962), grief involves a series of subjective responses to the loss of a significant love object. Individuals may describe feelings of helplessness, loneliness, hopelessness, anger, sadness, and guilt. The frequency and duration of these responses depend upon several factors:

1. Amount of support received from the lost object
2. Degree of ambivalence toward the lost object
3. Anticipatory preparation
4. Extent to which the loss alters life-style
5. Other supportive relationships available to the bereaved

Mourning encompasses the psychological processes or reactions a person uses to assist him in overcoming a loss. In the case of the loss of a family member or friend, mourning includes the funeral ritual, the wearing of somber, dark colors, or the draping of purple or black cloth over doorways and windows. As we will discuss later, such rituals permit the survivors to acknowledge the loss of the significant person and to share the loss with others.

Loss can be defined as the relinquishing of objects, status, persons, or functions that are identified as supportive. Loss is very much a part of the life cycle. It is imperative that nurses direct their energies toward helping people respond in a positive manner to the crises caused by loss. Obstacles to mental health generally arise when a person attempts to avoid intense distress and the expression of related emotions.

What does a bereaved person feel or experience? Is there an empathic route a nurse might select that would facilitate a genuine involvement with such a client? John Bowlby (1973) believes that the grieving process is set in motion by a loss or separation that leads to a feeling of emancipation from the lost object. The individual experiences a varying array of feelings, ranging from numbness and anger to healing and resolution. Eric Lindemann (1944), in his extensive studies of grief, has delineated four phases of the grieving process. The process is characterized by somatic distress, including tightness in the throat, an empty feeling, a loss of appetite, and even a lack of muscular power. A sense of unreality—that the loss has not actually occurred—is often described by a bereaved person. There is an accompanying sense of purposelessness, as well as an inability to maintain any patterns of organization.

Bowlby also describes four phases, which are similar to those of Lindemann. Each phase is characterized by a predominant form of behavior. The first phase incorporates Bowlby's concept of denial. A person experiencing a loss cannot believe what has occurred. He responds intellectually and appears to be in control; however, the emotional component is forced into the background. In modern society the emotional aspect is frequently not allowed to surface. Little emphasis is placed on attachment behavior. Rather, we encourage stoic behavior, particularly on the part of men. Crying is considered acceptable in most instances, and it is recognized as a means of asking for support. Yet this aspect of the grieving process may be inadvertently negated as well. We are not able to tolerate the anguish of others; therefore, we cut off the grieving person through such casual statements as "Wasn't he ill for a long time?" or "It's better that she didn't suffer." The grieving person does not often hear "It's all right to feel relieved" or "I can understand you're feeling angry because you are the person who is left." What must nurses possess to intervene in this initial response to loss? The answer lies primarily in themselves. It is the listening ear, the willingness to sit, the ability to share in the intensity of grief.

During the second phase, the bereaved person begins to experience the sensation of the loss itself. The distress symptoms previously described, such as an empty feeling and a sense of helplessness and frustration, are characteristic of this period. It is difficult to speak of the loss without crying. A young woman decribed her feelings after the death of her father: "It was as though I couldn't even think of him or things we did without bursting out in tears. I would see his face in my mind's eye and just begin to cry, no matter where I was."

"Rites de passage" provide an atmosphere in which the bereaved person can share his loss with others. Through the process of a Christian wake or the shiva of Judaism, the family and friends of the deceased person can recount old times together. It is this support and caring that carries the bereaved through a most crucial period, that of viewing the body and saying good-bye.

Mourning itself begins in the third phase, or restitution. The ego does not feel whole; it is vulnerable at this point. The bereaved person may demonstrate a lack of concern or consideration for others. It is often difficult to acknowledge the happy times that had been shared with the deceased person or the positive aspects of one's own life. Ambivalence is frequently a part of this phase. On the one hand, there is the belief that the person who has died is at peace. On the other hand, there is a feeling of anger. "Why couldn't I have more time with him? He saw his grandchildren born, but I wanted him to see them graduate from college." There is always more to be wanted.

Catharsis, or talking, particularly, in a repetitive fashion, is characteristic of this third, or restitution, phase of grief. Idealization of the deceased person, or of the previous functioning of the lost part, occurs; the bereaved person cannot accept negative aspects of the person who has died. Such negative thoughts are repressed until a future time when they can be dealt with. There is an identification with the positive traits of the deceased person. In some instances, maladaptive behavior, such as the total introjection of the deceased individual's personality, occurs. Strong guilt feelings are usually the precursor of the process of introjection. In such a situation, the ambivalence, hostility, and intense sadness do not decrease. Instead, the bereaved person is more likely to assume the negative attributes of the dead person then the positive aspects, with little regard for his own sense of self.

Resolution does not occur within any particular time frame. Some theorists believe that 6 to 12 months is a realistic period of time; however, this phase may extend for as long as 2 years. The length of time required depends on the nature of the relationship between the bereaved and the deceased. How does a nurse *know* when a bereaved person is beginning to resolve a loss? There is a feeling of solitude, of renewed investment in other objects and relationships. The person who died is not forgotten but assumes a different yet always special place in the bereaved person's memory. The initial reinvestments may be quite similar to the investment in the lost object or person. Eventually this is no longer the case. Healthy resolution involves the incorporation of some aspects of the dead person into the bereaved person's ego structure, coupled with a drive toward new relationships. A point to remember: even after healthy resolution, significant dates or events, such as birthdays, Christmas, or the anniversary of the death, may precipitate intense feelings of loss.

As a result of healthy adaptation by means of the mourning process, a person is able to remember both the pleasures and the disappointments of the lost relationship. The identity of the bereaved individual remains intact. He is able to reorganize his thoughts and consider new patterns of problem solving. The behavior of the bereaved in this fourth phase is characterized by readiness to move forward, openness to new avenues, and reconciliation with the fact that the loss has occurred.

The four phases occur not only in response to the death of a loved one but also in response to any situation involving loss. As was discussed previously (see Chapter 4), research demonstrates that loss may be a critical precipitating factor in both physical and emotional illness. For example, LeShan (1959) concluded that "the most consistently reported, relevant psychological factor [in the development of neoplasms] has been the loss of a major emotional relationship prior to the first-noted symptoms." Greene (1966) and Bahnson and Bahnson (1966) reported similar findings. Loss of a relationship through divorce, loss through change in job status, loss of a body part or alteration in body function, and loss of a particular life-style as a result of marriage or the birth of a child are examples of changes that may precipitate the grieving process. The response to such a change, however, is often not recognized as grieving. A vague feeling of distress, and sadness may occur, as well as somatic symptoms.

> A young business executive had been experiencing feelings of lethargy, frustration, and helplessness in his work situation, and he described muscle spasms in his neck and back. A discussion with a nurse revealed that the young man's superior had recently been transferred. He had had a close relationship with the superior and had expanded his role within the company while working for this individual. By identifying the feelings he was experiencing as valid responses to the loss of a relationship and to the possible loss of some of his current responsibilities, the young man was able to accept the feelings as normal. Healthy adaptation to the loss was facilitated, and the experience could then be integrated into the self as a basis for future adaptations to loss.

What characterizes a maladaptive response to loss? Should a depressive response to loss be considered normal? A maladaptive response may frequently be characterized as depression, yet such a characterization is not always accurate. Denial may be operating at such an intense level that thoughts and feelings relating to the lost object are repressed. Reality is often rejected as being too painful to cope with. Restlessness, withdrawal, and disorganized patterns of behavior are predominant themes. Disintegration of ego functioning results. Why are some individuals able to make healthy adaptations while others develop depression or physical illnesses? There is no one answer to this question. We must consider the individual as a system that is part of a larger system and that responds to that larger system. We must remember that diverse external and internal factors cause each of us to be unique and worthwhile.

Each of us responds to loss in a different manner. The life cycle of each of us is characterized by a series of losses, beginning with the loss of the breast or the bottle. Our reactions to loss are based on many factors, including previous experiences with loss, our repertoire of effective adaptive measures, support relationships, and changes in daily living patterns necessitated by the loss.

The emotions we experience when we are faced with loss are quite likely to be the most intense of our lives. Nurses, however, do not always recognize that clients are frequently responding to loss situations. Nurses do not readily view illness as a loss situation, even though clients routinely lose the ability to function in their own environments, to wear their own clothing, and to determine their own schedules. Depression occurs as a result of such loss, but this behavioral response often goes unrecognized.

Loss of a significant object, relationship, status, or the like is a common human experience. Depression in its mildest form is a natural response to loss. We will define depression in terms of a continuum, and we will discuss predominant themes, underlying dynamics, and intervention.

TYPES OF DEPRESSION

"I'm depressed." How many times have you heard this statement? When you cannot find a solution to a frustrating situation, do you sit down with head in hands and stare at your toes? Things are just not working out well. Is this clinical depression? What is the difference between feeling low and overwhelming sensations of helplessness, anger, anxiety, and self-doubt? The human personality is dynamic; it constantly reflects the many changes that occur at its interfaces with the environment. Thus, depression, as one form of human adaptive response, cannot be pigeonholed; it must be viewed as a continuum of behavior ranging from mild to severe.

During the past two decades depression, along with anxiety, has become one of the most prevalent disease entities. Interest in depressive states has also increased, perhaps as a result of increased coverage by the mass media of mental health in general. It has been widely publicized that significant persons in drama, art, and the professions have experienced depressive responses and have recovered—in the fullest sense of the word. There have been major new approaches to the treatment of depression, such as transactional analysis, family therapy, and milieu groups. Depression in some shape or form affects millions of people each year. According to Secunda (1973), 15% of the population of the United States between 18 and 74 suffers from significant depressive symptoms; only half of these people seek help. In a sense, depression occurs as frequently as the common cold. Some people develop depressive symptoms as an adaptive response, while other people respond through the autonomic nervous system. Still others make healthy adaptations. As has been mentioned previously, it is important that nurses realize that many variables may act to produce a depressive response. Intervention can then be directed toward identification of behavior that is indicative of a response to loss.

Depression should be thought of in terms of a continuum. For purposes of discussion, the continuum can be arbitrarily divided into three sections—depressive affect, mood disorder, and clinical depression.

Continuum of depression

Mild	Moderate	Severe
(affect)	(mood disorder)	(clinical syndrome)

— — — — — →   — — — — — →

A depressive affect is characterized by feelings of sadness, dejection, and disappointment. Such feelings are transitory, usually being relieved within a period of 4 to 6 weeks. These feelings are related to the here-and-now and do not impair the everyday functioning of an individual. These "low" periods in the life cycle are related to a loss of some kind, whether it be a change in job status or function. The intensity of these transitory feelings can be correlated with the intensity of the grief response.

If this response continues and becomes distorted, other changes occur to place a person farther along the continuum. A mood disorder is characterized by more intense feelings of self-doubt and dejection. A cluster of behavioral changes occurs. Bodily function slows to a bare minimum. Great effort is required to accomplish everyday activities. A person becomes less kempt, and household tasks are often not completed. (In some instances, however, the opposite occurs. Obsessional impulses lead to continuous housecleaning and to other seemingly purposeless activities.) Eating habits change. Some individuals in this stage of depression may drink and eat very little and therefore lose weight. Others eat very heavily, perhaps as a means of making up for the loss. Again, depending upon the individual, constipation or diarrhea may be present. Weakness and fatigue are common. The client describes feelings of "aching all over" and joint weakness.

Judy, a 25-year-old woman, came into a 24-hour emergency walk-in clinic at a large, urban hospital. She described herself as being a generally happy person; but during the past 2 weeks she had become increasingly more dejected. She awoke early in the morning and was unable to fall back to sleep. Everyday activities became monumental tasks to accomplish. She felt as though her whole body had come to a halt. Relationships with other people in her environment were also being affected. She no longer wanted to participate in social gatherings. She often found herself sitting alone, pondering her fate in life. She was prompted to come to the clinic by a co-worker who was concerned by her change in personality.

This woman is a typical example of an individual who is midway on the continuum of depression. After several sessions at the clinic, Judy acknowledged that she had lost her mother a year ago. She had been coping "well" until recently, when she lost her cat. When discussing the two loss experiences, she said, "I never really cried it all out when Mom died." But the loss of the cat triggered the revival of the past loss. Judy began to experience again the angry and helpless feelings she had experienced when her mother died. These feelings had been repressed, only to surface later. This is often the case. Loss is one of the cornerstones of the dynamics of depression. Judy, in this imaginary case history, not only felt the loss of her mother but also saw herself as no longer being important to anyone. These two factors acted as the foundation for the development of her depressive response.

The communication patterns of a person in the middle stage of depression tend to be limited. Most interactions with others are filled with self-deprecatory statements. A rigid, stereotypical pattern of responding to others develops. Feelings of low self-esteem manifest themselves: the client believes that he is incapable of succeeding. He believes that his failures in life result from personal inadequacy, no matter what the circumstances might be. When this fact is pointed out to him, he holds fast to the belief that he, and he alone, is responsible. As in Judy's case, social interactions are diminished. The sense of low self-esteem becomes so strong that the person truly believes that no one thinks much of him. The pattern then becomes cyclical. He isolates himself; he discourages anyone from approaching him. Others perceive him as being cold, uncaring, even hostile. In his depressed state, he is unable to perceive other people's needs. His energy is directed inward toward his own needs. Isolation continues to increase. He finds himself believing even less in his own worth; he believes that no one could possibly take an interest in him. Low self-esteem increases as isolation increases. A primary goal for nurses is to intervene in this cyclical pattern of interaction. Later in this chapter we will discuss specific aspects of nursing intervention and rationale.

The condition of a person in this middle stage of the continuum is referred to as exogenous or reactive depression. As the term implies, reactive depression involves a definite cause-and-effect relationship. In contrast, severe depression is referred to as endogenous or psychotic depression. Severe depression, the last of the three major types of depressive responses, is also known as clinical depression. There is no apparent triggering factor. Many variables—psychological, chemical, genetic, familial—may singly or in any combination cause an endogenous depressive response. Hopelessness, powerlessness, and worthlessness are predominant themes. The person perceives reality in a grossly distorted fashion. Delusions and hallucinations occur. Feelings of low self-esteem are reinforced by the delusions. The person becomes trapped in the tangled web of a delusional system, unable to sift fact from fantasy. He forms a shell to protect himself as he retreats farther into isolation. Tasks of everyday living are perceived as overwhelming. All available energy is channeled into a hate campaign against the self. Concentration narrows; problem-solving capabilities are poor at best. The person often does not react to environmental stimuli. If he does react, it is in an inappropriate fashion. There is a marked decrease in bodily functioning, a vegetative state ensues. As stated previously, the opposite may also occur—that is, agitated, purposeless, stereotypic behavior.) One of the primary characteristics of severe depression is its diurnal nature. The individual awakens early in the morning, usually preoccupied with unpleasant thoughts. As the day progresses, the depressive pattern tends to lift. An overall assessment of a severely depressed individual reveals a person who perceives himself as worthless; his every movement and his slouching posture reflect the low regard in which he holds himself. (These characteristics will be discussed at greater length later in this chapter.)

Another method of classifying affective disorders is being used with increasing frequency. "Bipolar" disorders involve a cyclical manic-depressive reaction, while "unipolar" disorders involve only depressive responses. These terms can be used to clearly separate clients who have episodes of mania and depression from those who only have depressive symptoms.

There are several reasons why it is important to differentiate bipolar disorders from unipolar disorders. Research demonstrates that relatives of clients with unipolar illnesses have increased incidences of depressive personalities and therefore of unipolar illnesses. Similarly, there is a high incidence of bipolar illness in families of clients who have been diagnosed as having such an illness.

Another rationale for the differentiation between bipolar and unipolar illnesses is that such a distinction facilitates the determination of an appropriate treatment plan. Dunner, Fleiss, and Fieve (1976) have studied the course of mania in clients with recurrent depression. These authors find that approximately 80% of clients with bipolar illnesses initially have symptoms of mania or hypomania. On the other hand, only 5% of clients who initially have depressive symptoms are later diagnosed as bipolar. These data suggest that clients experiencing bipolar disorders respond more positively to treatment with lithium carbonate than do clients with unipolar disorders. Depressive episodes in bipolar illness may also be treated with a tricyclic compound such as imipramine (Tofranil). Lithium carbonate and Tofranil may be administered concurrently to the client who has a history of bipolar illness. The client diagnosed as having a unipolar disorder can be treated most effectively with tricyclic compounds and, in some instances, electroconvulsive therapy. Supportive therapy is necessary for clients diagnosed as having either a bipolar or a unipolar disorder.

AGE DETERMINANTS
Childhood

Spitz and Wold (1946) and Bowlby (1973) each suggest that the early mother-child relationship plays a critical role in a child's response to separation and loss. Separation anxiety occurs in the child prior to the establishment of object permanence. Inadequate preparation for separation can be stressful for the child and can ultimately lead to depression. Characteristics of prepubertal depression include school phobia and fear of loss of parents through death, along with feelings of sadness and dejection, as in adult depression.

Adolescence

Adolescence has been described as "initiation into mourning." An adolescent loses his childhood and the dependent state that characterizes it, the implicit message is that he must grow up. Often the "all or nothing" principle operates in the development of independence. The adolescent believes that he must achieve independence immediately rather than accomplish it gradually over a period of time. Depression may result from a fear of failure—the fear of not being able to live up to the concept of self he has defined. Depression in an adolescent may resemble adult depression; however, a depressed adolescent frequently behaves impulsively, taking action against the environment. Restlessness, apathy, sulkiness, social isolation, grouchiness, and aggression characterize the depressed adolescent. His inability to gain approval or understanding may lead to feelings of rejection and to self-deprecation. He may then seek to run away to cope with feelings of inadequacy. Loss or lack of a significant other or a meaningful relationship often precipitates a depressive reaction. Suicide is the second leading cause of death among adolescents. The suicidal impulse may take the form of accident-prone behavior. Depression in adolescents, in whatever form it takes, needs to be recognized and assessed in order for appropriate nursing responses to be determined.

Middle age

See the discussion of involutional melancholia on pp. 390 and 391.

Old age

Depression is one of the most common syndromes found in the elderly. In this phase of the developmental process, loss occurs more frequently, leaving little time for appropriate grieving. The elderly person finds himself experiencing the loss of significant others at a time when physical health may be declining. This factor, coupled with a decrease in the elderly client's ability to cope with the emotional trauma of loss, places him at risk for depression. The elderly individual may feel that he is no longer able to tolerate emotional investments in others; he may believe that such investments would only allow him to be hurt again. Social isolation follows. But isolation, which is designed to defend against emotional pain, serves to reinforce depression.

Depression in the elderly may be expressed through angry, hostile responses. This behavior is often frustrating to a nurse if he or she is unable to fully assess the elderly client in the context of the client's environment. Angry outbursts by a client may mask the need for social contact and, again, serve to reinforce social isolation.

The suicide rate among the elderly is on the rise, a fact that reflects the increase in the incidence of depression in this age group.

ENDOGENOUS DEPRESSIVE REACTIONS
Involutional melancholia

Depressions that occur during the middle and later years of life are said to be "involutional." This term refers to the return to the nonsexual state of function of the female and male genitalia. Women in their early forties experience menopause, while men experience andropause. Andropause occurs at a much later age, usually beginning somewhere in the middle to late fifties. Menopause and andropause are part of the syndrome known as climacteric, which includes all the physical and psychological changes associated with the end of the reproductive years.

There are several theories as to the underlying dynamics of involutional melancholia. One of the most widely held beliefs is that this form of depression results from hormonal and/or biochemical changes. Sufficient data in support of this proposition has not been collected. However, the replacement of hormones—estrogens, to be specific—has been found to relieve the vasomotor symptoms that accompany climacteric.

What other variables come into play? Let us review what is happening developmentally, socially, and emotionally to a person who is reaching middle age. For a woman it may be a time of many role changes. A woman who has spent her entire life nurturing her children is left with no children. The proverbial "empty nest" syndrome begins. Where does she begin to "find" herself at this stage of life? Her primary support systems (children) may no longer be available. Her husband still has his job to provide him with a sense of accomplishment. He is at the top of his career; she may feel at the bottom.

There is less energy for investment in new friends and new adventures. The realization that it is literally impossible to meet remaining goals occurs for both men and women. There is less physical vigor available, and sensory function declines markedly. Chronic illness becomes a very real part of a person's life-style. For a man who has been a breadwinner all his life, the prospect of retirement may be an etiologic factor in the development of overwhelming depression.

The compulsive personality is considered most susceptible to the development of involutional melancholia. What characteristics are peculiar to involutional melancholia? The major distinguishing symptom is agitation. The behavior of a person who has this form depression is characterized by gross motor activity and anxiety. He paces back and forth, wrings his hands, moans loudly, and complains about each and every ache and pain. Somatic complaints occur more frequently in such agitated depression than they do other depressive responses. It is important to note that although agitation is present, the mood context is similar to that found in the other depressive responses.

A paranoid form of involutional melancholia is less common than the usual form, yet it is worth mentioning. Operating in such a clinical picture is a paranoid ideology, along with the depression. Often there is also a delusional system that includes many persecutory overtones.

Although involutional melancholia can be discussed as a separate entity, much of the clinical investigation completed thus far indicates that it is not clearly distinct from other forms of depression. Nursing intervention is similar to that provided in response to the predominant themes found in all forms of depression: milieu therapy and individual psychotherapy utilized in combination with pharmacological agents.

Manic depression

The manic-depressive reaction has become one of the most widely discussed depressive responses in Western society. It is characterized by mood swings; a manic-depressive person's moods range from profound depression to extreme euphoria, with periods of normalcy in between. It is important to point out that mania is considered to be the mirror image of depression. The term "bipolar" implies that mania is the opposite of depression: a defense *against* depression. This concept is in accord with the psychoanalytic viewpoint that mania is a defense against depression.

Various theories regarding the development of the manic-depressive response have been proposed. Familial and genetic studies by Kallman (1953) indicate that genetic predisposition may be involved. Kolb (1973) suggests that a dominant X-linked factor accounts for the presence of manic depression in families whose members have had manic and/or depressive disorders. He notes that manic depression occurs twice as frequently in females as in males and that maternal relatives of a manic-depressive person are affected much more frequently than paternal relatives.

The roles of norepinephrine and the catecholamines in the origin of the depressive response will be discussed later in this chapter. It can be said that since lowered levels of norepinephrine are apparent in a person experiencing a depressive response, the converse is true in a manic response. Lowered intracellular sodium levels are also common during a manic response. We will discuss the implications of sodium levels further in the section on psychopharmaceuticals, which appears later in this chapter.

The predominant themes in manic depression are similar to those encountered in the depressive response. The client in the manic phase is very outgoing; he easily involves himself in relationships with others. He can be quite manipulative and controlling if a situation is not satisfactory in terms of his own interests. In order for this type of individual to feel important, he often attacks the worth of other individuals. The manic-depressive person is extremely unsure of his own worth. For him, stepping on someone else is a maneuver guaranteed to make him feel powerful. Nurses need to be eclectic in their approach to a manic-depressive client; their primary concern is to identify predominant themes and appropriate forms of intervention.

The mother-infant relationship and its impact on the development of the depressive response has been discussed previously. This factor plays a significant role in the dynamics of manic depression. The early dependence of the infant on the mother is pleasurable for the mother. However, as the child becomes autonomous, he begins to pose a threat to the mother figure. If the child is thwarted and labeled as bad each time he acts to assert his independence, he learns that in order to survive he must fulfill parental expectations, no matter what the price. The child then continually strives to gain parental affection by complying with each request, negating his own needs and wishes. Ambivalent feelings arise, as the child resents the mother while at the same time strongly desiring her attention. The following is an operational definition of manic depression:

Ambivalent →	Ego gives up →	Punitive or	Strong id
feelings		superego	↓
towards love		anger turned	Uncontrollable
object		inward	impulsive
			behavior

Such a child carries with him low self-esteem and the resulting inability to actively problem solve to meet his own needs. Since the parent-child relationship had been fraught with unreasonable demands, the child in later life is unable to experience a trusting relationship. The possibility of open, free lines of communication between himself and others is never considered. Satir in her book *Peoplemaking* (1972), points out that direct, honest communication among family members is necessary in order for positive feelings about oneself and one's capabilities to develop.

What are the onset and general course of manic depression? Can nurses be alert to clues in the environment? Published reports indicate that manic episodes usually occur in persons between the ages of 20 and 35 and that depressive episodes usually occur in persons between the ages of 35 and 50. Cyclothymia, hypomania, and depressive behavior are usually characteristic of the premorbid personality. The cyclothymic personality is characterized by alternating periods of high and low spirits.

Manic-depressive behavior manifests itself in varying degrees. Responses can be entirely of one form—for example, all manic behavior. Responses may alternate with one another. For example, a first episode may be circular, a second depressive, and a third mainly manic. Following each attack, the person returns to his premorbid state; in some instances his condition is improved. Thus, mania can be viewed as a preventive measure against becoming depressed. It is literally a flight into reality. An interesting point is the fact that the onset of mania is not necessarily linked directly to any precipitating event.

Manic-depressive behavior can be divided into three general categories or phases: manic, depressive, and circular.

The first category, mania, can be divided into hypomania and acute mania. Hypomanic behavior is characterized basically by elation. The person is well liked by others; he is very outgoing; he is often identified as the life of the party. His energies seem boundless, and others often marvel at how much he can accomplish. Behavior at this point is purposeful and goal oriented. As the mood of elation increases, the client becomes more grandiose in his responses to others. No task is beyond accomplishment. He alludes often to his personal achievements and capitalizes on each opportunity to increase other people's awareness of them. Logic and rational thought processes are not within his scheme of things, although he may seem to be in command of all his faculties. The hypomanic client frequently engages in projects requiring large sums of money. These, however, are rarely seen to fruition. The spending of money is no object.

Mary K., a 34-year-old mother of three children, was admitted to a small, private psychiatric hospital. On admission, she was in a state of such hyperactivity that it required four people to assist her to her room. She was extremely hostile and was lashing out at all around her. Her husband described her as having progressed from being quite vigorous in her approach to tasks to being so aggressive in her actions that he could not control her. She had decided to build an addition to their house and had contacted four contractors. She had then ordered building supplies amounting to a total cost of $4,000. Flitting to another project, she had taken the children shopping to buy clothes for camp and in one afternoon had spent more than $5,000. It was at this point that her husband sought psychiatric help.

As the mood continues to escalate, the person's attention span shortens. He talks rapidly yet coherently or writes voluminous notes. The hypomanic has a great penchant for collecting items. He may save anything from bottle caps or old rags to scraps of paper. These collectibles may be hidden away in body orifices, particularly the vagina and the anus. Nurses must be acutely aware of such a client's need to have these items. Intervention should include saving the items and, if need be, assisting the client to find alternative caches for them.

Creativity is a primary theme in the hypomanic phase. Designs are drawn in a large, bold hand. There is much underlining for emphasis of pertinent points. It is obvious that the drawings correlate with the person's expansiveness.

As the person moves into the acute phase of mania, activity is speeded up to an even greater degree. Thought processes are characterized by flight of ideas; he speaks so rapidly that sentences are often incomplete. It is difficult to get a word in edgewise. This stream of verbiage often has at its base a central theme relevant to the person's needs—a theme that can be identified by a careful listener.

Motor activity increases to the point that the person spends most of his time in a constant flurry of motion. He involves himself in everyone else's interactions and becomes quite irritating to other people. He often has suggestions about how this or that activity should be conducted. He even interferes in the personal lives of others, often giving sexual advice. He has little time to sleep, eat, or groom himself, and his activity leads him to the point of physical exhaustion. However, there is little increase in sexual activity. Indiscreet sexual acts may occur, however, and the use of profanity may increase.

Inappropriate dress is quite common. The manic client uses heavy make-up, resembling that of a clown. Brightly colored baubles and beads accentuate every outfit. Clothing is usually mismatched and poorly fitting; often it is not appropriate to the climate. This type of behavior is observed in both men and women.

Ultimately, the acute manic phase may lead to complete physical and emotional exhaustion.

The most severe form of mania, delirious mania, is not frequently seen. A person in this phase exhibits hallucinations and delusions, and he may be dangerous to himself and others. Activity is purposeless and continuous. Speech is accelerated to such a degree that thoughts are presented incoherently.

The second category of manic-depressive behavior—the depressive response—has already been discussed at length. It is important to note that one of the major clinical problems of the depressive phase of manic depression is the possibility of suicide, which will be the next area of primary focus in this chapter.

The third category of manic-depressive behavior is the circular response, which is characterized by alternating periods of manic and depressive behavior. The person experiences a period of manic behavior, followed by a period of "euthymia," or normal mood responses. This period may then be followed by depressive behavior. The person is usually in a well-defined manic, depressive, or euthymic period. These recurrent periods or episodes may be separated by months to years of remission. It has been found that the longer the time between episodes, the smaller the chance that they will recur. Is it possible to experience a continuous series of mood swings? In some unusual instances, this has occurred, but it is not the common pattern of response.

In summary, there are both similarities and differences between manic depression and other types of depression. The influences of childhood on later life are significant in the understanding of any depressive state. The manic person is often "the life of the party" or the individual who has the energy to accomplish everything. But is this pattern of response being used to escape from reality? Is the pain of loss so great? As in depression, we see a diminished sense of worth, a loss of dependence, and a fear of not being loved. Yet these feelings are hidden beneath a mask of pseudohappiness. Relationships are characterized by superficiality; the manic-depressive person manipulates his environment in order to continually receive the gratification and support he needs. When anxiety increases, however, the mask no longer serves as an effective coping response. The person then turns to either the elative or the depressive response to preserve his ego integrity.

SUICIDE

Suicide is the ultimate response to hopelessness, helplessness, and low self-esteem. It is the final escape from reality. For a person who considers suicide, life has become so intolerable that previous mechanisms of dealing with stress are inadequate.

It is difficult to consider the possibility of ending one's life. Therefore, it is even more difficult to understand the dynamics of self-destructive behavior. Nurses who work with clients who have attempted suicide must understand their own feelings about and responses to such an individual. A relationship with a suicidal client can have a profound impact on a nurse. Health professionals devote much time and energy to the preservation of life. How can a nurse relate to a person who constantly deprecates himself, finds no happiness in living, and simply wishes to die? Working with such a client is a frustrating, anxiety-provoking, discouraging experience. The client's negative perceptions may lead to negative responses by the nurse. A pattern may emerge in the interaction that increases the client's feelings of worthlessness.

In the past decade the trend toward the study of suicide (suicidology) and the development of suicide prevention centers and hot lines has been growing. The National Institute for Mental Health's Center for Studies of Suicide Prevention directs its efforts toward increasing the scope and amount of research being done in the areas of assessment of clues to suicidal behavior and the etiological factors in suicide. Suicidal behavior has many sources—biological, psychological, and sociocultural. A nursing care plan should incorporate all of these factors. An integrated concept of depression, and of suicide as an outcome of depression, is essential to the assessment process.

Freud believed that the instinct for life (Eros) and the instinct for death (Thanatos) exist in every human being. Self-destructive behavior results in hatred toward an internalized lost object. There is marked ambivalence, however, in a suicidal person. If the hatred becomes overwhelming, the person literally has no choice but to kill himself. Freud correlated suicide with the death instinct: Thanatos turned inward may cause an individual to take his life.

Durkheim's (1951) sociological theory has been one of the fundamental constructs of suicide theory. He presents three basic forms of annihilative behavior: egoistic (finding life unappealing and killing oneself), altruistic (that which is demanded by society), and anomic (that which results from no longer feeling ties to the environment). This last form of behavior is engaged in by a person who feels powerless and alienated in a society that no longer has firm ground rules or structure.

Menninger, in his book *Man Against Himself* (1938), describes three basic components of the suicidal personality: the wish to kill (aggression), the wish to be killed (submission), and the wish to die (self-punishment). These components may be seen in overt acts or in the guise of addiction, frigidity, antisocial behavior, impotence, or a tendency to have serious accidents.

Schneidman and Farberow (1957) group individuals who attempt suicide into four general categories: those who commit suicide as a means of saving their reputations; those who regard suicide as a release—for example, the old and the chronically ill; those who commit suicide in response to hallucinations and/or delusions; and those who wish to hurt others in their environment.

Loss of self-worth and resulting helplessness and hopelessness are critical factors in the precipitation of suicidal behavior. The suicidal person perceives himself as a poor social risk, a failure in every aspect of his life. He places little or no value on his own existence. He has no hope for the future.

Wetzel (1976) pointed out that hopelessness, rather than depression, is positively correlated with suicidal intent. Wetzel found that when suicidal clients exhibited decreased hopelessness, depressive responses were no longer significant in the assessment of suicidal intent. Conversely, when depression was controlled but hopelessness continued to be a predominant theme, suicidal intent was high.

Nurses need to be cognizant of the many etiologic factors relevant to suicidal behavior. The decision to kill oneself is not the result of a simple choice; nurses need to remember that fact when they work with suicidal clients. Each client experiences many feelings, including a lack of worth and a sense that he is responsible for his own personal failures as well as the failures of persons around him. Unresolved grief for a lost love object, status, body part, or function, and internalized hostility toward the self also need to be considered as precipitators of a suicide attempt. A nursing assessment must identify all relevant precipitating factors in order for appropriate nursing interventions to be determined.

Demographic data

The suicide rate is highest among white males who have never been married. Divorced and widowed people have the next highest rate. The suicide rate increases with age. For women, however, the rate peaks at approximately age 55. There seems to be virtually no suicide among young children, although there is increasing evidence that accident-prone children may in fact be experiencing feelings of rage and helplessness. During adolescence the rate becomes markedly higher; suicide is the second leading cause of death among college students. Linden (1976) states that in the general population three times more males than females *commit* suicide but that females *attempt* suicide more frequently than males. Linden also points out that, generally, married people have the lowest suicide rates.

Although Linden states that suicide occurs predominantly among whites, there is evidence that suicide is increasing among blacks, particularly males. Farberow (1975) suggests that a history of rejection and abandonment in early mother-child relationships is often present in urban families. Abandonment may be a result of socioeconomic factors such as little or no income, poor shelter and clothing, and no means of support. In addition, feelings of low self-esteem may develop out of a continuing inability to meet one's most basic needs. A shortage of trusting relationships and feelings of hopelessness and alienation also serve as precursors to a suicidal act.

Familial determinants

Richman (1971) has identified several characterisitics of families with suicidal problems: family fragility, family depression, intolerance for separation, symbiosis without empathy, closed family relationships, scapegoating, poor patterns of dealing with aggression, double-bind communicating, and inflexibility in responding to crisis. Since the family network has profound effects on a person's integrative functioning, it plays a important role in the development of any maladaptive response. But the role of the family is especially important in the case of a suicidal client. Oftentimes, it is a perceptive family that identifies clues to impending suicidal acts.

Sociocultural context

American society is composed of various ethnic groups and subcultures. Each person is a unique being whose behavior reflects the environment from which he comes as well as biological and psychological factors (see Chapter 3). In this section the attitudes toward suicide held by three ethnic groups are discussed.

Navajo Indians. Suicide is not acceptable to the Navajo tribe, not because it is thought to be inherently bad but because of its effect on the members of the family.

Webb and Willard, in Farberow's *Suicide in Different Cultures* (1975), point out the Navajo's belief that any death other than that resulting from old age is unnatural. A violent death is certain to bring misfortune to the family of the person who died. The usual precipitating event is bad feelings between kin; frequently, a person who commits suicide does so near his own residence. Suicidal behavior is found most frequently in men between the ages of 25 and 39.

An intense fear of ghosts is an important element in the Navajo attitude toward suicide. Navajos believe that the dead person does not leave the situation but merely takes a new status—that of ghost.

The Navajo's fear of the dead, coupled with their attitude toward violent death, clearly makes suicide unacceptable.

Scandinavian-Americans. Scandinavian-Americans, proud of their Viking heritage, do not look favorably on suicide. To kill oneself is a sign of weakness, of an inability to cope with life's stresses. Survival of the fittest was a predominant theme among the Vikings, as was the idealization of the physically strong.

Scandinavian-Americans also carry with them the belief that suicide is a sin that cloaks the entire family with shame. Early Christian doctrine forbade the Church from giving a eulogy for a person who committed suicide or sprinkling the traditional earth on the coffin.

Petterstol (1975) sees a change of direction in Scandinavian-American attitudes toward suicide. There is still great concern for physical health, vigor, and life. However, there also is a more empathic attitude toward persons who attempted suicide and toward the survivors of persons who commit suicide. The survivors themselves are ashamed and unsure of how they should respond to others. There are still strong taboos against taking one's own life.

Italian-Americans. For Italian-Americans, suicide is regarded as a grave sin, a belief rooted in Catholic dogma. The family of a person who commits suicide is dishonored, the avenues to certain occupations are closed to his survivors, and his body cannot be buried in consecrated ground. This attitude is so strong that physicians and members of the clergy will falsify death certificates. For example, mental illness might be listed as the cause of death, for this is acceptable to the Church.

According to Farberow (1975), an understanding of the family is of utmost importance to an understanding of the dynamics of suicide among Italian-Americans. The family is the primary support system. A person is encouraged to depend on others in his family constellation; the family provides nurturing in the form of love, help, and protection. With such a constant support system it may be difficult for a person to feel worthless. Italian-Americans believe that each individual should be accountable for the welfare of others. Although the family is a support system, it often places great demands on its members. Since the family provides nurturance, it may also attach strings. Feelings of rage and helplessness may arise, leading to overt conflict and, in some instances, suicide.

Italian-Americans exhibit the characteristic ambivalence of persons who are considering suicide as a way of relieving overwhelming stress. Their ambivalence results from the strong doctrine of the Church and from an inability to escape the intricately woven net of family and Church. Members of third, fourth, and successive generations of Italian-Americans may no longer feel as constrained by Catholic dogma. Their concern for life, however, remains strong.

EPIDEMIOLOGY

Are some people more prone to depression than others? If so, do these individuals have similar characteristics? The person most likely to be depressed can be described as shy, perhaps oversensitive, self-conscious, and a worrier. Reaching a level of perfection is his ultimate goal. The results of not achieving this end are self-deprecation and self-doubt—primary characteristics of the depressed person.

Statistics indicate that depression occurs more frequently in females than in males. However, this may not be an accurate assessment. The overt expression of depression by males is frequently frowned upon. Statistics also show that the incidence of depression increases with age in both men and women. Depression cuts across social classes. Neurotic depression, however, may be more common in the middle and upper classes, while psychotic depression may be more common in the lower class. To understand the prevalence of depression, a nurse must consider socioeconomic factors, availability of mental health services, the attitude of each class toward mental health, and at what point treatment is sought.

General practitioners frequently treat depression as either a primary symptom or as a symptom that is secondary to a physical illness. According to Kolb (1977), less than 5% of persons who experience depression seek psychiatric care.

Depression affects all age groups, from childhood through senescence. A person may be born with a predisposition to depression; however, susceptibility to depression also depends on the many factors noted previously—familial, genetic, biological, and chemical—and on early life experiences.

THEORIES OF DEPRESSION
Psychoanalytic theory

Proponents of the psychoanalytic theory of depression believe that a depressive response has at its roots a significant loss, either real or imagined. Anger resulting from the loss is turned inward, and self-hate results. The original loss is repressed; however, subsequent losses reactivate the feelings associated with it. Freud, in "Mourning and Melancholia" (1917), postulates that the characteristics of the normal grieving process are similar to those of the pathological state of depression. Unlike the person experiencing normal grief, however, the person experiencing depression seems to be grieving over an inner loss that he is unable to resolve. It is this unresolved grief that the depressed individual carries with him.

Freud states that the initial lost love object is the parent. The person simultaneously feels both love and hate for the parent, yet it is the hatred that is incorporated or symbolically introjected into the self. The psychic mechanism of introjection serves as a basis for the development of the superego. For the person who later suffers from pathological depression, the embryonic superego is punitive in that it never permits that acceptance of praise. The individual never learns to value his own sense of self, a situation that is carried on throughout the life cycle.

The psychoanalytic literature holds that such a person's self-derogatory behavior is a sign that hostility toward the lost object has been internalized. He then becomes narcissistic. He believes that no one else cares enough about him to take care of his needs; therefore, he must care for himself. By not becoming involved in any relationship, the depressed individual limits the social failures he might experience. Strong dependence needs become apparent. It is literally impossible to meet the needs of such a person; they never seem to be fulfilled. A cyclical pattern develops: The dependent individual is disappointed in his attempts to gain recognition. He pulls back from relationships in order to save face while at the same time chastising himself for being so inadequate. The depressive response is adopted and promoted.

Melanie Klein (1934) suggests that the depressive response can be traced to the early mother-infant relationship. Feelings of rage and hostility characterize the infant's response to a lack of gratification of needs. A weakened ego state results; feelings of helplessness, sadness, and dejection arise as a result of tension between ego and superego. The introjective mechanism acts to internalize the persecutor. Klein points out that children need to feel fully assured that parental love is genuine. Without this assurance, sadness, dejection, lack of self-esteem, and a sense of loss result.

Rene Spitz and K. M. Wold (1946) and John Bowlby (1973) believe that the origins of depression can be found in the infant's responses to experiences of separation and loss. This "object loss theory," as it is commonly referred to, suggests that trauma results when separation from significant others occurs. Spitz and Wold, in their studies of mother-infant responses, point out a particular pattern of behavior that occurs following separation. (It is important to note that these authors argue that for the first 6 months of life a mother-infant relationship exists but that during the second 6 months of life the relationship is gradually severed.) Spitz and Wold describe infants reacting to separation as being withdrawn, stuporous, and anorectic; showing psychomotor retardation; and experiencing overall slowing of the normal growth and development process. They call this cluster of symptoms "anaclitic depression." Bowlby identifies similar patterns of response in older children. He proposes three phases:

1. Protest—crying, looking for mother
2. Despair—withdrawal from environment, apathy
3. Detachment—total lack of investment in any mothering figure

Bibring (1953), although psychoanalytically oriented, differs from other psychoanalytic theorists in his perception of the dynamics of depression. He suggests that depression is characterized primarily by a loss of self-esteem. This loss can be stimulated by inadequate fulfillment of needs for affection as well as by frustration of significant hopes and desires. Bibring's primary thesis is based on the assumption that all depressive reactions have one aspect in common—a sense of loss. He attributes much of the basis of depression to trauma during the oral phase. Bibring also postulates that attacks of the ego that result in feelings of loss can occur in any developmental phase. We know, for example, that during the toddler phase, the child is directing his energies toward increasing his mobility. Bibring believes that the inability to accomplish this task is viewed by the toddler as a personal failure, a loss. Nurses thus need to be alert to potential loss situations in any developmental phase. Primary prevention then can begin to make strides forward.

Cognitive theory

Cognitive theorists suggest that analysis of the depressive response too often becomes tangled in the web of the psyche. They point out that Freud's concept of hatred directed toward the introjected lost love object is difficult, if not impossible, to validate and that it seems to involve no actual connection between theoretical constructs and observable behavior.

Beck (1967) ascribes causal significance to illogical thinking processes. He believes that illogical thought patterns operate solely in relation to the self. These patterns generate self-doubt and self-deprecation. In essence, a person's thought processes determine his emotional reactions. Beck identifies a "primary triad" in depression—three major cognitive patterns that force the individual to view himself, his environment, and his future in a negativistic manner.

First, the individual perceives himself as unworthy and inadequate; he believes he is a failure. He attributes his failures to some nebulous flaw, whether physical, emotional, or moral. Rejection of self occurs as a result of these perceptions.

Second, he views his interactions with the social world as being poor at best. He is particularly sensitive to any barriers placed in the way of the attainment of his goals. Difficulties of any degree are interpreted as indicating total inadequacy on his part. (Depressed persons are programmed to respond with a sense of failure. A mildly depressed nursing student, for example, did poorly on one out of ten quizzes. She looked on this one quiz grade as an indication of total failure and considered dropping out of the nursing curriculum.)

Another facet of the negative interpretation of interactions is that of deprivation. The depressed person perceives seemingly trivial events as incurring serious losses. Beck gives the example of a depressed client on his way to visit his psychiatrist. The client felt he was losing valuable time by having to wait 30 seconds for the elevator.

He then regretted the loss of companionship by riding alone in the elevator. Then he discovered that he was not the psychiatrist's first patient, and he regretted not having the first appointment.

Other loss situations related to interactions with other people center around money or the comparison of others' possessions to one's own.

> A young woman had just moved to a lovely new home in a new neighborhood. She had been quite upset over this move initially. Her husband held a very good job, and she was finally able to purchase the kinds of things she desired for herself, her children, and her home. Yet when friends bought items for their homes, she felt as though she were being deprived.

This woman, and the man in Beck's example, automatically interpreted their experiences negatively, even though more plausible explanations were available.

The third, and final, component in Beck's triad is the depressed person's negative expectations of the future. Just as he holds negative interpretations of himself and his social relationships, so also does he perceive his future as being constantly overcast with large dark clouds. There are no silver linings for the depressed person. Even short-range predictions are negative. Each day is viewed with trepidation: there is not a chance in the world that events will turn out positively. Thus the power of thought is clearly an overwhelming factor in depression. This factor is of great importance in the assessment the depressed client and in the determination of nursing goals.

It is quite simple to predict a relationship between affect, motivation, and the cognitive triad. If a person thinks he is worthless and bases his behavior on this premise, his mood will be negative. In addition, he will experience a loss of motivation—a primary characteristic of depression. He consistently expects to meet with failure and humiliation; therefore, he attempts nothing. Hopelessness and self-doubt pervade his thought processes. Depressed individuals envision themselves as being overwhelmed by tasks they had previously been able to cope with. It has been demonstrated that by changing such a client's thought patterns to a more positive track, a nurse can enhance his ability to actively solve problems.

Psychodynamic theory

Arieti (1974) describes the depressed client as one who has experienced a nurturing relationship that was later withdrawn. In its stead came a provisional relationship—a relationship based on the stipulation that the child must meet the expectations of the parents. In this relationship, praise and gratification were given, for example, when good grades or other symbols of prestige were achieved. Feelings of self-worth were not enhanced, since rewards were in the far distant future.

The failure to receive positive feedback can be perceived as a loss, even though the significant other may have been physically present. Again, we can discern the early beginnings of the inability to form relationships. The expectations of an early significant relationship are not met; therefore, the individual believes that all other relationships will fail. Little by little, he stops trying to interact with his environment.

It is important to see depression as a reaction or response. It is something a person is doing rather than something that is happening to him. Depression is a behavioral interaction, a response to environmental stimuli.

The individual who suffers from depression is often a perfectionist whose few relationships are characterized by manipulation and control. He is unable to accept anything other than "black and white" solutions to problems. Underneath the veneer of this high-powered executive type is the fear of total failure and powerlessness. The depressive response becomes apparent when he feels he has not met his own goals or those of significant others in the environment.

Biological theory

As they have in many emotional disorders, investigators have looked for an alteration in physiological functioning as a possible etiological factor. The study of electrolyte metabolism has indicated that in persons suffering from depression there is a disturbance in the distribution of sodium and potassium from one side of a nerve cell to the other. Gibbons (1960), who worked with a group of 24 clients exhibiting depressive reactions, discovered that every client had an elevated sodium level within the nerve cells. During recovery from depression, the excess sodium was excreted.

These findings are consistent with what we know about the effect of the use of lithium compounds in the treatment of manic depression. Lithium interferes with sodium exchange at the cellular level. With the resolution of the mania, the tolerance of the body for lithium is lowered, and the lithium, along with the excess sodium, is excreted.

We need to be aware, however, that electrolyte changes may be a *result* of depression rather than a causative factor. Changes in diet and motor activity during depression could lead to electrolyte imbalance.

The biochemical theory described by Kicey (1974) is worth noting. Her research suggests that the supply of norepinephrine at receptor sites is lowered when a person is depressed. There is an inhibition of the transmission of impulses from one neural fiber to another. The purpose of the monoamine oxidase (MAO) inhibitors is to increase the availability of active norepinephrine.

These have been extremely simplified views of what are actually very complex biochemical operations.

Genetic and familial factors may play roles in the depressive response. Studies have shown that the incidence of affective disorders is higher among relatives of persons who have had such disorders than in the general population. One of the most striking results of genetic studies is the division of affective disorders into unipolar and bipolar groups. This development may lead to the ability to predict the occurrence of affective disorders among family members. However, the role of genetics in the development of depression has yet to be definitively determined.

Sociocultural theory

Learning theory. Can a depressive response be learned? Is assuming a helpless position a viable adaptive mechanism for some individuals?

Seligman (1973) proposes that depression is learned helplessness. In his study with dogs, he found that the experience of having no control over what was happening interfered with the dogs' adaptive response. The dogs actually learned that they were helpless, that no matter what the situation was, their actions did not matter. They could not succeed. Seligman suggests that, in humans, the precursor to depression may be the belief that one has no control over his situation—that he is unable to effect any change in his life experiences, to reduce suffering, or to gain praise. According to Seligman, if an individual has little success in mastering his environment, hopelessness, helplessness, and lack of assertiveness eventually become his primary characteristics. These themes, in combination with the small degree of environmental mastery, increase his susceptibility to depression.

Feminist theories. Published studies indicate that two to three times as many women experience depressive responses as men. There has been much investigation of the relationship between female hormones and the occurrence of depression. It is not unusual to hear a woman say she is "depressed" when she has her "period." In addition, depressive responses have been identified during times when changes in hormonal levels are marked—notably 2 to 3 days following childbirth, the general postpartum period, and menopause. However, there have been no data to validate these assumptions.

In previous sections of this chapter, we have discussed the various etiological factors in the manifestation of the depressive response. Common themes include powerlessness, helplessness, a sense of loss, and a negative view of self. These feelings are identical to those experienced by minority groups such as women, blacks, and the aged. Women, in particular, have assumed the depressive response as a natural part of their role.

According to Phyllis Chesler (1972), few women have been able to develop a true sense of identity outside of that of wife and mother. This fact can be seen vividly when the prestige levels of men and women in the male-oriented professional and business world are compared. Chesler proposes that "women are in a constant state of mourning, grieving for that which they never had or had too briefly." The concept of learned helplessness can be correlated with society's preconceived notion of how a woman is to respond. It is more acceptable for a woman to adopt a depressive response than for a male to do so.

Are women predisposed to depression? Dr. Pauline Bart (1971) studied depression in middle-aged women in relation to role loss. She suggests that women who have invested all their time and energy in their children and their homes are more likely to experience a depressive response than women who have not done so. These women are unable to find new roles for themselves. They have suffered the greatest loss—the loss of a purpose in life. Their self-doubt and low self-regard prevent them from seeing themselves as anything other than wives or mothers. The fear of attempting to adapt to new roles because they may fail in them becomes paramount. However, women who begin early to define roles outside of those of wife and mother will find it less difficult to adjust to the eventual loss of the nurturing role.

As a result of the women's movement, there has been increased recognition of rape and its implications for women.* Dr. Dorothy Hicks (1977) states that "rape is a violent crime that has nothing to do with sex except

---

*See Chapter 12 for further discussion of rape.

that the sex organs are involved." It is an act of aggression; the victim is assaulted and then left humiliated and isolated.

Courts in the United States have only recently become compassionate in their treatment of rape victims. The legal definition of rape can be traced back to the property rights of men. A woman belonged to her husband—if she were raped, *his* rights as property owner would have been violated. There was little, if any, consideration given to the woman.

Beginning in the early 1960s, the women's movement directed its attention toward consciousness-raising activities relating to rape. Feminists spoke out on rape as a political issue. Diane Russell (1975) proposed that the feminist movement might temporarily increase the amount of forcible rape. She believes the growing desire of women to be independent may threaten male egos, thus causing an increase in outwardly directed hostility. Susan Brownmiller (1975) addressed the theme of rape in much stronger tones: rape is the perpetuation of male domination over women by force. As a result of the efforts of these individuals and others, there has been an increased awareness of the crisis of rape and its impact on the victim. Myths surrounding rape, such as the belief that a woman "invites" an attacker or is responsible for the crime in some way, are slowly being dissipated.

Nurses may come into contact with rape victims in a variety of settings. A nurse may be the only person who has any type of sustained relationship with a rape victim. It is critical that the nurse recognize his or her own feelings as well as what the client is experiencing.

A woman who has been raped feels a sense of powerlessness, a sense of helplessness, and a sense of loss. She may feel unable to determine her life's course. She may also feel isolated from significant others, friends, and colleagues. She may be afraid to return to her home or to walk alone, whether it be day or night. The greatest assault, however, has been against the self. Her personal space has been violated by an aggressive act. Loss of her personhood, her self-esteem, results. The rape victim experiences a wide range of feelings, from anxiety and fear to profound depression. Rape victims should be allowed to grieve for the loss of self. A nursing assessment should identify loss of self-worth as a predominant theme, and intervention should be based on this theme.

Burgess and Holstrum (1974) describe a two-phase response to rape—rape trauma syndrome. The first, or acute, phase is characterized by disorganization. Feelings of embarrassment, anger, humiliation, fear, and self-blame are described by victims. Burgess and Holstrum identify two emotional styles characteristic of this phase. The first is the expressed style: the victim releases her angry, anxious feelings by talking, shouting, crying, or pacing. The second is the controlled style: the victim maintains a calm, subdued affect, acting as though nothing out of the ordinary has occurred. Burgess and Holstrum also describe the compounded reaction that can occur in women who have had previous psychological difficulties. This reaction is characterized by psychotic behavior, depression, acting-out behavior, and suicides.

The second, or reorganization, phase begins at a different time for each victim, depending on the availability of healthy coping measures and social support systems. This phase is characterized by changes of residences, changes of jobs, nightmares, fear of entering the house of apartment alone, fear of being followed, and sexual fears. Long-term studies indicate that rape vicimts benefit from extended follow-up periods, sometimes as long as 2 years after the rape.

The goal of nurses is to identify the feelings the rape victim is experiencing and to facilitate the grieving process as a normal response to loss. A nurse acts as a support person for the rape victim during the medical and legal procedures that follow the rape. The nurse also assists the victim in her re-integration into the community by mobilizing significant support systems.

Interrelationship of theories

It is important to point out that *no one* theory is sufficient to explain depression. Any client is a complex, unique human being who cannot be understood through an assessment of only one factor in his life. It would indeed by simple to say that a client is experiencing biochemical changes or that poor early relationships with his mother account for a depressive response. It would then be easy to develop a nursing care plan to facilitate the client's remediation of these problems. In reality, however, life is not that simple. A nursing approach based on one theory would not facilitate an understanding of the client as a total human being.

An integrated approach reflects the interaction of genetic, biochemical, cognitive, social learning, and object loss theories, as well as sex-role stereotyping. Akiskal and McKinney (1975) suggest that depression results from many variables, including biochemical responses, previous experiences, and learning and behavioral responses. According to these authors, a behavioral response such a social withdrawal is not an isolated factor but has direct impact on biochemical levels in the body. The reverse is also true: chemical imbalances may cause a person to perceive situations in a distorted manner, thus leading to social withdrawal.

Nursing strategies must be based on an understanding of the various etiologic theories and their interrelationship with precipitating factors in order to be reflective of the individual client—his personality, his expression of needs, and his method of adaptation.

TREATMENT MODALITIES
Psychopharmaceuticals

Antidepressants may be effective in the treatment of both endogenous and exogenous depressive states. These drugs produce the energy that a client needs in order to invest in his environment rather than retreat into isolation. Two basic categories of drugs are utilized—MAO inhibitors and tricyclic compounds. The drugs in each of these groups treat symptoms rather than underlying dynamics. The administration of medication is therefore not the total solution. Drugs must be utilized concurrently with a supportive relationship. A client must receive active support from the environment once the medication has enabled him to move out of isolation.

MAO inhibitors inhibit the production of the enzyme monoamine oxidase, which is present in several vital organs, including the brain. This enzyme reduces the levels of norepinephrine, epinephrine, and serotonin, all of which serve to activate the body. MAO inhibitors counteract this reduction, thus permitting the reactivation of normal levels of these vital hormones.

Side effects and idiosyncratic responses must be considered in a comprehensive assessment of a client. The drugs in this group of medications can be lethal if they are not administered properly. The following points must be remembered:

1. These drugs are long-acting; they require 3 to 4 weeks to initially take effect.
2. There is a cumulative effect.
3. When switching from MAO inhibitors to tricyclics, wait 1 to 2 weeks so that synthesis will have occurred. When MAO inhibitors and tricyclics are given simultaneously, twitching, general restlessness, and even death can occur.

4. MAO inhibitors potentiate the actions of many other drugs, such as morphine, meperidine (Demerol), barbiturates, sedatives, tranquilizers, atropine derivatives, anti-parkinsonian drugs, antihistamines, and corticosteroids.
5. MAO inhibitors enhance the hypotensive effects of diuretics and will sensitize clients to procaine (Novocain) and other anesthetic agents.
6. Do not administer MAO inhibitors with amphetamines or ephedrine-like compounds, such as cold tablets or sinus aids.
7. Be alert to the "Parnate-cheese" reaction. Individuals receiving MAO inhibitors must avoid cheese, wine, yeast products, beer, yogurt, fava beans, chicken livers, and pickled herring. Otherwise, an increased level of tyramine, which is found in cheeses as well as these other products, results. Normally, tyramine is destroyed by MAO. However, this does not happen when the MAO inhibitors are in effect. The rise in tyramine levels leads to a hypertensive crisis. If the crisis is not controlled, blood vessels in the brain rupture, and death ensues.

The tricyclics are much more widely used than the MAO inhibitors and have a much higher success rate. The greatest difficulty encountered with the tricyclics is the premature removal of the client from the medication. Physicians often feel that the depression has lifted when the symptoms have been alleviated. In many cases, however, after a period of a month or more the client is again experiencing symptoms of the depressive response. Maintenance of an adequate dosage is the key to successful control of depression.

Tricyclics seem to affect the brain amine levels, although the specific response is not actually known. Unlike MAO inhibitors, tricyclics have little potential for causing hypertensive crisis. Most side effects can be regulated by adjusting the dosage as necessary.

Table 11-1, which is based on data of the Department of Drugs of the American Medical Association, lists the most common MAO inhibitors and tricyclics along with their trade names, dosage levels, routes of administration, and common side effects.

Nurses must act to support clients as barriers are let down through the action of medication. Leaving a client to function on his own because symptoms have been relieved can cause an exacerbation of those same symptoms. Another point to remember is that medication acts to lift the mood of a client, to provide him with more available energy. This energy can then be turned toward self-destructive behavior.

TABLE 11-1. Antidepressants

Drug	Trade name	Method of administration	Usual daily dose (mg)	Side effects
Monoamine oxidase inhibitors				
Isocarboxazid	Marplan	Oral	10-30	Headaches, dizziness, blurred vision, dry mouth, postural hypotension, increased appetite, nausea and vomiting, constipation or diarrhea, weakness, edema, tremors, impotence, insomnia, dermatitis, nightmares
Nialamide	Niamid	Oral	12.5-200	
Phenelzine dihydrogen sulfate	Nardil	Oral	15-75	
Tranylcypromine sulfate	Parnate	Oral	20-30	
Tricyclics				
Imipramine	Tofranil	Oral Intramuscular	75-300	Palpitations, increased pulse rate, postural hypotension, dizziness, faintness, loss of visual accommodation, nausea and vomiting, increased perspiration, constipation, urine retention, aggravation of glaucoma, minor tremors, twitching (NOTE: These symptoms are mild and can be controlled by reducing the dosage.)
	Tofranil-PM	Oral		
Amitriptyline hydrochloride	Elavil	Oral Intramuscular	50-200	
Desipramine hydrochloride	Norpramin	Oral	75-150	
Nortriptyline hydrochloride	Pertofrane Aventyl	Oral	20-100	
Protriptyline hydrochloride	Vivactil	Oral	15-60	
Doxepin hydrochloride	Sinequan	Oral	25-300	

Lithium carbonate is utilized primarily for the manic phase of manic depression. Marked reduction in manic behavior has been demonstrated after a period of 2 weeks. Lithium carbonate interferes with the elevated levels of norepinephrine and also affects the electrolyte balance within the brain, particularly sodium and potassium levels. Studies have shown that levels of intracellular sodium are low during the manic phase. Lithium increases the ion exchange factor, thus leading to higher levels of intracellular sodium and less impulsive behavior. Sodium regulation and the use of diuretics must be carefully monitored while a client is receiving lithium. Blood levels of lithium should be checked weekly, since the toxic dose is dangerously close to the therapeutic levels. Kidney function is of utmost importance, since the kidneys are responsible for a large percentage of the excretion of lithium.

Prior to the administration of lithium, the client must have a complete physical, which will provide a complete data base. It is critical to determine whether the client has a history of cardiovascular or kidney disease; the administration of lithium is contraindicated in those instances. There is a lag period of approximately 1 week between the initial administration and the subsiding of symptoms. Other tranquilizers may be used until the lithium takes effect. The nurse's primary role in the administration of lithium is the education of the client to the side effects and the results of misuse of lithium. It is imperative that the client continue to take lithium even though he is "feeling fine." Too often, ceasing to take the medication sets the client back to the beginning in relation to establishing therapeutic blood levels and concurrent behavioral responses.

Individual and group psychotherapy

Individual psychotherapy initially is more fruitful than group psychotherapy. A depressed client has difficulty seeing himself as a worthwhile person. Becoming part of a group may precipitate stress and could be an overwhelming experience. The client's greatest need is to be accepted as a human being. By relating to another individual on a one-to-one basis, the depressed client can explore various ways to reach that goal. As he becomes more sure of himself and ceases to view trust as an unattainable goal, he will venture into a group setting. Groups can be strictly supportive or they may be analytical and insight-directed. An effective group leader facilitates growth through interaction within the group setting. Each person needs to become what he is capable of becoming. This can be accomplished only when a group leader is warm, sincere, and most important of all, sensitive to the nature of the client's depressive behavior. Through the group process, the depressed client can learn alternative approaches to problems he is encountering. He may even find that the areas he considered problematic are no longer of primary concern. Whether the approach is individual or group, nurse-therapists must place top priority on the worth of the human being and the uniqueness of his responses.

Electroconvulsive therapy

Electroconvulsive therapy (ECT) was introduced by Ugo Cerletti and Lucio Bini in 1938. It is basically the administration of electricity via electrodes placed on the temples. Theories of the action of this therapy vary, and none seems to be widely accepted. One theory proposes that a person who considers himself worthless views the shock as a punishment that he deserves. Another theory holds that the shock rearranges brain cells, causing neurotransmission changes that, in turn, reduce the barriers to the understanding of the origins of the depressive response. Another theory suggests that aggression is at last turned outward, through the tonic and clonic phases of the convulsion. Whatever the underlying dynamics, electroconvulsive therapy does seem to exert a profound effect on clients experiencing clinical depression.

The care of the client receiving electroconvulsive therapy parallels that of the client undergoing an operation. Prior to therapy, the nurse should explain the procedure thoroughly and simply. A complete physical, including spinal x-ray film, is required. A consent form must be signed. On the morning of the treatment, the client should eat or drink nothing. He should remove dentures, put on loosely fitting clothes, and void prior to the administration of the treatment. Tranquilizers may be given if anxiety levels are rising. Atropine may or may not be given to reduce secretions.

The client is placed on a stretcher in the treatment room, and a short-acting barbiturate is given intravenously, followed by a muscle relaxant. A rubber mouthpiece is inserted to maintain a patent airway. The shock is administered, and a grand mal seizure results. Nurses in attendance allow the client's body to move with the tonic and clonic spasms, rather than holding him down. Restraining the body often causes fractures rather than preventing them.

Following the treatment, routine postoperative care is the primary nursing goal. Positioning the client on the side, with the head tilted, facilitates the maintenance of an open airway and reduces the possibility of aspiration.

Although the client may be alert and awake immediately following the treatment, assessment of vital signs every 15 minutes for the first hour is necessary. Since periods of confusion may occur after the treatment, clients need to be protected from injuring themselves. Nurses should orient the client to his surroundings, to enable him to feel in control of himself and his environment to some extent.

Once the client is able to, he returns to his own room. Nourishment is provided as well as an opportunity to rest. Electroconvulsive treatments are given in a series, ranging anywhere from 12 to 60.

Electroconvulsive therapy alone is not the solution to depression. As in other treatments, the client must be supported by a relationship with a significant other. Once the client's defensive barrier has been lowered, nurses need to be there to welcome him.

NURSING INTERVENTION

All areas of prevention—primary, secondary, and tertiary—need to be reflected in a nursing assessment and successive interventions. A nursing diagnosis must be made, and long- and short-term goals must then be determined. This section discusses the levels of prevention and identifies the interventions appropriate to each level.

PRIMARY PREVENTION

Programs of primary prevention of depression are just beginning to be organized. Clinical research is providing nurses with steadily increasing amounts of data regarding the delicate interweaving of the etiological factors underlying loss and depression. The major goal of primary prevention is to promote positive feelings toward the self and to facilitate the healthy adaptation to loss. The focus of this level of prevention is the promotion of open lines of communication and freedom of expression of feelings. By learning to respond to one another's needs, each partner in a marriage, for example, can enhance his own feelings of self-worth and integrity. When one member of the dyad is not feeling "good" about himself, he can bring that feeling out into the open without fear of reprisal. Anxiety can be dealt with in a healthy manner, without the need to resort to maladaptive responses.

As a couple moves from dyad to triad, a new dimension is added. A child presents another set of needs to be fulfilled. More demands are placed on the couple. It is imperative that angry, frustrated, helpless feelings be shared before they become pervasive themes in the family relationship. Each individual must meet the others' needs in order to prevent a sense of loss of love and the resulting feelings of loss of self-esteem.

Where does primary prevention begin? Prenatal classes, well-baby clinics, even physicians' offices are important target areas. The central goal at this level is to facilitate the mothering response, not just physically but emotionally as well. Mothers who are anxious and fearful are unable to meet their own needs, let alone attend to those of their infants. Parents who feel positive about themselves are more capable of allowing their children the room to explore their territory, to develop a sense of their own personal space—in other words, to be! Children need positive reinforcement on a continuous basis—not sporadically, when expectations are fulfilled. Mistrust begins to develop, as do feelings of low self-worth, when reinforcement is only sporadic. The child, as he grows up in such an anxious, uncomfortable environment, does not become able to relate successfully to others in his social world. Relationships are characterized either by withdrawal or by aggressive, manipulative behavior. These responses tend to separate the individual from others even more.

Since loss is a fundamental theme in the origins of depression, primary preventive efforts need to be directed toward helping people to adapt to the various loss situations that occur throughout the life cycle. The crises of loss begin with the loss of the warm, uterine environment and end with the ultimate loss—the loss of one's own life. Programs such as those outlined in parent effectiveness training courses, health education curricula, and workshop presentations can identify potential loss situations and probable reactions to them. Individuals can learn to be managers of their lives rather than victims of circumstances. Loss situations can be turned into learning situations. Disappointments can be handled appropriately. Children can then be better equipped to react to crises in a healthy, adaptive fashion in later life. Through positive appraisals from significant others in his environment, a child's self-esteem can be enhanced at particularly crucial times of development. The child will learn that he is adept at using his problem-solving faculties, a discovery that in turn reaffirms positive feelings of self.

Primary preventive programs are still new, yet they serve as the basis for the healthy adaptation of tomorrow's generation.

Grieving is a healthy response to loss, whether it be of a love object, self-worth, status, or function. The resolution of this process ultimately leads to the investment of energy in new relationships and to positive feelings regarding the self. When grief is prolonged, however, and the loss is not resolved, anxiety arises. The depressive response is activated to contain and/or diminish the anxiety. Nursing intervention therefore needs to be directed toward facilitating healthy adaptation to loss. The following principles are important in such intervention:

1. The primary goal is to promote catharsis. Verbalization enables the client to work through feelings of anger, sadness, relief, and helplessness. Be particularly cognizant of nonverbal communication.

2. Recognize that ambivalence is common. There may be sorrow that the loss has occurred. Yet in the case of a client who is experiencing the loss of a relative, there may be a sense of relief that the process of dying is finally over. For example, a family may feel a sense of relief after the death of a loved one who has been chronically ill. These ambivalent feelings are quite common; however, they are also quite upsetting. Let the client know that these feelings are quite normal. Provide a setting in which these feelings can be shared.

3. Assess the client to determine what phase of the mourning process he has entered.

4. Assist the client to maintain contact with highly valued objects or people. This is not the time for the grieving client to sell all his belongings or give them away.

5. Support already existing coping mechanisms, such as denial. Denial is quite commonly utilized to deal with pain experienced in a loss situation. If this mechanism is removed, the client will replace it with another, more pathological one. Do not reinforce denial, however; present reality as it can be tolerated.

6. Help the client to control his environment to prevent additional losses. Encourage him to participate as much as possible in his normal activities of daily living. He will then be able to feel as though his lifestyle has not been irreversibly altered. He will see that he is still able to perceive events occurring in his environment and that he can actively deal with them as necessary.

7. Be patient and tolerant of the wide range of behavior that can be exhibited by the grieving client. Anger toward the lost object that is released into constructive channels during this phase will not likely be turned inward upon the self at a later time.

8. Provide a private, quiet room for the grieving client in order that he may feel comfortable in his unique expressions of grief.

9. Assist the grieving person and family to review previous encounters with loss and methods of coping with them. Often a person is unaware of his repertoire of adaptive mechanisms. The nurse can identify them for him. The grieving person thus can be helped to develop a healthy approach to loss rather than to perceive it as a totally negative situation each time it occurs.

10. Allow enough space and time for the individual to grieve. Each person is unique in his

responses, particularly in the response to loss. Healthy resolution may take as long as 2 years, depending on the extent and type of relationship with the lost object. Anniversaries, birthdays, a special song, or a type of food may cause a normal reactivation of sadness. It is important to point out that such a reaction is acceptable behavior and to encourage the sharing of feelings regarding the precipitating factor.

11. Since loss is inevitable in the developmental cycle, nursing intervention must involve anticipatory work, as was previously pointed out. Recognize that an individual is having a difficult time resolving a situation. There may be a continued state of denial; he may be unable to progress to the awareness phase. Further supportive therapy is then necessary. In addition, nurses may want to consult resource people in the event that a depressive response is prolonged.

Three basic situational crises—loss of love, loss of personal security, loss of self-esteem—can be discussed as separate entities, but they actually are interrelated in their ultimate impact on an individual. As previously noted, the most important etiological factor in the development of depression is a significant loss—of a person, a relationship, bodily function, role, or status. This loss, if not resolved, leads to feelings of low self-esteem as well as feelings of insecurity in

one's role. By concentrating their efforts on potential loss situations, such as the ones that have been discussed, nurses can facilitate healthy adaptation to them.

SECONDARY PREVENTION

Secondary prevention focuses primarily on the early diagnosis and treatment of depressive responses. Since a depressive response can have many underlying causes, nurses need to observe depressive behavior carefully and to assess its implications thoroughly. Too often, signs of depression are cast aside as being unimportant or relevant *only* to another condition. Nurses should encourage everyone to be cognizant of changes in his own patterns of response to life's events. For example, a housewife may begin to feel that each household duty is an insurmountable task that cannot be accomplished at any cost. A business executive may find that he lapses into daydreams that diminish his productivity. A college student's grades may take a steady turn for the worse. These clues to the development of depressive responses can be identified at an early point along the continuum of depressive behavior. Part of the nurse's role is to provide an atmosphere in which clients feel comfortable seeking help and in which they can be helped to make intelligent, rational decisions regarding their own life events.

Identification of themes. A nursing assessment must identify predominant themes; in other words, a nursing diagnosis must be made. Goals and interventions can then be based on each major theme.

Several major themes are significant in the understanding of depression: (1) dependence; (2) powerlessness, helplessness, and hopelessness; (3) anger and hostility; (4) guilt; (5) ambivalence; and (6) worthlessness or low self-esteem. Nursing actions in response to each of these themes follow.

Dependence
1. Assess the client's capability to perform routine activities for himself. Since a dependent client expects that a nurse is more capable than he is, he will attempt to shift responsibilities onto the nurse at every possible chance.
2. Be cognizant of the feelings that the dependence response evokes in you. Sometimes nurses either respond in an overprotective manner or become annoyed and frustrated. Neither of these responses is helpful to the client.
3. Avoid reinforcing "dependent" behavior. Take the time to permit the client to act. It may be much easier to take care of some task yourself, but doing so only reinforces the client's feeling that he is incapable of accomplishing the task himself. He could then turn around and say, "See, I really cannot manage alone!" Goals need to be defined in terms of what can be realistically accomplished at present.
4. Maintain open lines of communication at all times. This is often easier said than done. When angry tirades occur, permit the client to express his demands. Then spend time discussing them and explaining why they cannot be honored. In this way, you do not bow to his demands, yet you provide him the freedom to speak his own mind. He feels that he is worth something, that someone *is* willing to listen.
5. Recognize the secondary gains of depression and the need of the client to exploit the kindness and attention shown him. His depressive behavior affords him the attention that he believes he cannot obtain in any other manner. Explore with the client alternative ways of achieving gratification and praise.

Powerlessness, helplessness, and hopelessness. Powerlessness is the inability to effect change in one's environment. This in turn leads to feelings of helplessness and eventually hopelessness.

1. Assist the client to manipulate his environment so that he may effect change. For example, suppose that a client describes feelings of being unable to change her role from strictly mother and wife to mother, wife, and interior decorator. The task seems overwhelming to her. Nurses can break down the overall goal into short-term, attainable goals. The client can experience success, and the pattern can be broken.
2. Recognize that helplessness may be a learned response. Provide situations in which the client can exert some control over his environment.
3. In response to behavior that indicates hoplessness, do not become "Suzy Sunshine" and try to talk the client out of his depression. Instead, work with him to

develop experiences in which he will receive positive feedback.

4. Do not condemn the negative feelings of the client, since he has a right to those feelings. On the other hand, do not perpetuate those feelings by condoning them.

Anger and hostility
1. Encourage the client to verbalize feelings of anger rather than to internalize them. Provide safeguards in the event that the client acts out aggressive feelings against others or himself.
2. Act as a role model. Let the client see that anger can be handled constructively, that it can be a healthy response to a situation. Show him that an angry retort by another person can be a positive learning experience.
3. Provide physical outlets for angry feelings. Gross motor activity, such as jogging, playing volleyball or tennis, and hammering or pounding copper, serve as useful releases for pent-up anger.
4. Be direct and honest in communication, since the client's interactions in the past have been laced with innuendo and misperception.
5. Do not be intimidated by the client, since he in fact fears his anger will destroy all those around him. An empathic response by a nurse will help to alleviate anxiety.
6. Do not provoke the client into expressing anger by probing into emotionally charged areas. A depressed client walks a veritable tightrope in his attempt to keep his anger in check. A torrential outburst of anger may be a

devastating event, emotionally draining him and making him more vulnerable to his own feelings and those of others.

Guilt
1. Do not negate the guilt feelings that the client is experiencing, even though they seem totally unreasonable. The client feels that he has done wrong and should be punished for it. Some theorists have proposed that menial tasks assigned to a depressed client assist him in assuaging these guilt feelings. He perceives this treatment as being the punishment he rightfully deserves. However, at present such treatment is seldom considered appropriate, and it is not widely utilized.
2. Avoid closing off avenues of communication by refusing to listen to the constant degradation of self. Such a refusal will only serve to reinforce the client's already existing low self-esteem and self-doubt.
3. Encourage the client to accept the forgiveness of others and to look to the future instead of the past.
4. Explore alternatives to the client's self-inflicted punishment. Can he experience joy in any activities? If there is even the slightest kindling of interest in an activity, facilitate the client's participation in it.

Ambivalence
1. Recognize that opposing feelings are in existence within the depressed client. It is a frightening experience to feel both love and hatred toward another human

being. The client does not know which feeling to attend to. He is on the proverbial fence. On the one hand, it is very important to him to feel close to another person; on the other hand, it is difficult for him to invest in a relationship. The response of the client resembles lack of interest but should not be taken as such.

2. Leave the door open for the initiating of a relationship. Do not ask if the client wants you to stay with him. He is unable to make that decision. Instead, make a statement to the effect that you will come to see him at a designated time. You must be the positive, active force in the relationship. Leaving it up to the depressed client will result in no interaction at all. After a series of interactions, the client will begin to believe that you are truly interested in him. At this point, you and the client can develop a plan for increasing his feeling of worth.

Worthlessness or low self-esteem

1. Accept the client as a unique human being with needs specifically his own. The most devastating factor in the depressed client's life has been a lack of praise and gratification for *being!* Nurses must start at this most basic of points in order to be effective in intervening with any of the other themes.

2. Define goals that are attainable so that the client can begin to achieve positive feedback in relation to his capabilities. Do not make situations so easy that success is achieved with little effort. This will only serve to reinforce feelings of worthlessness and the inability to function.

3. Accept but do not condone the feelings of worthlessness exhibited. Avoid a power struggle. A shouting match between client and nurse as to the worth of the client will certainly not further any type of relationship.

4. Recognize the client's need for privacy—do not "crowd" him. You must maintain a delicate balance: let the client know that you are concerned yet do not overwhelm him with your presence. Safety measures must be considered, such as removing sharp objects and mirrors and having someone remain with the client. Which safety measures are necessary depends on the level of suicidal intent.

5. Attend to the nurturance and bodily functions of the client. Whether he is depressed or manic, he may be incapable of meeting nutritional needs, hygienic needs (eliminatory and bathing functions), and the need for rest and sleep. An individual cannot begin to develop a positive sense of self-esteem when perspiration is the pervasive odor, fingernails are caked with dirt, hair is matted, and clothing is torn and filthy. These most basic needs must be met before you can move on to the development of a positive concept of self.

Hygiene and safety needs. The depressed individual is often unable to care for himself. Individuals who are severely depressed have little energy left to direct outward. Coupled with overwhelming feelings of low self-esteem, such a client is unable to mobilize enough energy to care for himself. If left alone, the severely depressed person will neglect his bodily needs—for example, bathing, brushing his teeth, and using the toilet properly. Eating also is of significant concern. An individual in a severely depressed state may become extremely malnourished and eventually may even starve to death.

Nursing intervention for the depressed client in regard to hygiene and safety includes the following:
1. Bathe and comb the client's hair as necessary.
2. Provide well-balanced meals that are attractive and appetizing.
3. Remain with the client during meals, and encourage family and significant others to eat with him.
4. Watch the client who is shaving to be sure that he does not inadvertently harm self.
5. Be alert to situations in which the client might fall.
6. Maintain appropriate lighting levels.
7. Act as an advocate for the client, since he may be unwilling or unable to actively participate in his own environment.
8. Recognize changes in the client's level of participation in the activities of daily living. Lightening of a depressive mood and increased activity may be significant clues to possible suicidal intent.
9. Encourage the client to again take responsibility for own hygienic and safety needs, as appropriate.

Intervention in a suicidal crisis. A suicide attempt is a cry for help; there is no truth to the statement that someone who talks about suicide never really attempts it. The suicidal client radiates many clues as to his intent. It is critical that nurses be alert to these clues and respond actively. Nurses need to be acutely aware of potential loss situations throughout the life cycle that may decrease feelings of self-worth.

What happens when a person calls a suicide prevention center and says that he is going to commit suicide? Farberow (1967) has designated five steps in the treatment process: "(1) establishment of a relationship—maintain contact and obtain information; (2) identification of and focus on the central problem; (3) evaluation of suicidal potential; (4) assessment of strengths and resources; (5) formulation and initiation of therapeutic plans."

The primary goal is to evaluate the suicidal potential. This is accomplished through an assessment that includes the following components (Hatton et al., 1977):

Demographic data. The following information should be obtained: name, age, sex, race, education, religion, and living arrangements.

Hazard. What happened within the 2 to 3 weeks prior to entry into the health care system? Have there been any significant developmental or situational crises? Were there potential loss situations that might have precipitated the threat? The most crucial task is to identify the meaning the individual ascribes to such an event.

Crisis. What is the client experiencing internally? What are the psychological and somatic symptoms, and how severe are they? Be alert to the fact that as depression lifts, the client is more apt to attempt suicide, because he is able to view it as a way to resolve his problems. Is the level of hopelessness elevated to such a degree that the suicide potential is great?

Coping mechanisms. It is important to determine how the individual usually approaches a problem. What makes the present situation different from others he has encountered? Is there a dependence on alcohol or drug abuse present that might alter his level of impulse control? Find out what he perceives as helpful in reducing stress.

Significant others. Who constitutes the primary support system or systems in the client's environment? What does the client feel would be the reaction of significant others to his current behavior? Is this perception real or distorted? Contact may have to be made with these persons in order to obtain a complete data base.

Social and personal resources. What social resources, such as shelter, food, and clothing, are available? Personal resources include money, time, physical and mental abilities, and job. A client is more able to cope with a crisis when such resources are available.

Past suicide attempts. Any past suicide attempts must be evaluated. Their seriousness, the methods used, and the resources available prior to those attempts should be determined. The current risk may be great if past attempts have been frequent and serious.

History of psychiatric problems. If the person has been hospitalized for emotional difficulties in the past, the risk of suicide should be considered great. Has the client made contact with any other psychiatric agencies? How did the client respond to them? Such information gives the nurse an idea of what alternatives have been explored and of what has been useful and what has not.

Current medical status. Is the client being treated by a health professional at the present time? If so, why is he now seeking out other people for support? Counseling is an emotionally charged process and may engender many feelings that the client feels he cannot share with his current therapist. He may simply need another listening ear at this time. He then could be referred back to the original therapist. Does the client have any physical illnesses, acute or chronic, that may precipitate a stress response? If so, has this illness been going on for a long time? What were previous methods of coping, and were they effective? What has caused these coping mechanisms to be ineffective? Has there been any significant change in health status within the past 6 months? Has the client consulted a physician during that time? Often, a person's attempts at making his needs known fall upon deaf ears. We need to be acutely alert for the underlying theme "Please help me."

Life-style. Is the individual's life-style fairly stable? Or does he move from one job to another, from one location to another, and from one group of friends to another? Such a

TABLE 11-2. Assessing the degree of suicidal risk*

Behavior or symptom	Intensity of risk		
	Low	**Moderate**	**High**
Anxiety	Mild	Moderate	High, or panic state
Depression	Mild	Moderate	Severe
Isolation/ withdrawal	Vague feelings of depression, no withdrawal	Some feelings of helplessness, hopelessness, and withdrawal	Hopeless, helpless, withdrawn, and self-deprecating
Daily functioning	Fairly good in most activities	Moderately good in some activities	Not good in any activities
Resources	Several	Some	Few or none
Coping strategies/ devices being utilized	Generally constructive	Some that are constructive	Predominantly destructive
Significant others	Several who are available	Few or only one available	Only one, or none available
Psychiatric help in past	None, or positive attitude toward	Yes, and moderately satisfied with	Negative view of help received
Life style	Stable	Moderately stable or unstable	Unstable
Alcohol/drug use	Infrequently to excess	Frequently to excess	Continual abuse
Previous suicide attempts	None, or of low lethality	None to one or more of moderate lethality	None to multiple attempts of high lethality
Disorientation/ disorganization	None	Some	Marked
Hostility	Little or none	Some	Marked
Suicidal plan	Vague, fleeting thoughts but no plan	Frequent thoughts, occasional ideas about a plan	Frequent or constant thought with a specific plan

*From Hatton, Corrine, Sharon Valente, and Alice Rink. 1977. Suicide: Assessment and Intervention. New York: Appleton-Century-Crofts.

life pattern offers no consistency, no certainty as to where a person might be or what he might be doing. The client who has not had stable patterns of interaction with other people will be less able to cope with any significant crisis situations.

Suicidal plan. Four basic criteria are involved in the measurement of suicidal intent: method, availability, specificity, and lethality. Has the client selected a particular method? How available is that method? Assume, for instance, that a woman tells you she has four full bottles of barbiturates on the nightstand next to her and that she rattles them into the phone. This action alerts you to the fact that suicide could be readily attempted. If the individual has formulated a specific plan of action, right down to the exact time and place, then there is a marked increase in suicidal risk. How lethal is the method? Lethality can be expressed in terms of the time span between the suicidal act and death. The most lethal method is shooting; hanging is second. Slashing one's wrists is last. Ingestion of pills poses considerable danger, yet there is still time to get help to an individual. Gunshot wounds and hanging have a more immediate effect. Assessment of a suicidal plan cannot be a one-time activity; the criteria must continually be reviewed if a nurse is to act effectively to prevent suicidal acts.

Hatton et al. (1977) have developed a system for rating suicidal risk; this system appears in Table 11-2. The types of behavior listed are not mutually exclusive, nor are they arranged in a hierarchy. The types of behavior are evaluated in terms of a hypothetical scale from 1 to 9. A rating of 1 to 3 indicates low risk. A rating of 4 to 6 indicates moderate risk, and a rating of 7 to 9 indicates high risk. All criteria are not necessarily relevant to all clients.

•　•　•

This section has identified the underlying dynamics of suicide and has discussed epidemiological data and nursing intervention. Relating to a suicidal client may produce feelings of vulnerability to the loss of one's own life. Nurses need to be aware of their responses to the suicidal act. It is easy to become drained emotionally from working for long periods of time with suicidal clients. Nurses also need to recognize their own limitations and to have their emotional wells replenished from time to time.

TERTIARY PREVENTION

The use of therapeutic agents such as lithium and the MAO inhibitors requires great caution. Nurses need to be continually alert for alterations in psychodynamic factors that may ultimately increase the severity of a depressive response.

Continued research in the area of family dynamics and the interrelationship of etiological variables is an important concern of tertiary prevention. Nurses need to direct efforts toward modifying the environment to reduce the intensity of some of the stress factors that ultimately lead to depression.

What happens to an individual who has experienced loss? Where is the follow-up care? When symptoms disappear, the underlying dynamics may remain. A discussion of what significance the loss holds as well as its correlation with past losses can facilitate the individual's understanding of his coping measures. Nurses need to be acutely aware of the need to provide follow-up care for clients who have experienced depressive responses, even though symptoms may have subsided. It is quite easy and comfortable for these clients to revert to maladaptive methods of coping when stress again becomes overwhelming. It is therefore of utmost importance that such a client, who may possess little self-worth, feels that there is always a link with someone who cares. Contact with family members and others in the community can help him to develop a social network of support that can facilitate his reentry into the community.

CHAPTER SUMMARY

Loss occurs throughout the life cycle. The grieving process can be a healthy, adaptive response to loss. Individuals develop a pattern of response to loss that is based on early childhood experiences. It is important to understand the significance of these early experiences with loss in order to facilitate the open sharing of feelings. Grief is a normal response. Nurses can encourage people to participate actively in the grieving process, whether the grief be for the loss of a person, status, self-esteem, a body part, or a bodily function. Through such active involvement, a person can lay a foundation for adaptation to future losses.

Recurrently unhealthy or maladaptive responses to loss situations may lead to a delayed grief reaction, depression, or even suicide. Nurses need to recognize that many variables may be responsible for the development of a depressive response. Several major theories of depression, manic-depressive reactions, and suicide have been presented. A nursing assessment must reflect an integration of these theories, since no one theory can explain depressive behavior.

Individual and group therapy, the administration of psychopharmaceuticals, and electroconvulsive therapy have been discussed as treatment modalities.

Nursing intervention has been discussed in terms of the three levels of prevention. Primary prevention is directed toward facilitating an individual's adaptation to loss. Secondary prevention involves the use of specific techniques in response to each of the predominant themes of depression. The goals of tertiary prevention are to minimize the effects of loss, through discussion of an individual's adaptive (or maladaptive) mechanisms, and to facilitate the reentry of the client into his community.

We hope that as a result of the discussion of affective disorders presented in this chapter, nurses will be more aware of the wide range of etiological variables involved in the development of depression. Nursing assessment and intervention should reflect the fact that each human being is unique.

REFERENCES

Akiskal, H., and W. McKinney
  1975 "Overview of recent research in depression." Archives of General Psychiatry 32:285-290.
American Medical Association Department of Drugs
  1973 AMA Drug Evaluations (ed. 2). Acton, Mass.: Publishing Sciences Group, Inc.
Anthony, James, and Therese Benedek (eds.)
  1975 Depression and Human Existence. Boston: Little, Brown & Co.
Arieti, S.
  1974 "Affective disorders: manic-depressive psychosis and psychotic depression." In American Handbook of Psychiatry. S. Arieti (ed.-in-chief). New York: Basic Books, Inc., Publishers.
Bahnson, C. B., and M. B. Bahnson
  1966 "Role of the ego defenses: denial and repression in the etiology of malignant neoplasm." Annals of the New York Academy of Sciences 125:827-845.
Bart, Pauline
  1971 "Depression in middle-aged women." In Women in Sexist Society. Vivian Gornick and B. Moran (eds.). New York: Basic Books, Inc., Publishers.
Beck, Aaron
  1967 Depression: Causes and Treatment. Philadelphia: University of Pennsylvania Press.
Bibring, Edward
  1953 "The mechanism of depression." In Affective Disorders. P. Greenacre (ed.). New York: International Universities Press.
Bowlby, John
  1973 Attachment and Loss: Separation, Anxiety, and Anger, vol. 2. New York: Basic Book, Inc., Publishers.
Brownmiller, Susan
  1975 Against Our Will. New York: Simon & Schuster, Inc.

Burgess, Ann, and Lynda Holstrum
  1974 "Rape trauma syndrome." American Journal of Psychiatry 131(9):981-986.
Chesler, P.
  1972 Women and Madness. New York, Doubleday & Co., Inc.
Clark, Terri.
  1976 "Counseling victims of rape." American Journal of Nursing 76:1964-1966.
Court, J. H.
  1972 "The continuum model as a resolution of paradoxes in manic-depressive psychosis. British Journal of Psychiatry 120:133-141.
Dunner, D., J. Fleiss, and R. R. Fieve
  1976 "The course of development of mania in patients with recurrent depressions." American Journal of Psychiatry 133:907.
Durkheim, Emile
  1951 Suicide. New York: The Free Press.
Engel, George
  1962 Psychologic Development in Health and Disease. Philadelphia: W. B. Saunders Co.
Farberow, Norman (ed.)
  1975 Suicide in Different Cultures. Baltimore: University Park Press.
Fieve, R.
  1975 "Unipolar and bipolar affective states." In The Nature and Treatment of Depression. F. Flach and S. Draghi (eds.). New York: John Wiley & Sons, Inc., pp. 145-160.
Freud, S.
  1917 "Mourning and melancholia." In The Collected Papers, vol. 2. London: The Hogarth Press Ltd.
Gibbons, J. L.
  1960 "Total body sodium and potassium in depressive illness." Clinical Scientist 19:133-138.
Greene, W. A.
  1966 "The psychosocial setting of the development of leukemia and lymphoma." Annals of the New York Academy of Sciences 125:794-801.
Hatton, Corrine, Sharon Valente, and Alice Rink
  1977 Suicide: Assessment and Intervention. New York: Appleton-Century-Crofts.
Hauser, E., and F. Feinberg
  1976 "Operational approach to delayed grief and mourning process." Journal of Psychiatric Nursing 2:26-29.

Hicks, Dorothy
  1977 "Not a sex act—a violent crime."
       Modern Medicine 1:15-21.
Kallman, F. J.
  1953 Heredity in Health and Mental Disor-
       ders. New York: W. W. Norton & Co.,
       Inc.
Kicey, Caroline
  1974 "Catecholamines and depression: a
       physiological theory of depression."
       American Journal of Nursing 74:2018-
       2020.
Klein, Melanie
  1934 "A contribution to the psychogenesis
       of manic-depressive states." In Contri-
       butions to Psychoanalysis 1921-1945.
       London, The Hogarth Press Ltd.
Kolb, L.
  1973 Modern Clinical Psychiatry. Philadel-
       phia: W. B. Saunders Co.
LeShan, L.
  1966 "An emotional life-history pattern as-
       sociated with neoplastic disease." An-
       nals of the New York Academy of Sci-
       ences 125:780-793.
Lindemann, Eric
  1944 "Symptomatology and management
       of acute grief." American Journal of
       Psychiatry 101:141-148.
Linden, L., and W. Breed
  1976 "Epidemiology of suicide." In Suici-
       dology: Contemporary Developments.
       E. S. Schneidman (ed.). New York:
       Grune & Stratton, Inc.
Menninger, Karl
  1938 Man Against Himself. New York: Har-
       court, Brace & Co.
Richman, Joseph
  1971 "Family determinants of suicidal po-
       tential." In Identifying Suicidal Poten-
       tial. D. Anderson and L. McLean (eds.).
       New York: Behavioral Publications,
       Inc.
Russell, Diane
  1975 The Politics of Rape. New York: Stein
       & Day, Publishers.
Satir, V.
  1972 Peoplemaking. Palo Alto: Science and
       Behavior Books, Inc.
Schmagin, B., and D. Pearlmutter
  1977 "The pursuit of unhappiness: the sec-
       ondary gains of depression." Perspec-
       tives in Psychiatric Care 15(2):63-65.
Schneidman, E., and N. Farberow (eds.)
  1957 Clues to Suicide. New York: McGraw-
       Hill Book Co.

Secunda, Steven
  1973 "The depressive disorders: special re-
       port." In Department of Health, Edu-
       cation, and Welfare Publication.
       Washington, D.C.: U.S. Government
       Printing Office.
Seligman, M.
  1973 "For helplessness: can we immunize
       the weak?" Psychology Today, 73:90-
       95.
Selkin, James
  1975 "Rape." Psychology Today 75:71-76.
Spitz, Rene, and K. M. Wold
  1946 "Anaclitic depression." In The Psy-
       choanalytic Study of the Child. New
       York: International Universities Press.
Wetzel, R.
  1976 "Hopelessness, depression and suicid-
       al intent." Archives of General Psy-
       chiatry 33:901-908.

ANNOTATED SUGGESTED READINGS

Cohen, S.
  1977 "Helping depressed patients in general
       nursing practice." American Journal
       of Nursing 77:1007-1009.
       *This article directs its attention toward
       depression as it is experienced in the
       general hospital setting. The presenta-
       tion is in the form of programmed in-
       struction, which proves useful for the
       beginning undergraduate student.*
Seligman, M.
  1974 "Depression and learned helplessness."
       In The Psychology of Depression: Con-
       temporary Theory and Research. R.
       Friendman and M. Katz (eds.). Wash-
       ington, D.C.: V. H. Winston & Sons,
       Inc.
       *Seligman proposes a direct correlation
       between lack of control over one's envi-
       ronment and depression: Individuals
       who learn through repeated life experi-
       ences that they are unable to effect
       change eventually opt not to even at-
       tempt change. The inability to make
       changes in one's life and environment
       then leads to a sense of helplessness.
       Helplessness, in turn, becomes a
       learned life-style.*
Swanson, Ardis
  1976 "Communicating with depressed per-
       sons." Perspectives in Psychiatric Care
       13(2):63-67.
       Swanson suggests that therapeutic

communication with the depressed person requires theory as well as practice. The key concept presented is the nurse's use of self to facilitate the client's perception of communication (or lact of it) with the external environment. Problematic verbal and nonverbal messages are identified, and attempts are made to match these two components of the communication process. This article is valuable in that the active role of the nurse in the communication process is emphasized as a mechanism for assisting the client to communicate needs in an adaptive manner.

FURTHER READINGS

Crary, W., and G. Crary
  1973 "Depression." American Journal of Nursing 73:472-475.
Drake, R., and J. Price
  1975 "Depression: adaptation to disruption and loss." Perspectives in Psychiatric Care 13:163-166.
Flack, F., and S. Draghi (eds.)
  1975 The Nature and Treatment of Depression. New York: John Wiley & Sons, Inc.
Freedman, A. M., H. Kaplan, and B. Sadock
  1976 Synopsis of Comprehensive Psychiatry, vol. 2. Baltimore: The Williams and Wilkins Co.
Malmquist, C.
  1971 "Depressions in childhood and adolescence" New England Journal of Medicine 284:887-995, 995-1014.

12
COPING THROUGH
SOCIALLY DEVIANT
BEHAVIOR

CHAPTER
FOCUS

Everyone lives within a social system, and every social system is based on a set of values and rules. These values and rules serve as standards to which members of society are expected to conform.

Some people try to cope with tensions and conflicts by acting out against society. These people behave in ways that deviate from society's standards. Such socially aberrant behavior often harms others and is condemned by society.

Various theories have been formulated to explain the etiology of socially deviant behavior. These theories fall into three major categories: psychological conflict, biological defect, and sociocultural conflict. It is probable that a combination of factors leads to the development of socially deviant behavior. Some type of socially aberrant behavior is known to all societies, but its form, meaning, and incidence are culturally determined.

Persons who behave in socially aberrant ways are usually content with their behavior and may not seek treatment voluntarily. When treatment is instituted, a combination of therapies is usually indicated. The goals of therapy are to supplant the aberrant behavior with acceptable behavior and to facilitate an individual's reentry into society.

Although nurses may not directly participate in all treatment modalities, they do participate in all three levels of preventive intervention. When working with socially deviant persons, nurses need to be nondefensive, realistic, accepting, consistent, and firm. A nurse's insight into his or her own attitudes, values, and behavior is essential in helping socially deviant individuals confront their aberrant behavior. By clarifying their own attitudes and values, nurses can accept people who behave in socially aberrant ways without condoning their life-styles.

12

COPING THROUGH SOCIALLY DEVIANT BEHAVIOR

Socially deviant, or aberrant, behavior includes a large number of seemingly disparate and unrelated conditions. Such behavior is characterized by deeply ingrained personality patterns and restricted emotional responses. Many users of socially aberrant behavior have not internalized socially sanctioned values and rules—a situation that brings them into repeated conflict with society.

Underlying dynamics

    Alienation

    Anomie

    Manipulation

    Rationalization

    Blame placing

    Hostility

    Impaired judgment

Types of socially deviant behavior

    Antisocial behavior

    Addictive behavior

    Sexually deviant behavior

Epidemiology

Cross-cultural context

Theories of socially deviant behavior

    Psychological theories

    Biological theories

    Sociocultural theories

    Interrelationship of theories

Treatment modalities

    Aversion therapy

    Drug therapy

    Group therapy

    Social network therapy

    Educational therapy

    Meditation therapy

    Milieu therapy

Nursing intervention

    Primary prevention

    Secondary prevention

    Tertiary prevention

UNDERLYING DYNAMICS

Many people who behave in socially deviant ways have failed to internalize social values and standards; they may habitually operate outside the norms of society. Socially deviant individuals tend to be egocentric and oriented toward the immediate present. They strive for satisfaction of immediate needs and are unwilling to tolerate delayed gratification. They often perceive other people as objects through which personal strivings may be satisfied. Interpersonal relationships tend to be superficial. Such people attempt to cope with the world and the people in it through alienation, anomie, manipulation, rationalization, blame placing, hostility, and poor judgment.

Alienation

Alienation can best be defined as a failure in reciprocal connectedness between a person and significant others. Alienation is the estrangement of self from others. Hobart (1965) and Halleck (1967) ascribe the following characteristics to alienated people:
1. Present oriented
2. Uncommitted to people, ideas, or causes
3. Possessors of poor self-images
4. Convinced that people do not understand them
5. Unable to communicate with others
6. Possessors of poor powers of concentration
7. Active in promiscuous but unsatisfying sexual relationships
8. Users of marijuana and/or LSD

Alienation seems to arise from an interaction of several factors. Brown (1968) identifies these factors as urbanization, egalitarian disparity, a striving for success, and a lack of caring.

Urban life is marked by decentralized and depersonalized living. Work is a major source of economic gratification, social interaction, and personal esteem. With rising rates of underemployment and unemployment, however, many people are denied access to this primary source of life satisfaction.

Operating within this urban context is egalitarian disparity. There is a disjunction between actual behavior and idealized behavior. This is especially true for members of minority groups who are discriminated against and denied access to opportunities. The Glazer and Moynihan study (1963) has shown that all people do not have equal access to opportunity.

Coterminous with this egalitarian disparity is a need to succeed. Success is measured in terms of the possession of "things"—money, material goods, services, and education. In order to succeed, one must compete. If one is unable or unwilling to compete, success is usually unattainable.

Partially resulting from the aforementioned factors and certainly interrelated with them is a lack of caring. Modern society is technological. Technology often takes priority over people. Emphasis is on "doing," and succeeding is of paramount importance. Both men and women compete in this society. This competition often produces fatigue and irritability. There may be little time for meaningful interpersonal relationships. Within such a psychosocial context, alienation tends to develop.

Anomie

When prevailing social standards and values have little personal meaning, a state of anomie, or normlessness, develops. Anomie and alienation are closely related. McClosky and Schaar (1965) have found that alienation correlates positively with anomic responses. The loose social integration and impoverished interpersonal matrix associated with alienation provide a foundation for the development of anomie. Without significant interpersonal relationships, there is little internalization of social mores. A self-system of right and wrong does not develop. Freedom from norms not only means freedom from a socially sanctioned value system but also freedom from social constraints. An expectation usually develops that socially unacceptable behavior is required to attain desired goals (Clinard, 1964). Anomic responses are characteristic of many socially deviant persons.

Manipulation

Manipulation is the act of using the social environment for personal gain. Horney (1937) and Fromm (1947) refer to people who habitually manipulate as exploitative. People who are alienated and anomic tend to repeatedly use others to gratify their own needs and desires. Manipulation is a characteristic behavior of many socially deviant persons. Other people are perceived merely as means to ends. Socially deviant individuals usually manipulate others through force or guile. They may be domineering and ruthless, or they may be cunning and charming. Either approach is designed to allow them to use others. No one is exempt from being used. Family members, friends, and strangers are all fair game. Manipulative people feel little or no guilt about exploiting others and often behave as if they had a right to expect others to give them the good things in life.

Rationalization

Rationalization is a mechanism frequently used by socially deviant individuals. Rationalization is the process of constructing plausible reasons to explain and justify one's behavior. It allows a person to avoid looking at the actual reasons behind behavior. Underlying the rationalized explanation there is usually a shred of truth that is enlarged upon. For example, an alcoholic may tell himself that it is acceptable to drink three or four martinis at lunch: "Everyone has a drink at lunch. It relaxes a person." By accepting this explanation for his behavior, he denies the compulsive nature of his drinking; he denies the fact that he *must* have those martinis and that he becomes increasingly tense until he has had them.

Blame placing

Socially deviant persons tend to use the mechanism of blame placing in their interpersonal relationships. Responsibility for their behavior, and especially their misbehavior, may be placed on others. Such persons usually experience alienation in conjunction with the blame placing. They may feel alienated from the persons they blame. Harkins (1965) states that blame-placing individuals often view others as personifications of cultural disjunctions that are at the root of their alienation.

By placing blame on other people, socially deviant individuals are able to avoid dealing with their roles in and responsibility for what happens to them. Blame is assigned to other people rather than to themselves. Blame placing is a way of manipulating the social environment. Clark (1963) points out that people tend to project blame when they feel powerless to control their social environment to the extent they consider necessary. Since being blamed is an extremely uncomfortable experience, even the threat of being an object of blame can often effectively control the behavior of many people. Scheflen (1972) observes that certain members of society have learned to use blame as a habitual way of solving problems. For these people, blame placing is a way of life.

Hostility

Hostility underlies all the interpersonal themes mentioned thus far. Hostility is a state of animosity. It is a response that endures; it builds up slowly and dissipates slowly. By reducing anxiety that is engendered by threats to one's security, hostility functions as a self-preservatory mechanism. Hostility is expressed covertly in physical and verbal behavior that delivers some degree of injury or destruction to either animate or inanimate objects. Hostility is present in socially deviant behavior; the object of the hostility varies with the type of behavior. In some types of socially deviant behavior, such as rape, hostility is directed at others. In other types of behavior, such as alcoholism and drug addiction, hostility is directed both at oneself and at others. In all types of socially deviant behavior, because conflicts and tensions are acted out in socially unacceptable ways, hostility is directed at society.

Impaired judgment

People who behave in socially aberrant ways usually evidence poor judgment. Many do not show any insight into their behavior, nor do they indicate any concern about the consequences of that behavior. They may express little remorse or guilt for the damage they do to themselves or to others. Although socially deviant persons may convincingly promise to repent and mend their ways, at the first opportunity they usually repeat the same behavior. The socially aberrant acts tend to be impulsive, and their perpetrators often take unnecessary risks of being caught. One explanation for this impulsiveness and poor judgment is that such persons tend to have a low threshold for sameness; they are continually pursuing new sources of stimulation (Quay, 1965; DeMeyer-Gapin and Scott, 1977).

• • •

The dynamics of alienation, anomie, manipulation, rationalization, blame placing, hostility, and poor judgment interrelate. A hypothetical clinical situation will demonstrate this interrelationship.

A student nurse had established a therapeutic relationship with an adolescent male drug addict. Student and client had been interacting twice a week over a 12-week period. During one of these interactions the client lit up a reefer and began to smoke. Possession of any drug was grounds for being asked to leave the drug treatment center. When the student nurse reminded the client of the center's rules, he responded: "I've really been trying hard to get off drugs. I've just been so tense and pot helps me relax. It's harmless enough. It's even going to be legalized. Everyone smokes it. You or your friends might even smoke it. It's less harmful than cigarettes. Anyway, I promise I won't do it again. If you report me, I'll get kicked out of here and I won't be able to complete the program. You know if I'm sent out into the streets now I'll get hooked on drugs again."

The student nurse was faced with a dilemma: should she ignore the client's infraction of the drug center's rules, or, knowing that he might be made to leave the center for breaking the rules, should she report him?

This clinical situation demonstrates many themes common to people who behave in socially deviant ways. By smoking a reefer in front of the student nurse, the client was ignoring the center's rules (anomie) and was taking an unnecessary risk at being caught (poor judgment). The client had not learned from past experience and was repeating the same type of unacceptable behavior. The client's explanation that he was tense and needed to relax, that everyone does it, that marijuana is less dangerous than tobacco, and that marijuana might soon be legalized were rationalizations. Promising not to repeat the offense and reminding the student nurse that if she reported him he would be expelled from the treatment program were attempts at manipulation and blame-placing. To the client's way of thinking, his expulsion from the treatment center would be a result of the student nurse's action and not a consequence of his misbehavior. The client would not accept responsibility for what might ensue. He placed the student nurse in a dilemma and showed neither concern nor remorse for the anxiety he caused her. Underlying the client's behavior were hostility and alienation. This clinical situation shows the interplay of themes that characterizes the behavior of socially deviant individuals.

TYPES OF SOCIALLY DEVIANT BEHAVIOR

People who behave in socially deviant ways are responding to and trying to cope with tension and conflict. However, the techniques they use for reducing tension and conflict are usually socially unacceptable. This situation results in ongoing opposition from society. We will examine three categories of aberrant behavior that represent major social problems: antisocial behavior, addictive behavior, and sexually deviant behavior.

Antisocial behavior

Delinquency and criminal activity are the most common types of antisocial behavior. People who display antisocial behavior are estranged from society and its predominant cultural themes. *Juvenile delinquents* and *criminals* often have grown up in environments in which socially approved role models and societal values, purposes, and goals are weak or absent. This is not to say that antisocial individuals have no standards or values. Quite to the contrary, antisocial persons usually belong to a counter-society—a society that runs counter to or against the established society in which it exists. This counter-society has its own role models, goals, and system of values and norms (Lerman, 1968; Halliday, 1976).

Emerging from and reinforcing a counter-society is an anti-language. An anti-language contains special words that refer to the central activities of the counter-society—for example, words for "police" and "bomb". These anti-language words express meanings and values that are not shared with established society (Halliday, 1976).

While antisocial behavior can be engaged in alone, it is usually engaged in with at least one other person. Antisocial behavior is essentially a group activity (Barron, 1960). It has a tradition. Antisocial persons are the bearers of tradition, and anti-language is a major vehicle for socializing persons into the tradition. By conveying special "secret" meanings during verbal interaction, individuals establish ties of strong effective identification with significant others in the counter-society. These significant others serve as role models. Participants in a counter-society learn and pass on to others the rules, regulations, and modi operandi governing antisocial behavior. They learn how to engage in antisocial activities and how to avoid getting caught. They also learn about the social hierarchy of the counter-society and the rules governing loyalty to members of the counter-society (Barron, 1960; Yablonsky, 1963; Halliday, 1976).

In a sense, then, antisocial behavior can be viewed as adaptive. It helps a person obtain a positive self-concept and a sense of belonging and relatedness. It is an attempt to deal with frustrations, deprivations, and inadequacies. Antisocial behavior is adopted as a coping response when socially acceptable coping behavior has been thwarted (Shibano, 1961).

Addictive behavior

Some people compulsively use a substance or practice to cope with the stresses of daily living and to obtain a sense of well-being. The terms "addiction" and "dependence" are often used interchangeably, but they have distinct meanings. Dependence, also referred to as "habituation," is marked by *emotional withdrawal symptoms* when a practice or the ingestion of a substance is abruptly terminated. Addiction is marked by *physical withdrawal symptoms* in such a situation. Common types of addiction include compulsive gambling, compulsive eating, compulsive use of a substance (alcoholism, drug addiction, tobacco smoking), and compulsive working.

Compulsive gambling. Unlike people who occasionally gamble as a form of recreation and who usually frequent gambling spots with friends, compulsive gamblers bet excessively and uncontrollably and usually gamble in isolation. Bergler (1958) and Martinez (1978) identify some characteristics of the compulsive gambler: predisposition to risk taking; involvement with gambling to the exclusion of other interests; unrealistic optimism that is not altered by consistent losses; frequent fantasizing that he is prestigious, wealthy, or able to outsmart rivals; ability to derive an emotional "high," or euphoria, from gambling; powerlessness to stop gambling when he is winning; and compulsion to bet beyond his means.

Compulsive gamblers view money as an avenue to adulation. The development of a winning system and the winning of money are perceived as evidence of intelligence, shrewdness, and success. When compulsive gamblers are gambling, their energy and attention are devoted to the challenge of the minute and the fantasies of winning (Livingston, 1974).

Goffman (1969) describes four stages of a complete gambling transaction:

1. "Squaring off"—the decision to take a chance, the selection of a method of gambling, and the placing of a bet
2. "Determination"—production of a result (for example, though the spinning of a roulette wheel or the dealing of cards)
3. Disclosure—realization of an outcome (calling of the numbers or reading of the cards)
4. Settlement—Payment of losses or collection of winnings

Compulsive gamblers usually do not want to stop gambling but do wish that the undesirable side effects of losing could be changed (Moran, 1970). While there are no physical withdrawal symptoms associated with the cessation of compulsive gambling, the psychological withdrawal symptoms of depression and guilt may be experienced (Hyde, 1978). Gamblers cannot give up their compulsive gambling without assistance.

Compulsive eating. People who eat compulsively are sometimes referred to as *foodaholics*. Stunkard (1959, 1963) identifies two types of foodaholics. "Night-eaters" have no appetite in the morning, gorge themselves in the evening, and suffer from insomnia. Periodic spells of night-eating are related to periods of situational stress. "Binge-eaters" overeat in response to frustration. Overeating often occurs within minutes of the precipitating frustration.

Foodaholics do not eat because they are hungry. Compulsive eaters are stimulated to eat by such emotions as anxiety, happiness, anger, boredom, frustration, excitement, and depression (Holland et al., 1970; Leon et al., 1973; Greene and Jones, 1974). Compulsive eaters seem to experience "conceptual confusion" in differentiating between hunger and satiation and hunger and mood changes (Stunkard and Mendolson, 1961).

Foodaholics are well aware of the cardiovascular complications associated with obesity, such as heart disease and hypertension. Yet this knowledge is not an adequate motivator to keep them from overeating. Family members and friends who try to persuade foodaholics to lose weight for reasons of health or appearance soon become discouraged. If diets are imposed on them, compulsive eaters will often hide food and eat it surrepticiously. Foodaholics often diet in public and gorge in private. For foodaholics, life revolves around food: food that is low in calories and food that is high in calories, food that is permitted by a diet and food that is prohibited or restricted by a diet, food that will be consumed and food that will not be consumed, food that should have been eaten and food that should not have been eaten (Orbach, 1978). Compulsive eaters experience a loss of control when they are around food, they cannot give up their habit without assistance.

Abuse of substances. In an attempt to cope with the stresses of daily living and to achieve a feeling of well-being, a person may use chemical substances. These substances may be introduced into the body through inhalation, ingestion, or injection. People who use chemical substances beyond the point of voluntary control are referred to as *substance abusers.* If certain chemical substances are used often enough, tolerance is encountered. Larger and larger amounts of the substance are then required to produce the desired effect. The following are some of the chemical substances on which people become dependent:

Narcotics. The term narcotics refers to opium and its derivatives. Users commonly call these drugs "hard stuff." Included in this group are heroin ("horse," "smack"), morphine ("white stuff," "morpho"), and codeine ("pop," "school boy").

Sedatives and depressants. These drugs have a quieting and sometimes sleep-producing effect. Bromides and barbiturates are frequently used. Alcohol, which is a central nervous system depressant, is so widely used and abused that it will be discussed separately. Users refer to barbiturates as "goof balls," "barbs," or "birds".

Tranquilizers. These drugs reduce anxiety without producing sleep. Valium and Librium have become increasingly abused, and there is growing evidence of tolerance and habituation.

Stimulants. These drugs produce mood elevation and a feeling of boundless energy. Included in this group are cocaine ("speed," "coke") and amphetamines ("pep pills," "bennies," "cart wheels").

Hallucinogens or *psychedelics.* The effect obtained from these drugs is frequently referred to as "tripping." A sense of unreality is experienced, and distortion in time, hearing, vision, and distance perception is produced. Actual hallucinations and delusions may occur. LSD flashbacks may happen days, weeks or months after a dose. Included in this group are D-lysergic acid diethylamide ("LSD," "acid," "cubes," "royal blue"), mescaline ("mesc"), psilocybin ("God's flesh," "mushrooms"), and marijuana ("Mary Jane," "tea," "grass").

Solvents. Solvents include such substances as glue, gasoline, paint thinner, and lighter fluid. Their fumes are inhaled. The immediate effects that are produced are similar to those of alcohol intoxication. Thirty to forty-five minutes later, drowsiness, stupor, and sometimes unconsciousness occur. The user retains no memory of the episode. The majority of solvent inhalers are children between the ages of 10 and 15.

Because substance abusers do not necessarily restrict themselves to one category of drug, cross addiction is common. For instance, someone taking amphetamines during the day may take sedatives at night. Someone who drinks to "steady his nerves" may turn to tranquilizers when he is not ingesting alcohol. The substances that are most commonly used in combination are as follows: opiates and barbiturates; opiates and cocaine; opiates and marijuana; barbiturates and amphetamines; barbiturates and alcohol; marijuana, amphetamines, and hallucinogens; and tranquilizers and alcohol. These combinations are dangerous. Because they are both central nervous system depressants, alcohol and barbituates used together may be life threatening.

Some evidence suggests that abuse of chemical substances may be harmful not only to the user but also to his future offspring. For example, Kato et al. (1970) have found that the use of psychedelic drugs may cause chromosome changes in the user and may cause developmental anomalies in a fetus. However, other investigators believe that evidence relating chromosome damage to habitual use of psychedelics is inconclusive (Dishotsky et al., 1971; Leavitt, 1974).

People who use chemical substances in an attempt to cope with the stresses of daily living are usually engaging in illegal as well as socially aberrant behavior. Most of these substances are "controlled" drugs. Under the Controlled Substances Act of 1970, unless these chemical substances are prescribed by a licensed physician, their possession is illegal.

One very common type of substance abuse is *alcoholism*. Alcohol is a central nervous system depressant. Because alcohol decreases inhibitions, it produces a transient feeling of well-being. People who are addicted to alcohol are referred to as *alcoholics*. Alcoholics compulsively use alcohol to cope with conflicts and tension. According to Roueche (1962), for the past 5000 years there have been people in most human societies who have used alcohol as an anesthetic for psychic pain.

Once alcoholics start to drink, they tend to become progressively unable to control their consumption of alcohol. However, Marlatt et al. (1973) have found that all alcoholics do not necessarily "lose control" and go on a drinking "spree" after only one drink. In addition, alcoholics do not all follow the same drinking pattern. Some alcoholics periodically go on drinking sprees and become noticeably intoxicated. Others drink consistently day in and day out. These alcoholics rarely show signs of intoxication but are continuously under the influence of alcohol. Authorities agree that the development of alcoholism usually occurs in three stages.

1. Social drinking. A person starts to drink socially in order to relax, to be less inhibited, and to be more convivial.
2. Escape drinking. Gradually, a person progresses from drinking to be sociable to drinking to escape stress and feelings of insecurity, inadequacy, and anxiety.
3. Addicted drinking. Ability to control the consumption of alcohol decreases, and the need to ingest alcohol increases. At this point, interpersonal relationships, work, and health are noticeably affected.

For every alcoholic at least four other people are affected. Family members who try to cajole, beg, or intimidate alcoholics into sobriety soon become discouraged and frustrated. Alcoholics can only give up alcohol for themselves. Should an alcoholic decide to "swear off the bottle" for his spouse or children, at the first argument he will return to drinking.

Even though alcohol reduces tension, awareness of deteriorating interpersonal relationships, knowledge of alcohol-associated physiological damage, and the realization that one may be drinking to cope with tension tend to increase an alcoholic's stress (Polivy et al., 1976). Since use of alcohol is an alcoholic's primary way of coping, a vicious cycle is perpetuated.

If alcoholism is allowed to progress, an alcoholic may develop delirium tremens ("d.t.'s"), a form of acute psychosis sometimes precipitated by abrupt abstinence from alcohol. It is characterized by delirium, gross tremors, irritability, hyperactivity, and hallucinations. While the hallucinations may be of any type, they are most often visual, in color, and threatening. A "pink elephant" is a popular stereotype of an alcoholic hallucination. Alcohol-induced hallucinations differ from those experienced during a schizophrenic episode (see Chapter 13). Unlike most persons with schizophrenia, an alcoholic is usually aware that he is hallucinating. Prolonged alcoholism can also lead to Korsakoff's syndrome—a type of chronic brain syndrome characterized by amnesia, disorientation, confabulation, and peripheral neuropathy—or as Wernicke's syndrome—a type of encephalopathy characterized by amnesia, ophthalmoplegia, confabulation, and ataxia. Wernicke's syndrome sometimes culminates in coma.

These three disorders are usually seen only in chronic alcoholism. These syndromes seem to be related to the toxic effects of alcohol and the nutritional deficiencies (especially of thiamine and niacin) associated with chronic alcoholism. Alcohol consumption is especially harmful during pregnancy. Physical and mental birth defects are found more frequently in the babies of drinking women than in the babies of nondrinking women.

Compulsive tobacco smoking. In the wake of evidence that tobacco smoking is dangerous not only to smokers but also to nonsmokers who inhale smoke-filled air, tobacco smoking is encountering increasing social disapproval. Theaters and restaurants are beginning to segregate smokers from nonsmokers; and many establishments completely prohibit smoking. Smoking is beginning to be perceived as socially deviant behavior.

Thomkins (1966) identifies four types of smokers:
1. Habitual smokers—people who are psychologically dependent on tobacco and experience psychological withdrawal symptoms when tobacco is abruptly withheld
2. Positive-effect smokers—people who derive a stimulant effect from tobacco
3. Negative-effect smokers—people who derive a sedative effect from tobacco
4. Addictive smokers—people who are physically dependent on tobacco and experience physical withdrawal symptoms when tobacco is abruptly withheld

Psychological withdrawal symptoms consist primarily of craving (which may persist for years) and restlessness. Physical withdrawal symptoms include a decrease in vital signs, lowered basal metabolism rate, increased salivation, and weight gain (Hammond and Percy, 1958; Larson et al., 1961).

Studies have shown that smokers have more antisocial tendencies than nonsmokers (Stewart and Livson, 1966; Evans et al., 1967; Smith, 1967). Smokers are more apt to attribute what happens to them to chance, fate, or the actions of others than are nonsmokers. Smokers tend to perceive the locus of control as existing outside themselves; they may not readily see occurences as consequences of their own actions (Lilienfeld, 1959; Straits and Sechrest, 1963; James et al., 1965).

Addictive smokers, also known as *smokaholics*, experience a compulsion to continue smoking. Over time, most smokaholics develop tolerance for tobacco (especially the nicotine in tobacco) and therefore increase the amount of their smoking (Windsor and Richards, 1935; Johnston, 1942; Finnegan et al., 1945; Van Proosdij, 1960). Many smokaholics cannot give up smoking without assistance.

Compulsive working. Some people compulsively use work to control tension and to produce a feeling of well-being. *Workaholics* immerse themselves in work to the exclusion of other life activities. Immersion in work is one way of avoiding meaningful interpersonal relationships. Friedman and Rosenman (1974) and Jenkins (1975) describe workaholics as people who have an exaggerated sense of the work ethic and who suffer from environmental overburdening. Workaholics work long hours and often take work home on evenings and weekends. They seldom take vacations; when they do vacation, they frequently bring work along or cut their vacations short in order to return to work. Workaholics are very competitive. Their setting of extremely high standards of productivity places workaholics in competition not only with others but also with themselves.

Workaholics have a "type A" behavior pattern. According to Friedman and Rosenman (1974), a type A behavior pattern consists of the following constellation of attitudes, actions, and emotional responses: competitiveness, achievement orientation, aggressiveness, restlessness, impatience, a constant sense of time urgency, drive, persistence, polyphasic thinking, rapid and explosive speech, and hurried motor movements. Recent research suggests that type A behavior is a significant predictor of coronary heart disease (Rosenman et al., 1970; Wardwell and Bahnson, 1973; Rosenman et al., 1975).

Workaholics cannot *not* work. Because they do not direct their tensions and conflicts against society, their compulsion to work cannot be accurately classified as socially deviant behavior. However, today's world is marked by unemployment and underemployment. Unions are trying to obtain shorter work weeks for employees. Management is exploring the possibility of early retirement for employees. Society is espousing the merits of leisure time. While workaholics are not breaking society's norms, neither are they totally working within them. Workaholism may be a type of borderline socially deviant behavior.

Sexually deviant behavior

Some people engage in sexual behavior that differs significantly from society's norms. Underlying aberrant sexual behavior are overt or covert hostility and aggression. Prostitution and rape are two types of sexually deviant behavior that are of increasing social concern.

Prostitution. Persons who engage in coital or extracoital sex in return for money are engaged in prostitution and are referred to as prostitutes. Although much of the general public considers prostitution to be strictly an adult female activity, prostitutes may be children or adults, men or women, heterosexuals, homosexuals, or bisexuals (Masters, 1962; Anslinger and Oursler, 1962; Chesser, 1971). Today many prostitutes are youngsters (16 years of age and younger) who have run away from home in an attempt to escape from intolerable home situations that often include alcoholism or drug addiction on the part of parents (Morgan, 1975; Thomkins, 1977).

People engage in prostitution for many reasons. Broken homes, parental promiscuity, and a social network that accepts prostitution may predispose people to prostitution. Economic incentives, opportunity for diverse types of sexual activity, and the expectation of a more leisurely and exciting life may attract people to prostitution. Economic difficulties, inducement by a pimp or by other prostitutes, or ready opportunity may precipitate entry into prostitution. By examining the reasons why people become prostitutes, Benjamin and Masters (1964) have divided prostitutes into two types: voluntary and compulsive. Voluntary prostitutes freely select prostitution as a way to support themselves, because of the advantage associated with it. Compulsive prostitutes enter prostitution because of a strong impulse to engage in sex for money. The classifications of voluntary and compulsive prostitutes are based on the *predominant* reasons people become prostitutes. These categories are not mutually exclusive, and most prostitutes have a combination of reasons. The attractive features of prostitution play an important role in the case of voluntary prostitutes. Predisposing elements play an important role in the case of compulsive prostitutes. A precipitating event or events usually increases the strength of attractive and predisposing factors (Benjamin and Masters, 1964; Gregg, 1976).

Prostitution, by definition, is an activity that necessitates the involvement of at least one other person, the client. Much of the research on prostitution has focused on female prostitutes and male clients. The Kinsey report, *Sexual Behavior in the Human Male* (1948), found that 69% of white American men have had some type of experience with prostitutes.

Clients, like prostitutes, can be divided into voluntary and compulsive categories. Voluntary clients engage in sex with prostitutes for such utilitarian reasons as sexual unavailability of a mate due to distance or illness, limited opportunity (or no opportunity) to find a mate, and desire to prove one's "maleness" to male friends. Some such clients engage in sex with prostitutes as an alternative to birth control: if one's mate refuses to use contraceptives, intercourse with the mate may be avoided and a prostitute may be sought instead.

Compulsive clients engage in sex with prostitutes for such psychophysiological reasons as inability to compete with others for a mate because of age or physical handicap; need for variety; sadomasochism or fetishism; and desire to avoid interpersonal relationships (Ellis, 1959; Kirkendall, 1961; Benjamin and Masters, 1964; Donaldson, 1977).

An important aspect of prostitution is the prostitute-pimp relationship. Mutual exploitation is a predominant theme. Prostitutes turn their earnings over to their pimps and usually take their pimps as lovers. Pimps act as intermediaries between prostitutes and clients, drug dealers, police, and/or crime syndicate members. Pimps handle payoffs and protection money. From their relationship with pimps, prostitutes extract protection, the illusion of a caring figure, and a defense against loneliness. From their relationship with prostitutes, pimps extract money and the status symbols that money can buy. These status symbols plus the awareness of being a lover to a woman who has sexual relationships with many men increase the self-esteem of many pimps (Choisy, 1960; Benjamin and Masters, 1964; Donaldson, 1977).

In addition to the utilitarian nature of pimp-prostitute relationships, sadomasochism is a common theme. Pimps often viciously beat their prostitutes. The prostitutes, who in most cases have isolated themselves from family and friends, tend to interpret these beatings as evidence that their pimps "care" about them. Sexual intercourse between pimp and prostitute frequently follows beatings (Choisy, 1960; Benjamin and Masters, 1964; Chesser, 1971).

Most prostitutes have antisocial tendencies that are developed and reinforced by their experiences in jail and by society's attitudes toward prostitutes. Risk taking is engaged in daily. They face the risk of arrest, the risk of bodily harm, and the risk of encountering clients who will make bizarre demands. Prostitutes display hostility toward society by being contemptuous of any work that society sanctions. Most prostitutes do not perceive prostitution as work. Instead they believe that by engaging in prostitution they are violating the work ethic—living off the workers of society and thereby outsmarting society (Benjamin and Masters, 1964; Chesser, 1971; Donaldson, 1977). "Sex for sale" is more than the sale of sex. By breaking with sexual mores and engaging in prostitution, prostitutes display their hostility toward society.

Rape. Men who engage in forcible intercourse with an unwilling partner* are committing rape. Rapists not only act out their tensions and conflicts through sexually unacceptable behavior but also commit a crime. Rape is not an act of passion; it is an act of aggression. Rape serves the nonsexual purposes of venting anger and hostility and exercising control and power. These themes—anger, hostility, control, power—are present in every rape, but in any given rape one theme or combination of themes may predominate (Brownmueller, 1975; Burgess and Holstrom, 1974).

Burgess and Holstrom (1974) identify three types of rapists. The "anger rapist" displaces his anger toward a significant woman or women onto the rape victim. He uses more physical force than is needed to subdue his victim. He brutalizes her. This type of rapist may also degrade his victim by forcing her to engage in oral sex, by masturbating on her, or by urinating on her. The victim selected by such a rapist is usually old or in some other way vulnerable.

The "power rapist" is the most common type of rapist. He uses only the amount of force necessary to subdue his victim. His aim is to get his victim into his power. He wants to gain control, demonstrate his power, and thereby "prove" himself as a man. Intimidation rather than physical force is used to gain control over his victim. Often, this type of rapist fantasizes that his victim will be sexually attracted to

---

*See Chapter 11 for a discussion of the victim's reaction to rape.

him because of the sexual prowess he will show during the rape. He will frequently ask his victim, while raping her, if she is enjoying the experience. This is the type of rapist who may ask his victim for a date at the conclusion of the rape.

The third type of rapist, the sadistic rapist, seeks sexual gratification and an outlet for aggression through rape. Sexuality and aggression are blended together. This type of rapist receives his ultimate erotic excitement from the death of his victim. Instead of penetrating his victim with his penis, he may use an instrument. He may ejaculate at the moment of the victim's death, or he may have intercourse with the victim's body. In addition, there may be a ritualistic aspect to such a rape. The Boston Strangler and the Hillside Rapist are examples of sadistic rapists. Fortunately, this type of rapist is rare.

Selkin (1975) suggests that most rapists follow an identifiable pattern. First, a rapist selects a woman who is perceived as vulnerable (for example, old, living alone, or hitchhiking). Then he tests his potential victim. For example, a rapist may approach a woman, ask her for a match, make insinuating remarks, and then direct her to remove her clothes or tell her not to scream. In this way, he determines whether she can be intimidated. Next, he threatens her. He tells her what he wants her to do, that he will harm her if she does not submit, and that she will be spared if she cooperates.

EPIDEMIOLOGY

The exact incidence of socially deviant behavior is unknown. Hospitals usually treat only a small portion of the people who display socially aberrant behavior. Many such individuals are neither hospitalized nor treated by mental health practitioners but instead are sentenced to reform schools or imprisoned for their offenses against society.

An impressive amount of research has shown a correlation between socioeconomic environment and socially aberrant behavior. People who experience socioeconomic deprivation are often isolated from the mainstream of society. They may experience overcrowding, poverty, and scarcity of employment opportunities. They tend to have little access to information, goods, and services. Such an environment may lead to blocked aspirations and to the use of illegitimate means to achieve goals. A circular system of blocked aspirations and illegitimate ways of achieving goals may develop to maintain such people in a state of alienation and anomie. Drug addiction, alcoholism, gambling, prostitution, and violence are often commonplace in such an environment. Rather than being considered deviant, such behavior may come to be viewed as "adult" and to be considered part of a rite of passage from childhood to adulthood. Thus children who grow up in an environment of socio-economic deprivation may be socialized into a system of deviant norms, a situation that may lead to a high incidence of socially aberrant behavior (Langer and Michael, 1963; Bagely, 1967; Zusman, 1969, Ashcraft and Scheflen, 1976).

The incidence of socially deviant behavior is two to three times higher among men than among women. Chesler (1972) refers to various types of behavior as "male diseases." She points out that aggressive acts, sexual misbehavior, drinking, swearing, gambling, and even stealing are all part of an exaggerated stereotype of the male role. In order to be "masculine" in Western society, less powerful and secure men have to "prove" themselves by taking what more powerful and secure men either already have or can readily obtain. For example, the sociocultural environment surrounding the working-class male often equates risk taking, womanizing, and possession of money, cars, and clothes with "machismo." Gambling may be a routine aspect of the life-style of many adult men. Such an environment tends to reinforce a gambler's self-image as "action-seeker" and to contribute to his fantasies of power and prestige (Gans, 1962; Livingston, 1974). This is not to say that women do not behave in socially aberrant ways. For example, most prostitutes are women, and compulsive overeating occurs primarily in women. Orbach (1978) views compulsive overeating among women as a rebellion against culturally defined sex-role stereotypes. (For an in-depth discussion, refer to the sections on psychological and sociocultural theories in this chapter.)

Although many incidents of socially deviant behavior are not reported (for example, rape) or are recorded as crimes rather than as psychosocial disorders (for example, prostitution), the prevalence of two types of socially deviant behavior—drug addiction and alcoholism—has been estimated.

Drug abuse and addiction are found among all age groups. Drug use in general has increased in recent years. Even when the use of alcohol is excluded, there are still an estimated 60,000 to 1,000,000 drug addicts in the United States (MacLeod et al., 1975).

Alcohol is the most commonly abused drug in the United States. Alcoholism ranks with cancer and heart disease as a major health problem. Yet alcoholism is one of our most neglected health problems.

There are approximately 100 million persons aged 15 years or older who consume alcohol, and we know that many children younger than 15 drink. Of these users of alcohol, approximately 10 million are alcoholics. Violent behavior associated with alcohol intoxication is related to 64% of all murders, 41% of all assaults, 34% of all rapes, 29% of other sex crimes, and 60% of all cases of child abuse (Report of the National Council on Alcoholism, 1976). Alcoholism is therefore associated with many other types of socially aberrant behavior.

CROSS-CULTURAL CONTEXT

Socially deviant behavior must be viewed from a cultural perspective. Special attention should be paid to the fact that cultures define aberrant behavior in various ways.

Many anthropologists believe that violence is *not* universal. For example, adult violence is unknown among the Ifaluk of Micronesia (Burrows and Spiro, 1953). On the other hand, some societies have a high incidence of violence. The Yamana of Tierra del Fuego are almost continuously involved in brawls and interfamily murders (Gusinde, 1961).

Nash (1967) suggests a correlation between increased homicide rates and periods of social change. She has found that in response to social change among the Teklum, in Mexico, charges of witchcraft have increased, with an associated rise in homicide. Among the Teklum, murder is strictly a male activity. Both perpetrators and victims are men. Men who are murdered have usually been suspected of witchcraft. Most of this Indian community feel that these homicides are justified. This situation points to a correlation between social stress and social deviance. It also shows that while homicide might be perceived as a deviant form of behavior, members of a particular society might not always interpret it as troublesome.

In contrast to evidence suggesting that violence may not be a universal occurrence, the use of psychoactive substances is found in all societies. Each society decides which substances will be sanctioned and which will be condemned.

Even when socially acceptable drugs are used, certain rules must be followed. Persons who ignore the rules are considered just as deviant as those who use unacceptable drugs. This is best exemplified by a village in Rajasthan, India. In this village, members of different social castes approve of different intoxicants. Ragputs (members of rules and warrior caste) regularly indulge in "daru" (alcohol), while Brahmins regularly use "bhang" *(Cannabis indica).* Each caste condemns the use of the other's drug. However, both Rajputs and Brahmins also have rules governing the use of their own drugs. Persons who break the rules are regarded as drug abusers (Carstairs, 1954). In the United States, many Indian tribes use peyote in religious ceremonies. The Native American Church uses peyote as a sacramental (LaBarre, 1960, 1964; Slotkin, 1967). Thus, the way a society views a drug and its use determines that constitutes drug abuse.

Alcohol is one drug that is known to most societies. However, the amount of alcohol that is imbibed and the frequency with which people become alcoholics is strongly influenced by culture. Defining alcoholism as the ingestion of 5 or more ounces of alcohol per day, DeLint and Schmidt (1971) found that the rate of alcoholism varies greatly from country to country. France has the highest incidence of alcoholism, and Norway and Finland have the lowest. With approximately 2% of its inhabitants developing alcoholism, the United States falls in the midrange of DeLint's and Schmidt's international survey.

Drinking patterns in the United States are related to cultural background. Although Jewish Americans, Italian-Americans, and Chinese-Americans tend to drink alcoholic beverages more frequently than people from other ethnic groups, these three groups have low incidences of alcoholism. The low incidence of problem drinking is probably related to the family-oriented drinking patterns of these ethnic groups. In Jewish culture, the primary alcoholic beverage is the sweet wine served at family gatherings and especially on religious holidays. In Italian culture, drinking is usually limited to the wine served during meals and at social activities. Similarly, in Chinese culture, drinking is done within the family milieu. In these cultures, alcohol is viewed as a social beverage, and drinking patterns tend to be family-oriented. Rarely do persons of Jewish, Italian, or Chinese heritage view alcohol as a way to escape from personal problems (Bell, 1970).

Prostitution is another type of socially deviant behavior that is found in many societies. The stigma attached to prostitution is related to other aspects of a social system. For example, in Latin societies such as those of Italy and Spain, prostitution must be understood in terms of a group of cultural patterns known as the Madonna complex. The Madonna—the mother of Christ—represents the ideal woman: loving, tender, forgiving, and asexual. In Latin cultures, the virginity of women prior to marriage and the fidelity of women after marriage are extremely important. "Decent" women need to be protected from sexual advances; protection is provided through patterns of chaperonage. In addition, the life of women revolves around the home. The home symbolizes femininity, safety, and asexuality. In sharp contrast, it is socially acceptable for Latin men to engage in premarital and extramarital sex. Boys first engage in sex during their teens, and the occasion is a time for boasting rather than secrecy. The life of Latin men revolves around the street, the bar, and the café, which represent the public domain, a domain that is closed to all women except prostitutes. Thus there is a clear dichotomy between the "decent" woman and the prostitute. The prostitute has violated cultural taboos and has assumed the prerogatives of masculine behavior (Parsons, 1964; Buitrago-Ortiz, 1973; Martinez-Alier, 1974).

Some form of gambling is also found in many cultures. Even prior to the European colonization of the Americas, Indians engaged in dice matches (peach or other fruit stones were fashioned into dice). The form of gambling that is preferred by people is often influenced by their culture. For example, betting on cockfights is popular in Latin America and the Philippines, betting on jai alai is popular in Latin America and Southern Europe, betting on poker games is popular throughout the United States, betting on camel fights is popular in Turkey, and betting on scorpion races is popular in Arab countries.

While most societies outlaw some types of gambling (for example, cockfights are illegal in the United States), other forms of gambling may be sanctioned. For example, Mexico, Japan, Russia, and a majority of the states in the United States permit lotteries. Legal gambling casinos operate in such countries as Monaco, France, Germany, Puerto Rico, St. Martin, and the United States (Chafetz, 1960; Fleming, 1978).

Thus, some type of socially deviant behavior is known to all societies. The form it takes and the meaning it is given are related to other aspects of a social system. Socially deviant behavior is culturally influenced, and the incidences of particular types of socially aberrant behavior vary from society to society.

THEORIES OF SOCIALLY DEVIANT BEHAVIOR

It is probably true that people have always been trying to understand socially deviant behavior. In the 1600s, for example, Thomas Hobbes' became concerned with the origins of social order and social disorder—a concern that has come to be known as the "Hobbesian problem of order." Hobbes believed that human beings are basically morally abject and that human nature causes people to pursue their own self-interests through any means, even through the use of socially unacceptable behavior. Hobbes maintained that only through legitimized force, vested in government, could socially deviant behavior be controlled. John Locke disagreed with Hobbes. Locke believed that people are born with a "tabula rasa" (a clean slate) and that they are molded by their experiences. Locke maintained that social order can be fostered and social deviance kept in check through a shared system of values and interests.

Concern and speculation about the causes of social order and social disorder persist. Why do people deviate from society's standards? Why do people act out tensions and conflicts in socially unacceptable ways? There are almost as many theories to explain socially deviant behavior as there are types of socially deviant behavior. These theories fall into three major categories: psychological conflict, biological defect, and sociocultural conflict. It is important to keep in mind that no definitive "cause" of socially aberrant behavior has been found. It is probable that a combination of factors leads to the development of deviant behavior. We will look at some of these factors and at how they are interrelated.

Psychological theories

The consensus of psychological theorists is that socially deviant behavior patterns and life-styles can be traced back to adolescence or even earlier. Superego formation or "conscience" is acquired through identificaton with the values of significant others, especially parents. Fundamental to the process of identification is a relationship built on trust and affection. In individuals who display socially deviant behavior, this identification process has not occurred or identification has been made with socially undesirable traits. When a parent of the same sex is absent, weak, or feared, a child lacks a warm and trustworthy role model. In the case of a weak or absent parent figure, there is little opportunity for a child to identify with the parent. In the case of a feared parent figure, a child often internalizes socially undesirable characteristics.

In either event, without a relationship of love and trust between child and parent (especially the parent of the same sex), a child is unable to effectively identify with his parent and tends not to internalize socially approved roles or socially acceptable values. Such a child grows into adulthood with an inadequately socialized superego. Social acceptance and disapproval then prove to be ineffective motivators or constraints. The individual operates for pleasure. He is impulsive. He is unable to arrive at a successful compromise between society's standards and his own impulsive desires. This situation frequently places such an individual in direct conflict with society.

Psychoanalytic theories. The psychoanalyst Freud (1930, 1959) identified three agencies of the mind: id, ego, and superego (see Chapter 4). He believed that human infants are dominated solely by the id. Only through the process of socialization do the ego and superego develop. The ego, through its appraisal of reality, and the superego, through its use of guilt, make people conform to social standards and thereby curb id behavior.

According to Freud, socially deviant individuals have defective egos. Their egos are unable to control and regulate behavior. Freud also held that people who display socially aberrant behavior have weak or immature superegos: these people feel little guilt or remorse about their behavior.

Some neo-freudian research supports Freud's ideas. Studies show that smokers have stronger oral needs than nonsmokers and that, despite the health risks involved, smokers gratify these needs through smoking. In addition, smokers tend to be more impulsive or impetuous than nonsmokers (Jacobs et al., 1966; Lane et al., 1966; Kimeldorf and Giwitz, 1966). Dubitzky and Schwartz (1968) have found that smokers evidence poorer ego control than nonsmokers.

Interpersonal theories. Another psychoanalyst, Horney (1937), criticized Freud for not recognizing the role that anxiety and inner conflict play in the development of socially deviant behavior. Horney saw quests for power, prestige, and possessions as attempts to find reassurance against anxiety. She also realized that these quests are culturally specific and that they are not found in every society. She argued that in trying to obtain power, prestige, and possessions, some people become exploitative and manipulative.

More recently, psychoanalysts have found that the quest for power, prestige, and possessions is important in socially deviant behavior such as prostitution. Through the sale of sex, prostitutes and pimps are able to acquire money and improve their standard of living. Money is also symbolic of power and prestige. Choisy (1961) and Chesser (1971) suggest that a prostitute symbolically emasculates a client by taking both his erection and his money. However, not only do prostitutes use money to gain control over clients, but clients use money to exert control over prostitutes. Through the exchange of money for sex, clients make prostitutes purchasable items. Clients "thingify" and degrade prostitutes. Both prostitutes and clients have a need for power and prestige. The prostitute's sale of sex and the client's purchase of sex give each the illusion of power and prestige.

There are many ways in which human beings acquire and assimilate power, prestige, and possessions. They can be cooperative or competitive, egalitarian or authoritative, giving or exploitative. These orientations constitute basic character or personality patterns.

Fromm (1947) defined character or personality as the way human energy is "canalized" or directed in the process of living and relating to the world. Once energy is directed into a specific character orientation, behavior becomes fairly consistent or "true to character." Thus, personality orientation enables an individual to function in society, and personality orientation is itself molded by society. However, even within the same character orientation, individual differences exist. Because of constitutional differences, especially differences in temperament, no two people experience a situation in the same way.

Fromm's term "exploitative orientation" can be used to describe many socially deviant individuals. Such people perceive the source of good and bad to be outside themselves. The only way to obtain the good things of life is to take them—through manipulation, guile, and/or force. This orientation pervades an individual's life-style. Everyone and everything is subject to exploitation. People and things are valued only for their usefulness. Fromm believed that an exploitative orientation is so pervasive that it even affects one's facial expression and gestures. He asserted that hostility and manipulation underlie an exploitative life-style and that these characteristics may be reflected in a "biting mouth" and in aggressive, pointed gestures.

Some psychologists use Fromm's concept of exploitative orientation to explain the psychology of gambling. In gambling, winning and losing are matters of chance. Chance lies outside the control of gamblers. According to Lindner (1950) and Begler (1970), compulsive gamblers continuously rebel against logic, moderation, and morality. By gambling, compulsive gamblers are scorning socially approved rules for living and are relying on the rules of chance. Compulsive gamblers will use manipulation, guile, and force in order to continue gambling. These authors see gambling as an expression of hostility and aggression against those representatives of society (for example, parents, teachers, and clergymen) who have tried to inculcate socially approved rules for living.

When people gamble, there is always the possibility of getting rich without working. Compulsive gamblers are defying the work ethic. Chance determines how the die rolls, which card is dealt, or where the roulette ball stops. Compulsive gamblers thus are defying the idea that logic and reason prevail in the world (Lindner, 1950; Bergler, 1970).

No one psychological theory is adequate for explaining all types of socially deviant behavior or why different people display different types of such behavior. We cannot speak of a psychological "cause" for socially deviant behavior.

Biological theories

Biological theories purport that individuals become socially deviant because they are biologically predisposed to such behavior. On the basis of the cosmology of Empedocles, early scientists believed that people reflect the natural elements and that differences in temperament result from body structure, humors, and muscle tone. Phrenologists believed that it was possible to determine an individual's characteristics by observing the protuberances on the external surface of his skull. These ideas pervaded the study of human behavior for more than 2,000 years.

Then, for many years, a link between biology and social deviance was discredited. Recently, however, improper nutrition, brain defects, and physiological malfunctions have been suggested as possible causes of socially deviant behavior.

Biochemical theories. Diet, food colorings, sugar, and food allergies have all been cited as possible causes of hyperactivity and/or violent behavior. For example, Bolton (1972) has found a relationship between violent behavior and hypoglycemia among Peru's Quolla Indians. Feingold (1975) contends that the increased incidence of hyperactivity among children is directly related to increased consumption of "junk foods" containing food additives. However, some researchers investigating the effect of additive-free diets on the incidence of hyperactivity have not substantiated Feingold's contention (Kolbye, 1976).

Physiological theories. Some research indicates that early eating habits determine the number of fat cells an individual will have—that the number of fat cells becomes set early in a person's life and cannot be changed. Weight loss can only be accomplished by decreasing the size of fat cells. When people with large numbers of fat cells try to reduce, they experience energy deficits. Because it is very difficult for such people to curtail their eating, many of them may become compulsive eaters (Hirsch and Knittce, 1970; Nisbett, 1972).

Other studies indicate that neurological problems may cause socially deviant behavior. Mark and Ervin (1970) suggest that malfunctions in the brain may be responsible for such aberrant behavior. Brain mechanisms for controlling impulsive violence are believed to be located in the limbic system, especially in the amygdala. Removal of the amygdala in violent individuals, with ensuing control of violent behavior, has reinforced this theory.

At the 1979 annual meeting of the American Academy of Neurology, Pincus (1979), a neurologist on a research team, suggested that neurological disorders may contribute to violent behavior in juvenile delinquents. Pincus found that 96% of the violent delinquents studied had some neurological impairment, as compared to 22% of the nonviolent delinquents. The violent delinquents had such symptoms as memory lapses, dizzy spells, headaches, convulsions, and twitchy body movements.

Genetic theories. Genetic predisposition also may be involved in some types of socially deviant behavior. For example, animal studies indicate that, in mice and rats, an appetite for alcohol is genetically determined (Ericksson, 1968; Eimer and Senter, 1968).

Studies of human beings show a strong correlation between the genetic marker for color blindness and alcoholism or alcoholic cirrhosis (Cruz-Coke and Varela, 1965, 1966; Ugarte et al., 1970). Kaij (1960) reports a higher incidence of alcoholism among monozygotic twins than among dizygotic twins. Similar studies focusing on smoking among twins indicate that there is a higher incidence of smoking among identical twins than among fraternal twins (Fisher, 1959; Shields, 1962).

• • •

Although rapid advances in biochemistry, neurophysiology, and genetics are providing increasing amounts of evidence for a relationship between biology and socially deviant behavior, we cannot speak of a biological "cause" of such behavior. However, because man's perception of and response to his environment must be filtered through his brain and implemented by his total body, we should not negate the role of biology in social deviance.

Sociocultural theories

After observing behavior in many societies, Benedict (1934) theorized that although babies are born with a wide range of temperaments and personalities, each society sanctions only a certain few of these personality types. Only those personality types that conform to the society's cultural pattern are allowed to develop unimpeded. Since most personalities are malleable and responsive to socialization, the majority of persons in a society conform to the pattern and are accepted by the society. Those who do not conform are viewed as socially deviant.

Urbanization theory. Some years ago, Redfield (1947) developed a theory that deals with social deviance. He differentiated between "folk" and "urban" societies. A folk society is small, homogenous, non-literate, and isolated; it has a strong sense of community. An urban society is large, heterogeneous, literate, and non-isolated. While a folk society is characterized by a high degree of social integration and little deviant behavior, an urban society is characterized by a low degree of social integration and much deviant behavior. Redfield's theory would seem to explain the high crime rates in inner cities.

Travel and mass media have penetrated even the most remote parts of the world. As societies interact with one another, they tend to diversify and to take on each other's characteristics. As folk societies have disappeared, socialization has become less effective. Social integration has gradually weakened, and social deviance has increased. Mills (1950) believes that Redfield's ideas are important to the understanding of socially aberrant behavior.

While the folk-urban dichotomy continues to influence the study of social deviance, some anthropologists question the premise that social discord is absent in folk societies. Lewis (1951) found pervasive social conflict, mistrust, fear, and hatred among the villagers of Tepoztlan, in Mexico. Lewis' observations are especially significant, since Redfield's study of Tepoztlan (done before Lewis') had described tranquil, conflict-free people. It had been from his fieldwork in Tepoztlan that Redfield had derived many of his premises about the nature of folk societies.

Social strain theory. Another theory that attempts to explain social deviance is social strain (or anomie) theory. Social strain theory originated with Durkheim (1938) and has been advanced by Merton and Nisbet (1961, 1971), Srole (1962), and Reich (1970). Social strain theory views people as basically moral and desirous of following the rules of society. This theory maintains that since people want to internalize society's rule system, only a major inconsistency in society can produce frustration, alienation, and socially aberrant behavior. For example, Orbach (1978) views compulsive overeating among women as a rebellion against culturally defined sex-role stereotypes. In order to fulfill the female sex-role stereotype, women are socialized to be appealing to men. Emphasis is placed on dependence, nurturing, sensualness, coquettishness, and physical attractiveness. This idealized image of femininity is imposed by significant others, the media, and the fashion industry.

Much of a woman's self-image reflects her dual social role of sex object and nurturer. Orbach states that many women find these two roles unrealistic and conflicting. For many women, it is impossible to be both a thin, demure, dependent sex object/lover and a reliable, well-organized, giving wife/mother. For these women, fat symbolizes the sustenance necessary to fulfill the role of wife and mother.

Orbach goes on to explain that compulsive overeating also protects many women from the feelings of competitiveness and anger that women have been socialized to repress. Compulsive overeating diverts the energy associated with competitiveness and anger away from these feelings and toward the concern about obesity. Orbach suggests that being fat is one way that women rebel against the feminine stereotype.

Sociocultural disjunctions. While society stresses certain values, roles and standards of behavior, the social structure often makes it difficult for a person to act in accordance with them. There may be a disjunction between socially sanctioned goals and access to legitimized ways of achieving these goals, or the social situation may make the rules contradictory and meaningless. For example, while humanitarianism, honesty, and success are socially valued, many people find that they can only be successful through egocentric, aggressive, and cut-throat behavior.

Social strain theory speaks to the dilemma of people who have meager incomes but who, through the mass media, have been exposed to the revolution of rising expectations. These individuals often aspire to middle-class goals and life-style but are unable to achieve them. People with low access to legitimate means of achieving goals or high access to illegitimate means of achieving goals may develop socially aberrant behavior. For example, Bagley (1967) found a significant correlation between job opportunities and delinquency rates and between delinquency rates and services for children and adolescents.

Community integration vs. community disintegration. Technology, once the American dream, has become the American idol. Progress and success are measured in terms of the possession of the biggest and fastest machines and the most machines. In this technocratic society, each person has become just another productive unit. Most people no longer directly participate in the production of their own food, shelter, or clothing. Piecework and mass production rob people of a sense of relatedness to nature and of a sense of accomplishment. This noninvolvement often results in a loss of the sense of self.

Fromm (1955) explains that in our age of technology, social structure and social relationships have become complex and impersonal. People often feel powerless, noncreative, and stripped of their uniqueness as individuals. Labor is often repetitive and meaningless, with workers taking little or no pride in workmanship. Rather than viewing themselves as the originators of their own acts, people often view their acts as alien to themselves. In modern society, alienation is pervasive; it characterizes the relationship of people to work, to things, and to other people.

There seems to be a correlation between social integration and social order, on the one hand, and social disintegration, alienation, anomie, and socially aberrant behavior on the other hand. Leighton (1959) points out that a community will almost certainly become disorganized if it is suffering from a disaster such as war, extensive flooding, or widespread fire; if it is experiencing pervasive poverty, either chronic or acute; if it is experiencing significant cultural change, as when ethnic groups are in conflict or are undergoing acculturation; if it is experiencing heavy immigration or emigration; if it is moving away from organized religion; or if it is experiencing rapid and extensive technological change.

Since it is not possible to directly measure the integration-disintegration balance of a community, specific sociocultural indicators may be useful. By employing a set of indices, Leighton (1959) has operationally defined social disintegration. He believes that a community may be characterized as disintegrated if it has many of the following sociocultural disjunctions:

1. A high incidence of "broken" homes. Leighton defines broken homes as malfunctioning families.

2. Inadequate associations. There is little actual grouping of people around such common interests as religion, work, or recreation. Those groups that do exist are marked by low group cohesiveness.
3. Inadequate leadership. Leaders who live in the community are realtively ineffective.
4. Inadequate opportunities for recreation. Few opportunities exist for such group diversions as sports and hobbies. Recreation tends to take such individualistic forms as drinking and sexual promiscuity.
5. A high degree of hostility. There are many instances of physical and verbal abuse.
6. A high incidence of crime and delinquency. Criminal acts such as child abuse, robbery, physical aggression, and sexual assault are frequent.
7. Inadequate communication. Poor communication may be caused by such physically isolating factors as poor transportation systems or absence of telephones, or it may result from poor or nonexistent interpersonal relationships.

These disjunctions threaten the efficient functioning of a social system. Leighton (1959) and Yablonsky (1963) suggest that sociocultural disjunctions may result in inadequate socialization of children. Family patterns, kinship obligations, child-rearing practices, and economic activities may be disrupted. Value systems and role relationships may become confused, fragmented, or conflicting. Children may fail to learn socially sanctioned values, standards, and roles. Socially deviant behavior may develop. For example, Esselstyn (1967) found that violent behavior occurs predominantly among adolescents and young adults who live in urban slums, female-headed households, or middle-class homes in which adults are affectionally distant. In such situations, youths may become estranged from socially approved purposes and goals. Esselstyn concludes that violent behavior seems to be related to a system of socially deviant norms shared by population groups that are experiencing social disintegration.

Interrelationship of theories

It is likely that socially deviant behavior results from the interaction of psychophysiological and sociocultural factors. This view is born out in the research of Thomas, Chess, and Birch (1968). For 12 years, they studied 136 American children from 85 families. The temperaments of these children were periodically measured and recorded. The behavior of each child was classified as either negative or positive. "Negative" behavior included mood swings, easy distractibility, and overreaction. "Positive" behavior included mood stability, ready acceptance of change, and ability to concentrate. While the researchers considered all of these traits to be "neutral," or nonpathological, the terms "negative" or "positive" were used to denote society's view of the desirability of each trait.

The children with negative behavior patterns were seen as presenting many child-rearing problems. Those with positive behavior patterns were seen as presenting few child-rearing problems. At the end of twelve years, 70% of the children possessing negative behavior patterns had been labeled by society as social deviants, while only 18% of the children possessing positive behavior patterns had been so labeled. The researchers concluded that while all the measured personality traits were potentially neutral, society (especially significant others) had determined that certain of these traits were undesirable. The majority of the children possessing undesirable traits had developed socially aberrant behavior, while very few of the children with desirable traits had developed aberrant behavior.

On the basis of this study, we may conclude that people who possess culturally desirable traits are relatively unlikely to develop socially deviant behavior but that people who possess culturally undesirable traits are likely to become socially deviant.

To look only at sociological factors in explaining the etiology of socially deviant behavior is as dangerous as looking only at psychological factors or only at biological factors. A person's behavior is a product of his interaction with other people and with his environment. Inadequate interpersonal relationships, biological dysfunction, socially undesirable personality traits, a poorly socialized superego, and the perception that society's norms are ambiguous, weak, or conflicting are all probably involved in the development of socially deviant behavior.

TREATMENT MODALITIES

Before we discuss specific therapies for persons who behave in socially aberrant ways, we need to consider the question of *when* to institute treatment. Because many socially deviant individuals come into conflict with society and are subsequently arrested, they are often considered criminals rather than persons in need of treatment. Factors

that may precipitate the institution of treatment include the following:
1. Confrontation with the law
2. Impaired physical health
3. Medical emergencies
4. Psychiatric emergencies
5. Coercion by family, friends, or employer
6. Disenchantment with one's life-style
7. Desire to change one's life-style

Once a decision to begin treatment has been made, another question arises: *what type of treatment setting is appropriate?* Frequently, because of the medical problems associated with socially aberrant behavior (for example, malnutrition, veneral disease, infection, or personal injury), a general hospital may be chosen. Social deviants usually wish to have their medical problems treated and will cooperate with a medical regimen. Unfortunately, once the medical problems have been corrected, referrals are only infrequently made for psychosocial therapy.

Socially deviant individuals who are transferred to psychiatric treatment centers or who are remanded there by the courts are often poorly motivated to deal with their psychosocial problems. Since rationalization is a mechanism that is used frequently by such persons, they sometimes enter into treatment only half-heartedly. Ulterior motives may be operating. For instance, an addict may seek detoxification in order to reduce the severity of his habit rather than to kick it. A rapist may prefer the ambience of a treatment center to the environment of a jail.

Social deviants who are placed in psychiatric hospitals that also treat psychotic persons may resent being sent to a "booby hatch." In all probability, they not only will try to keep themselves apart from psychotic individuals but also may ridicule and attempt to provoke them.

Specialized treatment centers may be the best setting in which to treat persons who display socially aberrant behavior. In such centers, personnel are trained and experienced in working with specific types of socially deviant individuals. Very often, rehabilitated former offenders constitute part or most of the treatment team. This combination of professionals and former offenders is uniquely able to deal with the dynamics underlying much socially aberrant behavior.

Alternatives to hospitals and specialized treatment centers include such self-help groups as Alcoholics Anonymous, Gamblers Anonymous,

Overeaters Anonymous, and Narcotics Anonymous. The support and intervention offered by these groups have proven effective in helping many socially deviant individuals. Of course, not everyone is a candidate for such a group. Social deviants whose behavior poses serious threats to society cannot safely be treated on a voluntary basis. Self-help groups usually provide a support system that functions 24 hours a day and 7 days a week to help sustain members through the periods of treatment, recovery, and rehabilitation.

Once a decision has been made to treat rather than to jail a socially deviant individual, any combination of the options mentioned may be used.

> Laura was a middle-aged housewife. Her children were grown and had set up households of their own. She complained of feeling "edgy and jumpy." She would begin with one drink each morning to help her get started with her housework. By the time her husband, Jim, came home for dinner, she was usually drunk. Jim recognized that Laura drank too much but he did not want to "humiliate" her by placing her in an alcohol treatment center. Instead he consulted their family doctor, who had been Laura's physician for many years. The doctor told Jim that Laura was very tense and anxious, and he prescribed Valium to help her relax. Laura took the Valium but cut down on her drinking very little.
>
> One day, Jim came home and found Laura hemorrhaging from the mouth. She was rushed to their community hospital, where she underwent detoxification and was treated for esophageal varices, gastritis, and malnutrition.
>
> After her medical problems had been corrected, Laura was sent to a treatment center for alcoholics. There she was helped to recognize that she was cross-addicted to alcohol and Valium. While at the center, weekly Alcoholics Anonymous meetings were held. At discharge, Laura was referred to AA for rehabilitation.

This hypothetical situation demonstrates that a combination of medical, psychological, and social therapy may be indicated in treating socially deviant behavior. Once the decision to initiate treatment has been made, a number of settings may be used: general hospital, psychiatric hospital, specialized treatment center, and self-help groups. It is in these settings that the treatment modalities that facilitate recovery are instituted. We will now explore some of the most frequently used modalities.

Aversion therapy

Aversion therapy, or negative conditioning, makes use of learning theory to cause a person to stop behaving in a socially unacceptable way. Some unpleasant consequence is attached to the undesirable behavior. Aversion therapy is applied in a systematic manner. First, the unwanted behavior is identified. Next, its baseline frequency is established. Then, any environmental factors supporting the behavior are discerned.

A common type of aversion therapy for alcoholism involves the use of the drug disulfiram (Antabuse). Disulfiram remains inert in the body unless alcohol is ingested. Once an alcoholic beverage (or any medicine or food with an ethyl alcohol base) is taken, a physiological reaction, similar to a severe hangover, occurs. The reaction includes throbbing headache, dizziness, nausea, vomiting, facial flushing, heart palpitations, difficult breathing, and blurred vision. These symptoms last for 1 to 2 hours. Disulfiram must be taken regularly to be an effective deterrent to alcoholism. If a person wishes to drink, he simply has to discontinue the use of disulfiram and thereby avoid its effects.

John's employer had given him an ultimatum: either stop drinking or be fired. John decided to enter a veteran's hospital. He had heard about disulfiram and requested it. While he was in the hospital he took the drug regularly. After he was discharged, he continued to take disulfiram. John's job performance and interpersonal relationships improved. However, December came, and with it the office Christmas party. John decided to enter into the Christmas spirit—or should we say "spirits." He discontinued his use of disulfiram so that he would be able to "drink socially." He did not suffer any of the effects of disulfiram, but he did become intoxicated.

Thus there clearly are drawbacks to treatment with disulfiram. The use of the drug can be discontinued at any time. Disulfiram therapy requires self-motivation to be successful.

Aversion therapy is also used in treating compulsive gambling, drug addiction, smoking, and compulsive overeating. A combination of noxious stimuli and verbal imagery has been found to be most effective in cases involving these types of socially undesirable behavior (Seager, Pokorny, and Black, 1966; Goorney, 1968; Hunt and Matarazzo, 1973; Elliott and Denney, 1975; Kingsley and Wilson, 1977).

Aversion therapy is based on the premise that aberrant behavior has been learned and therefore can be unlearned. Nurses are faced with an ethical question: who decides what behavior is "normal" and what behavior is "sick"? Although, ideally, socially deviant individuals participate in this decision, sometimes therapists do not include their clients in the decision-making process. As in any other type of therapy, nurses should be vigilant client advocates. They should be certain that aversion therapy is administered only with a client's informed consent. They should also be alert to any sadistic tendencies in attending therapists.

Aversion therapy has been criticized because it inflicts noxious stimuli on clients without providing opportunities for pleasurable reinforcement of positive behavior. In addition, critics argue, only overt behavior is dealt with: aversion therapists are not concerned with the dynamics underlying behavior.

Proponents of aversion therapy emphasize that such therapy often works in cases in which other types of therapy have failed. They maintain that noxious stimuli are administered only in an attempt to change behavior that both the client and society have defined as unacceptable. Proponents argue that a short period of aversion therapy is preferable to a lifetime of socially unacceptable and inevitably self-destructive behavior.

The ultimate choice must be the client's. Nurses should ensure that candidates for aversion therapy have enough information to be able to weigh the advantages and disadvantages of negative conditioning and to compare it to other available treatments.

Drug therapy

Because of the addictive nature of much socially deviant behavior, the use of drugs as a treatment modality is extremely restricted. Many treatment programs are drug free: no drug, even aspirin, is permitted.

Some drugs have been found to have limited value in the treatment of specific types of acting-out behavior. In the discussion of aversion therapy, the use of disulfiram (Antabuse) for the treatment of alcoholism was mentioned. Two hundred fifty milligrams of disulfiram each day is an average maintenance dose. Disulfiram must be taken daily. Many alcoholics will intentionally discontinue use of the drug so that they can return to drinking. Therefore, motivation for sobriety is very important. If disulfiram therapy is to be effective, concurrent psychotherapy is usually advisable.

People who take disulfiram need to avoid all substances containing ethyl alcohol, including not only alcoholic beverages but many medications, mouthwashes, and food preparations. Even inhaling alcohol fumes can cause a disulfiram reaction.

John had been discharged from an alcohol treatment program. He was taking disulfiram. One day he became violently ill; he had all the symptoms of a disulfiram reaction. He telephoned a counselor at the treatment center and made an appointment for the next day. John swore that he had not been drinking, and the counselor believed him. After discussion and data collection that bordered on detective work, the counselor discovered that John had bought a new mouthwash and had begun using it the day before he became ill. The mouthwash had a high alcohol content. No one had thought to discuss such a potential problem with John before his discharge.

This vignette illustrates the importance of education. It is not enough to dispense medication; a medication's action and side effects, as well as any contingencies affecting the action, should be made known to a client.

Opiate-blocking drugs have been found to be useful in preventing the pleasurable, tension-reducing effects of narcotics. Methadone (Dolophine) and cyclazocine (WIN) are two opiate-blocking agents. Dolophine, the best known of these drugs, is a synthetic opiate. Like an opiate, it is an addicting drug. Treatment based on the administration of dolophine involves the substitution of a legal addiction (to dolophine) for an illegal addiction (to narcotics). Dolophine has two functions. It enables addicts to stop opiate usage without the usual painful withdrawal symptoms, and it helps addicts stay off opiates because they no longer get "high" from them. Dolophine is administered orally. It is long acting and has to be taken only once a day. An average maintenance dose is 140 mg daily. This dosage level effectively eliminates withdrawal symptoms, blocks the pleasurable effects of opiates, and lessens the desire for narcotics.

Dolophine maintenance has been instrumental in the successful treatment of many "hard core" addicts—those who have not responded to other therapies. Many such addicts have been able to resume their normal social roles and to remain gainfully employed. However, because their addictive personality patterns have not been altered, many of these addicts may take non-opiate drugs along with Dolophine. As opponents of treatment through Dolophine maintenance point out, a person using Dolophine is still addicted, even though his addiction is legal. Thus it is important that psychotherapy accompany Dolophine maintenance. Otherwise, addictive personality traits and socially deviant patterns of coping and communicating may remain unchanged.

Group therapy

One of the most commonly used treatment modalities for socially aberrant behavior is group therapy. The utilization of a group approach recognizes the need of socially deviant individuals for group identification.

Many socially deviant persons have not internalized social constraints. Identification with the needs and values of society has not resulted. For example, Barron (1960) maintains that delinquency develops when, in the course of social interaction, a person experiences more situations favorable to antisocial behavior than to socially acceptable behavior. In addition, socially deviant individuals may be unable to function effectively in group situations (Barron, 1960; Yablonsky, 1963).

Because socially deviant individuals demonstrate much hostile and aggressive behavior, they tend to threaten neurotic and psychotic persons. People who display socially aberrant behavior are better able to check one another's behavior than are outsiders. Therefore, socially deviant individuals may be treated more effectively in homogeneous groups than in heterogeneous groups. In a homogeneous group, limits are set by people who are experiencing or have experienced the same difficulties. Such a group setting permits socially deviant individuals to reveal their true selves without fear of retaliation. Authority, restraint, and controls arise from within the group. Because they may be deriving gratification from the group experience, socially deviant persons may begin to submit to group pressure. Satisfying group experiences may ultimately lead to the capacity to become integrated into groups. Rules and norms may be internalized, and, eventually, other people and society may no longer be perceived as antagonistic. (See Chapter 6 for a general discussion of group therapy.)

Social network therapy

A social network is a group of interconnected significant others, both relatives and nonrelatives, with whom a person interacts. Usually only a segment of a network is included in therapy. A small part of a network may be involved, as in couples therapy, or a somewhat larger part of a network may be included, as in family therapy. When a person's entire network is included in the therapeutic process, the process is known as social network therapy. In this type of therapy the support systems of society are utilized in the process of treatment (Speck and

Attneave, 1973). Social network therapy involves the gathering together of client, family, and other significant persons into group sessions for the purpose of problem solving.

Every socially deviant individual has at least one facilitator in his social network. A facilitator may be a wife who calls the office and says her husband is sick when he is really drunk. A facilitator may be a child who assumes the role of parenting younger siblings and thereby enables the mother to spend more time gambling. A facilitator may be a father who closes his nose to the smell of alcohol on his adolescent son's breath. A facilitator may be a friend who suspects his "buddy" is a rapist but does not want to get him into trouble. Facilitators may be of any age, of either sex, and of any relationship to a socially deviant person. Facilitators make it easier for people to engage in socially deviant behavior.

Socially aberrant behavior involves other people. Many of the patterns of communication and coping that are apparent in a socially deviant individual may be subtly present in some of his network members.

Matthew was in his final year of a nursing program. His college performance had always been poor. At one point, he had been failing a course and had decided to withdraw from it and repeat it at a later time.

Each time Matthew was offered academic counseling he would refuse it. He would insist that his present academic performance was good. He would blame past academic difficulties on personality clashes between himself and his instructors, but he would always add that his present instructor was "really good—cares about students." Matthew would then recount in detail his current nursing experiences. He would sound enthusiastic, knowledgeable, and sincere. By the time he left his advisor's office, his advisor would be questioning her own judgment. Was she making too much of past performance? Was she overlooking Matthew's ability to change? It certainly sounded as though he now had the situation under control. He always promised to return if problems arose. Then the semester's grades would come in, and he would again be on probation.

During his senior year, which involved a work-study experience, Matthew demonstrated unsafe nursing practices. Both Matthew's instructor and the hospital staff were in agreement. When confronted with this inadequacy, Matthew talked about the head nurse's dislike of him and about how she had influenced the rest of the staff. Matthew rationalized that it was almost impossible to perform under such pressure. He also became enraged at the head nurse for not evaluating his performance sooner. The head nurse insisted that she had spoken to him on several occasions. He accused her of lying.

Matthew's nursing instructor advised him to withdraw from the course before he failed it. He would then be eligible to repeat the course the following semester. The instructor also suggested that since he experienced so many personality conflicts he should consider psychotherapy. He became infuriated with the instructor. A few days later, Matthew's mother came to the university. She was enraged at the treatment her son had received, and she threatened to sue both the school and the head nurse. She explained that Matthew had worked very hard to get through the nursing program. "Even during the semester that he had to withdraw from that course, Matthew left the house at the same time each day so that his father would not suspect anything." Matthew had "conned" his father, and his mother had facilitated the deception.

When Matthew's mother realized that no amount of talk or threats would change the situation, she tried bribery. She said that if Matthew would be permitted to participate in the graduation ceremony, he would withdraw from the course and there would not be a lawsuit. This way no one, including Matthew's father, would have to know what had happened.

Matthew was obviously making use of deviant patterns of coping and communicating. He was charming, cunning, and manipulative; he engaged in rationalization and denial. Matthew's mother mirrored many of these mechanisms. Aberrant patterns of communicating and coping are often found in various members of a socially deviant person's network.

In addition, socially deviant individuals often precipitate problems in their social networks. For instance, a parent who feels guilty about a child's socially aberrant behavior may project this guilt onto a spouse. Conflict may develop between husband and wife. Couples therapy may be indicated. If one or both of a child's parents are socially deviant, the child may suffer role confusion and have difficulty finding role models who demonstrate socially acceptable behavior. Family therapy may be indicated. These are some of the problems that members of a socially deviant individual's social network might experience.

To date, therapy has focused on the socially deviant individual (individual therapy), on his relationship with his spouse (couples therapy), or on his relationship with his family (family therapy). Little has been done to implement a total social network approach. Yet social network therapy is essential to the treatment of socially aberrant behavior. Socially deviant individuals may not have internalized the standards of society. Since these values and ways of behaving are normally taught by family members and significant others, total network therapy includes both the family and these significant others. A social network is a microcosm of society. Social network therapy views the network as an open system.

Social network therapy should be designed to assist socially deviant individuals and their network members to cope with socially aberrant behavior. The purposes of network therapy may be summarized as follows:

1. To assess a socially deviant individual's communication patterns
2. To modify network patterns of communication (such as facilitating) that support a member's socially deviant behavior
3. To help a socially deviant individual's social network serve as a reference group for socially acceptable behavior
4. To facilitate a socially deviant individual's reentry into the community.

In most cases, the client and the members of his social network should meet together, but there may be times when network members will attend therapy sessions without the client being present. Special organizations, such as Alanon and Alateen, have been designed to help network members cope with the destructive and unacceptable behavior of a socially deviant individual.

Allison, a student nurse, was receiving poor grades. She did not hand assignments in on time, and she frequently fell asleep in class. She developed a good relationship with one of her teachers, to whom she revealed that she had many family problems. Allison's father was an alcoholic, and her mother was schizophrenic. Allison had two younger brothers. The 16-year-old was "running around with a loose group and drinking." The 12-year-old seemed well adjusted. Allison was trying to hold the family together, straighten out her 16-year-old brother, and protect the 12-year-old. She had assumed the parenting role. Allison had not spoken about her situation with anyone except her teacher. She was afraid that if her classmates knew about her parents, they would not want to associate with her.

Allison's teacher referred her to Alateen, where she was helped to express her feelings of guilt and anger. She also learned that her situation was not unique and that many adolescents were in similar predicaments. Allison learned that while she could not change her family's behavior, she could change the way she reacted. She found the Alateen group very supportive.

Educational therapy

People who behave in socially aberrant ways usually suffer from inadequate group identification and low self-esteem. Educational and vocational training programs offer opportunities for such persons to build self-esteem and to direct energy into socially acceptable channels (Winchester, 1972). Educational therapy also provides information that can facilitate personal and occupational adjustment.

Educational therapy should involve more than the teaching of subject matter. In an attempt to help socially deviant individuals reconstruct their lives, educational therapists should help clients to look at past failures in school and to ascertain what contributed to those failures. In this way, those experiences can provide opportunities for learning and growth. Educational therapy often also includes instruction in such personal matters as grooming, dress, and etiquette.

> Lisa, an adolescent girl, had been admitted to a drug treatment center. She had been doing poorly in school and thought of herself as a "dummy." She planned to drop out of school as soon as it was legally permissible. The treatment team decided that Lisa was definitely a candidate for educational therapy. While at the drug center, Lisa not only attended daily classes but also received tutoring in subjects of special weakness. She was shown how to budget study time, how to take notes, and how to outline chapters. In addition, she was placed in a personal development group that included other adolescent girls. With the assistance of a nurse, the group regularly discussed clothing styles and experimented with hairstyles and cosmetics. By the time Lisa was ready to leave the center, she felt able to return to junior high school and was confident that she could at least pass her courses. She also felt more comfortable with her appearance.

Many socially deviant individuals are children, adolescents and young adults. The preceding vignette shows how educational therapy can be designed to facilitate their social and adademic reentry into society.

Meditation therapy

Transcendental meditation is one way of achieving relaxation and consciousness expansion. A client is asked to focus his thoughts on a "mantra" (a word, a sound, or an image) and to relax. Some research on transcendental meditation indicates that it may be helpful in treating alcoholism and drug abuse. Studies have found that a large percentage of the people who practiced transcendental meditation over a 20-month period significantly reduced drug and alcohol consumption. Interviews with study participants indicated that because transcendental meditation reduced anxiety and tension and produced a sense of general well-being, the need for drug-induced experiences was diminished (Marzetta, Benson, and Wallace, 1972; Benson and Wallace, 1972). More research is needed to determine the validity of meditation as a treatment modality for socially deviant behavior.

Milieu therapy

A therapeutic community* is a form of milieu therapy. A therapeutic community attempts to correct socially deviant behavior and to prepare residents for reentry into society. Every activity is designed to teach residents to live by society's standards and to function in a socially acceptable manner. A therapeutic community serves as a real-life reference group. As one resident of such a community explained,

> We use a yardstick approach here. We figure that most of the people in society function at 24 inches. We try to bring ourselves up to 36 inches because we know when we leave here we'll slip back a little. But even with slipping back we'll be okay.

This "yardstick approach" explains why, in a therapeutic community for socially deviant persons, exacting behavior is expected and infraction of rules carries heavy penalties. A resident who does not clean his room may have to wear a sign that says "I'm a slob." A resident whose attitude is manipulative or sullen may verbally be "blown away." A resident who runs away from the community and then wants to return may receive a "haircut"—his head may literally be shaved as a constant reminder of his immature behavior. These measures are taken to inculcate society's values and norms into people who have been operating outside society's rule system. Society may expect its members to function at "24 inches," but because a socially deviant individual may start out with little or no social conscience, he has to be brought up to "36 inches."

A therapeutic community serves an important function in the treatment of people who are socially deviant. However, as in any treatment modality, problems may arise. Leone and Zahourek (1974) talk about the reentry shock that may accompany discharge from a therapeutic community. Life in a therapeutic community is characterized by group interaction and group activity. As much as 83% of a resident's time may be spent with other people. After leaving a therapeutic community, many former residents live alone and spend much time by themselves. Their lives may be characterized by "aloneness," which can be either a positive or a negative experience. When used for psychic rejuvenation and pleasure, aloneness is a growing experience. When it is marked by physical and emotional isolation, it becomes a regressive experience.

---

*See Chapter 6 for a general discussion of milieu therapy and the therapeutic community.

One way of not having to deal with aloneness and reentry into society is to become totally dependent on a therapeutic community. Synanon, for example, encourages such dependence (Yablonsky and Dederich, 1965; Deissler, 1970). Synanon bases its approach on the premise "once an addict, always an addict." Since an addict can never be "cured," he must live out his life in a setting in which he can have the support system of a therapeutic community. Synanon constructs new social networks for addicts. Former addicts are not encouraged to reenter society and to integrate themselves into their old social networks. When former addicts leave Synanon, they are expected to maintain close contact with the organization. Synanon has constructed Synanon City to house many former addicts. This ultimate extension of the organization into the lives of former addicts defeats the primary goal of a therapeutic community—reentry into society. It raises the question of whether Synanon's approach can be considered therapeutic.

Frequently, the staff of a therapeutic community for socially deviant persons is composed entirely of former offenders. Professionals may only be tangentially involved. The rationale for such a staffing policy includes three elements:

1. Former offenders have experienced the problem and have overcome it. They therefore can serve as role models.
2. Since former offenders have used all the mechanisms common to socially deviant behavior, they can recognize and confront these mechanisms in newcomers.
3. Former offenders are considered peers by residents of a therapeutic community. Structure, challenge, confrontation, and discipline are more readily accepted when meted out by peers.

Many socially deviant individuals have become expert manipulators. Some are highly skilled at manipulating groups and have even been "gang" leaders. Most professionals do not have this kind of personal history. Professional education often focuses more on intervention with individuals than on intervention with groups. Many professionals have not learned confrontation techniques. Therefore, a former offender is often better able to deal with socially aberrant behavior than is a health professional.

•   •   •

Socially deviant individuals may be treated in a variety of treatment settings and with a variety of treatment modalities. The goals of therapy are to supplant socially aberrant behavior with socially acceptable behavior and to facilitate reentry into society. Although nurses may not directly participate in all treatment modalities, they do participate in all levels of preventive intervention: primary, secondary and tertiary.

NURSING INTERVENTION

The behavior of socially deviant individuals often challenges a nurse's value system. Frequently, such persons not only resist treatment but also attack the treatment process. They may try to "con" their therapists and "work" the system. In view of these difficulties, what qualities should nurses who work with these people possess?

First, nurses should be *nondefensive.* They should expect that socially deviant individuals may question, argue against, and reject society's values and standards. It is through socially aberrant behavior that such persons try to cope with tension and conflict. Once nurses understand the dynamics underlying socially aberrant behavior, they will find it easier to be less defensive.

Second, nurses should be *accepting but firm.* Socially deviant individuals tend to resist treatment and do not readily ask for help. Often, the ways in which they try to communicate and cope alienate other people. Socially deviant individuals may try to charm, cajole, con, or dupe nurses. While it is necessary to set firm limits on such patterns of behavior, it is also important not to reject a person. Nurses can be ac-

cepting without condoning behavior; they can be firm without being punitive. Kimsey (1969) found that it is vital for therapists to assume a mature, "adult" role, rather than a peer role, if they are to teach impulse control and foster socially acceptable behavior.

Ruesch (1961) suggests that therapists find concrete ways to show concern and interest in socially deviant clients. Concern and interest may be demonstrated by treating somatic complaints or by alleviating stress-provoking situations. After such initial concrete demonstration of concern, therapists should be careful to avoid encouraging dependence. A socially deviant individual often tries to con his therapist into doing things for him. Every effort should be made to encourage self-reliant behavior.

Finally, nurses need to be *realistic* about the course of therapy. In the treatment of socially deviant individuals, relapses are common. For instance, alcoholics may "go on the wagon" only to begin drinking a few months later. Drug addicts may undergo detoxification but later revert to drug abuse. Compulsive eaters may diet and lose weight only to regain it later. The course of recovery for socially deviant individuals is often marked by periods of improvement and relapse. Once nurses recognize that this pattern is not uncommon and that it is often a prelude to true recovery, they are less apt to respond with anger and disappointment. They may be able to help socially deviant individuals identify stressors that precipitate relapses to socially aberrant behavior and thereby prevent them.

PRIMARY PREVENTION

Socially aberrant behavior patterns may be traced back to adolescence or to even earlier periods. It is during these periods that a social conscience is developed. Social networks in general and family systems in particular are primary socializing agents. These agents form the matrix for the internalization or the noninternalization of society's rules and value systems. Rules and value systems influence and are influenced by the prevailing social climate. For example, during times of social strain, society may stress certain standards of behavior, but the existing social structure may make it difficult for a person to act in accordance with those standards. A contradictory rule system or a disjunction between socially sanctioned goals and access to legitimized ways to achieve the goals may result. This situation is known as social strain or anomie. When social networks and family systems operate within a milieu of social strain, children may either *learn* socially unacceptable behavior or *fail to learn* socially acceptable behavior. They may grow into adulthood without developing social con-

sciences. The alleviation of conditions that produce crime (such as poverty, unemployment, and overcrowding) and the strengthening of family systems are essential elements in the primary prevention of social deviance (Minuchin, 1967; Ruben, 1972).

Only in recent years has socially aberrant behavior come to be viewed as a psychosocial problem. Emphasis is now being placed on treatment rather than on punishment. Such a wide range of disorders is included in socially aberrant behavior that no one cause can be singled out. The consensus is that the etiology of social deviance is multifactorial and that a multifactorial approach therefore needs to be taken in primary prevention. Several factors may predispose a person to socially aberrant behavior:

1. A family history of social deviance
2. Loss of one or both parents (through death, noninvolvement, or separation)
3. Brutality by parents
4. Parental psychopathology
5. A disorganized sociocultural environment (characterized by overcrowding, poverty, inadequate housing, and poor job opportunities) (Roth, 1972; Rubin, 1972)

However, not everyone with such risk factors in his background develops socially aberrant behavior. What are the implications of this fact for primary prevention? The primary prevention of social deviance involves two goals:

1. To minimize the effects of predisposing factors

2. To find ways to prevent high-risk individuals from becoming socially deviant and then to use this information to prevent others from developing socially aberrant behavior

Nurses can implement these goals by identifying high-risk individuals, initiating parental and family counseling, and modifying the social environment.

Identification of high-risk individuals. Reiner and Kaufman (1959) believe that a high percentage of families known to social agencies display extreme degrees of social deviance in their family and community interactions. These families usually are disorganized. One or both parents may be absent. If parents are present, they may be only marginally functional.

Community health nurses and school nurse–teachers work with families and observe family interactions. As nurses become more intimately involved with families, they are better able to identify important risk factors. If nurses are not knowledgeable, they may fail to recognize risk factors or may be unable to make appropriate referrals for treatment.

Parental counseling. Early exposure to parental brutality has been associated with the development of socially aberrant behavior in children. From a feared parent figure, children often internalize socially unacceptable characteristics. In fact, parents who are child abusers and who display identifiable social aberrations usually have histories of having been battered as children

themselves (Rubin, 1972). In addition, Myrna Weissman (1972) has found that socially deviant individuals often had depressed mothers. Depressed women may be unable to appropriately express their anger and may instead direct it toward their children.

Public health nurses, school nurse–teachers, and child health nurses need to be alert for symptoms of maternal depression and signs of child battering. Intervention at an early stage may prevent the development of socially aberrant behavior.

Women who appear lethargic, apathetic, indecisive, hopeless, and helpless and who complain of anorexia, weight loss, insomnia, amenorrhea, and constipation may be suffering from *maternal depression.** A nurse who recognizes this syndrome of maternal depression in a woman should refer her for therapy. Since a depressed person usually does not have the energy—physical or emotional—to ask for help or to initiate contact with a helping person, nurses need to enlist the support of family and social networks. Nurses should assess the potential of the woman and of her family to make the initial contact. If the family needs assistance, then help should be offered. In addition, nurses need to acquaint family and/or network members with the mother's depressed state, with her inability to handle anger, and with the possible need to protect children from mis-

---

*Refer to Chapter 11 for a general discussion of depression and nursing intervention for it.

directed angry outbursts. This intervention should be carried out with the mother's knowledge and, when possible, approval. Since all therapeutic relationships should be structured on the basis of qualified confidentiality—the principle that only in the event of potential harm to the client or to others will confidential material be divulged, and then only to appropriate persons—the question of breach of confidentiality should not arise.

Child abuse should be suspected when a child repeatedly has fractured bones, soft-tissue swelling, welts, subdural hematomas, bruises, or abrasions. In most cases of child abuse, the degree and type of injury do not correspond with parental explanations of how the "accident" occurred.

> Miriam and Jack were the parents of three children, aged 5 years, 3 years, and 3 months. The 3-month-old baby was a boy, Jackie Jr. Jackie physically resembled his father. Following the birth of Jackie, Miriam had become very depressed and was experiencing difficulty fulfilling her roles as wife and mother.
>
> Jack's employment pattern had been sporadic, and the family was living on unemployment benefits. Jack was preoccupied with looking for a job. He offered little emotional support or child-rearing assistance to Miriam.
>
> One day while Miriam was bathing Jackie, a public health nurse unexpectedly visited. Although Miriam hurredly dried and dressed Jackie, the nurse noticed what appeared to be burns on Jackie's back. Miriam explained the burns by saying that she often smoked while bathing the baby: "Ashes from my cigarette must have fallen on his back."

Child abuse may develop when a parent has inadequate support in the parenting role. An abusing parent is usually isolated from a supportive social network and is not receiving support from the marital relationship. Such a parent may have unrealistically high developmental expectations for a child and may become frustrated and angry when, at a young age, the child cannot be toilet trained, for example, or feed himself. In addition, many abusing parents have themselves been abused as children and have not personally experienced parental nurturing (Smith and Hanson, 1975).

Nurses who suspect battering need to assess parental attitudes. Accurate and well-documented records are also important. The name of anyone who has witnessed the abuse of a child should be noted in such records. Most importantly, suspected instances of child abuse should be reported to appropriate legal or social service agencies. Efforts need to be made to protect a child from further abuse. This may mean moving a child to a safe environment. In addition, abusing parents should be offered opportunities for treatment. Besides traditional psychotherapy, self-help groups composed of abusing parents are springing up in many communities (Collins, 1978). Since child-abusing parents often have low self-esteem, nonsupportive marital relationships, and unrealistically high developmental expectations of their children, treatment should focus on these areas. Ways should be explored to improve parental self-esteem, to develop a relationship of support and assistance between spouses, to educate parents about childhood growth and development, and to explore with parents alternative methods for coping with their children's disruptive behavior. The abused child is not the sole problem in the family relationship but represents a much larger problem: dysfunction in the family system.

Family counseling. Family disorganization predisposes a person to the development of socially aberrant behavior. Disorganized households are often characterized by insufficient income, food, fuel, and clothing. There may be instability regarding place of residence, time of meals, child-rearing practices, and interpersonal relationships. Because disorganized households may lack adequate space and furniture, families may be unable to eat meals together. Minuchin (1967) emphasizes that disorganized families usually attempt to control and inhibit their children's annoying behavior rather than try to consistently guide children and teach them socially acceptable behavior. Bad behavior is punished, but good behavior is rarely rewarded. Children in such families may soon learn to respond to parental moods and parental discipline (external controls), but they may not learn to develop internal controls or social consciences. These children frequently react with aggression and display socially aberrant behavior.

Nurses need to help disorganized families on several levels. If such families are not already involved with social service agencies, referrals should be made. If disorganized families are involved with social service agencies, it is very probable that they are experiencing difficulties in their relationships with the agencies. The agencies may be handling the families in a way that provokes feelings of frustration, anger, alienation, and avoidance. Nurses should assist these families to communicate with the social service agencies, and vice versa.

Because the social deviance of one member is usually reflected in or facilitated by the rest of the family, families may need to learn more effective and socially acceptable ways to communicate. Parents may need to develop some sense of their own self-worth. Parents may also need to learn socially acceptable child-rearing practices.

Modification of sociocultural environment. Leighton (1954) has discussed the correlation between community disorganization and socially deviant behavior. Inner cities experiencing widespread overcrowding and poverty and ethnic enclaves undergoing acculturation are examples of disorganized communities. Disorganized communities may be marked by broken homes, inadequate leadership, and frequent occurrences of violence, delinquency, and other forms of socially aberrant behavior. When neighborhoods begin to deteriorate, surrounding neighborhoods usually close their boundaries. Attempts may be made to keep ghetto residents in the ghetto. At the same time, there is usually a reduced flow of goods and services to the disorganized communities. The extent and condition of communication and transportation systems in ghetto areas may also be poor. Street maintenance, public transportation systems, and public telephones may be allowed to deteriorate. Buildings may fall into disrepair. Hallways, playgrounds, and streets may become extremely unsafe. In such disorganized communities, it is fairly common for abandoned buildings to become havens for youth gangs, "winos," and junkies (Freedman, 1975; Ashcraft and Scheflen, 1976).

Friends and relatives of persons who live in deteriorating communities are usually afraid to travel into the communities. At the same time, residents may not want to leave their neighborhoods. They may worry about what will happen to their apartments while they are away, or they may fear traveling on neighborhood streets after dark. Decreased interpersonal contact and bond servicing* erodes social networks. In addition, immigrants who live in inner-city ghettos usually have left supportive social networks in foreign lands and often find it difficult to develop new networks.

For residents of disorganized communities, scarcity of goods and services usually coexists wtih social isolation and alienation. Overcrowding, poverty, and scarcity of resources—all characteristics of disorganized neighborhoods—are inextricably associated with socially deviant behavior. Nurses, as concerned citizens and as client advocates, need to militate for social change. When fiscal budgets are streamlined, money for social services is

usually cut. Yet this type of economizing usually contributes to further disintegration of already disorganized communities. Social changes that prevent neighborhood disintegration or improve living conditions are essential components of primary prevention of socially deviant behavior.

A comprehensive approach to primary prevention of socially aberrant behavior is necessary. Since social deviance has many interrelated causes, only a multifactorial primary prevention program will be effective. Such a strategy has been used by one Eskimo community in Labrador, Canada.

> In 1960 it became legal for Eskimos to buy and consume alcohol. Alcoholism, especially spree drinking, became a community problem. Community leaders developed a four-pronged attack on the problem. Bars were forbidden to sell alcohol for home consumption; people who wanted to buy liquor for home consumption had to place their orders 3 weeks in advance; educational programs about alcoholism were developed and implemented; and laws against public drunkenness were strictly enforced. This comprehensive program effectively changed both the community's accepting attitude toward alcoholism and the pattern of spree drinking (Wilkinson, 1970).

Such a multifaceted approach, encompassing a range of strategies, is necessary for an effective program of primary prevention.

SECONDARY PREVENTION

What is the secondary level of prevention for people who display so-

---

*Refer to Chapter 5 for a discussion of bond servicing and interpersonal relationships.

cially deviant behavior? In the discussion of secondary prevention, two aspects will be stressed: case finding and direct intervention.

Case finding. Nurses—especially public health nurses, school nurse–teachers, occupational health nurses, and staff nurses in general hospitals–have unparalleled opportunities for case finding. Socially deviant individuals more readily seek help for physical problems, which may or may not be associated with their socially aberrant behavior, than for psychosocial problems.

Children. Rubin (1972) describes a childhood triad of behavior—firesetting, bedwetting, and cruelty to animals. When these types of behaviors appear *in combination* and *consistently*, some degree of socially aberrant behavior may be present.

> Johnny, a 7-year-old boy, was brought to the emergency room of a general hospital. Both his hands were severely burned. While taking a nursing history, the emergency room nurse discovered that this was not the first time that Johnny had "played with matches." Further exploration of his behavior revealed repeated enuresis and cruelty to animals. Both of Johnny's parents were concerned about his behavior.
> Once Johnny's burns were treated, the emergency room nurse referred him and his parents to the hospital's clinical nurse specialist. The clinical nurse specialist suspected that Johnny's actions were indicative of early antisocial behavior. Although this community hospital did not offer family therapy, the clinical nurse specialist gave the family the names of three local agencies that did offer family therapy. He helped the family make the initial

appointment. Three weeks later, he telephoned the parents to ascertain how they were managing. They confirmed that they had begun family therapy.

Separate and occasional appearances of any of the three types of behavior are often part of normal growth and development. However, when they appear in combination and consistently, they may indicate antisocial tendencies.

Nurses can be involved in early case finding and referral for treatment. Follow-up work to determine that referrals are being acted upon, to reinforce the need for treatment, and to facilitate contact with appropriate agencies are also important nursing functions.

Adolescents and adults. The presence of the following cluster of behavior in adolescents and adults may be indicative of emerging social deviance:
1. Violent outbursts against oneself and/or others
2. Repeated criminal behavior
3. History of poor work or school performance
4. Unsafe and aggressive automobile driving
5. Substance abuse or addiction
6. Repeated suicidal attempts (Bach-y-Rita, 1971; Roth, 1972)

In combination, these types of behavior express the interrelated dynamics of hostility, manipulation, alienation, anomie, poor judgment, and inability to learn from previous experience. These core mechanisms underlie and are manifested in most socially aberrant behavior. Once nurses recognize predictor or indicator behavior patterns, they can identify emerging social deviance and make appropriate referrals.

An occupational health nurse noticed that Mr. McCabe frequently called in sick on Mondays. His work performance during the rest of the week was sporadic. Mr. McCabe worked conscientiously in the morning, but in the afternoon he became lackadaisical about his work and irritable with his co-workers. During the past few months Mr. McCabe had experienced a number of minor industrial accidents. Each accident had occurred in the afternoon.

The occupational health nurse suspected that Mr. McCabe had a drinking problem. By observing his behavior and talking with him, the nurse confirmed this diagnosis. Mr. McCabe drank several beers with his lunch and took frequent afternoon work breaks for additional beers. He drank heavily on weekends "to relax and forget the rat race."

Mr. McCabe was told that if he did not seek treatment he would be fired. At the same time, he was assured that if he completed a treatment program his job would be waiting for him. The occupational health nurse helped Mr. McCabe find an appropriate treatment program.

This vignette illustrates how nurses may be able to identify incipient alcoholics (people who are still able to maintain some degree of control over their drinking behavior) and refer them for treatment. By involving alcoholics in treatment programs at this early stage, when they are still able to function in the community, nurses may prevent chronic alcoholism.

The Civil Service Commission (1971) has established a federal civilian employee alcoholism program. This program

1. defines alcoholism as an illness that directly affects job performance.
2. stresses that employees who are alcoholics should receive the same thoughtful attention and assistance received by employees suffering from other illnesses.
3. emphasizes that alcholic employees have the same right to medical record confidentiality that any other employees have.
4. urges that alcoholic employees requesting sick leave for treatment be given the same consideration as employees requesting sick leave for other illnesses.
5. stresses that employee requests for counseling or referral to alcohol treatment programs should not threaten job security.
6. emphasizes that all information, referral, or counseling should be provided on a confidential basis.

In their role as client advocates, nurses in occupational health settings need to be aware of these guidelines and to be active in implementing them. These guidelines can be adapted and applied to intervention in other settings and in situations involving other types of socially deviant behaviors.

Nursing responses to behavioral problems

Interpersonal themes. One predominant theme in the interpersonal relationships of many socially deviant individuals is *manipulation*. A socially deviant person may appear charming and ingratiating; he may try to identify with or flatter his therapist. These are attempts at manipulation.

Socially deviant individuals tend to perceive the loci of reward and control as being outside themselves. Therefore, they often do not accept responsibility for their behavior. They displace this responsibility onto people and things in the environment. When things go wrong, other people are at fault. Instead of recognizing the consequences of their own actions, socially deviant persons tend to *rationalize* and to engage in *blame placing*.

According to Sullivan (1953), low self-esteem* underlies all manipulative behavior. People with low self-esteem do not feel good about themselves and cannot feel good about others. This sense of worthlessness generates anxiety. Socially deviant individuals channel this anxiety into exploitative behavior.

Nursing intervention in cases of manipulative behavior involves two goals: increase self-esteem and teach socially deviant individuals to rely on themselves. Nursing intervention should be based on an awareness that exploitation arouses anxiety and hostility in the people being exploited. These feelings may lead to rejection of socially deviant individuals. Nurses should work with the entire health team in recognizing and discouraging the use of manipulative behavior. If the health team is consistent in refusing to be used, a manipulative person will have to learn other ways of interacting with people.

---

*At this point it may be useful to refer to Chapter 11 and the discussion of dynamics of low self-esteem.

The following are ways in which nurses can facilitate the learning of new, nonmanipulative behavior:
1. Practice nonreinforcement of any attempted manipulation.
   a. Identify manipulative behavior.
   b. Set limits on manipulative behavior.
   c. Communicate to the client what behavior is expected.
   d. Explain reasons for limits that have been set.
   e. Enforce these limits.
   f. Encourage the client to express his feelings about the limits.
   g. Evaluate with the client the effectiveness of the limits.
   h. Assist the client to establish his own limits.
2. Help the individual acknowledge that he uses and takes advantage of others.
   a. Explore the client's preception of how needs are gratified.
   b. Discuss ways in which other people gratify their needs.
   c. Point out instances in which the client uses rationalization and blame placing.
   d. Point out instances in which the client tries to con people.
3. Help the individual recognize that manipulation is not an effective way of coping or interacting.
   a. Point out instances of poor judgment and failure to learn from experience.
   b. Explore the damaging ef-

fects of manipulation on interpersonal relationships.

   c. Explore the client's feelings when he perceives that others may be trying to manipulate him.

4. Assist the individual to develop alternative, constructive and nonmanipulative ways to approach his problems and needs.

   a. Help him identify personal strengths and effective communication skills.

   b. Help him develop new skills and abilities.

5. Support the individual while he tests out his new, nonmanipulative approach to life.

6. Help him evaluate the effectiveness of this new behavior.

7. Remind the individual when he is slipping back into manipulative patterns.

When clients use ingratiation and charm, nurses or other team members may not recognize that they are being manipulated.

> Mrs. Graff, who had been admitted to a hospital with drug-related hepatitis, was very charming and witty. She confided to one of the nurses, "You are the only one in this hospital who treats me like a person. All the other nurses try to avoid me. They don't like me very much." The nurse was flattered by this comment. Even though he did not approve of Mrs. Graff's drug abuse, he felt that of all the staff, he alone was able to relate to Mrs. Graff as a person. In an attempt to compensate for the rejecting attitudes of the other nurses, he tried to be available to Mrs. Graff and to comply with her requests. One day over coffee, several nurses began discussing Mrs. Graff's feeling of rejection. They discovered that Mrs. Graff had told each of them that the other nurses were avoiding her and that he or she was the only nurse who cared. Each had felt flattered and had responded by going out of the way to give Mrs. Graff extra attention.

Thus, when nurses fail to recognize manipulation, they may unwittingly reinforce it.

When nurses or other team members do recognize manipulative tendencies in clients, they sometimes respond defensively. They may begin to see manipulation in the actions of all clients, or they may reject or show hostility toward manipulative clients. If a staff member possesses manipulative tendencies, he or she may try to manipulate the client and rationalize that the client is "being taught a lesson" or "being given a dose of his own medicine." It is important for nurses and other health team members to be aware of these possible responses to manipulative clients. Such responses may reinforce a client's sense of low self-esteem and increase his need to engage in exploitive behavior.

Most nurses explain to clients that confidential material is shared with other health team members. This sharing minimizes client manipulation of staff and facilitates consistency in approach among staff members.

Alienation and *anomie* are also frequent themes in the life-styles of socially deviant individuals. Alienation is a failure in reciprocal connectedness between an individual and his environment. Alienation is experienced as a sense of estrangement of self from others. Out of this loose social integration and impoverished inter-personal matrix anomie develops.

Srole (1956) uses a continuum to describe alienation and anomie. On one end is a sense of belonging. On the other end is a sense of alienation. Between these opposites are various degrees of distance between oneself and others. Personality factors interrelate with elements of societal dysfunction to produce anomie. Socially deviant individuals often are alienated and view society's rule system as something that exists to be broken.

The goal of nursing therapy for alienated and anomic clients is twofold: to build a sense of relatedness to others (rapport) and to facilitate the internalization of social norms. Consistency, acceptance, and firmness are keys to implementing these goals.

Nurses should be consistent in approach, and they should be consistent in setting and reinforcing limits. In conjunction with the rest of the health team, nurses should be consistent in sanctioning socially acceptable behavior and constraining socially unacceptable behavior. The message to a client should be clear: it is not you, but rather your behavior, that is unacceptable.

A structured setting, with opportunities for gradual increases in independence, facilitates the learning of socially acceptable behavior. Violation of rules should result in firm and consistent penalties. Step by step, the socially deviant individual should be taught to live within society's rule system. As his behavior becomes more acceptable and he demonstrates a sense of responsibility for his behavior, he should be allowed more opportunity for independence.

A unit for socially deviant adolescents used a card system to reinforce socially acceptable behavior. The unit's environment was highly structured; strict adherence to routine and rules was required. When an adolescent was admitted to the unit, he had no privileges. Through the card system, privileges could be earned. Card 1 meant that an adolescent could use free periods (nontherapy periods) for activities of his choice. Card 2 carried grounds privileges: during free periods an adolescent could go outside unaccompanied by a staff member and could participate in sports, take walks, or lounge about. Card 3 carried weekend privileges: it allowed an adolescent to go home for weekends.

Just as cards could be earned for socially acceptable behavior, they could be lost for socially deviant behavior. If a card was taken away, a nurse would discuss the reasons for the penalty with the adolescent. The possibility of rearning the card and the behavior required to accomplish this were discussed. In this way, an adolescent was made aware of his socially disapproved behavior and of the penalty accompanying it. At the same time, the nurse did not reject the adolescent as a person.

Because many socially deviant individuals have not internalized society's standards, nurses often find their own attitudes and values are under assault. For instance, a nurse who has been raised to be law-abiding and considerate of others may react to the alienation and anomie of a client with rejection, anger, derogation, or moralizing. Nurses should try, with the aid of peer supervision, to clarify their own values and attitudes.* In this way, they may gain greater insight into their own behavior and may be better able to therapeutically intervene in the cases of alienated and anomic clients.

Hostility is a state of animosity. It develops slowly and dissipates slowly. Unlike anger, hostility does not generate measurable autonomic responses.

When a socially deviant client is confronted with his behavior, he usually responds with evasiveness, denial, or anger. This response serves the dual purpose of venting hostility and focusing attention away from himself.

Hostility functions as a coping mechanism by reducing anxiety associated with threats to security. If a socially deviant individual is confronted with his hostile feelings before he is ready to deal with them, he may become increasingly anxious, deny his hostility, and displace his hostility onto people or objects in his environment.

Hostility is expressed *indirectly*, and it may be aimed at either animate or inanimate objects. Because hostility is not directly expressed, it is not easily depleted. Hostility under-

lies socially deviant behavior, and society is often the object of the hostility.

The goal of nursing intervention is threefold:

1. Help the individual realize that he feels hostile.
   a. Be alert for indirect expressions (clues) of hostility, and point them out to the client. You might say, "You sound upset about . . ." or "You seem annoyed with . . .."
   b. Encourage the client to validate your assessment of hostility: "Yes, I feel annoyed" or "No, I'm not upset.
2. Help the individual identify and describe the object of his hostility.
   a. Because many socially deviant individuals have difficulty verbalizing their feelings, activity therapy may be used to facilitate the expression of hostility.
   b. Assist the client to gradually verbalize his hostile feelings and the object of his hostility.
3. Help the individual learn to express hostility in a socially acceptable manner.
   a. Explore with the client alternative ways of dealing with hostile feelings. For example, activities such as gardening, tennis, and woodworking channel hostile energy into socially acceptable behavior.
   b. Support the client as he tries out new coping behavior.

---

*Refer to Chapter 2 for a discussion of attitude clarification.

c. Assist the client in evaluating the effectiveness of new coping behavior.

Because hostility is often unconscious, many people find it very difficult to express. Nurses may easily recognize overt hostility (such as sarcasm, vulgarity, or physical acting out) but may fail to recognize covert hostility (such as excessive politeness, obsequiousness, or ingratiation.) Nurses should also realize that what socially deviant clients initially identify as the objects of their hostility may not be what actually bothers them.

Hostility, like anxiety, can be communicated from person to person. A nurse may begin to feel hostile toward a client, or a nurse may become so caught up in a client's hostility that he or she begins to feel hostile toward the object of the client's hostility.

Many nurses may be unaccustomed to acknowledging their own hostile feelings. They may fear the repercussions of dealing with their hostility. They may repress hostility, or they may try to diffuse it through griping. Occasionally, nurses may be fearful of hostile feelings in themselves or others. This apprehension may interfere with a client's expression of hostility.

A student nurse who was working with a socially deviant individual began to realize that hostility was one of the client's predominant interpersonal themes. Although the student frequently assured the client that it was "all right to feel hostile" and encouraged him to talk about his hostile feelings, the client continued to deny any feelings of hostility. An instructor helped the student nurse look at her mode of intervention. Even though the student verbally encouraged the client to express hostility, her nonverbal communication (which included a very soft voice, crossed legs, and arms clenched around herself) amounted to "I'm afraid of your hostility." Once this situation was pointed out, the student nurse was able to talk about her fear of expressed hostility. She said that her family had always repressed and denied hostile feelings.

With this newly gained insight into her own behavior, the student nurse's nonverbal communication no longer belied her words. The client then began to express his hostile feelings. The instructor was able to support the student nurse through the experience, and the student nurse was able to tolerate and understand the client's expression of hostility—even when it was verbally directed at her.

Thus, when nurses are unaware of their own feelings about hostility or are afraid of hostile feelings, they may be unable to understand or intervene in a client's hostility.

Social networks. To date, therapy has focused on the socially deviant individual (individual therapy), his relationship with his spouse (couples therapy), or his relationship with his family (family therapy). Little has been done to implement Speck and Attneave's (1973) total social network approach. Yet social network therapy is essential to the treatment of socially deviant persons.

A socially deviant individual's social network may mirror his behavior or may facilitate and reinforce his behavior. It is thus necessary to work with a social network so that it can serve as an agent for socially acceptable behavior. The central goals of social network therapy are as follows:

1. Identify the most destructive conflict or fear.
2. Decrease the severity of this conflict, within the matrix of social network relationships.
3. Increase the level of communication and interdependence among network members.

The primary role of a therapist should be to help modify the perceptual field of network members so that they will realize that change is possible. This may be accomplished through exploration of and intervention in the patterns of communication and coping that are evidenced during network therapy. When individual network members alter their perceptions, it follows that their responses may also change. Consequently, the network as a whole may alter both its perceptual field and its reactions. Patterns of coping and communication may change. A network that in the past may have facilitated the socially aberrant behavior of a member may no longer tolerate the maladaptive interpersonal mechanisms used by the socially deviant member. As a consequence, he may change his mode of interaction with his social network.

With the support of the therapist, the socially deviant individual may learn to use more desirable ways of communicating and coping. New, socially acceptable behavior may supplant the old, socially deviant behavior.

Most nurse-therapists have concentrated on individual, group, couples, and family therapy. Few, if any, nurses are working with entire social networks. One reason may be the overwhelming size of a network, which is potentially much larger than the six to ten members that usually form a group. Cotherapists probably could best handle the numbers of people and the multiple dynamics involved in network therapy. Despite the difficulties involved, Speck and Attneave (1973) have shown that network therapy is not only possible but therapeutic.

Some psychiatric nurses are beginning to realize that treatment of socially deviant individuals cannot be truly effective unless it involves working with their reference groups —their social networks. Nurses have traditionally been accepted as deliverers of health care in community settings. With the movement toward short-term hospitalization and convalescent care in the community, nurses are especially well suited to assume the role of network therapist.

Intervention in the social networks of socially deviant individuals should not be restricted to the efforts of psychiatric nurse-therapists. School nurse–teachers, occupational health nurses, and public health nurses have unparalleled opportunities to promote and reinforce good mental health practices in healthy social networks and to refer networks in distress for treatment. Nurses in general hospitals also have prime opportunities for assisting members of distressed social networks. General duty nurses are often the first to see the destructive effects of socially aberrant behavior on network members. Socially deviant individuals are usually receptive to treatment for the physical problems associated with their behavior. For instance, very few alcoholics will refuse treatment for gastritis; few addicts will refuse treatment for infection; few juvenile delinquents will refuse treatment for traumatic injuries. Thus, nurses in general hospitals often see or hear about the devastation that is occurring within a socially deviant individual's social network. Relatives and friends might confide to a receptive staff nurse just how difficult it is to live with the person.

> Sharon had been admitted to her community hospital for cirrhosis of the liver. While she was hospitalized, some relatives and friends visited. Family members seemed annoyed with her. When a nurse asked if anything was the matter, the family denied having any problems. However, a neighbor confided to the nurse that Sharon's children (aged 15, 12, and 9) were "running wild." The neighbor said that Sharon was drunk most of the time and that the children were left on their own from the time they came home from school until their father came home. The children usually prepared their own meals and got themselves off to school. Any household chores that were done were done by the children. The oldest child, a boy, tried to keep an eye on the younger children but found it difficult. The younger children usually would not listen to him. In order to make ends meet, the husband/father was working at two jobs. Although some neighbors tried to help out and to keep an eye on the children, they often felt overwhelmed by

the situation, believed that they were intruding, or felt imposed upon.

> The nurse arranged an opportunity to talk with Sharon and her husband about how they were managing at home. Although Sharon denied that there were any problems, her husband later confided to the nurse, "I'm at my wits' end, and I'm thinking of divorcing Sharon and getting custody of the children." The nurse arranged for Sharon's husband to talk with the hospital's psychiatric clinical nurse specialist. Although Sharon refused to participate, her husband, her children, and some of the neighbors who had been helping the family entered into the therapy. In addition, the children began attending Alateen.

The behavior of a socially deviant individual can be very destructive to his social network. At the same time, the behavior of network members can facilitate and reinforce a member's socially deviant behavior. For change to occur, the social network should be part of the therapeutic process.

Substance intoxication and addiction. Substance intoxication exists when a person has ingested a toxic amount of a drug or alcohol. If a person frequently combines substances, adulterates substances, or experiments with new substances, it may be difficult to assess and intervene in substance intoxication.

Nurses, especially public health nurses, school nurse–teachers, occupational health nurses, and emergency room nurses, are often the first to recognize signs of substance intoxication. A person experiencing

TABLE 12-1. Usual reactions to drugs

Signs and symptoms	Sedatives and depressants	Stimulants	Narcotics	Hallucinogens	Tranquilizers	Solvents
Behavioral						
Aggression	A*	A		A		
Depression	A	W				
Disorientation	A, W	A		A		
Euphoria		A	A	A		A
Drowsiness	A		A	A¹	A	W
Hallucinations	A, W	A		A		
Inattentiveness	A		A			
Irritability	A	A				
Suspicion	W	A		A		
Restlessness	W	A	W	A		
Physical						
Slurred speech	A		A			
Gastrointestinal			A		A	
Respiratory	A	A	A			
Nasal			W²		A³	A
Lacrimation			W	A		A
Pinpoint pupils			A			
Dilated pupils	A	A	W	A		
Tachycardia		A	W	A	A	
Hypotension	A, W		A		A	
Skin rash	A	A			A	

*A, Acute phase; W, Withdrawal phase.
¹Occasional
²Runny nose
³Nasal stuffiness

substance intoxication may appear disoriented, depressed, giddy, excited, inattentive, sleepy, or irritable. Body functions may be altered.

Different substances produce different effects. Table 12-1 summarizes some of these reactions. However, frequent mixing of substances often produces a combination of seemingly unrelated reactions (The Desk Reference on Drug Abuse, 1970).

In all instances of suspected substance intoxication, it is necessary for nurses to assess three levels of functioning: behavioral, physical, and contextual.

Behavioral level
1. State of consciousness
2. State of orientation
3. Mood or affect
4. Thought and sensory functioning
5. Motor activity
6. Perception of time and space

Physical level
1. Vital signs
2. Skin color
3. Appearance of eyes
4. Odor of breath
5. Muscle tremors
6. Urine output
7. Gastrointestinal functioning
8. Speech patterns

Contextual level
1. Substance or substances used
2. Method of administration
3. Alterations in life-style
4. Changes in personality
5. Deterioration in physical appearance

Even in emergency situations, these assessments are important. However, in such situations it is sometimes necessary to intervene with a less than ideal data base.

In addition to assessment, nurses intervene in substance intoxication by administering antidotes and medications.

If substance addiction is suspected, a physician should be summoned immediately. If the substance is known, nurses can make use of standing orders for antidotes. (Because of the danger of cross addiction, all medications should be administered judiciously.) Otherwise, nursing therapy involves the relief of symptoms or the administration of life-sustaining measures (for example, maintenance of an airway). In cases of alcohol or barbituate addiction, abrupt withdrawal from the substance may precipitate convulsions. It is especially important for nurses in general hospitals to keep this in mind.

Mr. Frink was admitted to his community hospital after he had suffered a stroke. He was placed in an intensive care unit, and his condition was closely monitored. He became increasingly restless, and muscle tremors began. Suddenly, he had a convulsion.

Mrs. Johnson was admitted to a hospital the day before gall bladder surgery. The next morning, when a nurse brought Mrs. Johnson her preoperative medication, he noticed that she was restless, shaky, and speaking rapidly. The nurse attributed Mrs. Johnson's condition to preoperative anxiety.

In both situations, delirium tremens was neither anticipated nor recognized, but it was present. These vignettes illustrate the importance of thorough history taking and of being alert for substance abuse.

Nurses, in their roles as clinicians and client advocates, need to be sure that the possibility of substance addiction is not overlooked and that signs of withdrawal are not misinterpreted.

Self-inflicted injury. Several types of self-inflicted injury are commonly found among substance abusers: inadvertent injury, which generally occurs during either the acute phase or the withdrawal phase of substance abuse; intentional injury for secondary gains; and injury resulting from suicide attempts. (The acute phase is the period of maximal physical and/or behavioral effects caused by substance abuse. The withdrawal phase is the period of physical and/or behavioral symptoms caused by abrupt termination of substance abuse, especially if the the body has become physically dependent on the substance.)

Nurses should be sure that substance abusers are treated in a protective environment. Every effort should be made to prevent them from injuring themselves. During the acute and withdrawal phase, substance abusers may be disoriented and restless. Protective measures such as side rails on beds, rounded corners on furniture, and padded rooms may be necessary. During the treatment phase, it is not uncommon for substance abusers to intentionally injure themselves or to exaggerate their discomfort. Such behavior is usually designed to gain sympathy and to force the prescription of sedatives, tranquilizers, narcotics, or other drugs that reduce anxiety or produce pleasurable effects. Nurses need to be especially careful that addictive substances are not carelessly left within an addict's reach. Even cough medicines and alcohol-based mouth washes fall into this category.

There is a high incidence of suicide among substance abusers (Bell, 1970). Alternating moods of euphoria or omnipotence ("high") and severe depression ("letdown") usually accompany substance abuse. When coming out of the phase of depression, many addicts commit or attempt to commit suicide. Nurses therefore need to be alert for direct and indirect clues to suicidal intent. (Refer to the discussion of suicide in Chapter 11.)

Poor health patterns. To determine the state of a socially deviant individual's health, a nurse should conduct a physical examination. Nurses should help clients establish routines regarding exercise, diet, sleep, and hygiene. Often, socially deviant individuals are in poor physical health. For example, hepatitis may develop in main line drug users, and avitaminosis may occur in alcoholics. Foodaholics may be overweight but undernourished. Rapists may contract venereal diseases. Narcotic users may never feel the pain of dental caries. Discussion of health problems associated with specific types of socially deviant behavior is an educative goal of nursing therapy.

For more than a year, Joanna had been using psychedelic drugs. In addition, after she had run away from home and joined a commune, much of her food supply had been coming from begging and scavangering. Joanna's physical examination revealed malnutrition and gonorrhea. A nurse talked with her about nutrition and sexually transmitted diseases. Joanna was unaware that untreated gonorrhea could cause permanent sterility. She was also surprised to learn that long-term patterns of poor nutrition could limit her body's ability to fight infection, affect the health of any children she might bear, and eventually shorten her life.

Nurses can be instrumental in educating socially deviant clients about good health practices. The ultimate goals are to improve a client's current health status and to restore him to a normal or near-normal state of health.

TERTIARY PREVENTION

Because social networks and communities change slowly, socially deviant individuals may be discharged from treatment centers and returned to the environments that contributed to the development of their unacceptable behavior. Following discharge from treatment centers, ongoing support in the form of *rehabilitative* or *after-care* services may be needed.

While most people agree that tertiary prevention is a necessary part of treatment for socially aberrant behavior, after-care is not a major priority in the United States. Many people fear that they or their children will be seduced by former prostitutes, assaulted by former juvenile delinquents, or "turned on" to drugs by former addicts. Everyone supports the idea of rehabilitation, but few people want an after-care center located in their neighborhood.

A drug treatment center purchased a large house in a suburban community. The plan was to establish a drug-free day care program for former addicts. Community members, however, were concerned and angry; they did not want former addicts passing through the streets on their way to the day care center. Parents, clergymen, and educators feared that the former addicts would serve as anti-establishment role models, try to peddle drugs, or in some other way adversely influence children and adolescents. After three fires of suspicious origin occurred, the treatment center sold the house and dismissed the idea of establishing a day care program.

Limited tertiary prevention programs are available in the following settings.

Transitional services. Transitional services involve the gradual severing of ties with a treatment center. Socially deviant individuals spend ever-increasing amounts of time away from the center. They may start with an overnight pass, go on to weekend privileges, and finally work up to a week away from the center. Skills for community living and help in locating work and housing are provided. Once socially deviant persons are living in a community, many transitional programs encourage them to return to the treatment center for weekly, semimonthly, or monthly "rap" sessions. At these sessions, problems of adjustment and daily living and ways of coping are discussed.

After-care centers. After-care centers are designed for socially deviant persons who have a place to live and an accepting, supportive family or social network but who are not yet ready to return to work. At a day center, some clients receive medication (such as methadone or Antabuse). All clients receive structure and organization. Social skills and activities of daily living are taught, and assistance is given in looking for a job and preparing for a job interview. Opportunities for socializing are provided. Many day care centers achieve a high degree of autonomy. A system of peer group control may develop, and members may actively set and reinforce rules. If a member experiences a crisis, other members may institute a 24-hour-a-day support system.

Night hospitals. Night hospitals are designed for socially deviant individuals who demonstrate a high degree of impulse control, judgment, and social conscience but who are not yet ready to function full time in the community. Clients work during the day and return to the treatment center each evening. Nightly supportive therapy sessions may be part of the program. Some prisons and drug treatment centers are experimenting with the night hospital approach.

Educational training. Depending on the age, interests, and abilities of a socially deviant individual, continued education, including college and vocational training (retraining in old skills or teaching of new skills) may be indicated. Education increases self-esteem and prepares a client to be as financially self-reliant as his potential permits.

Self-help groups. Self-help groups support socially deviant individuals in their readjustment to community living and intervene in crisis situations. Such groups are composed of former socially deviant persons who have successfully learned to live by society's standards. Alcoholics Anonymous, Narcotics Anonymous, Gamblers Anonymous, and Overeaters Anonymous use a repressive-inspirational approach (see Chapter 6). Women for Sobriety attempts to teach women to live without alcohol. The Fortune Society helps former criminals learn to operate within society's standards, assists them to support themselves legitimately, and helps them to cope with the social stigma attached to imprisonment. A self-help group known as Scapegoat helps prostitutes leave their pimps, learn marketable skills, and find employment.

Voluntary rehabilitation groups. The purpose of voluntary rehabilitation groups is similar to that of self-help groups. What differentiates these groups from self-help groups is that most of the members of voluntary rehabilitation groups have not had socially deviant life-styles. The Salvation Army and the St. Vincent de Paul Society are examples of voluntary rehabilitation groups. Emergency aid in the form of financial assistance, housing, and food is usually available. In addition, counseling, assistance in finding employment and housing, work projects, and leisure time activities may be offered.

Family and social networks. Family and social networks are an essential part of tertiary prevention of socially deviant behavior. Counseling of family members and friends helps to decrease their feelings of guilt, frustration, and anger. Counseling also teaches network members how to avoid facilitating socially aberrant behavior and encourages them to remain involved with the socially deviant individual. Network members are helped to develop an honest, open, consistent, firm approach to the client and to identify and resist attempts at manipulation. Family and social network counseling may be done by professionals or by members of such self-help groups as Alanon, Alateen, (for the network members of alcoholics), Gam-Anon, and Gam-A-Teen (for the network members of gamblers).

CHAPTER SUMMARY

Socially deviant or aberrant behavior includes a large number of seemingly disparate and incongruous ways of relating to people. Socially deviant persons are characterized by such deeply ingrained maladaptive personality patterns and restricted emotional responses that they develop life-styles that often bring them into conflict with society.

Many theories have been formulated to explain the etiology of socially aberrant behavior. These theories fall into three major categories: psychological conflict, biological defect, and sociocultural conflict. It is likely that a combination of factors leads to the development of socially deviant behavior. Some type of socially aberrant behavior is known to all societies, but its form, meaning, and incidence are culturally determined and culturally relative.

Socially deviant individuals may be treated in a general hospital, a psychiatric hospital, a specialized treatment center, or a self-help group. Some of the most frequently used treatment modalities include aversion therapy, milieu therapy, individual therapy, and group therapy. A combination of therapies is usually indicated. The goals of therapy are to supplant socially deviant behavior with socially acceptable behavior and to facilitate reentry into society.

Although nurses may not directly participate in all treatment modalities, they do participate in all three levels of preventive intervention.

Primary prevention focuses on identification of and intervention for such high-risk individuals as depressed mothers and the victims of child abuse. Attempts are also made to rectify overcrowding, community disorganization, and other contributory social or environmental conditions. Secondary prevention involves case finding and intervention in socially deviant behavior. Secondary prevention is most effective when it involves a collaborative and consistent team approach. Nurses function as integral and important members of the mental health team. However, socially deviant life-styles are not easily changed. The course of recovery is often marked by relapses. Tertiary prevention of socially aberrant behavior requires that mental health workers, former socially deviant individuals, clients, and network members work toward a unified rehabilitative approach.

When working with socially deviant persons, nurses need to be *nondefensive, realistic, accepting, consistent,* and *firm.* Insight into their own values and behavior is essential in helping socially deviant individuals confront their unacceptable behavior. By clarifying their own attitudes and values, nurses can accept people who behave in socially aberrant ways, without condoning their lifestyles.

REFERENCES

Anslinger, Harry, and Will Oursler
  1962 The Murderers. New York: Farrar, Straus & Cudahy
Ashcraft, Norman, and Albert E. Scheflen
  1976 People Space: The Making and Breaking of Human Boundaries. New York: Anchor Press
Bach-y-Rita, George, et al.
  1971 "Episodic control: a study of 130 violent patients." American Journal of Psychiatry 127:1473-1478.
Bagley, Christopher
  1967 "Anomie, alienation and the evaluation of social structures." Kansas Journal of Sociology 3:110-123.
Barron, Milton L.
  1960 The Juvenile In Delinquent Society. New York: Alfred A. Knopf, Inc.
Bell, D. S.
  1970 "Drug addiction." Bulletin on Narcotics 22: 21-32.
Bell, R. Gordon
  1970 Escape from Addiction. New York: McGraw-Hill Book Co.
Benedict, Ruth
  1934 Patterns of Culture. Boston: Houghton Mifflin Co.
Benjamin, Harry, and R. E. L. Masters
  1964 Prostitution and Morality. London: Souvenir Press Ltd.

Benson, Herbert, and Robert Keith Wallace
  1972 "Decreased drug abuse with transcendental meditation: a study of 1,862 subjects. In Drug Abuse: Proceedings of the International Conference. Chris J. D. Zarafonetis (ed.). Philadelphia: Lea & Febiger.
Bergler, Edmund
  1970 The Psychology of Gambling. New York: International Universities Press, Inc.
Bolton, R.
  1972 Aggression and Hypoglycemia Among the Quolla: A Study in Psychobiological Anthropology. Sterling Award paper in culture and personality. American Anthropological Association.
Brown, William N.
  1968 "Alienated youth." Mental Hygiene 52:330-336.
Brownmiller, Susan
  1975 Against Our Will: Men, Women and Rape. New York: Simon & Schuster, Inc.
Buitrago-Ortiz, C.
  1973 Esperanza: An Ethnographic Study of a Peasant Community in Puerto Rico. Tucson: University of Arizona Press.
Burgess, Ann, and Lynda Holmstrom
  1974 Rape, Victims of Crisis. Bowie, Maryland: Robert J. Brady.
Burrows, E. G., and M. E. Spiro
  1953 Atoll Culture: Ethnography of Ifaluk in the Central Carolines. New Haven, Conn: Human Relations Area Files Press, Yale University Publications.
Carstairs, G.
  1954 "Daru and bhang: cultural factors in the choice of intoxicant." Quarterly Journal of Studies on Alcohol 15:220-237.
Chafetz, Henry
  1960 Play the Devil: A History of Gambling in the United States from 1492 to 1955. New York: Clarkson N. Potter, Inc.
Chesler, Phyllis
  1972 Women and Madness. New York: Avon Books.
Chesser, Eustace
  1971 Strange Loves: The Human Aspects of Sexual Deviation. New York: William Morrow & Co., Inc.
Choisy, Maryse
  1960 A Month Among the Girls. New York: Pyramid Communications, Inc.
  1961 Psychoanalysis of the Prostitute. New York: Philosophical Library, Inc.

Clark, John P.
  1963 "Acceptance of blame and alienation among prisoners." American Journal of Orthopsychiatry 3:557-561.
Clinard, Marshall B.
  1964 Anomie and Deviant Behavior: A Discussion and Critique. New York: The Free Press of Glencoe.
Collins, M. C.
  1978 Child Abuser. Littleton, Mass.: PSG Publishing Co.
Cruz-Coke, R., and A. Varela
  1965 "Color blindness and alcohol addiction." Lancet 2:1348.
  1966 "Inheritance of alcoholism." Lancet 2:1282.
Deissler, K. J.
  1970 "Synanon—its concepts and methods." Drug Dependence 5:28-35.
DeLint, J., and W. Schmidt
  1971 "The epidemiology of alcoholism." In Biological Basis of Alcoholism. Y. Israel and J. Mardones (eds.). New York: John Wiley & Sons, Inc.
DeMeyer-Gapin, S., and T. J. Scott
  1977 "Effect of stimulus novelty on stimulation-seeking in antisocial and neurotic children." Journal of Abnormal Psychology 86:96-98.
Desk Reference on Drug Abuse
  1970 New York: New York State Department of Health.
Dishotsky, N., W. Loughman, R. Mogar, and W. Lipscomb
  1971 "LSD and genetic damage." Science 172:431-440.
Donaldson, William
  1977 Don't Call Me Madam—The Life and Hard Times of a Gentleman Pimp. New York: Mason/Charter Publishers, Inc.
Dubitzky, M., and J. Schwartz
  1968 "Ego-resiliency, ego-control and smoking cessation." Journal of Psychology 70:27-33.
Dukheim, Emile
  1938 The Rules of the Sociological Method. New York: The Free Press.
Eimer, E. O., and R. J. Senter
  1968 Alcohol Consumption in Domestic and Wild Rats. Psychosomatic Science 10:319
Elliott, C., and D. Denney
  1975 "Weight control through covert sensitization and false feedback. Journal of Consulting and Clinical Psychology 43:842-850.

Ellis, Albert
  1959 "Why married men visit prostitutes." Sexology 25:344-347.
Ericksson, K.
  1968 "Genetic selection for voluntary alcohol consumption in the albino rats." Science 159:739.
Esselstyn, T. C.
  1967 "The violent offender and corrections." Paper submitted to the President's Commission on Law Enforcement and Administration of Justice. Washington, D.C.: U.S. Government Printing Office.
Evans, R. R., E. F. Borgatta, and G. W. Bohrnstedt
  1967 "Smoking and MMPI scores among entering freshmen." Journal of Social Psychology 73:137-140.
Feingold, Benjamin F.
  1975 Why Your Child is Hyperactive. New York: Random House, Inc.
Finnegan, J. K., P. S. Larson, and H. B. Haag
  1945 "The role of nicotine in the cigarette habit." Science 102:94-96.
Fisher, R. A.
  1959 Smoking—The Cancer Controversy. Edinburgh: Oliver & Boyd.
Fleming, Alice
  1978 Something for Nothing—A History of Gambling. New York: Delacorte Press.
Freedman, J. L.
  1975 Crowding and Behavior. New York: The Viking Press Inc.
Freud, Sigmund
  1930 Civilization and Its Discontents. Joan Riviere (trans.). London: The Hogarth Press Ltd.
  1959 Collected Papers of Sigmund Freud. Ernest Jones (ed.). New York: Basic Books, Inc., Publishers.
Friedman, M., and R. H. Rosenman
  1974 Type A behavior and your heart. New York: Alfred A. Knopf, Inc.
Fromm, Erich
  1942 Man for Himself. New York: Holt, Rinehart and Winston, Inc.
  1955 The Sane Society. New York: Holt, Rinehart and Winston, Inc.
Gans, Herbert
  1962 The Urban Villagers. New York: The Free Press of Glencoe.
Glazer, Nathan, and Daniel Patrick Moynihan
  1963 Beyond the Melting Pot. Cambridge, Mass. The M.I.T. Press.

Goffman, Erving
   1969 Where The Action Is. London: Allen
        Lane.
Goorney, A. B.
   1968 "Treatment of a compulsive horse-race
        gambler by aversion therapy. British
        Journal of Psychiatry 114:329-333.
Greene, Herbert, and Carolyn Jones
   1974 Diary of a Food Addict. New York:
        Grosset & Dunlap, Inc.
Gregg, G.
   1976 "From masseuse to prostitute in one
        quick trick: a study by A. Velarde. Psy-
        chology Today 10:27-28.
Gusinde, M.
   1961 The Yamana. New Haven, Conn.: Hu-
        man Relations Area Files Press, Yale
        University Publications.
Halleck, Seymour L.
   1967 "Psychiatric treatment for the alien-
        ated college student. American Jour-
        nal of Psychiatry 124:642-650.
Halliday, M. A. K.
   1976 "Anti-language." American Anthropol-
        ogist 78:570-584.
Hammond, E. C., and Constance Percy
   1958 "Ex-smokers." New York State Jour-
        nal of Medicine 58:2956-2959.
Harkins, Arthur N.
   1965 "Alienation and related concepts."
        Kansas Journal of Sociology 1:78-89.
Hirsch, J., and J. L. Knittle
   1970 "Cellularity of obese and non-obese
        adipose tissue." Federal Process
        29:1516-1521.
Hobart, Charles W.
   1965 "Types of alienation: etiology and in-
        terrelationships." Canadian Review of
        Sociology and Anthropology 2:92-107.
Hobbes, Thomas
   1965 Leviathan. Oxford: Clarendon Press.
Holland, J., J. Masling, and D. Copley
   1970 "Mental illness in lower class normal,
        obese and hyperobese women." Psy-
        chosomatic Medicine 32:351-357.
Horney, Karen
   1937 The Neurotic Personality of Our Time,
        New York: W. W. Norton & Co., Inc.
Hunt, W., and J. Matarazzo
   1973 "Three years later: Recent develop-
        ments in the experimental modifica-
        tion of smoking behavior." Journal of
        Abnormal Psychology 81:107-114.
Hyde, Margaret O.
   1978 Addictions: Gambling, Smoking, Co-
        caine Use and Others. New York:
        McGraw-Hill Book Co.

Jacobs, M. A., et al.
   1966 "Orality, impulsivity and cigarette
        smoking in men: further findings in
        support of a theory." Journal of Ner-
        vous and Mental Disease 143:209-219.
James. W. H., A. B. Woodruff, and W. Werner
   1965 "Effect of internal and external control
        upon changes in smoking behavior."
        Journal of Consulting Psychology
        29:184-186.
Jenkins, C. D.
   1975 "The coronary-prone personality." In
        Psychological Aspects of Myocardial
        Infarction and Coronary Care. W. D.
        Gentry and R. B. Williams, Jr. (eds.).
        St. Louis: The C. V. Mosby Co.
Johnston, L. M.
   1942 "Tobacco smoking and nicotine." Lan-
        cet 2:742.
Kaij, L.
   1960 Studies on the Etiology and Sequels of
        Abuse of Alcohol. Lund: University of
        Lund Press.
Kato, T., et al.
   1970 "Chromosome studies in pregnant rhe-
        sus macaque given LSD-25." Diseases
        of the Nervous System 31:245-250.
Kimeldorf, C., and P. J. Geiwitz
   1966 "Smoking and the Blacky orality fac-
        tors. Journal of Projective Techniques
        and Personality Assessment 30:167-
        168.
Kimsey, L. R.
   1969 "Out-patient group psychotherapy
        with juvenile delinquents. Distur-
        bances of the Nervous System 30:472-
        477.
Kingsley, R. G., and G. T. Wilson
   1977 "Behavior therapy for obesity: a com-
        parative investigation of long-term ef-
        ficacy. Journal of Consulting and Clin-
        ical Psychology 45:288-298.
Kinsey, Alfred, et al.
   1948 Sexual Behavior in the Human Male.
        Philadelphia: W. B. Saunders Co.
Kirkendall, Lester A.
   1961 Premarital Intercourse and Interper-
        sonal Relationships. New York: Julian
        Press, Inc.
Kolbye, A. C.
   1976 First Report of the Preliminary Find-
        ings and Recommendations of the In-
        teragency Collaborative Group on Hy-
        perkinesis. Washington, D.C.: Depart-
        ment of Health, Education, and
        Welfare; U.S. Government Printing Of-
        fice.

LaBarre, Weston
  1960 "Twenty years of peyote studies." Current Anthropology 1:45.
  1964 "The peyote cult." Hamden, Conn.: The Shoe String Press, Inc.
Lane, N. E. A., et al.
  1966 The Thousand Aviator Study: Smoking History Correlates of Selected Physiological, Biochemical and Anthropometric Measures. Bureau of Medicine and Surgery MF 022.03.02-5007.11. Washington, D.C.: U.S. Government Printing Office.
Larson, P. S., H. B. Haag, and H. Silvette
  1961 Tobacco: Experimental and Clinical Studies. Baltimre: The Willams & Wilkins Co.
Leavitt, F.
  1974 Drugs and Behavior. Philadelphia: W. B. Saunders Co.
Leighton, Alexander H.
  1959 My Name is Legion. New York: Basic Books, Inc., Publishers.
Leon, G. R., and K. Chamberlain
  1973 "Emotional arousal, eating patterns, and body image as differential factors associated with varying success in maintaining a weight loss." Journal of Consulting Clinical Psychiatry 131:423-427.
Leone, Delores, and Rothlyn Zahourek
  1974 "'Aloneness' in a therapeutic community." Perspectives in Psychiatric Care 12:60-63.
Lerman, Paul
  1968 "Individual values, peer values and subcultural delinquency." American Sociological Review 33:219-235.
Lewis, Oscar
  1951 Life in a Mexican Village: Tepoztlan Restudied. Urbana, Ill.: University of Illinois Press.
Lilienfeld, A. M.
  1959 "Emotional and other selected characteristics of cigarette smokers and nonsmokers as related to epidemiological studies of lung chancer and other diseases." Journal of the National Cancer Institute 22:259-282.
Lindner, Robert M.
  1950 "The psychodynamics of gambling." Annals of the American Academy of Political and Social Science 269:93-107.
Livingston, J.
  1974 "Compulsive gamblers: a culture of losers." Psychology Today 7:51-55.

Locke, John
  1967 Two Tracts on Government. Philip Abrams (trans. and ed.). London: Cambridge University Press.
Mark, V. H., and F. R. Ervin
  1970 Violence and the Brain. New York: Harper & Row, Publishers, Inc.
Marlatt, G. A., B. Demming, and J. B. Reid
  1973 Loss of control drinking in alcoholics: an experimental analogue. Journal of Abnormal Psychology 81:233-241.
Martinez, Tomas
  1978 Cited in Addictions: Gambling, Smoking, Cocaine Use and Others. Margaret O. Hyde. New York: McGraw-Hill Book Co.
Martinez-Alier, Verena
  1974 Marriage, Class and Colour in Nineteenth-Century Cuba. London: Cambridge University Press.
Marzetta, B. R., H. Benson, and R. K. Wallace
  1972 "Combating drug dependency in young people: a new approach. Medical Counterpoint 4:13-37.
Masters, R. E. L.
  1962 Forbidden Sexual Behavior and Morality. New York: Julian Press, Inc.
McClosky, Herbert, and John Schaar
  1965 "Psychological dimensions of anomy." American Sociological Review 30:14-40.
Merton, Robert King, and Robert A. Nisbet
  1961 Contemporary Social Problems: An Introduction to the Sociology of Deviant Behavior and Social Disorganization. New York: Harcourt, Brace and World.
  1971 Contemporary Social Problems. Robert K. Merton and Robert A. Nisbet (eds.). New York: Harcourt Brace Jovanovich, Inc.
Mills, C. W.
  1950 The Sociological Imagination. New York: Oxford University Press.
Minuchin, S.
  1967 Families of the Slums. New York: Basic Books, Inc., Publishers.
Moran, E.
  1970 "Pathological gambling." British Journal of Hospital Medicine 4:59-70.
Morgan, T.
  1975 "Little ladies of the night: runaways in New York." New York Times Magazine, November 16, pp. 34-38.
Nash, June
  1967 "Death as a way of life: the increasing resort to homicide in a Maya Indian community." American Anthropologist 69:455-470.

Nisbett, R. E.
1972 "Hunger, obesity, and ventromedial hypothalamus." Psychological Review 79:433-453.

Orbach, Susie
1978 Fat Is A Feminist Issue—The Anti-Diet Guide to Permanent Weight Loss. New York: Paddington Press.

Outwater, Alice D.
1978 "Addictions to food." In addictions: Gambling, Smoking, Cocaine Use and Others. Margaret O. Hyde. New York: McGraw-Hill Book Co.

Parsons, Anne
1964 "Is the oedipal complex universal? The Jones-Malinowski debate revisited and a southern Italian 'Nuclear Complex.'" In The Psychoanalytic Study of Society. W. Muensterberger and S. Axelrad (eds.). New York: International Universities Press.

Pincus, Johanthan H.
1979 "Neurologic abnormalities in violent delinquents." Neurology 29(4):586.

Polivy, J., A. L. Schueneman, and K. Carlson
1976 "Alcohol and tension reduction: cognitive and physiological effects." Journal of Abnormal Psychology 85:595-600.

Quay, H. C.
1965 "Psychopathic personality as pathological stimulus seeking." American Journal of Psychiatry 122:180-183.

Redfield, Robert
1947 "The folk society." American Journal of Sociology 52:298-308.

Reich, Charles A.
1970 The Greening of America: How the Youth Revolution is Trying to Make America Livable. New York: Random House, Inc.

Reiner, Beatrice, and Irving Kaufman
1959 Character Disorders in Parents of Delinquents. New York: Family Service Association of America.

Report of the National Council on Alcoholism
1976 Long Island Council on Alcoholism Fact Sheet. Garden City, N.Y.

Rosenman, R. H., et al.
1970 "Coronary heart disease in the Western Collaborative Study: a follow-up experience of four and one half years." Journal of Chronic Diseases 23:173-190.

Rosenman, R. H., et al.
1975 "Coronary heart disease in the Western Collaborative Group Study: final follow-up experience of eight and one half years. Journal of the American Medical Association 233:872-877.

Roth, Martin
1972 "Human violence as viewed from the psychiatric clinic. American Journal of Psychiatry 128:1043-1056.

Roueche, B.
1962 Alcohol: Its History, Folklore, and Effects on the Human Body. New York: Grove Press, Inc.

Rubin, Bernard
1972 "Prediction of dangerousness in mentally ill criminals." Archives of General Psychiatry 17:397-407.

Ruesch, Jurgen
1961 Therapeutic Communication. New York: W. W. Norton & Co., Inc.

Scheflen, Albert
1972 Body Language and Social Order—Communication as Behavioral Control. Englewood Cliffs, N. J.: Prentice-Hall, Inc.

Seager, C. P., V. M. Pokorny, and D. Black
1966 "Aversion therapy for compulsive gambling. Lancet 1:546.

Selkin, James
1975 "Rape." Psychology Today 8:70-76.

Shibano, Sholan
1961 "The meaning of alienation in juvenile delinquency from the integrative viewpoint of delinquent conditions and mechanisms." Journal of Educational Sociology 16:209-237.

Shields, J.
1962 Monozygotic Twins Brought Up Apart and Brought Up Together. London: Oxford University Press.

Slotkin, J. S.
1967 "Religious defenses (the Native American Church)." Journal of Psychadelic Drugs 1:80.

Smith, G. M.
1967 "Personality correlates of cigarette smoking in students of college age. Annals of the New York Academy of Sciences 142:308-321.

Smith, S. M., and R. Hanson
1975 "Interpersonal relationships and child-rearing practices in 214 parents of battered children." British Journal of Psychiatry 127:513-525.

Speck, Ross V., and Carolyn L. Attneave
1973 Family Networks. New York: Pantheon Books, Inc.

Srole, Leo
1956 "Social integration and certain corollaries: an explorative study." American Sociological Review 21:709-716.

Srole, Leo, et al.
1962 Mental Health in the Metropolis: The Midtown Manhattan Study. New York: McGraw-Hill Book Co.

Stewart, L., and N. Livson
1966 "Smoking and rebelliousness: a longitudinal study from childhood to maturity. Journal of Consulting Psychology 30:225-229.

Straits, B. C., and L. Sechrest
1963 "Further support of some findings about the characteristics of smokers and nonsmokers." Journal of Consulting Psychology 27:282.

Stunkard, A. J.
1959 "Eating patterns and obesity." Psychiatric Quarterly 33:284-295.
1963 "Obesity." In Encyclopedia of Mental Health, vol. 4. A Deutsch (ed.). New York: Franklin Watts, Inc., pp. 1372-1385.

Stunkard, A. J., and M. Mendelson
1961 "Disturbances in body image of some obese persons." Journal of the American Dietetic Association 38:328.

Sullivan, Harry Stack
1953 The Interpersonal Theory of Psychiatry. New York: W. W. Norton & Co., Inc.

Thomas, A., S. Chess, and H. Birch
1968 Temperament and Behavior Disorders in Children. New York: Holt, Rinehart and Winston, Inc.

Thomkins, S. S.
1966 "Psychological model for smoking behavior." American Journal of Public Health 56:17-20.
1977 "Youth for sale on the streets." Time 110:23, November 28.

Ugarte, G., et al.
1970 "Relations of color blindness to alcoholic liver damage." Pharmacology 4:308.

Van Proosdij, C.
1960 Smoking, London: Elsevier.

Wardwell, W. I., and C. B. Bahnson
1973 "Behavioral variables and myocardial infarction in the South Eastern Connecticut Heart Study." Journal of Chronic Disease 26:447-461.

Weissman, Myrna
1972 "The depressed woman: recent research." Social Work 17:19-25.

Wilkinson, Rupert
1970 The Prevention of Drinking Problems. New York: Oxford University Press.

Winchester, Harley V., Jr.
1972 "Educational therapy for adolescents in the short-term psychiatric hospital." Perspectives in Psychiatric Care 10:37.

Windsor, A. L., and S. J. Richards
1935 "The development of tolerance for cigarettes." Journal of Experimental Psychology 18:113-120.

Yablonsky, Lewis
1963 The Violent Gang. New York, MacMillan, Inc.

Yablonsky, Lewis, and C. E. Dederich
1965 "Synanon: an analysis of some dimensions of the social structure of an antiaddiction society." In Narcotics. D. M. Wilner and G. G. Kassebaum (eds.). New York: McGraw-Hill Book Co.

ANNOTATED SUGGESTED READINGS

Ashcraft, Norman, and Albert E. Scheflen
1976 People Space: The Making and Breaking of Human Boundaries. New York, Anchor Press.
The authors explore the use of space by people and the consequences of the human use of space. Within this context, such social problems as poverty, crowding, ethnic differences, scarcity of resources, deterioration of living conditions, and violence are examined.

Hyde, Margaret O.
1978 Addictions: Gambling, Smoking, Cocaine Use and Others. New York: McGraw-Hill Book Co.
Addiction is defined as a characteristic, habitual way of coping with life stresses. Within this framework such addictions as compulsive eating, compulsive drinking (alcohol, coffee, tea, and cola), compulsive gambling, drug abuse, compulsive working, cigarette smoking, and jogging are discussed. This book includes a list of associations and clearing houses that may serve as sources for further information.

Merton, Robert K., and Robert A. Nisbet (eds.)
1971 Contemporary Social Problems. New York: Harcourt Brace Jovanovich, Inc.
This book looks at the characteristics of social structure that generate social order and socially conforming behavior and that also have the potential for producing social disorganization and socially deviant behavior. Social disorganization and social deviance are viewed as untoward and tangential consequences of institutionalized behavior

patterns of society. The book is divided into two parts: "Deviant Behavior" (juvenile delinquency, mental disorders, alcoholism) and "Social Disorder" (family disorganization, poverty, violence, race relations).

Reich, Charles A.

1970 The Greening of America: How the Youth Revolution is Trying to Make America Livable. New York: Random House, Inc.

Reich discusses the current social structure of the United States and the impact of this social structure on the quality of life. He relates contemporary social problems to the coercive influence of the corporate state on values and life-style. Reich anticipates the emergence of a new life-style out of a revolution of consciousness that emphasises creativity, love, and community.

FURTHER READINGS

Drabman, R. S., and M. H. Thomas

1976 "Does watching violence on television cause apathy? Pediatrics 57:329-331.

Halleck, Seymour, L.

1974 "Legal and ethical aspects of behavior control." American Journal of Psychiatry 131:381-385.

Rachman, S., and J. Teasdale

1969 Aversion Therapy and Behavior Disorders: An Analysis. Coral Gables, Fla: University of Miami Press.

13
COPING THROUGH
WITHDRAWAL
FROM REALITY

CHAPTER
FOCUS

Schizophrenia is the most perplexing of all the psychopathies. More has been written about its etiology, course, and treatment than about any other emotional disorder.

Schizophrenia is more properly called a syndrome than a disease. It can involve any of several combinations of symptoms, disturbances, and reactions. Some writers and investigators have suggested that it would be more accurate to refer to the schizophrenias rather than to a single entity. The condition has probably always been with mankind, at least since man became a social animal.

Because of the complexity of schizophrenia, many theories of its etiology have been proposed and many treatment modalities have evolved

and are still evolving. This chapter will summarize several of the etiological theories, including the psychodynamic, sociological, and biological views. Current and past treatment methods will be reviewed as well as the many dimensions of primary, secondary, and tertiary prevention.

Nursing intervention for schizophrenic individuals is based not on a reaction to a diagnostic category but on a therapeutic response to specific types of behavior. These forms of behavior, while maladaptive, are not unexplainable and awesome derivatives of madness, as they have been thought of in the past. They represent an individual's attempts to deal with a threatening environment and a disintegrating sense of self.

13

COPING THROUGH WITHDRAWAL FROM REALITY

. . . a syndrome characterized by a final common path of disturbances of the ego, with a primary etiology of chemogenic, histogenic, genogenic or psychogenic nature or a combination thereof, different in each individual case, but probably identifiable as clusters or subgroups.

Bellak, 1958

HISTORICAL ASPECTS

There are ancient tomb writings that graphically describe what was most likely schizophrenia. Undoubtedly, many of the witches who were burned at the stake in medieval times for being possessed by the devil were suffering from schizophrenia.

The syndrome was termed "dementia praecox" by Morel, a contemporary of Sigmund Freud. Dementia praecox, as Morel used it, meant youthful (precocious) insanity. It was thus distinguished from the dementias of later life, such as senility. Kraepelin, who has been called the "Great Classifier" of mental disturbances, used the term when he set about developing his taxonomy. Another contemporary of Freud, Eugen Bleuler, reacted to the primary symptom of dementia praecox—a splitting off of the emotions ordinarily connected to thoughts—by inventing the term "schizophrenia." The word comes from the Greek "schizo" (to split) and "phren" (mind). Schizophrenia is the term now in popular use.

SOCIOCULTURAL ASPECTS OF LABELING

The label "schizophrenia" has caused some difficulties. A minor difficulty is the confusion many people experience over the meaning of the word. Many have understood the word to mean "having more than one personality." This is really a description of another psychological disturbance—a severe psychoneurotic condition of the dissociative type called *multiple personality* (see Chapter 10). *The Three Faces of Eve* and *Sybil* are both accounts of persons with the disorder of multiple personality. *Dr. Jekyll and Mr. Hyde* is a fictional account of a person with multiple personality.

The difficulty in the average person's understanding of the term schizophrenia is inconsequential when compared to the problems it has caused for most of the people who suffer from the disorder. These problems are inherent in the process of labeling. The fear and utter hopelessness associated with schizophrenia, which have grown throughout the history of the disease, remain with us even after more effective treatments for controlling the symptoms have evolved. Schizophrenia is still the most dread of all psychiatric disorders (Grinker, 1969). Being told that one is schizophrenic is akin to receiving a diagnosis of cancer. Yet, if one were to compare the prognosis for successful adaptation to life, a diagnosis of schizophrenia is more hopeful than one of *sociopathy*.

Another problem with the label of schizophrenia is that, as defined by Bleuler, it suggests "OK, here it is—live up to it!" In other words, expectation of pathological behavior tends to elicit pathological behavior. Through the expectations and interpretations of other people, symptoms that had been dormant or even nonexistent may be manifested. Any of a therapist's biases or distortions may be projected onto a client during a therapeutic relationship; the effects of such projection should never be underestimated. It is particularly important to remember this point, in view of the studies (such as Sarbin, 1972) that have shown that many persons who have been labeled schizophrenic do not demonstrate one or more of the cardinal symptoms of schizophrenia. It has also long been known that anyone—schizophrenic, neurotic, or normal—who is under sufficient stress may demonstrate any of these symptoms.

Another problem arising in connection with the use of diagnostic categories has to do with cultural differences between the labeler and the person who gets labeled. For example, it is well known that in Great Britain, where the average citizen is more reserved than the average American, the label most frequently given at the time of admission to psychiatric facilities is manic-depressive psychosis. In the United States, where dynamic, gregarious characters are more common and withdrawal is less acceptable, the most frequent diagnosis upon admission to state hospitals is schizophrenia.

The economic factor is also important in the diagnosis of schizophrenia. Psychiatrists are reluctant to give their private patients that label on admission. Upper- and middle-class patients admitted to psychiatric units in general hospitals are less apt to be called schizophrenic than the lower-class patients of the state hospital systems.

Much of the discontent with the diagnostic term schizophrenia is reflected in one prominent psychiatrist's statement:

> The term schizophrenia should be abandoned. It has no priority, it misleadingly implies an understanding of a supposed basic disorder, and its two main subdivisions (process and reactive) are defined by responses to therapy, which is absurd! (Altschule, 1970)

The validity of labeling people with psychiatric terms has been questioned for many. For example, Laing (Boyers and Orrill, 1971) and Szasz (1961) have both pointed out that such labeling has served a purpose for society—it has allowed society to explain away as "sick" any behavior that deviates from accepted norms.

A nurse working with psychiatric clients usually has an aversion to putting people into pigeonholes. Nurses are aware that such a practice can be destructive. However, there is another side to this question, and other factors need to be examined. Some would argue that it is not the label itself but the stigma attached to it that causes the damage. They see the label as potentially *helpful* device. For example, proponents of the medical model of the etiology of schizophrenia suggest that we say to a client: "You have a biochemical disorder called schizophrenia. We have medications and other treatments to help you control your symptoms. We will work together." Proponents of the medical model thus believe that confronting the client with his disorder, in the same way in which a diabetic person must be confronted with his metabolic disorder, is more helpful than shrouding the term "schizophrenia" in mystery. They accuse the "radical therapists"* of not providing any real help to a person trying to cope with schizophrenia when they deny that it is a disease, as Szasz does, or define it as "the only way to be sane in an insane world," as Laing views it. Whichever side of the debate you agree with, an understanding of terms and diagnostic categories is necessary if you are going to be able to read the enormous amount of literature about the schizophrenic experience. With this point in mind, we will review several classification systems, along with the underlying dynamics and common symptoms of the schizophrenic syndrome.

UNDERLYING DYNAMICS
The schizoid personality

The development of schizophrenia often follows a predictable course. The first stage of this course is the assumption of the schizoid personality. The schizoid personality is characterized by a tendency toward isolation and withdrawal, a bland affect, vagueness in communicating, and an overuse of the defense mechanism of projection. There seems to be an emptiness or poverty of personality, and the individual may appear rather eccentric to other people. While most schizophrenic processes may be shown to have developed in persons who have schizoid personalities, it does not follow that everyone who demonstrates a schizoid personality will necessarily develop schizophrenia.

---

*R. D. Laing is considered one of the "radical therapists" because of his beliefs, for example, that schizophrenia is a liberating experience. Thomas Szasz is also counted among the radical therapists because of such views as his denial of schizophrenia as a disease.

The preschizophrenic state

The next stage of the process is the preschizophrenic state. This stage, which may last 1 or 2 years, is characterized by excessive daydreaming, an aloof and withdrawn attitude, and indifference to others.

The need-fear dilemma. The individual has low self-esteem and a basic feeling of rejection combined with a fear of relating to others. This fear is a factor in the conflict that has been termed the "need-fear dilemma" (Burnham, 1969). The preschizophrenic person seems to suffer from an inordinate *need* for interpersonal closeness and an inordinate *fear* of that closeness. Since we all suffer from the need-fear dilemma, it is the adjective *inordinate* that sets the preschizophrenic person's experience apart from that of everyone else. Leopold Bellak (1958) has illustrated this dilemma by citing the philosopher Schopenhauer's parable of the porcupines:

> On a cold winter day the porcupines move close to each other in order to take advantage of the warmth from their body heat. As they move closer and closer, they hurt each other with their quills. The porcupines had to move back and forth to find the best distance between each other in order to get the maximum body warmth while minimizing the hurts from their quills.

We only have to think of the instances when the need-fear dilemma has operated in our own lives. For example, we fall in love and experience fear because the loved one now has the power to hurt by leaving. An expectant mother experiences the need-fear dilemma: her desire for the new baby is combined with a fear of the baby's power to hurt her by becoming sick or dying.

The "as-if" phenomenon. Feeling rejected by others leads to increased and painful isolation from others, which leads in a circular fashion to increased feelings of rejection. Gradually the person's whole existence takes on an "as if" quality (Laing, 1959). He may go through the necessary actions related to his job, family, and friends in a mechanical way—acting *as if* he were an interested worker, a loving husband and father. But he does not feel involved in what he is doing.

Inappropriate affect. The person's affect may be inappropriate. A few preschizophrenic persons may be depressed or euphoric, but most seem to have a bland affect. The bland, shallow affect that accompanies the preschizophrenic and schizophrenic states may be an indication of a withdrawal into the individual's inner world.

There is not always a clear line of demarcation between the preschizophrenic state and the schizophrenic state. Often an insidious development from one stage to the next occurs. With some individuals, however, there *is* a dramatic shift. Usually, when there is a florid and sudden psychotic "break with reality," the prognosis is better than it is when the break is gradual.

The schizophrenic state

The symptoms of many emotional problems can be viewed as unconscious attempts to make the best of a bad situation; so can the symptoms of schizophrenia. They are unconsciously mediated attempts to halt the destructive process of the disease. It is useful to divide the symptoms of schizophrenia into primary and secondary groups. (The difference between primary and secondary symptoms becomes clear if we consider some examples from pathophysiology. In the physical disorder of rheumatic heart disease, the primary symptom is the stenosed mitral valve of the heart. Secondary or accessory symptoms include orthopnea, decreased renal function, and fatigue. In cirrhosis, a fibrotic, nodular and therefore inefficient liver is the primary symptom. Secondary symptoms include jaundice, bone demineralization, cholesterol lesions of the skin due to high serum levels, and a tendency toward bleeding. In both rheumatic heart disease and cirrhosis, the secondary symptoms result from the primary symptom and are ways the organism compensates for the primary symptom.)

Primary symptoms. The primary symptoms of schizophrenia were delineated by Bleuler and are usually remembered as *Bleuler's four A's.* They are: autism, a associative looseness, ambivalence, and affective indifference or inappropriateness.

Autism. The term autism refers to thought processes that are not used by the normal person in his conscious thinking. They are similar to the thought processes of very young children or to those found in dreams. The ego judgments of time and place, of possible and impossible, are not used, and there is a strong element of unreality. In a case of autism that is so extreme that it leads to a break with reality, a person might construct his own inner world, complete with characters. He then might live in this dream world, which could become a nightmare. Cameron (1963) has termed this phenomenon the *pseudocommunity.*

Autism is a compensating maneuver of the ego. It may be an attempt to deal with the pain of failing to relate to other people (Mendel, 1976). Autism is closely tied to the ability to think abstractly. When this function is impaired, as is often the case in schizophrenia, autism results. Words, objects, events, and even people may take on private, symbolic meaning for a schizophrenic person, and communication may therefore become difficult. Autism may be manifested in personally symbolic communication, concrete thinking (inability to think abstractly), or associative looseness, another of Bleuler's A's.

Associative looseness. Associative looseness is characterized by verbalizations that are very difficult and sometimes impossible to understand. Associative looseness may seem similar to the *flight of ideas* that is seen in the manic phase of manic-depressive psychosis (see Chapter 11). Flight of ideas, however, is different in that even though it involves rapid jumping from one topic to another, there is some connection between one phrase or idea and the next. In associative looseness, the connection between one phrase and other is apparent to the speaker but not the listener. Associative looseness may be diagramed as follows:

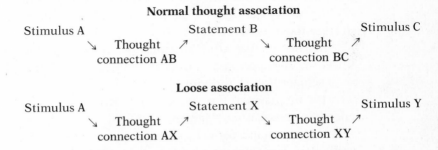

The logical sequence of A to B to C makes the normal thought processes easy to understand and follow. The esoteric or autistic connections of thought that characterize associative looseness make conversation difficult or impossible. Consider the following sample conversations:

Both persons normal
Person 1: "I'm late because the phone was ringing." (A)
Person 2: "Did you answer it in time?" (AB)
Person 1: "Yes." (B)
Person 2: "Who was it?" (BC)
Person 1: "My mother." (C)

One person schizophrenic
Person 1: "Im late because the phone was ringing." (A)
Person 2: "Are you engaged?" ("ringing" is associated with getting a ring and being engaged.) (AX)
Person 1: "Excuse me?" (X)
Person 2: "I cannot teach you." (The association is that one is dismissed or "excused" in class by a teacher.) (XY)
Person 1: "I don't understand you." (Y)

Loose association is not limited to individuals who are suffering from schizophrenia. Anyone may at times demonstrate this defect in communication—especially under conditions of stress. You may have witnessed this symptom if you have taken part in a lengthy telephone conversation in which the other person's way of communicating was unclear to you. Perhaps that person was upset about something, and you slipped into agreeing with his points along the way because of your reluctance to admit that you did not quite understand all of what he was saying. At the end of the conversation you may have been disturbed to find yourself agreeing with a point he was making when you were not at all sure that you actually did agree. At that point you may have been embarrassed to admit that you had not been "tuned in." It is quite possible that one reason you found yourself in this uncomfortable position was that the person you were listening to was demonstrating loose association.

Ambivalence. We all experience ambivalent feelings at times. The difference between this "normal" ambivalence and that experienced by a schizophrenic individual lies not so much in the frequency or even the intensity of the ambivalence. It lies in the effect the ambivalence has on behavior (Mendel, 1976).

A schizophrenic person may experience a powerful combination of conflicting emotions of love and hate toward his signficiant others. These strong and opposing emotions neutralize each other, leading to psychic immobilization and difficulty in expressing other emotion. The result is often inactivity and *apathy,* an extreme, defensive "blunting" of the emotions. Apathy is always a defense against possible pain—it has been described as the defense mechanism of the concentration camps (Frankl, 1959). Apathy is evident when a person is indifferent to what might be expected to cause emotional arousal. Affective indifference is part of another of Bleuler's four A's.

Affective indifference or inappropriateness. A schizophrenic person often displays indifference or apathy or expresses feelings that do not fit a situation. For example, he might begin to laugh loudly after being notified that his mother has just died.

The term "inappropriate" may be misleading. Mendel maintains that if we were to understand the purely personal logic and thought processes of a schizophrenic individual, his behavior would not seem inappropriate. He suggests that a better term would be "socially inappropriate" (Mendel, 1976).

Secondary symptoms. The secondary symptoms of schizophrenia can be viewed as disturbances in thought, speech, mood, behavior, sensation, and perception.

Anxiety. Anxiety, of course, is more than a secondary symptom. It is the basis for all emotional disturbances, and in that sense it might be considered the most primary, or fundamental, of all symptoms. However, it is a secondary symptom in schizophrenia because much anxiety is generated by the trauma and the social consequences of being schizophrenic. In addition, anxiety can occur in response to other secondary symptoms. For example, the experience of hallucinating can be very anxiety-producing. Anxiety often occurs at various points in the natural history of schizophrenia, such as hospital admission and discharge, initial diagnosis, and exacerbations of symptoms.

Depression. Because depression is in itself a psychiatric entity or category, nurses sometimes lose sight of the fact that schizophrenic clients can be and usually are depressed. Like anxiety, depression can occur in response to the schizophrenic experience. To feel that one is a failure in interpersonal relationships can be extremely depressing. In addition, schizophrenia is most often a chronic condition, and depression naturally accompanies chronicity.

Social withdrawal. Shyness, isolation, fear of others, and withdrawal can be expressed on a continuum on which the extreme situation would be characterized by *mutism* and *stupor.*

Loosening of external ego boundaries. Inappropriate identification, depersonalization experiences, and gender identity confusion can occur as a result of a loosening of external ego boundaries. External ego boundaries are those mental processes that help us differentiate between our inner, subjective thoughts and stimuli that are coming from the outer environment.

INAPPROPRIATE IDENTIFICATION. A client might begin to dress like the nurse who is caring for him, verbalize a decision to become a nurse, smoke the same cigarettes, use identical phrases, and so on. Again, this behavior should be viewed on a continuum; an extreme example would be a client who is unable to distinguish his wants and needs from those of the other person or to make his own decisions.

DEPERSONALIZATION. Depersonalization results from feelings of change in self or environment. These feelings may be relatively mild— expressed by such phrases as "I don't look like I usually do" or "Somehow the room has changed—it seems completely different." The feelings and experiences may, however, be more extreme; believing that one has been "transformed" or that one has entered another dimension of the universe would be examples. The delusion* that one is someone else would be an even more extreme situation. Delusions of this kind and others often follow current cultural trends and facts. For example, it is not likely that a person would have the delusion of being Napoleon, as is often portrayed in comic situations. He would be more apt to believe that he is the President, the Godfather, Martin Luther King, or Elvis Presley, reincarnated. The most common delusions of this kind are for a male to believe he is Jesus Christ and for a woman to believe she is the Virgin Mary. Many factors are operating within such delusions; feelings of evil versus good and of power versus impotence are among them.

GENDER IDENTITY CONFUSION. Sexual identification might become weak or confused. Instead of a comfortable acceptance of one's sexual orientation (heterosexual, homosexual, or bisexual), a labile, primitive, guilt-ridden stance in relation to sexuality might develop. In some instances this situation may be characterized by a wish to become a member of the opposite sex or by a fear that such a transformation might occur spontaneously and magically. In extreme cases there may be delusional and symbol-laden beliefs that one is actually half male and half female.

Loosening of inner ego boundaries. Inner ego boundaries are the borders between the repressed unconscious of an individual and his conscious mental life. They help us to differentiate "real" from "unreal." Defective inner ego boundaries can lead to the *attribution of supernatural powers to self and others.* Symptoms of this phenomenon include ideas or delusions of reference, ideas or delusions of control, and religiosity.

IDEAS OR DELUSIONS OF REFERENCE. Ideas or delusions of reference occur when a person believes that others are referring to him or communicating with him through newspapers, television broadcasts, or books (even books published many years ago) or in passing conversations. A mild form of this condition would be for someone to believe that the people across the hall are talking about him (something that perhaps most of us have experienced). An extreme form would be for a person to believe that the headline of this morning's paper is actually a coded message about him.

IDEAS OR DELUSIONS OF CONTROL AND INFLUENCE. Ideas and delusions of control or influence are demonstrated when an individual believes

---

*A delusion is a belief that is contrary to fact.

that he can control and influence other people through supernatural means or that other people are influencing his mind or controlling his behavior in some manner. The following letter illustrates such a delusion.

Dear Sir:

My name is _____. I am writing to you in hope of some answers. My wife, three sons, and myself are being bugged by some kind of electronics, which I believe is in your field. I went to electronics experts for consultation, and they told me it would cost about $3,000 for them to help me. I don't have that kind of money, so I'm writing to you and pray that you can help me and my family. Here are some of the things that are taking place: (1) Using some kind of transmission to our heads, they can jam our memory so we can't think straight. (2) The equipment they're using can induce personality changes, such as increased friendliness or aggression. (3) They can keep us awake or make us sleep. (4) They can put words in our mouth, and make us say things we don't want to say. (5) At times I hear a high ringing noise in my ears that causes great pain. (6) It affects us mainly on our heads. (7) It appears that I can hear voices from the liquid in my stomach. (8) The frequency they use affects our equilibrium and causes pain to our spinal column.

I would appreciate any help you can give me.

Thank you,

_____

(name and address)

RELIGIOSITY. Religiosity is a difficult symptom to assess in another person, since religious belief and degree of commitment are exceedingly personal and variable. It has been pointed out that it is extremely difficult for people to agree on the line of demarcation between normal and pathological religious investment (Field and Wilkerson, 1973).

An individual in a preschizophrenic state that is becoming steadily more severe may seek out religion to compensate for the cruelty of an increasingly alien world and to provide structure and guidelines for his behavior. Religion and God thus become good parents, substituting for the real, "bad" parents (Arieti, 1955).

Field and Wilkerson view the schizophrenic's use of religiosity as a restitutive attempt to deal with two major pathological processes that are operating in the disorder—tendency toward withdrawal and lability of affect. They suggest that religious preoccupation helps support and rationalize this withdrawal and that it also helps to stabilize or control emotions (Field and Wilkerson, 1973).

Autistic thinking and acting

SYMBOLIC DISTORTIONS AND NEOLOGISMS. Schizophrenic individuals may exhibit any of several forms of symbolic distortions: overuse of generalization and universal pronouns (for example, "they" said . . .), vagueness, and inaccuracy are all relatively common patterns of communication. Neologisms are words that are invented to describe people, things, and events. They have completely personal meanings, and they may be egocentrically symbolic in nature. In extreme disorders of communication it may be necessary to "decode" the verbalizations of a client. This requires the establishment of a trusting relationship and may take a fairly protracted period of time.

CONCRETE THINKING. Symbolic distortion often has its roots in another autistic form of thinking—concrete thinking. Concrete thinking involves the fairly consistent use of literal interpretation of others' communication; it is a regression to an earlier form of thinking. A person who thinks such a way has great difficulty in thinking abstractly. The belief that this symptom is frequently associated with schizophrenic thought disorders has led to the use of a "proverb test" in the diagnosis of schizophrenia. The individual is asked to guess the meanings of some common proverbs, such as "A new broom sweeps clean" or "A rolling stone gathers no moss." Inability to give the abstract meanings of the proverbs is viewed as evidence of concrete thinking and becomes one of the factors in a diagnosis of schizophrenia.

PRIMARY PROCESS THINKING. Primary process thinking, a freudian term, is an early, prelogical form of thinking that incorporates such elements as concrete thinking, the post-hoc fallacy,* and paralogical or paleological thinking. Dreams are examples of a type of primary process thinking that is considered normal experience. During a psychotic experience, a person may seem to be dreaming while in a waking state.

PARALOGICAL OR PALEOLOGICAL THINKING. Paralogical thinking is a term that has been adopted by clinicians (Von Damarus, 1944) to denote a type of logic that accepts identity based upon identical predicates—in contrast to normal logic, which only accepts identity based upon identical subjects. Arieti prefers to designate this type of thinking, which is a frequent correlate of schizophrenia, as "paleologic," from the Greek word for ancient: "palaios." This form of thinking is

---

*"After this; therefore because of it." The post-hoc fallacy is also an element in Sullivan's concept of *parataxic distortion* (Arieti, 1967).

illogical according to normal logic, but it is really a logic of its own (Arieti, 1955, 1967). The following is an example of normal, or Aristotelian, logic:

All men are mortal.
Socrates is a man.
Therefore, Socrates is mortal.

Compare this with the following example of paralogical or paleological thinking:

The Blessed Mother Mary is a virgin.
I am a virgin.
Therefore, I am the Virgin Mary.

For a more detailed examination of this complex and interesting phenomenon, see *Language and Thought in Schizophrenia*, edited by J. S. Kasanin, *Interpretation of Schizophrenia*, by Sylvano Arieti, or *The Intrapsychic Self*, also by Sylvano Arieti.

STEREOTYPICAL ACTIONS, ECHOPRAXIA, ECHOLALIA. Stereotypical actions involve the persistent repetition of a motor activity. A "normal" example of this is thumb twiddling or finger tapping. Such actions are often much more bizarre when used by a psychotic client; they may include posturing, intricate hand gestures, or facial grimacing. A stereotypical action is used to control anxiety, but it may also have symbolic, personal meaning. Echopraxia, which is also characterized by persistent movement, is the imitation of someone or something a person is observing; it thus involves the element of loose ego boundaries. Echolalia is the pathological repetition of the words or phrases of another person.

LACK OF SOCIAL AWARENESS. A withdrawn, self-preoccupied person may exhibit some degree of social insensitivity and crudeness. He may engage in such activities as nose picking and masturbation in public places, with little or no awareness of the impact on other people. The activities of daily living (ADL), such as body cleanliness, grooming, and proper attire, may be completely neglected. In a very extreme situation, there may be bizarre, repulsive behavior, such as coprophagia, the desire to eat feces. In fact, the habitual ingestion of various objects (for example, knives and spoons) is a symptom of the extreme or regressed stage of schizophrenia, which is not often seen today. This behavior is sometimes symbolic for the schizophrenic person. Before the advent of psychotropic drugs, it was not as rare an occurrence as it is now.

SOMATIC PREOCCUPATIONS. A person who is either preschizophrenic or schizophrenic may exhibit overconcern about his body functions and health. This behavior may be demonstrated anywhere on a continuum from vague fears about one's health, to hypochondria, to the extreme situation wherein the person suffers from bizarre somatic delusions. The following are some somatic delusions that have been expressed by schizophrenic patients:

1. Complete body infestation by worms
2. Body infestation by snakes
3. Electrical wiring throughout the body
4. Electrical wiring of the brain
5. Depletion of energy and life force by others and through the eyes
6. Exposure of one's inner thoughts, to be read as if in a book, through the eyes
7. One side of the body being female, the other male
8. One side of the body being clean and healthy, the other filthy and diseased.

It is evident that these delusions, like most other secondary symptoms of schizophrenia, may serve more than one purpose for a person with a threatened and crumbling ego. Symbolic statements, expressions of guilt, projection of blame onto others and outside forces, and rationalization of weaknesses and fear of others are a few explanations that are possible.

CLASSIFICATIONS OF SCHIZOPHRENIA
Classic

Several systems for categorizing schizophrenia have been devised. The oldest one—the classic one—was first described by Kraepelin. It included several types, four of which are still in use today: *catatonic, paranoid, hebephrenic,* and *simple.* Before Kraepelin devised this classification system, all the types of schizophrenia were considered to be one disease and were seen as that particular kind of madness that strikes at a young age—dementia praecox. Three of these four types (catatonic, paranoid, and hebephrenic) can be shown to involve specific patterns of defensive reactions to the threat of the ego-disintegrating schizophrenic process.

Catatonic schizophrenia. Catatonic schizophrenia is associated with motor disturbances. There are two stages to this type of schizophrenia: the *catatonic excitement* and *catatonic stupor.* Someone who is in the excited stage may exhibit a frenzied overactivity that is in many ways similiar to the extreme state of mania that is part of the manic-depressive psychosis (see Chapter 11). There is, however, more personality disorganization evident in this schizophrenic condition than in mania. Before the antipsychotic drugs were available, a person in the excited stage of catatonic schizophrenia was in danger of dying from exhaustion.

In catatonic stupor, the motor disturbance is underactivity, which can occur in varying degrees. In severe cases, a person may exhibit the symptom of cerea flexibilitas, or "waxy flexibility." The phrase describes a situation wherein the person's arms, legs, or any other body part can be moved about by another person and will remain in any position in which they are placed. The childhood game of "statues" is a little like this situation—it is as if the person had relinquished voluntary movement as being no concern of his. Catatonic stupor was a fairly common occurrence in psychiatric wards before the availability of the major tranquilizers; there was an ever-present danger of such conditions as leg ulcers, because of the impaired circulation that results from remaining in any one position too long. Hypostatic pneumonia was also a danger, as were accidental burns from radiators that were leaned against during the stuporous phase.

Hallucinations and delusions may be present in catatonic schizophrenia; the delusional system may be persecutory or mystical and magical. Catatonia, of all of the four Kraepelinian types, is most often the one to come on and clear up suddenly—it is thought to have the best prognosis of the four. Denial is the defense mechanism that is pathologically overused—the individual denies reality and the environment through complete withdrawal or through frenzied overactivity that shuts out the world and everyone in it.

Paranoid schizophrenia. The defense mechanism being used in a pathological manner by a paranoid schizophrenic person is projection. Fear, insecurity, or a hostile and threatening inner world is projected or blamed on the outside environment and on other people. Delusions are often persecutory or grandiose, and suspicion is a predominant theme. The paranoid schizophrenic often appears more organized and better able to function within his psychosis than the catatonic schizophrenic, but the prognosis is considered less favorable.

Hebephrenic schizophrenia. Hebephrenic schizophrenia is thought to represent massive regression to a primitive, childlike state. The word comes from the name for the Greek goddess of youth—Hebe. It is a more extreme condition than the previously mentioned types of schizophrenia; there is a rapid disintegration of the personality. Hebephrenic schizophrenia is considered to have the poorest prognosis of the four types. Hallucinations and delusions are common, and it often involves childishness, silly giggling, and bizarre facial grimacing. Speech may be garbled—a person may exhibit "word salad," an unintelligible jumbling of words and phrases. Sometimes complete disorganization and dissociation from the self take place, and the person believes he is someone else.

Simple schizophrenia. There is no predominant pattern of defensive reaction in simple schizophrenia—only the primary symptoms of schizophrenia appear. Loose association and poor attention span are usually present. Persons with simple schizophrenia are seen less often in psychiatric units and hospitals than in jails, skid rows, and isolating jobs. Such persons sometimes become "neighborhood eccentrics." Some heroin addicts may actually be simple schizophrenics, since heroin can have an encapsulating effect on a person's life. Simple schizophrenia is often described as a "poverty of personality."

The newer types

Kraepelin's classification system has been enlarged and refined throughout the years. Several additional types of schizophrenia have been delineated.

Schizoaffective schizophrenia. Schizoaffective schizophrenia includes a pronounced affective element—there is much similarity to manic-depressive psychosis. The underlying thought disorder that characterizes schizophrenia is present, along with a marked lability of mood.

Pseudoneurotic schizophrenia. Pseudoneurotic, borderline, latent, residual, ambulatory, nonpsychotic—these are all terms that have been used by various writers and clinicians to describe approximately the same state. An affected person seems to have moderately severe neurotic problems, but there is actually an underlying schizophrenic process. Sometimes treatment that is traditionally used for neurotic symptoms (for example, psychoanalysis) will uncover the schizophrenic process.

Childhood schizophrenia. There is some debate in clinical circles as to whether early infantile autism and childhood schizophrenia are the same thing. However, most writers do distinguish between the two disorders. While the etiology of early infantile autism is not known, several theorists believe that it has a definite organic basis.

Childhood schizophrenia, which has also been termed "pathological symbiosis," it is thought to involve a pathological fusion of mother and child. Each is dependent upon the other, and independence in one is a threat to the other.

Chronic, undifferentiated schizophrenia. Recently, in tribute to the commonsense idea that no one ever fits into neatly delineated categories, the term "chronic, undifferentiated schizophrenia" has come into common use. A sort of wastebasket term, it is probably the most common diagnosis for schizophrenia that is currently being made in large psychiatric facilities. "Burned-out schizophrenia" is another term that is used to describe chronicity in schizophrenia. While it means that the condition has become chronic, it also implies that the rather dramatic, florid aspects of the process are not especially evident. There may be an element of docility in an affected person's approach to life. For this reason, many clinicians feel that such a person is more amenable to rehabilitation than someone who is actively psychotic.

Process schizophrenia and reactive schizophrenia

A recently devised way of categorizing schizophrenia is to describe it as either "process" or "reactive." This broad system looks at schizophrenia in terms of the parameters of premorbid adjustment, timing and quality of onset of symptoms, progress, and prognosis.

Process schizophrenia. A person with process schizophrenia has had a relatively poor premorbid adjustment. In terms of ability to form and maintain interpersonal and sexual relationships, to function at school or in an occupation, or to master the environment, he has had little success. The onset of symptoms is early (most commonly, at or just after puberty), and the onset of the schizophrenic condition tends to be slow and insidious rather than sudden and dramatic. The precipitating events in the environment are not particularly obvious. This disorder is characterized by a steady, progressive worsening rather than an abrupt, florid exacerbation followed by remission. The prognosis for a person with process schizophrenia is considered to be poorer than that for a person with reactive schizophrenia.

Reactive schizophrenia. A person with reactive schizophrenia probably has made a fairly adequate—in some cases, a rather good—premorbid adjustment. There is usually evidence of accomplishment in the areas of social, sexual, educational, and occupational adjustment.

Perhaps the person has graduated from high school or college, for instance. The events that lead to diagnosis or hospitalization are fairly obvious, and the onset tends to be abrupt and dramatic. Often, remissions will follow acute exacerbations—there is a periodic quality to the course of the disorder. There is often evidence that the person has developed insight into the effects of his behavior on the quality of his life. The prognosis for an improved adjustment to life is much more promising in reactive schizophrenia than in process schizophrenia.

Orthomolecular psychiatry

A group of psychiatrists has adopted a system for categorizing schizophrenia that is based on the principles of orthomolecular medicine, a term that was coined by the biochemist and double Nobel laureate Linus Pauling. Orthomolecular medicine involves the provision of "the proper quantities of nutrients for the individual" (Pfeiffer, 1975). Orthomolecular psychiatrists believe that in schizophrenic persons, the blood (and therefore the brain) contain abnormal levels of histamine: *histapenic schizophrenics* have abnormally low levels, and *histadelic schizophrenics* have abnormally high levels. Histapenic schizophrenics comprise 50% of all schizophrenics, and histadelics comprise 20%. The remaining 30% are *mauve factor schizophrenics,* so called because of an abnormal factor that is excreted in the urine in greater frequency than is the case with normal persons (Pfeiffer, 1975). Orthomolecular psychiatrists have characterized persons who have schizophrenia-like clinical pictures as "facsimile schizophrenics." Facsimile schizophrenia can result from such conditions as brain syphilis (dementia paralytica), pellagra, thyroid hormone deficiency, amphetamine psychosis, vitamin B_{12} deficiency, or wheat gluten sensitivity.

Persons with histapenic schizophrenia are apt to be excessively affected by inner stimuli and thus to have misperceptions of place, time, self, and other people, which result in confusion and distortion. They often hallucinate and suffer from delusions. There is hyperactivity and a high pain threshold.

Histadelic schizophrenia is characterized by suicidal depression, obsessive rumination, and loss of contact with reality. Hallucinations and delusions are much less frequent, but there is difficulty in thinking and an inability to concentrate. Frequent headaches may be a symptom.

In mauve factor schizophrenia, the classical symptoms of schizophrenia are often present, but insight and affect are better than in the other two types. This condition is sometimes called *pyroluria* because pyrroles are found in the urine. Other symptoms may include white spots on the fingernails, stretch marks on the skin, memory problems, sweet breath odor, constipation, photosensitivity, impotence, and intolerance for barbiturates. The illness is viewed as stress induced (Pfeiffer, 1975).

EPIDEMIOLOGY AND SOME SOCIOCULTURAL ASPECTS OF THE SCHIZOPHRENIC SYNDROME

While schizophrenia can strike at almost any age, the usual range for onset is 15 to 45, and especially 25 to 35. For some unknown reason, significantly more schizophrenic persons are born in the first quarter of the year than in any other quarter (Cancro, 1976). Schizophrenia is a major health problem. Of all of the hospital beds in the country, roughly 50% are located in facilities designed for the treatment of mental illness, and 50% cent of these are occupied by schizophrenic patients (Henley, 1970). Many more schizophrenics function with varying degrees of success outside of hospitals. It has been estimated that as many as 4,000,000 people in the United States may suffer from schizophrenia. Estimates range from .85% to 2% of the population (Trotter, 1977).

Schizophrenia is found in all cultures throughout the world and in all socioeconomic groups. However, the distribution is not equal: there is a definite correlation between poverty and the incidence of schizophrenia. The possible reasons for this are complex and debatable. Various workers cite economic, sociological, and genetic factors. For one thing, schizophrenia depletes financial resources, as any debilitating and chronic disorder does. Roman and Trice found, in their synthesis of several studies of the etiology and epidemiology of schizophrenia, that one generalization was possible—the positive correlation among life in the lower socioeconomic strata, excessive psychological stress, and schizophrenia (Roman and Trice, 1967). Certainly, the effects of poverty are felt in many areas of living. Poor people generally do not receive proper nutrition and health care, and they lack adequate living space. They also have little opportunity for socialization and self-actualization. These conditions may increase the chances that a person will develop a schizophrenic psychosis. Finally, there is an element of subjectivity inherent in the act of diagnosing: many clinicians are reluctant to condemn their middle-class patients with the label of schizophrenia, even when they believe it to be present.

Sociocultural factors must be considered integral parts of the schizophrenic process. For example, which etiology is accepted depends on culture. The Awilik Eskimos may attribute a case of catatonia to the machinations of a vengeful ancestral spirit (Carpenter, 1953), while a Washington psychiatrist may proclaim it to be the result of an escalation of multigenerational psychopathology.

Treatment also is related to sociocultural forces. In Israel, where a premium is placed on being a productive citizen, even the most passive, chronic psychotic is considered capable of some personal and social regeneration and is treated accordingly. Communal philosophy in China fosters the development of self-help groups for patients, and reintegration into family and community groups is an important goal of treatment (Howells, 1965).

The content of delusions and hallucinations is shaped by sociocultural trends and current events. Presidential assassinations, moon landings, or the popularity of a movie star are all possible influences.

The severity of and prognosis for a case of schizophrenia depend in large part upon a socioeconomic or cultural group's reaction to the disorder. Since medieval times, ambulatory schizophrenic patients in the village of Gheel, Belgium, have easily made the transition from hospital to community because of the villagers' acceptance of them.

Anthropologists have pointed out that the incidence of mental illness seems to increase during the social unrest that accompanies periods of change and acculturation (Carpenter, 1953). Sometimes, according to medical anthropologist Edward F. Foulks (1975), schizophrenia may even be helpful to an individual or to society during times of social upheaval. The hallucinations and delusions of an individual can help to explain catastrophic events to the people or provide guidelines for change when social change is required. Foulks describes a New York Seneca Indian, called Handsome Lake, whose stress-induced hallucinations in the mid–eighteenth century told him of a new and useful code for his people to adopt. His society was in a period of rapid change and therefore of social disorganization, with its potential for destructive trends. Thus, through his hallucinatory experience Handsome Lake was able to assume the role of prophet or shaman.

The syndrome of schizophrenia has a long history in the development of mankind and a wide incidence throughout the world. Symptoms of the syndrome can be viewed as restitutional; they are extreme exaggerations of the defense mechanisms we all use. Useful definitions of schizophrenia acknowledge the complexity of the syndrome and of the etiological factors surrounding it. While several systems of classification have been devised and are used by clincans and writers, it remains crucial to recognize and remember the concept of individuality in the treatment of schizophrenic clients. Mendel and Green (1967) have pointed this out succinctly:

> Obviously, the patient does not have a diagnosis; we the physicians, have the diagnosis. When the diagnosis and the patient do not fit we must feel free to abandon the diagnosis and return to the patient.

THEORIES OF SCHIZOPHRENIA

The exact etiology of schizophrenia is unknown. There are, however, many theories about the origin of the disorder, and several of them will be reviewed here.

Genetic theories

Many studies concerned with the genetic basis of schizophrenia have been carried out, with various results. Some early studies reported a concordance as high as 76% (Slater, 1953) or 86% (Kallman, 1938) for monozygotic twins as compared to 14% to 15% for dizygotic twins. Other studies have reported lower degrees of concordance. Possible explanations for this variability in findings in studies of twins include the use of differing statistical methods, research designs, and diagnostic criteria.

Recently, more adequately controlled studies of schizophrenic persons were carried out in Denmark. These studies, which involved schizophrenics who had been raised by adoptive families, showed a significant incidence of schizophrenia in the biological parents (Kety et al., 1976). This incidence was close to that described in earlier studies, which had shown an expectation of 16.4% that children of one schizophrenic parent would become schizophrenic (versus .85% for the general population) and an expectation that ranges from 38% to 68% when both parents are schizophrenic (Jackson, 1960).

Both early and recent studies show that nonschizophrenic relatives of schizophrenic persons have significantly more of the conditions, such as eye-tracking disorders, that are associated with schizophrenia than the general population (Holzman et al., 1974).

Most theorists, whether they are concerned with organic, psychodynamic, or sociocultural bases for schizophrenia, do agree that a genetic factor is operating. There is no conclusive evidence as to the mode of genetic transmission—schizophrenia, like many other disorders, seems to be polygenetic.

At least one aspect of the genetic controversy that needs to be refined is the differentiation of genetic factors from perinatal and prenatal influences.

Biochemical and physical theories

Prenatal and perinatal influence theory. Prenatal and perinatal influences have been cited as factors in the etiology of schizophrenia. Explanations include a possible alteration of the fetal oxygen supply, passage of endocrine and toxic substances across the placental barrier, and the effects of maternal emotions on fetal endocrine balance and nervous system.

Birth trauma of one sort or another has been suggested as an explanation for schizophrenia. Significantly more prenatal and perinatal complications have been found in the histories of schizophrenics than in those of nonschizophrenics (Taft and Goldfarb, 1964), and stillbirth rate, rate of premature births, and incidence of serious congenital malformations in offspring have been found to be higher in schizophrenic mothers (Campion and Tucker, 1973). Some investigators suggest that some sort of trauma present at or before birth is the agent that interacts with a genetic predisposition to result in schizophrenia.

Anatomical or physiological defect theories. One physiological defect that has been identified as a possible etiological factor is an abnormally responsive autonomic nervous system. One group of researchers, which verified this finding in a large-scale study, found an overresponsive autonomic nervous system to be especially evident in schizophrenics who had suffered complications at birth. The researchers hypothesized that this overreactivity combines with a genetic predisposition for schizophrenia and results in expression of the disorder (Trotter, 1977).

In the past, anatomical, and physiological defects have been hypothesized as the basis of schizophrenia. Until recently there has been no evidence to support these hypotheses. Now, however, investigators have announced findings that they view as a breakthrough in our understanding of the physical basis of schizophrenia. *Amphetamine psychosis* is a condition that closely mimics the schizophrenic process and symptomatology. In this disorder, amphetamine stimulates the release of dopamine (a neurotransmitter catecholamine), and a possible flooding of the brain with dopamine may occur. Also consistent with the anatomical or physiological defect theory are aspects of another disorder—Parkinson's disease. In this disease the problem is that the individual's brain lacks many of the dopamine-producing cells, resulting in a scarcity of the substance. Treatment with L-dopa alleviates symptoms of parkinsonism. Another fact linking schizophrenia to a physiological defect is that antischizophrenic drugs, which are believed to act on the neurotransmitters in some way, possibly reducing the level of dopamine or blocking its transmission, also produce side effects that mimic the symptoms of Parkinson's disease.

Another etiological model (Stein and Wise, 1971) suggests a possible deficiency in the level of the enzyme that converts dopamine to norepinephrine, while yet another model (Potkin et al., 1978) postulates decreased activity of the enzyme monoamine oxidase, which is involved in the degradation of chemicals such as dopamine. In addition, it was recently discovered through autopsy studies that the brains of schizophrenics contain about twice the normal number of receptor sites for dopamine. They theorize that schizophrenics are overstimulated with their own brain signals and thus are flooded with strange thoughts, hallucinations, and misperceptions (Science News, Vol. 112, p. 342, 1977).

The *dopamine hypothesis* was the second hypothesis to be derived from attempts to understand the physical bases of schizophrenia. The first was the *transmethylation hypothesis*, which was derived from the study of psychotomimetic drugs such as mescaline. Mescaline, which is a methylated catechol, produces symptoms that mimic schizophrenia. It was theorized that a transfer of a methyl group to neurotransmitters or their precursors changes them into psychotomimetic substances. Methylated catecholamines and methylated indoles were looked for, but so far there has been no definitive evidence of elevated levels in schizophrenic persons. The difficulty of separating the effects of diet, drugs, stress, and environmental conditions has complicated the picture. It seems likely that excess dopamine is a fundamental factor in schizophrenia. The dopamine hypothesis currently is probably the most widely accepted biochemical theory.

Toxic substance theories. A theory suggested by Heath et al (1958) concerned a toxic or abnormal protein, called *taraxein*, in the blood of schizophrenics. When injected into nonschizophrenics, it produced behavior and symptoms similar to those of schizophrenia. This substance has been isolated by three different researchers, but it is not generally considered to be the fundamental factor in schizophrenia. The dopamine hypothesis seems more widely accepted as the biochemical basis for schizophrenia.

It has been hypothesized that food might contain a toxic substance—specifically, the protein gluten that is found in wheat. A research team found that when wheat was removed from the diet of schizophrenics, their symptoms improved dramatically. While the research team cautioned that this is not a simple cause-and-effect situation, it concluded that wheat gluten is a pathogenic factor in schizophrenia (Singh and Kay, 1976).

It has been suggested that a slow viral infection process may be responsible for the subsequent development of schizophrenia. This theory has received support because of the discovery that the organic brain syndrome known as Jakob-Creutzfeldt disease may be of viral origin and because of the fact that individuals suffering from herpes encephalitis have a clinical picture that is very similar to an acute schizophrenic episode (Wynne et al., 1978).

Orthomolecular theory. "Orthomolecular," a word invented by the scientist and Nobel laureate Linus Pauling, means "the right molecules in the right concentrations."

Mescaline psychosis has been used as a model by the proponents of the orthomolecular theory of schizophrenia. Osmond and Hoffer studied mescaline psychosis and saw similarities to the delirium associated with the vitamin deficiency disease pellagra (Pfeiffer, 1975). They noted that earlier findings had shown that vitamin B_3 (in the form of niacin or nicotinic acid) not only cured the physical symptoms of pellagra but also provided complete relief from the mental symptoms. They hypothesized that perhaps schizophrenia, with symptoms that are also similar to mescaline psychosis, represents an abnormally high requirement for vitamin B_3. They began treating patients with megadoses of the vitamin—usually 3 gm combined with 3 gm of vitamin C and trace mineral supplements.

The orthomolecular psychiatrists prefer to designate the disorder in the plural—the schizophrenias. They have categorized them as histadelic schizophrenia, histapenic schizophrenia, and mauve factor schizophrenia. The histapenic schizophrenics are the ones who are treated with vitamin B_3. Vitamin therapy is not the sole treatment; a combination of vitamins, psychotropic drugs, and psychotherapy is used. Young schizophrenic persons, whose symptomatology is still labile, are viewed as the most likely candidates for the treatment.

The theory is not widely accepted in established medical circles; and conflicting claims are made by proponents and skeptics.

Perceptual and cognitive disturbance theories

Sensory input dysfunction. Several theories have been postulated and explored concerning a possible defect in the schizophrenic's ability to perceive and organize his experience effectively. The defect in controlling incoming stimuli from the environment results in overload. According to those theories, a schizophrenic person has an ineffective barrier between his inner self and the parade of events he is exposed to in his environment. One theorist (Cameron, 1963) has termed this situation "overinclusiveness" and has described it as a failure to weed out irrelevant material, with a resultant flooding of the ego. The person is unable to organize his perceptions appropriately. Such theories are consistent with several studies of the effects of sensory deprivation, which indicate that chronic schizophrenics tolerate sensory deprivation much better than nonschizophrenics.

Another way of looking at sensory input dysfunctions and schizophrenia is to view the schizophrenic as being deficient in the ability to modulate sensory input. Two manifestations of this defect are possible—the overresponsiveness of the acute stage of schizophrenia and the underresponsiveness of the chronic schizophrenic (Epstein and Coleman, 1971).

Learning theory. One hypothesis concerning schizophrenia holds that the disorder is learned. According to this theory, an overresponsive autonomic nervous system, a genetic predisposition for schizophrenia, and a harsh environment combine to encourage a person to learn to avoid stress by displaying schizophrenic symptoms—hallucinations, delusions, withdrawal, isolation from others, and so on (Trotter, 1977).

Psychodynamic theories

Generally, the psychodynamic theorists argue that the roots of schizophrenia are in the oral stage of psychosocial development—the stage in which a child develops an ability to trust other people. These theorists believe that schizophrenia originates in problems in the mother-child relationship that develop during this period. There is a faulty development of the ego. In particular, the defense mechanism of repression is ineffective, a situation that constitutes the underlying psychodynamic problem. Clinicians have long noted that the schizophrenic's unconscious seems very close to the surface. Since the defense mechanism of repression is weak and ineffective, unconscious material threatens to flood the ego and thus stimulates the psychotic symptoms as defense mechanisms. Freud viewed schizophrenia as a regression to a state of infantile narcissism, with a withdrawal of the libido from the external world to the internal self. Freud did not work with many schizophrenics—most of his patients were neurotics. In fact, he was rather pessimistic about the value of psychotherapy for schizophrenics.

Harry Stack Sullivan did a good deal of his work with schizophrenic persons. His "interpersonal" theory of psychiatry pointed to an unhealthy relationship between the schizophrenic and his parents. His view of schizophrenia was more hopeful than Freud's; he believed that a later, more satisfying relationship could do much to erase the harm of the early, unhealthy ones.

Carl Jung viewed schizophrenia as centripetal (inner-directed) in their relationships with the world rather than centrifugal (outer-directed).

Sylvano Arieti, a contemporary American authority on schizophrenia, sees schizophrenia basically as a defensive reaction to severe anxiety that originates in childhood and recurs in later life. It is a restitutive attempt to make the best of a bad situation.

Eric Berne's transactional analysis system defines schizophrenia as a situation in which the "child ego state," rather than the "adult ego state," is in command of the ego functions. The child is frightened and "not OK." In the schizophrenic person the "parent ego state" participates sporadically, mostly in a harsh and oppressive manner. Berne believed that the only way to proceed with psychotherapy for a schizophrenic is to engage the child ego state and obtain his cooperation.

Family systems theories

Family systems theorists have identified communication patterns and family relationship patterns (see Chapter 6) that may be etiological factors in schizophrenia. Murray Bowen, a leading family systems theorist who did his original work with schizophrenic clients, argued that a *multigenerational transmission* may be operating in the disorder. He postulated that in some families, a process that is based on the defense mechanism of projection is passed down from one generation to the next. If two people who are neurotic marry and have a child, their neuroses may "mesh" in such a way as to produce a more severe neurosis in the child. If this child eventually marries a neurotic person, once again neuroses will mesh to produce an even more severely impaired offspring. Bowen views schizophrenia as a severe emotional disorder. While others see neurosis and schizophrenia as discrete entities, he considers schizophrenia to be on a continuum with neurosis and other emotional disorders. According to Bowen's theoretical system, schizophrenia is a product of several generations of escalating impairment, with increasing use of a *family projection process* and decreasing levels of differentiation between family members. As a treatment goal, Bowen stresses increased differentiation of each family member from the family system, as opposed to unhealthy "fusion" among family members. He sees a tendency to fuse or merge with others operating in all families. This is the "undifferentiated family ego mass." If this tendency is strong enough and pervasive enough, it can be pathological for individual family members, who lose their sense of self.

Thus, some family systems are viewed as being pathological to the point of being *schizophrenogenic*. That is, the family system itself fosters schizophrenia. The person who is identified as the patient is simply the carrier of the family's illness.

Certain *family configurations* have been singled out by Lidz (1973) as being schizophrenogenic. According to Lidz, the *skewed family pattern* is most often seen in the development of male schizophrenics. While the mother is most apt to be termed schizophrenogenic, the father, through his ineffective role modeling and inability to counteract the actions of his wife, plays an equally important role. The mother is described as domineering and egocentric. She is unable to differentiate her own feelings and anxieties from those of the other members of the family—particularly those of her son. In the beginning she has great difficulty relating to her infant son. This situation leads to overprotection and then to symbiosis. Eventually, she begins to use her son to make up for her own failures and disappointments in life.

In the *schismatic family pattern* there is usually overt conflict between the spouses—the father is dominant and perhaps overtly paranoid. He tends to downgrade his wife and her role as mother and wife. Both spouses undercut each other, and the child is competed for and used as a pawn in the conflict between his parents. Lidz believes that this pattern is more apt to produce schizophrenia in a girl than in a boy. There is overprotection, great concern about morality, and intrusiveness into the child's sexual behavior during adolescence.

There are some similarities between these two patterns—overprotection, a poor relationship with the parent of the same sex, and parental failure to establish proper and healthy boundaries between self and child. The child is unconsciously used by the parent of the opposite sex to fulfill needs and make up deficiencies.

Other patterns that family theorists see as particularly important in the development of schizophrenia include emotional divorce, coalition across generation boundaries, vagueness in communicating, tangentiality, double-bind communication, family myths, and mystification. (See Chapter 6.)

Existential theories

The existential psychologist Binswanger believed that the great philosopher Kierkegaard referred to schizophrenia when he described sickness of the mind as "the sickness unto death" (May, 1967). Existentialists point to the schizophrenic's altered perceptions of time, space, and causality as essential ingredients in the creation of his world. Themes that existential psychologists and psychotherapists mention when they discuss schizophrenia include emptiness, nothingness, and painful internal vacuum. The schizophrenic's defect resembles a hole that requires constant filling; he is in constant fear of annihilation. This need for constant filling and the fear of nonexistence are cited as reasons for obesity in some schizophrenics and latent schizophrenics. It has been suggested by clinicians, existential and otherwise, that a certain percentage of obese individuals should not attempt to reduce, since doing so may prescipitate a schizophrenic break with reality.

The internal emptiness of the schizophrenic, or lack of identity, leads to strained interpersonal relations; his whole existence takes on the "as if" quality described earlier in this chapter. R. D. Laing, considered to be an existential psychiatrist, believes that schizophrenia is not an illness but a way of being in the world. He views it as a potentially growth-promoting state, a change to correct a developmental problem. He sees the submerging into a psychotic state as beneficial, with a higher and more insightful level of development being the eventual compensation. His Kingsley Hall experiment allowed patients to enter psychotic states, in a tolerant and drug-free atmosphere. This philosophy of treatment is not shared by more conventional therapists, who see the potential for residual damage to the personality inherent in each psychotic break.

Sociocultural theories

R. D. Laing also suggests that schizophrenia may be the only way to be sane in an insane world. Thus he implicates society in the etiology of schizophrenia.

Other theorists, notably Thomas Szasz, have proposed that schizophrenia is not a disease or a psychological disorder at all but rather a construct that has been invented by society to serve some of its needs—for example, to explain behavior that is deviant from the mainstream and to segregate persons who, in their deviance, make us uncomfortable. Proponents of this view remind us of the historical beginnings of care for the mentally ill, when the so-called mentally ill included the dregs of society—beggars, paupers, the physically disabled, and the diseased. They were an embarrassment to the more privileged classes, so they were warehoused in large institutions—at first mixed in with criminals. Szasz and theorists who agree with him maintain that the "treatment"—the warehousing of people—existed first and that it then became necessary to have the "patients" to fit the treatment. The furtherance of the modern mental health industry, which does indeed provide financial support and security for many workers, is pointed to as one of the purposes the mentally ill serve for society.

One facet of society that has been implicated in the etiology of schizophrenia is poverty: poverty and schizophrenia are strongly correlated. Several explanations for this are possible. One that has been postulated is that poverty is an etiological agent through the medium of increased stress. Crowded living conditions, poor nutrition, inadequate or nonexistent prenatal care, and lack of meaningful recreation are only some of the concomitants of poverty that increase stress in everyday living. In their review of the massive literature on schizophrenia and social class, Roman and Trice hypothesized that a combination of child socialization patterns and patterns of environmental stress and social disorganization is related to the high incidence of schizophrenia in the lower social strata (Roman and Trice, 1967). One well-controlled study comparing schizophrenics with normal persons found that schizophrenics experience significantly greater stress in dealing with life events than do nonschizophrenics (Serban, 1975). An animal study that incorporated increasingly stressful conditions resulted in the delineation of three groups of animals—those that remain relatively disease-free, those that suffer from various psychosomatic disorders, and those that exhibit behavior that could well be described as psychotic (Stroebel, 1969).

Stress-diathesis theory

While environmental stress is considered to be the most important etiological factor by many—just as genetic predisposition, metabolic disorders, psychodynamic weaknesses, and family dysfunction each have their advocates—current psychiatric opinion favors a multifactorial etiology or a stress-diathesis model for the genesis of schizophrenia. The disorder is considered to be the final outcome of many complex factors. Eisenberg (1973) describes the stress-diathesis model as follows:

> Psychobiological stress acts on an individual with a genetic predisposition to psychosis and eventually leads to abnormal metabolic processes that cause disorders of mood and thought. Predisposition probably varies on a continuum.

Within this etiological model, psychobiological stress and genetic predisposition both vary on a continuum. An individual with a strong genetic predisposition might succumb to moderate or even minimal stress—for example, the stress of adolescence (the process schizophrenic described earlier). A person with relatively little genetic predisposition might react to severe stress with a psychotic break (the reactive schizophrenic). This continuum model for stress and genetic predisposition is compatible with Murray Bowen's view that schizophrenia exists on a continuum with neurosis and other psychological disorders (Bowen, 1976). While some theorists disagree and consider schizophrenia and neurosis as discrete and unrelated phenomena, Karl Menninger also views neurosis and schizophrenia on a continuum of mental health and mental illness (Menninger, 1963).

Schizophrenia and psychophysiological complementarity

Carrying the continuum model a step further, Bahnson and Bahnson view all of the human individual's disorders, psychological and physiological, as being on a continuum—a continuum of psychophysiological complementarity. This particular construct seeks to identify alternate forms for the discharge of energy associated with stress experienced by the human organism. As the degree of stress increases, an individual becomes more vulnerable to physical or psychological disorders. Which type of disorder he "chooses" depends on habitual patterns of response. The extreme manifestation of disorder in a person who tends to somatize is cancer, while in an individual with a tendency toward emotional lability, it is schizophrenia. The Bahnsons point to various studies that demonstrate an inverse relationship between cancer and schizophrenia (Bahnson and Bahnson, 1964). This approach represents an attempt to develop a monistic theory rather than a false splitting of "mind" and "body" (Bahnson, 1969, 1974).

· · ·

The exact etiology of schizophrenia is not known. The many theories that have been postulated focus on such areas as genetic endowment, biochemical abnormalities, anatomical differences, psychodynamic defects, family dysfunction, and social disorganization. The schizophrenic syndrome is a complex disorder, and the most generally accepted view is that it is a multifactorial disorder incorporating many or all of the elements that have been discussed in this section.

TREATMENT
History

The treatment of schizophrenia has a history as long as the history of the disease itself. In ancient times, treatment was quite enlightened; it involved music, poetry, and dance therapy; rest; and "talking therapy." In ancient Greece temples were set aside for such treatments. In medieval times, when madness was thought to indicate possession by evil spirits or to be evidence of the practice of witchcraft, treatment took the form of exorcism and burning at the stake. After this period, but before any scientific approach to mental illness had evolved, treatment consisted of segregation from society in places like Bedlam in England or the prototype of the modern mental hospital, the Hôpital Général in France. In these large institutions people were kept in crowded, filthy conditions, and they were watched over by keepers who were at best apathetic and often cruel. Even at the beginning of the twentieth century, families of schizophrenics were told to forget about their hospitalized relatives. There was little hope for improvement.

When psychiatrists began to treat schizophrenia, their approach was mainly somatic. *Prefrontal lobotomy* is a brain operation that was used on many schizophrenics before the discovery of the phenothiazine drugs. In this procedure the tracts between cortex, subcortex, and basal ganglia are severed. It often resulted in a mitigation of aggressive, violent behavior, but it also left the patient in a fairly deteriorated condition—docile, unmotivated, and demonstrating regressive, crude behavior. Thousands of lobotomies were performed on schizophrenics during the 1940s and early 1950s.

Hydrotherapy was a much less destructive modality. The purposes of hydrotherapy included sedation of the overactive patient (continuous tub baths and wet sheet packs) and production of tonic effects (needle spray and alternate jet showers). The wet sheet packs did seem to have a highly sedating action, and before effective psychotropic drugs were available, some patients would ask to be put into the packs when they realized that tension and anxiety were building up.

Isolation from others in seclusion rooms was a common treatment. There is a legitimate rationale for reducing environmental stimuli and allowing the hyperactive patient to calm down. Unfortunately, the seclusion rooms were sometimes used as punishment in the manner of solitary confinement in prisons. Seclusion also became the easiest way to treat excited patients; some were kept in the same small, bare seclusion rooms for long periods—sometimes for years.

Insulin coma therapy, or *insulin shock*, was used—for the most part, in the 1940s and early 1950s. The patient was given insulin to induce coma; he became somnolent and pacified in the hypoglycemic state. There appeared to be some successes with the treatment, particularly in cases of young schizophrenics who had just experienced their first psychotic breaks. There were also some very real dangers attached to insulin coma therapy, and some fatalities resulted—one reason why it is no longer used as a treatment for schizophrenia. The apparent remissions that sometimes occurred were later attributed to the intensive and intimate nursing care required during the coma period—care that was described as a healthier and more loving re-parenting (Schwing, 1954). Perhaps some of the remissions were ones that would have occured in any group of young schizophrenics undergoing their first psychotic breaks.

Electroconvulsive therapy

Electroconvulsive therapy is sometimes called *electric shock therapy* or *electrostimulative therapy*, which is the currently preferred term. The rationale for using this treatment in cases of schizophrenia was originally based on a misconception. It was thought that schizophrenia and epilepsy do not occur together and that convulsions perhaps prevent schizophrenia (Rowe, 1975). This view was later shown to be untrue, since schizophrenia and epilepsy can occur in the same person. While the reason for the treatment was inaccurate, the treatment was helpful in some cases. Today electroconvulsive therapy is considered useful for schizophrenics who are in severe, life-threatening catatonic stupors (Redlich and Freedman, 1966) or for severely depressed and suicidal schizophrenics (Goldfarb and Goldfarb, 1977; Mendel, 1976; Redlich and Freedman, 1966; Rowe, 1975). It also seems to be helpful for extremely confused and agitated postpartum psychosis patients. A woman who is suffering from postpartum psychosis is actually experiencing an acute schizophrenic reaction.

Psychotropic drugs

The somatic treatment most widely used for schizophrenia today is the administration of psychopharmaceuticals. The major tranquilizers, which came into widespread use in the early 1950s, are called *antipsychotic drugs,* or *antischizophrenic drugs* by some. In some ways, "tranquilizer" is a misnomer, since the action of such a drug is to decrease the severity of psychotic behavior more than it is to sedate. In fact, the tranquilizers will stimulate or energize persons who are withdrawn and apathetic and calm those who are hyperactive—in other words, these drugs tend to normalize levels of activity. Chlorpromazine was the first of the phenothiazine drugs to be used. Other drugs were developed from the prototype. Some common phenothiazines that are used today include chlorpromazine (Thorazine), promazine (Sparine), butaperazine (Repoise), triflupromazine (Vesprin), trifluoperazine (Stelazine), perphenazine (Trilafon), prochlorperazine (Compazine), fluphenazine (Prolixin), and thioridazine (Mellaril). Haloperidol (Haldol), chlorprothixene (Taractan), and thiothixene (Navane) are not phenothiazines but are examples of some other major tranquilizers or antipsychotic drugs. Haldol is a butyrophenone, and Taractan and Navane are thioxanthenes.

A psychotropic drug that was used in India for several centuries, *Rauwolfia serpentina,* is used today to make the calming agent reserpine (Serpasil). However, the use of reserpine as a psychotropic drug is infrequent—it is more often used to lower blood pressure.

While it must be remembered that any drug can demonstrate a paradoxical reaction in any one person, some of the major tranquilizers tend to be sedating and some tend to be activating (see Table 13-1).

Characteristics specific to some of these drugs are as follows:

Haldol is believed to be especially helpful in decreasing the severity of hallucinations and delusions. It is also the drug of choice in *Gilles de la Tourette's syndrome,* a physiologically based disorder that is characterized by bizarre choreiform movements and the compulsive and uncontrollable utterance of obscene words—coprolalia. The syndrome is believed to be related to excess dopamine in the brain, and antipsychotic drugs are thought to somehow block the transport of dopamine.

Prolixin, in the form of Prolixin Enanthate, is a long-lasting phenothiazine. Intramuscular injections can be given in dosages that will last for 1 to 3 weeks, with an average of 2 weeks' duration. For this reason, Prolixin is believed to be an especially appropriate drug for persons who, for various reasons, resist taking their medication or are unreliable self-medicators. Among schizophrenics, failure to take drugs is one or the main reasons for readmission to hospitals.

TABLE 13-1. Sedating and activating tranquilizers*

	Daily dose	
	Outpatients	**Inpatients**
Sedating tranquilizers (used with overactive patients)		
Chorpromazine (thorazine)	50-400 mg	200-1600 mg
Thioridazine (Mellaril)	50-400 mg	200-800 mg
Chlorprothixene (Taractan)	30-60 mg	75-600 mg
Promazine (Sparine)	Range: 25-1000 mg	
Activating tranquilizers (used with withdrawn patients)		
Trifluoperazine (Stelazine)	4-10 mg	6-30 mg
Prochlorperazine (Compazine)	15-60 mg	30-150 mg
Perphenazine (Trilafon)	8-24 mg	16-64 mg
Haloperidol (Haldol)	2-6 mg	4-15 mg
Thiothixene (Navane)	6-15 mg	10-60 mg
Fluphenazine (Prolixin)	1-3 mg	2-20 mg
Butaperazine (Repoise)	Range: 30-50 mg	

*Data adapted from Dimascio, Alberto, and Richard I. Shader. 1970. Clinical Handbook of Psychopharmacology. New York: Science House.

Dosages of *Mellaril* should not exceed 800 mg per day. In high doses, Mellaril can cause pigmentary retinopathy and eventual blindness. Any complaints of decreasing visual acuity from clients who are taking phenothiazines should be investigated immediately, and this is particularly important for those who are taking Mellaril.

The major tranquilizers are relatively safe drugs for long-term use, and they are not addicting. Minor or moderate side effects occur fairly frequently; serious and life-threatening side effects are rare. (See Table 13-2.)

Psychotherapy

Forms of psychotherapy representing all of the various schools of psychology have been used in the treatment of schizophrenic clients. Many clinicians believe, as Freud did, that psychoanalysis is not the treatment of choice for schizophrenics because of its goal of freeing unconscious conflicts. They argue that the psychodynamic defect in schizophrenia is an impaired ability to repress and that the unconscious is all too close to the surface. It is the threat that unconscious material will flood the ego that stimulates the psychotic symptoms as defenses.

TABLE 13-2. Side effects of the major tranquilizers

Side effects	Nursing intervention
Minor	
Menstrual irregularities	Inform client of possibility
Changes in libido	Inform client of possibility
Increased weight, increased appetite	Nutritional counseling
Constipation	Increased ingestion of bulk-producing foods; exercise; laxatives as needed
Dry mouth	Rinse with water; give sugarless gum (however, not advisable for elderly clients because of increased danger of choking—the phenothiazines can effect the swallowing reflex)
Postural hypotension	As a preventative, client should learn to sit up gradually from a lying position; to combat: have client lie down with feet elevated
Photosensitivity	Use sun hats and sunscreening lotions during the summer months
Allergic rash	May require an order to change to another drug
Contact dermatitis in staff members dispensing the drug in liquid form	Use of rubber gloves when the drug is being dispensed
Moderate	
Extrapyramidal symptoms: drugs act on limbic area of brain to promote muscular dysfunctions (see Table 13-3)	Extrapyramidal symptoms, if they persist, require drugs to counteract them. Such drugs as benztropine (Cogentin), procyclidine (Kemadrin), trihexyphenidyl (Artane), and biperiden (Akineton) may be used. These drugs, however, are not without side effects of their own (e.g., constipation). The automatic prescribing of one of these is not an advisable practice, since extrapyramidal symptoms are sometimes transitory and thus may disappear after a few days.

Continued.

TABLE 13-2. Side effects of the major tranquilizers—cont'd

Side effects	Nursing intervention
Serious	
Agranulocytosis (often is manifested as a sore throat or high fever)	Stop giving the drug immediately. Notify a physician when a client complains of a sore throat or has a fever. Total and differential white cell counts are done, and in some cases, reverse isolation may be used.
Drug-induced jaundice (begins like influenza)	Periodic liver function tests should be carried out when patients are receiving phenothiazines
Tardive dyskinesia (Although one of the extrapyramidal symptoms, it is included here because unlike the other extra-pyramidal symptoms it can become irreversible. It is a disfiguring and disabling syndrome characterized by involuntary twitching of the face, tongue, arms, and legs. Abnormally low levels of acetylcholine are believed to be responsible.)	Some success has been reported recently at M.I.T. with the treatment of tardive dyskinesia. Researchers used lecithin, a natural food substance and a major source of choline, which is a precursor of the neurotransmitter acetylcholine.

TABLE 13-3. Extrapyramidal symptoms

Akinesia	Akathisia	Dyskinesia	Pseudo-parkinsonism
Usually has slow onset	Usually has slow onset (most often occurs in middle-aged people)	May have sudden onset (most often occurs in younger people)	Slow onset (most often occurs in older people)
Reduced physical activity	Restlessness, pacing	Torticollis	Shuffling gait
Listlessness	Jittery movements	Carpal spasms	Masklike facies
Apathy (often not recognized)	Fine hand tremor	Opisthotonos	Increased salivation
Development of painful muscles and joints	Facial tics	Oculogyric crisis	Stooping posture
	Insomnia		"Pill rolling" tremor Cogwheel rigidity

Some notable clinicians, however, have worked with schizophrenics in a psychoanalytic manner: Harry Stack Sullivan, Gertrud Schwing, John Rosen, Marguerite Sechehaye, Harold Searles, and Frieda Fromm-Reichmann are examples. All have written about their work. A well-known psychiatric nurse who works within the psychosis of a client is June Mellow. She calls her in-depth approach *nursing therapy*. Mellow helps the client to relive the original mother-child symbiotic attachment, but the new emotional experience is a corrective one.

Therapists who do work in this manner with schizophrenic clients point out that the clinician must himself be a healthy, well-integrated person in touch with his own thoughts, feelings, and reactions. The ethical practice of psychoanalysis mandates that the therapist be analyzed as part of the training process. Psychoanalysis is not an economical form of treatment, since one therapist can treat only a limited number of clients and there are many schizophrenics in need of help. Psychoanalysis is a specialized and expensive form of therapy. In comparison to the number of schizophrenics in need of treatment, there are *very* few psychoanalysts willing and able to treat them in this esoteric manner. Aside from this fact, as was mentioned before, many clinicans and writers believe that psychoanalysis, with its goal of uncovering unconscious conflicts, is not a useful or even safe treatment for schizophrenics, whose faulty use of repression may be the basic defect of the disorder.

Several mental health workers point to relationship or supportive therapy as the most appropriate form of psychotherapy for schizophrenics. Such therapy can be long term, and it can be crisis oriented at intervals when necessary. It can be modified over time to match the needs and the growth of the client. Rather than attempting to uncover the unconscious, the goal of relationship or supportive therapy is to gain insight into the effects of one's behavior on one's life and to encourage the development of ego strengths through the realization of successful changes in behavior. Mendel and Green (1967) describe this type of treatment and suggest that while the beginning stages of a relationship may require frequent meetings with the client, the number of meetings may gradually decrease. Eventually—perhaps after several years, in some instances—once-a-year phone calls to "check in" with the therapist may be sufficient.

Mendel and Green take the "as if" phenomenon, described earlier, and turn it around to use it therapeutically. For example, they suggest encouraging a person who feels he cannot get up and face the world and a daily job as other people do, to act "as if" he could do so. After acting this way for a period of time, the client gains some ego strength from the realization that he *has* been able to accomplish this task every morning.

In relationship therapy, the nurse lends ego strength to the client in order to provide support while they both work toward the goal of developing the client's own ego strength. The nurse-patient relationship in psychiatric nursing is ideally suited to relationship therapy.

Family therapy

Therapy that involves the families of schizophrenics is focused on clarifying mystifying forms of communication, such as double-bind communicating and tangentiality, which were discussed in Chapter 6. Family therapy is also concerned with strengthening appropriate boundaries between family members. For instance, one approach to decreasing the debilitating hold of a mother and a son's symbiotic relationship might be to improve the relationship between the two spouses and the relationship between the son and his father. Insight into communication and relationship patterns within the family is encouraged, and alternate patterns are explored.

The initial and primary goal of the family therapist, according to Murray Bowen (1977), is to decrease the level of anxiety within the family system, since it is this anxiety that fosters development of the various types pathological behavior. Bowen's definition of a mental health professional is "someone who helps decrease anxiety."

Pittman and Flomenhaft have described a marital configuration that is characterized by an unequal relationship between the spouses. One spouse's incompetence is required and encouraged by the other spouse, in order to verify his own competence. This "doll's house marriage"—the name comes from the situation portrayed in Ibsen's play *The Doll's House*—usually involves a child-like wife and a masterful husband, although the roles can be reversed. Each spouse needs this system of relating to maintain his own inner equilibrium and the equilibrium of the marriage. Pittman and Flomenhaft view this type of unequal relationship as common in a potentially schizophrenic population; they suggest that one or both spouses may be latent schizophrenics maintaining stability through the marriage. With the development of crises such as severe financial difficulties or the addition of children to the family, such an individual may come into a treatment situation. It is then that the tendency of a therapist to push for too much and too rapid change can precipitate a psychotic break. The great importance that the therapist places on individual growth may cause him to attempt to promote more change than is necessary, thus destroying the family and precipitating illness in one or more family members. Pittman and Flomenhaft suggest that the therapist work with caution and develop an ability to tolerate a certain degree of inequality within a marriage, which may be the wiser choice for some couples (Pittman and Flomenhaft, 1970).

Group therapy

As is the case in individual psychotherapy, few clinicans advocate psychoanalytically oriented group therapy for schizophrenics. Group therapy should be focused not on probing the unconscious but rather on the development of insight into behavior. A more comfortable adjustment to life is a legitimate goal of group therapy for schizophrenic clients. Group therapy can promote socialization—or resocialization for a regressed schizophrenic—and can provide opportunities for a client to become more outer-directed. Concern for other people can be positively reinforced, a development that can lead to increased self-esteem. Sharing of experiences and problems can provide the reassurance that comes from knowing that others have lived through similar situations. Support from a peer group during periods of crisis and attempted change can help to make experiments with new behavior less frightening.

The leader in group therapy for schizophrenics—particularly withdrawn schizophrenics—needs to take a more active role than the leader of another type of group might take, especially in the beginning stages of the group. But the same principles of group dynamics apply. Besides psychotherapy groups, various activity therapy groups, such as dance, music, and poetry groups, are helpful. *Remotivation groups* are often used to bring severely regressed schizophrenics back to a here-and-now orientation; such groups constitute a particularly useful tool for psychiatric nurses.

Certain self-help community groups are available for discharged schizophrenics; giving a client information about them would be an appropriate and helpful. Recovery Inc. is one such group—its method is a type of self-mediated behavioral modification combined with peer group support. Schizophrenics Anonymous is another self-help group that is available in many communities.

Milieu therapy

Since disorganization in living is a major aspect of the schizophrenic experience, milieu therapy can provide schizophrenic clients opportunities to learn or relearn interpersonal skills and to become competent in the activites of daily living. Milieu therapy can also provide opportunities for satisfying recreation. An ideal milieu for schizophrenics is one that provides the structure that is so badly needed in a disorganized life.

Milieu therapy of a specific kind has been used in combination with regressive electroconvulsive therapy, a procedure that induces confusion, amnesia, and a decreased ability for self-care. A milieu is set up to recapitulate a family situation, with the goal being a healthy reparenting of the schizophrenic client. This treatment, however, has not gained wide acceptance.

Brief hospitalization versus institutionalization

Many clinicians believe that much of the apparent deterioration in chronic schizophrenics is due not to the disease process but to the effects of long-term institutionalization. Some of the dangers of institutionalization have been pointed out by Mendel and Green (1967) in their excellent book on the treatment of chronic schizophrenics:

1. The client loses his "place" in his family and community. It is not so unusual for a person who is discharged after many years of hospitalization to go back to his "roots" and find that a parking lot or a high rise has been built where his old neighborhood stood.
2. The fact that the person has failed in his developmental task is reified. Secondary guilt is an accompaniment of this realization.
3. The role of the person as a passive receiver of treatment is reinforced instead of the role of active participant in his own treatment plan.
4. The person's energy and resources (for example, financial) go toward his adaptation to the hospital rather than toward his adaptation to living in society.

Mendel and Green argue that short-term hospitalization should be viewed as a coping mechanism or safety valve that can be used when a person's anxiety approaches unbearable heights. They suggest that his knowing the hospital is there when he needs it may help to reduce his anxiety.

Cancro (1970) has outlined criteria on which the decision to hospitalize a schizophrenic person should be based:

1. Safety—the person is endangering himself or others.
2. Crisis times—coping mechanisms are strained, and anxiety is high in the person or his family (death in the family or divorce are possible examples).
3. Stabilization of treatment and observation of the client—(for example, stabilization of a medication regimen or administration of electroconvulsive therapy) may be necessary.

• • •

Many forms of treatment are used to help schizophrenic clients live more comfortably in the world. While a few specially trained clinicians provide psychoanalytical therapy for schizophrenics, psychoanalysis is a comparatively rare form of treatment in schizophrenia, and the value and safety of it for schizophrenics are questioned by many clinicians. Supportive individual and group therapy, in combination with psychotropic drugs and, if possible, family therapy seems to be the treatment of choice for schizophrenic clients.

NURSING INTERVENTION

PRIMARY PREVENTION

Primary prevention of schizophrenia includes modification of the environment and strengthening of coping abilitites. It is only in recent years that much has been attempted or even written as far as prevention of schizophrenia is concerned. This is probably because there has never been agreement on the etiology of the disorder. Since the consensus is that it is of multifactorial etiology, a multifactorial prevention program must be developed. Some work has begun. Clinicians have identified high-risk groups—this process is termed *vulnerability research*. Basically, it is the selection and study of children who are at risk of developing schizophrenia. This determination is based on the presence of the following factors:

1. Genetic predisposition
2. History of deprivation of some kind in the prenatal or neonatal period
3. Evidence of excessive disorganization in the family
4. A disordered sociocultural environment such as that found in poverty-stricken inner-city areas or that occurring after a massive natural or man-made disaster (Garmenzy, 1972).

Through study of the vulnerable children, a group of children classified as "invulnerables" has been delineated. These are people who, through every indication, should have developed schizophrenia but did not—in fact, many excelled in various life tasks. The goal of researchers is to try to determine what factors helped to prevent these children from becoming schizophrenic and then to use this information to help prevent other children from developing the disorder.

Several areas have in the past been defined as providing possible approaches to the prevention of schizophrenia. *Premarital counseling* has been employed to help ensure a strong base for the future family or, in some instances, to prevent marriages from taking place. Most marriages are the result of "falling in love," which is an interweaving of the unconscious and often neurotic needs of two people. Later, it is the projection of these needs by one spouse onto the other that causes many marital problems. Some insight into the potential hazards may help to minimize marital discord or at least set a pattern for individual self-awareness and open communication between the spouses. Perhaps people need lessons in how to be married—it is not something that we know instinctively.

Marital counseling has been used for marriages that are showing signs of strain because of discord or dysfunctional family members. Alleviation of anxiety between married persons may prevent the conflict from being projected onto a child, a situation that can, according to family theorists, result in a schizophrenic reaction.

Family therapy that is instituted in the preschizophrenic stage of a child or adolescent's disorder may prevent a full-blown schizophrenic break. Alleviating anxiety within the family system, fostering insight into disordered patterns of communicating and relating, and encouraging the learning of new patterns are all parts of the family therapist's goal.

Prenatal care and *neonatal care* should be optimal in order to prevent the possible damage to fetus and infant that is significantly correlated with the incidence of schizophrenia.

Genetic counseling may be appropriate for families that are at extremely high risk of having schizophrenic offspring because numerous family members have the disorder. However, the exact mode of genetic transmission is unknown.

Child-rearing counseling can help alleviate such problems as "poor fit" between mother and child as far as stimulus barriers are concerned. A mother who enjoys giving and receiving stimuli might have a child with a low tolerance for stimuli, or vice versa. Developmental stages and the mother's need for rest, recreation, and time away from her children are also important aspects of this type of counseling. Just as people may need lessons in how to be married, preparation in parenting might prevent potentially harmful family discord.

The preceding list of possible avenues for preventative intervention makes it obvious that there is an important role for nurses in the prevention of schizophrenia, whether they work in the community, in maternal and child-focused agencies, in psychiatric settings, or in traditional hospital settings.

Traditionally, the allocation of funds for research into the etiology and treatment of schizophrenia has been sparse—this area is sometimes called the stepchild of research in this country. Perhaps one of the reasons for this situation is that chronically ill schizophrenics have very little political power, they have neither the personal nor the financial resources to mount much of a protest movement. As concerned and informed citizens and as advocates of their clients, nurses can make their voices and their votes count. Social changes that lead to improved living conditions and to the availability of optimum health care for all people may be viewed as primary preventive measures for all mental illnesses, including schizophrenia. The reason for the strong correlation between poverty and schizophrenia is unclear, but that there is a strong correlation is undisputed.

SECONDARY PREVENTION

What constitutes nursing care for the schizophrenic client? Just as no person fits exactly into any of the diagnostic categories, there is no exact set of rules or techniques that nurses use to intervene in cases of schizophrenia. It is best to deal with the behavior manifested rather than with the client as a psychiatric category. According to Freud, all behavior has meaning and the psychotic behavior of the schizophrenic is a form of communication.

The two areas that nurses can be particularly helpful in are interpersonal relationships and communication—these are usually the two areas that the schizophrenic has the most problems with in his life. A well known psychiatric nurse, Marguerite Holmes, believes that in the nurse-patient relationship, the nurse should concentrate on learning about and understanding the way the client is experiencing his world. The client will then have been *heard* and *understood*, and because this communication will have taken place, he may be able to move toward changing his behavior.

The skills required of the nurse then, are that she be able to (a) help the patient accept and appreciate his own inner experiences, which means that she has to be able to tolerate sharing in some of these experiences, and (b) meet the patient in real encounter. (Holmes, 1971)

Many things can happen to the nurse and the client through their attempts to relate to each other in a meaningful way. An important development is that the client may be able to increase his trust in other people. One relationship is rarely, if ever, the remedy for many years of social withdrawal, but one relationship can lead to another.

A therapeutic four A's. Bleuler's "four A's"—his delineation of the primary symptoms of schizophrenia—were reviewed earlier in this chapter. While they may be helpful as a mnemonic device, they are basically a negative concept, since they focus on pathology. There is a danger in this. Expectation of pathological responses is a powerful stimulus for the production of pathological responses in people. A more helpful way of viewing the interaction between the nurse and the schizophrenic would be to focus on four A's of therapeutic intervention (Arnold, 1976). Unlike Bleuler's four A's, which are concepts that are often projected onto the client, the therapeutic four A's apply to both partners in the relationship. The therapeutic four A's are as follows:

1. Acceptance. Crucial to the relationship is the nurse's acceptance of self, of the client as he is in the present stage of his development, and of the world as *he* sees it.
2. Awareness. Before nurse and client can begin to communicate effectively, the nurse must be aware of his or her own thoughts, feelings, and actions. This self-understanding, combined with an awareness of the client's verbal, nonverbal, and symbolic communication, is an essential part of the therapeutic relationship.
3. Acknowledgement. The existence of a person whose communication is not acknowledged is disconfirmed. People need to know that they have been heard, and they need to know whether they have been understood.
4. Authenticity. Most important of all of the elements of a therapeutic relationship, whether they begin with "A" or not, is authenticity. The tool of a psychiatric nurse is *self*. The self can only be a useful tool if it is real. Because of the nature of their disorder, it is not unusual for schizophrenic clients to have a history of many hurtful relationships. For this reason they tend to be very sensitive interpersonally and can quickly detect any signs of dissembling or deceit.

Nursing responses to behavioral problems. Many approaches to the etiology and treatment of schizophrenia have been discussed. Psychiatric nursing is based on an eclectic theoretical approach and on appropriate responses to behavioral problems.

Underactivity and withdrawal. Years ago, before psychotropic drugs and under conditions of inadequate care, withdrawal could progress to the point that some patients actually became ankylosed into a fetal position. Conditions have improved, but the tendency toward withdrawal is always present. The "good" patient, who makes no trouble for the staff, and the "unpleasant" one, whose behavior feeds into a pattern of mutual withdrawal between client and staff, are examples of clients whose interpersonal isolation may be reinforced by the hospital experience. Remotivation groups and activities such as art, exercise, and dance are important therapeutic interventions. The nurse's encouragement and support of the client as he begins to participate in unit activities can make a crucial difference.

The withdrawn schizophrenic may be neglectful of personal hygiene. Direction given in a way that protects his self-esteem, as well as positive reinforcement of his efforts through praise, can help facilitate his learning.

One way that withdrawal may be manifested is through varying degrees of mutism. Intervention for a nonverbal client requires an attitude of patience and quiet optimism on the part of a nurse. The communications from the nurse to the client should be simple and precise, and they should be phrased so as to require an answer from the client. Excessive detail and the introduction of many topics may be overwhelming and should be avoided. Orientation as to the proposed length of time for the interaction and the schedule of future interactions should be part of each exchange. Asking for a description of actions and events is probably less threatening to the nonverbal client than asking for thoughts or feelings (Oden, 1963). While fear is most often involved in the client's need to be mute, a need to control interpersonal situations may also be present. For this reason it is important to avoid making the client's mute behavior part of a power struggle with the nurse.

Nursing supervision and maintenance of physical health are necessary in the treatment of many withdrawn clients. Since subjective reports of physical condition are not always reliable in the case of a preoccupied, autistic schizophrenic, the nurse needs to be vigilant in observing his state of health. Nutrition, regular exercise, rest, and necessary medical examinations may all be neglected by the schizophrenic who copes with the world through withdrawal and isolation. While the nurse may take on a "mothering" role for the withdrawn client as an appropriate intervention, the fostering of excessive de-

pendence in the client should be avoided. The good mother is one who allows her child to grow and leave the dependent state.

Overactivity and anxiety. Some clients may block out harsh reality through frenzied overactivity. As in the case of the withdrawn, underactive client, nursing intervention may be necessary for maintenance of physical health. Many of the principles used in working with the manic client will apply here. Exercise and games that do not involve a great deal of concentration may help dissipate the tension and energy associated with the state of anxiety. The client's need for adequate rest and nutrition may be ignored by him. The same is true of the symptoms of physical illness—one young schizophrenic man was developing a serious case of pneumonia, but his hyperactivity belied his temperature of 105°.

Sometimes an overactive client's behavior and rapid speech can prove overwhelming to the staff member assigned to work with him. For this reason it may be necessary to plan staff involvement on a rotating basis, which will help ensure a therapeutic approach rather than one that is influenced by negative countertransference.

Anxiety is often a part of the schizophrenic experience. The times when a client is particularly vulnerable to acute anxiety attacks are as follows:

1. On admission to a psychiatric facility (and particularly on first admission—depression is

more apt to accompany subsequent readmissions)

2. When he begins to participate in any new activity, such as group therapy
3. When the staff member of therapist he is accustomed to working with goes on vacation, is transferred, or resigns
4. Just before he is discharged from the hospital. Many hospitalized schizophrenics express feelings of ambivalence and anxiety about being discharged. The hospital may seem less threatening to him and more accepting of him than the outside world, he may feel overwhelmed by the thought of increased responsibility.

In working with an anxious client, a nurse must remember that anxiety can interfere with the client's hearing and comprehension; a nurse may have to repeat much of what he or she says. Complete but concise directions are best. The nurse's support of the client through his or her presence as the client begins to participate in new activities or try out new behavior may help ease discomfort. Adequate preparation, with opportunities for the expression of concerns, will help a client during the anxiety-provoking predischarge period or when a trusted staff member is leaving.

Underactivity and overactivity, besides being indications of a client's psychological state, may be extrapyramidal symptoms resulting from the use of psychotropic drugs. The client should be evaluated for appropriate medication.

Verbal hostility and physical aggression. It is not unusual for a nurse working in a psychiatric setting to witness a client's verbal hostility. The nurse may also be the recipient of such hostility. Verbal hostility may be displaced anger that the client actually feels for someone else. Quite often the nurse is viewed as a less threatening object for displacement of feelings. However, there are times (such as when maintenance of the therapeutic milieu interferes with the wishes of the client) when angry feelings are indeed felt toward the nurse. In dealing with verbal hostility, a nurse must keep certain important facts in mind.

The expression of anger serves a purpose. It substitutes a more comfortable feeling for feelings of anxiety, and it provides relief from the tension that comes from being frustrated or disappointed or from a threat to self-esteem (Hays, 1963). Also, verbally expressed anger may be viewed as a more mature form of behavior than the *physically* expressed anger that previously may have resulted in many unpleasant situations for the client. Jurgen Ruesch, who is an expert in the field of human communication, views communication as a continuum. Acting out one's feelings—a primitive form of communicating—is situated on one end of the continuum. Verbalizing one's feelings—a more developed form of communicating—is situated on the other end. Interestingly, Ruesch views psychosomatic illness as being situated in the middle, between acted-out feelings and verbalized feelings (Ruesch, 1957):

Acted-out	Psychosomatic	Verbalized
feelings	illness	feelings

Continuum of communication

The client who is able to express feelings of anger and hostility is demonstrating a healthier, more mature form of communicating. It is important to remember, however, that it may be necessary at times to intervene in order to protect the self-esteem of a client who is the recipient of the angry feelings.

When a client expresses anger toward the nurse, the *nondefensive stance* is the most therapeutic way of dealing with the behavior. If the nurse becomes defensive in reacting to hostility, he or she may lose complete control of the situation. The nurse's defensive reaction tends to escalate the defensive behavior of the client, and little real communication takes place. If the nurse instead remains nondefensive, he or she may be able to disarm the client and defuse the situation. The vicious circle of escalating feelings will then be broken, and nurse and client can explore the situation together in an authentic learning experience.

The optimal way to deal with physical aggression is to prevent it from happening in the first place. Careful observation of the levels of tension and anxiety and early, judicious use of medication may do much in this area. If a client must be restrained because of his physical aggression, chemical restraints are much more acceptable and protective of self-esteem than any physical restraint. The use of seclusion or "quiet" rooms, where threatening environmental stimuli can be controlled, is preferable to such devices as camisole restraints. It is best to work with a client in a way that will encourage him to communicate his need for sedation before the tension becomes unbearable.

When a situation has reached the point where a client is clearly exhibiting signs of assaultiveness, some points are helpful to remember:

1. A unit should have a pre-planned way of dealing with such incidents; all staff members should know what it is.
2. The self-esteem of the client should be protected, through the nurse's attitude and communication.
3. Since anxiety is contagious, a calm attitude the nurse's part may also help to soothe the client.
4. Nurses should avoid smiling at the client. A suspicious, paranoid person may feel he is being laughed at.
5. A sufficient number of staff members should be available to deal with the problem physically. Even the frailest of psychotic clients can exhibit tremendous strength under conditions of panic. But a nurse should *not* automatically use all staff members present at the scene to surround the client at close quarters. Sometimes the very sight of a number of staff members in the background will quiet an assaultive client, while his feeling that he is surrounded can be a threat that increases his panic.

Suspicion and fear of interpersonal relationships. A client who is habitually suspicious of other people requires a thoughtful and consistent nursing approach. The following are some helpful points:

1. A matter-of-fact attitude is better than one that is overly warm. While a nurse's warmth may be an asset with other clients, in this situation it can arouse even more of the client's feelings of suspicion ("Why is she pretending to be my friend?" "What does she really want?").

2. In situations in which an apology may be appropriate (for example, a nurse is delayed because of another client or a necessary procedure and thus is late for a scheduled appointment) it is best to offer the apology in a matter-of-fact way and to avoid overdoing it. Profuse apologies may elicit increased suspicion.

3. Physical contact should be avoided—it can be interpreted by a paranoid client as a sexual advance or threat.

4. Too much eye contact can be threatening, while too little can arouse suspicion.

5. The nonverbal behavior of a nurse is important—smiling, as mentioned earlier, may be misinterpreted by a suspicious client.

6. A nurse should speak clearly and concisely and with sufficient loudness. There should be no chance for a client to misinterpret what is being said. The use of the communication technique of *consensual validation* may be helpful.

7. A nurse should never hide medications in the food of *any* client but particularly that of a client who has difficulty trusting others.

8. In situations in which the nurse is taking notes while talking with the client, the nurse should be prepared to let the client read them at any time he seems concerned.

9. The *need to control* and the *fear of being controlled* often characterize a suspicious client. Nurses should avoid power struggles or situations wherein nurse or client is required to be dominant or submissive. The client should be allowed as many opportunities for decision making as possible. But a nurse should avoid a situation wherein efforts to provide such opportunities result in his or her being manipulated or feeling controlled by the client.

10. A nurse must always be aware of, and allow for, the *need-fear dilemma* of the client. The client should be allowed to set the pace for the closeness of the relationship and to backtrack whenever the degree of closeness becomes threatening.

11. Nurses should be as honest as possible about their own feelings when asked about them by clients. A suspicious person is usually very sensitive in interpersonal situations; he may "test" a nurse in this way to see if the nurse really can be trusted.

Autistic behavior

SYMBOLIC COMMUNICATION. The verbalizations of schizophrenics are often quite difficult to follow. Loose association of thoughts, the use of neologisms, a tendency to use pronouns in unusual ways, and paleological thinking all are elements in a way of communicating that is disguised, confusing, and ineffective in facilitating interpersonal relationships. Decoding this communication pattern and helping the client to learn clearer ways of communicating with others are important nursing problems. Some particularly helpful communication techniques include consensual validation, asking for clarification, exploring content, and asking for amplification (Hays and Larson, 1963).

The most important aid in communicating with a schizophrenic client is the attitude of the nurse who wants to learn to decode the client's communication system and who conveys this interest to the client. Autistic communication may be used as a defense against threatening interpersonal closeness. As trust grows within a therapeutic relationship, however, the client may begin to translate his personal language for the nurse.

It is essential that the nurse let the client know when he or she does not understand—the nurse should not let things slip by because of the fear of alienating the client by asking for his meaning frequently. The client may be testing the nurse to see if he or she is interested enough to ask for clarification. Also, a nurse who does not ask for clarification may reinforce a client's ineffective way of communicating with others.

It is important to avoid fostering the notion that either the nurse or the client can read the other's mind. Such notions are not at all uncommon among schizophrenics. Responding to hints, inferring meanings that are not obvious or intended, offering interpretive statements, and finishing the other person's sentences are all examples of communication techniques that are not therapeutic.

INAPPROPRIATE BEHAVIOR. Some types of behavior of regressed schizophrenics, while serving very real purposes, may get them into trouble in social situations. For example, a client who is very anxious may masturbate openly in a crowded day room. Masturbation, besides providing relief from tension for a psychotic client, may be a substitute for interpersonal relatedness and a way of maintaining reality contact (Gibney, 1972). This statement suggests several possible elements of nursing intervention:

1. The rest of the client population may need to be protected from a scene that could be anxiety provoking. The needs of the entire group are important to consider.
2. The client's need to masturbate and his need for increased social awareness can best be served by suggesting, in a nonjudgmental way, that he seek a more private place.
3. A nurse can respond to the message that the client may need or wish greater interper-

sonal contact by increasing his or her efforts to relate to the client and by encouraging the client to relate to others in the unit.

4. Masturbation that has become compulsive may indicate severe regression.

RITUALISTIC OR STEREOTYPICAL BEHAVIOR. Another form of socially inappropriate behavior was demonstrated by a young schizophrenic girl who felt compelled to touch other females or stroke their hair. The behavior may have had its roots in an exceptionally strong symbiotic relationship with her mother. She would make such statements as "My mother is my only reason for living." The touching and stroking aroused anger among other clients—particularly those who felt threatened by physical closeness. She was sometimes assaulted. At best, her behavior alienated her from many of the ward residents. The nursing staff members used a firm but gentle approach. They conveyed their expectations that she could indeed control her behavior. After a student nurse taught her how to crochet as a possible substitute activity for her hands, she was able to decrease the touching significantly, resorting to it only when anxiety was extremely high.

An elderly and chronically ill woman greeted every morning with her ritual of placing a cloth packet of salt she had made on her head and facing the east for 15 minutes. Her need for this strange but harmless ritualistic behavior was accepted by the nursing staff. After this ritual she would go about her business of the day. One burly, middle-aged man controlled his anxiety by twirling about the room like a ballet dancer. Staff members responded by accepting his need for this behavior, but they also focused on developing his ability to control it at times. Eventually, the frequency of the behavior decreased to a point where the success of his placement in the community was ensured. His substitute behavior was an unspoken slogan that he would recall during times of increased anxiety.

A helpful, cooperative nurse-client plan for dealing with such ritualistic and stereotypical behavior should include the following:

1. Nonjudgmental acceptance of the client
2. Awareness of the purpose the behavior serves on the part of both client and staff (usually the behavior is used to help decrease anxiety and/or to communicate something)
3. Expectations on the part of the staff that the client can control behavior
4. Protection of other people from the client's behavior, when necessary
5. Substitution of activities for the behavior (helpful in some cases)

Feelings and thoughts of unreality
DEPERSONALIZATION. Feelings of strangeness and estrangement or thinking that one's body or objects in the environment have changed are all highly anxiety provoking. They are also anxiety based. Such situations are examples of anxiety feeding upon itself. A nurse can combat this escalation by explaining the phenomenon to the client.

By explaining that depersonalization is a by-product of increased anxiety, the nurse can remove the unknown, frightening quality and interrupt a vicious circle. Things that are unknown or unexplained are always frightening to the person experiencing them. Depersonalization increases with increasing anxiety, and it is a part of the phenomenon of loose ego boundaries.

LOOSE EGO BOUNDARIES. No clear concept of self, getting one's needs and desires "mixed up" with other people's, difficulty in forming opinions on any subject, and problems in differentiating internal stimuli from environmental stimuli are all manifestations of loose ego boundaries. The phenomenon can be thought of as a continuum on which manifestations range from indecisiveness and lack of clarity about one's own feelings to having a delusion that one has been transformed into someone else.

Sometimes loose ego boundaries will result in mild or intense identification with another person. For example, expressing a desire to be a nurse, stating that he really is a nurse, wearing the same sort of clothes, copying a hairstyle, and so forth may all be indications that a client is identifying with the nurse. Saying things like "You'd like to go down to the music room" when he really means *he* would is also an indication. It is important that a nurse use correcting, clarifying statements such as "Did you mean that *you* would like to go to the music room?" Differences between the nurse and the client should be pointed out whenever appropriate.

More extreme feelings of unreality that are based in loose ego boundaries include delusions and hallucinations. In responding to these experiences of the client, the nurse can act as a bridge to reality.

DELUSIONS. Delusions are ideas that are contrary to culturally accepted facts. Delusions can be persecutory, grandiose, of control or of influence, somatic, or religious. There is a kernel of truth somewhere in a delusion, although, if it is a long-standing delusion that has been embellished through the years into a complex delusional system, it may be difficult to find. A delusion may be difficult to dispel. If a delusion is just beginning to form and is still rather fluid, it may be possible to intervene in order to prevent its adoption by the client. In the case of a rigid delusional system, however, some researchers suggest that the best way to work with it is to help the client see the importance of keeping his delusional beliefs to himself so that he can function acceptably in society.

The difference between these two approaches to the treatment of delusional beliefs can be illustrated by a comparison of the cases of clients with whom a student nurse worked. One client was an elderly woman who had had numerous admissions to the hospital. She usually remained in the hospital for 3 to 4 months and then was able to function quite adequately in the community for several months. Her delusion was complex and quite fixed. Among other things, she believed that pigeons carried secret messages about her to the Nazis and that they, in collaboration with a Puerto Rican political group, carried out experiments on human beings in the apartment beneath her—no matter where she lived. When she was less anxious and ready for discharge, she was able to keep quiet about these beliefs. But they never really left her, and she would start to talk about them more as her anxiety began to increase.

In contrast to this woman, the other client the student was involved with had experienced her first psychotic break and was exhibiting obsessive-compulsive behavior and indications of low self-esteem. She washed her hands constantly after touching anyone or anything in her unit, and she dusted off any chair she intended to sit on. One day she greeted the student in an excited, worried state: "Don't touch me! I have all of these worms growing inside of me and you might catch them!"

By spending time with her and asking for details and clarification, the student learned the basis for this belief. The client had been eating almost constantly (probably because of a combination of anxiety and the appetite-increasing effects of thorazine), and an aide in the unit had jokingly said, "You must have a tapeworm, you eat so much!" Interpreting this remark concretely and in the light of her low self-esteem, she began to believe that she had worms growing inside of her. The student was able to explain what the aide really meant, and the client was able to accept the explanation.

In responding to a delusion that is already formed, a logical, rational confrontation is usually not helpful. In fact, in the cases of some clients it may stimulate a defensive argument. Usually it is best to respond to what is at the "core" of the delusion and to the feelings associated with it (Donner, 1969). For instance, at the core of a delusion of grandeur one might expect to find feelings of low self-esteem and powerlessness. Most likely at the core of a persecutory delusion are projected feelings of hostility toward other people. The following are some points to consider in responding to the client who is experiencing delusions:

1. Collect data before formulating a response; in the beginning, noncommittal responses may be necessary. In some situations you may only suspect that a client is making a delusional statement. It is easy to make a judgment when the client she is the Virgin Mary and that she is being controlled from the planet Mars, but a client who tells you she has 16 children may be telling you the truth. Then again, she may not be, since this is a fairly common sort of delusion. Give the client the benefit of the doubt until you know whether she is suffering from a delusion, but remain fairly noncommital in your responses.

2. In responding to the client, convey your acceptance of his need for the belief while letting him know you do not agree with the delusion.

3. Do not argue with the client about his belief—incorporating

reasonable doubt as a communication technique is more effective.

4. If possible, connect the belief to the client's feelings (for example, "It's possible to misinterpret things when anxiety is very high" or "Things can seem like they're out of control when you're frightened").

5. Respond to the core of the delusion. If low self-esteem is at the core, try to help the client build his self-esteem in a realistic way. An individual who thinks that there is a complex and well-controlled plot against him may need to express his anger appropriately in everyday situations.

HALLUCINATIONS. Hallucinations are false sensory perceptions. They can be auditory, visual, tactile, olfactory, gustatory, or kinesthetic. The majority of schizophrenic hallucinations are auditory. In fact, the occurrence of auditory hallucinations is correlated so strongly with schizophrenia that some suggest that it be considered a fifth "A" to be tacked on to Bleuler's original "four A's" (Hofling, Leininger, and Bregg, 1967).

Approaches to hallucinations depend upon the need that the hallucinations are serving and upon the length of time the client has been experiencing them. If a client has been hearing voices for a short time, it is important to know *what* the voices say, since they could be *command hallucinations* (commands to commit suicide or homicide, for example). It is helpful to know if the hallucinations are frightening, degrading, or kind and helpful to the client. The therapeutic response in each situation would be different.

In the case of a client who has hallucinated over a long period of time, a nurse might not be as concerned with content as with *when* he tends to hallucinate. This information is useful if the nurse intends to distract him back to reality or to attempt to decrease his anxiety and thus his need for hallucinations. Also, continually focusing on content that is already well known might reinforce the hallucinations.

In general, the following points are helpful in the treatment of the hallucinating client:

1. An accepting approach will encourage the client to share the content and the times of his hallucination. It is important to accept the client and his need for the hallucinations and to accept the fact that while you do not share his perceptions, the client does indeed experience them.

2. Determine the content of the hallucinations in order to prevent possible injury to client or to others from command hallucinations.

3. When discussing hallucinations, phrase your comments in such a way as to avoid reinforcing the hallucinations.

4. Respond to and reinforce the aspects of reality that the client reacts to. Connect the hallucinations to anxiety as an explanation that might prevent the

escalating sequence of increased anxiety, increased hallucination, increased anxiety.

5. Be alert for times of hallucinating. Arieti has identified a "listening pose" that a schizophrenic who is hallucinating may assume.

6. Distract the client at times of hallucinating. Bring the client back to reality through interpersonal involvement and activities.

7. In cases of clients who have hallucinated chronically, instructions to "talk back" to voices, telling them to "shut up," have sometimes helped, since they can give the client a feeling of control over his symptoms and thus decrease his anxiety. This technique *must* be used with a clear message that the voices are not awesome realities but merely symptoms of anxiety.

Low self-esteem, depression, and suicide. Schizophrenia is often accompanied by *anhedonia*, the inability to experience pleasure. The schizophrenic is quite apt to be depressed. The symptoms of the disorder, its incapacitating effects, the inhibition of personal growth, and the drain on financial resources are some of the reasons for depression. As in any chronic illness, depression is part of the process of the individual's acceptance of his disorder. In addition, low self-esteem is the common denominator of *all* emotional illnesses.

The therapeutic response to depression in the schizophrenic is the same as that for any depressed client. Realistic emotional support, activity, and gradually increasing interpersonal involvement are all helpful. Since depression can produce symptoms of psychomotor retardation, nurses must allow clients enough time to react to questions or statements and to verbalize. Like any depressed person, a depressed schizophrenic may attempt suicide. But factors other than depression may also lead to suicide attempts. Suicide attempts by schizophrenic persons are sometimes bizarre and are often quite unpredictable. A suicide attempt may occur in response to a hallucinated voice, or it may be a response to a delusional system. Since a break with reality affects an individual's judgment, the impossible—for example, "flying" out of a window of a tall building—may seem possible. A suicide attempt might be precipitated by loose ego boundaries. For example, a young, very psychotic man reacted to the successful and just-completed suicide of his roommate by jumping out of a window after him. He was badly injured, but he lived. His explanation of why he jumped was that the crumpled body lying on the ground was really *him* and that he was jumping to put himself back together again.

Since the suicides of schizophrenics are so unpredictable, with few if any "clues" given, it is particularly important for nurses to be vigilant. A vague, subjective uneasiness about the possibility of the client committing suicide may be an important clue and should not be dismissed lightly.

TERTIARY PREVENTION

While an individual may experience one schizophrenic break, recover, and perhaps never have another, schizophrenia is most often a chronic disorder.

According to Mendel and Green (1967), two elements that are most needed in the lives of chronic schizophrenics and that can be fostered through supportive relationship therapy are *organization* and *structure*. A chronic schizophrenic's whole life is unstructured and disorganized; the ordinary activities of daily living seem overwhelming to him. The goals of relationship therapy are to foster remission, to prevent complications, and to support the functioning of the schizophrenic patient. Mendel and Green transform the "as if" phenomenon, a symptom that appears in the pre-schizophrenic state, into a concept that can be used as a therapeutic aid for the chronic schizophrenic. They suggest that a therapist say to a client, "OK, so you *don't* feel like you have the ability to get up, get dressed, and go to work every morning—act *as if* you can." After the client has done so for a number of mornings, he will gain some ego strength from having accomplished something he thought he was not capable of.

Mendel and Green also advocate long-term involvement between a helping professional and the chronic schizophrenic. In some cases the amount of this involvement may be decreased, during times of low anxiety and adequate functioning, to a monthly or even yearly "check in"

with the therapist. Of course, at times of developmental or situational crises, involvement would be increased again.

The schizophrenic, the community, and tertiary prevention. What was probably one of the most ideal communities for discharged schizophrenics ever to be devised existed at one time in the village of Gheel, Belgium. This town is situated near a shrine to St. Dymphna, the patron saint of the mentally ill, and a psychiatric hospital dedicated to her. During the Middle Ages and later, people from all over the world came to the shrine and hospital, hoping for saintly intervention in their illness. After treatment at the hospital they were often discharged into the town. Some lived in the village while they awaited admission to the hospital. The villagers were quite accepting of them; eccentric behavior was tolerated, and individuals were allowed to participate in the community to the degree that they were able.

Unfortunately, in the United States today there are no such friendly and accepting communities. A discharged schizophrenic too often faces a harsh, intolerant, and unwelcoming community situation. *Aftercare* of mental illness has not been a major priority in our country; it can only be described as inadequate. We have the knowledge of what is required to provide optimum aftercare services for chronic schizophrenics, but most often only lip service is paid to the ideals. Services that are available to a limited degree include the following:

Coping through withdrawal from reality   **557**

1. *Transitional services*—a concept that includes a gradual lessening of the client's dependent ties with the hospital. Clients are given lessons and help in tasks of everyday living. Particularly in the case of a client who has been institutionalized for a long time, many skills may not have been learned or they may have been long since forgotten. Helping a client to arrange for suitable living accomodations is another transitional service.

2. *Day care centers*—for the client who has a supportive, accepting home environment but who cannot yet function in a job. This service provides structure to his day, opportunities for socialization, and a chance to learn some skills. In addition, medication may be supervised in such a center.

3. *Night hospitals*—for the client who can function in a job but has no suitable living arrangements. Perhaps, as is so often the case with the chronic schizophrenic, there are no family ties. The client may also benefit from supportive therapy within the night hospital. For instance, group therapy sessions may be held in the evening as part of the hospital's program.

4. *Halfway houses and foster homes*—for the client who does not have a family or whose family can no longer support him. Such a client needs some supervision in such areas as diet, medication, recreation, and activities of daily living. Some foster homes in a com-munity may be excellent; others may be deplorable. A system of inspection before placement is therefore crucial to the protection of the client's welfare.

5. *Rehabilitation, vocational training, and sheltered workshops*—retraining in old skills and training in new skills in order to help the client function to the maximum of his potential and strengthen his self-esteem.

6. *Token economy programs*—for severely regressed schizophrenics. These programs, which have been used in some psychiatric inpatient and outpatient facilities, involve a form of behavior modification. Tokens that can be exchanged for goods (cigarettes, food, or clothing) or privileges are given in return for participation in certain activities. For example, a token may be given for making one's bed in the morning or for attending group therapy sessions. Such a program can be useful if it is carried out in a way that protects the dignity of the client. Unhappily, this is not always the case.

Working with family and client. An important aspect of the tertiary care of schizophrenics is the supervision of medications. Failure to take prescribed drugs is one of the most common reasons for readmission to hospitals (Van Putten, 1974). A drug like prolixin, which can be given in 2-week intervals, is very often useful. But the most important aspect of tertiary care is the continuing and regular involvement of the community mental health nurse with the client and his family. Some hospitals provide "crisis teams" of hospital personnel—people the client has known while in the hospital. Home visits at times of increased anxiety for the client may prevent rehospitalization. It is essential that a nurse engage the family of the chronic schizophrenic, along with the client, as part of the treatment team. It is especially important to avoid arousing any feelings of guilt in family members, since such feelings can lead to a withdrawal from involvement with helping professionals and perhaps to a withdrawal from the client. Family members can be helpful in alerting professionals to increasing anxiety in the client, and they can assist in the supervision of medications. In addition, they can help modify environmental stress in the client's life and facilitate the client's necessary acceptance of his illness.

CHAPTER SUMMARY

Schizophrenia is a disorder of thought, mood, feeling, sensation, and behavior. It is characterized by a disturbed ego, no clear concept of self, and inadequate ways of communicating with and relating to other people. Schizophrenia is a major health problem. It affects 0.5% to 2% of the population of the United States, and there is some evidence that the incidence is increasing (Kramer, 1978).

Schizophrenia was originally called "dementia praecox" (dementia of the young); its incidence seems to be highest among young adults, but it can occur at any age. "Schizophrenia," the term invented by Bleuler, means "split mind"; it refers to a splitting apart of some of the functions of the mind. For instance, thoughts and feelings that normally go together may be split apart.

The disorder occurs in all cultures and all socioeconomic groups, but for complex reasons it is strongly correlated with poverty.

Several systems for classifying schizophrenia are in existence. Some writers believe that schizophrenia is actually several disorders and therefore refer to "the schizophrenias."

The etiology of schizophrenia is unknown, but several theories have been postulated. These include genetic, biochemical, intrapsychic, interpersonal, family, communication systems, sociological, and adaptation theories. An eclectic or multifactorial approach to the etiology of schizophrenia is most widely accepted.

Treatment for schizophrenia includes somatic approaches (particularly the use of drugs), psychotherapy, group and family therapy, and occupational and recreational therapy. Primary prevention at this time is limited mainly to the identification of high-risk groups. Secondary prevention currently focuses on the belief that much of the deterioration in the condition of a schizophrenic may result from institutionalization rather than from the disorder itself. A more active treatment approach has provided a much better prognosis for recovery. However, schizophrenia is often a chronic disorder. Tertiary prevention of schizophrenia involves a cooperative, rehabilitative effort from health workers, client, and family. Providing support and helping to add structure and organization to the client's life are very important.

In working with a schizophrenic client, a nurse helps most by assisting in the improvement of *communication skills* and *interpersonal skills. Therapeutic use of self* in an authentic relationship with the client is the most important component of nursing intervention.

REFERENCES

Altschule, M.
  1970 In The Schizophrenic Reactions: A Critique of the Concept, Hospital Treatment and Current Research. R. Cancro (ed.). New York: Brunner/Mazel, Inc.
Arieti, S.
  1955 Interpretation of Schizophrenia (ed. 1). New York: Basic Books, Inc., Publishers.
  1967 The Intrapsychic Self. New York: Basic Books, Inc., Publishers.
  1975 Interpretation of Schizophrenia (ed. 2). New York: Basic Books, Inc., Publishers.
Arnold, H.
  1976 "Working with schizophrenic patients, four A's: a guide to one-to-one relationships." American Journal of Nursing 6:941-943.
Bahnson, C. B.
  1969 "Psychophysiological complementarity in malignancies: past work and future vistas." Annals of the New York Academy of Sciences 125(3):827-45.
  1974 "Epistemological perspectives of physical disease from the psychodynamic point of view." American Journal of Public Health 64(11):1036.
Bahnson, C. B., and M. B. Bahnson
  1964 "Cancer as an alternative to psychosis: a theoretical model of somatic and psychological regression." In Psychosomatic Aspects of Neoplastic Disease. D. M. Kissen and L. L. LeShan (eds.). Philadelphia: J. B. Lippincott Co.
Bellak, L.
  1958 "The schizophrenic syndrome: a further explanation of the unified theory of schizophrenia." In Schizophrenia: A Review of the Syndrome. L. Bellak (ed.). New York: Logos Press.
  1970 In The Schizophrenic Reactions: A Critique of the Concept, Hospital Treatment and Current Research. R. Cancro (ed.). New York: Brunner/Mazel, Inc.
Bowen, M.
  1976 "Theory in the practice of psychotherapy." In Family Therapy. P. J. Guerin (ed.). New York: Gardner Press, Inc.
  1977 Workshop in Family Therapy, Mercy Hospital, Rockville Center, N.Y.
Boyers, R., and R. Orrill (eds.)
  1971 R. D. Laing and Anti-Psychiatry. New York: Harper & Row, Publishers.
Burnham, D. L., A. I. Gladstone, and R. W. Gibson
  1969 Schizophrenia and the Need-Fear Dilemma. New York: International Universities Press.
Cameron, N.
  1963 Personality Development and Psychopathology: A Dynamic Approach. Boston: Houghton Mifflin Co.
Campion, E., and G. Tucker
  1973 "A note on twin studies, schizophrenia and neurological impairment. In Annual Review of the Schizophrenic Syndrome. R. Cancro (ed.). New York: Brunner/Mazel, Inc.
Cancro, R. (ed.)
  1970 The Schizophrenic Reactions: A Critique of the Concept, Hospital Treatment and Current Research. New York: Brunner/Mazel, Inc.
Carpenter, E.
  1953 "Witch-fear among the Aivilik Eskimos." The American Journal of Psychiatry 110(3):194-199.

Donner, G.
1969 "Treatment of a delusional patient." American Journal of Nursing 12:2642-2644.

Eisenberg, L.
1973 "Psychiatric intervention." Scientific American 229(3):117-127.

Epstein, S., and M. Coleman
1971 "Drive theories in schizophrenia." In the Schizophrenic Syndrome: An Annual Review. R. Cancro (ed.). New York: Brunner/Mazel, Inc.

Field, W. E., and S. Wilkerson
1973 "Religiosity as a psychiatric symptom." Perspectives in Psychiatric Care 11(3):99-105.

Foulks, Edward F.
1975 "Schizophrenia held useful for evolution." New York Times, December 9.

Frank, V.
1959 Man's Search for Meaning: An Introduction to Logotherapy. New York: Washington Square Press.

Fromm-Reichman, F.
1950 Principles of Intensive Psychotherapy. Chicago: University of Chicago Press.

Garmezy, N.
1971 "Vulnerability research and the issue of primary prevention." American Journal of Orthopsychiatry 41:101-116.

Gibney, H.
1972 "Masturbation: an invitation for an interpersonal relationship. Perspectives in Psychiatric Care 10(3):128-134.

Goldfarb, C., and S. Goldfarb
1977 "Multiple monitored electroconvulsive treatment." In Current Psychiatric Therapies, vol. 17. J. H. Masserman (ed.). New York: Grune & Stratton, Inc.

Grinker, R., Sr.
1969 "An essay on schizophrenia and science." Archives of General Psychiatry 20:1-24.

Hays, D. R.
1963 "Anger: a clinical problem." In Some Clinical Approaches to Psychiatric Nursing. S. Burd and M. Marshall (eds.). New York: Macmillan, Inc.

Hays, J. S., and K. H. Larson
1963 Interacting with Patients. New York: Macmillan, Inc.

Heath, R., et al.
1958 "Behavioral changes in nonpsychotic volunteers following the administration of tarexein, the substance obtained from the serum of schizophrenic patients." American Journal of Psychiatry 114:917-920.

Henley, A.
1971 "Schizophrenia: current approaches to a baffling problem. Public Affairs Pamphlet No. 460. New York: Public Affairs Committee, Inc.

Hofling, C. K., M. M. Leininger, and E. Bregg
1967 Basic Psychiatric Concepts in Nursing (ed. 2). Philadelphia: J. B. Lippincott Co.

Holmes, M. J.
1971 "Influences of the new hospital psychiatry on nursing." In The New Hospital Psychiatry. New York: Academic Press, Inc.

Holzman, P., et al.
1974 "Eye-tracking dysfunctions in schizophrenic patients and their relatives." In Annual Review of the Schizophrenic Syndrome. R. Cancro (ed.). New York: Brunner/Mazel, Inc.

Howells, J. G.
1975 World History of Psychiatry. New York: Brunner/Mazel, Inc.

Jackson, D.
1960 The Etiology of Schizophrenia. New York: Basic Books, Inc., Publishers.

Kallman, F. J.
1938 The Genetics of Schizophrenia. New York: Augustin.

Kasanin, J. S. (ed.)
1944 Language and Thought in Schizophrenia. New York: W. W. Norton & Co. Inc.

Kety, S.
1978 "Heredity and environment." In Schizophrenia: Science and Practice. J. C. Shershow (ed.) Cambridge, Mass.: Harvard University Press.

Kramer, M.
1978 "Population changes in schizophrenia, 1970-1985." In The Nature of Schizophrenia: New Approaches to Research and Treatment. L. C. Wynne et al (eds.). New York: John Wiley & Sons, Inc.

Laing, R. D.
1960 The Divided Self. Chicago: Quadrangle Books.
1965 "Mystification, confusion and conflict." In Intensive Family Therapy: Theoretical and Practical Aspects. I. Boszormenyi-Nagy and J. L. Framo (eds.). New York: Harper & Row, Publishers, Inc.

Lidz, T.
1973 The Origin and Treatment of Schizophrenic Disorders. New York: Basic Books, Inc., Publishers.

May, R.
1958 "The origins and significance of the existential movement in psychology." In Existence: A New Dimension in Psychiatry and Psychology. R. May et al (eds.). New York: Simon & Schuster, Inc.

Mellow, J.
1968 "Nursing therapy." American Journal of Nursing 68(11):2365-2369.

Mendel, W.
1976 Schizophrenia: The Experience and Its Treatment. San Francisco: Jossey-Bass, Inc., Publishers.

Mendel, W. M., and G. A. Green
1967 The Therapeutic Management of Psychological Illness: The Theory and Practice of Supportive Care. New York: Basic Books, Inc., Publishers.

Menninger, K.
1963 The Vital Balance. New York: The Viking Press, Inc.

Oden, G.
1963 "There are no mute patients." In Some Clinical Approaches to Psychiatric Problems. S. Burd and M. Marshall (eds.). New York: Macmillan, Inc.

Pfeiffer, C.
1975 Mental and Elemental Nutrients: A Physician's Guide to Nutrition and Health Care. New Canaan, Conn.: Keats Publishing, Inc.

Pittman, F. S., and K. Flomenhaft
1970 "Treating the doll's house marriage." Family Process 9(2):143-155.

Potkin, S. G., et al
1978 "Are paranoid schizophrenics biologically different from other schizophrenics?" New England Journal of Medicine 298(2):61-66.

Redlich, F. C., and D. X. Freedman
1966 The Theory and Practice of Psychiatry. New York: Basic Books, Inc., Publishers, pp. 480-481, 512-513.

Roman, P., and H. M. Trice
1967 Schizophrenia and the Poor. Ithaca, N.Y.: Cayuga Press.

Rosen, J.
1953 Direct Analysis: Selected Papers. New York: Grune & Stratton, Inc.

Rosenbaum, C. P., and J. E. Beebe
1975 Psychiatric Treatment: Crisis/Clinic/Consultation. New York: McGraw-Hill Book Co., p. 213.

Rowe, C. J.
1975 An Outline of Psychiatry (ed. 6). Dubuque, Iowa: William C. Brown Co., Publishers, p. 246.

Ruesch, J.
1957 Disturbed Communication: The Clinical Assessment of Normal and Pathological Communicative Behavior. New York: W. W. Norton & Co., Inc.

Sarbin, T.
1972 "Schizophrenia is a myth, born of metaphor, meaningless." Psychology Today 6(June):20-27.

Schwing, G.
1954 A Way to the Soul of the Mentally Ill. New York: International Universities Press.

Searles, H. F.
1965 Collected Papers on Schizophrenia and Related Subjects. New York: International Universities Press.

Sechehaye, M. A.
1956 A New Psychotherapy in Schizophrenia. New York: Grune & Stratton, Inc.

Serban, G.
1975 "Stress in schizophrenics and normals." British Journal of Psychiatry 126:397-407.

Singh, M., and S. Kay
1976 "Wheat Gluten as a pathogenic factor in schizophrenia." Science 191:401-402.

Slater, E.
1953 Psychotic and Neurotic Illnesses in Twins. London: Her Majesty's Stationery Office.

Stein, L., and C. D. Wise
1971 "Possible etiology of schizophrenia: progressive damage to the noradrenergic reward system by 6-hydroxy dopamine. Science 171:1032-1036.

Stroebel, C. F.
1969 "Biological rhythm correlates of disturbed behavior in the rhesus monkey." In Circadian Rhythms in Nonhuman Primates. F. H. Rohles (ed.). New York: Skrager.

Szasz, T. S.
1961 The Myth of Mental Illness. New York: Dell Publishing Co., Inc.

Taft, L. T., and W. Goldfarb
1964 "Prenatal and perinatal factors in childhood schizophrenia. Developmental Medicine and Child Neurology 6:32-34.

Trotter, R. J.
1977 "Schizophrenia: a cruel chain of events." Science News, June 18, 1977, p. 394.

Van Putten, T.
1974 "Why do schizophrenic patients refuse to take their drugs?" Archives of General Psychiatry 31:67-72.

Von Domarus, E.
1944 "The specific laws of logic in schizophrenia." In Language and Thought in Schizophrenia, Collected Papers. J. S. Kasanin (ed.). Los Angeles: University of California Press.

Wynne, L. C., et al
1978 The Nature of Schizophrenia: New Approaches to Research and Treatment. New York: John Wiley & Sons, Inc.

ANNOTATED SUGGESTED READINGS

Kasanin, J. (ed.)
1944 Language and Thought in Schizophrenia. New York: W. W. Norton & Co., Inc.
A compilation of the works of several well-known authors, this classic book describes and analyzes various aspects of the thought and communication processes in schizophrenia. For example, the schizophrenic's tendency to use paralogical thinking is examined.

Lidz, T.
1973 The Origin and Treatment of Schizophrenic Disorders: New York: Basic Books, Inc., Publishers.
This book presents a unified theory of schizophrenia that views disorders in the family system as the primary causative factor. Family settings (schismatic or skewed) are described, the thought disorder is examined, and appropriate family treatment is discussed.

Mendel, W.
1976 Schizophrenia: The Experience and Its Treatment. San Francisco: Jossey-Bass, Publishers.
The most prominent etiological theories are reviewed, including the genetic, the physical, and various psychological theories. Mendel's own comprehensive theory is described as well as his suggested method of treatment for the schizophrenic client.

Mendel, W., and G. Green
1967 The Therapeutic Management of Psychological Illness: The Theory and Practice of Supportive Care. New York: Basic Books, Inc., Publishers.
Mendel and Green describe helpful long-term treatment methods for the chronic schizophrenic client. Emphasis is placed on helping the client remain in the community through supportive relationship therapy.

Snyder, S.
1974 Madness and the Brain. New York: McGraw-Hill Book Co.
This book traces the new breakthroughs in research into brain function and the effects of various chemicals on the brain. Snyder attempts to shed some light on the mystery of schizophrenia by explaining how schizophrenic symptoms and the effects of psychotropic and psychotomimetic drugs are related.

FURTHER READINGS

Moser, D. H.
1970 "Communicating with a schizophrenic patient." Perspectives in Psychiatric Care 8(1):36-45.

Shershow, J. C. (ed.)
1978 Schizophrenia: Science and Practice. Cambridge, Mass.: Harvard University Press.

14
COPING WITH IMPAIRED BRAIN FUNCTION

CHAPTER FOCUS

Mental disorders have historically been attributed to a variety of natural and supernatural forces. In our own era, many people, including prominent research scientists, have come to believe that most, if not all, psychiatric disturbances are the result of altered physiological processes within the central nervous system. Such a belief has even been attributed to Freud, the father of dynamic psychiatry.

The neuropsychiatric conditions to be discussed in this chapter—the organic brain dysfunctions—have long been known to have their etiology in disturbances in central nervous system functioning. Research in neurophysiology during the last quarter-century has led to increased knowledge of neuronal functioning and to a better understanding of the complex metabolic processes of the central nervous system. This advancement in knowledge has made possible the improvement in treatment for many conditions, including organic brain dysfunctions, although treatment of organic conditions has not always kept pace with the expanding knowledge. Wells (1978) points out that in the early stages of organic brain dysfunction, when treatment could be most effective, the proper diagnosis often is not made.

Organic brain dysfunction, in either the acute form or the chronic form, may occur at any point in the life cycle, although it is more common in the later years of life. The organic brain disorders are believed to be among the most prevalent of psychiatric disorders. There is some evidence that the incidence of the acute form of organic brain dysfunction is increasing as more complex medical treatments become possible with advances in medical technology and that it may even be endemic in acute health care settings. Since nurses are frequently the health professionals in the most direct and continuous contact with persons experiencing organic brain dysfunction, they are often in the best position to identify early manifestations and to set in motion the early treatment measures that are essential to a client's health—and at times, his survival. This chapter will focus upon the symptoms and etiology of organic brain dysfunction and upon the therapeutic modalities that are used in the treatment of these conditions. In addition, attention will be given to primary, secondary, and tertiary prevention in both the acute and the chronic forms of organic brain disorders.

14

COPING WITH IMPAIRED BRAIN FUNCTION

Organic brain syndromes are neuropsychiatric disorders which are caused by any interference with the complex neurophysiological processes essential to mental functioning.

Classifications of organic dysfunctions

Characteristics and underlying dynamics

    Acute brain syndrome

    Chronic brain syndrome

    Factors that influence coping ability

Epidemiology and sociocultural aspects

Etiology

    Acute confusional states

    Chronic brain syndrome

Treatment modalities

Nursing intervention

    Primary prevention

    Secondary prevention

    Tertiary prevention

CLASSIFICATIONS OF
ORGANIC DYSFUNCTIONS

Psychiatric disorders are frequently broadly classified as either *functional* or *organic*. The functional disorders include the mood, thought, and personality disorders that have been discussed in previous chapters; they are believed to have their origins in psychogenic or psychological processes. The term "functional," in this context, refers to psychosocial or psychodynamic functioning, rather than to biological functionings. The symptoms of functional disorders are viewed as defensive responses to stress and anxiety; they differ from symptoms of organic conditions in that disturbances in cognitive functioning either are not present or are secondary to such symptoms as delusions or hallucinations. The term "organic" refers to psychiatric conditions, both chronic and acute, that are known to have their origins in disturbances in neurophysiology or brain tissue functioning. Disturbances in cognitive functioning characterize these disorders.

Current research strongly suggests that there is some neurophysiological contribution to the etiology of such disorders as schizophrenia (see Chapter 13) and the affective disorders (see Chapter 11). These findings therefore cause some confusion in the use of the terms "organic" and "functional" in the classification of psychiatric disorders.

Organic brain dysfunction is usually classified as either *acute* or *chronic*. Factors that cause alterations in normal brain functioning may produce an acute, temporary dysfunction that responds readily to appropriate therapy and the normal physiological reparative processes, leaving no residual effects. For such conditions the terms "acute" and "reversible" are used. In some instances of organic brain dysfunction, there are residual deficits that result from diffuse alterations of neuron structure or from some continuing interference with neurophysiological processes. The terms "chronic" and "irreversible" are often used to categorize this type of dysfunction. The terms acute and chronic can be misleading, however, since some brain dysfunctions can progress from acute to chronic, often depending upon the etiology of the disorder and the effectiveness of treatment. In addition, chronic disorders of unknown origin can appear with a gradual or insidious onset, without an acute phase. Chronic disorders may also be classified as mild, moderate, or severe, depending upon the degree of cognitive dysfunction.

The neuropsychiatric disorders associated with impaired brain function may also be classified according to etiology. Organic brain dysfunction has been associated with systemic disorders; infections; chemical, drug, and alcohol intoxication; nutritional deficiencies; intracranial trauma and neoplasms; neurological disorders; iatrogenic disorders; and genetic factors. Organic syndromes of unknown etiology are termed *primary*, signifying the absence of any known etiology. Organic disorders of known etiology are termed *secondary*, to indicate an association with some known pathophysiological process.

CHARACTERISTICS AND UNDERLYING DYNAMICS

The clinical manifestations that make up the syndrome, or symptom complex, that results from organic brain disorders are disturbances in attention, comprehension, memory, orientation, and judgment. Emotional instability, or lability of affect, may also be present. These disturbances in cognitive or intellectual functioning are always indicative of brain dysfunction.

Acute brain syndrome

Symptoms of delirium or an acute confusional state generally have an acute onset that is associated with some underlying pathophysiology. These symptoms are indicative of a serious level of brain dysfunction, and they require immediate treatment of the underlying pathology, often as a life-saving measure.

Difficulty in focusing attention and in comprehending incoming stimuli are often the most prominent features in acute brain dysfunction (Seltzer and Sherwin, 1974). The difficulty in focusing or maintaining attention will be reflected in an inability to grasp an idea or a simple communication. There will be difficulty in comprehending the facts of a situation and in responding to questions or other verbal communication. Even when grasped or understood, information or ideas will not be retained. There may be a lack of clarity or a fuzziness in thinking, and an inability to recall or remember pertinent information. Difficulties in focusing attention also lead to an inability to screen out irrelevant stimuli, so that anything going on around the person readily distracts his attention. Persons who are experiencing delirium often convey their confusion and lack of comprehension through facial expressions and other forms of nonverbal communication.

In a health care setting, a person with an acute brain dysfunction may have difficulty in comprehending and cooperating with monitoring and treatment activitites. People who are regaining consciousness after general anesthesia often display a similar difficulty in sustaining attention and a similar distractibility. They also may experience the fluctuations in levels of consciousness that may appear in acute brain dysfunction. Disturbances in levels of consciousness may vary from a clouding of consciousness, in which the individual is not fully conscious and responsive, to intermittent periods of stupor or coma.

Emotional instability may or may not be present in acute brain dysfunction. Some people respond with sustained fearfulness, apprehension, irritability, and restlessness. In others, such emotions may alternate with periods of calm and lethargy. Other symptoms may appear, often in association with the underlying pathophysiology. Hallucinations and delusions, for example, may appear in dysfunction that is associated with withdrawal from alcohol or drugs.

Chronic brain syndrome

The onset of symptoms in chronic brain dysfunction is usually insidious in those cases termed senile or presenile dementia, in which the causative factor is unknown. Some chronic dysfunctions may, however, directly follow an acute phase, when the causative agent has resulted in irreversible brain tissue damage, as in some cases of prolonged anoxia, or when a disturbance in neurophysiology persists. Although chronic brain syndrome may occur at any age, the majority of cases appear in the geriatric population and are of unknown etiology.

The prominent symptoms of chronic organic brain dysfunction are disturbances in intellectual abilities—particularly memory, orientation, and judgment. Disturbances in attention are reflected in the distractibility that is often present. Fluctuations in emotional tone—that is, lability of affect—are often present. Additional neurological symptoms may also occur, depending upon the kind of neurophysiological impairment.

The extent to which chronic organic brain dysfunction disrupts a person's ability to function in society varies considerably. Some people are able to adapt to the deficit and continue to function adequately. Others may be so severely impaired in functions of daily living that they are unable to care for themselves. Disturbances in memory, for example, may be so mild as to be imperceptible to anyone other than the affected person himself or a close family member. Forgetting where one put down one's eyeglasses or reading material, or not remembering the names of people recently met, are lapses of memory that most of us experience from time to time. More serious defects in memory, such as a tendency to forget appointments or details of important events, may be compensated for by such special efforts as note taking and association tricks. In severe memory loss, there may be difficulty in recalling what, if anything, one had for breakfast or in the ability to recognize friends and family members. In chronic brain syndrome memory of recent events is often more impaired than remote memory, or memory of earlier phases of life.

Severe memory disturbances are apt to be accompanied by disturbances in orientation—in the ways in which we relate to and in our environment. Disturbances in orientation may involve time, place, or people. Disturbances that involve time are usually of a gross nature, such as an inability to distinguish night from day or to identify the season, the year, or even the decade. The hour of the day or the day of the month may very possibly, however, be unknown to a client who is shut off from ongoing events. Many of us, when on vacation, may ignore the clock or the calendar. People from cultures that are not highly time oriented may pay little attention to precise times, days, and dates. It is important, therefore, that an evaluation of time orientation take into account an individual's circumstances.

Disturbances in orientation to place may vary from a recognition of where one is, but an inability to recall how one got there, to an inability to accurately perceive one's present location. The former type is often seen in persons who have suffered head injuries followed by a period of coma. A period of amnesia or total loss of memory of events immediately preceding the trauma often occurs. Disorientation in relation to place may also appear spontaneously and for no known reason in persons who suffer from chronic organic dysfunction.

Disorientation in relation to other people is an inability to accurately perceive or comprehend the identity of persons who are in the immediate environment. In a hospital setting, a person may mistake health care providers for family members. A nurse may be perceived as a mother, for example. In an extreme case of this form of disorientation, there may be a lack of recognition of a close family member.

Disturbances in judgment are manifested by impairment of the ability to perceive, interpret, and respond appropriately or effectively to situations in the environment. Judgment will usually be impaired to the degree or extent to which the other cognitive functions are impaired. Behavioral manifestations may vary from mild peccadilloes that embarrass family and friends to a failure to observe social mores or to use economic and other resources prudently. In some instances, impaired judgment is so extreme that a person can endanger his own life or other's lives through imprudent acts. Goldfarb (1974) uses the phrase, "disorientation to situation," which may more accurately describe the disturbances in judgment noted here.

Certain communication and speech patterns may be found in chronic brain disorders. Among them are circumstantiality, confabulation, and (to some extent) recall and association difficulties.

Circumstantiality is the name given to a speech pattern in which a person has difficulty in screening out relevant from irrelevant material in describing an event. There is a tendency to include every detail, often in sequential order. While a raconteur may delightfully embellish a story with interesting details that bring it to life, circumstantiality often has the opposite effect, arousing impatience in the listener, which may cause him to tune out or lose interest. In a busy health care setting, there may be a tendency on the part of health care providers to complete a story for a person who displays circumstantiality, or to intervene in other ways. This tendency may arouse anxiety and anger. If the person is under stress and vulnerable to any additional frustration, pressure to have him get to the point of the story or omit unnecessary detail may increase confusion or even result in a catastrophic anxiety reaction.

Circumstantiality may, at times, cause the individual who is affected to lose the point of a story or a question, as one association leads to another and the main thread is forgotten. Very often the person will realize that the main point has been lost; he may say so and ask to have a question repeated.

The following vignette illustrates circumstantiality in an older woman who has mild to moderate brain dysfunction. In the situation described here, pain and fear played an important role.

> Mrs. M., who lived alone in her own home, phoned a niece and told her that she had hurt her foot and did not know what to do. The niece took her aunt to the emergency room of the local hospital for treatment. Mrs. M. was in pain from the injured foot, and she was very anxious about what would happen if she were unable to walk for any length of time. When asked by a nurse to tell her what had happened, Mrs. M. responded: "I was going to the department store to buy a shower gift for my neighbor's daughter. She's getting married to a very nice boy, and my neighbor across the street is having a shower, and all the people on the block are invited. I am all alone, you know, and have to do everything for myself, and the girl's family have been very good to me. So I wanted to get something nice

for the shower. I was reading the paper last night and saw an ad for a coffee pot on sale. I don't have too much money, you know, so I rushed out early this morning to buy it before they were all gone. I don't have anyone to drive me, so I have to do everything for myself. It's awful to be alone." Prodded a bit by the nurse, Mrs. M. continued to explain how, in her rush to get on the bus, she had turned her ankle as she stepped off the curb.

Although Mrs. M. was able to arrive at the appropriate end point in her description of the event, she also included many ramifications that were irrelevant to the immediate situation in the emergency room. The story had been told in the same detail, and almost identical language, earlier, when Mrs. M. told the niece about the accident. The astute observer will also note an underlying theme of dependence, or fear of dependence and helplessness. These emotions and the uncertainty they indicate may have a higher priority of concern for Mrs. M. than the physical injury and pain in this situation.

Another symptom of brain dysfunction that may be demonstrated in speech patterns is difficulty in recalling words, ideas, or events and in making associations with other words, ideas, or events. Difficulties in *recall* and *association* are not uncommon, nor are they limited to persons with brain dysfunction. Who among us has not forgotten words or things that, in retrospect, we should have remembered? When memory is impaired by brain dysfunction, however, the ability to recall or make associations may inhibit communication ability. The symptom may be severe in the more extreme forms of chronic brain syndrome. In Pick's disease, for example, in which cerebral insufficiency is related to damage to the areas of the brain having to do with speech and association, there may be an inability to name such commonly used items as pencils. An affected person may, however, be able to state the purpose for which such an item is used. Even in such a situation, the association loss may be selective; the amount of loss depends on the familiarity and value to the individual of a particular object or idea. For example, Mrs. L. was unable to recall the word for a wristwatch when she was asked to name this commonly used item during an examination, but she could readily identify coins by their monetary value.

Confabulation is a commonly observed phenomenon in chronic brain syndrome, one that is often seen in residents of nursing and adult homes and psychiatric hospitals. In confabulation, an individual who cannot recall specific aspects of an event will often fill in the gaps in memory with relevant but imaginary information. For example, a man whose recent memory was being tested responded to a question about what he had eaten for breakfast by saying a soft-boiled egg and toast, when, in fact, he had been given oatmeal and coffee cake. Confabulation is occasionally viewed by health care providers as a wish-fulfilling fantasy, as a deliberate attempt to deceive, or as evidence of severely impaired memory. It is often none of these, but represents a face-saving device or ego defense mechanism, in which the person copes by filling in gaps in memory with substitutions. Thus, confabulation can represent a strength: it can be an attempt to cope with and adapt to an intolerable situation. A recognition of the defensive nature of confabulation can serve a useful purpose in the provision of needed emotional support for such clients.

Factors that influence coping ability

Disturbances in cognitive abilities always reflect a disturbance in brain tissue functioning, which to some degree influences a person's ability to cope with life's experiences. However, the degree to which such dysfunction is disorganizing to a person is influenced by a variety of factors. Although the extent of neuronal damage or dysfunction may be a factor in some instances, other factors may be of even greater significance as a person attempts to cope with the stress of life. Among these factors are the developmental era in which an organic dysfunction begins and the psychodynamic and sociocultural forces that have an influence on the functioning of everyone.

Developmental factors

Acute brain syndrome. The age of onset of organic dysfunction, particularly when it is early in life, may have a profound influence on the ability to cope with life. A young child who has not yet mastered language and logical thinking will respond to brain dysfunction quite differently from the way an older person, who has mastered these developmental tasks, responds. In a hospitalized child, the failure to focus attention and the irritability or apathy that may be symptomatic of acute organic dysfunction can be confused with the psychological coping process of regression, which often accompanies the stress of illness and separation from home and family. In an older person the symptoms of acute brain dysfunction may mistakenly be attributed to a degenerative process associated with aging. Conversely, deficits in the sensory apparatus, particularly that involving sight and hearing, may be mistaken for a disturbance in comprehension, especially when such deficits are severe enough to promote a level of isolation that leads to illusions or hallucinatory experiences. Culture shock (see Chapter 2), which many people experience when first admitted to a hospital, may also influence adaptive responses to the hospital setting. This is particularly true when there is a language barrier, or when there is a marked cultural difference between the client and the health care providers. Severe pain, apprehension, and anxiety may also distort or be mistaken for symptoms of acute brain dysfunction. The picture is further confused when an organic dysfunction is superimposed upon a functional psychiatric disorder. Because symptoms may be distorted by such factors, a history of an individual's patterns of functioning and ways of coping with stress, prior to the onset of the medical problem underlying the acute brain dysfunction, is an important aspect of nursing assessment and intervention. Taking such a history will be discussed later in this chapter, in the section on nursing intervention.

Chronic brain syndrome. The characteristics of chronic brain dysfunction will, of course, be affected by the age of onset. Up to this point we have focused primarily upon the older adult, because the largest number of people with chronic brain syndrome is in this age group. However, since chronic cerebral dysfunction can occur at any age, it is important to briefly mention its effects upon the child and the young adult. If organic dysfunction has its onset in the early adult years, the individual has already mastered the language and the learning tasks necessary for adaptation to his culture. He has educational and living experiences to fall back upon in coping with the deficit, and he has a variety of coping and adaptive measures to aid him. The young child, in contrast, must learn language and must negotiate the developmental crises upon which personality and cultural adaptation are founded. He must also master the knowledge, skills, and other requirements essential to adapting to the people and mores of a complex culture.

Organic brain disease can occur at any point during the developmental process, from conception to the end of life. When the onset is in the prenatal or perinatal period, the child may fail to master language and may be so impaired in the ability to function or learn, that he may be severely mentally retarded.

Onset later in childhood also may have a profound effect upon the child and his family. The memory disturbance makes learning difficult, and the shortened or altered attention span increases the learning difficulties. Such a child has a very low tolerance for frustration, and he is often restless and hyperactive. The following excerpt from a history illustrates some of the aspects of such brain damage in a child:

> Thomas was brought to a mental health clinic by his parents when he was 6 years old. He was of average size for his age and physically well developed and well nourished. He did not respond to any questions or directions, and was extremely restless and hyperactive. He had a very pained facial expression, and he exhibited stereotypical movements of the hands: he would hold them in front of him and shake them up and down. He had been excluded from all schools, even those for emotionally disturbed children. The mother reported that he had frequent, severe temper tantrums at home, in which he would break anything in sight. He required constant and direct supervision. The family was very devoted to him and willing to make any sacrifice to get help for him and to care for him at home.
>
> The parents described Thomas' early development as normal. He was a very happy, responsive child whose language development was normal. The father, who was a professional photographer, had taken many movies of the son from birth until the onset of the present symptoms when he was 3 years of age. A review of these movies tended to confirm the parents' assessment of Tommy's early development. Between the ages of 2 and 3, he developed an acute infectious illness, from which he appeared to have an uneventful recovery. But shortly following the illness, language development stopped and his personality changed from that of the happy, responsive child he had been to the hyperactive, anxious, and unresponsive picture he presented upon admission to the clinic. Neurological, psychological, and other testing measures confirmed a diagnosis of organic brain dysfunction.

In the young adult, the symptoms closely resemble those in the older adult, although the social and psychological impact may be more devastating in the young adult. Cognitive defects inhibit learning of new material, thus often interfering with career plans. Even previously mastered knowledge and skills are affected. For example, a computer programmer may no longer be able to function in his field. In severe cases, the memory defect may be so embarrassing in relationships with peers that it promotes isolation and withdrawal. In instances in which the functional deficit is mild or moderate, a young adult may be more resilient in compensating for and adapting to the cognitive defect than an older person is.

Disturbances in cognitive functioning that result from organic brain dysfunction may, of course, be superimposed upon such functional disorders as the thought and mood disturbances. Depression and elation frequently accompany organic brain disease. Goldfarb (1974) points out that such mood disorders are functional disturbances secondary to brain dysfunction. He notes that they are often the "emotional responses to the organic deficit and to the loss of an important part of the self." Depression often represents a grief and mourning process similar to that which occurs after the loss of a body part. Such depression responds to appropriate therapy. Depression, particularly in the elderly, may be mistaken for brain dysfunction. Anger, apathy, and depression are often misperceived by health care providers as organic dysfunction.

> Mrs. S. had been active all of her life, participating in running a small store that she and her husband owned. When her husband died, Mrs. S. was in her early seventies. The store was sold, and she was moved to a small apartment near her only son, in a community far removed from the one in which she had lived for many years and where she knew many people. Alone much of the time, and isolated from old friends and acquaintances, Mrs. S. became severely depressed. She was taken to a mental health center, where she was diagnosed as having chronic brain syndrome. After a few weeks, Mrs. S. was transferred to an adult home, where she came to the attention of a community mental health nurse. Working with Mrs. S. over a period of time, the nurse became aware that her cognitive abilities were intact but that she was depressed and lonely. Her mental state was exacerbated by a physical infirmity that was not being treated and was somewhat immobilizing. The immobilization increased her feelings of helplessness and abandonment. Working with the son and community agencies, the nurse was instrumental in having Mrs. S. transferred to a health-related facility that was more suitable to her needs. Her medical and psychological problems were treated there. In the new setting, where she felt more safe and secure, Mrs. S. made excellent progress and began to take part in and enjoy social and other activities.

Sociocultural factors. Many sociocultural factors influence each of us in our ability to cope with the normal stresses of life. The psychosocial needs for love, approval, acceptance, status, recognition, and achievement are important to the mental health of everyone. Economic security and the availability of family, friends, and other social support systems are essential to meeting these needs.

For the individual with organic brain dysfunction, many factors may combine to limit the ability to satisfy these normal human needs. In an older person, as Goldfarb (1974) points out, organic brain dysfunction often occurs at a time of sociocultural stress. Loss of family and friends through marriage, death, illness, and change of residence frequently coincides with physical ailments that contribute to organic dysfunction. Forced retirement from productive employment conflicts with one's need to be a useful, constructive member of society. In addition, retirement often leads to economic insecurity and isolation from friends and coworkers.

Although these factors are especially pertinent to older persons, a young person with some cognitive deficits may suffer very similar deprivations. Work and earning capacity can be limited by the disability, and isolation from family and peers often occurs.

All of these factors influence a person's ability to adapt. The person who can maintain close ties with family and friends and who experiences little disruption in life-style may adapt more effectively to the disability.

Psychodynamic factors. Stress and emotional responses to it can be disruptive of anyone's ability to function (see Chapter 4). For an individual with some organic brain dysfunction, such emotional factors as anxiety, anger, hopelessness, and depression may cause greater disorganization of behavior than would be the case for a person with normal brain functioning. This exacerbation of symptoms may be erroneously attributed to cerebral damage (Goldfarb, 1973). For example, an individual with a mild degree of organic brain dysfunction, when confronted with interpersonal, economic, social, or other crises, frequently experiences increased fear, anxiety, anger, frustration, and feelings of helplessness. These emotions in turn may cause restlessness, inattention, and difficulty in comprehension and memory. All of these symptoms are characteristic of organic dysfunction, but easily become exaggerated under emotional stress. Thus, assessment on the basis of cognitive function alone, without the level of anxiety and coping responses to it being taken into account, may easily lead to an inaccurate assessment of the degree of brain dysfunction and to an overlooking of the strengths of a client.

Clients with organic brain dysfunction are very often quite aware of their disability and of their emotional responses to pressure, stress, or assaults upon their self-concept and security. Such individuals will often voluntarily mention that they become very nervous and confused when pressured. They also frequently respond with embarrassment and anger when deficits in memory or other cognitive abilities are pointed out to them.

• • •

Thus, many factors in addition to the cognitive dysfunction influence the adaptive abilities of persons who have organic brain syndrome. The following brief case summaries point up some of the differences in the ways people adapt.

Mrs. M., who is in her mid-seventies, has lived alone in a single-family dwelling since the death of her husband, which occurred when she was 60. She has no children, but she maintains close family ties with her four siblings and their children. Although she had to drop out of school after the eighth grade to help support her immigrant family, Mrs. M. is fluent in and able to read and write both English and the language of her ethnic group. She is in good physical health, and she is economically secure. Mrs. M. is able to do her own housework, shopping, and cooking. She also maintains a small yard and flower garden, and takes great pride in her home. Always socially active, Mrs. M. continues to entertain family and friends and participates in various social and religious activities with them.

Mrs. M. has several complaints that she associates with aging, which shows a degree of insight. She complains of having trouble remembering things. If one observes her carefully, however, one finds the memory defect to be selective and related to new material or to areas that have little value for her. For example, she cannot remember where her favorite nephew's wedding will be held, although she has heard the plans many times and in detail. But she has no need to remember, since she will be taken there and brought home by a family member. She can, however, remember in detail the previous day's soap opera episode in order to recount it to a friend who missed the broadcast. In the retelling and in other social interactions, her speech is somewhat stereotypical and circumstantial.

She also complains that she becomes very nervous and upset when she is under any pressure or when she is confronted with a problem in her home that requires maintenance from service people in the community. But she is very effective in using problem solving techniques and in appealing to appropriate family members or friends for assistance. And she meets the need to feel useful by doing minor alterations and repairs of clothing for family members and close friends.

Mrs. G., also a widow, is in her late seventies. In many ways, her situation is similar to that of Mrs. M. She is also economically secure and owns her own home. Although she has several married children and a large extended family, her home is at some distance from any of them, so any immediate support or contact with her family is limited. In addition Mrs. G. speaks little English, and since she does not live in a neighborhood where her language is spoken, her community contact is more limited.

She is a strong-willed woman, however, and for several years had been able to manage her affairs and care for herself fairly effectively. Gradually, however, her family had begun to notice changes in her ability to function. Her memory had become progressively poorer. She would forget where she had put her money and other things, and whether or not a tenant had given her a check for the rent of an apartment. She also had begun to make errors in judgment, such as renting the apartment to a second family after she had already rented it and giving to strangers articles of furniture that she needed. When Mrs. G. had begun steadily to lose weight, a daughter had suspected that she had been forgetting to prepare meals or eat an adequate diet. A physical check-up had revealed no disease, but the physician convinced the family that Mrs. G's cognitive difficulties were making it impossible for her to continue living alone. At this point, she had moved into her daughter's home.

Although immediately following the change she would become somewhat disoriented during the night, when she would awaken and think she was still in her own home, Mrs. G.'s condition has become more stable. She continues to have some defects in memory, but in the protective and supportive environment, with adequate nutrition and the presence of family members, the cognitive defects have become less disabling.

Mrs. A. was also a widow in her late seventies who was economically secure and in good physical health. She lived in a stable ethnic community throughout her lifetime, and had many relatives and friends nearby. Within a period of 3 years Mrs. A. lost both her husband and her only daughter, and her grandsons married and moved away. Much of Mrs. A.'s social activity prior to their deaths had centered around the husband, the daughter, and the daughter's family. The husband had been retired for many years; he did all the shopping for the family and made all of the major decisions. Although he was several years older than Mrs. A., he had, over a period of time, kidded her about her forgetfulness. A few months after the husband's death, Mrs. A.'s neighbors began phoning a son, who lived some distance from his mother, with complaints about Mrs. A.'s behavior. They described her as confused and said she was harassing them about not paying rents, which they had indeed paid. The son and his wife visited Mrs. A. and hired someone to stay with her, but her condition continued to deteriorate. She became increasingly disoriented to time, confusing the night with the day and summer with winter, often appearing outside on very cold days clad only in a sweater. She also began to confuse her neighbor's children with the grandsons, who were grown and married. She began to cook large pots of food for the deceased husband and daughter, which she stored in the refrigerator to await their arrival. She continued to harass the tenants about the rents and, at times, to confuse them with people from her youth. On one occasion, she left home, saying she was going to visit her mother. She was found some distance from her home, and in a very confused state, by the police. They took her to a psychiatric hospital, where she was admitted with a diagnosis of chronic brain syndrome. In the hospital her general health and cognitive abilities deteriorated until her death about 6 months later.

EPIDEMIOLOGY AND SOCIOCULTURAL ASPECTS

Organic brain dysfunctions are the most ubiquitous of all mental health problems. Acute forms occur with regularity in many health facilities as complications of physiological and traumatic disorders and their treatment. The chronic forms constitute one of the major mental health problems. Despite, or perhaps because of, this prevalence, definitive data about the incidence of organic brain dysfunction are not currently available. The multiplicity of etiological factors that may contribute to organic dysfunction, however, suggests a very high and possibly increasing incidence, and also is an indication of some of the problems involved in gathering demographic data.

When acute confusional states occur as complications of medical conditions, data are often not compiled on such complications or, when collected, are related to specific underlying diagnoses. In addition, delirium often goes undiagnosed by physicians, although nursing staffs are often more aware of the symptoms and record them in their notes (Butler, 1975; Heller and Kornfeld 1974).

The incidence of organic dysfunctions of both acute and chronic nature is highest in people over 65 years of age. Persons in the older age groups are more susceptible to the major health problems (cancer, cardiac and respiratory diseases, and so on), with which organic dysfunctions are often associated. There is also empirical evidence that susceptibility to delirium is high among persons who experience illness and injury in the later years of life. Many individuals with some degree of chronic organic impairment are living in the community and do not come into contact with any data collection system. In some instances, a diagnosis of chronic brain syndrome is made purely on the basis of behavioral assessment. Butler (1975) terms chronic brain syndrome a "wastebasket" diagnosis that is made when anyone starts acting "senile."

The diagnosis of chronic brain syndrome frequently arouses feelings of hopelessness in physicians, nurses, and other health professionals and leads to a lack of interest in the active treatment of such disorders in the elderly (Butler, 1975). Such responses may have contributed to the historical paucity of research in this area of psychiatry (Wells, 1978). There is, however, a growing interest in the neuropsychiatric conditions associated with impaired cerebral functioning, and there has been an increase in the amount of research into the causes and treatment of such conditions (Wells, 1978).

Organic brain disturbances occur in all social classes and ethnic groups. Many sociocultural factors contribute, directly or indirectly, to the incidence of organic brain dysfunction. Poverty, with its concomitant poor housing, overcrowding, and malnutrition, may increase the incidence of infectious and other diseases, which can be complicated by organic brain disorders of either an acute or a chronic nature.

Leighton (1974) notes that "societal malfunction" or "social disintegration" increases the frequency of organic disease, in part through malfunctioning of the health care network and the resulting disruption of preventive and treatment services.

Spector (1979) points out that lead poisoning is a serious health problem among black and Hispanic Americans. When untreated, it results in chronic brain dysfunction. Many victims of lead poisoning live in old houses in which lead-base paints had been applied to exterior and interior surfaces. Current legislation has fairly well eliminated the use of lead in paints for most purposes, and many states have directives for preventing inhalation of lead when old paint is removed. In some older dwellings, however, lead paint remains on walls, where it becomes a source of lead poisoning as a result of flaking, paint removal efforts, and children chewing on painted surfaces.

Social stress and the competitive pressures of highly industrialized society are experienced by people of all classes, ages, and ethnic groups. Pressures upon the adolescent to achieve in school, upon the adult in many work situations, upon the older person forced into retirement and often into isolation, and upon minority group members who are excluded from the job market and meaningful participation in other aspects of life are commonplace.

The ways in which people cope with social stress often contribute, directly or indirectly, to organic disease. Social pressures contribute significantly to drug and alcohol abuse, as people increasingly turn to such chemicals in an effort to cope with the pressures of modern life. Suicide attempts may also result in brain damage, depending upon the particular method employed and other factors.*

Prejudice, another source of social stress, may contribute indirectly to organic brain dysfunction in a variety of ways, including the failure to provide early or preventive treatment of disorders that can lead to chronic organic dysfunction when they are untreated. Raskus et al. (1979) note "the sense of futility" of health professionals toward treatment of emotional disturbances in older people. Butler (1975) speaks of the "profound prejudice against the elderly which is found to some degree in all of us." To be elderly and from a minority ethnic group places the person in "multiple jeopardy." (Butler, 1975).

The technological era in which we live may contribute to the incidence of organic dysfunction. Environmental pollution from industry

---

*Sociocultural aspects of alcohol and drug abuse are discussed in Ch. 12; sociocultural aspects of suicide are discussed in Chapter 11.

and other sources is an ever-present danger. Advances in medical technology, which have been so effective in prolonging life and functioning ability, have also contributed to the increase in the incidence of organic dysfunction. Heller and Kornfield (1974) discuss the delirious states associated with cardiac and general surgery, intensive care units, and treatment of renal diseases.

High-speed transportation, another aspect of our advanced technology, has increased the incidence of head injury—through automobile and other accidents. While improved treatment has decreased mortality from head trauma, organic dysfunction is an increasingly common sequela of severe head injury (Tuerk et al., 1974).

ETIOLOGY

Organic brain dysfunction is not a disease entity in itself. The brain syndromes represent complex responses of the central nervous system to disturbances in neurophysiological processes that maintain normal functioning. Brain tissue is highly dependent upon a constant supply of oxygen, glucose, and certain amino acids to maintain normal functioning. Any systemic or local condition that interferes with these essential elements or that inhibits or alters the normal metabolic processes can produce brain dysfunction of either an acute or a chronic nature. It should be noted that the present state of our knowledge of neurophysiology is not suffcient to explain all of the mechanisms through which systemic disorders affect brain function.

Acute confusional states

"Acute confusional state" is a term used by Seltzer and Frazier (1978) to describe the acute brain dysfunction that often accompanies physical illness and injury. Many other diagnostic terms are also used, among them "delirium," acute delirious states, "acute brain syndrome," and "toxic psychosis." The following are some of the major causes of an acute confusional state, but it should be borne in mind that any condition that interferes with complex biochemical or metabolic functions may result in brain dysfunction of a temporary or permanent nature.

Systemic disorders. Among the systemic disorders that may be associated with an acute confusional state are chronic heart and lung diseases, hepatic and renal insufficiencies, acute forms of diabetes, and severe anemias. The specific etiological factors that such systemic disorders produce vary with the underlying pathological process. Among these factors are hypoxia, which is particularly prevalent in chronic heart and lung disorders and in severe anemias. Hypoglycemia often occurs in severe diabetes. Disturbances in acid-base and electrolyte balances and in the water-sodium balance may be present in any of these physical ailments and in many others. Toxic substances in the blood that accompany renal and hepatic dysfunction can also contribute to brain dysfunction. Uremic toxins may cause such neurological symptoms as seizures and asterixis— a characteristic flapping tremor of the hands—in addition to acute brain dysfunction (Seltzer and Frazier, 1978).

Infectious disorders. Acute confusional states frequently occur in systemic infectious disorders such as typhoid fever, malaria, pneumonia, and infectious hepatitis. Central nervous system infections such as meningitis and encephalitis may also cause delirium. In the systemic infectious conditions, brain dysfunction is believed to be associated with the high temperature and level of toxicity that are symptomatic of the diseases. The debilitating effects of such an illness may also be a contributory cause. Encephalitis may be followed by a chronic syndrome. Immunization against the communicable diseases of childhood and effective treatment of syphilis with penicillin have nearly eliminated the encephalitis often associated with these diseases. Antibiotic treatment of viral and bacterial encephalitis has also been effective in preventing chronic brain dysfunction as a result of these diseases.

Chemical intoxication. Chemical intoxication is becoming an increasing hazard in industrial societies. The presence of numerous chemical additives in foodstuffs and the chemical pollution of our air, water, and soil have received wide attention because of their potential for the production of cancer and birth defects. There has, however, been far less attention paid to the potential hazard of such chemicals to the normal physiological processes of the central nervous system and the rest of the body.

Two chemicals that have long been associated with brain dysfunction are carbon monoxide and lead, although other chemicals may produce similar effects. Carbon monoxide poisoning can come about suddenly, from breathing automobile exhaust fumes in a suicide attempt or as a result of a faulty automobile exhaust system combined with poor ventilation of a car's interior. In current model cars in which ventilation depends upon a system that brings air into the car when it is in motion and windows are closed, idling a motor when the car is stopped in order to provide heat or air conditioning is particularly hazardous. In addition, incomplete combustion of fuels, particularly coal, may cause toxic levels of carbon monoxide to be emitted into the air of a home.

Carbon monoxide causes anoxia by combining with blood hemoglobin to form a stable substance, carboxyhemoglobin. This condition prevents the uptake of oxygen by the hemoglobin. When severe or prolonged enough, carbon monoxide poisoning can cause death or permanent brain damage. The symptoms of confusion and a clouding of consciousness may be early indications of carbon monoxide poisoning. Mild cases may appear in persons working in such industries as auto repairing, in which a constant level of carbon monoxide results from motors being run in inadequately ventilated garages.

Several of the heavy metals—lead, mercury, and manganese—may cause brain dysfunction. Lead has received the greatest attention and may be the most commonly found of the heavy metals. The ingestion of lead by children has been greatly reduced as a result of government actions that ban the use of lead in paints, particularly in paints used on toys, children's furniture, and other items that young children may suck or chew on. The habit of pica, or the craving of unnatural foods such as plaster from walls, may still be a hazard to children, and occasionally to adults, who live in older dwellings in which lead paint remains on the walls.

In adults, lead poisoning is usually caused by inhalation associated with industrial activities. Workers in the construction industry are particularly vulnerable when they are dismantling or removing paint from older structures on which lead paints had been used over a period of time. A study conducted during the dismantling of one of the elevated railway structures in Manhattan found lead intoxication in some of the workers despite the fairly extensive safety measures that had been employed to prevent it (Fishbein et al., 1978). Removal of lead paint from older houses by homeowners can also result in lead inhalation.

Lead intoxication may produce an acute delirious state, or it may result in chronic brain syndrome—particularly if treatment is delayed or ineffective. Lead produces a fragility of the red blood cell membrane, with subsequent destruction or hemolysis of the cell. Lead may be stored in the bones, which can lead to symptoms recurring as it is later released without further inhalation or ingestion (Luckmann and Sorensen, 1974).

Pharmacological agents. Many pharmaceuticals may cause an acute confusional state in some people. This side effect may occur in susceptible individuals at normal therapeutic dosage levels, as well as in high dosage levels and overdoses. Among the drugs that may cause such a response are anticholinergics, diuretics, digitalis, levodopa, hypnotics, sedatives, and some of the hormonal substances. Kolb (1974) points out that some children may develop delirium following a single application of atropine eye drops. The reason why some children are so affected is not known.

Other drugs may produce acute confusional states when taken in overdoses or in combination with other chemicals such as alcohol or other central nervous system depressants. A synergistic or potentiating effect takes place when such drugs are taken in combination. Baldessarini (1977) mentions the tricyclic antidepressants and lithium salts as drugs that cause delirium and other neurologic symptoms when they are taken in toxic levels. He also notes that the tricyclic drugs are increasingly being used in suicide attempts. Mild intake of alcohol, in combination with such drugs as the phenothiazines, the antidepressants, the barbiturates, may produce an acute intoxication and may even lead to coma and death as a result of depression of the respiratory centers.

Many therapeutic procedures may produce an acute confusional state. Diruetic therapy and low sodium diets, for example, unless carefully monitored, can produce fluid electrolyte imbalances that may lead to symptoms of delirium. Anesthesia and prolonged surgical procedures may also cause an acute brain dysfunction.

Alcohol and drug withdrawal. There are two ways in which alcohol may produce an acute brain syndrome. First, excessive ingestion produces acute alcoholism. Second, for people who habitually consume large quantities of alcohol and who are physiologically addicted, the abrupt withdrawal of the substance may produce the symptom picture known as delirium tremens. This condition is often encountered in persons admitted to a general hospital for treatment of a physical illness or injury. Very often it is not known that the individual is physically addicted to alcohol until the symptoms appear. Withdrawal symptoms, including brain dysfunction, may also occur in individuals addicted to such drugs as opiates, meprobamates, and barbiturates.

Nutritional deficiencies. A deficiency in the B vitamins (particularly thiamine) is the most common nutritional deficiency associated with psychiatric and neurological disorders. The condition known as Wernicke's syndrome is caused by a deficiency of thiamine in the diet (Seltzer and Frazier, 1978). Because of the addition of the B vitamins to many foods, most people in the United States have an adequate intake of these essential substances. Deficiencies of B vitamins are seen most often in chronic alcoholics, because of the poor nutritional habits and the interference with intestinal absorption that are associated with chronic alcoholism. Thiamine deficiency may, however, occur in cases of hyperemesis gravidarum and pernicious anemia and in elderly persons who have inadequate nutritional intake. Delirium may be one of the early symptoms of the syndrome. Prolonged deficiency of thiamine may cause permanent neurological damage and chronic dysfunction. The chronic condition is known as Korsakoff's psychosis.

Severe dehydration may also produce delirium. Elderly people living alone may be especially vulnerable in hot summer weather, because of inadequate fluid intake and-or excessive loss of fluids.

Head injuries. An acute confusional state is often associated with head injuries, particularly in instances involving a concussion and loss of consciousness. The delirium may result from neuronal injury from the concussion, but prolonged or recurring delirium may indicate hemorrhage and intracranial pressure (Kolb, 1977).

Chronic brain syndrome

Like acute brain dysfunction, chronic brain dysfunction may be secondary to many pathological processes. In addition to the toxic, metabolic, and circulatory disorders that may underlie chronic brain dysfunction, examples of which have been noted, intracranial neoplasms and infections, normal-pressure hydrocephalus, and Huntington's chorea (a genetic disorder) are among other causative factors.

In the majority of cases, however, symptoms of chronic brain dysfunction cannot, in our present state of knowledge, be attributed to any such pathological processes. The disorders are, then, somewhat arbitrarily as Seltzer and Frazier (1978) point out, considered to be primary and labeled presenile or senile dementia, depending upon age of onset. When the onset occurs in the sixth decade of life or later, the condition is considered senile dementia. An earlier onset, often in the fourth decade of life, results in the condition being termed presenile dementia. Presenile dementia may be further classified as Alzheimer's disease or Pick's disease, after the physicians who first described these organic dysfunctions that have their onset in midlife.

TREATMENT MODALITIES

The treatment of acute brain dysfunction depends upon the underlying medical condition with which the dysfunction is associated. Aspects of treatment will be discussed further in the section on nursing intervention.

Many of the chronic brain dysfunctions associated with underlying pathological disorders may be reversed or ameliorated through proper treatment during the early stages. In a few disorders, advances in the treatment of the acute stages have virtually eliminated the appearance of chronic brain disease. For example, early and effective treatment of syphillis with penicillin has prevented the general paresis associated with syphilis, which was at one time a common cause of dementia. Early diagnosis of Wernicke's syndrome and treatment with thiamine cure this acute organic disorder and prevent the development of a chronic dysfunction.

Increased knowledge and better diagnostic procedures have enhanced the possibility of recognition and treatment of underlying pathology. For many years a diagnosis of psychosis with cerebral arteriosclerosis was almost routinely made for persons older than 65 who were admitted to large state mental hospitals. At the present time this diagnosis is being increasingly questioned as a valid cause of chronic brain syndrome. As Seltzer and Sherwin point out, cerebral arteriosclerosis would be more apt to cause an acute condition such as a cerebral vascular accident. There is, however, possibility of brain damage from multiple cerebral infarcts occurring over a period of time. Such a condition is associated with hypertension; if hypertension is recognized and treated early, such multiple infarctions could be prevented (Seltzer and Sherwin, 1978).

Normal-pressure hydrocephalus is another disorder that has received increased attention during the past decade. Normal-pressure hydrocephalus is characterized by a progressive dementia, accompanied by incontinence and a peculiar gait. As the name indicates, the cerebrospinal fluid pressure is normal in this condition. Diagnosis is made by pneumoencephalogram and other neurological diagnositc measures. A history of head trauma, infection, or another brain disease has been associated with the condition in some cases. A cerebrospinal shunt has been effective in reversing the symptoms in some patients (Seltzer and Sherwin, 1978).

The psychiatric treatment modalities utilized in therapy for clients with chronic organic brain dysfunction include individual, group, and family psychotherapy; occupational, recreational, and work therapies; activity therapies, including dance and movement therapies; crisis intervention; brief hospitalization; and administration of psychopharmaceuticals. Since most of these forms of treatment have been dealt with in earlier chapters, discussion in this chapter will be limited to aspects that are particularly relevant to clients who have organic insufficiency.

The utilization of individual and group psychotherapy in the treatment of clients with organic brain syndrome has been increasing since World War II. The extent to which these forms of therapy are available to such clients will depend upon a variety of factors. Among those factors are the socioeconomic status of the individual, the availability and interest of psychotherapists, the willingness of the client to accept these forms of therapy, and so forth. Perhaps major inhibiting factors are attitudes toward chronic brain dysfunction and toward the elderly population, who make up the largest number of potential clients. Many professionals, including therapists and nurses, experience feelings of hopelessness and helplessness in response to chronic brain dysfunction and to elderly people. Such emotional responses inhibit the ability of the health professional to function or to maintain an interest in working with such clients. Goldfarb (1974) points out the importance of psychotherapy for the elderly person with organic brain dysfunction and the importance of setting realistic goals. Many such people suffer from anxiety, fear, depression, and anger, which in themselves can be disorganizing to the personality. Goldfarb (1974) notes that the therapeutic relationship can be made more effective if the client who feels dependent and helpless is offered an opportunity to achieve, or feel that he has achieved, mastery and gratification. Such mastery or feelings of mastery, Goldfarb points out, come about as a result of the need of the client to ally himself with a powerful person or parent surrogate, in this case the therapist. The therapist, in Goldfarb's method, does not act out the powerful role ascribed to him, but accepts the client's perception by neither confirming nor denying it. In the ongoing therapeutic sessions, the interest, concern, and appropriate approval expressed by the therapist provide emotional support that meets the needs of the client. This form of therapy, like any other form of psychotherapy, should be used only by professionals with adequate training and preparation.

Psychopharmaceuticals are widely employed in the treatment of people with organic dysfunction to control such symptoms as agitation, anxiety, and depression. In addition, many substances have been used and studied in relation to their effect on cognition. Among these are stimulants such as amphetamines, vasodilators, anticoagulants, hormones, vitamins, and procaine. The anticoagulants continue to be widely used in the geriatric population in the treatment of circulatory and cognitive disorders. The possibility of hemorrhage, from even a minor injury, when anticoagulants are used, requires close monitoring of blood levels and close health supervision. In the case of persons who have organic dysfunctions with memory defects, which may interfere with the ability to follow through prescribed treatment and medication instructions, monitoring by community health nurses is important. Some drugs have been used in an attempt to improve or affect cognitive function, but studies have not supported their effectiveness. The use of vitamins, particularly for clients whose nutritional intakes may not provide adequate amounts of vitamins, has shown some promise (Eisendorfer and Fridel, 1977).

The use of antipsychotic and antidepressant drugs in older people has a higher risk of toxic side effects than it does in younger people. The absorption, metabolism, and excretion of many of these drugs are altered in the older age group. The side effects that may appear include confusion, disorientation, lethargy or agitation, and aggression. Since confusion and disorientation are common symptoms in organic brain dysfunction in both the acute and the chronic states, antipsychotic or antidepressant drugs may exacerbate these symptoms. Although lower-than-average doses may prevent such side effects, it is important that nursing staff be alert to toxic side effects in assessing client behavior (Baldessarini, 1977).

NURSING INTERVENTION

PRIMARY PREVENTION

Primary prevention in organic brain dysfunction is a serious and multifaceted problem that involves many aspects of our complex social system. The importance of the prevention of a condition that in many instances is preventable and that often has a devastating effect upon the individual, his family, and the community cannot be overemphasized. The nurse, as a member of a health profession and as a citizen, has an opportunity and a responsibility to participate in the primary prevention of organic disorders.

Primary prevention in organic disorders focuses upon individuals, families, and groups who may be at risk and upon factors in the environment that contribute to the disease process. Because the etiology of organic disorders may lie in a broad range of causative factors, and because the etiology is closely interrelated with other health problems, primary prevention activities will often be an integral part of general health promotion. The prevention of suicide through "hot lines," for example, or programs that enable nurses to prevent and intervene in alcohol and drug abuse may have an impact on the incidence of organic brain disorders.

Social and political action related to such community concerns as environmental pollution, consumer products safety, and highway and transportation safety may also be part of primary prevention of organic disorders. Although Ralph Nader has demonstrated that one committed individual can have an impact upon public safety, the most effective action has come about through persistent and informed group action.

The degree to which environmental pollution contributes to organic brain disease is not known. It is known, however, that certain chemcals—heavy metals and carbon monoxide, for example—play a very direct role. The ever-increasing number of reports in the news media of severe environmental pollution by industry is alarming. Reports of the long-term pollution of a town in Italy after a single emission of a toxic chemical from a factory and of buried chemicals seeping to the surface in the Love Canal in Niagara Falls, New York, and their destructive impact on the health of residents, are but two examples. Whether or not people have a right to pure drinking water is an issue

that the United States Supreme Court may soon confront.

Professional nurses working in industry have long been involved in occupational health and safety. They have been effective in the early identification of health and safety hazards and in early diagnosis and treatment of health problems. Such nurses also have had an opportunity to work with environmental and safety engineers and with the Occupational Safety and Health Administration to identify and eliminate potential hazards to health in industry and to assist in the promotion of safety measures through health teaching and health supervision of workers.

Since brain dysfunction is often a secondary response to underlying metabolic or other systemic disorders, any advances in the prevention of such conditions would automatically have a preventive effect on the incidence of acute brain syndrome caused by them. Immunization against communicable diseases is an example of such prevention. Early diagnosis and effective treatment of many systemic disorders—treatment of pneumonia with antibiotics, for example—has also been important. Efforts to prevent alcohol abuse, drug abuse, and toxic substance use have been less than successful despite the expenditure of much effort toward this end. Early identification of people at risk and the availability of community services for effective treatment are important aspects of these efforts. Public education, particularly of the younger population, can play a role. Research into the underlying causative factors may eventually lead to more effective preventive measures.

Primary prevention in chronic brain syndrome is more complex, since the etiology is not known in the majority of cases. Wells (1978) points out that the increasing interest in such conditions and the awareness that they are disease processes and not the normal concommitants of aging are hopeful signs for further research and treatment of these disorders. He further points out that the greatest advances to date have been in the fields of neuropathology and neurochemistry. Wells (1978), Seltzer and Sherwin (1978), and others have noted that a number of people, labeled as having chronic brain syndrome, have symptoms that represent an underlying disorder that in many instances can be alleviated or ameliorated through appropriate treatment. Improved diagnostic measures, including neurological evaluation, could lead to the institution of such treatment. Normal-pressure hydrocephalus, for example, is a neurological condition that is often mistaken for senile dementia when the diagnosis is based on the symptom picture alone, without an aequate neurological evaluation.

Depression in an older person is also often misdiagnosed as senile dementia. Goldfarb (1974) points out that "many older people labeled as having chronic brain syndrome, are often angry, depressed and apathetic." Treatment for the depression alleviates the symptoms in such cases. The prevalence of such conditions in the elderly has become widely enough recognized to have spawned the term "pseudodementia" to describe them.

Professional nurses working in hospitals and communities can be effective in many aspects of primary prevention of chronic brain dysfunction. Early identification and treatment of physical and psychological health problems often rest with the community health nurse, who may be the first health professional to become aware of the existence of such health problems. Differentiating between symptoms of depression and chronic brain dysfunction may be more possible for a nurse, who frequently has greater contact with a client, than for a physician, who may see the person only briefly. Communication of such observations to other health professionals is important in obtaining appropriate treatment. Case finding among people living alone and somewhat isolated in a community and providing information about resources for recreation, crisis intervention, and social interaction are also appropriate nursing functions that may play a part in prevention.

The frequency with which many health problems coincide with some degree of organic brain dysfunction, particularly in elderly people, points up the need for and importance of ongoing health supervision and teaching for clients with these health problems. Many such people are receiving medical care and have had drugs prescribed for the treatment of the physical disorders. However, even a mild degree of organic dysfunction, and the memory deficit that accompanies it, often makes it difficult for a person to understand, remember, or carry out prescribed treatment. This situation can be complicated by anxiety, attitudes toward taking drugs, ethnic beliefs about illness, food preferences, and a variety of other factors.

Several aspects of health supervision and teaching are particularly relevant preventive measures in working with such clients. *Counseling* that is oriented toward helping a person identify the concerns he may have about medications and other treatments, whether these be lack of understanding of purpose, ethnic beliefs about illness, or whatever, will provide a baseline of mutual understanding for nursing intervention and also will serve to communicate interest in and concern for the client as a person.

Frequently, prescribed medical treatment is not followed because a person does not understand or remember the purpose of the therapy or because he is confused by the variety of pills and capsules ordered by a physician. An understanding of the purpose of each medication and/or treatment usually overcomes such difficulties. Helping the person to devise an organized system for taking medication can help combat a medication error or omission resulting from a memory deficit. Adapting special diets to accommodate ethnic food preferences may provide a person the incentive necessary to maintain a prescribed dietary regimen. Consultation with family, friends, or people of the same ethnic background as a client can be utilized for a variety of purposes.

Acting in support of or on behalf of a client—client advocacy—has long been a part of professional nursing practice, and it is currently receiving renewed attention as a part of mental health practice. Client advocacy is particularly important when nurses are working with clients who may be at risk of developing organic brain dysfunction. The objective in both prevention and treatment is to help a person maintain an optimal level of independent functioning. Attempting to cope with the bureaucracies of social agencies, the isolation that confronts older people, and other aspects of our society often requires that a client have the support and assistance of a nurse or other health professionals.

Service as a client advocate can involve a variety of activities or actions carried out in cooperation with a client or, with a client's permission, on his behalf. Maintaining contact and cooperation with a physician, clinic, or health agency serving a client can help the nurse to reinforce, clarify, or amplify prescribed medical or other treatment. Assisting a client to contact social, recreational, and other community services and to follow through on appointments are often important aspects of working with people with organic brain disorders. Seeking out social support systems in the community and helping a client to make use of them can help him to overcome isolation and loneliness.

In carrying out an advocacy role for a client, a nurse must protect the client's rights, and any actions must have the full support and approval of the client. Client advocacy may also be carried out in cooperation with or on behalf of a group, class, or community to achieve social goals, through social and political action.

SECONDARY PREVENTION

Secondary prevention in organic brain dysfunction is oriented toward early diagnosis and effective treatment so that a person may be restored to the optimal level of functioning. The professional nurse performs an important function in both aspects of this objective.

For a client in the acute confusional state, early recognition of symptoms of organic dysfunction and prompt treatment of the underlying pathological condition are often essential to preserving the integrity of the brain and, at times, the life of the client. Since the nurse is frequently the health professional in closest contact with the client, he or she may be the first to identify early signs of cognitive dysfunction and thus to take action (including communication of findings to medical and nursing staff) to initiate early treatment. Which treatment is appropriate will depend upon the underlying pathology or upon the causative agent. But it is important to note that symptoms of cognitive dysfunction may, in some instances, be the first indications of systemic and other disorders. Shear and Sacks (1978) point out that delirium may be the earliest manifestation of a toxic level of digitalis.

Nursing intervention in acute confusional states is based upon the nurse's ability to utilize the nursing process in assessment and correlation of data and to protect the client and prevent chronicity. Kolb (1978) points out that delirium can be progressive. Early symptoms may be shifting levels of awareness, difficulty in focusing attention, and an inability to screen out irrelevant stimuli. These symptoms may be accompanied by clouding of consciousness or an inability to think clearly or to comprehend what is said. There may be a haziness or vagueness of perception. In later stages there is confusion and disorientation and evidence of memory impairment. In severe stages there may be loss of motor control. Kolb also notes that shifts in degrees of awareness and orientation and changes in emotional responses, from calmness to restlessness, fearfulness to apathy, or irritability to placidity, are always suggestive of delirium.

Nursing intervention in an acute confusional state often depends on the ability of the nurse to assess and interpret symptoms. The nursing history is an important part of the assessment process in delerious states. An understanding, obtained from the family or the client, of the person's functioning prior to the onset of the illness and of the ways in which the person coped with stress may be important in distinguishing chronic from acute brain syndrome and in identifying early symptoms of organic dysfunctions, particularly in the elderly. Pertinent information about many other factors that can contribute to delirium, such as medication, drug and alcohol use, and diet, may be a part of such a history. Correlation of the symptoms with the medical history, the diagnosis, and the laboratory data is also an important aspect of assessment. Communication of findings to other members of the health team, particularly the physician and the nursing staff, is essential to appropriate intervention.

Treatment of a person in an acute confusional state depends upon the etiology. In view of the fact that such a state may be precipitated or caused by a broad range of medical problems, therapeutic measures may encompass a broad range of treatments. In some conditions, such as drug and alcohol withdrawal, chemical intoxication, head trauma, and intracranial neoplasms or infections, an acute confusional state may be an anticipated complication. In other conditions, an organic dysfunction is far less predictable. Some people may be more vulnerable to organic brain dysfunction than other people are. Older people, for example, may be more vulnerable to the toxic effects of prescribed medications or a fluid electrolyte imbalance. A low-grade fever in an elderly person may not be indicative of the degree of an inflammatory process, because the normal physiological responses to inflammation (elevated temperature, elevated white blood count and so on) may be altered in older people. The temperature for example, may be only slightly elevated in the presence of a severe inflammatory process. In such a situation, the severity of the disease process may go unrecognized.

Nursing intervention will, of course, include participation in the diag-

nostic and therapeutic measures employed to care for the client in each situation. Ongoing assessment of the client's responses to the therapeutic measures employed is an important component of intervention. But regardless of the etiology, some aspects of nursing intervention are applicable to any client with delirium, since they provide protection and aid the client in maintaining cognitive abilities to the extent possible. In order to achieve these objectives, nursing team planning, in an ongoing process, is essential. These aspects include the following:

1. The number of people providing direct care to the client should be limited; a group should consist of the smallest number possible to provide adequate care. Nurses and other members of the group should function as a team, sharing information and offering guidance and support to each other. A small number of people providing continuity of care to the client will be less demanding of his cognitive abilities than a large number and will aid in maintaining orientation to people. Consistency in the staff caring for the client, which is implied in this team concept, will also promote the establishment of supportive relationships.

2. Close supervision of client by team members is important in order to protect safety.

3. The atmosphere should be as quiet as possible, in order to limit distracting external stimuli. Placing a client in a room near the call box results in dis-

traction, as does placing him in a room in which or near which there is a high level of activity.

4. Communication with clients in acute confusional states should be brief and clear, and abstractions should be avoided. Questioning should be limited to essential information, and it should be terminated if the client becomes more confused or appears frustrated. Staff members should call patients by name and should also identify themselves by name, avoiding asking if clients remember them.

5. Since clients in acute confusional states are often frightened or anxious, reassurance appropriate to the situation can help allay fears. When it is known that a condition is temporary and directly related to a physical condition, a simple explanation of this fact can be reassuring to a client. Often, the presence and understanding of the nurse are the most important factors in helping allay fears.

6. When possible, the presence of a familiar and caring family member can be a stabilizing factor. This is particularly important when ethnic and language differences exist between the client and the health staff.

7. Disorientation is often more severe during the night, when energy levels are lower and darkness increases the possibility of visual distortion. Keeping the room of a client with delirium well lighted at night may prevent the increase in cognitive dysfunction and development of illusions (visual misperceptions).

In addition to these forms of intervention, which are applicable to anyone experiencing an acute confusional state, there are some conditions in which particular kinds of intervention are indicated. For example, Kolb (1974) points out that in brain injuries, treatment should be started as soon as the individual has regained consciousness. He notes that such clients are often extremely fearful and suggestible. He recommends that an explanation of the injury be given the client and that providing an expectation of the outcome can reassure him. Because of the suggestibility of the client, Kolb (1977) recommends that questions concerning symptoms that the client has not raised should be avoided. He further suggests that, as soon as it is medically feasible, a carefully planned program of progressive physical activity should be instituted. Kolb cautions against overtaxing the client physically, intellectually, or emotionally.

Another condition to which special attention should be given is in intracranial neoplasm. Often, the earliest symptoms of brain tumor are symptoms of brain dysfunction. Acute, temporary disturbances in memory, levels of awareness, and ability to pursue a thought or line of communication may precede other symptoms. The affected person recognizes these disturbances in memory and level of consciousness and becomes terrified. "What is happening to me?" "What does it mean?" "When is it going to happen again?" Such thoughts run through the mind of the sufferer, arousing fear and even panic.

Complicating the picture is the fact that a diagnosis often cannot be made until the intracranial neoplasm is fairly well advanced, especially when the primary site of the neoplasm is the brain. The prevalence of brain tumors may be far greater than demographic data suggest, and many such clients may be found among people in hospitals. Burgess and Lazare (1973) point out that brain tumors are found in 2% of all persons on whom autopsies are performed, regardless of the cause of death. Only a portion of these can be attributed to metastasis (15% to 20% of all brain tumors are metastatic).

Although nursing intervention is focused upon the nursing, rather than the medical, diagnosis, an awareness of the symptom picture, particularly when it is persistent or progressive, can enable the nurse working in the community to make referrals to appropriate diagnostic resources. In addition, a supportive nurse-client relationship may provide an individual with needed emotional support.

The nature of secondary intervention in chronic brain syndrome depends upon the identified needs and the circumstances of the particular client. Needs and circumstances may vary among persons with chronic organic dysfunction as much as they vary in any other group of people. People with chronic brain dysfunction have the same physical, psychological, social, cultural, and spiritual needs as everyone else. The degree to which a client is able to meet these needs depends, to some degree, upon the extent of cognitive dysfunction, the state of physical and mental health, the availability of social support networks and community resources, and the individual's economic situation. Needs vary with the age of onset.

The major objective in secondary intervention in organic brain syndrome is to promote and sustain, to the maximum degree possible, a client's ability for independent functioning. The following services are essential to meeting this objective.

1. Adequate medical care and health supervision. Treatment and rehabilitation of existing physiological disorders and/or disabilities are essential. Preventive intervention through health supervision and teaching in such areas as nutrition and hygiene are particularly important for such clients.
2. Early identification and treatment of emotional disorders such as depression, which can complicate organic dysfunction
3. Preventive measures to promote emotional security and comfort through utilization of such resources as family, friends, social, religious, and ethnic groups, and community agencies
4. Provision of economic security
5. Availability in the community of resources to provide such services as crisis intervention and emergency medical and psychiatric care and to meet economic and social needs

6. Providing information to the client on the availability and location of health, social welfare, recreational, and other community services and serving as client advocate in securing and utilizing these resources

As noted earlier in this chapter, stress and the emotional responses to it may increase the degree of cognitive dysfunction and the usual ability of an individual to cope with daily living. For this reason assessment in chronic brain disturbances must have a multiple focus in the collection and interpretation of data. That is, in addition to assessment of the cognitive functions of comprehension, memory, and orientation, there is also a need to assess mood or affect and the status of physical health and nutrition, as well as to be alert for the presence of psychosocial factors that may be serving as stressors.

For example, a person living alone who develops an abscessed tooth or suffers pain from ill-fitting dentures may become extremely anxious and depressed because he lacks means of transportation to a dentist or the necessary funds to pay for dental services. In addition, the pain and discomfort he experiences may make it impossible for him to eat a normal diet, so that nutrition becomes inadequate. A failure to take into account all of these factors could easily lead to an erroneous impression of the degree of cognitive dysfunction.

A combination of social, economic, health, and other problems, and the

fear, anxiety, helplessness, and depression that they often arouse, may distort the symptoms of organic brain dysfunction, making a mild or moderate degree of disability appear more severe. Anxiety, for example, can be disorganizing to any personality. For the individual with some degree of organic dysfunction, there may be less ability to cope with the anxiety or with the stress factors that aroused it.

Identification of these variables and intervention to reduce psychosocial stress and/or provide treatment for physical health problems and emotional disorders can restore a person to his optimal level of functioning. In situations in which there has been an ongoing relationship with a nurse and other members of the health team, sudden changes in the person's ability to function may be readily apparent to those who know the client well. The stress factors that are contributing to the client's anxiety level may also be known to the health team. In other instances, a nurse working in the community, for example, may need to make an initial assessment of the degree of cognitive dysfunction of a new client. This assessment may have to be made in the home, where little information is available about such variables as psychosocial stress.

Goldfarb (1974) points out that two tests, when used in combination, are effective tools for measuring organic brain dysfunction: the "Mental Status Questionnaire—Special Ten" and the "Face Hand Test." The Mental Status Questionnaire—Special Ten is a brief (10 questions) questionnaire designed to test orientation to time and place and recent and remote memory of personal and general information. The test is scored on the basis of number of errors given in the responses, to indicate the degree of dysfunction. The Face Hand Test assesses the ability of a client to identify double nonverbal stimuli (touch) as he is simultaneously touched on one cheek and one hand in an alternating pattern (left hand, right cheek, and so on).

Both tests have been well validated (Goldfarb, 1974); when given together and properly administered and interpreted, they may be useful in determining the degree of cognitive dysfunction in instances in which emotional problems are present. Since many factors in addition to organic disorders can influence responses to questions on a mental status examination, a discrepancy between the findings of the Mental Status Questionnaire and the Face Hand Test may be indicative of depression or other emotional factors. In such an instance, assessment of cognitive functioning may be more difficult.

Although these measurement tools are designed for medical use, familiarity with them could help a professional nurse in the community make an initial assessment of a client's cognitive dysfunction prior to referral or consultation.

Health teaching and supervision are important aspects of nursing intervention for persons with organic brain dysfunctions. Since the majority of such clients are in the older age groups, they are more vulnerable to the degenerative diseases that require close health supervision and adequate medical treatment of underlying physical disorders. A client's economic status may limit the availability of such services. This situation is often complicated by a lack of knowledge of the existence and location of community resources.

Maintaining adequate nutrition is often a problem for clients with organic dysfunction, whether they are treated in the home or in a community agency. Psychosocial factors such as poverty, ethnic background, and lack of transportation, as well as lack of knowledge of nutritional needs, may contribute to poor nutrition. Health teaching for such clients should incorporate an understanding of ethnic food preferences; nutritional teaching and planning should be adapted to these preferences, as well as to economic status.

Diagnostic labeling of children is at least as controversial as diagnostic labeling of adults. However, a significant number of children with behavior and learning difficulties is diagnosed as having minimal brain dysfunction. The term "hyperactive syndrome" is sometimes preferred. The terms are used interchangably. The incidence may be as high as 5% to 10% of children who have not reached the age of puberty (Cantwell, 1977). The symptoms that make up the minimal brain dysfunction or hyperactive syndrome include "hyperactivity, distractibility, excitability," and a shortened attention span (Cantwell, 1977).

Whether or not such behavioral manifestations are due to organic dysfunction is debatable. Such symptoms have, in the past, been attributed to a variety of emotional disorders in children. Cantwell (1977) observes that we lack the ability to determine the degree of brain dysfunction in children. Others observe that we lack diagnostic criteria for assessing brain dysfunction in children. A major disadvantage of attributing these behavioral manifestations in children to organic dysfunction is the connotation of irreversibility that often accompanies such a diagnosis, and the possibility that less effort may, therefore, be expended in treatment.

Despite the controversy, we have included a brief discussion of secondary prevention for such children and their families in this chapter on organic dysfunction. It should be remembered that treatment measures and nursing functions are applicable whether or not the symptoms are regarded as evidence of brain dysfunction.

The major objectives in secondary intervention in cases involving children are to promote normal development, including education, of the children to the extent possible and to provide the supportive services to their families that are essential to achieving the goals for the children. These objectives are dependent upon the availability of human services to meet the needs of the children and families. Among these services are the following.

Schools for special education. Schools for special education offer very small classes, with teachers who have special training in work-ing with hyperactive children. An essential ingredient in schools providing special education is the availability, at least on a part-time basis, of a mental health team with special preparation in pediatric psychiatry. The availability of a psychiatrist, a psychologist, a social worker, and a child mental health nurse is important in planning, implementing, and evaluating the coordination of therapeutic and educational objectives for each child. The mental health team is also a resource for supportive measures with teachers, parents, and teacher assistants working with the children.

Comprehensive health services. In addition to providing health supervision and teaching, comprehensive health services can provide family counseling, crisis intervention, and group and family therapy to families of hyperactive children. The treatment objectives for the child are to reduce hyperactivity, to change disruptive behavioral patterns, and to promote mental health. Various therapeutic modalities are utilized in combination to achieve these objectives. Reducing the hyperactivity and excitability of a child is often essential to the promotion of health development and to the child's participation in the educational process. Medication is often prescribed to reduce hyperactivity. It is somewhat paradoxical that central nervous system stimulants are more effective in reducing hyperactivity in children than are sedative drugs. Cantwell (1977) recommends the use of methylphenidate (Ritalin) or d-amphetamine as the drugs of choice. Behavior therapy is often employed to change patterns of behavior that may be disruptive in the home and school. Play therapy and other forms of psychotherapy are employed in combination with the other therapies to promote normal development.

Comprehensive social services. Maintaining a hyperactive or emotionally disturbed child in the home may cause social and economic problems for a family far beyond those involved in raising a normal child. Although it is generally agreed that home care of such a child is far superior to institutional care, government funding in many areas tends to favor the institutions. Providing social services to families to meet economic and other social problems is essential. Social and political action to achieve this goal is an important aspect of secondary prevention in meeting the needs of families with hyperactive children. Assisting families in the utilization of the resources that do exist is an important aspect of client advocacy.

Nursing intervention for hyperactive children may involve working with the children, their families, and often teachers and other members of the educational system involved with the children. Collaboration and cooperation between schools providing special educational services and facilities providing comprehensive health services is essential to meeting health and educational objectives. Coordination of these services is often a function of the community health nurse. Health supervision on the part of the school nurse–teacher or community health nurse offers an opportunity for case finding and refer-

ral of children in whom learning and behavioral difficulties may be indicative of organic dysfunction or hyperactive syndrome. Health supervision of children also includes identifying physical health problems that may only be expressed through such behavioral manifestations as increased hyperactivity and excitability.

Nursing intervention for families of hyperactive children might include group discussions with parents or groups of parents, with the objective being to assist the parents in identifying problems and developing strategies for coping with their hyperactive children. Participation, in the home, to help families to follow behavior therapy programs designed to shape behavior patterns in children is often an important nursing function. Close cooperation between the nurse and the behavior therapist is essential to this kind of endeavor. Crisis intervention and home visits to provide support for parents are additional nursing activities that can assist parents of hyperactive children.

The nurse working in a school serving hyperactive children has opportunities beyond those related to health supervision. Direct participation in the classroom with the teacher offers an opportunity for assessment of behavior, through observation in the class setting, and for participation with one or more children in meeting mental health and education objectives. Such a nurse may want to establish nurse-client relationships with individual children. Participation in group meetings with teachers and other staff members offers the opportunity to share experiences and insights and to plan strategies for meeting mental health and educational objectives.

TERTIARY PREVENTION

As noted earlier, some individuals adapt to the cognitive impairment associated with organic brain dysfunction and are able to function adequately in their culture, except at times of crisis, when supportive services may be needed. In this respect, such individuals differ little from the general population, with the possible exception of a greater vulnerability to stress and a somewhat diminished capacity to cope with stress without assistance.

In other individuals the cognitive dysfunction and associated psychosocial factors may inhibit the ability to care for oneself and may become progressively incapacitating. Perception, memory, orientation, and judgment may be so impaired that an individual cannot be responsible for his own care. Such individuals require a fairly constant level of care and supervision by other people. They may be found living with families who are willing and able to care for them or in mental hospitals or other institutions.

Whether it is given in the home or in a community agency, care for such individuals has the following major objectives:

1. Promoting and maintaining the optimum level of functioning possible for the individual
2. Promoting a sense of dignity and worth

3. Maintaining physical health and well-being by means of adequate diagnostic measures so that treatment may be instituted for those conditions that may respond to treatment
4. Maintaining and promoting reality orientation
5. Encouraging independent functioning to the degree possible.
6. Providing opportunity to meet psychosocial needs, such as recreation, intellectual stimulation, and socialization
7. Providing support when needed

Meeting such treatment objectives necessitates close cooperation between the health team members and, when possible, between the family and the health team. Since the nurse is often the health professional in the most direct and continuous contact with the client, some responsibility for promoting interdisciplinary team functioning often rests with nursing members of the health team. The role of liaison between the client and family and between members of the health team is an important function of the nurse, whether the client resides in an agency or in his home.

A therapeutic environment is especially important in meeting objectives for providing protection, support, and rehabilitation for clients. The therapeutic milieu as a treatment modality that employs all aspects of the environment to promote health has been discussed in earlier chapters. Special emphasis in a milieu treating clients with brain dysfunction should be placed upon providing physical and emotional support, encouraging independent functioning to the extent possible for the individual, and promoting reality orientation.

Maintaining orientation can be encouraged through the placement of large-faced clocks and calendars in prominent places and through individual and group discussions focused upon events associated with daily living and affairs of interest in the broader community. Contact between the community and the hospital or agency unit may also be utilized to stimulate interest and interaction between clients and the broader environment. Utilization of community resources for recreation, health care, support systems, and so on is important in preventing the isolation of a client.

Recreational, occupational, and movement therapies are important in promoting mental and physical health. Such therapies should be adapted to the interests and physical abilities of clients.

Interpersonal therapies, both individual and group, are important modalities in maintaining emotional security. The nurse-client relationship, which has been discussed at length in earlier chapters, provides opportunity for emotional support.

CHAPTER SUMMARY

The organic brain disorders are a group of complex conditions that involve disturbances in cognition caused by disruptions in the normal neurophysiological processes essential to intellectual functioning. Behavioral manifestations of cognitive impairment include disturbances in levels of awareness, comprehension, memory, association, orientation, and judgment, that interefere with a person's ability to perceive, interpret, and respond effectively to his environment. The cognitive dysfunction may range from mild to severe, and it is often accompanied by emotional responses of fear, anger, feelings of helplessness, and depression.

Organic brain dysfunction may be acute and temporary, in which case the individual recovers completely in a relatively brief period of time with appropriate treatment and effective restorative processes. In other instances, the brain dysfunction may be chronic and irreversible because of a continuing disturbance in metabolic functioning or a diffuse destruction of brain tissue.

The etiology of organic brain dysfunction may lie in any systemic or central nervous system pathological condition, including metabolic disorders, systemic and central nervous system infections, trauma, and conditions caused by chemicals and drugs. In some chronic forms, the etiology is unknown, in which case the onset is often slow and insidious, rather than acute.

Organic brain disorders may occur at any age along the life span. When the causative agent results in chronic dysfunction early in life, the inhibition in learning ability often results in mental retardation. The highest incidence of organic brain disorders, however, is in the older age groups, in which there are often functional impairments in sensory, motor, and homeostatic mechanisms and in central nervous system integrative efficiency. Persons in this age group are also more susceptible to chronic metabolic or systemic disorders and to psychosocial problems related to changes in role and status that are contributory factors. The emotional responses of grief, anger, and depression may distort the degree of cognitive dysfunction; in older persons particularly, such symptoms are often mistaken for signs of an organic disorder.

Therapeutic modalities in the treatment of acute organic brain dysfunction include the early diagnosis and treatment of the underlying pathological condition so that cognitive dysfunction may be reversed or ameliorated. In some acute disorders, early diagnosis may be essential to preventing progressive dysfunction, which can lead to coma and death. Which specific treatment is used depends upon etiology. For the client with acute brain dysfunction, who is most often seen in a general hospital, nursing assessment of cognitive dysfunction may be very important to early diagnosis.

Treatment modalities in chronic brain dysfunction have the objective of promoting independent functioning to the maximum degree possible. They include adequate medical and nursing care for treatment and rehabilitation of physical and emotional disorders and preventive intervention through health teaching and supervision. Preventive measures to promote emotional security and comfort include client advocacy in the utilization of community resources to meet psychosocial needs and in the development and strengthening of social networks. In addition, a protective therapeutic environment, all of the forms of psychosocial therapy, and chemotherapy are employed.

Treatment settings include general hospitals, private homes, foster homes, nursing homes, and mental hospitals.

Clients with organic brain dysfunction may be found in almost every area in which professional nurses practice. Nursing intervention spans both the preventive and the therapeutic aspects of organic brain disorders, although not every nurse will be involved in every area. Primary prevention encompasses the nurse's role both as a citizen and as a health professional. As a citizen, participation in social, political, and community action groups that seek to reduce environmental pollution, promote occupational safety, or provide community facilities to meet the needs of vulnerable individuals is an important preventive activity. Professional roles include health education, genetic counseling, case finding, and client advocacy in meeting health and psychosocial needs.

Secondary prevention and tertiary prevention include collaboration with the health team, participation in therapeutic modalities, health supervision and promotion, and participation in individual and group activities that promote the emotional comfort and the cognitive functioning of clients.

REFERENCES

Adams-Woodward, Carolyn
1978 "Wernicke-Korsakoff syndrome: a case approach." Journal of Psychiatric Nursing and Mental Health Services 16(4):38-41.
Baldessarini, Rose J.
1977 Chemotherapy in Psychiatry. Cambridge, Mass: Harvard University Press.
Butler, Robert N.
1975 "Psychiatry and the elderly: an overview." American Journal of Psychiatry 132(9):893-900.

1975 Why Survive? Being Old in America. New York: Harper & Row, Publishers, Inc.
Cantwell, Dennis P.
1977 "Drug treatment of the hyperactive syndrome in children." In Psychopharmacology in the Practice of Medicine. Murray E. Jarvick (ed.). New York: Appleton-Century-Crofts.
Carter, Frances Monet
1976 Psychosocial Nursing. New York: Macmillan, Inc.
Covert, Anthony B.
1979 "Community health nursing: the role of the consultant in the nursing home." Journal of Psychiatric Nursing and Mental Health Services 17(7):15-19.
Davidhizar, Ruth, and Elizabeth Gunden
1978 "Recognizing and caring for the delirious patient." Journal of Psychiatric Nursing and Mental Health Services 16(5):38-41.
Eisdorfer, Carl, and Robert O. Friedel
1977 "Psychotherapeutic drugs in aging." In Psychopharmacology in the Practice of Medicine. Murray E. Jarvik (ed.). New York: Appleton-Century-Crofts.
Epstein, Charlotte
1974 Effective Interaction in Contemporary Nursing. Englewood Cliffs, N.J.: Prentice-Hall, Inc.
Feldman, R. G.
1978 "Urban lead mining: lead intoxication among deleaders." New England Journal of Medicine 298:1143.
Goldberg, Connie, and Mary Anne Stanitis
1977 "The enhancement of self-esteem through the communication process in group therapy." Journal of Psychiatric Nursing and Mental Health Services 15(12):5-8.
Goldfarb, Alvin I.
1964 "The evaluation of geriatric patients following treatment." In Evaluation of Psychiatric Treatment. P. Hoch and J. Zubin (eds.). New York: Grune & Stratton, Inc.

1974 "Minor maladjustments of the aged." In American Handbook of Psychiatry (ed.2), vol. 3. Sylvano Arieti and Eugene Brody (eds.). Sylvano Arieti (ed.-in-chief). New York: Basic Books, Inc., Publishers, Ch. 37.
Haber, Judith, et al.
1978 Comprehensive Psychiatric Nursing. New York: McGraw-Hill Book Co.
Haraguchi, Kay L.
1978 "Nurses can take the heat off workers." Occupational Safety and Health 47:4.
Heller, Stanley S., and Donald S. Kornfeld
1974 "Delirium and related problems." In American Handbook of Psychiatry (ed. 2), vol. 4). Morton F. Reiser (ed.). Sylvano Arieti (ed.-in-chief.). New York: Basic Books, Inc., Publishers.
Hendler, Nelson, and William Leahy
1978 "Psychiatric and neurologic sequelae of infectious mononucleosis." American Journal of Psychiatry 135(7):842-844.
Hoch, P. H., and J. Zubin (eds.)
1964 Evaluation of Psychiatric Treatment. New York: Grune & Stratton, Inc.
Hoff, Lee Ann
1978 People in Crisis. Understandstanding and Helping. Menlo Park, Calif.: Addison-Wesley Publishing Co.
Howard, Jean Stoltz
1978 "Liaison nursing." Journal of Psychiatric Nursing and Mental Health Care 16:4
Jarvik, Murray E.
1977 Psychopharmacology in the Practice of Medicine. New York: Appleton-Century-Crofts.

Kalb, Melvyn, and Morton S. Propper
1976 "The future of alcohology: craft or science." American Journal of Psychiatry 133(6):641-645.

Kolb, Lawrence. C.
1973 Modern Clinical Psychiatry (ed. 8). Philadelphia: W. B. Saunders Co.
1977 Modern Clinical Psychiatry (ed. 9). Philadelphia: W. B. Saunders Co.

Leighton, Alexander H.
1974 "Social disintegration and mental disorders." in American Handbook of Psychiatry (ed. 2), vol. 2. Gerald Caplan (ed.). Sylvano Arieti, (ed-in-chief). New York: Basic Books, Inc., Publishers, Ch. 28.

Lipkin, Gladys B., and Roberta G. Cohen,
1973 Effective Approaches to Patients' Behavior. New York: Springer Publishing Co., Inc.

Luckman, Joan, and Karen Sorensen
1974 Medical-Surgical Nursing: A Psychophysiologic Approach. Philadelphia: W. B. Saunders Co.

Morse, R.
1970 "Postoperative delirium: a syndrome of multiple causations." Psychosomatics 11:164-168.

Moses, Dorothy V.
1970 "Reality orientation in the aging person." in Behavioral Concepts and Nursing Intervention. Carolyn E. Carlson (ed.). Philadelphia: J. B. Lippincott Co.

Mueller, John F., and Terrie Schwerdtfeger
1974 "The role of the nurse in counseling the alcoholic." Journal of Psychiatric Nursing and Mental Health Services 12(2):26-32.

Raskind, Murray A., Hubert Orenstein, and T. Graham Christopher
1975 "Acute psychosis, increased water ingestion, and inappropriate antidiuretic hormone secretion." American Journal of Psychiatry 132(9):907-910.

Raskus, Richard S., Stephen Lerner, and Bruce E. Kline
1979 "The elderly patient in a therapeutic community." Comprehensive Psychiatry 20:4.

Robinson, Lisa
1972 Psychiatric Nursing as a Human Experience. Philadelphia: W. B. Saunders Co.

Schneideman, Jean
1976 "Remotivation: involvement without labels." Journal of Psychiatric Nursing and Mental Health Services 14(7):41-42.

Seltzer, Benjamin, and Shervert H. Frazier
1978 "Organic mental disorders." In The Harvard Modern Guide to Psychiatry. Armand M. Nicholi, Jr. (ed.). Cambridge, Mass.: Belknap Press of Harvard University Press.

Seltzer, Benjamin, and Ira Sherwin
1978 "Organic brain syndromes: an empirical study and critical review." American Journal of Psychiatry 135(1):13-21.

Shear, Katherine M., and Michael H. Sacks
1978 "Digitalis delirium: report of two cases." American Journal of Psychiatry 135(1):109-110.

Shraberg, David
1978 "The myth of pseudodementia: depression and the aging brain." American Journal of Psychiatry 135:5.

Spector, Rachel E.
1979 Cultural Diversity in Health and Illness. New York: Appleton-Century-Crofts.

Strob, Richard L.
1980 "Alzheimer's disease—current perspectives." Journal of Clinical Psychiatry 41(4):110-112.

Strosser, Alexander L.
1978 "Engineering, sampling and surveillance: a team approach to respiratory protection" Guest editorial in Occupational Safety and Health 47:4.

Tuerk, Kenneth, Irving Fish and Joseph Ransohoff.
1974 "Head injury." In American Handbook of Psychiatry (ed. 2), vol. 4. Morton F. Reiser (ed.). Sylvano Arieti (ed.-in-chief). New York: Basic Books, Inc., Publishers, Ch. 7.

Ujhely, Gertrud Bertrand
1963 The Nurse and Her "Problem" Patients New York: Springer Publishing Co., Inc.

Wells, Charles E.
1978 "Chronic brain disease: an overview." American Journal of Psychiatry 135(1):1-12.

Wender, Paul H., and Leon Eisenberg.
1974 "Minimal brain dysfunction in children." In American Handbook of Psychiatry (ed. 2), vol. 2. Gerald Caplan (ed.). Sylvano Arieti (ed.-in-chief). New York: Basic Books, Inc., Publishers, Ch. 8.

ANNOTATED SUGGESTED READINGS

Davidhizar, Ruth and Elizabeth Gunden
1978 "Recognizing and caring for the delirious patient." Journal of Psychiatric Nursing and Mental Health Services 16(5):38-41.
This article focuses upon nursing assessment and intervention in acute organic dysfunction. The importance of early intervention in this acute condition and the role of the nurse in early identification and treatment are stressed.

Goldfarb, Alvin I.
1974 "Minor maladjustments of the aged." In The American Handbook of Psychiatry (ed 2), vol. 3. Sylvano Arieti and Eugene B. Brody (eds.). Sylvano Arieti (ed.-in-chief). New York: Basic Books Inc., Publishers, Ch. 37.
The author, an expert in problems of the aging, takes a holistic view of the aging process and its impact upon the individual. Particular emphasis is placed upon recognizing and distinguishing between depression (or other psychiatric conditions) and organic brain dysfunction in the older person. The author includes measurement tools that have proved useful in distinguishing between organic brain syndrome and depression.

Seltzer, Benjamin, and Shervert H. Frazier
1978 "Organic mental disorders." In The Harvard Modern Guide to Psychiatry. Armand M. Nicoli, Jr. (ed.). Cambridge, Mass.: Belknap Press of Harvard University Press.
The authors provide a background for understanding the neuropsychiatric disorders that are caused by diffuse impairment of brain tissue functioning. The entire range of organic dysfunction—from the acute confusional states to severe organic brain syndromes—is discussed in relation to newer developments in neurophysiology and brain function.

Wells, Charles E.,
1978 "Chronic brain disease: an overview." American Journal of Psychiatry 135:1.
This article provides an overview of current thinking about organic brain disease of a chronic nature. The importance of adequate diagnostic and treatment measures is stressed, and the need for basic research in relation to organic brain disease is emphasized.

15
POWER, POLITICS, AND PSYCHIATRIC NURSING

CHAPTER FOCUS

Power is a dynamic of interpersonal relationships. Power arises from many sources, has many forms, and comprises many strategies. In order to influence the nature and direction of mental health care and professional nursing, nurses must understand the interrelationship between power, politics, and planned change. Institutions, consumers, and nurses are major components of the contemporary mental health delivery system. Within this system, power strategies and power struggles sometimes arise around such issues as quality of care, client rights, and allocation of resources. Trends in mental health often portend the issues around which future power strategies and power struggles may revolve. In the United States today, the major trends in mental health are deinstitutionalization, consumerism, and decreased funding for mental health research.

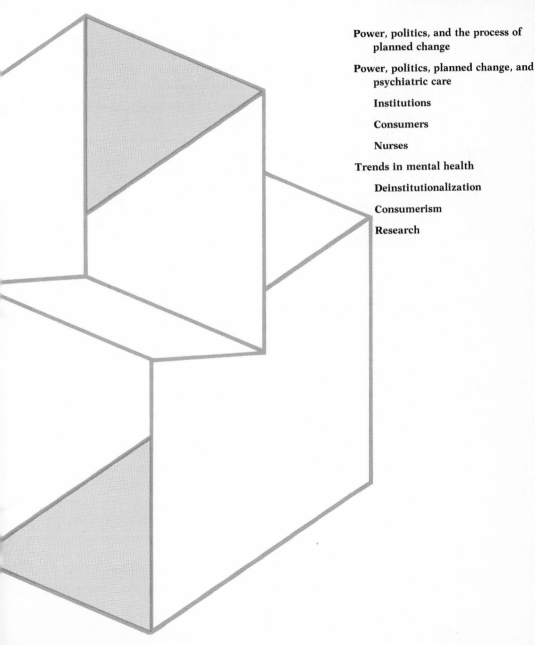

15
POWER, POLITICS, AND PSYCHIATRIC NURSING

Power is the ability to act, to do, and/or to control others. Everyone needs to experience some form of power. Peplau (1953) states that the need for power enters into every nursing situation. Whether a nursing situation involves clients, families of clients, health team members, or agency administrators, interacting participants are usually striving for, relinquishing, exerting, or submitting to power. Certain basic assumptions underlie this concept of power:

1. Power is a resource. It is neither innately good nor innately evil. Power may be used constructively to solve social problems or destructively for corrupt and selfish purposes.
2. Power is an essential dynamic of human interaction. In order for power to operate in an interaction, it must be acknowledged through "empowering responses."
3. Power is dynamic. Its supply is constantly being increased, decreased and redistributed (Votaw, 1979).

There are many different types of power. Power may be exerted covertly or overtly. People may be subtly influenced (covert power) or coerced (overt power) into complying with the wishes of others (Ashley, 1975; Leininger, 1975). Power may be used either rationally or irrationally. Rational power structures behavior in a manner that allows a person to act in accordance with his thoughts and feelings. Irrational power structures behavior in such a way that a person's actions conceal his thoughts and feelings (Peplau, 1953).

Power arises from various sources. Power derived from one's role, status, or position is called legitimate power. Power based on one's expertise and knowledge is called expert power. Power founded on one's intimate relationship with a powerful person or persons is referred to as associative power. Power arising from one's admired personal attributes is known as referent power (McFarland and Shiflett, 1975; Zaleznik, 1979). An individual's power may originate from one source or from a combination of sources. For example, the power base of a nurse administrator who is a charismatic leader may be largely founded on referent power, while the power source of another nurse administrator may arise from legitimate and expert power.

Power may be used either constructively or destructively (Ashley, 1975; Leininger, 1975). The constructive use of power facilitates the functioning of those subject to it. For instance, a nursing care coordinator may use power to enable nurses to work toward specific goals of nursing care or to achieve desired results of nursing actions. The destructive use of power inhibits the functioning of those who must submit to it. For example, a director of nurses may decide, in collaboration with a medical director, that only psychiatrists, psychologists, and social workers should hold therapy groups. Nurses prepared in group therapy would not be permitted to function as group therapists. Such destructive use of power may be repressive, suppressive, and demoralizing.

Martin and Sims (1956) identify the following power strategies:

1. Formation of alliances
2. Development of maneuvers
3. Control of information
4. Utilization of self-dramatization
5. Employment of compromise
6. Use of decisiveness
7. Utilization of inaction (deciding not to act or make a decision)

The right to use power to command behavior, enforce rules, and make decisions is referred to as *authority* (Leininger, 1979; McFarland and Shiflett 1979). Authority is often based on rank or position in a social hierarchy. Authority may be either of two types: line authority or staff authority. Line authority is based on job status. People with line authority have a position of power that enables them to hire, fire, and command. Overt use of power tends to predominate. Staff authority is based on interpersonal relationships. People with staff authority do not have the power to hire, fire, or command. A relatively nonthreatening environment is created, and the covert use of power tends to predominate.

Power is a complex concept; it has many sources and forms. There are various types of power strategies and various ways in which power can be used. In order to influence the nature and direction of mental health care and professional nursing, nurses need to understand that power, politics, and planned change are interrelated. We will explore this interrelationship.

POWER, POLITICS, AND THE PROCESS OF PLANNED CHANGE

Politics is the process of achieving and using power for the purpose of influencing decisions and resolving disputes between dissenting factions. A political system is a network of ideas and interpersonal relationships that effectively influences the thoughts, decisions, and behavior of people within formal, organized institutions (Leach, 1954; Ashley, 1975; Leininger, 1975). Each political system contains ideologies, goals, loyalties, interests, norms, and rules that foster cohesion within the political system and differentiate it from other political systems (Scheflen, 1972). For example, a neighborhood drug rehabilitation program will have a political system that is different from that of a neighborhood crisis center. The political system of a federal psychiatric hospital will differ from that of a state psychiatric hospital. An agency operated by a board of directors composed of community residents will have a political system that is different from that of an agency operated by a board of directors composed of mental health professionals.

In order to apply knowledge about power processes and strategies and influence the nature and direction of mental health care and professional nursing, nurses must understand the process of planned change. Planned change involves the formulation of a program or scheme for altering the status quo. There are three basic types of planned change: collaborative, coercive, and emulative. Collaborative change involves mutual goal setting and planning. Interactions are characterized by the covert use of power. In contrast, coercive change involves the overt use of power in order to impose goals and plans on others. Emulative change is characterized by people identifying with an authority figure and adopting the goals and plans of the authority figure. The authority figure usually uses power covertly and serves as a role model.

Planned change is characterized by four phases:
1. Unfreezing the present level
   a. Development of need for change
   b. Identification of need for change
2. Establishing a change relationship
   a. Clarification of problems and situations requiring change
   b. Examination of alternative procedures
3. Moving to a new level
   a. Establishment of goals and a plan of action
   b. Transformation of the plan of action into actual change efforts
   c. Incorporation of change efforts into the system
4. Freezing at the new level
   a. Achievement of the desired goals
   b. Establishment of a state of equilibrium (Lewin, 1974; Lippitt et al., 1958).

Essential to the success or failure of planned change are motivational and resistive factors. *Motivational factors* include desire for alleviation of an intolerable situation, disparity between a hoped for situation and an actual situation, external demands for change, and internal demands for change. *Resistive factors* include reluctance to accept any change, refusal to accept a particular change, satisfaction with the status quo, conflict in the relationship between an agent for change and a health delivery system, and transformation of initially obscure factors into major obstacles to change (Lippitt et al., 1958).

When planned change is contemplated, it is essential that the people who will be affected by the change be involved in all aspects of the process of change. Whenever responsibility is given for effecting change, it is necessary that the authority to implement change also be delegated. Otherwise the persons trying to effect change will be powerless, and their efforts will be frustrated.

When faced with a need for change, a person can either adapt to a situation, leave a situation, or change a situation. If either of the first two options is selected, the status quo is maintained. If the last option is selected, change occurs. People who try to influence the making and implementing of decisions in a way that fosters change are referred to as change agents.

Change agents act as resource people, as catalysts for change, and as educators in techniques of planned change. In order to fulfill these roles, change agents need to be skilled in the following areas:

1. Identifying and helping others recognize a need for change
2. Assessing factors that may facilitate or impede change
3. Helping people view themselves as a group that can effect change
4. Helping a group explore its mode of interaction and correct disruptive interaction patterns
5. Helping a group establish goals for change
6. Selecting appropriate roles and techniques to assist a group in achieving goals
7. Helping a group develop methods for achieving goals
8. Supporting and guiding a group through the phases of change
9. Maintaining channels of communication within the health delivery system
10. Helping a group evaluate change efforts and results (Lippitt et al., 1958; Bennis, 1969; Argyris, 1972)

Argyris (1972) believes that people who are committed to effecting change need to possess high degrees of candor and trust and that they must be willing to take risks. These personal attributes are especially important when change requires the adoption of deviant behavior (for example, promoting a policy that differs markedly from previous agency policy) or self-corrective behavior (self-evaluation or self-improvement), the unfreezing of present behavior, and/or a high degree of interdependence among participants in a group or situation.

Power, politics, and planned change are complex and interrelated processes. We will now look at the utilization of these processes in mental health care.

POWER, POLITICS, PLANNED CHANGE, AND PSYCHIATRIC CARE
Institutions

Institutions* are organizations that fulfill normative functions and purposes in society. An institution is a subsystem of a larger system (Blase 1973). Federal, state, and local psychiatric hospitals and community mental health agencies are examples of institutions.

Institutions are characterized by bureaucracy and hierarchy. The aim of a bureaucracy is efficiency. In a bureaucracy rules are established by authority figures, work is impersonally defined in terms of job descriptions, and activities are recorded and monitored by means of such written documents as timesheets, data cards, and monthly reports. Authority is vested in a hierarchy that can be displayed as an organizatonal chart. At the top of the hierarchy is a board of directors, which establishes rules. These rules are interpreted and applied by administrators. Division heads and supervisors enforce the rules, and staff members are expected to comply with the rules.

Establishment, interpretation, application, and enforcement of rules, and compliance with them, are facilitated by an institution's communication system. A communication system also serves two important political functions: regulation of vertical mobility and behavior and indoctrination of staff members into the ideology of the institution (Scheflen, 1972).

Regulation of vertical mobility is facilitated by a dominance hierarchy. Even though an institution may have a philosophy of egalitarianism, in practice a dominance hierarchy may be present, and upward mobility may be limited to persons who demonstrate loyalty to the institution, who possess certain educational qualifications, or who belong to the "right" social class or ethnic group (Scheflen, 1972).

---

*Refer to Chapter 2 for a discussion of institutions and culture shock.

Regulation of behavior may be accomplished nonverbally,* through the use of symbols and kinesic monitors (Scheflen, 1972). An institution usually officially communicates its philosophy of health care in verbal and written statements. However, an institution's unofficial philosophy may be reflected in symbols (for example, use or nonuse of uniforms, locked or unlocked psychiatric units). Institutions also officially and unofficially state expectations about members' performance. These expectations define acceptable behavior for all members—(both staff members and clients). Members are then evaluated on the basis of their desire and ability to fulfill these expectations. Staff members who satisfy these expectations may be promoted or given salary increases. Clients who fulfill the expectations may be judged mentally healthy and discharged from the institution. Scheflen (1972) emphasises that kinesic monitors, especially those that convey negative feedback, are very effective in evaluating and controlling behavior.

> A clinical nurse specialist thought that the wearing of uniforms in a psychiatric setting conveyed messages of control and authority, reinforced the passive client role, and contributed to an interaction theme of dominance (nurse)–submission (client). When she discussed this issue with the director of nurses, the director took a deep breath and rolled her eyes upward toward the ceiling. The director's kinesic monitor conveyed the message: "Here we go again. I've heard this before. I don't approve of the idea." The clinical nurse specialist felt intimidated and did not pursue the idea any further.

Because staff members and clients, to differing degrees, depend on an institution for gratification of security needs, negative kinesic monitors tend to be very effective in controlling behavior.

Often there is incongruity between the verbal and kinesic levels of institutional communication. For instance, an administrator's verbal philosophy of care may emphasize client participation in the setting of treatment goals, while his kinesic behavior may severely restrict client input into the treatment program. Such inconsistency between verbal and kinesic messages tends to confuse staff members and render them powerless to change the system. Kinesic monitors derive much of their power from the incongruity produced in the communication system (Scheflen, 1972).

A system of reinforcement that includes both kinesic monitors and

---

*Refer to Chapter 5 for a discussion of nonverbal communication.

negative and positive sanctions helps regulate the behavior of an institution's members. For instance, staff members who display institutionally approved behavior may be rewarded with job security, job advancement, and salary increments. Staff members who deviate markedly from institutionally approved behavior may be threatened with demotion, firing, and negative references for future jobs, or they may actually be demoted or fired.

Members of an institution may be, to varying degrees, indoctrinated into institutional *ideology*. An ideology projects an institution's ideas and purpose for existing outward onto its social environment. Indoctrination into institutional ideology promotes cohesion and commitment among members and minimizes the need for overt use of power in the implementation of programs and the delivery of services. The more controversial an institution's programs and services, the greater the importance of ideology in defending and supporting its activities (Downs, 1967; Zentner, 1973).

Members who are fully indoctrinated into institutional ideology tend to believe and think along institutional lines—to engage in "institutional think". When institutional think occurs, members are apt not to recognize discrepancies, problems, or alternatives. At this point, a member may so closely identify with the institution that an attack on it becomes an attack on him (Scheflen, 1972).

Any discussion of planned change in institutions must include three elements: institutional variables, networks, and transactions.

Institutional variables include leadership, ideology, programs, resources, and internal structure. Leadership must be displayed by the people who are actively involved in making policies and decisions and in directing institutional operations. Ideology consists of an institution's stated philosophy and its purpose for existing. Programs are methods for translating institutional ideology into actions and for allocating resources for accomplishing those actions. Resources include money, materials, labor, and political support, all of which may be necessary for implementation of programs. Internal structure, the organizing and channeling of power, authority, and decision-making within an institution, may be either lateral or hierarchical* (Perrow, 1970; Argyris, 1972; Bumgardner et al., 1972; Blase, 1973; Zaltman et al., 1973).

Networks are interrelationships between an institution and its so-

---

*Lateral structure involves a dispersed locus of authority, with all members presumably enjoying equal power and authority. Hierarchical structure involves a centralized locus of authority and a chain of command.

cial environment that influence and maintain the institution and provide it with a capacity for change. Blase (1973) and Bumgardner et al. (1972) describe several types of networks:

1. Enabling network—composed of organizations that give an institution both legal authority and resources for its existence. For example, the Community Mental Health Centers Act of 1963 authorized establishment of community mental health centers, and Title II provided funds for their establishment.
2. Normative network—composed of interrelationships between an institution and an organized body of people who determine norms and standards for the operation of the institution. For example, the Community Mental Health Centers Act amendments of 1975 established standards and guidelines for the operation of community mental health centers.
3. Diffuse network—composed of interrelationships between an institution and the public. For example, the National Association of Mental Health and organized consumer groups may be component linkages in a normative network.
4. Functional network—composed of interrelationships between an institution and a body of people who provide the institution with such resources as clients and professional staff.

Transactions are the actual interactions between an institution and the component linkages in its network, which both influence and are influenced by the institution. Transactions involve planning and strategy decisions. These plans and strategies comprise the matrix of planned change in institutions (Bumgardner et al., 1972; Scheflen, 1972; Blase, 1973).

Institutional variables, networks, and transactions may interrelate to produce planned change within an institution. When institutional ideology is not viable, impetus for change tends to develop from forces outside the institution (from component linkages in the institution's networks). The internal structure of the institution will then either respond to or resist pressure for change. If institutional structure is of a lateral type, all members will presumably be equally involved in the process of change and will respond to pressure for change. However, if institutional structure is of a hierarchical type, pressure from outside the institution for change will usually be met by resistance (Perrow, 1970; Argyrus, 1972; Bumgardner et al., 1972; Blase, 1973).

When institutional ideology is viable, impetus for planned change tends to develop from forces within the institution. For instance, professional staff may realize that mental health services do not meet the needs of the catchment population. If commitment to institutional ideology is weak, then a hierarchical structure will be most effective in mandating and effecting planned change. If commitment to institutional ideology is strong, a lateral structure will be most effective in initiating and implementing planned change (Bumgardner et al., 1972; Blase, 1973).

Consumers

A consumer is an individual, a group, or a community that utilizes a product or service. In the area of mental health, consumerism refers to the utilization of all levels of mental health services (services designed for primary, secondary, and tertiary prevention of mental illness). Gonzalez (1976) points out that consumer groups have been organized on all levels—local, state, national, and international. These groups which may operate either independently or corporately, often grow out of special interest movements in schools, health agencies, government, and industry. The Mental Patients' Liberation Movement—composed of people who have at some time in their lives been treated for mental illness—and the Federation of Parents' Organization—composed of parents of people who are mentally ill, as well as other concerned relatives and citizens—are examples of consumer groups that are actively involved in client advocacy and in upgrading the quality of mental health care.

Consumers, individually and organized as groups, serve two functions: to monitor and to regulate. In their function as monitors, consumers ascertain the need for and the accessibility, availability, and effectiveness of health care services; check into the cost effectiveness of health care activities; and observe for unethical behavior on the part of mental health professionals. In their function as regulators, consumers are concerned with the credentials and competence of mental health professionals and with standards of professional practice (Gonzalez, 1976).

In order to carry out these functions, consumers assume roles as planners, advisors, and educators. Consumers are actively involved in the following areas:

1. Lobbying for legislation that will upgrade mental health care
2. Lobbying for adequate funding of mental health programs
3. Reordering of local, state, and national priorities
4. Utilizing community resources for the planning and implementation of programs that will meet the mental health needs of the community

5. Contributing to the preparation of mental health workers by acquainting them with the needs, values, and goals of the community that the workers are servicing (National Commission on Community Health Services, 1966; Health Task Force of the Urban Coalition, 1970; National Association for Mental Health, 1974)

Consumers, individually or in groups, tend to have certain basic concerns. Fundamental to these concerns is the idea that mental health professionals have too much power over clients. Consumer groups point out that even the courts usually accept a psychiatrist's observations or predictions of dangerous behavior over a client's request for discharge from a psychiatric institution. Consumers also express concern that, once a person is labeled mentally ill, the focus of mental health professionals is on abnormal rather than normal behavior. In addition, consumers are concerned that some psychiatric institutions do not provide adequate treatment and that transitional and aftercare facilities are insufficient.

Consumers of mental health services do not have the vested interest in protecting a mental health agency or program that mental health professionals may have. Moreover, consumers are the people who experience the health delivery system. For these reasons, it is often easier for consumers to identify areas where change is needed than it is for mental health professionals. Some mental health professionals may become accustomed to the status quo and may not be aware of a need to change practices. Other mental health professionals may fear the effect change will have on their role status and functioning and may therefore deny a need for change.

Consumers often have a better understanding of their mental health needs or of the mental health needs of their community than do mental health professionals. Epstein (1974) observes that the social class and life-style of mental health professionals often differ from those of their clients. Epstein suggests that even mental health professionals who originally came from backgrounds similar to those of the majority of their clients usually drastically alter their life-styles once they achieve the position of mental health professional. It becomes the function of indigenous workers, who still share the same life-style as the clients, to serve as liaisons between clients and professionals. Indigenous workers may help professionals view clients within the sociocultural context of the community, facilitate communication between clients and practitioners, and articulate needs for change from the perspective of the client (Ruiz and Behrens, 1973; Epstein, 1974).

If change is to occur in the mental health delivery system, consumers must be involved in the decision-making process. In order to effectively participate in decision-making, consumers are demanding information about mental health care. They want to know about the efficacy of various therapeutic approaches, the comparative costs of therapies, and the anticipated therapeutic results and side effects of various treatment modalities (Gonzalez, 1976).

Comprehensive health care programs operated by boards of directors composed of consumers have demonstrated that consumers are able to

1. make decisions and policies based on an intimate knowledge of a community's health needs.
2. identify areas that require professional expertise and seek consultation in those areas.
3. evaluate services and staff behavior from the perspective of the client.
4. identify areas that need change and effectively use power to achieve change in a mental health program (Ruiz and Behrens, 1973; Epstein, 1974).

The consumer movement has successfully used power to effect changes in the field of mental health that range from research to delivery of care. For example, in one year, consumers

1. initiated a lawsuit that resulted in release of $126 million for research, alcoholism, and manpower programs.
2. influenced the amending of a health maintenance organization bill to include basic mental health coverage.
3. helped amend a rehabilitation act so that affirmative action in hiring would include the "mentally handicapped."
4. succeeded in getting the United States Civil Service Commission to remove a question about previous treatment for mental illness from employment applications.
5. instituted and awarded National Association for Mental Health Research Fellowships.
6. successfully lobbied so that the Federal Education Act would allocate funds to states for the establishment of programs for mentally ill children.
7. sponsored a conference, under the auspices of the National Association for Mental Health, on critical issues related to mental health research (National Association for Mental Health, 1974).

Nurses

Nurses are important members of the interdisciplinary mental health team. Many nurses work in psychiatric agencies. Some clinical specialists work independently or in group practice situations. Chapters 6 and 8 emphasize the role and functions of nurses as care providers in an interdisciplinary mental health setting and define the various levels of practice in psychiatric nursing. In this section, we will focus on the nursing role of client advocacy.

Nurses as client advocates. As client advocates, nurses are responsible for the following functions:

1. Ensuring ethical practice. Nurses need to be committed to basic human rights, able to assess possible consequences of actions, and sensitive to situations that may influence the application of principles pertinent to accountable nursing practice (Nations, 1973; Annas and Healey, 1974; Curtin, 1978).

2. Ensuring client rights. Nurses assist clients to learn about, protect, and assert their rights. Nurses may explain civil rights, retention status, and institutional procedures to clients and may help them to obtain legal counsel. In addition, nurses act as monitors to assure that client rights are not violated.

3. Acting as liaisons. Nurses help clients and staff members develop effective interpersonal relationships, investigate clients' complaints, and assist clients in using institutional resources for problem solving (refer to Chapter 8).

4. Ensuring quality care. Nurses participate in and cooperate with quality assurance programs. Data is collected, analyzed, and utilized for planning, assessing, and improving the quality of mental health care.

Ensuring ethical practice. Nursing is a "moral art." Nursing combines a concern for a person's well-being with the technical skills needed to achieve that end. Basic ethical dilemmas encountered by nurses center around two major areas: institutional policies and/or physicians' orders that affect quality of client care and the appropriation of nurses' legitimate authority to make decisions about nursing care (Curtin, 1978). Rouslin (1976) states that mental health nurses should be guided by two rules: (1) optimal behavior concerning client welfare and (2) optimal professional conduct.

Nurses should use a *code of ethics* to direct their professional conduct. The International Code of Nursing Ethics (1953) and the American Nurses' Association Code of Ethics (1968) state that the need for nursing care is universal and should not be denied because of a person's race, color, creed, politics, nationality, or social status. These codes emphasize that the primary responsibilities of nurses are the preservation of life, the relief of suffering, and the promotion and maintenance of health. These codes also stress the responsibilities that nurses have as citizens to follow laws, to carry out the duties of citizenship, and to work with other citizens to improve and preserve the health of communities on local, state, national, and international levels.

Some nurses' associations have adopted *codes of ethics for psychiatric nurses.* One such code of ethics includes the following provisions:

1. The promotion of mental health is a primary responsibility of psychiatric nursing.
2. Through continuing education, psychiatric nurses must increase their professional knowledge and competencies.
3. Maintenance and utilization of professional competencies are essential to the provision of optimal mental health care.
4. Regardless of the color, race, religion, or gender of clients, clients should be respected as individuals and should be the focus or nursing concern both during and after therapy.
5. Client-nurse interaction should be confidential except when there is a possibility of harm to self or others.
6. Psychiatric nurses are accountable for their own psychiatric nursing decisions and actions.
7. Psychiatric nurses work with and sustain confidence in other health professionals.
8. Psychiatric nurses should report incompetency or unethical conduct of health team members to appropriate authorities.
9. Psychiatric nurses assume responsibility as concerned citizens for promoting efforts to meet the mental health needs of a community.
10. Psychiatric nurses collaborate with other health professionals in informing clients of treatment plans and of the anticipated outcomes and side effects of treatment procedures.
11. Psychiatric nurses follow laws that relate to the practice of mental health nursing.
12. Psychiatric nurses should not engage in a nursing practice that violates the code of ethics (Psychiatric Nurses Association of Canada, 1977).

In making use of mental health nursing codes of ethics, psychiatric nurses must learn to critically analyze situations. Curtin (1978) has developed a model for critical ethical analysis. Using Curtin's model, we can extrapolate the following steps:

1. Obtain an adequate data base of relevant information. This information should pertain to the situation, circumstances, and factors that directly influence the situation.

2. Identify ethical constituents. Sort out ethical from nonethical issues. Ethical issues may include alleviation of aggressive behavior vs. loss of ability to generate and express ideas (as with psychosurgery) and freedom vs. restriction of rights (as in the treatment of mental illness).

3. Identify ethical agents and their role in the situation. Ethical agents include people who are or will engage in or be affected by a decision. Clients, families, clergymen, court judges, and health team members are examples of ethical agents. The rights, responsibilities, and duties of each ethical agent, as well as factors that may facilitate or impede his freedom to make and carry out a decision, should be explored.

4. Explore alternative actions. The possible consequences of each action should be considered. Instances in which duty or responsibility conflict with consequences of an action are especially difficult to resolve. For example, a nurse may be confronted with the following dilemma: "If I intervene to prevent a client from committing suicide (my responsibility as a nurse), I am denying the client's right to self-determination (the client's right to take his own life)."

5. Develop an approach based on ethical principles. Ethical principles include ideas about the nature of human beings and self-determination and the manner of ethical thinking and decision making. For example, nurses who rely on the authority of the Scriptures may hold that the taking of life is always wrong and therefore may view suicide as wrong. On the other hand, nurses who hold that actions that deny human freedom are wrong may view suicide as an act of self-determination and therefore as a rightful act.

6. Resolve the dilemma. After engaging in the process of obtaining pertinent information, identifying ethical agents and components, exploring alternative courses of action, and developing an approach based on ethical principles, nurses may more readily arrive at a decision or assist clients and/or families to decide on a course of action.

Utilization of these steps may help psychiatric nurses analyze and resolve client-care situations that present ethical dilemmas.

Ensuring client rights. Ensuring client rights is a primary responsibility of nurses. In order to fulfill this responsibility, nurses should be knowledgeable about the legal aspects of mental health nursing practice. Nurses need to be aware of retention procedures, client rights, and client advocacy services.

There are three reasons for retaining a person in an institution: danger to self, danger to others, and need for psychiatric treatment. Each state in the United States has its own statutes or mental health code on which retention procedures are based. The purpose of legally defined retention procedures is to protect against retention abuses. A person may be retained in a psychiatric hospital or in a psychiatric unit of a general hospital. Retention procedures generally involve three steps: application, assessment and evaluation, and commitment to an institution. Most states recognize four types of retention: informal, voluntary, emergency, and involuntary.

To be informally retained, a person verbally requests admission to an institution for psychiatric treatment. In most states, a person who is being informally retained may leave the institution simply by notifying the director of the institution (through the professional mental health staff) of his plan to leave. If the mental health professionals think the client needs to remain in the institution, then application must be made to convert the client's status from informal to involuntary.

Voluntary retention has two components: a written request for admission to an institution and a voluntary seeking of psychiatric treatment. People who are voluntarily retained usually do not relinquish their civil rights and may vote, manage property, and conduct business (Lindman and McIntyre, 1961). If a client wants to leave the institution before he has been discharged, he must make a written request to the director of the institution. The director must either honor the client's request or get a court order authorizing involuntary retention. Each state specifies the length of time a voluntary client may be retained after requesting discharge. For example, in New York and Pennsylvania, the director of an institution has 72 hours to either honor a client's request for discharge or to obtain a court order converting the client's status to involuntary.

A person who is acutely mentally ill may be admitted to an institution on an emergency status. This type of admission is time limited. For example, in New York, emergency retention is only valid for 48 hours. If at the end of the time period it is felt that the client is not ready to be discharged, the client may either agree to voluntary retention or the director of the institution may petition the court to convert the client's status to involuntary.

There are two avenues to involuntary retention:

1. Medical certification. A specified number of physicians certify that a person is mentally ill and *potentially dangerous to himself or others*. The number of physicians required for certification is established by state statue and varies from state to state. In many states the assessment of two physicians is necessary for certification. The director of the institution then presents this assessment to the court and requests a court order for involuntary retention.

2. Status conversion. By court order, retention status is converted from informal, voluntary, or emergency to involuntary.

A court order for involuntary retention is time limited. The time period may vary from state to state. If, at the expiration of the first court order it is felt that a client still needs to be retained in the institution, the director of the institution may petition the court for an extension of the involuntary retention order. Each time the order for involuntary retention is extended the time period may be increased. For example, in New York the first court order is valid for 60 days, the second for 6 months, and the third for 1 year. In many states, when the court is considering a retention order of 1 year or more, the client must be physically present in court. At any time, by using a habeas corpus procedure, a client or a client's family may petition the court for repeal of the retention order and discharge from the institution.

Ensuring client rights encompasses more than knowledge about retention procedures. A person with mental illness is the only "patient" who has to be granted, by state statutes, rights previously guaranteed to him as a citizen. These rights include the right to vote (by absentee ballot, if necessary), the right to personal freedom unless convicted of a crime, the right to a court hearing (in cases of involuntary retention), and the right of appeal and review by a higher court (Szasz, 1968; Ennis, 1972; Offir, 1974). Even persons certified as insane* retain the civil rights of citizenship. In addition, no instutional regulation may deprive mentally ill clients of rights guaranteed them by state mental health statutes or codes (Lindman and McIntyre, 1961). Although state statutes may vary, most state mental hygiene codes guarantee the following rights of mentally ill adults:

1. Right to know one's retention status

---

*Refer to Chapter 7 for a discussion of insanity.

2. Right to the least restrictive conditions that will meet the aims of retention
3. Right to periodic review of one's mental health status if one is involuntarily retained
4. Right to an explanation of one's psychiatric condition and treatment plan and of any untoward reactions that may occur as a result of treatment
5. Right to treatment. An individualized treatment plan must be established by a qualified mental health professional within a specified period after admission (for example, 5 days in New York State). There must be prompt and adequate treatment of any physical illness. A discharge plan must be developed by a qualified mental health professional, and, when needed, transitional care after discharge must be provided.
6. Right to accept or refuse a course of treatment
7. Right to judicious use of medication. Medications must be prescribed in writing, have a maximum termination date, and be reviewed periodically. Medications cannot be administered as a form of punishment, for staff convenience, in lieu of a treatment program, or in dosages that conflict with a treatment program.
8. Right to judicious use of physical restraints and isolation. Physical restraints and isolation may only be used in a situation in which a client is deemed dangerous to himself or others. Physical restraints and isolation can only be ordered by a physician who has personally seen the client. The order must be in writing and cannot exceed a specified time period (for example, 24 hours). The client's physical and psychiatric status must be closely monitored and recorded (for example every hour). Bathroom privileges must be allowed, and the client must be bathed regularly (for example, every 12 hours).
9. Right to privacy and to be treated with dignity
10. Right to communication with people outside the institution. Mentally ill clients have the same rights of access to telephones and visitors as clients in general hospitals. This right can be denied only by written order from a qualified mental health professional who is responsible for the client's therapeutic regimen. The order must be reviewed at regular intervals. Mentally ill clients have the right to visits from lawyers, private physicians, and other health professionals. Mentally ill clients

have the right to receive sealed mail from attorneys, health professionals, courts, and government officials. The right to receive mail from other persons may be restricted or denied only by written order from a qualified mental health professional responsible for the client's treatment program.

11. Right to informed consent. Clients must give informed consent and/or have legal counsel prior to administration of such potentially dangerous treatment modalities as electroconvulsive therapy, psychosurgery, and aversion therapy or prior to experimental research. Research must be reviewed and approved by a human subjects committee. If a client is incompetent to consent, a judge or lawyer may become a proxy consenter.

12. Right to confidentiality. A client has the right to confidentiality about his diagnosis, type of treatment, and the fact that he is receiving treatment. "Privileged communication" is a legal term referring to a client's right not to have information gained through psychiatric therapy divulged in court. A client may waive, in writing, the right of privileged communication.

13. Right to be adequately clothed. Unless such a right is denied or restricted in writing by a qualified mental health professional, a client has the right to wear his own clothes and keep personal belongings. If a client does not have adequate clothing, he has the right to be clothed by the institution.

14. Right to regular physical exercise. The institution must supply facilities and equipment for exercising. Unless he is physically ill, a client has the right to go out of doors on a regular basis.

15. Right to be paid the minimum wage for any work that contributes to the operation and maintenance of the institution

16. Right to engage in religious worship (Lindman and McIntyre, 1961; Shapiro, 1974; Miller et al., 1976; Stone, 1979).

Nurses also are responsible for ensuring the *rights of mentally ill children and adolescents*. Although these rights may vary from state to state, most state mental health statutes guarantee the following:

1. Right to free educational services.
2. Right to be free from involuntary sterilization. Parents cannot authorize the sterilization of their child.
3. Right to have legal counsel for any retention procedures
4. Right to the least restrictive conditions that will meet the aims of retention.
5. Right to treatment. A child or an adolescent has the right to an

individualized treatment plan that considers the developmental stage of the child or adolescent and to treatment by a qualified mental health professional who is a specialist in child and/or adolescent mental health. There should be interaction between mental health personnel and the child or adolescent's family. When parents deny treatment for a child or an adolescent, the court may act as an advocate and make a decision on the child or adolescent's behalf.

6. Right to informed consent. Whenever possible, informed consent should be obtained from a child or an adolescent.

7. Right to confidentiality. A child of any age has the right not to have detailed information derived from therapeutic relationships disclosed to parents. An adolescent over 16 years of age usually can decide what information he wants disclosed. When a child is unable to give consent, because of age or other reasons, parents have the right to know the type of treatment their child is receiving and their child's progress in treatment and the right to decide about releasing information to a third party (Lindman and McIntyre, 1961; Burgdorf, 1979).

Nurses may function as formal or informal child advocates. Formal advocacy involves appearing in court as a witness or primary initiator of a lawsuit on a child's behalf. Informal advocacy involves educating parents, administrators, and health team members about the rights of mentally ill children and adolescents and guaranteeing these rights (Burgdorf, 1979).

State statutes usually provide a client advocacy service that is under the jurisdiction of the state courts. The purpose of a client advocacy service is to safeguard the rights of child and adult clients. For example, in New York State the Mental Health Information Service informs clients of their retention status and rights, including their right to counsel from the Service. It reviews annually the status of involuntarily retained clients. If there is any doubt about the need for retention, the Mental Health Information Service must request a court hearing to resolve the issue.

Nurses are responsible for guaranteeing client rights, for educating others about the rights of mentally ill individuals, and for acting as liaisons between clients and a state-established client advocacy service. Nurses may be directly or indirectly involved in safeguarding client rights. For example, when a nurse performs a nursing procedure (for example, administers a medication), he or she must explain the purpose, anticipated results, and possible side effects of the procedure to the client. If the client then allows the nurse to perform the procedure, the client is implicitly giving consent. If the client refuses the procedure, the nurse should comply with the client's refusal and should then inform the psychiatrist. For nonnursing procedures (such as aversion therapy), nurses are responsible for ascertaining that clients are giving informed and voluntary consent. Occasionally, nurses are asked to ensure that a client's consent is voluntary and informed. This entails detailed recording of the discussion with the client. The questions and responses of both nurse and client and the client's mental status should be indicated. These are instances of direct involvement of nurses in the safeguarding of client rights (Creighton, 1970; Willeg, 1970).

Sometimes, nurses are indirectly involved in the protection of client rights. Education of nonprofessional staff about the rights of clients is an example of indirect protection of client rights. If a staff member does not believe in a particular right, he probably will not be vigilant in guaranteeing it. In a study of psychiatric aides, Daugherty (1978) found that aides supported rights that concerned abstract concepts or basic human needs (for example, adequate nutrition and treatment of medical problems) but had reservations about rights that might affect ward management or give increased responsibility to clients (for example, the right to be paid for work necessary to the operation of a psychiatric center and the right to judicious use of physical restraints and medications).

Nurses, as client advocates, are responsible for ensuring client rights. In order to fulfill this responsibility, they should be aware of retention procedures, the nature of client rights, client advocacy services, and the attitudes of the mental health staff members with whom they work.

Ensuring quality of care. As client advocates, nurses should be concerned with the quality of care provided, and they should be active participants in quality assurance programs. *Quality assurance* refers to activities designed to indicate the quality of health care and efforts aimed at improving the quality of health care (Towery and Windle, 1978).

In 1975, the Community Mental Health Centers Amendment (Public Law 94-63) made three stipulations concerning quality assurance in community Mental Health centers:

1. Development of national standards for community Mental Health centers
2. Development of quality assurance programs

3. Collection of data for the evaluation of quality assurance programs. Data should include operating costs and patterns of service utilization (acceptability of services, accessibility of services, and responsiveness of services to the needs of the catchment population).

A minimum of 2% of the previous year's operating expenses of a center must be allocated and used for implementation and evaluation of quality assurance programs (Towery and Windle, 1978).

Depending on the level of program development, either a formative or a summative evaluation may be used. Scriven (1967) explains that a formative evaluation involves the collection of empirical data for the purpose of developing a program. To date, designs for formative evaluation have not been well developed. A summative evaluation involves the collection of data for the purpose of assessing the effectivenss of an already existing program. A summative evaluation may be conducted internally by the personnel responsible for the program, or it may be conducted externally by individiuals or groups outside the program. Whether a summative evaluation is internal or external, it has the following objectives:

1. To establish outcome criteria for specific populations of clients. Comparing results of health care with outcome criteria gives an indication of the effectiveness of services.

2. To determine the least number of cost-effective activities and resources required to accomplish outcome criteria. Relating the expense incurred for required activities and resources to outcomes serves as a measure of efficiency.

3. To ascertain the degree to which a health delivery program meets the needs of the catchment population. Identifying factors that facilitate or inhibit the use of program services provides a measurement of accessibility of services (Zimmer, 1974; Towery and Windle, 1979).

Nurses may participate in formative and summative evaluations of Mental Health programs. The collection and analysis of data for the purpose of planning, assessing, and improving the quality of mental health care is a vital component of client advocacy.

Nurses and planned change. The effectiveness of nurses as client advocates is often hampered by inadequate knowledge about the process of change and the use of power. Nursing education often poorly prepares nurses to understand change and provides them with limited experience with power strategies.

Within an agency or institution, the power structure usually comprises three groups: administrative personnel, medical personnel, and nursing personnel. Power tends to shift continuously, through negotiation, among these three groups and the individuals within these groups. It is not unusual for a given person (for example, a director of nurses) to belong to more than one group. The intergroup power system creates a balance of power. In order to participate effectively within this balance of power, nurses, especially nurse-leaders, should learn to negotiate for power. When power is controlled by one group or when one group has little power, there may be diminished morale, ineffective functioning of the group having little power, or abuse of power by the group controlling power (McFarland and Shiflett, 1979).

Conflicts in the vested interests of the individuals and groups that make up the health delivery system may result in a *power struggle* (Ashley, 1979). A power struggle often occurs between nurses and other professionals within the health delivery system. In mental health settings, power struggles often are related to such advocacy functions as ensuring ethical practice and quality care. Struggles may be centered around issues such as the following:

1. Agency or institutional philosophy and delivery of mental health care
2. Negotiation for limited strategic resources (human and material)
3. Autonomy in mental health nursing practice
4. Roles and functions of nurses within the mental health delivery system

In a broader social context, power struggles sometimes exist between nurses, special interest groups, and legislators, on local, state, or federal levels. Such power struggles often center around client advocacy issues such as the following:

1. Allocation of money for mental health research and preventive intervention
2. Legislation concerning client rights and affirmative action programs for children and adults with a history of mental illness
3. Legislation forbidding discrimination against children and adults because of a history of mental illness
4. Insurance coverage for the treatment of mental illness (including third-party payment).

Political nursing is the use of knowledge about power processes and strategies to influence the nature and direction of health care and professional nursing (Ashley, 1975; Leininger, 1975). In order to be effective client advocates, nurses need to learn how to use power for planned change. The goals of political nursing are the same as the goals of the mental health care system: the availability, quality, accessibility, and funding of mental health care (Brown et al., 1978; McFarland and Shiflett, 1979). The constituency of political nursing is clients: communities, groups, and individuals—both diagnosed and potential.

Through political nursing, nurses attempt to provide input into power systems and to establish power strategies that can be used to regulate information and influence people in power. Methods for regulating information include rapid acquisition and distribution of accurate information by organizations to members, verification of information so that people do not have to act on the basis of rumor, and dissemination of knowledge about who to contact, how to initiate contact, and methods for conveying ideas to people in power. Involvement in local government, participation in public hearings, and lobbying are ways of influencing people in power (Van Steeg, 1979).

Knowing how to regulate information and influence people in power is important in effecting change. Nurses may be instrumental in effecting change in their own mental health agencies or in the broader social contexts of community, state, and nation. In order to effect change, nurses should explore the following avenues for expanding their bases of power and authority:

1. Increase nursing knowledge and clinical expertise in order to provide a base for expert power.
2. Develop strong, creative, and knowledgeable nursing leadership. Such leadership serves as a source for role models, gives novices an opportunity to develop power strategies and to be socialized into leadership roles, and provides a foundation for assertive and effective action.
3. Recognize that power is a component of interpersonal relationships. Identify the source of one's own power, and learn to use power strategies effectively.
4. Develop alliances that will increase support and power. Such alliances tend to diminish power struggles and to increase associative power.
5. Understand the channels of communication and authority. Nurses need to know about people who can serve as intermediaries in expediting change (Leininger, 1979; McFarland and Shiflett, 1979).

Because of the risks to personal security (for example, job security), nurses are sometimes hesitant to initiate change in their own agencies or institutions. However, these risks can be minimized. Epstein (1974) suggests that nurses minimize risks to personal security by identifying with like-minded colleagues, by expanding their power bases, and, whenever possible, by utilizing supportive agency policy. Identification with people who view the need for change in a similar way creates a network of support and action. Within this network, nurses can develop power strategies, evaluate progress, revise plans for change, and support one another in both success and failure. By talking with other members of the mental health team and with administrators, nurses can broaden their support bases both quantitatively and qualitatively. In addition, if an agency has a clearly and concisely written policy that supports a proposed change, nurses should use the policy in effecting change. If the policy is violated, violators may be confronted with the written policy. Whenever possible, such confrontation should be done by a group of people who are committed to the change. Confrontation by a group reduces the risk of retaliation against an individual.

Effecting change in the broader social contexts of community, state, and nation involves the use of many of the same strategies that are used in effecting change in an individual mental health agency. Burke (1979) suggests that nurses apply the interpersonal skills utilized in nurse-client relationships to relationships with community leaders and legislators. She suggests that a nurse should first establish a working relationship and then should identify appropriate contact people. Often local community leaders and their staffs can act as liaisons with other people and agencies. Maintaining an ongoing relationship is important. Even when a nurse is not lobbying for change, he or she should keep in touch with community leaders and legislative staff. Nurses must be knowledgeable: they should learn the names and functions of leaders who are involved with health issues, and they should be well informed about those issues. They should support lobbies and special interest groups that share their concerns. A nurse should provide community leaders and legislators with the local perspective— the way people in the community feel about an issue. Community leaders and legislators tend to be politically sensitive to this type of feedback (Burke, 1979; Donely, 1979).

Through political nursing, nurses utilize power processes and strategies to influence the nature and direction of health care and professional nursing. Political nursing is an essential element in client advocacy. McFarland and Shiflett (1979) caution nurses to consider the ethical implications of power strategies, not to use power solely for self-serving ends, and to be mindful of the responsibilities and obligations associated with the use of power.

Institutions, consumers, and nurses are the major components of the contemporary mental health delivery system. Within this delivery system, power strategies and power struggles sometimes arise around such issues as quality of care, client rights, affirmative action, and allocation of resources. We will now examine some major trends in mental health that may indicate the issues around which future power strategies and struggles will revolve.

TRENDS IN MENTAL HEALTH

Trends in mental health develop within a social context and need to be examined within that social context. Deinstitutionalization, consumerism, and decreased funding of mental health research are trends that affect and are affected by such social factors as inflation, political activism, and community attitudes. As these trends evolve and ramify, implications for the future are suggested.

Deinstitutionalization

In the past 20 years, state mental hospitals have experienced a decline of 66% in the number of residents. The total of all client populations has decreased from approximately 559,000 to 191,000 people (Bachrach, 1979). The practice of discharging chronically mentally ill clients into the community is known as deinstitutionalization. According to the Report of the Task Panel on Deinstitutionalization (1978), planning for deinstitutionalization is often inadequate. The desire to shift the cost of care for chronically mentally ill clients from the state to the federal government often results in discharging clients into the community without ascertaining whether community service facilities exist. There is usually little assessment of client needs and level of functioning and little consideration of whether hospital or community is the best treatment setting for a particular client. Clients are frequently discharged from a state institution into a hostile community. The lack of aftercare and support services to facilitate the transition from a highly structured hospital setting to a less structured community setting may have a devastating effect on a client.

Organizational stressors. Factors inherent in providing care to chronically mentally ill clients in the community may produce organizational stress and ineffective and inefficient delivery of care. Stern and Minkoff (1979) identify six organizational stressors:

1. Goal of community mental health. The goal of the community mental health movement—to reintegrate clients into the community—is not compatible with the needs of most deinstitutionalized clients. Many chronically mentally ill clients do not have access to social networks, community support, or aftercare services necessary for reintegration into the community. Nurses and other mental health professionals who are strongly committed to the community mental health movement may experience stress when reintegration into the community cannot be effectively implemented for deinstitutionalized clients. Mental health professionals may try to deal with this conflict by engaging in blame placing (blaming clients and/or the community) and rejecting deinstitutionalized clients.

2. Ideal of community mental health. Many nurses and other mental health professionals hold that community mental health centers should serve the entire community. Treating deinstitutionalized clients is time consuming. If community mental health professionals work with deinstitutionalized clients, they have less time to serve the rest of the community. This dilemma may cause conflict and stress. Many nurses and other mental health professionals resolve the conflict by concentrating on primary and secondary prevention, to the exclusion of tertiary prevention. This approach results in the abandonment of deinstitutionalized clients.

3. Threat to professional esteem. Among nurses and other mental health professionals, status and professional recognition tend to be associated with the care of acutely ill, rather than chronically ill, clients. Acutely ill clients may be viewed as more challenging and more satisfying to work with then chronically ill clients. In addition, the education of most mental health professionals has not developed the special skills needed to work with chronically mentally ill clients. These factors tend to threaten professional esteem.

4. Threat to professional ability. There is a dearth of research dealing with chronic mental illness. Those treatment strategies that are available are often ineffective with deinstitutionalized clients. Craig and Hyatt (1978) find that when nurses work with deinstitutionalized clients, they may experience frustration,

helplessness, and hopelessness. For this reason, nurses and other mental health professionals often try to avoid treating deinstitutionalized clients and may delegate this responsibility to nonprofessionals.

5. Reality of chronicity. Chronic mental illness is rarely cured. Many nurses and other mental health professionals judge their effectiveness by their ability to cure clients. In order to satisfy their need for client progress, many mental health professionals may pressure deinstitutionalized clients to alter their behavior, may establish short-term goals that deal only with dysfunction, and may ignore long-term goals that would deal with problems related to chronicity. A power struggle between client and therapist may develop over control or the definition of the therapeutic relationship (Craig and Hyatt, 1978).

6. Reality of deinstitutionalization. The discharge of chronically mentally ill clients into the community may present many problems. Communities may be hostile and resistent. Families may feel overwhelmed. Clients may feel isolated and insecure in their new community surroundings and may wish for the security associated with hospital routine. After-care facilities for deinstitutionalized clients may be lacking or inadequate.

Implications for the future. The gestalt of the community mental health movement may need to be altered to include the hospital as an integral part of the community. The hospital and the community mental health agency will need to cooperate with and complement each other. The hospital may need to introduce creative approaches to chronicity and to increase the type and number of services for chronically mentally ill clients. In order to prevent duplication of services, hospitals and community mental health agencies may need to cooperate in planning programs geared to the problems associated with chronicity. This approach necessitates a recognition of such unique service needs of chronically mentally individuals as resocialization, housing, vocational rehabilitation, and employment opportunities.

The goal of reintegrating all mentally ill clients into the community may need to be reexamined. Long-term institutionalization may be indicated for people who are so severely chronically ill that the structure and nursing care available in hospitals are necessary. For people who are mildly or moderately chronically ill, reintegration into the community may be a viable alternative to institutionalization. However, it will be necessary to provide adequate aftercare and supportive services and to involve communities in planning and delivering services. In addition, in order to obtain continuous information about the needs of chronically mentally ill individuals, outreach programs for deinstitutionalized clients may need to be developed (Schulberg, 1977; Stein and Test, 1978; Bachrach, 1979).

The education of nurses and other mental health professionals may also need to be examined. Clinical specialization and in-service education programs for the care of chronically mentally ill individuals will need to be encouraged. Development of skills that are effective in the treatment of chronically mentally ill clients may lessen the threat to professional esteem that many nurses and other mental health professionals often experience and may help to keep professionals involved in the care of chronically mentally ill clients (Stern and Minkoff, 1979).

Consumerism

Consumer power. A philosophy is emerging that encourages equal participation in decision making between consumers and providers of mental health care. The trend toward increased involvement of and power for consumers is moving ahead on two levels—individual and community.

On the first level, individuals are being given knowledge that will make them educated consumers of and effective participants in the therapeutic process. Clients have a right to, and are being given, explanations about their psychiatric conditions, treatment plans, alternative types of treatment and their costs, and any untoward reactions that may occur as a consequence of treatment. Within the therapeutic relationship, mutuality between clients and nurses (or other mental health professionals) is also being encouraged. Stone (1979) notes that the introduction of mutuality between client and therapist restructures the therapeutic relationship from a status relationship (a relationship based on hierarchical positions) to a contract relationship (a relationship based on voluntary individual arrangements). Clients have an opportunity for more autonomy in contractural than in status relationships (Main, 1907; Durkheim, 1933; Barth, 1959).

Many clients are turning for assistance to self-help groups composed of people who have recovered from specific psychosocial problems. Alcoholics Anonymous, Gamblers Anonymous, and Overeaters Anonymous are examples of such groups. In many instances, these self-help groups constitute the major treatment modality. In other instances, self-help groups are used in conjunction with other therapies. Client decisions to utilize the therapeutic properties of self-help groups and the assumption of care-provider roles by some recovered clients exemplify the increasing autonomy of consumers in the mental health delivery system.

The second level of the trend in consumerism is characterized by collaboration between the community and nurses and other professionals in community mental health centers. Increasingly, community representatives are sitting on the boards of community mental health centers. Community mental health boards thereby become a point of articulation between community residents and care providers. Such collaboration between community representatives and mental health professionals is a potentially educational experience. Community representatives may learn firsthand about the community mental health movement—its philosophy, goals, and problems. This educational process helps to demystify mental health and mental illness, to teach consumers (and potential consumers) about treatment modalities and the roles and functions of members of the mental health team, and to sensitize residents to the mental health problems in their community.

Community residents may become aware of the influence their involvement and support can have on a community mental health program. Community representatives may develop an increased understanding of their sources of power and of how power relationships affect budgeting, service priorities, and programing.

Nurses and other mental health professionals may better view clients within the sociocultural context of the community. The values, ideology, and traditions of subgroups (such as ethnic groups and classes) composing the community may be better identified and understood. Nurses and other mental health professionals may also increase their awareness of the perceptions that subgroups within the community have about the definition, cause, and treatment of mental illness (Ruiz and Behrens, 1973; Borus and Kiermen, 1976; Landsberg and Hammer, 1978).

The trend towards including community representatives on the boards of community mental health centers can be very beneficial in assessing the mental health needs of a community, evaluating services, and identifying areas that need improvement.

Implications for the future. The role of consumers (actual and potential) in the mental health delivery system will probably continue to expand. Presently, people who have recovered from specific psychosocial problems (such as alcoholism, drug abuse, and compulsive eating) are effectively intervening in the treatment of people who have not yet recovered. Gonzalez (1976) suggests that this trend may grow to include other psychosocial problems (for example, depression, phobias, and compulsive working).

In addition, consumers are becoming more vocal about their perceptions of effective treatment for mental illness, and nurses and other mental health professionals are becoming more responsive to the ideas of consumers. Gonzalez (1976) and Warner (1977) note that many consumers rely on the native healers and folk medicines of their cultures. Client belief in folk medicine and confidence in native healers need not rule out treatment by nurses and other mental health professionals. Torrey (1973), a psychiatrist who is associated with the National Institute of Mental Health, explains that both native healers and mental health professionals function as therapists in the treatment of mental illness and that both achieve therapeutic results. Native healers are important mental health resources and should be actively integrated into mental health programs.

Research

In the United States, the National Institute of Mental Health (NIMH) is the major source of funding for mental health research. Over the past decade, the combination of budgetary cuts and inflation has resulted in a 50% decrease in the purchasing power of monies invested in mental health research. With the current rate of inflation, every 25% cut in funding translates into more than 50% decrease in purchasing power (Brown, 1976).

Status of mental health research. Because trained researchers are having difficulty obtaining research grants, many researchers are entering other fields of mental health, such as practice or teaching. Brown (1976) predicts that not only will the scarcity of research grants affect the current level of mental health research, but, because young scientists have limited research opportunities, there will be a dirth of prepared researchers for the next 10 or 20 years.

There is also a trend in American society toward evaluating the worth of a program in terms of its cost effectiveness. Mental health researchers have difficulty translating their results into a dollar amount. While dollar savings can be attached to decreases in the number of people hospitalized for mental illness, similar cost effectiveness cannot as readily be demonstrated for such improvements in human functioning as increased sense of well-being or more effective coping behavior. The difficulty of translating research results into cost-effectiveness formulae plus the stigma that much of the general public still attaches to mental illness result in a lack of public support for mental health research (Brown, 1976).

Implications for the future. Nurses and other mental health professionals will need to become more politically active and politically effective in educating legislators and the general public about the importance of mental health research. Brown (1976) suggests that such an educational program should encompass the crisis in mental health research, as well as the process, purpose, and importance of mental health research. Public support will be essential if mental health professionals are to successfully compete for scarce research resources. The National Association for Mental Health, a consumer citizen group that in the past used its political influence to engender support for mental health services, is beginning to use its political influence to engender support for mental health research.

Nurses and other mental health professionals are becoming politically active. They will need to direct some of their political activity toward influencing legislation concerning mental health research. Such political activity should involve more than lobbying and contacting legislators. Ver Steeg (1979) believes that mental health professionals who are experts in their fields and who are also politically active are more apt to be asked to serve on advisory committees. Serving on advisory committees may increase the opportunities for mental health professionals to influence legislation concerning research in mental health.

In addition, nurses and other mental health professionals will need to learn the art of grantsmanship. Donley (1974) stresses that it is not enough to write a grant; an application for a grant must be followed up with telephone calls and visits to regional offices in order to clarify the purpose and the importance of the proposal.

CHAPTER SUMMARY

Power, which is a dynamic of all interpersonal relationships, has many sources and forms, and it is the basis of many strategies. In order to have input into power systems that affect the direction of mental health care and professional nursing, nurses need to understand the interrelationship between power, politics, and planned change. Institutions, consumers, and nurses are major elements of the contemporary mental health delivery system. Within this system, issues related to quality of care, client rights, and allocation of resources often lead to power strategies and power struggles. Trends in mental health may indicate the issues around which future power struggles will revolve. Currently, the major mental health trends are toward deinstitutionalization, consumerism, and decreased funding for mental health research.

REFERENCES

Annas, G., and J. Healey
1974 "The patient's rights advocate." Vanderbilt Law Review 27:243-269.

Argyris, Chris
1972 The Applicability of Organizational Sociology. Cambridge: Cambridge University Press.

Ashley, J. A.
1975 "Power, freedom and professional practice in nursing." Supervisor Nurse 1:12-29.

Bachrach, Leona L.
1979 "Planning mental health services for chronic patients." Hospital and Community Psychiatry 30(6):387-393.

Barth, Fredrik
1959 Political Leadership Among Swat Pathans. London. Athlone Press.

Beigel, Allan
1977 "The politics of mental health fundings: two views." Hospital and Community Psychiatry 28(3):194-195.

Bennis, Warren, et al.
1969 The Planning of Change. New York: Holt, Rinehard & Winston.

Blase, Melvin G. (ed.)
1973 Institution-Building, A Source Book. Washington, D.C.: U.S. Department of State, U.S. Government Printing Office.

Borus, Jonathan F.
1976 "Neighborhood health centers as providers of primary mental health care." New England Journal of Medicine 295(3):140-145.

Borus, Jonathan F., and Gerald L. Klerman
1976 "Consumer-professional collaboration for evaluation in neighborhood mental health programs. Hospital and Community Psychiatry 27(6):401-404.

Brown, Barbara J., Kristine Gebbie, and Joan F. Moore
1978 "Affecting nursing goals in health care." Nursing Administration Quarterly 2(3):17-31.

Brown, Bertram S.
1976 "The crisis in mental health research." Address presented at the 1976 Annual Meeting of the American Psychiatric Association.

Bumgardner, Harvey L., et al
1972 Institution Building: Basic Concepts and Implementation. Chapel Hill, North Carolina, University of North Carolina at Chapel Hill (mimeographed).

Burgdorf, Marcia Pearce
1979 "Legal rights of children: implications for nurses." Nursing Clinics of North America 14(3):405-416.

Burke, Sheila
1979 "What the Washington professionals expect." American Journal of Nursing 79(10):1949.

Code for Nurses with Interpretive Statements.
1968 Prepared by American Nurses' Association Committee on Ethical, Legal,

and Professional Standards. Kansas City, Mo.: The Association.

Craig, Anne E., and Barbara A. Hyatt
1978 "Chronicity in mental illness: a theory on the role of change." Perspectives in Psychiatric Care 16(3):139-144.

Creighton, Helen
1970 Law Every Nurse Should Know. Philadelphia: W. B. Saunders Co.

Curtin, Leah L.
1978 "Nursing ethics: theories and pragmatics." Nursing Forum 17(1):4-11.
1978 "A proposed model for critical ethical analysis." Nursing Forum 17(1):12-17.

Daughtery, Lynn B.
1978 "Assessing the attitudes of psychiatric aides toward patients' rights." Hospital and Community Psychiatry 29(4):225-229.

Donley, Rosemary
1979 "An inside view of the Washington health scene." American Journal of Nursing 79(10):1946-1949.

Downs, Anthony
1967 Inside Bureaucracy. Boston: Little, Brown & Co.

Durkheim, Emile
1933 Division of Labor in Society. G. Simpson, trans. New York: Macmillan, Inc.

Ennis, Bruce J., and Loren Siegel
1978 The Rights of Mental Patients: The Basic ACLU Guide to a Mental Patient's Rights. New York: Richard W. Baron Publishing Co., Inc.

Epstein, Charlotte
1974 Effective Interaction in Contemporary Nursing. Englewood Cliffs, N.J.: Prentice-Hall, Inc.

Gonzalez, Hector H.
1976 "The consumer movement: the implications for psychiatric care." Perspectives in Psychiatric Care 14(4):186-190.

Gordon, Marjory
1969 "The clinical specialist as change agent." Nursing Outlook 17:37-39.

Health Task Force of the Urban Coalition.
1970 Rx. for Action. Washington, D.C.: The Urban Coalition, U.S. Government Printing Office.

International Code of Nursing Ethics.
1953 Adopted by the Grand Council of Nurses of the ICN. Sao Paulo, Brazil.

Landsberg, Gerald, and Roni Hammer
1978 "Involving community representatives in CMHC evaluation and research."

Hospital and Community Psychiatry 29(4):245-247.

Leach, Edmund
1954 Political Systems of Highland Burma. Boston: Beacon Press.

Leininger, Madeline
1978 "Political nursing: essential for health service and education systems of tomorrow." Nursing Administration Quarterly 2(3):1-16.
1979 "Territoriality, power, and creative leadership in administrative nursing contexts." In Nursing Dimensions: Power in Nursing. Dalton E. McFarland and Nola Shiflett (eds.). Wakefield, Mass.: Nursing Resources, Inc. 7(2):33-42.

Lewin, Kurt
1947 "Frontiers in group dynamics." Human Relations 15-41.

Lindman, F., and D. McIntyre
1961 The Mentally Disabled and The Law. Chicago: University of Chicago Press.

Lippitt, Ronald, et al.
1958 The Dynamics of Planned Change. New York: Harcourt, Brace & World, Inc.

Maine, Henry
1907 Ancient Law. London: John Murray.

Martin, N. H., and J. H. Sims
1956 "Thinking ahead: power tactics." Harvard Business Review 34:25-29.

McFarland, Dalton E., and Nola Shiflett
1979 "The role of power in the nursing profession." In Nursing Dimensions: Power in Nursing. Dalton E. McFarland and Nola Shiflett (eds.). Wakefield, Mass.: Nursing Resources, Inc. 7(2):1-13.

Miller, W., R. O. Dawson, and R. I. Parnas
1976 The Mental Health Process. New York: New York Foundation Press.

National Association for Mental Health
1974 "Citizens making a difference." M. H. 58(4):16-17.

National Commission on Community Health Services.
1966 "Health is a community affair. Cambridge, Mass. Harvard University Press.

Nations, W.
1973 "Nurse lawyer is patient advocate." American Journal of Nursing 73:1039-1041.

Offir, Carol Wade
1974 "Civil rights and the mentally ill: revolution in Bedlam." Psychology Today 8(5):60-62.

Peplau, Hildegard E.
  1953 "Themes in nursing situations." American Journal of Nursing 53:1221-1223.
Perrow, Charles
  1970 Organizational Analysis: A Sociological View. Belmont, Calif.: Wadsworth, Inc.
Psychiatric Nurses Association of Canada
  1977 "Code of ethics." Canadian Journal of Psychiatric Nursing 18(6):8.
Report of The Task Panel on Deinstitutionalization, Rehabilitation, and Long-Term Care.
  1978 In Task Panel Reports Submitted to the President's Commission on Mental Health, vol. 2. Washington, D.C.: U.S. Government Printing Office, pp. 356-375.
Rouslin, Sheila
  1976 "Commentary on professional ethics." Perspectives in Psychiatric Care 14(1):12-13.
Ruiz, Pedro, and Manfred Behrens
  1973 "Community control in mental health: how far can it go?" Psychiatric Quarterly 47 (3):317-324.
Scheflen, Albert E.
  1972 Body Language and Social Order. Englewood Cliffs, N.J.: Prentice Hall, Inc.
Schulberg, H. C.
  1977 "Community mental health and human services." Community Mental Health Review 2(6):1-9.
Scriven, M.
  1967 "The methodology of evaluation." In Perspectives on Curriculum Evaluation. AERA Monograph Series on Curriculum Evaluation, no. 1. Chicago Rand McNally & Co.
Shapiro, M.
  1974 "Legislating the control of behavior control: autonomy and coercive use of organic therapies. Southern California Law Review 47:237-356.
Stein, L. I., and M. A. Test
  1978 "An alternative to mental hospital treatment." In Alternatives to Mental Hospital Treatment. L. I. Stein and M. A. Test (eds.). New York: Plenum Publishing Corp., pp. 43-55.
Stern, Robert, and Kenneth Minkoff
  1979 "Paradoxes in programming for chronic patients in a community clinic." Hospital and Community Psychiatry 30(9):613-617.

Stone, Alan A.
  1979 "Informed consent: special problems for psychiatry." Hospital and Community Psychiatry 30(5):321-326.
Szasz, Thomas
  1963 Law, Liberty and Psychiatry; An Inquirey Into the Social Uses of Mental Health Practices. New York: Macmillan, Inc.
Torrey, E. Fuller
  1973 Cited in "Tending the spirit." Wall Street Journal, March 26, pp. 1, 17.
Towery, O. B., and Charles Windle
  1978 "Quality assurance for community mental health centers: impact of P.L. 94-63. Hospital and Community Psychiatry 29(5):316-319.
Ver Steeg, Donna F.
  1979 "The political process, or, the power and the glory. In Nursing Dimensions: Power in Nursing. Dalton E. McFarland and Nola Shiflett (eds.). Wakefield, Mass.: Nursing Resources, Inc. 7, 2:20-27.
Votaw, Dow
  1979 "What do we believe about power?" In Nursing Dimensions: Power in Nursing. Dalton E. McFarland and Nola Shiflett (eds.). Wakefield, Mass.: Nursing Resources, Inc. 7, 2:50-63.
Warner, Richard
  1977 "Witchcraft and soul loss: implications for community psychiatry." Hospital and Community Psychiatry 28(9):686-690.
Willeg, Sidney H.
  1970 The Nurse's Guide To The Law. New York: McGraw-Hill Book Co.
Zaltman, Gerald, Robert Duncan, and Jonny Holbek
  1973 Innovations and Organizations. New York: John Wiley & Sons, Inc.
Zentner, Joseph L.
  1973 "Organizational ideology: some functions and problems." International Review of History and Political Science 10(2):75-84.
Zimmer, Marie J.
  1974 "Quality assurance for outcomes of patient care." Nursing Clinics of North America 9(2):305-315.

ANNOTATED SUGGESTED READINGS

Donley, Rosemary
  1979 "An inside view of the Washington health scene." American Journal of Nursing. 79(10):1946-1949.

The author discusses some of the insights gained into Washington politics as a result of her experience as a Robert Wood Johnson Health Policy Fellow. She suggests approaches for nurses who want to develop political power.

Gonzalez, Hector H.
1976 "The consumer movement: the implications for psychiatric care." Perspectives in Psychiatric Care 14(4):186-190.
Gonzalez discusses the historical development of the consumer movement in health care and then focuses on consumerism in mental health care. Implications are explored for utilizing consumers as active participants in mental health care: as mental health care providers, as doctors of the people, and as evaluators of treatment modalities. Issues and problems associated with consumerism in mental health are discussed.

McFarland, Dalton E., and Nola Shiflett (eds.).
1979 Nursing Dimensions: Power in Nursing. Wakefield, Mass.: Nursing Resources, Inc. 7, 2:1-86.
The process of power and its implications for health care and nursing are discussed. Special emphasis is given to strategies for acquiring and exerting power; these strategies are compared to the usual nursing strategies in power situations. An annotated bibliography is included.

Ruiz, Pedro, and Manfred Behrens
1973 "Community control in mental health: how far can it go?" Psychiatric Quarterly 47(3):317-324.
Ruiz and Manfred discuss the role of consumer representatives in developing knowledge about community mental health programs, learning how to effectively use power to achieve results, and determing what type of mental health services are most valuable for their community. The authors focus on Lincoln Community Mental Health Center in Bronx, N.Y.

GLOSSARY

accommodation—A Piagetian term referring to the identification and elimination of disequilibrium. As accommodation occurs, more accurate perceptions result.

acculturation—The process of reciprocal retentions, losses, and/or adaptations of culture patterns that results when members of two or more ethnic groups interact

acute confusional state—Acute brain dysfunction caused by any interference with the complex biochemical or metabolic processes essential to brain functioning. Symptoms include disturbances in cognition, levels of awareness, memory, and orientation, accompanied by restlessness, apprehension, irritability, and apathy. SYNONYMS: delirium, acute delirious state, acute brain syndrome, toxic psychosis

adaptation—Adjusting one's responses in order to cope with internal or external stress

addictive personality—characterized by compulsive and habitual use of a substance or practice to cope with psychic pain engendered by conflict involving aggressive, sexual, or dependent feelings

affect—Mood, emotion, or feeling tone

agoraphobia—Irrational fear of open spaces or of entering public places alone, because of a psychic phenomenon in which internal fears or anxiety are projected onto an aspect of the environment

alienation—A failure in reciprocal connectedness between a person and significant others; estrangement of self from others

ambivalence—The simultaneous existence of strong feelings of both love and hate toward a person, an object, or a situation

amnesia—An emergency response to stress and anxiety in which a part or all of a person's past life is forgotten or forced out of awareness through repression

anal phase—In psychosexual development, the stage that encompasses ages 15 months to 3 years. Libidinal energy is shifted from the mouth as a source of gratification to the anus.

andropause—The return to the nonsexual state of function of the male genitalia. Andropause occurs later than menopause, usually beginning in the middle to late fifties.

anger—A sense of intense tension or discomfort that arises when a goal is thwarted

anhedonia—An inability to find pleasure in situations that would normally be pleasurable

anomie—A state of alienation and disassociation from social values and beliefs; normlessness

anorexia nervosa—A condition characterized by excessive dieting, which is often carried to the point of severe malnutrition and emaciation and which, in some instances, leads to death through starvation

anticipatory planning—The identification of possible stressors in one's life—for example, pregnancy or change in job—and the initiation of the problem-solving process to reduce or eliminate a crisis situation before it occurs

antisocial personality—Characterized by impulsive and asocial behavior, poor judgment, irresponsibility, and lack of insight into the consequences of one's behavior

643

anxiety—A diffuse feeling of apprehension and of dread of being threatened or alienated. The threat may be real or perceived. Anxiety can maintain one's alertness, or it can immobilize an individual.

anxiety reactions—Overt physiological and psychological manifestations of anxiety in which there is a lack of any stable defense mechanisms or symptom formation to cope with the anxiety

apathy—A blunting of affect; an absence of feeling from a psychological point of view

approximation—The movement of one individual toward another in the development of an interpersonal relationship

associative looseness—A thinking disorder in which relationships among ideas are autistically determined

assimilation—A Piagetian term referring to an individual's ability to comprehend and integrate new experiences

asthenic personality—Characterized by constant and extreme fatigue, listlessness, and indecisiveness. Asthenic personality is believed to be a precursor of neurasthenia.

attitudes—Major integrative forces in the development of personality that give consistency to an individual's behavior. Attitudes are cognitive in nature, formed through interactions with the environment. Attitudes serve to direct an individual's commitments and responsibilities; they reflect innermost convictions about what is good or bad, right or wrong, desirable or undesirable.

authority—The right to use power to command behavior, enforce rules, and make decisions. Authority is often based on rank or position in a social hierarchy, and it may be either of two types: line authority or staff authority.

autism—Exclusive focus is on the self. Subjective, introspective thinking and a good deal of fantasy are prominent aspects of autism.

aversion therapy—A type of negative conditioning that uses learning theory to change behavior from maladaptive to adaptive

basic group identity—Shared social characteristics such as world view, language, and value and ideological system. Basic group identity evolves from membership in an ethnic group.

biogenic—Motivated by physiological states

bipolar depressive response—An affective disorder that is characterized by symptoms of both depression and mania

blame placing—Process of placing responsibility for one's behavior, and especially misbehavior, on others

body image—An individual's conscious and unconscious perceptions of his body. Body image is an integral component of one's self-concept.

boundary maintenance mechanisms—Behavior and practices that exclude members of other ethnic groups from the customs and values of a particular ethnic group

castration—Removal of the testes in a male or the ovaries in a female

catatonic schizophrenia—A type of schizophrenia. In the catatonic stupor form, prominent symptoms may include stupor, stereotypical behavior, cerea flexibilitas (waxy flexibility), and negativism. In the catatonic excitement form, there may be hyperkinesia, stereotypical behavior, mannerisms, and impulsivity.

catharsis—A therapeutic outpouring of repressed ideas or conflicts through verbalization and working through of conscious material. An appropriate emotional reaction accompanies catharsis.

cerea flexibilitas—Waxy flexibility—a symptom often seen in catatonic schizophrenia. The individual's muscular system is in a condition that permits the molding of arms and legs into any position where they will remain indefinitely.

change agent—A person who tries to influence the making and implementing of decisions in the direction of change

character neuroses—Character neuroses are personality organizations characterized by excessive anxiety and unconscious conflict in which the compromise solutions needed to maintain adjustment or adaptation result in rigidity of personality and inhibit interpersonal relations, although there are no overt clinical symptoms.

childhood triad—Three types of behavior (firesetting, bedwetting, and cruelty to animals) that when used in combination and consistently may predict emerging sociopathy.

chronic, undifferentiated schizophrenia— The symptoms of more than one of the classic types of schizophrenia (simple, paranoid, catatonic, hebrephrenic) are demonstrated in this category.

circum-speech—Behavior characteristic of conversation. Instrumentals, markers, interactional behavior, demonstratives, and stress kinesics are types of circum-speech.

circumstantiality—A speech pattern in which there is difficulty in screening out irrelevant material in describing an event. The inclusion of many irrelevant details results in a lengthy and rambling account before the end point is reached. This speech pattern may be found in chronic brain dysfunction.

coding—The process of categorizing information. Information is sorted and then stored in various types of memory codes.

cognition—The processing of information by the nervous system. This processing structures reality and gives meaning to human experience.

cognitive dissonance—A state of disequilibrium and tension produced when two or more sets of information are at variance with one another

command hallucination—An hallucinated voice that an individual experiences as commanding him to perform a certain act. Command hallucinations may influence a person to engage in behavior that is dangerous to himself or to others.

communication theme—A recurrent idea or concept that underlies and ties together communication. There are three types of communication themes: content theme (the idea that underlies or links together seemingly varied topics of discussion), mood theme (the affect or emotion an individual communicates), interaction theme (the idea or concept that best describes the dynamics between communicating participants).

community mental health—The prevention, early diagnosis, effective treatment, and rehabilitation of mental disorders and disabilities in geographically defined communities, through a network of collaborative health and social welfare systems, community organizations, and consumers

compulsion—A persistent, irrational need or urge to perform a particular act or acts. A compulsion, which often has the quality of a ritual, serves a defensive purpose by controlling anxiety, guilt, and other noxious feelings.

concrete thinking—Part of the thought disorder characteristic of schizophrenia. Concrete thinking is a primitive way of thinking in which an individual tends to take the literal meanings of ideas. It is indicative of a difficulty in abstracting.

confabulation—An adaptive or defensive phenomenon in which a person with memory deficits fills in gaps in memory with relevant but imaginary information

conscience—The part of the superego system that monitors thoughts, feelings, and actions and measures them against internalized values and standards

conscious—The conscious level of experience includes those aspects of experience that are in awareness at any given time. Consciousness is a psychodynamic concept that embraces three levels of awareness, each of which influences behavior.

These levels are the conscious, the preconscious, and the unconscious.

consensual validation—A term coined by Harry Stack Sullivan that refers to a method for diminishing interpersonal and communication distortions. It involves a comparison of one's evaluations of experience with those of another person.

consumer—An individual, group, or community that utilizes a product or service. In the area of mental health, consumerism refers to the utilization of all levels of mental health services (services designed for primary, secondary, and tertiary prevention of mental illness).

conversion—The transformation of unacceptable, anxiety-provoking impulses into sensorimotor sysmptoms such as paralysis or blindness. There is no organic basis for such impairment. Conversion is an emergency response to stress.

coping mechanisms—Measures utilized to reduce tension. These measures are often learned through early interactions with significant others in the environment.

coprolalia—Excessive use of profane language

countersociety—A society that runs counter to or against the established society in which it exists

countertransference—An emotional and often unconscious process in the helping person that is related to the client and that has an effect on the therapeutic interaction between therapist and client

crisis intervention—Provision of immediate treatment for individuals undergoing acute psychological distress

cultural event—The communication of meaning that takes place each time one member of a society interacts with another member

culturally specific—Unique to a particular culture and a function of that cultural context

culture—An ordered system of shared and socially transmitted symbols and meanings that structures world view and guides behavior

culture shock—A drastic change in the cultural environment that is both precipitated by and a response to cognitive dissonance

cyclothymic personality—Characterized by vacillation between depression and elation. Differentiation between cyclothymic personality and manic depressive psychosis is a matter of degree of symptomatology.

day hospital—A psychiatric facility where formerly hospitalized clients participate in a therapeutic program during the normal working hours

deinstitutionalization—The practice of discharging chronically mentally ill clients into the community

delirium—See *acute confusional state*

delusion—A false belief (other than a commonly believed myth or superstition of a culture)

dementia praecox—An outdated term used to describe schizophrenia. Dementia (insanity) praecox (youthful) was used to distinguish schizophrenia from the dementias of later life, such as senility.

demonstrative—A type of circum-speech that accompanies and illustrates speech

denial—Unconsciously motivated behavior that manifests itself as evasion or negation of objective reality

dependence—Reliance on others in the environment to meet needs for nurturance, security, love, shelter, and sustenance

dependent personality—Characterized by excessive or compulsive needs for attention, acceptance, and approval from other people in order to maintain security and self-esteem and to resolve neurotic conflict. Dependent personality is a concept of Karen Horney.

depersonalization—A state in which an individual feels that he has lost his personal identity. The feeling that the environment is also changed and unreal may also be present. This latter feeling is termed *derealization.*

depression—An extension of the grieving process that is considered abnormal. Depression can be described in terms of affect, mood disorder, and a cluster of clinical symptoms.

developmental crisis—A period of vulnerability encountered as one progresses from one developmental stage to the next

displacement—Unconscious transferal of strivings or feelings from the original object to a different object, activity, or situation

dissociative reaction—Characterized by psychiatric symptoms that represent a form of psychological flight from the self. A part or all of the personality is denied or dissociated from present reality.

distance regulation—Behavior that marks off a quantum of space. Three types of distance are maintained: flight distance (distance that a wild animal will tolerate between itself and an enemy before fleeing), personal distance (the normal spacing maintained between animals of the same species), and social distance (maximal distance before a social animal begins to feel either psychologically threatened or physically and socially isolated from the group).

dyad—A combination of two (for example, husband and wife, parent and child)

echolalia—Imitating and repeating the speech of another person. Echolalia is a pathological form of speech that is demonstrated by some schizophrenic individuals.

echopraxia—Imitating and repeating the body movements of another person. Echopraxia is a symptom demonstrated by some schizophrenic individuals.

educational therapy—Educational and vocational training programs designed to develop self-esteem, group identification, and school and occupational adjustment

ego—The part of the personality that is in interaction with the external environment and with somatic and psychic aspects of the internal environment. Ego functions, which encompass intellectual and social abilities, maintain an equilibrium between id and superego, as well as the integrity of the personality in coping with stress.

egocentricity—The tendency to view one's own thoughts and ideas as the best possible, without considering the views of others

electroconvulsive therapy (ECT)—A somatic therapy in which electric current is applied to the brain through electrodes placed on the temporal areas of the skull. The desired generalized convulsion is precipitated by applying 70 to 130 volts for 0.1 to 0.5 seconds. The treatment is used in mania, depression, and certain cases of schizophrenia. SYNONYMS: Electrostimulation therapy (EST), Electric shock therapy

enculturation—The process of learning the conceptual and behavioral systems of one's culture

equilibration—The balancing and integrating of new experiences with those of the past as an individual progresses along his developmental course

Eros—According to Freud, the instinct for life

ethnic enclave—An area in a city, town, or village that is populated by a minority ethnic group

ethnic group—A collectivity of people organized around an assumption of common origin

ethnocentrism—The attitude that one ethnic group's folkways are superior and right and those of other ethnic groups are inferior and wrong. Each ethnic group uses its culture as a standard for judging all other cultures.

euthymism—Normal mood responses

explosive personality—Characterized by episodes of uncontrollable rage and physical abusiveness in response to relatively minor pressures

extended family—A family unit consisting of three or more generations

family—A group of people who are united by bonds of kinship, at least two of whom are conjugally related

family therapy—Simultaneous treatment of more than one family member in the same session. The family's communication patterns and their patterns of relating are considered the focus of the treatment.

feedback—A regulatory mechanism of the communication process. All interpersonal systems are viewed as feedback loops. Behavior of one person affects and is affected by the behavior of another person.

fixation—The concentration of libidinal energies in one psychosexual stage of development, because of over gratification or under gratification in that stage.

flight of ideas—Communication that is characterized by rapid movement from one idea to another. There is a connection between the ideas, but it is tenuous and often influenced by the immediate environment. This phenomenon is sometimes demonstrated in manic-depressive psychosis.

formation—A cluster of people that occupies, and thereby defines, a quantum of space

frame of reference—An individual's personal guidelines, taken as a whole. A person's frame of reference reflects his social situation, his cultural norms, and his ideas.

grief—A series of subjective responses that follow a significant loss—for example, loss of body function, a body part, status, or a relative.

guilt—Tension between ego and superego that occurs when one falls short of standards set for oneself.

hallucination—A false sensory perception; a perception for which there is no external stimulus. Any of the senses may be involved: individuals have experienced hallucinations that are auditory, visual, tactile, olfactory, gustatory, or kinesthetic.

hebephrenic schizophrenia—A type of schizophrenia that is characterized by severe thinking and emotional disorders. Behavior is bizarre, silly, and inappropriate. *Regression* is the main defense mechanism that is used in an exaggerated form. Hallucinations and delusions are present. This form of schizophrenia is generally believed to have the poorest prognosis. The age of onset tends to be young—before the twenties.

helplessness—A state characterized by the existence of an unfulfilled need and the inability to meet that need. Helplessness can be a learned response.

homeostasis—The maintenance of equilibrium or a steady state in a system. The term can be used in relation to physiological systems and social systems.

hopelessness—A situation characterized by the belief that all efforts to alter one's life situation will be fruitless

hostility—The tendency of an organism to do something harmful to another organism or to itself. Hostility may be passively rather than actively expressed.

hydrotherapy—The form of treatment for mental illness that involved the use of water at various temperatures. Hydrotherapy is mostly of historical interest; it included such measures as continuous tub baths, application of wet sheet packs, and use of shower sprays.

hypochondriasis—A morbid preoccupation with the state of one's health, usually accompanied by physical symptoms or the conviction that some disease process is present that cannot be substantiated by medical evidence

hypomania—A state of elation. A hypomanic individual has boundless energy; he is witty and outgoing, and he is considered the life of the party. Hypomanic behavior is purposeful and goal-directed.

hysterical personality—Characterized by extremely excitable, emotionally labile, and overly dramatic behavior

hysterical reaction—An emergency psychological response to overwhelming anxiety. Hysterical reactions include a variety of symptom formations, such as conversion reactions, amnesias, and fugue states.

id—In psychoanalytical theory, one of three interacting systems of the personality. The id represents the early or archaic parts of the personality. Id functioning occurs on an unconscious level, the existence of which can only be inferred through dreams, impulsive acts, and some psychiatric symptoms, as primitive or unacculturated drives, needs, and so forth seek expression.

ideas of reference—Pathological belief that the actions and speech of others have reference to oneself. For example, an individual who is experiencing ideas of reference may believe that what a television announcer is saying is actually a coded reference to him. Since ideas of reference can occur in degrees, this example might be termed a *delusion of reference*.

identification—The process whereby an individual imitates the desired qualities of a significant person in the environment

impotence—Inability of the male to achieve or maintain an erection

inadequate personality—Chraacterized by faulty judgment and poor physical and emotional endurance

institutional think—Tendency of people who are fully indoctrinated into institutional ideology to believe and think along institutional lines. When institutional think occurs, people may so closely identify with the institution that an attack on the institution becomes an attack on them.

instrumental—A type of circum-speech that is task oriented. Walking, smoking, and eating, when carried on while a person is speaking, are examples of instrumentals.

insulin coma therapy—The production of a coma, with or without convulsions, through intramuscular administration of insulin. The treatment, introduced by Sakel, was once used with schizophrenic persons. It is now of historical interest only.

intellectualization—A defense mechanism in which reasoning is used as a defense against the conscious realization of an unconscious conflict

interactional behavior—A type of circum-speech that includes body shifts or movements that increase, decrease, or maintain space between interacting individuals

intrapsychic—Taking place *within* the mind

introjection—The incorporation of qualities of a loved or hated object or individual into one's own ego structure. Introjection is an unconscious mechanism.

involutional melancholia—A form of depression that occurs during the middle to later periods of life. One of its primary characteristics is agitation.

isolation—A state in which the linkage between facts and emotions has been broken. Facts are allowed into the individual's experience, yet the emotional component is excluded from awareness.

kinesics—The use of body movements to communicate meaning

labeling—The attachment of a term to a cluster of behaviors that does not represent each identifiable behavior as separate and discrete

latency—The stage of development, according to Freud and Erikson, that encompasses ages 6 to 12.

liaison nursing—Provision, by clinical specialists in psychiatric nursing, of consultation services for nursing colleagues and members of other disciplines working in medical-surgical, parent-child, and geriatric settings.

libido—According to Freud, one's sexual drive

lithium carbonate—Compound utilized primarily for the manic phase of a manic-depressive reaction

loss—The relinquishing of supportive objects, persons, functions, or status

mania—An extreme state of elation characterized by rapid motor activity, inappropriate dress, and illogical thought processes.

manic-depressive response—A cluster of behaviors characterized by mood swings, ranging from profound depression to euphoria, with periods of normalcy in between

manipulation—The habitual use of others to gratify one's own needs and desires

markers—A type of body movement that aids in communication. Markers act as punctuation points and indicators.

meditation therapy—A way of achieving relaxation and consciousness expansion by focusing on a mantra (a word, sound, or image)

menopause—The return to the nonsexual state of function of the female genitalia; usually begins in the early forties

mental health–mental illness continuum—A graduated scale of physical, emotional, and social wellness along which a person's overall condition fluctuates according to internal and external environmental factors. Individuals function at varying levels of wellness during the course of a lifetime. There is no static state of "illness" or "wellness."

metacommunication—Communication that indicates how verbal communication should be interpreted. Metacommunication may support or contradict verbal communication.

milieu therapy—Treatment of a hospitalized person that makes use of the entire hospital environment: workers, scheduled and unscheduled activities, the physical plant, and so on.

monoamine oxidase (MAO) inhibitors—Sub-stances that counteract the reduction of norepinephrine, epinephrine, and serotonin levels in the body. The reactivation of these hormones to normal levels has an antidepressant effect.

monopolization—Domination of the discussion within a group by one member of the group

motivation—The reasons for one's actions, for what one experiences, and for the way one experiences his actions. These reasons can be on a conscious, preconscious, or unconscious level.

mourning—The psychological processes or reactions activated by an individual to assist him in overcoming a loss. The process is finally resolved when reinvestment in a new object relationship has occurred.

multifactorial—Having a variety of causes

mutism—Inability or unwillingness to speak

neologism—An invented word that has an obscure and purely subjective meaning. Neologisms are very often symbolic for a person; they are sometimes demonstrated in the speech of schizophrenic individuals.

neuroses—A group of disorders characterized by excessive anxiety and unconscious conflict. Although there is no gross distortion of the personality, the compromise solutions and defense mechanisms needed to cope with anxiety and conflict can inhibit personality functioning and may result in pathological symptoms. The terms "neuroses" and "psychoneuroses" are used synonymously.

non-with spaces—Spaces in which interacting persons use body parts and regions to show that they have different spatial orientations and thus are unaffiliated with one another.

nuclear family—A family unit composed of a man, a woman, and their children

obsession—A state in which a repetitive thought or thought pattern keeps recurring despite the individual's efforts to banish it or prevent it from recurring.

obsessive-compulsive personality—Characterized by orderly, methodical, ritualistic, inhibited, and frugal behavior

obsessive-compulsive reactions—A psychiatric disorder characterized by repetitious performance of ritualistic behavior and the presence of obsessive thoughts that cannot be banished

Oedipus complex—Direction of a child's erotic attachment toward the parent of the opposite sex, during the phallic stage of development. Concurrently, there is jealousy toward the parent of the same sex.

open charting—A charting system in which a client has access to his chart. The more progressive mental health facilities have open charting in varying degrees.

oral phase—The freudian developmental phase that encompasses approximately the first 15 months of life. This period is characterized by a concentration of libidinal energies in the oral zone, particularly the mouth and lips.

organic brain dysfunctions—Neuropsychiatric conditions caused by any disturbance in brain tissue functions and characterized by the following syndrome: disturbances in comprehension, memory, orientation, and judgment and lability of emotional responses. Brain dysfunctions may be either acute or chronic. SYNONYM Organic brain syndromes.

organic brain syndromes—See *organic brain dysfunctions.*

overinclusiveness—An association disturbance seen in the thought disorder of schizophrenia. The individual is unable to think in a precise manner because of an inability to keep irrelevant elements outside of perceptual boundaries.

paranoid personality—Characterized by extremely sensitive, rigid, suspicious, and jealous behavior. An individual makes exaggerated use of projection in an attempt to cope with insecure and negative feelings.

paranoid schizophrenia—A form of schizophrenia in which the paramount symptoms include suspicion, hallucinations, and delusions. The delusions are often grandiose or persecutory.

parataxic mode—In Sullivanian theory, perception of the whole physical and social environment as being illogical, disjointed, and composed of inconsistent parts. This process is common during childhood and the juvenile period.

passive-aggressive personality—Characterized by both independent and hostile behavior. Aggressiveness is usually covertly expressed through obstinateness, procrastination, vacillation, and helplessness.

patient (client) government—An organization, composed of clients, through which clients have some influence in the running of a unit

perceptual deprivation/restriction—Absence of or decrease in the meaningful grouping of stimuli, caused, for example, by an ever-present hum or constant dim lighting

perceptual monotony—A state characterized by a lack of variety in the normal pattern of everyday stimuli. Perceptual monotony can result, for example, from having the television on all day.

phobia—An irrational or illogical fear of some object or aspect of the environment, because of the externalization of inner fears or anxiety

phobic reaction—A psychiatric condition in which internal anxiety and conflict are displaced or externalized onto some object in the environment, which can then be avoided

planned change—Altering the status quo by means of a carefully formulated program or scheme. There are three basic types of planned change: collaborative, coercive, and emulative. Planned change is characterized by four phases: unfreezing the present level, establishing a change relationship, moving to a new level, and freezing at the new level.

point behavior—Orienting body parts in some direction within a quantum of space

polarization—Within a group, the concentration of members' interests, beliefs, and allegiances around two conflicting positions

political nursing—The use of knowledge about power processes and strategies to influence the nature and direction of health care and professional nursing. The constituency of political nursing is clients: communities, groups, and individuals, both diagnosed and potential.

political system—A network of ideas and interpersonal relationships that effectively influences people's thoughts, decisions, and behavior. Each political system contains ideologies, goals, loyalties, interests, norms, and rules that foster cohesion and differentiate it from other political systems.

politics—The process of achieving and using power for the purpose of influencing decisions and resolving disputes between factions

positional behavior—Orienting body regions in order to claim a quantum of space. Positional behavior involves four body regions: head and neck, upper torso, pelvis and thighs, and lower legs and feet.

power—The ability to act, to do, and/or to control others. Power may arise from various sources, and it may be of various types (for example, expert power, associative power, and legitimate power).

powerlessness—Inability to effect change in one's environment

preconscious—Those areas of mental functioning in which information is not in immediate awareness but is subject to recall

prefrontal lobotomy—A psychosurgical procedure in which some of the connections between the prefrontal lobes of the brain and the thalamus are severed. The procedure was used as a treatment for longstanding schizophrenia involving uncontrollable, destructive behavior. After surgery, individuals were often apathetic, docile, and lacking in social graces. The procedure is rarely used today, and it is frowned upon by many mental health professionals. The operation is called a lobotomy if tissue is removed; if only white fibers are severed, the procedure is called prefrontal leucotomy.

preoperational thought phase—According to Piaget, the phase of development during which the child focuses on the development of language as the tool to meet his needs. This period encompasses ages 2 to 7.

preschizophrenic state—The period before psychosis is evident. The individual deviates from normality but does not demonstrate grossly psychotic symptoms such as delusions, hallucinations, or stupor.

primary prevention—Health promotion in the areas of individuals, families, groups, and communities through the identification and alleviation of stress-producing factors

primary processes—Unconscious processes, originating in the id, that obey different laws from those of the ego (reality, logic, and the environment influence the ego). These processes are seen in the least disguised forms in infancy and in the dreams of the adult. Much of the distorted thinking of an acutely psychotic person is based on primary process thinking.

primary triad—In Beck's theory of depression, the three major cognitive patterns that force the individual to view himself, his environment, and his future in a negativistic manner

process schizophrenia—In contrast to the situation in reactive schizophrenia, organic, inborn factors are seen as paramount. The premorbid adjustment is usually poor, and onset is early in life. The process develops gradually and progresses to irreversibility.

projection—An unconscious mechanism that involves the attributing of one's own unacceptable thoughts, wishes, fears, and actions to another person or object

prototaxic mode—According to Sullivanian theory, the mode, occurring in infancy, that is characterized by a lack of differentiation between the self and the environment.

proxemics—The use of space to communicate meaning

pseudomutuality—A term used in family therapy theory and practice. It denotes an atmosphere, maintained by family members, in which there is surface harmony and a high degree of agreement with one another. The atmosphere of agreement covers deep and destructive intrapsychic and interpersonal conflicts.

pseudoneurotic schizophrenia—A form of the schizophrenic syndrome characterized by defenses that are, at least superficially, neurotic. On closer investigation, a schizophrenic process becomes evident.

psychodrama—A type of group treatment in which an individual is encouraged to act out his conflicts and problems in a supervised setting. Other people in the group take on the roles of significant others in the person's life. Insight and/or catharsis may develop through the use of psychodrama as a therapy.

psychoneuroses—See *neuroses.*

psychosomatogenic—Causing or leading to the development of psychophysiological coping measures that are learned as responses to stressful situations. Minuchin describes the "psychosomatogenic family" as one in which a child receives positive reinforcement for his symptoms.

psychotic insight—A stage in the development of psychosis that follows the initial experience of confusion, bizarreness, and apprehension. When the individual reaches the point of psychotic insight, everything begins to fit together and to become understandable. He then understands his external world in terms of his new system of thinking: his delusional system explains all of the things he had been confused by. The individual experiences this development as the attainment of exceptionally lucid thinking. The defensive nature of this phenomenon is obvious.

quality assurance—Activites designed to indicate the quality of health care or to improve the quality of health care

rape—Sexual intercourse without the partner's consent

rationalization—The process of constructing plausible reasons to explain and justify one's behavior

reaction formation—The unconscious assumption of behavior patterns that are in direct opposition to what a person really feels or believes

reactive depression—Depression that is exogenous—in other words, depression that has a definite cause

reactive schizophrenia—In contrast to process schizophrenia, reactive schizophrenia is attributed more to environmental factors than to inborn factors. There is usually a fairly good premorbid adjustment, onset is rapid, and the psychotic episode is usually brief.

reality—The culturally constructed world of preception, meaning, and behavior that members of any given culture regard as an absolute

reciprocal—A type of body movement that aids in communication. A reciprocal indicates affiliation between people.

reductionism—An approach that tries to explain a form of behavior or an event in terms of a particular category of phenomena (for example, biological, psychological, or cultural), negating the possibility of an interrelation of causal phenomena

reference group—A group with which a person identifies or to which he wishes to belong

regression—A return to an earlier stage of behavior, where modes of gratification had been more satisfying and needs had been met and where the ego had been acted upon rather than initiating the action

relationship therapy—Therapy that emerges out of the totality of a client-therapist relationship. The therapist *begins where the client is* and encourages the growth of self in the client. Relationship therapy is an experience in living that takes place within a relationship with another person.

relativism—An attitude or belief that all cultures are logically consistent and viable and can only be understood and examined in terms of their own standards, attitudes, values, and beliefs. Relativism is the opposite of ethnocentrism.

religiosity—A psychiatric symptom characterized by the demonstration of excessive or affected piety

remotivation group—A type of treatment group that is often used to stimulate the interest, awareness, and communication of withdrawn and institutionalized clients

repression—A defense mechanism through which unpleasant thoughts, memories, and actions are pushed out of conscious awareness involuntarily. Repression is the cornerstone of defense mechanisms.

resistance—Conscious or unconscious reluctance to bring repressed ideas, thoughts, desires, or memories into awareness

retention procedure—A method established by state statute or mental health code for committing a person to a psychiatric institution. Most states recognize four types of retention: informal, voluntary, emergency, and involuntary.

role blurring—The tendency for professional roles to overlap and become indistinct

scapegoating—Projecting blame, hostility, suspicion, and so forth onto one member of a group by the other group members in order to avoid self-confrontation. This behavior may be demonstrated in groups or families.

schizoaffective schizophrenia—Schizophrenic illness in which affective symptoms (depression, elation, and excitement) are prominent.

schizoid personality—Characterized by eccentric, introverted, withdrawn, and aloof behavior. The differentiation between schizoid personality and schizophrenia is a matter of degree of symptomatology.

schizophrenogenic—Adjective used to describe behavior that is believed by some family therapy theorists to cause schizophrenia

secondary prevention—Early diagnosis and treatment through the provision of referral services, the facilitation of the use of these services, and the rapid initiation of treatment

self-concept—A mental picture that includes an individual's identity—his strengths, his weaknesses, and how he perceives himself—based on reflected appraisals from the environment

self-esteem—The amount of worth and competence an individual attributes to himself

self-fulfilling prophecy—A distortion of an event or situation that eventually leads an individual to behave as he is expected to behave by others in his social setting

self-system—The organization of experiences that acts as a protective mechanism against anxiety

sensorimotor phase—According to Piagetian theory, the developmental phase encompassing the period from birth to 2 years

sensory deprivation/restriction—The reduction of environmental stimuli to a minimum

sensory-perceptual overload—A state characterized by an increase in the intensity and amount of stimuli to the point that a person loses the ability to discriminate among varying incoming stimuli

sexism—An attitude or belief that one sex is inferior or superior to the other

sex role—The expectations held by society about what constitutes appropriate or inappropriate behavior for each sex

sexually deviant personality—Characterized by sexual behavior that significantly differs from society's norms. Either the quality of sexual drives or the object of sexual drives is at variance with cultural norms for adults. While these forms of sexual behavior are considered deviant for adults, most of them are part of normal psychosexual growth and development.

significant other—A person in the environment who is considered by another as being special and as having an impact on that individual

simple schizophrenia—The form of schizophrenia in which impoverishment of emotions, intellect, and will is evident but in which secondary symptoms such as hallucinations and delusions are absent. The person is often viewed as eccentric, isolated, and dull.

site—The quantum of space occupied and defined by a cluster of people

situational crisis—A crisis that occurs when a person is confronted with a stressful event of such unusual or extreme intensity or duration that the habitual methods of coping are no longer effective. SYNONYM: Incidental crisis

social class—A grouping of persons who have similar values, interests, income, education, and occupations

social mobility—The process of moving upward or downward in the social hierarchy

social network—An interconnected group of cooperating significant others, both relatives and non relatives, with whom a person interacts

social network therapy—The gathering together of client, family, and other social contacts into group sessions for the purpose of problem solving

social order—The way in which a society is organized and the rules and standards of behavior that maintain that organization

social sanctions—Measures used by a group to enforce acceptable behavior or to punish unacceptable behavior

sociogenic—Motivated by social values and constraints

spatial zones—Spatioperceptual fields in which people interact. There are four spatial zones: intimate zone (distance of 18 or fewer inches), personal zone ($1\frac{1}{2}$ to 4 feet), social zone (4 to 12 feet), and public zone (12 to 25 feet or more).

spot—The small quantum of space that becomes the territorial object and extension of point behavior

stereotype—A generalization about a form of behavior, an individual, or a group

stereotypical behavior—A pattern of body movements that has autistic and symbolic meaning for an individual

stress kinesic—A type of circum-speech that serves to mark the flow of speech and that generally coincides with linguistic stress patterns

stupor—A condition in which an individual's senses are blunted and in which he is, to some degree, unaware of his environment

sublimation—The directing of unacceptable libidinal energies into socially acceptable channels

substance intoxication—A state that results when a person ingests toxic amounts of a substance—for example, alcohol or a drug.

suicide—The infliction of bodily harm on self that results in death

superego—In psychoanalytical theory, the system of the personality that represents the internalized ethical precepts and taboos of parents and others who are responsible for the enculturation of the child. The ego ideal and the conscience are aspects of the superego system.

symptom neuroses—Psychological disorders in which dysfunctional coping mechanisms appear as clinical symptoms that represent direct manifestations of anxiety or the unconscious defenses utilized to cope with anxiety

syntaxic mode—In Sullivanian theory, the ability to perceive whole, logical, coherent pictures as they occur in reality

tangentiality—An association disturbance characterized by the tendency to digress from one's original topic of conversation. Tangentiality can destroy or seriously hamper a person's ability to communicate effectively with other people.

territorial—A type of body movement that aids in communication. A territorial frames an interaction and defines a territory.

territory—The area claimed or occupied by an animal or a human being and over which it maintains some degree of control

tertiary prevention—The rehabilitative process. Its goals are the reduction of the severity of a disability or dysfunction and the prevention of further disability.

Thanatos—According to Freud, the instinct for death

therapeutic community—The concept that every aspect of hospitalization should be used as treatment for a client. In a therapeutic community all staff members work together as a team, and the environment is structured to be of maximum benefit to clients.

token economy—A therapeutic program that uses reward procedures (or positive reinforcement) in order to effect desirable behavioral change in individuals. This therapy is sometimes used in day hospitals, half-way houses, and wards for chronically ill persons in psychiatric hospitals.

toxic psychosis—See *acute confusional state.*

transference—The displacement of feelings and attitudes originally experienced toward significant others in the past onto persons in the present

triad—A combination of three—for example, two parents and a child

tricyclics—A group of medications that are effective in the treatment of depression

trust—A risk-taking process whereby an individual's situation depends upon the future behavior of another individual

unconscious—A psychodynamic concept that refers to mental functioning that is out of awareness and cannot be recalled. Drives, wishes, ideas, and so forth that are in conflict with internalized standards and ideals are maintained in the unconscious level through repression and other mental mechanisms.

undoing—Performing a specific action that is intended to negate, in part, a previous action or communication. Undoing is related to the magical thinking of childhood.

unipolar depressive response—An affective disorder that is characterized by symptoms of depression only

verbal language—A culturally organized system of vocal sounds that communicate meaning

with spaces—Spaces in which interacting persons use body parts and regions to show that they share a similar spatial orientation and thus are affiliated.

word salad—A type of speech characterized by phrases that are confusing and apparently meaningless. A word salad may contain neologisms. Only the client can provide the meaning of such highly personal, coded communication.

worthlessness—A component of low self-esteem; a feeling of uselessness and inability to contribute meaningfully to the well-being of others or to one's environment

ASSESSMENT GUIDES

The following assessment guides have been developed to assist students to

1. identify high-risk factors that may contribute to and/or precipitate the development of mental illness.
2. determine the need for intervention when high-risk factors are present in order to prevent the development or recurrence of mental illness.
3. understand the interrelationship of biological, psychological, and social factors in the maintenance of mental health and the prevention of mental illness.
4. assess mental health status.
5. assess clients' strengths and weaknesses.
6. develop nursing strategies designed to utilize strengths.
7. develop nursing strategies designed to minimize weaknesses.
8. assess psychocultural perceptions and orientations concerning health and illness.
9. establish mental health goals consistent with clients' perceptions and orientations about health and illness.
10. assess the dynamics of group and family systems.
11. view individuals, families, and groups as integral subsystems of a larger social system.

GUIDE FOR ASSESSMENT OF MENTAL HEALTH

I. Demographic data
  A. Name
  B. Address
  C. Age
  D. Sex
  E. Education
  F. Ethnicity (optional)*
  G. Religion (optional)*
  H. Living arrangements
  I. Marital status
II. Admission data
  A. Date and time of admission
  B. Manner of admission
    1. Self
    2. Relatives
    3. Police
    4. Other (describe)

---

*Legislation protects people from being required to reveal ethnicity and religion.

C. Form of retention (if hospitalized)
   1. Informal retention
   2. Voluntary retention
   3. Involuntary retention
   4. Emergency
   5. Comments
D. Reason for admission
E. Client's primary complaint
F. Client's premorbid personality

III. History of psychiatric problems
   A. Previous condition: date; problem
   B. Assistance sought: native healer; therapist; agency; clergyman; other (describe)
   C. Current levels of functioning and coping

IV. Behavioral observations
   A. Thought patterns
      1. Delusion: grandeur; persecution; somatic; self-accusatory
      2. Obsession
      3. Ideas of reference
      4. Phobia
      5. Looseness of association
      6. Flight of ideas
      7. Fugue
      8. Impaired judgment
      9. Impaired insight
      10. Impaired orientation to time, place, or person
      11. Impaired memory
      12. No observable thought disturbance
      13. Comments
   B. Sensory processes
      1. Hallucination: olfactory; auditory; tactile; gustatory; visual
      2. No observable sensory disturbance
      3. Comments
   C. Speech patterns
      1. Blocking
      2. Word salad
      3. Echolalia
      4. Circumstantiality
      5. Irrelevancy
      6. Confabulation
      7. Mutism
      8. Neologism
      9. Perseveration
      10. Stuttering
      11. No observable speech disturbance
      12. Comments
   D. Affect
      1. Elation
      2. Depression
      3. Ambivalence
      4. Apathy
      5. Anger
      6. No observable disturbance of affect
      7. Comments
   E. Motor activity
      1. Hyperactive
      2. Hypoactive
      3. Stereotypical: persistent; aimless; repetitive
      4. Perseveration
      5. Catalepsy: stupor; waxy flexibility
      6. Compulsion
      7. No observable disturbance in motor activity
      8. Comments
   F. Level of consciousness
      1. Confusion
      2. Stupor
      3. Delirium
      4. Alert
      5. Comments

---

*Legislation protects people from being required to reveal ethnicity and religion.

V. Physical appearance
  A. Posture
    1. Sagging
    2. Rigid
    3. Curled into fetal position
    4. Bent
    5. No observable disturbance in posture
    6. Comments
  B. Facies
    1. Drooping or sagging: deflected eyes; lusterless eyes; drooping eyelids; deep nasolabial folds
    2. Uplifted or retracted: smiling; retracted brow; wide open eyes; darting eyes
    3. Blank: staring into space; distant expression in eyes
    4. Mask-like or ironed-out
    5. Facial tic
    6. No observable disturbance in facies
    7. Comments
  C. Mode of dress
    1. Overly neat
    2. Disheveled
    3. Bizarre
    4. Appropriate
    5. Comments
VI. Physical status
  A. Vital signs: pulse; temperature; respirations; blood pressure
  B. Physical condition
    1. Medical problems: acute; chronic
    2. Physical aids (describe)
    3. Medications: date and time of last dose
    4. Allergies (describe)
    5. Comments
  C. Patterns of daily living
    1. Sleep patterns: restlessness; insomnia; narco-plexy; average number of hours of sleep
    2. Eating patterns: number of meals a day; compulsive eating; anorexia
    3. Drinking patterns: beverage; quantity consumed; frequency of consumption
    4. Sexual patterns: sexual orientation or preference; attitudes about sexuality; sexual activity
    5. Elimination patterns: constipation; diarrhea; urinary frequency; urinary retention
    6. Social patterns: recreation; work; intimacy; community involvement
    7. Comments
  D. Level of self-care
    1. Personal hygiene
    2. Activites of daily living
    3. Comments
VII. Cultural orientation
  A. Place of residence: interethnic neighborhood; ethnic enclave
  B. Family organization: nuclear; extended; members composing family unit; members vested with authority; members involved in child rearing; sense of obligation of family members to one another
  C. Sex-defined roles: stereotyped male and female roles; amount of independence permitted men and women; degree of intimacy permitted between married men and women, unmarried men and women
  D. Communication patterns: language spoken at home; language spoken outside

home; use of touching and/
or gesturing; interpersonal
spacing
E. Type of dress: traditional
ethnic dress; Western-style
dress
F. Type of food: ethnic food;
American food
G. Relationship to people:
individualistic; group-oriented; egalitarian; authoritative
H. Relationship to time: past-
oriented; present-oriented;
future-oriented
I. Relationship to the world:
personal control; goal directed; fatalistic
J. Health care patterns: ideas
concerning causes of men-
tal illness; ideas concerning treatment of mental illness; people consulted for
treatment of mental illness
(e.g., family member, na-
tive healer, mental health
therapist, other [describe])
K. Comments
VIII. Effective social network
A. Family
B. Household members (if different from family)
C. Friends
D. Associates: employer; co-
workers; neighbors; oth-
ers
E. Religious affiliates: clergyman; church elders; con-
gregants
F. Comments
IX. Stressors
A. Culture shock
1. Communication (foreign
verbal, kinesic, and
proxemic systems)
2. Mechanical environ-
ment (i.e., different

types of food, housing,
clothing, utilities)
3. Social isolation from
family and friends
4. Foreign customs, stan-
dards, and/or values
5. Different or new role relationships
B. Life changes
1. Affectional: marriage;
birth; death; divorce;
abandonment
2. Socioeconomic: promo-
tion; demotion; unem-
ployment; change of
employment; change of
residence; increased re-
sponsibilities
3. Biophysical: serious illness (acute or chronic);
surgery; accident; loss
of body part; sexual
trauma (e.g., rape, in-
cest)
C. Other (describe)
D. No significant stress
E. Comments
X. Coping mechanisms
A. Coping mechanisms used
(describe)
B. Effectiveness of coping
mechanisms
C. Client's perception of
mechanisms that are effective in reducing stress
D. Comments
XI. Resources
A. Personal: interests; leisure
time activities; physical
and mental abilities; educational achievement;
other
B. Social: interpersonal networks; economic support
systems (e.g., health insurance, sick leave, union ben-

efits); food, shelter, cloth-
ing; other
C. Comments
XII. Candidacy for active involve-
ment in treatment program
A. Developmental level
B. Interactional ability
C. Willingness to participate
in treatment program
D. Areas of anticipated need
for assistance from nursing
staff
E. Comments

GUIDE FOR ASSESSMENT
OF FAMILY PROCESS

I. Demographic data
A. Names of members
B. Age of members
C. Sex of members
D. Relationship between
members: affinal; consan-
guineous
E. Educational levels of mem-
bers
F. Occupations of members
G. Ethnicity (optional)*
H. Religion (optional)*
I. Family members living in
another household (de-
scribe relationship)
J. Nonfamily members living
in the household (describe
living arrangement)
K. Other (describe)
II. Family organization
A. Type of family: nuclear; ex-
tended
B. Type of system: open;
closed; boundary main-
taining mechanisms (de-
scribe); norms; rules
C. Members involved in child
rearing

D. Members vested with authority
E. Sense of obligation of family members—roles: peace-
maker; protector; attacker;
provider; interpreter; res-
cuer; other
F. Sex-defined roles: stereotyped male-female rela-
tionships; amount of independence permitted men
and women
G. Other (describe)
III. Family world view
A. Relationship to people: individualistic; group-ori-
ented; egalitarian; authoritarian
B. Relationship to time: past-
oriented; present-oriented;
future-oriented
C. Relationship to the world:
personal control; goal-directed; fatalistic
D. Comments
IV. Family perceptions and definitions
A. Family
B. Privacy
C. Intimacy
D. Health (mental and physical)
E. Illness (mental and physical)
F. Other (describe)
V. Family health care patterns
A. Ideas concerning causes of
illness (mental and physical)
B. Ideas concerning treatment
of illness (mental and phys-
ical)
C. People consulted in times
of crisis or for treatment of

---

*Legislation protects people from being required to reveal ethnicity and religion.

mental and physical illnesses (e.g., family member; native healer; mental health therapist; pharmacist; physician; other)

D. Comments

VI. Family living arrangements

A. Type of residence: multifamily dwelling; single-family dwelling; one-room dwelling; other

B. Environment of residence: urban; surban; rural; inter-ethnic neighborhood; ethnic enclave

C. Time in residence: length of time in present residence; length of time in previous residences

D. Sleeping arrangements: number of rooms serving as bedrooms (differentiate between rooms functioning solely as bedrooms and those that have other functions)

E. Eating arrangements: family members eat together; eat alone; eat in shifts

F. Privacy arrangements: Rooms or sections of rooms reserved for specific family members; furniture (e.g., chairs) reserved for specific family members

G. Other (describe)

VII. Family interaction patterns

A. Communication patterns
1. Verbal
   a. Language spoken at home
   b. Language spoken outside home
2. Kinesic
   a. Touching
   b. Gesturing
3. Proxemic
   a. Interpersonal spacing
   b. Fixed and/or built space
4. Themes
   a. Double-bind messages
   b. Manipulation
   c. Scapegoating
   d. Intellectualization
   e. Blame placing
   f. Validation
   g. Other (describe)

B. Behavior patterns
1. Physical acting out
2. Isolation
3. Detachment
4. Cooperation
5. Competition
6. Overdependency
7. Other (describe)

C. Social patterns
1. Alliances
   a. Among family members
   b. Between family members and members of social network
   c. Conflict between alliances
   d. Resolution of conflict between alliances
2. Authority
   a. Nominal authority figure(s)
   b. Actual authority figure(s)
   c. Patterns of authority
   d. Implementation of authority: direct; delegated
3. Decision making
   a. Nominal decision-making figure(s)
   b. Actual decision-making figure(s)
   c. Patterns of decision making

d. Implementation of decisions
4. Dissemination of information
   a. Sources of information
   b. Pattern of communicating information
5. Social interaction
   a. Social network: relatives; friends; employers; co-workers; neighbors; clergy; other (describe)
   b. Community involvement: school; church; union; neighborhood; other (describe)
   c. Patterns of recreation
   d. Patterns of intimacy
6. Other (describe)
VIII. Family stressors
   A. Culture shock
      1. Communication: foreign verbal, kinesic, and proxemic systems
      2. Mechanical environment (i.e., different types of food, housing, clothing, utilities)
      3. Social isolation from family and friends
      4. Foreign customs, standards, and/or values
      5. Different or new role relationships
   B. Life changes
      1. Affectional: marriage; birth; death; divorce; abandonment
      2. Socioeconomic: promotion; demotion; unemployment; change of employment; change of residence

3. Biophysical: Accident or serious illness involving a family member (acute or chronic)
   C. Other (describe)
   D. No significant stress
IX. Family coping mechanisms
   A. Coping mechanisms used (indicate whether mechanisms are used only by specific family members)
   B. Effectiveness of coping mechanisms
   C. Family's perception of mechanisms that are effective in reducing stress
   D. Comments
X. Family resources
   A. Familial: interests; leisure time activities; physical and mental abilities; other
   B. Social: interpersonal networks; economic support systems (e.g., health insurance, sick leave, union benefits); food, shelter, clothing; other

GUIDE FOR ASSESSMENT OF GROUP PROCESS

I. Description of group
   A. Type of group (e.g., activity, encounter, remotivation, psychodrama)
   B. Goals of group
   C. Size of group
   D. Composition of group
      1. Age of members
      2. Sex of members
      3. Ethnic backgrounds of members (optional)*
      4. Behavior exhibited by members

---

*Legislation protects people from being required to reveal ethnic background.

5. Educational levels of members
6. Communicational levels of members (e.g., verbal; mute; speak a foreign language)
7. Reality testing levels of members
8. Other (describe)

II. Characteristics of group
A. Group phase or stage (orientation, working, termination)
B. Level of cohesiveness
C. Level of anxiety
D. Level of conflict
E. Level of resistance
F. Other (describe)

III. Patterns of group interaction
A. Communication patterns
1. Silence
2. Semantic argument
3. Intellectualization
4. Monopolization
5. Scapegoating
6. Other (describe)
B. Behavior patterns
1. Physical activity
2. Withdrawal
3. Detachment
4. Cooperation
5. Competition
6. Other (describe)
C. Social patterns
1. Group norms
2. Group rules
3. Roles (e.g., peacemaker, leader, protector, attacker, interpreter)
4. Alliances among members (subgroups)
5. Conflict between alliances
6. Other (describe)

IV. Patterns of leadership

A. Approach of leader(s)
1. Laissez-faire
2. Democratic
3. Power struggle
4. Authoritarian
5. Other (describe)
B. Competence of leader(s)
1. Provides relaxed, non-judgmental atmosphere
2. Protects group members from disruptive communication patterns (scapegoating)
3. Accepts all feelings, attitudes, and ideas as valid themes for group discussion
4. Responds to verbal and nonverbal communication
5. Facilitates communication and problem solving by
   a. encouraging group members to clarify and describe feelings, attitudes, and ideas
   b. summarizing as needed
6. Facilitates group cohesiveness by
   a. asking for feedback and validation
   b. giving responsibility to the group
   c. encouraging the group to make decisions
   d. permitting the group to review and revise goals as indicated
   e. developing leadership among group members
7. Other (describe)

DSM-III CLASSIFICATION: AXES I AND II CATEGORIES AND CODES*

The *Diagnostic and Statistical Manual of Mental Disorders* is published by the American Psychiatric Association and is periodically revised. The third edition (DSM-III) appeared in 1980.

The *Manual* categorizes and codifies psychiatric diagnoses. A description of diagnostic criteria accompanies each diagnosis. Categories and codes are used by physicians when they make diagnoses and by institutional personnel when they compile statistics and complete insurance forms.

All official DSM-III codes and terms are included in ICD-9-CM. However, in order to differentiate those DSM-III categories that use the same ICD-9-CM codes, unofficial non-ICD-9-CM codes are provided in parentheses for use when greater specificity is necessary.

The long dashes indicate the need for a fifth-digit subtype or other qualifying term.

DISORDERS USUALLY FIRST EVIDENT IN INFANCY, CHILDHOOD OR ADOLESCENCE

Mental retardation

Code in fifth digit: 1 = with other behavioral symptoms (requiring attention or treatment and that are not part of another disorder), 0 = without other behavioral symptoms.

317.0(x) Mild mental retardation, _____
318.0(x) Moderate mental retardation _____
318.1(x) Severe mental retardation, _____
318.2(x) Profound mental retardation _____
319.0(x) Unspecified mental retardation, _____

Attention deficit disorder

314.01 with hyperactivity
314.00 without hyperactivity
314.80 residual type

Conduct disorder

312.00 undersocialized, aggressive
312.10 undersocialized,
     nonaggressive
312.23 socialized, aggressive
312.21 socialized, nonaggressive
312.90 atypical

Anxiety disorders of childhood or adolescence

309.21 Separation anxiety disorder
313.21 Avoidant disorder of
     childhood or adolescence
313.00 Overanxious disorder

Other disorders of infancy, childhood or adolescence

313.89 Reactive attachment
     disorder of infancy
313.22 Schizoid disorder of
     childhood or adolescence
313.23 Elective mutism
313.81 Oppositional disorder
313.82 Identity disorder

Eating disorders

307.10 Anorexia nervosa
307.51 Bulimia
307.52 Pica
307.53 Rumination disorder of
     infancy
307.50 Atypical eating disorder

Stereotyped movement disorders

307.21 Transient tic disorder
307.22 Chronic motor tic disorder
307.23 Tourette's disorder
307.20 Atypical tic disorder
307.30 Atypical stereotyped
     movement disorder

Other disorders with physical manifestations

307.00 Stuttering
307.60 Functional enuresis
307.70 Functional encopresis
307.46 Sleepwalking disorder
307.46 Sleep terror disorder
     (307.49)

Pervasive developmental disorders

Code in fifth digit: 0 = full syndrome present. 1 = residual state.
299.0x Infantile autism, _____
299.9x Childhood onset pervasive
     developmental disorder, ____
     299.8x Atypical, _____

Specific developmental disorders

> **Note: These are coded on Axis II.**
>
> 315.00 Developmental
>   reading disorder
> 315.10 Developmental
>   arithmetic disorder
> 315.31 Developmental
>   language disorder
> 315.39 Developmental
>   articulation disorder
> 315.50 Mixed specific
>   developmental disorder
> 315.90 Atypical specific
>   developmental disorder

ORGANIC MENTAL DISORDERS

Section 1. Organic mental disorders whose etiology or pathophysiological process is listed below (taken from the mental disorders section of ICD-9-CM).

Dementias arising in the senium and presenium
Primary degenerative dementia, senile onset

290.30 with delirium
290.20 with delusions
290.21 with depression
290.00 uncomplicated
  Code in fifth digit: 1 = with delirium, 2 = with delusions, 3 = with depression, 0 = uncomplicated.
290.1x Primary degenerative dementia, presenile onset, ____
290.4x Multi-infarct dementia, ____

Substance-induced
Alcohol

303.00 intoxication
291.40 idiosyncratic intoxication
291.80 withdrawal
291.00 withdrawl delirium
291.30 hallucinosis
291.10 amnestic disorder
  Code severity of dementia in fifth digit: 1 = mild, 2 = moderate, 3 = severe, 0 = unspecified.
291.2x Dementia associated with alcoholism, _____

Barbiturate or similarly acting sedative or hypnotic

305.40 intoxication (327.00)
292.90 withdrawal (327.01)
292.00 withdrawal delirium (327.02)
292.83 amnestic disorder (327.04)

Opioid

305.50 intoxication (327.10)
292.00 withdrawal (327.11)

Cocaine

305.60 intoxication (327.20)

Amphetamine or similarly acting sympathomimetic

305.70 intoxication (327.30)
292.81 delirium (327.32)
292.11 delusional disorder (327.35)
292.00 withdrawal (327.31)

Phencyclidine (PCP) or similarly acting arylcyclohexylamine

305.90 intoxication (327.40)
292.81 delirium (327.42)
292.90 mixed organic mental disorder (327.49)

Hallucinogen

305.30 hallucinosis (327.56)
292.11 delusional disorder (327.55)
292.84 affective disorder (327.57)

Cannabis

305.20 intoxication (327.60)
292.11 delusional disorder (327.65)

Tobacco

292.00 withdrawal (327.71)

Caffeine

305.90 intoxication (327.80)

Other or unspecified substance

305.90 intoxication (327.90)
292.00 withdrawal (327.91)
292.81 delirium (327.92)
292.82 dementia (327.93)
292.83 amnestic disorder (327.94)
292.11 delusional disorder (327.95)
292.12 hallucinosis (327.96)
292.84 affective disorder (327.97)

292.89 personality disorder (327.98)
292.90 atypical or mixed organic
mental disorder (327.99)

**Section 2. Organic brain syndromes
whose etiology or pathophysiological process is either noted as an additional diagnosis from outside the
mental disorders section of ICD-9-
CM or is unknown**

293.00 Delirium
294.10 Dementia
294.00 Amnestic syndrome
293.81 Organic delusional
syndrome
293.82 Organic hallucinosis
293.83 Organic affective syndrome
310.10 Organic personality
syndrome
294.80 Atypical or mixed organic
brain syndrome

SUBSTANCE USE DISORDERS

Code in fifth digit: 1 = continuous, 2 = episodic, 3 = in remission,
0 = unspecified.
305.0x Alcohol abuse, _____
303.9x Alcohol dependence
(Alcoholism), _____
305.4x Barbiturate or similarly
acting sedative or hypnotic
abuse
304.1x Barbiturate or similarly
acting sedative or hypnotic
dependence, _____
305.5x Opioid abuse, _____
304.0x Opioid dependence, _____
305.6x Cocaine abuse, _____
305.7x Amphetamine or similarly
acting sympathomimetic
abuse, _____
304.4x Amphetamine or similarly
acting sympathomimetic
dependence, _____

305.9x Phencyclidine (PCP) or
similarly acting
arylcyclohexylamine
abuse, _____(328.4x)
305.3x Hallucinogen abuse, _____
305.2x Cannabis abuse, _____
304.3x Cannabis dependence, _____
305.1x Tobacco dependence, _____
305.9x Other, mixed or unspecified
substance abuse, _____
304.6x Other specified substance
dependence, _____
304.9x Unspecified substance
dependence, _____
304.7x Dependence on combination
of opioid and other
nonalcoholic substance, _____
304.8x Dependence on combination
of substances, excluding
opioids and alcohol, _____

SCHIZOPHRENIC DISORDERS

Code in fifth digit: 1 = sub-
chronic, 2 = chronic, 3 = sub-
chronic with acute exacerbation, 4
= chronic with acute exacerbation,
5 = in remission, 0 = unspecified.

Schizophrenia

295.1x disorganized, _____
295.2x catatonic, _____
295.3x paranoid, _____
295.9x undifferentiated, _____
295.6x residual, _____

PARANOID DISORDERS

297.10 Paranoia
297.30 Shared paranoid disorder
298.30 Acute paranoid disorder
297.90 Atypical paranoid disorder

PSYCHOTIC DISORDERS NOT ELSEWHERE CLASSIFIED

295.40 Schizophreniform disorder
298.80 Brief reactive psychosis
295.70 Schizoaffective disorder
298.90 Atypical psychosis

NEUROTIC DISORDERS

These are included in Affective, Anxiety, Somatoform, Dissociative, and Psychosexual Disorders. In order to facilitate the identification of the categories that in DSM-II were grouped together in the class of Neuroses, the DSM-II terms are included separately in parentheses after the corresponding categories. These DSM-II terms are included in ICD-9-CM and therefore are acceptable as alternatives to the recommended DSM-III terms that precede them.

AFFECTIVE DISORDERS
Major affective disorders

Code major depressive episode in fifth digit: 6 = in remission, 4 = with psychotic features (the unofficial non-ICD-9-CM fifth digit 7 may be used instead to indicate that the psychotic features are mood-incongruent), 3 = with melancholia, 2 = without melancholia, 0 = unspecified.

Code manic episode in fifth digit: 6 = in remission, 4 = with psychotic features (the unofficial non-ICD-9-CM fifth digit 7 may be used instead to indicate that the psychotic features are mood-incongruent), 2 = without psychotic features, 0 = unspecified.

Bipolar disorder

296.6x mixed, _____
296.4x manic, _____
296.5x depressed, _____

Major depression

296.2x single episode, _____
296.3x recurrent, _____

Other specific affective disorders

301.13 Cyclothymic disorder
300.40 Dysthymic disorder (or Depressive neurosis)

Atypical affective disorders

296.70 Atypical bipolar disorder
296.82 Atypical depression

ANXIETY DISORDERS

Phobic disorders (or Phobic neuroses)

300.21 Agoraphobia with panic attacks
300.22 Agoraphobia without panic attacks
300.23 Social phobia
300.29 Simple phobia

Anxiety states (or Anxiety neuroses)

300.01 Panic disorder
300.02 Generalized anxiety disorder
300.30 Obsessive compulsive disorder (or Obsessive compulsive neurosis)

Post-traumatic stress disorder

308.30 acute
309.81 chronic or delayed
300.00 Atypical anxiety disorder

SOMATOFORM DISORDERS

300.81 Somatization disorder
300.11 Conversion disorder (or Hysterical neurosis, conversion type).
307.80 Psychogenic pain disorder
300.70 Hypochondriasis (or Hypochondriacal neurosis)
300.70 Atypical somatoform disorder (300.71)

DISSOCIATIVE DISORDERS (OR HYSTERICAL NEUROSES, DISSOCIATIVE TYPE)

300.12 Psychogenic amnesia
300.13 Psychogenic fugue
300.14 Multiple personality
300.60 Depersonalization disorder (or Depersonalization neurosis)
300.15 Atypical dissociative disorder

PSYCHOSEXUAL DISORDERS
Gender identity disorders

Indicate sexual history in the fifth digit of Transsexualism code: 1 = asexual, 2 = homosexual, 3 = heterosexual, 0 = unspecified.
302.5x Transsexualism, _____
302.60 Gender identity disorder of childhood
302.85 Atypical gender identity disorder

Paraphilias

302.81 Fetishism
302.30 Transvestism
302.10 Zoophilia
302.20 Pedophilia
302.40 Exhibitionism
302.82 Voyeurism
302.83 Sexual masochism
302.84 Sexual sadism
302.90 Atypical paraphilia

Psychosexual dysfunctions

302.71 Inhibited sexual desire
302.72 Inhibited sexual excitement
302.73 Inhibited female orgasm
302.74 Inhibited male orgasm
302.75 Premature ejaculation
302.76 Functional dyspareunia
306.51 Functional vaginismus
302.70 Atypical psychosexual dysfunction

Other psychosexual disorders

302.00 Ego-dystonic homosexuality
302.89 Psychosexual disorder not elsewhere classified

FACTITIOUS DISORDERS

300.16 Factitious disorder with psychological symptoms
301.51 Chronic factitious disorder with physical symptoms
300.19 Atypical factitious disorder with physical symptoms

DISORDERS OF IMPULSE CONTROL NOT ELSEWHERE CLASSIFIED

312.31 Pathological gambling
312.32 Kleptomania
312.33 Pyromania
312.34 Intermittent explosive disorder
312.35 Isolated explosive disorder
312.39 Atypical impulse control disorder

ADJUSTMENT DISORDER

309.00 with depressed mood
309.24 with anxious mood
309.28 with mixed emotional features
309.30 with disturbance of conduct
309.40 with mixed disturbance of emotions and conduct
309.23 with work (or academic) inhibition
309.83 with withdrawal
309.90 with atypical features

PSYCHOLOGICAL FACTORS AFFECTING PHYSICAL CONDITION

Specify physical condition on Axis III.
316.00 Psychological factors affecting physical condition

PERSONALITY DISORDERS

> **Note: These are coded on Axis II.**
>
> 301.00 Paranoid
> 301.20 Schizoid
> 301.22 Schizotypal
> 301.50 Histrionic
> 301.81 Narcissistic
> 301.70 Antisocial
> 301.83 Borderline
> 301.82 Avoidant
> 301.60 Dependent
> 301.40 Compulsive
> 301.84 Passive-Aggressive
> 301.89 Atypical, mixed or other personality disorder

V CODES FOR CONDITIONS NOT ATTRIBUTABLE TO A MENTAL DISORDER THAT ARE A FOCUS OF ATTENTION OR TREATMENT

V65.20 Malingering
V62.89 Borderline intellectual functioning (V62.88)
V71.01 Adult antisocial behavior
V71.02 Childhood or adolescent antisocial behavior

V62.30 Academic problem
V62.20 Occupational problem
V62.82 Uncomplicated bereavement
V15.81 Noncompliance with medical treatment
V62.89 Phase of life problem or other life circumstance problem
V61.10 Marital problem
V61.20 Parent-child problem
V61.80 Other specified family circumstances
V62.81 Other interpersonal problem

ADDITIONAL CODES

300.90 Unspecified mental disorder (nonpsychotic)
V71.09 No diagnosis or condition on Axis 1
799.90 Diagnosis or condition deferred on Axis I

> V71.09 No diagnosis on Axis II
> 799.90 Diagnosis deferred on Axis II

AMERICAN NURSES' ASSOCIATION STANDARDS OF NURSING PRACTICE*

Standard I. The collection of data about the health status of the patient is systematic and continuous. The data are accessible, communicated, and recorded.

Assessment factors:

1. Health status data include:
   Growth and development
   Biophysical status
   Emotional status
   Cultural, religious, socioeconomic background
   Performance of activities of daily living
   Patterns of coping
   Interaction patterns
   Patient's perception of and satisfaction with his health status
   Patient health goals
   Environment (physical, social, emotional, ecological)
   Available and accessible human and material resources
2. Data are collected from:
   Patient, family, significant others
   Health care personnel
   Individuals within the immediate environment and/or the community

3. Data are obtained by:
   Interview
   Examination
   Observation
   Reading records, reports, etc.
4. There is a format for the collection of data which:
   Provides for a systematic collection of data
   Facilitates the completeness of data collection
5. Continuous collection of data is evident by:
   Frequent updating
   Recording of changes in health status
6. The data are:
   Accessible on the patient records
   Retrievable from record-keeping systems
   Confidential when appropriate

Standard II. Nursing diagnoses are derived from health status data.

Assessment factors:

1. The patient's health status is compared to the norm in order to determine if there is a deviation

---

*Published by the American Nurses' Association, Kansas City, Mo. Reproduced with permission.

from the norm and the degree and direction of deviation.
2. The patient's capabilities and limitations are identified.
3. The nursing diagnoses are related to and congruent with the diagnoses of all other professionals caring for the patient.

Standard III. The plan of nursing care includes goals derived from the nursing diagnoses.
Assessment factors:
1. Goals are mutually set with the patient and pertinent others:
   They are congruent with other planned therapies.
   They are stated in realistic and measurable terms.
   They are assigned a time period for achievement.
2. Goals are established to maximize functional capabilities and are congruent with:
   Growth and development
   Biophysical status
   Behavioral patterns
   Human and material resources

Standard IV. The plan of nursing care includes priorities and the prescribed nursing approaches or measures to achieve the goals derived from the nursing diagnoses.
Assessment factors:
1. Physiological measures are planned to manage (prevent or control) specific patient problems and are related to the nursing diagnoses and goals of care, e.g., ADL, use of self-help devices, etc.
2. Psychosocial measures are specific to the patient's nursing care problem and to the nursing care goals, e.g., techniques to control aggression, motivation.
3. Teaching-learning principles are incorporated into the plan of care and objectives for learning stated in behavioral terms, e.g., specification of content for learner's level, reinforcement, readiness, etc.
4. Approaches are planned to provide for a therapeutic environment:
   Physical environmental factors are used to influence the therapeutic environment, e.g., control of noise, control of temperature, etc.
   Psychosocial measures are used to structure the environment for therapeutic ends, e.g., paternal participation in all phases of the maternity experience.
   Group behaviors are used to structure interaction and influence the therapeutic environment, e.g., conformity, ethos, territorial rights, locomotion, etc.
5. Approaches are specified for orientation of the patient to:
   New roles and relationships
   Relevant health (human and material) resources
   Modifications in plan of nursing care
   Relationship of modifications in nursing care plan to the total care plan
6. The plan of nursing care includes the utilization of available and appropriate resources:
   Human resources—other health personnel
   Material resources
   Community
7. The plan includes an ordered sequence of nursing actions.
8. Nursing approaches are planned on the basis of current scientific knowledge.

Standard V. Nursing actions provide for patient participation in health promotion, maintenance, and restoration.

Assessment factors:
1. The patient and family are kept informed about:
   Current health status
   Changes in health status
   Total health care plan
   Nursing care plan
   Roles of health care personnel
   Health care resources
2. The patient and his family are provided with the information needed to make decisions and choices about:
   Promoting, maintaining, and restoring health
   Seeking and utilizing appropriate health care personnel
   Maintaining and using health care resources

Standard VI. Nursing actions assist the patient to maximize his health capabilities.

Assessment actions:
1. Nursing actions:
   Are consistent with the plan of care
   Are based on scientific principles
   Are individualized to the specific situation
   Are used to provide a safe and therapeutic environment
   Employ teaching-learning opportunties for the patient
   Include utilization of appropriate resources
2. Nursing actions are directed by the patient's physical, physiological, psychological, and social behavior associated with:
   Ingestion of food, fluid, and nutrients

Elimination of body wastes and excesses in fluid
Locomotion and exercise
Regulatory mechanisms—body heat, metabolism
Relating to others
Self-actualization

Standard VII. The patient's progress or lack of progress toward goal achievement is determined by the patient and the nurse.

Assessment factors:
1. Current data about the patient are used to measure his progress toward goal achievement.
2. Nursing actions are analyzed for their effectiveness in the goal achievement of the patient.
3. The patient evaluates nursing actions and goal achievement.
4. Provision is made for nursing follow-up of a particular patient to determine the long-term effects of nursing care.

Standard VIII. The patient's progress or lack of progress toward goal achievement directs reassessment, reordering of priorities, new goal setting, and revision of the plan of nursing care.

Assessment factors:
1. Reassessment is directed by goal achievement or lack of goal achievement.
2. New priorities and goals are determined and additional nursing approaches are prescribed appropriately.
3. New nursing actions are accurately and appropriately initiated.

INDEX

A

Abroms, 212, 216
Abstract thought, 111
  autism and, 508-509
  disturbance in, 514-515
Abuse
  of children, 89
    nursing intervention and, 476-478
  of drugs; *See* Substance abuse
  verbal, group therapy and, 221
Academy of Certified Social Workers, 286
Acceptance, 239
  of community mental health concepts, 276-277
  of depressed person, 417, 421
  dying process and, 135
  of health care, 354-355
  resistance and, 204
  schizophrenia and, 546
  socially deviant behavior and, 474, 484
  therapeutic communication and, 198
Accidents, adolescents and, 389; *see also* Safety
Accommodation, 42
Acculturation, 34, 43-49, 522
Acid-base balance, 582
Ackerman, N., 311
A. C. S. W.; *see* Academy of Certified Social Workers
ACTH; *see* Adrenocorticotropic hormone
Acting-out, 430, 548-549; *see also* Socially deviant behavior
  group therapy and, 224, 226
Action, plan of, 196
Action for Mental Health: a Program for Meeting the National Emergency, 259-260
Activities
  of daily living, 515
  group therapy and, 226-227
    organic brain syndromes and, 586
  occupational therapists and, 287-288
  recreational therapist and, 288
  therapeutic milieu and, 212, 214
Acute anxiety attack, 147, 149, 338-340; *see also* Anxiety
  nursing intervention and, 365-366

Acute brain syndromes; *see* Organic brain syndromes, acute
Acute confusional states, 581-585; *see also* Organic brain syndromes, acute
Adaptation, 147-149
  cultural, 148-149
  diseases of, 310
  evolutionary concepts of, 148
  inward-directed, 148
  to loss, 161, 417; *see also* Loss
  mechanisms for
    crisis intervention and, 249
    formation of, 92-93
    loss and, 161, 417; *see also* Loss
  nursing intervention and, 149-150
  outward-directed, 148
  physiological, 147-148
  psychological, 149
  psychophysiological dysfunctions and, 310-311
  and stress, 8, 140-167; *see also* Stress
  understanding behavior and, 26
Addiction; *see* Substance abuse
Addington vs. Texas, 272
Adjustment disorders classification, 670
ADL; *see* Activities of daily living
Admission assessment, 245-246
Adolescence, 126-127; *see also* Children; Infancy
  accidents and, 389
  addiction and, 480; *see also* Substance abuse
  aggressive driving and, 480
  anorexia nervosa and, 299; *see also* Anorexia nervosa
  case finding and, 480-481
  classification of disorders of, 665-666
  crime and, 480
  delinquency and, 436-437, 467
  depression and, 388-389
  early, 111
  educational therapy and, 470-471
  late, 107, 111
  neuroses and, 362-363
  personality development and, 102-103, 107
  pressures and, 580

Hall, E. T., 23, 179, 187
Halleck, S. L., 432
Hallucinations
command, 555
delirium tremens and, 442
group therapy and, 221
hallucinogens and, 440
manic-depressive reactions and, 395
nursing responses and, 555-556
sociocultural aspects of, 522
Hallucinogens, 440, 489
Haloperidol, 535, 536
Hand-washing rituals, 342-345, 368-369
Harkins, A. N., 434
Harmon, M., 62
Hatton, S. V., 424, 425
Hazzard, 23
Head injuries, 581, 585
nursing intervention and, 593, 594
Headaches, 301
Health
morbid preoccupation with, 346, 369-370, 516
physical
anxiety and, 354-355
dependence and, 357
organic brain syndromes and, 581-585
schizophrenia and, 547
social deviants and, 491-492
Health, Education, and Welfare Department
guidelines for Medicaid, 263
Health care, acceptance of, 354-355
Health needs of society, 2
Health professionals; see Staff
Health Task Force of the Urban Coalition, 617
Health team; see Team
Heart, diseases of, 152-153, 301-302
organic brain syndromes and, 581
Heart clubs, 162
Heart failure, congestive, 301
Heath, R., 525
Heavy metals, 583, 589
Hebephrenic schizophrenia, 517-518
Hediger, H., 182
Heller, S. S., 581
Helplessness
depression and, 396-400
learned, 406
neuroses and, 329
nursing intervention and, 419-420
organic brain syndromes and, 571
Hepatic disease, 491, 581, 582
Hepatitis, 491, 582

Heroin abuse, 439; see also Substance abuse
schizophrenia and, 518
Herpes encephalitis, 526
Heterogeneous groups, 228
Heterosexuality, 87; see also Sexuality
Hicks, D., 407
Hierarchy
of needs, 114-115, 238-239
in organizational structure, 612
High-commitment configurations, 184
Hippocrates, 256
Hispanic Americans, 580
Hispanic women, 178-179, 450-451
Histadelic schizophrenics, 520, 526
Histamine, 520, 526
Histapenic schizophrenics, 520, 526
History
of client, nursing, 592-593
of mental health care, 255-258
psychophysiological response studies and, 294
schizophrenia and, 504, 533-534
sexual, 87-88
suicidal clients and, 423
Hobart, C. W., 432
Hobbes, T., 451
Hobbesian problem of order, 451-452
Hoffer, 526
Holistic approach, 2, 208, 254
Hollingshead, 323
Holmes, M., 243, 545
Holmes, T. H., 158, 159, 160
Holstrum, L., 408, 446
Home visits
hyperactive child and, 599
schizophrenia and, 559
Homeostasis, Cannon's theory of, 15
Homer, 255
Homicide, 449
Homogeneous group, 228
Homosexuality, 87
Hopelessness
depression and, 387, 396-400, 406
nursing intervention and, 419-420
organic brain syndromes and, 576
Hôpital Général, 533
Hormones
arthritis and, 303
climacteric and, 390
depression and, 406-407, 410
development and, 80
organic brain syndromes and, 584, 588

Hormones—cont'd
  sexuality and, 83
  stress and, 147
Horney, K., 18, 320, 323, 324, 325, 331, 348
  manipulation and, 433
  neurosis theories and, 325-330
  socially deviant behavior and, 453
Horowitz, D. L., 46
Hospitalization
  children and, 362
  community mental health services and, 269
  culture shock and, 56-59
  current status and, 275
  deinstitutionalization and, 632
  expanding populations and, 258-259
  long-term, 268-269; see also Institutionaliza-
    tion
  networks and, 614-615
  neuroses and, 351
  organic brain syndromes and, 587
  partial, 269
  schizophrenia and, 542-543
Hospitalized Adolescent Anxiety Tool, 363
Hostility; see also Anger
  neuroses and, 329
  nurses' feelings about, 486
  nursing responses to, 316-317, 420, 485-486,
    548-549
  old age and, 389
  psychophysiological responses and, 295, 316
    arthritis and, 303
    cardiovascular dysfunctions and, 301
    headaches and, 301
    hypertension and, 302-303
    sexual dysfunction and, 305, 306
  rape and, 408, 446
  toward self, nursing intervention and, 420
  sexually deviant behavior and, 408, 444, 446
  socially deviant behavior and, 434-435
    nursing intervention and, 485-486
Hoy, W. K., 90
Human behavior, theories of, 9-25; see also Be-
    havior
Human development; see Development
Human resources departments, 270
Human rights; see Rights
Human services departments, 270
Human sexuality; see Sexuality
Human spacing, properties of, 182-187
Humanism, 2, 256-257
Huntington's chorea, 585
Hyatt, B. A., 633

Hydrocephalus, 585, 590
Hydrotherapy, 533
Hydroxyzine, 352
Hygiene
  depressed client and, 421-422
  schizophrenia and, 546
Hyperactivity in children, 455, 574, 597-600
  comprehensive health services and, 598-599
Hyperemesis gravidarum, 585
Hypertension, essential, 302-303
Hypnosis, 163, 346
Hypnotics, 584; see also specific drug
Hypochondriasis, 346, 369, 516
  nursing intervention and, 369-370
Hypoglycemia, 455, 582
Hypomania, 393-394
Hypothalamus, 83, 147
Hypoxia, 581
Hysterical reactions, 340-341
  classification of, 670
  nursing intervention and, 367-368

I

Id, 14, 15, 94-95
  anxiety and, 143
Idealization, grief and, 382
Idealized images, 329
Ideas
  of control and influence, 512-513
  of reference, 512
Identification
  of adaptive mechanisms for loss, 417
  of anxiety, 354-357
  with culture of another ethnic group, 48
  ego boundaries and, 553
  family relationships and, 75
  of high-risk groups; see also Case finding
    neuroses and, 353, 363-364
    for psychophysiological dysfunctions, 313
    for social deviants, 476, 480-481
  inappropriate, 511
  latency period and, 102
  personality development and, 101-102, 106
  psychological theories of socially deviant be-
    havior and, 452
  sexual, confusion of, 512
  of stressors, psychophysiological dysfunctions
    and, 313
  of themes, 192-193; see also Interactions,
    theme of
  depression and, 418-421
  neuroses and, 354-357

Maslow, A. H., 114
Maslow's hierarchy of needs, 114-115, 238-239
Masochism, 345
Mason vs. Superintendent of Bridgewater State Hospital, 262
Mastectomy, 152, 162, 227
Mastectomy groups, 162, 227
Masters, R. E. L., 444
Master's in social work, 286
Masturbation, 84, 515, 551
Maternal depression, 476-477; *see also* Mother
Matheney, R., 239
Maturation concept, 80-81
Maturational crises, 247
Maturity
  development and, 80-81, 108
  psychological, 6
Mauve factor schizophrenics, 520-521
McCaffery, M., 155
McClosky, H., 433
McFarland, D. E., 632
McKinney, W., 409
McNaughton Rule, 273
McNeil, M., 159
Medicaid, 263
Medical model for community mental health, 254
Medical orders, defiance of, 358
Medications; *see* drugs; Psychopharmaceuticals
Medication therapy, 471
Mediterraneans, 185 ; *see also* Italy; Spain
Mehrabian, A., 168, 169
Mellaril; *see* Thioridazine
Mellow, J., 539
Memory
  anxiety and, 356
  organic brain syndromes and, 567-578; *see also* Organic brain syndromes
Memory codes, 49
Mendel, W. M., 7, 510, 523, 539, 542, 557
Meningitis, 582
Menninger, K., 397, 532
Menominee Indians, 55
Menopause, 390
Menstrual periods, 299
Mental health; *see also* Mental illness
  assessment of, 657-661
  characteristics of, 116-117
  crises and, 248; *see also* Crisis intervention
  definitions of, 5-9
  integration of concepts of, in health care delivery, 4-5

Mental health—cont'd
  laws and; *see* Legal aspects
  and mental illness, continuum of, 115-133
  nursing and, 3-5; *see also* Nurses
  research and, 637-638
  scope of problem and, 258
  trends in, 632-638
Mental Health Information Service, 626
Mental Health Studies Act, 259, 261
Mental health team; *see* Team
Mental hospitals; *see* Hospitalization; Institutionalization
Mental hygiene codes, state, 623-624, 625
Mental illness; *see also* Mental health
  chronic
    community and, 632-635
    future trends and, 634-635
  classification of, 665-671
  culture and, 54-56, 116; *see also* Culture
  definitions of, 5-9
  geography and, 323
  history of care for, 255-258; *see also* Community mental health
  and mental health, continuum of, 115-133
  social status and, 323; *see also* Social class
  state mental hygiene codes for, 623-624, 625
Mental Patients' Liberation Movement, 616
Mental Status Questionnaire-Special Ten, 596
Meperidine, 411
Meprobamate, 352, 584
Mercury, 583
Merton, R. K., 21, 457
Mescaline, 440, 525
Messick, 248, 249
Metabolic dysfunctions, 151
Metacommunication, 136, 177-178
  neuroses and, 354
Metals, heavy, 583, 589
Methadone, 466
Methyl groups, 525
Methylphenidate, 598
Mexican Indians, 449, 451, 457
Meyer, A., 255, 257
Micronesians, 449
Middle age, 130-131
  depression and, 390-391
Migraine headaches, 301
Migration, 54-55
Milieu therapy; *see* Therapeutic community
Military psychiatry, 258
Mills, C. W., 457
Miltown; *see* Meprobamate

Neighborhood; *see also* Ethnic group
  enculturation and, 39-40
  peer groups and, 39-40
Nemiah, 322
Neo-Freudians, 18
Neologisms, 514
Neoplasms, intracranial, 585, 593, 594-595
Nervous system
  autonomic, 147
    abnormally responsive, 524
  body image and, 151
  central
    depressants of, 584; *see also* specific drug
    organic brain syndromes and, 564; *see also*
      Organic brain syndromes
  socially deviant behavior and, 456
  stimulants of, 598; *see also* specific drug
Networks in institutions, 614-615
Neurochemistry, development and, 80
Neurofibrillary tangles, 12
Neurological function; *see* Nervous system
Neurophysiological theories of behavior, 11-12
Neuroses, 320-376
  anxiety and, 144, 338-345
    nursing intervention and, 364-368
  cardiac, 302
  character, 320, 322, 334-337
  characteristics and dynamics of, 332-347
    personality patterns in, 334-337
    symptom neuroses in, 337-347
  classification of, 669, 670
  compromise solutions in, 327-328
  culturally specific, 324
  dissociative reactions in, 345-346, 368-369
  emotional tone and, 354
  epidemiology and, 322-324
  flexibility and, 327, 328, 333-334
  Horney's theory of, 18
  incidence of, 322
  information about procedures and, 361
  normal behavior and, 333
  nursing intervention in, 353-373
    primary prevention in, 353-363
    problems in, 372-373
    secondary prevention in, 363-372
    tertiary prevention in, 372
  Oedipus complex and, 102
  schizophrenia and, 518
  sociocultural aspects of, 322-324
  somatiform reactions in, 346-347, 369-370
  symptom, 337-347
    culture and, 331

Neuroses—cont'd
  symptom—cont'd
    nursing intervention and, 364-372
    term of, 320-321, 322
  theories of, 324-332
    intrapsychic, 325-330
    sociocultural, 331-332
  treatment of, 347-353
Neurotic conflicts, 326-330; *see also* Neuroses
Neurotic trends, 332-333
Neurotransmitters, 11
Niacin, 442, 526
Nialamide, 412
Niamid; *see* Nialamide
Nicotinic acid, 442, 526
Night-eaters, 438; *see also* Compulsive behavior,
  eating as
Night hospitals, 493, 558
NIMH; *see* National Institute of Mental Health
Nisbet, R. A., 457
Nondefensiveness as nursing response, 474, 549
Nonverbal communication, 22-23, 172-191
  kinesics in, 173-181; *see also* Kinesics
  neuroses and, 354
  proxemics in, 181-191; *see also* Proxemics
Non-with space, 183
Norepinephrine, 147, 391-392, 406, 410, 413
Normative network, 615
Normlessness, 433; *see also* Anomie
Norpramin; *see* Desipramine hydrochloride
Nortriptyline hydrochloride, 412
Norway, 450
Nose picking, 515
Not-me concept, 109
Novak, M., 36
Novocain; *see* Procaine
Nuclear family, 38-39
Nurses; *see also* Nursing; Nursing intervention
  as advocates
    for clients; *see* Client advocacy
    for social change, 545
  attitudes of
    clarification of, 484-485
    toward socially deviant behavior, 430, 483,
      484-485
  code of ethics for, 619-620, 672-674
  and community health centers, 636
  dependent clients and, 315-316; *see also* De-
    pendence
  education of, 3-4, 635
    neuroses and, 364-365
  emotional responses of, neuroses and, 372

Observation; *see* Assessment
Obsessive-compulsive reactions, 342-345, 368-369
Occupational health and safety, 589
Occupational therapist, 287-288
Occupational therapy, 287-288
  group, 226-227
  organic brain syndromes and, 586
O'Connor vs. Donaldson, 263, 274
Oedipus complex, 101
  conflicts and, 306
Ogionwo, W. W., 50
Older age, 132-133
  depression and, 389
  organic brain syndromes and; *see* Organic brain syndromes
  retarded ejaculation and, 307
  suicide and, 389
Open-ended groups, 227-228
Open-mindedness, 51-52
Open social system, 23
Operant conditioning, 19, 20; *see also* Behavior modification
Opiate-blocking drugs, 466
Opiates
  abuse of, 439; *see also* Substance abuse
  withdrawal from, 584
Oral gratification, 96-97
Oral stage of development, 95-99
  schizophrenia and, 527
Orbach, S., 448, 458
Orders, defiance of, 358
Organic brain syndromes, 564-605
  acute, 566
    characteristics of, 567-568
    developmental factors and, 572-573
    etiology of, 581-585
  age at onset of, 572, 573, 585
  alcoholism and, 442, 585
  at risk persons and, 589
  attention span and, 567-578
  characteristics of, 567-578
    acute, 567-568
    chronic, 568-572
    coping ability and, 572-578
  chronic, 566
    characteristics and dynamics of, 568-572
    developmental factors and, 573-575
    etiology of, 585
  classifications of, 566-567, 667-668
  competition and, 580
  as complications of medical conditions, 578-579, 581

Organic brain syndromes—cont'd
  dynamics of, 567-578
    acute, 567-568
    chronic, 568-572
    coping ability and, 572-578
  early treatment of, 564, 586
  elation and, 574
  emotional instability and, 567-578
  endemic, 564
  epidemiology of, 578-581
  etiology of, 581-585
    classification and, 566-567
  health supervision and teaching and, 590-591, 597
  incidence of, 579
  irreversible, 566, 568
  nursing intervention in, 588-601
    primary prevention and, 588-592
    secondary prevention and, 592-600
    tertiary prevention and, 600-601
  prejudice and, 580
  primary, 567
  reversible, 566
  secondary, 567
  social action and, 589
  sociocultural aspects of, 578-581
  superimposed on functional disorders, 574
  treatment of, 585-588
    early, 564, 586
    objectives in, 600
Organization
  of mental health services, 27
  of nursing intervention, 28-31
  schizophrenia and need for, 557
  structure of, 609, 612, 614
Organizational stressors, 632-634
Orgasmic dysfunction, 305, 308
Orientation; *see also* Disorientation
  group therapy and, 223
  milieu therapy and, 212
  nursing intervention and, 594, 601
  organic brain syndromes and, 567-578; *see also* Organic brain syndromes
  space and, 183-184
  therapeutic interview and, 194
Orthomolecular psychiatry, 520-521, 526
Osmond, 526
Ostomy clubs, 162
Out-migration, 43
Outpatient services, 246, 269
Outreach programs, 635
Outward-directed adaptation, 148
Overeaters Anonymous, 223-224, 463, 493, 635

Overeating, compulsive; *see* Compulsive behavior, eating as
Overinclusiveness, 527
Overinvolvement, 243
Oxazepam, 352

P

Pain, 154-157
  culture and responses to, 155-156
  duration and intensity of, 154-155
  nursing intervention and, 163
  organic brain syndromes and, 573
  overt and covert expressions of, 157
  rewards or gains from, 156-157
  sensory restriction and, 155
  sleep and, 155
  theories of, 154
Pairing, 228, 229
Paleological thinking, 514-515
Paralogical thinking, 514-515
Paranoia, 98
Paranoid disorders classification, 668
Paranoid involutional melancholia, 391
Paranoid schizophrenia, 517, 549-550
Parasympathetic nervous system, 147
Parataxic distortion, 373, 514
Parent ego state, 528
Parents; *see also* Mother
  abusing, 477-478
  anxiety and, 144
  deleterious influences of, 75-76
  depressed client and, 405, 416
  good influences of, 75-78
  neuroses and, 325-326
    prevention of, 361-362
  personality development and, 75-78
  psychophysiological dysfunctions and, 310-311, 313, 314, 315
  rights of, 626
  social deviance and, 476
  unsure, 77
Paresis, general, 586
Parker, 362
Parkinson's disease, 12, 525
Parnate; *see* Tranylcypromine sulfate
Parsons, 21
Partial hospitalization, 269
Pathological symbiosis, 519
Pattern theory of pain, 154
Pauling, L., 520, 526
Pavlov, I., 13, 18
Peer groups, 39-40, 110

Pellagra, 526
Peplau, H., 5, 144, 145, 146, 170, 608
Peplau theory of anxiety levels, 144, 145
Peptic ulcer, 296
Perception
  disturbances in
    anxiety and, 356
    schizophrenia and, 510-516, 527
  immobilization and, 163
  of space, 187
Perceptual disturbance theory of schizophrenia, 527
Perinatal period
  organic brain syndromes and, 573
  schizophrenia and, 524
Permanence of objects, 113
Pernicious anemia, 585
Perphenazine, 535
Personal distance, 182
Personal hygiene
  depressed client and, 421-422
  schizophrenia and, 546
Personal priorities, setting of, 61
Personal zone, 187
Personality
  compulsive, involutional melancholia and, 390; *see also* Compulsive behavior
  cultural, 74
  cyclothymic, 393
  development of; *see* Development
  disorders of
    body image and, 151
    classification of, 670
  emptiness of, 506, 518
  immature
    hypochondriasis and, 369
    hysterical symptoms and, 368
  neuroses and, 334-337; *see also* Neuroses
  poverty of, 506, 518
  profile of, 309
  restructuring of, 348
  schizoid, 506
  socialization and, 70-74
  socially deviant behavior and, 454
  types of
    A, 301, 309, 443
    culture and, 457
    psychophysiological responses and, 294, 309
Pertofrane; *see* Desipramine hydrochloride
Peru, 455
Pesznecker, B., 159
Peterson, J. H., 43

Psychiatric aide, 288

Psychiatric care, 612-632
  consumers and, 616-618
  institutions and, 612-616; *see also* Hospitalization; Institutionalization
  nurses and, 619-632; *see also* Nurses
    client advocacy and, 619-628; *see also* Client advocacy
    planned change and, 628-632; *see also* Planning and change

Psychiatric disorders, 27-28; *see also* specific disorder
  functional, 566
    organic brain syndromes superimposed on, 574
  organic, 566; *see also* Organic brain syndromes

Psychiatric nurses; *see also* Nurses
  code of ethics for, 620
  as practitioners, 4
  terminology and, 289

Psychiatric nursing; *see* Nursing; Nursing intervention

Psychiatric nursing specialist, 4

Psychiatrists, 287

Psychiatry
  forensic, 271
  military, 258
  preventive, 29, 266-269

Psychic immobilization, 510

Psychoanalysis, 13
  educational preparation and, 348
  group therapy and, 223, 349
  neuroses and, 348
  psychotherapy and, 348; *see also* Psychotherapy
  schizophrenia and, 539

Psychoanalytic theory
  of depression, 401-403
  of psychophysiological dysfunctions, 308-309
  of socially deviant behavior, 453

Psychobiological stress, 532

Psychocultural model of society, 22

Psychodrama, 230-231, 350-351

Psychodynamic theory; *see also* Psychological theories
  of behavior, 13-18
  of depression, 404-405
  of psychophysiological dysfunctions, 309
  of schizophrenia, 527-528

Psychological adaptation, 149

Psychological conversions, 144

Psychological factors
  personality development and, 75-80
  physical illness and; *see* Psychophysiological responses
  sexuality and, 83-84

Psychological flight
  from anxiety, 340
  from self, 345

Psychological maturity, 6; *see also* Maturity

Psychological testing, 287

Psychological theories; *see also* Psychodynamic theory
  of behavior, 13-18
  of psychophysiological dysfunction, 308-310
  of socially deviant behavior, 452-455

Psychologists, 287

Psychoneuroses; *see* Neuroses

Psychoneurotic schizophrenia, 518

Psychopharmaceuticals
  depression and, 388, 410-413
  in neuroses, 351-353
  organic brain syndromes and, 583-584, 587-588
  psychophysiological dysfunctions and, 311-312
  schizophrenia and, 534-536, 537-538
    supervision and, 558-559

Psychophysiological complementarity, 532

Psychophysiological responses, 144, 292-319
  classification of, 296-308, 670
    anorexia nervosa in, 299-300; *see also* Anorexia nervosa
    arthritis in, 303-304
    asthma in, 297
    cancer in, 304-305
    cardiovascular dysfunctions in, 301-302
    essential hypertension in, 302-303
    migraine headaches in, 301
    obesity in, 298-299
    peptic ulcer in, 296
    sexual dysfunction in, 305-308
    ulcerative colitis in, 296-297
  as communication, 548-549
  dynamics of, 294-295
  etiology of, 308-311
  families and, 311
  high-risk groups and, 313
  history and, 294
  hypochondriasis and, 346, 369, 516
    nursing intervention and, 369-370
  multifactorial interrelationship of, 293, 295, 311
  nursing intervention in, 313-317

Recall, difficulties in, 571
Reciprocals, 175-176
Records; *see* Charts
Recovery, Inc., 541
Recreational therapist, 288
Recreational therapy, 226-227, 228
  organic brain syndromes and, 586
Redfield, R., 457
Redlich, 323
Reentry shock, 472
Referees, 219
Reference, ideas or delusions of, 512
Reference groups, 45
Referent power, 608
Referrals
  after case finding, 364
  disorganized families and, 478
Refusal for treatment, 358
  rights and, 274
Regression, 100
  nursing responses and, 551
  organic brain syndromes and, 572
  schizophrenia and, 517, 528
  in therapy for psychophysiological dysfunc-
    tions, 312
Rehabilitation, 31
  community mental health services and, 271
  as essential service, 269
  preventive psychiatry and, 267-268
  schizophrenia and, 558
  social deviants and, 492-494
Reich, C. A., 457
Reichman, F. F., 191
Reiner, B., 476
Reinforcement, 19, 20; *see also* Behavior modifi-
    cation
  kinesic monitors and, 613-614
Rejection
  anorexia nervosa and, 299
  as-if phenomenon and, 507
  feelings of, 299, 507
Relationship therapy, 539, 540, 541, 545; *see also*
    Nursing intervention; Therapeutic inter-
    view
Relationships; *see also* Interactions
  anxiety and, 144-145
  with community leaders, 631, 636
  conflicts in
    dying person and, 137
    sexual dysfunction and, 306
  contract, 635
  disorganized communities and, 479

Relationships—cont'd
  with dying person, 135-138
  early; *see also* Mother and infant relationships
    obesity and, 298
    psychophysiological dysfunctions and, 313
    ulcerative colitis and, 296
  family, 234, 235-236; *see also* Family
    personality development and, 75-78
    schizophrenic child and, 519, 527, 529, 540-
      541, 544
  flexibility in, neuroses and, 327, 328, 333-334
  in-group-out-group, 44-47
  with legislators, 631, 638
  loss and; *see* Loss
  mother-infant; *see* Mother and infant relation-
    ships
  need-fear dilemma and, 507, 549-550
  nurse-client; *see also* Nursing intervention;
    Therapeutic communication
    anxiety and, 145-147; *see also* Anxiety
    in schizophrenia, 545, 560; *see also* Second-
      ary prevention in schizophrenia
  pace of, 177
  power and, 608
  role; *see* Roles
  sadomasochistic, 229
  social deviance and, 481-483
Religion
  enculturation and, 40
  personality development and, 90
  schizophrenia and, 513
Religiosity, 513
Remotivation, 267, 541, 546
Renal disease, 581
Repetition of ritualistic acts, 342-345, 368-369,
    552
Repoise; *see* Butaperazine
Report of the President's Commission on Mental
    Health, 264-265
Repression, 14, 100
  dissociative reactions and, 345
  of hostility, psychophysiological responses
    and, 295
    cardiovascular dysfunctions and, 301
    headaches and, 301
    hypertension and, 302-303
    nursing intervention and, 316-317
    sexual dysfunction and, 305, 306
  obsessive-compulsive reactions and, 343
  resistance and, 203-205
  weak and ineffective, 527
Repressive-inspirational group therapy, 223-224

Research, 637
  community mental health services and, 269
  future trends in, 637-638
  organic brain syndromes and, 579
  schizophrenia and, 543, 544
  vulnerability, 543
Reserpine, 535
Resistance
  anxiety and, 147, 149
  as communication barrier, 203-205
  hypochondriasis and, 370
  planned change and, 611
Resocialization, 267, 268, 541
Resolution
  of crises, 249
  of grieving process, 382
Respondent conditioning, 19; *see also* Behavior
    modification
Restitution, 381-382
Restraints, 240-241, 533, 549
  rights and, 624
Restructuring of personality, 348
Retarded ejaculation, 305, 307
Retention
  civil commitment and, 272-273
  criminal proceedings and, 273
  involuntary, 272-273, 622, 623
  legal apsects of, 622-623
Rewards; *see also* Secondary gains
  behavior modification and; *see* Behavior mod-
    ification
  pain and, 156-157
Rhythm therapy, 232-233
Richman, J., 398
Rights, 2, 619, 622-627
  advocacy groups and, 286
  of children and adolescents, 625-626
  civil, 623
  to communication, 274, 624-625
  to confidentiality, 625, 626
  education of nonprofessional staff about, 627
  informed consent and, 625, 626; *see also* In-
    formed consent
  to legal counsel, 625, 626
  medications and, 624
  of parents, 626
  physical restraints and isolation and, 624
  to privacy, 274
  to refuse treatment, 274
  to treatment, 262, 263, 264, 273-274, 624, 625-
    626
    in least restrictive setting, 274

Ritalin; *see* Methylphenidate
Rites de passage, 381
Ritualistic behavior, 342-345
  nursing intervention and, 368-369, 552
Rogers, C., 219
Rokeach, M., 51
Role playing, 222, 231, 350; *see also* Roles
Roles
  blurring of, team and, 284, 290
  hospitalization and, 58
  inter-ethnic, 46-47
  loss of, depression and, 406
  models for
    group therapy and, 218
    psychophysiological dysfunctions and, 310-
      311
  reversals of
    group therapy and, 222
    psychodrama and, 231, 350
  sex, 85-86
  social interaction and, 53
Roman, P., 521, 531
Rosen, J., 539
Rosenberg, B., 45
Rosenman, R. H., 443
Roueche, B., 441
Rouse vs. Cameron, 262
Rousseau, 73
Ruesch, J., 168, 178, 474, 548
Rules
  institutions and, 612
  violation of, 484
Rural population, 323
Rush, B., 256, 257
Russell, D., 408
Russians, 188, 451

S

Sacks, M.H., 592
Sadism, 229
  obsessive-compulsive reactions and, 345
  prostitutes and, 445-446
  rape and, 447
Sadomasochism, 229, 445-446
Safety, 240
  delirium and, 593
  depression and, 421-422
  needs for, 115
  neuroses and, 366
  socially deviant behavior and, 491
St. Martin, 451
St. Vincent de Paul Society, 493

Salvation Army, 493
Sapir, E., 116
Satellite clinics, 270-271
Satir, V., 76, 310, 393
Saunders, J. M., 52
Scandinavian-Americans, 399
Scapegoat, 493
Scapegoating, 221, 228, 235
Schaar, J., 433
Scheflen, A. E., 23, 168, 174, 176, 177, 178, 179,
    180, 181, 182, 183, 184, 185, 186, 188, 189,
    190, 191, 434, 613
Schiff, S. K., 6
Schismatic family pattern, 529
Schizoaffective schizophrenia, 518
Schizoid personality, 506
Schizophrenia, 502-563
  age at onset of, 521
  anatomical defects and, 524
  burned-out, 519
  cancer and, 532
  catatonic, 516-517
  childhood, 518-519
  chronic undifferentiated, 519
  classic types of, 516-518
  classifications of, 516-521, 668
  continuum model of, 528-529, 532
  crisis teams and, 559
  discharge and, 548
  dynamics of, 506-516
    preschizophrenic state and, 507-508
    primary symptoms and, 508-510
    schizoid personality and, 506
    secondary symptoms in, 510-516
  epidemiology of, 521-523
  etiological theories of, 523-533
    biochemical, 524-526
    cognitive disturbance, 527
    existential, 530
    family systems, 528-530
    genetic, 10-11, 523-524
    multifactorial, 531-532, 533
    perceptual disturbance, 527
    physical, 524-526
    psychodynamic, 527-528
    psychophysiological complementarity and,
      532
    sociocultural, 530-531
    stress-diathesis, 531-532
  facsimile, 520
  hebephrenic, 517-518
  histadelic, 520, 526

Schizophrenia—cont'd
  histapenic, 520, 526
  history and, 504
  incidence of, 521
  mauve factor, 520-521
  motor disturbances and, 516-517
  multifactorial prevention program in, 543
  multigenerational transmission of, 528-529
  neonatal care and, 544
  newer types of, 518-519
  nursing intervention in, 543-559
    primary prevention in, 543-545
    secondary prevention in, 545-556; *see also*
      Secondary prevention in schizophrenia
    tertiary prevention in, 556-559
  overprotection and, 529
  paranoid, 517
  physiological defects and, 524
  poverty and, 521, 531
  premorbid adjustment and, 519
  process, 519
  prognosis of, 504, 517, 518, 519, 522
  psychoneurotic, 518
  reactive, 519-520
  schizoaffective, 518
  simple, 518
  social awareness lacks and, 510, 515
  sociocultural aspects of, 504-506, 521-523
  stigma and, 506
  term of, 504
  theories of, 523-533; *see also* Schizophrenia,
    etiological theories of
  therapy for, 533-543
    electroconvulsive, 534
    family, 540-541
    group, 541
    history of, 533-534
    hospitalization or institutionalization in,
      542-543
    milieu, 542
    psychopharmaceuticals in, 534-536, 537-538
    psychotherapy in, 536-540
Schizophrenics Anonymous, 541
Schizophrenogenic family, 236-237, 529
Schlemmer, J. K., 371
Schmidt, W., 450
Schneidman, E., 397
School nurses, 364, 371
Schoolage child, 124-125; *see also* Children
Schools; *see also* Education; Teachers
  enculturation and, 40-42
  performance and, 480